PUBLIC
Speaking

FINDING YOUR VOICE

TENTH EDITION

PUBLIC
Speaking

FINDING YOUR VOICE

Michael Osborn
University of Memphis

Suzanne Osborn
University of Memphis

Randall Osborn
University of Memphis

Kathleen J. Turner
Davidson College

PEARSON

Boston   Columbus   Indianapolis   New York   San Francisco   Upper Saddle River
Amsterdam   Cape Town   Dubai   London   Madrid   Milan   Munich   Paris   Montreal   Toronto
Delhi   Mexico City   São Paulo   Sydney   Hong Kong   Seoul   Singapore   Taipei   Tokyo

Publisher, Communication: Karon Bowers
Director of Development: Sharon Geary
Development Editor: Hilary Jackson
Editorial Assistant: Jennifer Nolan
Senior Marketing Manager: Blair Zoe Tuckman
Marketing Assistant: Karen Tanico
Program Manager: Anne Ricigliano
Project Manager: Barbara Mack
Project Coordination, Text Design, and Electronic Page Makeup: Cenveo® Publisher Services
Art Director Cover: Blair Brown
Cover Designer: Kathryn Foot
Cover Image: © Andres Rodriguez / Alamy
Operations Manager: Mary Fischer
Operations Specialist: Mary Ann Gloriande
Digital Media Editor: Lisa Dotson
Digital Media Project Manager: Sean Silver
Printer and Binder: Courier/Kendallville
Cover Printer: Lehigh-Phoenix Color/Hagerstown

Credits and acknowledgments borrowed from other sources and reproduced, with permission, in this textbook appear on appropriate page within text or on page 440.

Library of Congress Cataloging-in-Publication Data

CIP data is available upon request from the Library of Congress.

10 9 8 7 6 5 4 3 2

Student Edition:
ISBN-13: 978-0-205-93109-5
ISBN-10: 0-205-93109-X
Á la carte Edition:
ISBN-13: 978-0-205-99694-0
ISBN-10: 0-205-99694-9

This edition is dedicated to our students, from whom we have learned so much.

Brief Contents

Contents

PART TWO   Preparation for Public Speaking   79

5 Adapting to Your Audience and Situation 79

6 Finding Your Topic 104

PART FOUR   Types of Public Speaking   283

13 Informative Speaking   283

Informative Speaking: An Overview   285

Forms of Informative Speaking   286
  Speeches of Description   286
  Speeches of Demonstration   286
  Speeches of Explanation   287

Helping Listeners Learn   288
  Motivating Audiences to Listen   288
  Maintaining Audience Attention   289
  Promoting Audience Retention   291

Speech Designs   292
  Categorical Design   292
  Comparative Design   293
  Spatial Design   294
  Sequential Design   296
  Chronological Design   297
  Causation Design   298

Rising to the Challenge of the Informative Speech   299

Briefings: An Application   300

FINAL **reflections**   Bringing Fire to Your Listeners   302

14 Persuasive Speaking   306

The Nature of Persuasive Speaking   308

The Types of Persuasive Speaking   310
  Speeches That Focus on Facts   310
  Speeches That Emphasize Attitudes and Values   312
  Speeches That Advocate Action and Policy   313

The Persuasive Process   314
  Awareness   315
  Understanding   315

  Agreement   316
  Enactment   317
  Integration   317

The Challenges of Persuasive Speaking   318
  Convincing a Reluctant Audience to Listen   319
  Removing Barriers to Commitment   324
  Moving from Attitude to Action   325
  The Challenge of Ethical Persuasion   327

Designs for Persuasive Speeches   328
  Problem–Solution Design   329
  Motivated Sequence Design   330

FINAL **reflections**   The Case for Persuasion   332

15 Persuasion in Controversy   337

Reasoned Persuasion Versus Manipulative Persuasion   339
  Forming Evidence   339
  Developing Proofs   341

The Master Proof   345
  Defining Major Issues   345
  Deductive Reasoning   346
  Inductive Reasoning   347
  Analogical Reasoning   348

Refutative Design   350
  Design Combinations   351

Avoiding Defective Persuasion   352
  The Gallery of Fallacies   352

FINAL **reflections**   Persuasion That Has Legs   357

16 Ceremonial Speaking on Special Occasions   362

Techniques of Ceremonial Speaking   364
  Identification   364
  Magnification   366

Preface

What's New in This Edition?

Each new edition offers the chance to improve our book, and the tenth edition takes full advantage of this opportunity. Those familiar with previous editions will recognize at least seven major changes:

- **New Coauthor.** We are proud to welcome a dedicated teacher, distinguished scholar, and officer of the National Communication Association to our writing team. Professor Kathleen J. Turner of Davidson College has assumed responsibility for updating, revising, and refreshing the chapter on the use of presentation aids (Chapter 10) and the chapter on presenting (Chapter 12), which gives greater emphasis to impromptu and extemporaneous presentations. The successful results of her work are self-evident in these significantly revised chapters.

> **After Reading This Chapter, You Should Be Able To Answer These Questions**
> 1 What are the three levels of meaning involved in "finding your voice"?
> 2 What is ethnocentrism?
> 3 What are the three major forms of public speaking and the three main kinds of appeals named by Aristotle?

- **New Features.** We have developed a self-test, "After Reading This Chapter…," at the end of each chapter to review and reinforce the major concepts introduced and developed. These reviews measure Learning Outcomes that relate to the Learning Objectives provided at the beginning of each chapter. In addition, "For Discussion and Further Exploration" questions and projects at the end of each chapter encourage the extension and application of chapter content. In addition, the book offers new material on presentation media and cutting-edge technologies, such as presentation programs for tablets, as well as discussion of research resources from the library to the Internet to social media.

> **For Discussion and Further Exploration**
> 1 Complete the listening problems checklist in Figure 4.1. Working in small groups, discuss your listening problems with your classmates. Develop a listening improvement plan for the three most common listening problems in your group. Report your findings to the rest of the class.
>
> 2 Review your class notes from one of your lecture courses. Were your notes coherent? Were you able to identify the main points, or did you try to write down everything that was said? Was the material easy to follow and understand? How might you change your note-taking behavior?
>
> 3 One way to improve your concentration is to keep a listening log in one of your other classes. As you take class notes, put an X in the margin each time you notice your attention wandering. By each X, jot down a few words pinpointing the cause: for example, "used *men* as generic signifier." After class, count the number of times your mind drifted, and note the causes. Can you identify a pattern of reactions? This exercise will help you identify the conditions that bring on inattention and will make you more aware of your tendency to daydream. Once you realize how often and why you are drifting away, you can more easily guard against this.

> **Reasoned persuasion** concentrates on building a case that will justify taking some action or adopting some point of view with regard to a public controversy. The case rests upon arguments carefully constructed out of evidence and patterns of reasoning that make good sense when carefully examined. Reasoned persuasion invites rather than avoids careful inspection. It appeals to our judgment rather than to our impulses. It aims for long-range commitments that will endure in the face of counterattacks. It honors civilized deliberation over verbal mudslinging.

- **Clearer Approach to Persuasion**. Development of a clearer conceptual approach to persuasion: Chapter 14 covers the nature of persuasion, and Chapter 15 focuses on the social role of persuasion in the resolution of controversy. New material emphasizes that reasoned persuasion is the ethical, enlightened alternative to manipulative persuasion.

- **Expanded Horizons**. Expansion of the book's horizons reflects the reach of public speaking beyond the classroom. A new case study of speaking and persuasive practices related to the nationally honored Wellness Program of Nabholz Construction Services company has been added to Chapters 14 and 16. Numerous new examples from the workplace, including motivational speakers such as Biz Stone, the founder of Twitter, and the late Steve Jobs, appear throughout. Examples from the courtroom have been added to Chapters 10 and 12.

- **More Compact and Student Friendly**. For many students, this has become the Age of Multi-Tasking, a time in which many demands are being made simultaneously on their time. Partly to help such students, and partly (we admit!) because shorter is usually better, we have sought to tighten the writing, and streamline and condense certain sections without sacrificing the quality many have come to associate with our book. Examples of this greater accessibility are the revised discussion of the "Historical Roots of Public Speaking" in Chapter 1 and the explanation of persuasion in Chapters 14 and 15.

- **Social Media Connections**. Connections between public speaking and social media have been added in the "Finding Your Voice" boxes and end-of-chapter activities, as well as thought-provoking questions and examples throughout. Students will find these applications particularly relevant to their daily lives and interactions.

- **Development of "Finding Your Voice" Theme**. The ninth edition of *Public Speaking* introduced a subtitle. "Finding Your Voice" focused on a theme that had been implicit from the first edition: that developing as a speaker can also help one develop a sense of purpose and mission. Finding your voice in the public speaking class means developing on at least three levels. On the first and most basic level of *competence*, the student learns how to analyze audiences, find good topics, conduct research, design messages, word them for maximum effect, and present them so that they achieve the desired communication goals. The second level of finding your voice involves *self-discovery*: helping students gain confidence so that they can communicate successfully and find those causes that most deserve their personal commitment. The third level begins the process of *finding your place in society*, helping students develop a sense of the communication roles that they might play in their communities or in the global workplace.

Steve Jobs, speaking at Stanford graduation ceremonies, gave an inspiring commencement address that described how past career frustrations ultimately led to his current successes.

FINDING YOUR

voice   Persuasion in the Raw

The "Letters to the Editor" section of the Sunday newspaper is often a rich source for the study of persuasive material. Using a recent Sunday paper, analyze the persuasion attempted in these letters. You might also check blogs with which you're familiar or that discuss a topic of interest to you. Do you find the ideas expressed in these persuasive? Why or why not? Do you evaluate these comments differently from letters to the editor or from other media sources? Which do you think are most and least effective, and why? How might these help you find your voice on a topic? Report your findings in class discussion.

> *Give me the right word and the right accent, and I will move the world.*
>
> —JOSEPH CONRAD

A legislator was asked how he felt about whiskey. He replied, "If, when you say whiskey, you mean the Devil's brew, the poison scourge, the bloody monster that defiles innocence, dethrones reason, creates misery and poverty—yes, literally takes the bread from the mouths of little children; if you mean the drink that topples Christian man and woman from the pinnacle of righteous, gracious living into the bottomless pit of degradation, despair, shame and helplessness, then certainly I am against it with all my power.

"But if, when you say whiskey, you mean the oil of conversation, the philosophic wine, the ale that is consumed when good fellows get together, that puts a song in their hearts and the warm glow of contentment in their eyes; if you mean Christmas cheer; if you mean the stimulating drink that puts the spring in an old gentleman's step on a frosty morning; if you mean that drink, the sale of which pours into our treasury untold millions of dollars which are used to provide tender care for our crippled children, our blind, our deaf, our dumb, pitiful, aged and infirm, to build highways, hospitals, and schools, then certainly I am in favor of it.

"That is my stand, and I will not compromise."[1]

The new edition develops, integrates, and refines this idea throughout the book. Each chapter begins with stories and examples that illustrate finding your voice and concludes with an expanded "Final Reflections" section that places in context the importance of what you have learned. As each chapter develops, the "Finding Your Voice" feature offers short exercises, questions, and applications that challenge students to think about and apply what they are learning, providing opportunities for class discussion and a stimulus to learning.

FINAL
reflections   "And in Conclusion Let Us Say"

We began our book by encouraging your quest to find your voice. We hope that your quest has been successful and that you have benefited, are benefiting, and will continue to benefit from it. We end our book with our own speech of tribute, this time to you. Public speaking may not have always been easy for you. But it is our hope that you have grown as a person as you have grown as a speaker. Our special wishes, expressed in terms of the underlying vision of our book, are

■ that you have learned to climb the barriers that people sometimes erect to separate themselves from each other and that too often prevent meaningful communication.

■ that you have learned to weave words and evidence into eloquent thoughts and persuasive ideas.

■ that you have learned to build and present speeches that enlighten others in responsible and ethical ways.

■ above all, that you have found subjects and causes worthy of your voice.

Some Things Don't Change; They Just Get Better

So it is, we think, with our book. For all the changes from one edition to another, core values remain. With each edition, we try to state them a little more clearly, a little more powerfully. Among these values are the following:

■ From ancient times, educators have recognized that *the study and practice of public speaking belongs at the foundation of a liberal education.* What other discipline requires students to think clearly, be attuned to the needs of listeners, organize their thoughts, select and combine words artfully and judiciously, and express themselves with power and conviction, all while under the direct scrutiny of an audience? The challenge to teach such a complex range of abilities has always been difficult, but it also suggests the potential value of the course to many students. This book represents our best effort to help teachers and students rise to this challenge.

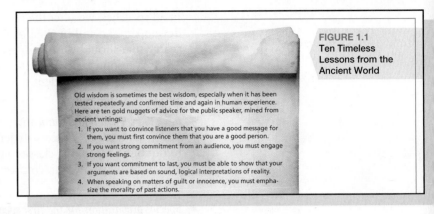

FIGURE 1.1
Ten Timeless Lessons from the Ancient World

Old wisdom is sometimes the best wisdom, especially when it has been tested repeatedly and confirmed time and again in human experience. Here are ten gold nuggets of advice for the public speaker, mined from ancient writings:

1. If you want to convince listeners that you have a good message for them, you must first convince them that you are a good person.
2. If you want strong commitment from an audience, you must engage strong feelings.
3. If you want commitment to last, you must be able to show that your arguments are based on sound, logical interpretations of reality.
4. When speaking on matters of guilt or innocence, you must emphasize the morality of past actions.

■ Another core objective of our book is to illuminate *the role of public speaking in a diverse society*. Adjusting to a diverse audience is a challenge ancient writers could not have anticipated. The increasing cultural diversity of our society adds to the importance of public speaking as a force that can express the richness of a diverse society, as well as counter the growing division and incivility that are the disease eating away at diversity. Our renewed emphasis on identification as the antidote to division, on the importance of shared stories that express universal values, and on the ethical importance of reasoned discourse as a preferred mode of public deliberation, all respond to the vital importance of diversity in our society. Thus, cultural diversity is a theme that remains constant in our book.

■ We continue to believe that a major goal of the public speaking course is *to make students more sensitive to the ethical impact of speaking on the lives of others*. We discuss ethical considerations throughout the book. For example, we direct the attention of students to ethical concerns as we consider listening, audience analysis and adaptation, cultural variations, topic selection, research, ways of structuring speeches, presentation aids, uses of language, and the consequences of informing and persuading others. Often we use a "Finding Your Ethical Voice" feature to highlight these concerns.

■ We continue to believe that *a college course in public speaking should offer both practical advice and an understanding of why such advice works*. We emphasize both the *how* and the *why* of public speaking—*how* so that beginners can achieve success as quickly as possible, and *why* so that they can manage their new skills wisely. Our approach is eclectic: we draw from the past and present and from the social sciences and humanities to help students understand and manage their public speaking experiences.

■ The Roman educator Quintilian held forth the ideal of "the good person speaking well" as a goal of education. Two thousand years later, we join him in stressing *the value of speech training in the development of the whole person*. In addition, *understanding the principles of public communication can make students more resistant to unethical speakers and more critical of the mass-mediated communication to which they are exposed*. The class should help students become both better consumers and better producers of public communication.

In addition to these core values, we continue to offer features that have remained constant and distinctive across the many editions of our book.

■ *Responsible knowledge as a standard for public speaking*. In order to develop a standard for the quality and depth of information that should be reflected in all speeches, we offer the concept of *responsible knowledge*. This concept is developed in detail in Chapter 7, in which we discuss the foundation of research that should support speeches and provide an *updated* account of current research resources available to speakers, as well as a new system for recording information as the student conducts research and personal interviews to find supporting materials.

- *How to cope with communication anxiety.* A separate chapter early in the book addresses communication anxiety and how to control it. Many students come to our public speaking classes with anxiety that amounts sometimes to terror. Our book helps them to confront their feelings and to convert their fear into positive energy.

- *Special preparation for the first speech.* As teachers, we realize the importance of the first speaking experience to a student's ultimate success in the course. Yet much useful advice must be delayed until later chapters as the subject of public speaking develops systematically over a semester. Having experienced this frustration ourselves while teaching the course, we include an overview of practical advice early in the book that previews later chapters and prepares students more effectively for their first speeches. This overview is provided in Chapter 3. The step-by-step approach to preparing the first speech offered in this chapter has been strengthened and restructured.

YOUR ethical VOICE   Guidelines for the Ethical Use of Evidence

To use evidence ethically follow these guidelines:

1. Provide evidence from credible sources.
2. Identify your sources of evidence.
3. Use evidence that can stand up under critical scrutiny.
4. Be sure evidence has not been tainted by self-interest.
5. Acknowledge disagreements among experts.
6. Do not withhold important evidence.
7. Use expert testimony to establish facts, prestige testimony to enhance credibility, and lay testimony to create identification.
8. Quote or paraphrase testimony accurately.

- *Situational approach to communication ethics.* We have always discussed ethical issues as they arise in the context of topics. The "Finding Your Ethical Voice" feature helps highlight these concerns as they develop chapter by chapter.

- *The importance of narrative in public speaking.* We discuss narrative as an important form of supporting material and as a previously neglected design option. This material is initially presented in Chapter 3. We also identify appeals to traditions, heroic symbols, cultural identity, and legends—all built upon narrative—as an important, emerging form of proof in persuasive speaking.

SPEAKER'S notes   Deciding What Presentation Media to Use

Let the following suggestions guide your selection of presentation media.

When you need to . . .	try using . . .
■ adapt to audience feedback	■ flip charts or chalk or marker boards
■ display maps, charts, graphs, or textual graphics	■ posters or computerized programs
■ present complex information or statistical data	■ handouts
■ display graphics or photos to a large audience	■ slides or transparencies
■ authenticate a point	■ audio and video resources
■ make your presentation appear more professional	■ computerized programs

- *Speaker's Notes as a major pedagogical tool.* When our first edition appeared some twenty-five years ago we introduced to the field a feature we called "Speaker's Notes." This feature serves as an internal summary that helps highlight and bring into focus important concepts as the student reads the text. In the new edition, this traditional feature works in collaboration with the new "Finding Your Voice" and "Finding Your Ethical Voice" features to encourage learning and enrich the student's reading experience.

■ *Improving language skills.* We introduce students to the power of language, help them apply standards so that this power is not diminished, and demonstrate special techniques that can magnify this power at important moments in speeches. Among the standards is learning how to avoid grammatical errors that make listeners cringe.

■ *Enhanced understanding of ceremonial speaking.* We provide coherence and respect for the study of ceremonial speaking by pointing out the importance of such speaking in society, and by indicating how two powerful concepts, one offered by Aristotle and the other by Kenneth Burke, can combine to generate successful ceremonial speeches, especially speeches of tribute and inspiration.

Plan of the Book

Public Speaking: Finding Your Voice is designed to help beginning students build cumulative knowledge and skills. Positive initial speaking experiences are especially important. For this reason, Chapter 2 helps apprehensive students manage communication anxiety as they stand to speak for the first time. Chapter 3 offers an overview of advice to help students design and present successful first speeches.

In the chapters that follow, students learn how to listen critically and empathetically; analyze their audiences; select, refine, and research speech topics; develop supporting materials; arrange these materials in appropriate structures; and create effective presentation aids. They also learn how to use language effectively and present their messages well. Students become acquainted with the nature of information and how to present it, the process of persuasion and how to engage it, and the importance of ceremonial speaking in its various forms. Appendix A, "Communicating in Small Groups," describes how to use public communication skills to participate effectively in small group interactions.

Teachers may adapt the sequence of chapters to any course plan, because each chapter covers a topic thoroughly and completely.

Detailed Plan of the Book

Part One, "The Foundations of Public Speaking," provides basic information that students need for their first speaking and listening experiences. Chapter 1 defines public speaking and the significance of "finding your voice," highlights the personal, social, and cultural benefits of being able to speak effectively in public, and emphasizes the ethical responsibilities of speakers. Chapter 2 helps students come to terms with communication anxiety, so that they can control this problem early in the course. Chapter 3 offers practical advice for organizing, practicing, and presenting first speeches. Chapter 4 identifies common listening problems and ways to overcome them, helps students sharpen critical listening skills, and presents criteria for the constructive evaluation of speeches.

Part Two, "Preparation for Public Speaking," introduces the basic skills needed to develop effective speeches. Chapter 5 emphasizes the importance of the audience, indicating how to adapt a message and how to adjust to factors in the speaking situation. Chapter 6 provides a systematic way to discover, evaluate, and refine speech topics. Chapter 7 shows how to research these topics, emphasizing the importance of acquiring *responsible knowledge.* Chapter 8 identifies the major types of

Objectives

This chapter will help you

1 Understand how persuasive speaking differs from informative speaking.

2 Master the types of persuasive speaking

3 Grasp how the persuasive process works

4 Soften the opposition of reluctant listeners

5 Remove barriers that block commitment

6 Turn agreement into action

7 Select appropriate designs for your persuasive speeches

OUTLINE

The Nature of Persuasive Speaking

The Types of Persuasive Speaking

The Persuasive Process

The Challenges of Persuasive Speaking

Designs for Persuasive Speeches

Final Reflections The Case for Persuasion

Listen to Chapter 14 at MyCommunicationLab

306

14 Persuasive Speaking

supporting materials fashioned from such research, including facts and statistics, examples, testimony, and narratives. Chapter 9 shows how to develop simple, balanced, and orderly speech designs, select and shape main points, use transitions, prepare effective introductions and conclusions, and develop outlines.

Part Three, "Developing Presentation Skills," brings the speaker to the point of presentation. Chapter 10 explains the types, media, and preparation of presentation aids. Chapter 11 provides an understanding of the role of language in communication and offers practical suggestions for using words effectively. Chapter 12 offers concepts and exercises for the improvement of voice and body language to help students develop an extemporaneous style that is adaptable to most speaking situations.

Part Four, "Types of Public Speaking," discusses informative, persuasive, and ceremonial speaking. Chapter 13 covers speeches designed to share information and increase understanding. The chapter discusses the types of informative speeches and presents the major designs that can structure them. Chapter 14 describes the persuasive process, focusing on how to meet the many challenges of persuasive situations. Chapter 15 examines the work of persuasion in controversy. The chapter encourages reasoned persuasion, helping students develop strong arguments to support their positions. The chapter also identifies the major forms of fallacies so that student speakers can avoid them and detect them in the messages of others. Chapter 16 explains how to prepare effective ceremonial presentations, including speeches of tribute and inspiration, speeches introducing others, eulogies, after-dinner speeches, and speeches presenting and accepting awards. The chapter shows how to use narratives and narrative design, often found in ceremonial speeches.

Appendix A, "Communicating in Small Groups," introduces students to the problem-solving process and to the responsibilities of both group leaders and group participants. This appendix also provides guidelines for managing meetings, including virtual meetings, and explains the basic concepts of parliamentary procedure. Appendix B provides a number of student and professional speeches for additional analysis.

Learning Tools

To help students master the material, we offer a number of special learning tools.

- We open each chapter with a chapter outline and learning objectives that prepare students for productive reading.

- The epigrams and vignettes that start each chapter help point out the topic's significance and motivate readers to learn more.

- We conclude each chapter with a "Final Reflections" summary, a self-test to review key concepts and assess how the learning objectives were met, and questions and activities to explore chapter content in greater detail.

- We use contemporary artwork and photographs to illustrate ideas, engage student interest, and add to the visual appeal of the book.

- Examples illustrate the content in a clear, lively, and often entertaining way.

- Special embedded features help students read productively. "Speaker's Notes" offer guidelines to help students focus on the essentials; "Finding Your Voice" offers exercises and applications that stimulate the learning process; and "Finding Your Ethical Voice" heightens ethical sensitivity.

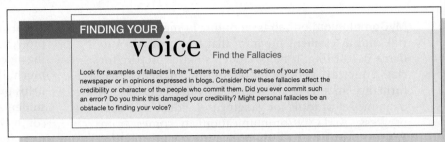

FINDING YOUR

voice Find the Fallacies

Look for examples of fallacies in the "Letters to the Editor" section of your local newspaper or in opinions expressed in blogs. Consider how these fallacies affect the credibility or character of the people who commit them. Did you ever commit such an error? Do you think this damaged your credibility? Might personal fallacies be an obstacle to finding your voice?

---

ples are not available or when their use would not be appropriate. While generally not as authoritative as their factual counterparts, hypothetical examples can still be very effective. They can be the fiction that reveals reality. Consider the following hypothetical example, which illustrates the growing problem of childhood obesity:

▶ **extended example** A more detailed example that speakers use to illustrate or develop a point.

▶ **factual example** An example based on something that actually happened or really exists.

▶ **hypothetical example** An example offered not as real but as representative of actual people, situations, or events.

- A Glossary runs through the book at the bottom of each page, helping students focus on key terms as they are introduced. In addition, all the key terms and their definitions are gathered in a complete Glossary at the end of the book.

- Sample classroom speeches found at the end of many chapters illustrate important concepts. The annotated speech texts show how the concepts apply in actual speaking situations. Appendix B contains additional speeches that offer an interesting array of topics, contexts, and speakers.

SAMPLE CEREMONIAL SPEECH

Simone Mullinax presented this speech of tribute to her grandmother in a public speaking class at the University of Arkansas. The speech develops a master narrative based on an extended metaphor and paints an endearing portrait of a complex person who–like key lime pie—combines the qualities of sweetness and tartness.

Baked-In Traditions

SIMONE MULLINAX

Have you ever baked a pie? No, I don't mean one you get from the freezer section at the grocery store—I'm talking about one you bake from scratch. I learned to bake a pie at an early age. And what I learned, early on, is that there are three things you have to master: the crust, the filler, and the topping. You can't have a pie if you lack any of these.

So where do you start? You start of course in the kitchen, which is where I meet my grandmother every time we get together. I would like to tell you she's that sweet, picturesque, grandmotherly grandmother you see on television, but she's not. Rather, she's that opinionated, bold, "her-way-or-the-highway" type that scares some people off. Her salvation is that she's also insanely funny and you fall in love with her stories, her cooking, and her opinions, even when you don't agree with all of them. Just when you're ready to pack up and move on, she does or says something that makes you want to hang around.

◀ This brief opening does a great deal of work. Simone opens with a rhetorical question and a definition and establishes her personal ethos. She then hints of a clever categorical design that will follow the three main ingredients of a pie.

◀ This paragraph completes

MyCommunicationLab®

www.mycommunicationlab.com

MyCommunicationLab is an online homework, tutorial, and assessment program that truly engages students in learning. It helps students better prepare for class, quizzes, and exams—resulting in better performance in the course—and provides educators a dynamic set of tools for gauging individual and class progress. And MyCommunicationLab comes from Pearson, your partner in providing the best digital learning experiences.

- **Assessment** tied to videos, applications, and chapter content enables both instructors and students to track progress and get immediate feedback—and helps instructors find the best resources with which to help students.

- **The Pearson eText** lets students access their textbook anytime, anywhere, and any way they want—including listening online or accessing on a smartphone or tablet device.

- **Videos and Video Quizzes:** Sample student and professional speeches offer students models of the types of speeches they are learning to design and deliver. Many interactive videos include short, assignable quizzes that report to the instructor's gradebook.

- **PersonalityProfile:** Pearson's online library for self-assessment and analysis provides students with opportunities to evaluate their own and others' communication styles. Instructors can use these tools to show learning and growth over the duration of the course.

- **MediaShare:** A comprehensive file upload tool that allows students to post speeches, outlines, visual aids, video assignments, role plays, group projects, and more in a variety of formats including video, Word, PowerPoint, and Excel. Structured much like a social networking site, MediaShare helps promote a sense of community among students. Uploaded files are available for viewing, commenting, and grading by instructors and class members in face-to-face and online course settings. Integrated video capture functionality allows students to record video directly from a webcam to their assignments, and allows instructors to record videos via webcam, in class or in a lab, and attach them directly to a specific student and/or assignment.

- **Class Preparation Tool:** Finding, organizing, and presenting your instructor resources is fast and easy with Pearson's class preparation tool. This fully searchable database contains hundreds of resources such as lecture launchers, discussion topics, activities, assignments, and video clips. Instructors can search or browse by topic and sort the results by type. You can create personalized folders to organize and store what you like or download resources as well as upload your own content.

- **Pearson's Writing Space:** The best way to develop and assess concept mastery and critical thinking is through writing. Writing Space provides a single place within MyCommunicationLab to create, track, and grade writing assignments; access writing resources; and exchange meaningful, personalized feedback quickly and easily. In addition, Writing Space will have integrated access to Turnitin, the global leader in plagiarism prevention.

Instructor and Student Resources

Key instructor resources include an Instructor's Manual (ISBN 0-205-99689-2), Test Bank (ISBN 0-205-99693-0), and PowerPoint Presentation Package (ISBN 0-205-99688-4). These supplements are available at www.pearsonhighered.com/irc (instructor login required). MyTest online test-generating software (ISBN 0-205-99692-2) is available at www.pearsonmytest.com (instructor login required).

For a complete list of the instructor and student resources available with the text, please visit the Pearson Communication catalog, at www.pearsonhighered.com/communication.

Acknowledgments

Many people have helped our book evolve and succeed over its twenty-five years of existence. Margaret Seawell and George Hoffman, communication editors at Houghton Mifflin, and Nader Dareshori, president of the company, were warm and helpful friends who enjoyed early good fortune with us.

More recently, for special assistance in the preparation of the tenth edition, we especially thank the following:

- Anne Osborn Tomasso, who offered creative, dedicated, and extended help in revising our chapter on research.

- Jayme Mayo, Chris Goldsby, and all the gang at Nabholz for their patience and enthusiasm in supporting our case study of persuasion at work in their workplace.

- David Horan, who helped us at the last minute enhance some photographs we really wanted to use in the book.

- Pat Baker, who constantly energizes her colleagues with her innovation and passion.

- And (most especially) Hilary Jackson, our brilliant development editor, who guided us, encouraged us, inspired us, and occasionally goaded us to complete this revision. Revising a book is not quite like going on the Lewis and Clark expedition, but to the extent that it is, Hilary has been our Sacagawea!

- We also thank our colleagues over all the years who have reviewed our book and helped us to make it better.

For the tenth edition, we are grateful to those listed below whose critical readings have inspired improvements:

Richard Armstrong, Wichita State University
Haley Draper, Odessa College
Sheryl Hurner, CSU Stanislaus
Nick Linardopoulos, Rutgers University
Mark May, Clayton State University
Crystal Rolison, Cisco College
David Testone, University of Bridgeport

Public Speaking: Finding Your Voice welcomes the following new student contributors to the pages of the tenth edition:

Lindsey Yoder, The University of Memphis

Nick Orobello, Davidson College

Maria Tomasso, Texas State University

Landon West, The University of Memphis

Olivia Jackson, Phillips Exeter Academy

Brandon Marshall, The University of Memphis

Jessica Floyd, The University of Memphis

Geron Johnson, The University of Memphis

Objectives

This chapter will help you

1 Understand the personal benefits of the course

2 Understand the social benefits of the course

3 Understand the cultural benefits of the course

4 Appreciate the historical roots of public speaking

5 Understand the seven elements of interactive public speaking

6 Understand public speaking as a dynamic process

7 Appreciate the importance of public speaking ethics

OUTLINE

What Public Speaking Has to Offer You

Introduction to Communication

What Public Speaking Asks of You

Final Reflections A Quest That Deserves Commitment

1 Finding Your Voice

((Listen to Chapter 1 at MyCommunicationLab

I wanna be somebody that somebody listens to. I wanna be a voice.

—GERON JOHNSON

Carolyn didn't see why she needed to take a public speaking course. She was majoring in engineering and didn't plan on being active in politics. She wondered what this course would offer her. At the first class meeting, Carolyn saw twenty-five other students who looked like they weren't sure they wanted to be there either.

Her first assignment was a speech of self-introduction. As she prepared her speech, it dawned on her why a career in engineering was important to her. She had initially thought it was because jobs were readily available. But now she recognized that she found the subject fascinating and wanted to prove she could succeed in a nontraditional field for women. Her journey toward finding her voice had begun. As she spoke, she became more enthusiastic about her topic. This helped ease her nervousness.

After the course, Carolyn found many uses for the skills she had learned. Along with some other female students in the engineering courses, she took the lead in organizing a campus support group for females in nontraditional disciplines. She felt more at ease making oral presentations in other classes. When she interviewed for an internship, she was able to present her ideas clearly and concisely. She had found her voice.

What does finding your voice mean? Clearly, it goes beyond opening your mouth and making sounds. There are at least three different aspects of finding your voice: becoming a competent speaker, discovering your self-identity, and finding your place in society.

The first aspect involves learning to be a competent speaker. To "find your voice" you have to know how to make a speech. Despite popular beliefs, speakers are made, not born. They have to learn—through study, practice, and experience—the art and principles that go into speech-making. Every chapter in this book elaborates an important dimension of this knowledge.

The second level of meaning involves self-discovery: As you "find your voice," you become more confident in yourself. You develop self-esteem and your own style as a speaker. You also develop an increased understanding of why you are speaking. As she spoke successfully, Carolyn not only found her voice but also developed a renewed appreciation for her career goals, which enhanced her sense of identity.

At a third level, "finding your voice" means finding your place in society, learning the value of the views and contributions of others, and discovering your ethical obligation to listeners. As you listen to others and as they respond to your words, you develop a sense of your mutual dependency. You learn, as the conservative intellectual Richard Weaver once noted, that "ideas [and the words that convey them] have consequences," and that what you say (or don't say) can be important.[1] We do live in a social world, and our speech or our silence can improve or degrade our surroundings.

"Finding your voice" is a quest that deserves your commitment. This chapter will explain further what this course has to offer and what it asks of you in return.

What Public Speaking Has to Offer You

The ability to communicate well in public settings will help establish your credentials as a competent, well-educated person. Learning to present yourself and your ideas effectively can help prepare you for some of the important moments in your life: times when you need to protect your interests, when your values are threatened, or when you need approval to undertake a project. The principles you will learn in this class should also make you a more astute consumer of public messages. They will help you sort through the information and misinformation that bombard us on a daily basis. Beyond these important considerations, the public speaking course also offers other personal, social, and cultural benefits. This chapter will introduce these and will help you understand the tradition and processes of public communication.

Personal Benefits

As you put together speeches on topics that you care about, you will explore your own interests and values, expand your base of knowledge, and develop your skills of creative expression. In short, you will be finding your own voice as a unique individual—a voice distinct from all others. As Roderick Hart has put the matter: "Communication is the ultimate people-making discipline. . . . To become eloquent is to activate one's humanity, to apply the imagination, and to solve the practical problems of human living."[2]

Your public speaking course should help you develop an array of basic communication skills, from managing your communication anxiety to expressing your ideas with power and conviction. These skills should help you succeed both in school and in your professional life. Each year, the National Association of Colleges and Employers (NACE) surveys hundreds of corporate recruiting specialists. According to this organization,

> Employers responding to NACE's survey named communication ability and integrity as a job seeker's most important skills and qualities. "Communication skills have topped the list for eight years." NACE advises: "Learn to speak clearly, confidently, and concisely."[3]

In its *Job Outlook 2013* report, NACE confirms: "What sets two equally qualified job candidates apart can be as simple as who has the better communication skills."[4]

Paul Baruda, an employment expert for the Monster.com jobs site, agrees that "articulating thoughts clearly and concisely will make a difference in both a job interview and subsequent job performance":

> The point is, you can be the best physicist in the world, but if you can't tell people what you do or communicate it to your coworkers, what good is all of that knowledge? I can't think of an occupation, short of living in a cave, where being able to say what you think cogently at some point in your life isn't going to be important.[5]

So unless you plan to live in a cave, what you learn in this course can be vital to your future.

Social Benefits

The benefits of developing your public speaking skills also extend to your life as a responsible citizen. All of us feel compelled to "speak out" from time to time to defend our interests and values. As you speak out on topics of concern, you will be enacting the citizenship role envisioned for you by those who framed the Constitution of the United States:

> Congress shall make no law respecting an establishment of religion, or prohibiting the free exercise thereof, or abridging the freedom of speech, or of the press; or the right of people peaceably to assemble, and to petition the government for a redress of grievances. (Amendment I to the U.S. Constitution)

The political system of the United States is built on faith in open and robust public communication. Indeed, Thomas Jefferson emphasized the importance of allowing freedom of speech as basic to the health and survival of a democratic society. He reasoned that if citizens are the repositories of political power, then their understanding must be nourished by a full and free flow of information and exchange of opinions so that they can make good decisions on matters such as who should lead and which public policies should be adopted.

SPEAKER'S
notes
Personal Benefits of the Public Speaking Course

This course can

- help reveal you as a competent, well-educated person.
- help you prepare for important communication situations.
- help you become a better communication consumer.

- help you develop basic communication skills.
- help you control communication anxiety.
- help you succeed in college and career.

In your classes, you might speak for or against stronger immigration laws, government domestic surveillance policies, the rights of gay people to marry, or the staging of public rallies by "hate" groups such as the Ku Klux Klan. On campus, you might find yourself speaking out about attempts to alter your college's affirmative admissions policy, to fire a popular but controversial professor, or to allow religious groups to stage protests and distribute literature on school grounds. In the community, you might find yourself wanting to speak at a school board meeting about a proposal to remove "controversial" books such as the Harry Potter series or *The Adventures of Huckleberry Finn* from reading lists or the school library. Or you may wish to speak at a city council meeting concerning attempts to rezone your neighborhood for commercial development.

Public speaking classes therefore become laboratories for the democratic process.[6] Developing, presenting, and listening to speeches should help you develop your citizenship skills. Preparation for your role as citizen is a benefit that serves not just you but also the society in which you live.

Cultural Benefits

As you learn to adapt to diverse audiences, you will also develop a heightened sensitivity to the interests and needs of others—what one might call an "other-orientation." The public speaking class teaches us to listen to one another, to savor what makes each of us unique, and to develop an appreciation for the different ways people live. Your experiences should bring you closer to meeting one of the major goals of higher education: "to expand the mind and heart beyond fear of the unknown, opening them to the whole range of human experience."[7]

This is not only an ethical concern; it is also quite practical. In the world beyond the classroom, as you begin your career, you may well encounter diversity in the workplace. How well you can relate to others of different cultural backgrounds may well influence the speed and the extent of your success.

As you expand your cultural horizons, you will gain a richer and more sophisticated appreciation of the world around you. You will be encouraged to seek out and consider multiple perspectives on controversial issues before committing yourself. Public speaking classes are unique in that they make you an active participant in your own education. You don't just sit in class, absorbing lectures. You communicate. And as you communicate, you help your class become a learning community. It is no accident that the words *communication* and *community* are closely connected.

Barriers to Cultural Growth.

Today's typical college public speaking class will expose you to a sampling of different races, religions, and cultural backgrounds from which you can learn. However, there are barriers that may stand in the way of your cultural growth.

One barrier might be **ethnocentrism**, our tendency to presume that our own cultural ways of seeing and doing things are proper and that other worldviews and behaviors are, at best, suspect and, at worst, inferior. There is nothing inherently wrong with being a proud American or a proud Native American or a proud Californian. But if we allow this pride to harden into arrogance, condescension, and hostility toward others, it becomes a formidable barrier to communication.

Public speaking is vital to the maintenance of a free society. The right to assemble and speak on public issues is guaranteed by the Bill of Rights.

Watch at **MyCommunicationLab** Video: "One Hundred Years of Empowerment and Communication"

Read at **MyCommunicationLab** Reading: Full transcript of "One Hundred Years of Empowerment and Communication"

FINDING YOUR

voice
The Story of Your Quest

Keep a diary in which you record your experiences as you navigate this class. As one of your first entries, consider what you think "finding your voice" might mean in your life and career. Formulate at least three personal-growth goals that you hope to reach during the course. Then for each of your speeches, keep a record of how you select your topic, develop your ideas, and prepare your presentation. What are your feelings as you plan and present your speech? Are you making progress toward your goals?

▶ **ethnocentrism** The tendency of any nation, race, religion, or group to believe that its way of looking at and doing things is right and that other perspectives are wrong.

Sensitivity toward and appreciation of cultural diversity will help you speak effectively to a wide range of audiences.

Watch at **MyCommunicationLab Video:** "Intercultural Listening"

A few decades ago, you might have encountered the assumption that our country is a "melting pot" that fuses the cultures of immigrants into a superior alloy called "the American character." The "ideal American" suggested by this phrase often had a white, male face. Historically, women and many minority groups were excluded from the public dialogue that shaped our values and policies. Moreover, the idea of a melting pot may not prepare us for the diversity of audiences we encounter both in classes and in later life. Elizabeth Lozano criticizes the melting pot image and proposes an alternative view of American culture:

> The "melting pot" is not an adequate metaphor for a country which is comprised of a multiplicity of cultural backgrounds . . . . [W]e might better think of the United States in terms of a "cultural bouillabaisse" in which all ingredients conserve their unique flavor, while also transforming and being transformed by the adjacent textures and scents.[8]

A public speaking class is an ideal place to savor this rich broth of cultures. As we hear others speak, we discover the many different flavors of the American experience. And as you examine your own identity and that of the people around you, you may discover that most of us are indeed "multicultural," a blend of many voices and backgrounds. If you want to speak effectively before American audiences, sensitivity toward and appreciation of cultural diversity is truly necessary.

A second barrier can arise in the form of **stereotypes**, those generalizations that purport to represent the essential nature of races, genders, religious affiliations, sexual orientations, and so on. Before we get to know the individual members of our audience, we may use such stereotypes to anticipate how they might react to our words. Even positive stereotypes—Asian Americans are good at math, Mexican Americans have a strong devotion to family—can be hurtful if they block us from experiencing the unique humanity of someone different from us. So pack your stereotypes away as you experience the public speaking class.

One of our favorite ways of depicting the complex culture of the United States was introduced in the conclusion of Abraham Lincoln's first inaugural address, as Lincoln sought to hold the nation together on the eve of the Civil War:

> The mystic chords of memory, stretching from every battlefield, and patriot grave, to every living heart and hearthstone, all over this broad land, will yet swell the chorus of the Union, when again touched, as surely they will be, by the better angels of our nature.[9]

Lincoln's image of America as a harmonious chorus implied that the individual voices of Americans will create a music together far more beautiful than any one voice alone. Lincoln's vision holds forth a continuing dream of a society in which individualism and the common good not only will survive but also will enhance each other.

In your class and within this book, you will hear many voices: Native Americans and new Americans, women and men, conservatives and liberals, Americans of all different colors and lifestyles. Despite their many differences, all of them are a part of the vital chorus of our nation. Public speaking gives you the opportunity to hear these voices and add yours to them.

▶ **stereotypes**   Generalized pictures of a race, gender, or group that supposedly represent its essential characteristics.

FINDING YOUR

voice   Ways of Thinking About the American Identity

Examine your personal tendencies toward ethnocentrism and stereotyping. Have these ever helped you communicate more effectively, or have they been a barrier? What can you do to change or manage these tendencies?

Introduction to Communication

Historical Roots of Public Speaking

The study of public speaking goes back thousands of years, perhaps to those moments when leaders, sitting around ancient campfires, learned that they could influence and convince others through the spoken word. Especially noteworthy in advancing our understanding were those who built—more than two thousand years ago—a civilization in Athens we still admire as the Golden Age of Greece.

These are the people who introduced democracy to Western civilization. They also left us a deep appreciation for the importance of public speaking, which served them as the major means of disseminating ideas and information. There were no professional lawyers in that era, and citizens were expected to speak for themselves in legal proceedings and to join in the deliberations that shaped public policy. One of their leaders, Pericles, concluded that the ability to speak and reason together was the key to their great civilization:

> For we alone think that a man that does not take part in public affairs is good for nothing, while others only say that he is "minding his own business." We are the ones who develop policy, or at least decide what is to be done, for we believe that what spoils action is not speeches, but going into action without first being instructed through speeches. In this too we excel over others: ours is the bravery of people who think through what they will take in hand, and discuss it thoroughly; with other men, ignorance makes them brave and thinking makes them cowards.[10]

We are heirs to this tradition of "participative democracy" enabled by "participative communication."[11] When citizens gather today to discuss and debate the policies that may govern their lives, they are enacting Pericles' dream of an empowered citizenship. As we explore ideas together, we often enrich our options, learn what causes are important to us, and shape our positions on vital issues. In essence, we are "finding our voices."

Perhaps the most important contribution of the Greeks to the study of communication was Aristotle's *On Rhetoric*, which taught the art of public speaking to the citizens of Athens. Aristotle brought system and order to the study of public speaking.

Greek philosopher Aristotle shaped the study and practice of public speaking with his influential work *On Rhetoric*.

He described three major forms of speeches: **deliberative**, used in law-making; **forensic**, used in the courts; and **ceremonial**, used during public ceremonies that celebrated great deeds and honored heroes. He also identified three major types of appeals: **logos**, appeals based on logic; **pathos**, appeals based on emotion; and **ethos**, appeals based on the character of the speaker. Aristotle also stressed the importance of using evidence, examples, and stories to support conclusions. He made it clear that "finding your voice" means not only finding yourself but also learning more about those with whom we communicate.

Another influential Greek, the philosopher Plato, wrote two dialogues that deal specifically with the power of the public oration. The first, *Gorgias*, offers Plato's dark vision of the subject. (Read the *Gorgias* online.) He charged that the public speakers of his time pandered to the ignorance and prejudices of the masses instead of advancing the truth. Too often, these orators told their listeners what they *wanted* to hear rather than what they *needed* to hear. Sound familiar?

In a second dialogue, *Phaedrus*, Plato paints his ideal of the virtuous speaker whose words will help listeners become better citizens and people. (Read this classic online.) Such speakers can be both ethical and effective, even though, Plato observed wryly, this balance may be hard for many speakers to achieve. Plato's vision of the ideal speaker would remain a challenge for the ages of communicators that would follow.

Throughout this book, we draw upon the classic tradition to help us understand both *how to communicate* and *how we ought to communicate*. The ancients can help us develop both the techniques and the ethics of speaking in public, whether face-to-face or in cyberspace (see a sampling of this wisdom in Figure 1.1). For more on the history and meaning of communication study, see the speech by Michael Osborn in MyCommunicationLab.

Communication: Interactive and Dynamic

Contemporary scientists and philosophers continue to enrich our understanding of the communication process: how communication works as an interactive and dynamic force in shaping our lives.

Public Speaking as an Interactive Process.   Our natural tendency is to think of a speech as words imposed by one person upon others. Actually, a speech is a complex interaction among seven elements: speaker, message, channel, interference, setting, audience, and feedback.

Speaker. The **speaker** initiates the communication process by framing an oral message for the consideration of others. Speakers should have a message of value that has been carefully prepared and that deserves serious attention from listeners in face-to-face communication situations. Because the fate of speeches depends on how listeners respond, effective speakers must be audience-centered, alert to the needs, interests, and capacities of their listeners. Ethical speakers believe their messages will improve the lives of listeners, helping their audiences think critically, creatively, and constructively about issues.

Whether listeners accept a speaker as credible is crucial to the interaction: If listeners think a speaker is competent, likable, and trustworthy and shares their

---

▶ **deliberative speeches**   Used to propose, discuss, debate, and decide future policies and laws.

▶ **forensic speeches**   Used to determine the rightness and wrongness of past actions, often in courts of law.

▶ **logos**   Appeals based on logic and evidence.

▶ **ceremonial speeches**   In ancient Greece, used to celebrate and commemorate heroic deeds, great events, and the honored dead.

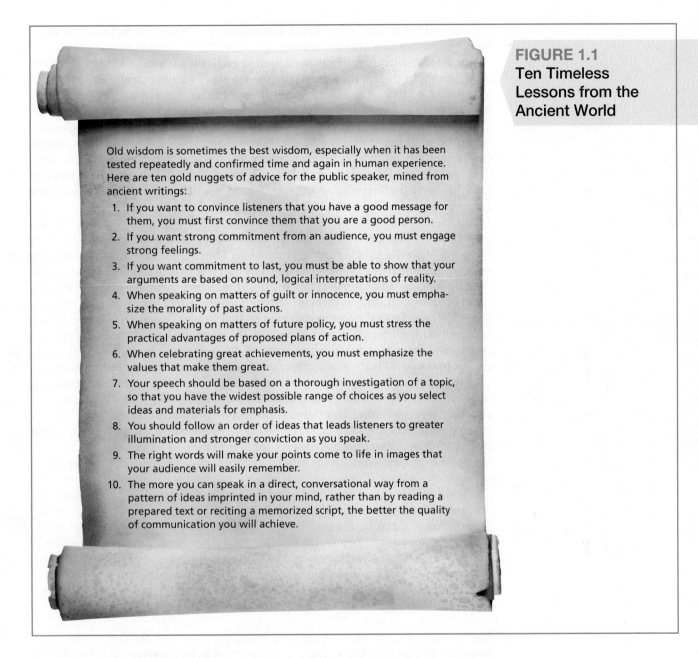

FIGURE 1.1
Ten Timeless Lessons from the Ancient World

Old wisdom is sometimes the best wisdom, especially when it has been tested repeatedly and confirmed time and again in human experience. Here are ten gold nuggets of advice for the public speaker, mined from ancient writings:

1. If you want to convince listeners that you have a good message for them, you must first convince them that you are a good person.
2. If you want strong commitment from an audience, you must engage strong feelings.
3. If you want commitment to last, you must be able to show that your arguments are based on sound, logical interpretations of reality.
4. When speaking on matters of guilt or innocence, you must emphasize the morality of past actions.
5. When speaking on matters of future policy, you must stress the practical advantages of proposed plans of action.
6. When celebrating great achievements, you must emphasize the values that make them great.
7. Your speech should be based on a thorough investigation of a topic, so that you have the widest possible range of choices as you select ideas and materials for emphasis.
8. You should follow an order of ideas that leads listeners to greater illumination and stronger conviction as you speak.
9. The right words will make your points come to life in images that your audience will easily remember.
10. The more you can speak in a direct, conversational way from a pattern of ideas imprinted in your mind, rather than by reading a prepared text or reciting a memorized script, the better the quality of communication you will achieve.

interests and goals, they will be more likely to accept the message. We discuss establishing your credibility as a speaker in Chapter 3.

Message. A speaker must have a clear idea of what a speech is to accomplish—this is called its **message**. You should be able to state your specific purpose in one clear, simple sentence—the simpler, the better. To promote a message, your speech should follow a design and strategy appropriate to the subject and to the needs of listeners. To make the message clear and attractive, your speech must use words artfully and often may use presentation aids such as graphs, charts, or photographs projected on a large screen. To make the message credible, your speech should offer convincing evidence drawn from reputable sources and sound reasoning. To make your message

▶ **pathos** Appeals based on feelings.

▶ **ethos** Appeals based on the character, competence, and personality of the speaker.

▶ **speaker** Initiates the communication process by framing an oral message for the consideration of others.

▶ **message** What the speaker wishes to accomplish.

forceful and impressive, your speech will require presentational skills—your voice, body language, and platform presence.

In addition to their main messages, speeches also communicate secondary messages about the speaker, especially the speaker's attitudes and opinions about the particular topic. It is essential that these primary and secondary messages be harmonious and mutually supportive: "She cares passionately about this subject" or "She has really prepared this speech" or "She's really excited about speaking today" would be an example of a harmonious secondary message conveyed by a speech. On the other hand, if the audience concludes, "He couldn't really care less about this," or "He hasn't researched these ideas very carefully," the secondary message would subvert the intended message. Creating a positive relationship among the messages of a speech is vital to the art of public speaking.

Channel.   The channel conveys your message to listeners. It may be radio, television, Facebook or YouTube, or it may be face-to-face. The channel is normally something we take for granted until something happens that blocks it or reveals its inadequacy.

This blockage indicates the close relationship between channel and interference. Competing sounds drift in through open doors and windows to distract listeners. Acoustical "dead spots" occur in auditoriums that garble the pattern of sound waves, making listening difficult, if not impossible. The sheer size of audiences may make it necessary to amplify and distort sound waves through microphones and loud speakers. We may have to learn new techniques to overcome these channel difficulties.

Fortunately, the channel in use in most public speaking classrooms, engaging small audiences in fairly confined spaces, normally presents few difficulties. The possible impact of other communication channels upon the messages that flow through them, however, can be very interesting. The channel of radio focuses great attention upon the voice, isolated from the appearance, facial expressions, and gestures of the speaker. Television features a kind of faux-familiarity, in which speakers can appear as though they were sitting in our living rooms, talking to us one-on-one (but without direct feedback). The television channel emphasizes facial expressiveness and physical attractiveness, especially of news announcers and commentators.

Some new social media may have also rearranged profoundly the channels of public communication. Twitter, for example, forces us to wrap messages in very small bundles, limiting communicators to messages with 140 characters, called "tweets." But communicators are apparently not discouraged by this limitation: In 2012, they exchanged some 340 million tweets daily![12] Does such limitation force us to essentialize our thinking, or does it simply glorify the trivial? The jury remains out.

Interference.   Occasionally, as we have noted, the flow of a message can be interrupted by distractions. These distractions function as **interference** that can disrupt the communication process. Outside the classroom, in cyberspace or in community meetings, interference in the form of relentless heckling and even verbal abuse has become an occasional but appalling feature of the communication practices of our time. Such lack of civility is an enemy of the free and open flow of communication that is essential to democratic forms of government.

Fortunately, you should experience little, if any, such willful interference in your classroom presentations. But what if you have just started your speech and you are drowned out by laughter in the hall? What if the classroom door opens and someone late for class walks up to a seat in the front row? Whatever happens, don't let such thoughtless interference disturb your composure. Usually, if you pause and smile, the distractions will fade. Often a little impromptu humor will disarm the situation and show that you are still in control. We discuss interference problems in greater detail in Chapters 4 and 5.

▶ **channel**   Medium that conveys the message to listeners.

▶ **interference**   Distractions that can disrupt the communication process.

Setting. A speech is always presented in a **setting** that can affect profoundly how it is designed, presented, and received. The setting of a speech refers to the physical arrangements of the space in which the speech is presented. The setting also includes the psychological mindset of listeners, their knowledge and feelings about your subject and recent events relevant to it, and their expectations concerning you and the occasion.

The *physical setting* includes the actual place where the speech is presented, the time of day, and the size and arrangement of the audience. Usually, the speaker simply makes the best on-the-spot adjustments possible in light of such factors. At other times, arranging the physical setting for a speech can be artful and challenging.

One of your authors, while managing an election campaign, wanted to use the "free speech" platform on a nearby university campus as the dramatic setting for his candidate's speech on education reform. To make this happen he had to (1) obtain permission from university officials for an "outsider" to use the platform, (2) arrange for sound equipment so that the candidate might be heard, (3) decorate the platform so that it would be visually appealing, (4) ask some colleagues to announce the event in their classes to assure a "live" audience, and (5) urge local media—especially television stations—to "cover" the event. The open and outdoor physical setting of the free speech platform called for a speech with a simple structure of ideas, vivid and concrete language, colorful examples that would catch and hold attention from passersby, and good sound amplifiers.

Similarly, but on a much grander scale, when Martin Luther King, Jr., described his "dream" of people of color participating fully in the promise of America, he spoke under the watchful eyes of Lincoln's statue to a vast audience gathered at the Lincoln Memorial in Washington, D.C. The very setting of the speech affected how these listeners—hundreds of thousands of them in the actual audience and millions more listening on radio or watching on television—would respond.

The *psychological setting* for a speech can obviously be more complicated and often varies from one listener to another. Among the factors that can influence the psychological setting of your speech are these:

1. *Individual beliefs*—a conservative member of the "tea party" might bring a much different mindset to listen to your speech than a "Move On" liberal would.

2. *Listener awareness of recent events*—if you plan a speech for (or against) gun control, the psychological setting might change dramatically should there be mass murders in a public school on the eve of your presentation.

3. *Listener anticipations of your speaking performance*—these anticipations, based on your previous speaking efforts, can create a positive or negative climate of expectations for your speech that you either can take advantage of or must work to change.

4. *Listener expectations because of the occasion*—listeners gathered for a Memorial Day celebration may react quite negatively if a speaker decides, instead of honoring the dead, to present her views on tax reform.

We consider the setting of a speech in detail in Chapter 5.

Audience. The **audience** for a message includes potential listeners the speaker hopes to reach. We often equate the audience with listeners who are actually present for a speech, but questions about the audience can become rather complicated. In planning the free speech platform occasion, we had to arrange for a live audience as the excuse for giving the speech to begin with, providing a reason for television news stations to attend. But this apparent audience of a few students was not the actual target audience for the speech. Rather, the intended audience was the much larger

Explore at
MyCommunicationLab
Activity: "Speech
Setting"

▶ **setting** Physical and psychological context in which a speech is presented.

▶ **audience** Includes potential listeners the speaker hopes to reach.

group of viewers who might catch a few "sound bites" on the evening news, giving us free exposure to a mass audience. We designed the message with this target audience in mind, developing brief, colorful statements that might invite inclusion in local news broadcasts as representing the message of the speech.

Similarly, "speakers" may broadcast overheated messages on YouTube, hoping to engage a portion of the global audience that congregates on the World Wide Web. They cast their speeches like nets into that vast undifferentiated sea of listeners and occasionally enjoy spectacular catches. Representative Alan Grayson (D-FL) reproduced on YouTube his congressional speech accusing Republicans of offering one health plan on the theme "Don't get sick" and another plan for the sick: "Die quickly." Ten thousand viewers offered a total of more than $250,000 to his reelection campaign after that effort. According to *Time*, Representative Michele Bachmann (R-MN) wondered whether health reform "would allow a 13-year-old girl to use a school 'sex clinic' to get a referral for an abortion and 'go home on the school bus that night.'" She raised the question of whether President Obama "may have anti-American views" and accused him of creating a "gangster government." She received a cascade of contributions after these rhetorical efforts.[13]

Questions about what constitutes an audience can be interesting. All teachers know that students can sometimes feign listening, while absorbing little of what they are hearing. Are they an "audience" just because they are seated in front of the speaker? Occasionally, speakers may "perform" a speech, enjoying their own contrived gestures and artificial vocal patterns. They seem to care little about whether others might actually benefit from what they are saying. So do these speakers constitute their own audience?

Finding your voice as a speaker can also require that you discover your ears as an audience member. If you want others to give you encouragement and a fair hearing, you must be a good listener in return. What are others saying that you can use? How can you help them grow as a speaker by being a good listener? We shall say more about what constitutes a good audience later in this chapter and in Chapter 4.

Feedback.   As you speak, you should be picking up cues from your audience that will help you adjust to the ongoing situation. These cues constitute **feedback** that helps you monitor the immediate effectiveness of your message. The need for feedback is one reason why you should maintain eye contact with listeners and not be focusing on your notes or gazing out the window or up at the ceiling.

This charismatic speaker seems dynamic and likable.

What if listeners are straining forward in their seats? This suggests they may not be able to hear you. You may have to increase the loudness of your voice and raise the energy level of your presentation. What if they look puzzled? You may need to provide an example to clarify your point. What if they are frowning or shaking their heads? Offer additional evidence to convince them.

On the other hand, suppose they are smiling and nodding in agreement. You are on the right track! Sometimes you will sense that listeners are so caught up in what you are saying that you know you are getting through to them. That's the moment when you know you are finding your voice! We discuss feedback further in Chapter 12.

These seven elements—speaker, message, channel, interference, setting, audience, and feedback—all interact in the adventure of public speaking. Figure 1.2, Speech as an Interactive Process, offers a visual model of the interplay of these elements.

▶ **feedback**   Speaker's perception of audience reactions to the message.

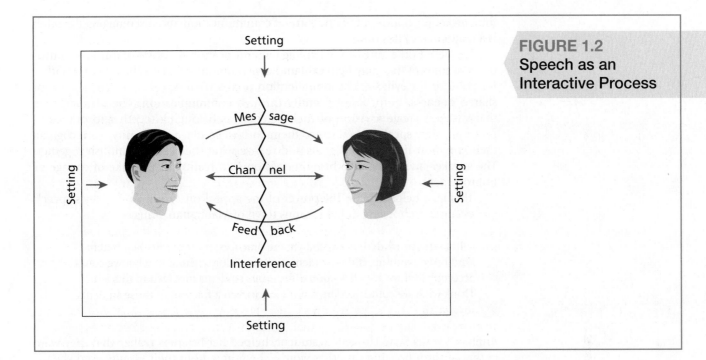

FIGURE 1.2
Speech as an Interactive Process

Communication as a Dynamic Process. Communication is dynamic as well as interactive. That is, communication can *change* the people who interact in it—speakers, listeners, and the community they form.

The concept of communication as dynamic is largely ethical in its impact. It suggests that people can be enlarged and enhanced by communication that informs them, makes them wiser, touches their humanity, and thus appeals to what Lincoln called "the better angels of our nature." Plato painted a classic vision of such communication in the *Phaedrus*. On the other hand, people can be diminished and degraded by communication that deceives them, arouses irrelevant passions, and reinforces a view once offered by Alexander Hamilton in an argument with Thomas Jefferson: "Your people, Sir, is nothing but a great beast." Plato depicts such communication in

FINDING YOUR

voice   Communication as Interaction

Attend a scheduled speaking event on campus, and observe the interaction of the seven elements discussed above and illustrated in the model. Was the speaker sensitive to the interplay of these elements? Did the message seem to come through without distortion? Did the speaker respond to feedback? Might the communication process have been improved? If so, how?

the *Gorgias*. Encouraging the one form of communication and discouraging the other is a major aim of this book.

Kenneth Burke, one of the leading communication theorists of our time, introduced a concept that may help explain how communication can be dynamic, either for good or for evil. Burke's **identification** occurs when speakers create a sense of shared oneness, purpose, or identity through communication. The idea suggests that speakers create a vision of their listeners as belonging together to one community.[14] The speaker then urges them to *become* that community, to recognize their common interests and goals and realize what they can accomplish together. The speaker invites them to bring the vision into reality for the sake of change or improvement.

This idea helps explain the power of the appeal offered in Anna Aley's speech protesting slum housing in her campus town of Manhattan, Kansas:

> What can one student do to change the practices of numerous Manhattan landlords? Nothing, if that student is alone. But just think of what we could accomplish if we got all 13,600 off-campus students involved in this issue! Think what we could accomplish if we got even a fraction of those students involved!

Anna, a Kansas State University student, helped her listeners realize that they were *victims* of slum housing. In other words, she pointed out their *identity*. And she offered a new, dynamic vision of themselves acting together to correct these abuses. (See Anna Aley's complete speech in Appendix B.)

Identification also helps explain the power of public speaking on the wider stage of public affairs. When Martin Luther King, Jr., strove to change racial practices in America, he offered a redress for the legacy of humiliation and segregation that continued to divide Americans. In his celebrated speech, "I Have a Dream," King offered a vision of brotherhood and sisterhood to bring the nation together.[15] As his leadership emerged, King's own image seemed to grow and expand. His followers also became heroic figures as they marched through one ordeal after another. These transformations indicate how people can grow and enlarge when they interact in ethical communication that inspires and encourages them.

What Public Speaking Asks of You

Watch at MyCommunicationLab Video: "The Ethics of Deception"

Explore at MyCommunicationLab Activity: "Ethical Speaking"

A course that offers so much requires a great deal in return. It asks that you make a serious commitment of time and dedication to finding your voice as a speaker. It asks also that you respect **public speaking ethics**, standards that determine the rightness or wrongness of public communication behaviors, in both your speaking and your listening. The National Communication Association in its "Credo for Ethical Communication" offers a list of principles that may guide you (see Figure 1.3).

Moral issues can arise in every phase of speech-making, from selecting the topic to making the actual presentation. For this reason, you will encounter situation-grounded discussions and "Your Ethical Voice" features throughout this text. In this final section, we discuss two major considerations that underlie ethical public speaking: respect for the integrity of ideas and information and a genuine concern for consequences.

▶ **identification** The feeling of closeness between speakers and listeners that may overcome personal and cultural differences.

▶ **public speaking ethics** Standards for judging the rightness or wrongness of public speaking behaviors.

Questions of right and wrong arise whenever people communicate. Ethical communication is fundamental to responsible thinking, decision making, and the development of relationships and communities within and across contexts, cultures, channels, and media. Moreover, ethical communication enhances human worth and dignity by fostering truthfulness, fairness, responsibility, personal integrity, and respect for self and others. We believe that unethical communication threatens the quality of all communication and consequently the well-being of individuals and the society in which we live. Therefore we, the members of the National Communication Association, endorse and are committed to practicing the following principles of ethical communication.

- We advocate truthfulness, accuracy, honesty, and reason as essential to the integrity of communication.

- We endorse freedom of expression, diversity of perspective, and tolerance of dissent to achieve the informed and responsible decision making fundamental to a civil society.

- We strive to understand and respect other communicators before evaluating and responding to their messages.

- We promote access to communication resources and opportunities as necessary to fulfill human potential and contribute to the well-being of families, communities, and society.

- We promote communication climates of caring and mutual understanding that respect the unique needs and characteristics of individual communicators.

- We condemn communication that degrades individuals and humanity through distortion, intimidation, coercion, and violence and through the expression of intolerance and hatred.

- We are committed to the courageous expression of personal convictions in pursuit of fairness and justice.

- We advocate sharing information, opinions, and feelings when facing significant choices while also respecting privacy and confidentiality.

- We accept responsibility for the short- and long-term consequences for our own communication and expect the same of others.[16]

FIGURE 1.3
Credo for Ethical Communication

Respect for the Integrity of Ideas and Information

In an age when misinformation and outright lies often circulate unchallenged on the Internet, when passion and prejudice—loudly asserted—too often take the place of sound reasoning, and when people may "tweet" more than they think, it is good to remind ourselves that respect for the integrity of ideas and information is a basic principle of ethical communication. This respect requires that you speak from responsible knowledge, use communication techniques carefully, and avoid academic dishonesty.

Speaking from Responsible Knowledge   No one expects you to become an expert on the topics you speak about in class. You will, however, be expected to speak from **responsible knowledge**. As we discuss in detail in Chapter 7, responsible knowledge of topics includes

- knowing main points of concern about your topic.
- understanding what experts say about it.
- acknowledging differing points of view on controversial topics and giving these due respect.
- being aware of recent events or discoveries concerning your topic.
- realizing how what you say might affect the lives of listeners.

In short, responsible knowledge is an advanced state of awareness concerning a topic. It is the goal of sound speech preparation.

Consider how student Stephen Huff acquired responsible knowledge for an informative speech. Stephen knew little about earthquakes before his speech, but he knew that Memphis was located on the New Madrid fault and that this could mean trouble. He also knew that there was an earthquake research center on campus.

Stephen arranged for an interview with the center's director. During the interview, he asked a series of well-planned questions: Where was the New Madrid fault, and what was the history of its activity? What was the probability of a major quake in the near future? How prepared was Memphis for a major quake? What kind of damage could result? How could listeners prepare for it? What readings would the expert recommend?

All these questions were designed to gain knowledge that would interest and benefit his listeners. Armed with what he had learned, Stephen went online and then to the library, where he found other valuable sources of information. He was well on his way to speaking from responsible knowledge.

Using Communication Techniques Carefully.

Unethical speakers can misuse valuable techniques for communicating ideas and information in order to confuse listeners or to hide a private agenda. Consider, for instance, **quoting out of context**. In Chapter 8, we encourage you to cite experts and respected authorities to support important and controversial assertions. However, this technique is corrupted when speakers twist the meanings of such statements to support their own views and to endorse positions these respected persons would never have accepted.

Speakers sometimes invoke Martin Luther King's "dream" of a color-blind society to roll back reforms that he helped to inspire. In his "I Have a Dream" speech, for example, King offered his vision of a world in which we would judge people by their character and not by their color. A governor used King's dream to explain why he was appointing only white men to the board running the university system in his state. A theater critic in New York invoked the vision to condemn the formation of black theatrical companies.[17] These people applied King's words out of the context of his speech, if not of his life, to defeat his actual purpose.

Throughout this text, we warn you in specific situations how evidence, reasoning, language, humor, visual aids, and other powerful communication techniques can be abused to deceive audiences and undermine constructive communication.

Avoiding Academic Dishonesty.

In the public speaking classroom, the most disheartening form of academic dishonesty is **plagiarism**, presenting the ideas or

---

▶ **responsible knowledge** An advanced state of awareness concerning a topic, understanding its major features, issues, latest developments, and local applications.

▶ **quoting out of context** An unethical use of a quotation that changes or distorts its original meaning.

▶ **plagiarism** Presenting the ideas and words of others as though they were your own.

words of others as though they were your own[18] Plagiarism mutates into specific forms of intellectual abuse, such as "parroting" an article or speech from a newspaper, magazine, or Internet site without crediting the source in your speech. In effect, you offer the work as though it were your own creation. Another corrupt form is "patchwork plagiarism," cutting passages from multiple sources and splicing them together as though they were one speech, *your* speech. Then there is a kind of "social plagiarism," in which students collude to produce one speech, which is then presented in different sections of the public speaking course.

There are many good reasons for you to avoid such behaviors. Most colleges and universities regard plagiarism as *a threat to the integrity of higher education* and stipulate penalties ranging from a major grade reduction to suspension or even expulsion from the university. You can probably find your university's policy in your student handbook or on your college website. Your communication department or instructor may have additional rules regarding academic dishonesty.

Another reason to avoid plagiarism in its various forms is the good possibility that *you will get caught.* Instructors are better at spotting academic dishonesty than students may think. Many departments keep files of speeches and speech outlines, instructors do talk to each other, and there are online resources that instructors can use for looking up "stock" speeches that have been lifted from the Internet. Professional associations are constantly updating speech instructors on how to detect plagiarism.[19]

An even better reason for avoiding plagiarism is that it is an *intellectual crime,* the theft and/or abuse of other people's ideas. Just as you would not steal the physical property of others, you should not steal the creative products of their minds. If you credit the thinking of others in your speech by citing your sources honestly, you honor them and at the same time build your credibility. If you plagiarize, you abuse them and convict yourself of a deep character flaw.

YOUR ethical VOICE   Avoiding Plagiarism

Avoiding plagiarism is a matter of faith among you, your instructor, and your classmates. Be especially alert to the following:

1. Don't present or summarize someone else's speech, article, or essay as though it were your own.

2. Draw information and ideas from a variety of sources; then interpret them to create your own point of view.

3. Don't parrot other people's language and ideas as though they were your own.

4. Always provide oral citations for direct quotations, paraphrased material, or especially striking language, letting listeners know who said the words, where, and when.

5. Credit those who originate ideas as you introduce their statements in your speech: "Studs Terkel has said that a book about work 'is, by its very nature, about violence—to the spirit as well as the body.'"

6. Allow yourself enough time to research and prepare your presentation responsibly.

7. Take careful notes as you do your research so that you don't later confuse your own thoughts and words with those of others.

The most compelling reason for avoiding plagiarism is that *you are cheating yourself*. The plagiarized voice is a fraud. When you plagiarize, you give up your search for your authentic voice and prevent yourself from growing into the communicator you might have become. When you do not prepare your own work, you likely will not speak very well anyway. You end up compromising all the benefits we have described.

So don't plagiarize!

A Genuine Concern for Consequences

Finding your voice also means developing concern for those who listen to you. You become more aware of how your words can impact the lives of your audience.

We have at present a crisis of civility in public communication. Robust and spirited debate of ideas is an ideal of democracy, but negative practices such as the verbal abuse of opponents and heckling that drowns out other voices are democracy's nightmare. In such an age, we personally need to set a high standard of honorable communication practices. In a world of increasing incivility, we must preserve and protect the goal of informed and rational decision making made possible only by open, tolerant, and respectful discussion of ideas.[20]

FINDING YOUR

voice
Becoming a Critic of Public Speaking

"Finding Your Voice: The Story of Your Quest" (p. 5) suggests that you keep a diary in which you describe your experiences as you find your voice. Add speech evaluation to your diary by commenting on effective and ineffective, ethical and unethical speeches as you hear them both in and out of class, whether through local and national media, on YouTube, or from other sources. As you listen to speeches, ask yourself these questions:

1. Was the speaker credible?
2. Was the speech well adapted to listeners' needs and interests?
3. Did the speech take into account the cultural makeup of its audience?
4. Was the message clear and well structured?
5. Were the language and presentation effective?
6. How did listeners respond, both during and after the speech?
7. Did the setting have any impact on the message?
8. Did the speech have to overcome any interference problems?
9. Did the speech promote identification between speaker and listeners?
10. Did the speaker demonstrate responsible knowledge and an ethical use of communication techniques?
11. Did the audience members meet their responsibilities as listeners?

FINAL reflections   A Quest That Deserves Commitment

Paleontologists tell us that a dramatic moment in the story of human evolution occurred several hundred thousand years ago when our early ancestors developed the capacity for speech. It is interesting to consider that each of us—as we discover our voices through preparation, practice, and ultimate success in presentation—replicates in miniature the experience of our species as humans discovered their voices and the incredible power of communication.

In some of us, this experience can be quite dramatic. In his biography of President Lyndon Johnson, Robert Caro tells the story of Johnson's mother, who taught communication skills to isolated Hill Country children, and of Johnson's cousin, Ava, who studied public speaking with her. When Mrs. Johnson began assigning speech topics, Ava recalls,

> I said "I just can't do it, Aunt Rebekah." And she said, "Oh, yes, you can. There's nothing impossible if you put the mind to it. I know you have the ability to deliver a speech." And I cried, and I said, "I just can't do it!" Aunt Rebekah said, "Oh, yes, you can." And she never let up, never let up. Never. Boosting me along, telling me I could do it. She taught me speaking and elocution, and I went to the state championships with it, and I won a medal, a gold medal, in competitions involving the whole state. I owe her a debt that I can never repay. She made me know that I could do what I never thought I could do.[21]

Our hope for you is that you win your own gold medal, whatever form it may take, as you find your voice as a public speaker.

After Reading This Chapter, You Should Be Able To Answer These Questions

1 What are the three levels of meaning involved in "finding your voice"?

2 What is ethnocentrism?

3 What are the three major forms of public speaking and the three main kinds of appeals named by Aristotle?

4 What seven elements are central to the nature of public speaking as an interactive process?

5 How are identification and community related?

6 How can a speaker meet the challenge of responsible knowledge?

7 What is plagiarism, and why should it be avoided?

Study and **Review** at **MyCommunicationLab**

For Discussion and Further Exploration

1 What personal and social benefits may be lost to societies that do not encourage the free and open exchange of ideas? To prepare for this discussion, read online John Stuart Mills' classic treatise, *On Liberty*. See especially his Chapter II: "Of the Liberty of Thought and Discussion."

2 Communication has been likened to, among other things, a game, a dance, a battle, and a difficult climb over barriers. Which analogy do you prefer, and why? Do the analogies people prefer reveal something about them?

3 Look for evidence of ethnocentrism in the "Letters to the Editor" section of the local newspaper or in a blog or website over a week's time. Bring what you find to class. Be prepared to defend your findings.

4 Identify film or television characters that stereotype race, ethnicity, or gender. What is accurate and inaccurate in these stereotypes? Might they be damaging if applied to individuals? Have others ever stereotyped you? How did you feel about that? ESL students: Are citizens of the United States stereotyped in your cultures?

5 Is it better to think of American culture as a "bouillabaisse" or "chorus" rather than as a "melting pot"? Can you think of other ways of expressing American identity? What are the strengths and weaknesses of these various perspectives?

6 Bring to class advertisements that illustrate ethical problems in communication. Do the ads make outlandish claims that they fail to prove? Do they make use of demeaning stereotypes?

7 As you read the "Credo for Ethical Communication" on page 15, think of situations in which one or more of these principles may have been threatened or violated. What keeps these principles from being observed and respected more widely?

8 Choose a recent "freedom of speech" controversy from the following options: (1) allowing cartoons, films, and books to depict the Prophet Muhammad; (2) "reforming" the Internet in order to protect children from pornography; (3) allowing "hate groups" such as the neo-Nazis or the KKK to stage public rallies; (4) permitting religious expression in public schools; (5) publishing university "speech codes" that regulate on-campus expression; (6) amending the Constitution to ban flag burning; and (7) restricting freedom of speech in times of war. Research your chosen issue, and identify the major arguments involved in this controversy, both pro and con. Which of these arguments do you find most persuasive, and why?

9 The social media have provided numerous new forms of communication, both private and public. How are these similar to and different from traditional public speaking as it is defined here? In your answer, be sure to consider the following qualities:

- The spoken aspects of the message
- The extent to which the message has been carefully designed and prepared
- Whether the message has been tuned for face-to-face presentation to a particular audience
- The size of the audience
- Whether speaker and listeners have distinct, separate roles in the communication process
- Whether body language plays a role in the delivery of a message
- The form of feedback, whether it is instantaneous or delayed

2 Managing Your Fear of Speaking

((• Listen to **Chapter 2** at **MyCommunicationLab**

> *Bravery is being the only one who knows you're afraid.*
> —DAVID HACKWORTH

Betsy Lyles enjoyed success in her public speaking class at Davidson College. After completing the class, she became a Speaking Center tutor, helping other student speakers. Clearly, Betsy never suffered from communication anxiety, right? Listen to her story:

I felt like I was experienced with public speaking—I had given speeches in high school and had lots of experience reading the lectionary at church. I normally heard positive responses from people about my public speaking; however, standing up to give my first COM 101 speech made me realize that my prior experience didn't mean I was immune to anxiety. When I stood up to give my first speech, I wanted to look confident, but my face was red, my body felt hot, and I began to fidget. I was less than graceful to say the least! It was a problem for me because I didn't want to think of myself as a poor public speaker. I wanted to begin with a high standard for myself and get better from there.

For my next speech, I knew I had to do something to counteract the apprehension. One of the most noticeable things I did was pin my hair back so I couldn't fidget or mess with it. Seems simple I know, but it's amazing how much an ethos can be helped by none other than not twirling hair! Also, I volunteered to make the first presentation (this became what I did for every speech I gave). It helped me to come to class with the mindset that the first thing I would be doing was presenting. I found that when I sat around or listened to other speeches, I made myself nervous when I didn't need to be. As I grew comfortable with the class, I felt like I gained control of my anxiety.

Betsy's struggles with **communication anxiety** suggest that apprehensive speakers are not alone. Most undergraduates are nervous when they have to speak to a class. International students and those from marginalized groups often have a great deal of apprehension. Students who work toward overcoming this problem are on the way to finding their voices.

Many well-known people also have problems when in front of an audience. Athletes may experience anxiety before or during a competition. Sometimes they control this through rituals such as bouncing a ball three times before attempting a free throw or crossing themselves before kicking a field goal.[1] The best athletes learn to channel their nervousness into positive energy. For example, Joe Montana, the legendary San Francisco 49ers quarterback who led his team to four Super Bowl

Explore at **MyCommunicationLab** **Activity:** "Willingness to Communicate"

▶ **communication anxiety** Those unpleasant feelings and fears you may experience before or during a presentation.

championships, noted, "Nerves are good. I want to be nervous. If you don't care, I hope you're on the other side."[2]

Actors and musicians often have similar problems. Kim Basinger had intense communication anxiety that she had to work hard to overcome. She narrated the HBO film *Panic: A Film About Coping,* which features her struggles with this problem.[3] Elvis Presley had similar problems. He noted, "I've never gotten over what they call stage fright. I go through it every show."[4]

Your speech instructor may even have some communication anxiety, but you probably won't be able to detect it. Even your authors have experienced this problem. Here is our story:

> As college professors and authors, we have done a lot of speaking both in and out of the classroom. Being the authors of a public speaking text puts special pressure on us. When you earn your bread and butter by telling others how to do something, they expect you to be able to do it yourself—and do it much better than most other people. Even with all our experience, every time we speak to a new group—a college class, a community meeting, or colleagues at conventions—we feel this pressure.

Still think that everyone else is more confident than you are? The late Edward R. Murrow, a famous radio and television commentator, once said, "The best speakers know enough to be scared. . . . The only difference between the pros and the novices is that the pros have trained the butterflies to fly in formation."[5]

The first step in controlling communication anxiety is understanding it. The second step is learning to manage it. Our goal is not to rid you of communication anxiety but to help you control your butterflies. Channeling your nervous energy into something constructive will help you find your voice. Communication anxiety shows up in many speaking situations. Figure 2.1 illustrates which situations are typically most problematic.

Many celebrities have problems with communication anxiety.

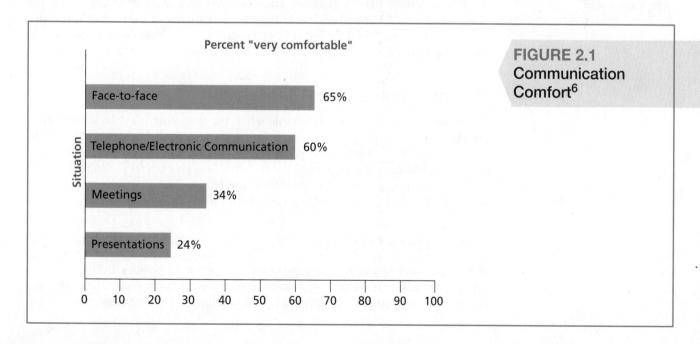

FIGURE 2.1
Communication Comfort[6]

Percent "very comfortable"

Situation	Percent
Face-to-face	65%
Telephone/Electronic Communication	60%
Meetings	34%
Presentations	24%

Understanding Communication Anxiety

On the day of your first presentation, you sit waiting for your turn to speak. You are not really listening to the speeches before yours because you feel worried. You hear your name called. Your stomach drops. Your hands start to sweat. Your heart races. Your ears feel hot. Your mouth feels dry. You plod to the podium and look up at the audience. Your knees start to shake. You grab the lectern for support.

Any of these symptoms sound familiar? Most likely, you may have some of these symptoms—not *all* of them, but some of them. If you didn't, you wouldn't be normal. *Remember, a little bit of nervousness is a good thing.* It can help you "psych up" for your presentation. You can learn to channel your nervousness into positive energy that enlivens your presentation.

About now you may be thinking, "Okay, so I'm not alone, but I'm still uptight." What is causing this problem and what can I do about it?

An Unfamiliar Situation

Almost everybody is somewhat ill at ease in unfamiliar situations, and addressing a large number of people is not an everyday event for most of us.[7] Fortunately, as you become more familiar with a situation, your anxiety will become less debilitating. What steps can you take to increase the familiarity of a situation? Practice your speech before a group of friends. If you can arrange it, practice in the room where you will give your speech. If your computer has a video camera, tape yourself practicing your speech. Let it rest, view it, and then tape yourself again. Can you see the improvement? Be patient with yourself. You will become more confident as the class progresses.

If you would like to evaluate your own communication anxiety, take the "Evaluating Your Public Speaking Anxiety" questionnaire at the end of this chapter. You may be surprised to find that you didn't score as high on this scale as you thought you might.

The Importance of the Occasion

People also tend to feel uncomfortable when the stakes are high. In school, most presentations (in this class and others) are graded. Outside the classroom, public speaking may have personal or professional consequences. To help reduce such discomfort related to the importance of the situation, give yourself plenty of time to prepare your speech. Don't wait until the night before your presentation to prepare your speech. The better prepared you are, the more confident you will be.

The Power of Negative Thinking

How often have you heard the expression "the power of positive thinking." Well, negative thinking can be powerful, too—in the opposite direction! One of the major causes of communication anxiety is that you have the wrong movie running in

FINDING YOUR voice   What Makes Me Afraid?

List the major fears that may make you afraid of giving a speech. Complete the sentence "I'm afraid that . . ." or "I'm afraid because . . . ." As you read this chapter, go over your list, and classify each of these fears as rational or irrational; then develop a plan to counter them, based on the techniques described here. Which of these techniques proves most and least useful in controlling your fears?

your head. You're playing and replaying *Titanic* when you should be playing *It's a Wonderful Life.* Your personal catastrophe film may include such scenes as these:

I'll be so scared I'll pass out.

I'll embarrass myself.

My mind will go blank.

I won't be able to finish my speech.

I'll shake so much my classmates will laugh at me.

Listeners are waiting to pounce on my mistakes.

I'm going to fail this class if my speeches aren't perfect.

If you run this movie through your head enough times, you are going to start accepting it as inevitable. Thinking that it's real can make it real for you. Psychologists call such scripts "suicidal predictions" (related to self-fulfilling prophecies) that literally bring about what you fear most. Dwelling on possible but highly improbable catastrophes may lead to self-defeating behaviors such as

- putting off registering for the course until you have no other option.

- registering for the course and dropping it before you attend.

- starting to attend the class and then dropping the course.

- failing to show up the day you are scheduled to speak.

- putting off preparation until the night before your speech.

- repeatedly asking your instructor to reschedule your speech for a later date.

Managing Your Communication Anxiety

You've probably heard a lot of advice about how to control communication anxiety. For example, someone may have told you to picture the audience sitting there naked (distracting advice at best!). Another pearl of wisdom is to take a really deep

Explore at **MyCommunicationLab** **Activity:** "Overcoming Nervousness"

breath each time you feel yourself getting anxious. Or—and this is probably the worst advice we've heard—cut back on your preparation because the more you prepare, the more anxious you will be. As one expert suggests, this becomes a vicious circle: If anxious people prepare less, their anxiety will increase because they don't feel well prepared.[8] People who offer such wisdom may mean well, but such quick-fix techniques usually don't work.

You also may have been told that taking a public speaking class will cure you of your communication anxiety. *There is no cure for communication anxiety, but there are ways to help you control it.* The techniques we discuss in this chapter do help, and they work best when used in combination. Start with one technique and move on to another until you find what helps you the most. The techniques that we will consider are reality testing, cognitive restructuring, selective relaxation, attitude adjustment, and visualization.

Reality Testing

Remember that disaster movie running in your head? When you engage in **reality testing**, you subject its negative aspects to rational scrutiny. To see things realistically you have to step back from your emotions and look for answers to three basic questions:

1. What has actually happened in the past?
2. What is the worst thing that might happen?
3. How bad would it be if it did happen?

For example, suppose one of the fears is "I'll be so scared I'll pass out." Have you ever passed out from fear? Is this likely to happen? How bad would this be? What would be the consequences? Let's reality test some of the other possible scenes in your personal horror film.

I'll Embarrass Myself.   What can you possibly do in a speech that would be all that embarrassing? Little blunders do not make a catastrophe. Save being embarrassed for the truly ludicrous things in your life. And keep in mind that you will survive even those.

The first class one of your authors taught was held in a large auditorium. While she was monitoring a test one day, a student asked her to cut off the noisy air conditioners. She shut off the air conditioner on one side of the stage and was walking across to the other side, not looking where she was going, and tripped over the base of the free-standing chalkboard, falling flat on her face in front of 250 students.

Now, that's embarrassing! To her amazement, no one was laughing. In her students' faces, she could see concern. She picked herself up, brushed the dirt off her clothes, and muttered something like "Grace is my middle name!" To her surprise, the sun rose as usual the next morning. And regardless of how embarrassed she had felt, she had to show up to teach the next class.

My Mind Will Go Blank.   Most of us can remember a time when we memorized a passage to recite in class—the Gettysburg Address, a scene from Shakespeare, or a poem—and drew a blank about halfway through our performance.

Having your mind go blank is one of the major pitfalls of memorized presentations. That is why most classroom speeches are presented extemporaneously:

▶ **reality testing**   Subjecting negative messages you send yourself to rational scrutiny.

prepared and practiced but not memorized. And if by chance you do forget what you were going to say next, repeat what you just said in different words. Audiences expect summaries in speeches, and going back over your material usually can help get you back on track.

I Won't Be Able to Finish My Speech.

On very, very rare occasions, a speaker may experience a panic attack. Let's say this happens to you. You're presenting your speech, and everything is going well when you suddenly feel overwhelmed with fear for no apparent reason. Not only are you afraid, but also you realize that your fear is irrational and you think maybe you're "losing it." All you want to do is run for the door.

We once had a student who had such a problem:

During Beverly's first presentation, she bolted from the room in the middle of her speech to try to compose herself. While she was out of the room, we discussed with the class how we might help her. She came to our office after the speech, and we encouraged her to focus on her message and her audience. Her second effort was a little better. She stopped during her presentation to try to pull herself together, but she managed to finish without leaving the room. Her third speech was a totally different story.

Beverly worked during the day as a dispatcher for a major interstate trucking firm. Her persuasive speech urged her classmates to lobby their congressional representatives to vote for a pending truck safety bill. This topic was very important to her. Her speech was filled with interesting examples of near catastrophes that this legislation would make less likely. She knew her topic. She knew it was important. She really cared about it. Consequently, she got so caught up with what she was talking about that she forgot to be anxious. The audience was spellbound. When she finished, there was a moment of silence while it all sank in; then there was spontaneous applause—applause for a good speech well presented and applause for a speaker who had conquered her personal demons. She had become other-centered and message-centered. Beverly came up to us after the class and asked if there was an advanced public speaking class she could take. She had found her voice by overcoming her anxieties and speaking on a topic of importance to her. She felt better about herself because of it.

If you feel a panic attack coming on, take comfort in knowing that such an attack seldom lasts more than a few seconds (although it may feel like it's going on for hours). Keep talking. Look for friendly faces in the room, and direct your words to those listeners. Accept your fear for what it is—a temporary aberration. Chances are it will never happen again.

I'll Shake So Much My Classmates Will Laugh at Me.

You may worry that everyone in the audience will know how nervous you are. Actually, most listeners won't know this unless you tell them. They are not clairvoyant!

We once had a student tape a presentation for us. She got through the first half of her speech quite well but then stopped and said she couldn't finish; she was too nervous. We would show this speech in class, stopping it right before she quit. When we asked the class how nervous she was, they would respond with statements like, "She's quite comfortable" or "She's not really nervous at all." When we turned the player back on and they saw her stopping, they were all quite surprised.

Even if your hands are trembling or your leg is twitching, is this all that bad? If listeners do notice, what will they think? That you're incompetent? Or that you— like them—are somewhat uncomfortable in front of a group? If you think you are prone to trembling, plan some purposeful activity such as gesturing or walking closer to the audience. Integrate a presentation aid into your speech. As you point out the features of a model or refer to the figures in a chart, you give yourself a positive way to work off some tension.

Listeners Are Waiting to Pounce on My Mistakes. You may picture your listeners as predators lying in wait, ready to pounce on any little mistake and eager to make fun of you like middle school kids. In reality, most audiences want speakers to succeed. This is especially true in the college classroom. If you see someone frowning, that listener is more likely worried about a personal problem, an upcoming test, or his or her own presentation. Don't second-guess your audience!

I'm Going to Fail This Class If My Speeches Aren't Perfect. As a beginning speaker, you may believe that your speech has to be perfect for it to be effective. No presentation is ever perfect. If you look at the speech evaluation forms that may be used in your class, you probably won't see perfection anywhere in the criteria. It's all right if you make a few mistakes—if you flub a word or leave out something you meant to include. Your listeners probably won't even notice these flaws unless you call attention to them. It's fine to want to do your best, but cut yourself some slack.

Cognitive Restructuring

Cognitive restructuring goes hand in hand with reality testing. Because the disaster scenario in your head sends you negative messages about your ability to present an effective speech, you need to consciously change these messages to their positive, more constructive counterparts. Psychologists call this **cognitive restructuring**. Positive messages can help boost your self-confidence.

To practice cognitive restructuring, begin by making a list of the irrational negative messages that you are sending yourself. Write these out in full, and then determine their positive counterparts. For example, instead of telling yourself "I'm going to sound stupid," say, "I've done my research and I'm going to sound knowledgeable." Replace "Everyone else is more confident than I am" with "I am as confident as anyone in this class." For "I really don't want to give this speech," try "This is my chance to share my ideas with the class." Use these positive messages as a pep talk to yourself. Figure 2.2 provides suggestions for how to cope with your concerns about communication apprehension.

Selective Relaxation

Another technique for handling your anxiety is the art of **selective relaxation**. Begin practicing this technique well before your first speech. Practice relaxing several times a day until it becomes second nature to relax on cue. Follow the sequence outlined here:

1. Find a quiet place where you can be by yourself. Sit in a comfortable chair or lie down, close your eyes, and breathe deeply, in through your nose and out through your mouth. You should feel yourself beginning to relax.

▶ **cognitive restructuring** Replacing negative thoughts with positive, constructive ones.

▶ **selective relaxation** Practicing muscle control techniques to help you reduce physical tension by relaxing on cue.

Concerned About . . .	Try This . . .	FIGURE 2.2 **Coping with Your Concerns**
Unfamiliarity of the situation?	Practice before an audience	
Importance of the occasion?	Prepare well in advance	
Afraid you'll be scared?	Remember you'll be "psyched up"	
Embarrassing yourself?	Don't sweat the little things	
Drawing a blank?	Paraphrase what you just said	
Won't be able to finish?	Keep talking, look for a friendly face	
I'll shake uncontrollably?	Use gestures and purposeful movement	
Predatory listeners?	Classmates want you to succeed	
I'll fail if my speech isn't perfect?	No speech is perfect, cut yourself some slack	

2. Once you feel yourself relaxing, begin slowly repeating a positive cue word, such as *yes*, each time you exhale. Let your mind drift freely. You should soon feel quite relaxed.

3. While you are relaxed and breathing deeply, tense and relax different muscle groups. Begin by tensing your feet and legs: Curl your toes, tighten your calves, lock your knees, and contract your thigh muscles. Hold this tension for several seconds, and think about how it feels. Not very comfortable, is it?

4. Concentrate on breathing deeply again, saying your special word, and feeling yourself relax.

5. Now, repeat steps 1 through 4, moving the focus of tensing and relaxing through your body: Move it first to your abdominal muscles, then to your hand and arm muscles, and finally to your neck and head muscles. After you have done this a number of times, simply repeating your selected word should trigger a relaxation response.

One good thing about this exercise is that once you have mastered the technique, you can practice it unnoticed in many situations. While you are sitting in class waiting to speak, tense your feet and leg muscles; then relax them. If you find yourself getting nervous while you are speaking, say your cue word to yourself. The word alone may be enough to help you relax and return your concentration to your message. If this technique doesn't work as well as you would like, try tensing and relaxing a hand as you speak. (Just be sure it's down at your side where it can't be seen.)

Attitude Adjustments

If you look over the scenes from your catastrophe movie about giving a speech, you'll find that most of them begin with "I." You think things like "I'm going to

---

FIGURE 2.3
Practicing Positive Thinking

Negative thoughts . . .	Constructive alternatives . . .
I really don't want to give this speech.	This is my chance to offer my ideas to others.
I'm the only one who is nervous.	Other students are just as nervous as I am.
My speech is going to be boring.	I have good examples and stories to liven up my speech.
I'm not an expert on my topic.	I've done enough research to be knowledgeable about my topic.
I know I'm going to blow it.	I'm ready and I'm going to do a good job.

---

really screw this up" or "I'll never remember what I want to say." You are focusing on yourself and not your message. You should make **attitude adjustments** to help you become more audience- and message-centered. Figure 2.3 suggests a variety of ways that you can practice positive thinking.

As you prepare and practice your speech, keep your audience in mind. What can I give to my listeners? How can I help them understand this issue? To help you focus on your message, choose a meaningful topic that you can get excited about. Learn all you can about the topic so that you have something of value to give to your listeners.

SPEAKER'S notes   Techniques for Handling Communication Anxiety

1. Reality testing helps you apply rational thinking to negative ideas.

2. Cognitive restructuring changes negative self-messages to more positive ones.

3. Selective relaxation reduces tension by training you to relax on cue.

4. Attitude adjustments help you focus on your listeners and your message.

5. Visualization puts a positive script in your mind.

Visualization

Early on the morning of October 9, 2009, President Barack Obama was awakened with the news that he had won the Nobel Peace Prize. He was scheduled to make a presentation from the Rose Garden at about 11 that morning. He didn't have much

▶ **attitude adjustment**   Shifting your focus from yourself to your listeners and message.

time to prepare his remarks acknowledging the award. CNN coverage was set up before he appeared to speak. In the time leading up to his speech, the television cameras zoomed in on the window where he was putting the finishing touches on his remarks and getting ready to deliver them. His head would bend down, presumably as he was looking at his manuscript; then it would rise up, and his eyes would close in contemplation of what he was going to say. He was visualizing his presentation. Clearly, **visualization** is not simply a tool for the communication apprehensive but also a vital part of speech preparation.

Musicians and athletes also use visualization to prepare for success.[9] Watch a basketball player preparing for a free throw; watch a football player getting ready to kick a field goal; watch a singer on *American Idol* just before she begins a song. Chances are all of these people are visualizing themselves succeeding.

You can help control your communication anxiety by visualizing yourself as a successful speaker.[10] As you prepare your visualization script, you will be rewriting the movie that has been playing in your head, moving from a disaster to a feel-good film. Begin by going through your horror movie and writing down the negative messages you are sending yourself. Do a reality check on these messages, asking yourself how likely they are to happen and what the consequences would be if they did. Restructure these messages into their positive counterparts. Use these new messages to develop your visualization script, keeping in mind that you want to be concerned mainly about reaching your listeners with a message that you communicate effectively and enthusiastically.

A sample visualization script might read as follows:

> I am walking to the podium in a self-assured manner. I pause and look at my audience, identifying friendly, receptive listeners. I begin with my well-prepared and practiced introduction to my speech. This good start increases my self-confidence. During my speech I concentrate on my message. I make and maintain eye contact with my audience. I look for feedback from them to tell me if they are remaining interested and if they seem to understand what I am saying. I grow in confidence as I speak. I deliver my well-prepared and well-practiced conclusion, knowing that I have done well on my speech.

Now write your own visualization script. As you write it, picture it as it will happen on the day of your speech. Take this glowing image of success with you as you enter the classroom on the day of your speech.

Putting It All Together

Think back to a time in your childhood when you acquired a new skill. It might have been learning to swim or to ride a bicycle. The more you learned and the more you practiced, the more confident you became. The more confident you became, the less afraid you were. Before too long, you were jumping into the deep end of the pool without hesitation or riding without training wheels.

The same type of learning relationship exists among knowledge, practice, confidence, and public speaking. When you learn how to prepare a speech and have practiced your presentation, you will feel more confident and have less apprehension.

Athletes often use visualization as a means of preparing for success.

▶ **visualization** Systematically picturing yourself succeeding as a speaker and practicing your speech with that image in mind.

Keep in mind that practicing is an important part of your preparation. Highly anxious students often spend a lot of time researching and organizing their speeches, but then they don't spend enough time actually practicing their presentations.[11] So practice, and then practice some more. The more you master the presentation of your message, the more confident you will be.

A final word of advice: When you rise to speak, *act confident* even if you may not feel that way. Walk briskly to the front of the room, look at your audience, and establish eye contact. Unless you are speaking on a very grim topic, smile at your listeners. Whatever happens during your speech, remember that your listeners cannot see or hear what's happening inside you. They know only what you show and tell them. Show them a poised speaker presenting a well-researched speech. Maintain eye contact for a short time, and then walk confidently back to your seat. Even though you may feel relieved that your speech is over, don't say, "Whew!" or "I made it!" And never act disappointed with your presentation. You probably did better than you thought.

Watch at **MyCommunicationLab**
Video: "Fear of Public Speaking"

SPEAKER'S notes   Ten Ways to Control Communication Anxiety

1. Select a topic that excites you.
2. Carefully research and organize your message.
3. Master your topic so you can speak with authority.
4. Practice your presentation until it flows smoothly.
5. Focus on communicating with your audience.
6. Learn how to relax on cue.
7. Think positively.
8. Visualize success.
9. Act confident even if you aren't.
10. Take advantage of opportunities to speak in public.

Do these techniques really work, and is such advice helpful? Research related to communication anxiety has established the following conclusions: (1) *Such techniques do work*, and (2) *they work best in combination*.[12] Heed the suggestions of Davidson College student Betsy Lyles, whose account of her communication anxiety opened this chapter:

> To incoming students, I would suggest a couple of things—the first being it doesn't matter how much experience you've had with speaking in the past. Taking a public speaking course and learning about the theories at work behind what you do can be illuminating. And, there's no way not to improve. If possible, have your speeches filmed so you can watch them after your presentation. Make note of what you like and also what you can improve upon. Unfortunately, communication anxiety is a universal problem faced by public speakers *without* a universal solution. Commit yourself to finding solutions that work for you. They might be different from what your classmates do.

Controlling anxiety takes time. As you become more experienced at giving speeches and at using the suggestions in this chapter, you will find your fears lessening, and you will be able to convert your mild anxiety into positive, constructive energy.

How You Can Help Your Classmates

As you may have noticed, many of the speech anxiety issues you may experience revolve around how listeners respond to you. Keep in mind that your classmates have similar concerns. You can help relax speakers by the way you listen to them.[13] Come to class prepared to listen. Give speakers your whole-hearted attention. Look pleasant and encouraging. Make it easy for them. If you know students who are extremely anxious, volunteer to serve as a listener when they practice their speeches. Encourage them and compliment them on what they do well. Be the kind of supportive listener you would like to face as you make your own presentations.

Finding your voice allows you to speak with confidence.

FINAL reflections CLIMBING FEAR MOUNTAIN

Before you can find your voice, you must gain control of your communication anxiety. For many people, communication anxiety can seem like a steep mountain that stands between them and their communication goals. But as this chapter indicates, there are many things you can do to climb this mountain successfully:

- Pick your speech topic early, and research it carefully.
- Keep your focus on your listeners and what you can give them through your speech rather than on your own anxieties.
- Practice your speech until you are confident how you will say things.
- Get a good night's rest before your speech, and go easy on the coffee the next morning.
- Form a vivid image in your mind of succeeding as you speak.
- Practice the art of selective relaxation to avoid becoming too tense.
- Appear confident as you walk to the podium, pause for a moment to arrange your notes, establish eye contact with listeners, smile at them, and get off to a strong start.
- Set a good pace—not too slow, not too fast. Let everything about you say, "I'm in control."

As you climb Fear Mountain, following these guides, you will discover something remarkable: What had looked like a mountain is actually only a hill you can master. The view from the top as you finish your speech can be exhilarating!

After Reading This Chapter, You Should Be Able To Answer These Questions

Study and
Review at
MyCommunicationLab

1 How can reality testing reduce communication anxiety?

2 How does cognitive restructuring work?

3 How can you master the art of selective relaxation?

4 What major changes can help you achieve attitude adjustment as you speak?

5 How can visualization help you control communication anxiety?

For Discussion and Further Exploration

1 Invite other students to join you in a support team to improve the quality of assigned speeches. Your support team should

- work to reduce communication anxiety and increase self-confidence.
- brainstorm possible topics and discuss strategies for effective speech designs and techniques for audience adaptation.
- serve as practice audiences.
- offer constructive criticism.

2 Consider your recent activity with social media such as tweets, Facebook posts, blog entries, or perhaps YouTube clips. Do you experience communication anxiety when communicating in this way? Why or why not? In what ways is this social media communication a form of public communication? In what ways is it different from public speaking? Be prepared to share your thoughts and discuss them with your classmates.

3 Professor Lou Davidson Tillson of Murray State University developed the following case study of acute communication anxiety. (His narrative has been shortened for presentation here.)

> It was the first day of graded speeches in Public Speaking 101. Scott, the football team captain and a 4.0 student, was near the end of his speech on the dangers of steroid use in high school athletics. He efficiently reviewed his main points and concluded with a poignant story about a teenager who died because he wanted to play football, even if that meant taking drugs to do so. The speech was a resounding success.
>
> The next speaker would be Lisa. A petite, blonde girl wearing wire-rimmed glasses and clasping note cards stood, took a few audible gulps of air, and walked toward the front of the classroom. Twenty-seven pairs of eyes looked in her direction. Lisa cleared her throat and placed the note cards on the podium. Her hands immediately grabbed the edge of the podium in a white-knuckled, death grip. A flush slowly inched its way from her chest to her throat. As her cheeks turned a blotchy, fire-engine red, she cleared her throat again and began to talk in a faltering, timid voice.

"My speech is on…why children who commit violent crimes…should be tried as adults in the court system," she stumbled. "There are three reasons why children who commit violent crimes should have to face adult penalties for their actions…."

Lisa fumbled on through her preview. As she arranged her note cards, one fell off the podium and slid under a nearby desk. No one else seemed to notice—except Lisa. She appeared to freeze in time as she apparently pondered whether to retrieve the card or try to continue without it.

Several seconds passed before Lisa decided what to do. As she stepped out from behind the podium she bumped into it and the rest of the cards fluttered to the floor. That mishap was the last straw. With a dumbstruck expression on her face, Lisa abandoned her search for the cards, turned, and ran out of the room. Tears of frustration and embarrassment stained her blotchy cheeks. The classroom was uncomfortably quiet except for the haunting sound of Lisa's footsteps running down the tile hallway outside.[14]

Fortunately, this kind of "worst case scenario" happens rarely, but many of us experience this sort of misery to some degree, and the incident deserves serious consideration. Exchange ideas in class discussion in response to the following questions:

- What might have caused Lisa to react the way she did?
- Pretend you were one of her classmates. How would you have felt?
- What could Lisa have done to ameliorate her response to the public speaking situation?
- What advice would you give Lisa to help her prepare emotionally for the next speech assignment?
- How could you show support for Lisa when she returns to class?
- Can you think of ways you might help her as a listener?

4 Use the self-examination on public speaking anxiety found on the following page to diagnose your communication apprehension.

Directions: Put a check next to any statements that apply to you.

____   I put off registering for this course as long as I could.

____   Everyone else in this class is less anxious than me.

____   I put off preparing speeches because thinking about them makes me nervous.

____   I felt very anxious the first day of class.

____   Practicing my speeches makes me nervous.

____   I know I'll forget what I want to say during my speech.

____   I am sure I will shake during my speech presentation.

____   My listeners will laugh at me if I make a mistake.

____   I have problems when I'm asked a question in other classes.

____   My mind will go blank during my speech.

____   I wish I could drop this class.

____   I'm afraid I'm going to sound foolish.

____   I won't be able to finish my speech.

____   I have trouble sleeping the night before I am scheduled to speak.

Consider the items you checked and develop a plan for addressing the problems you identified.

3

Your First Speech: An Overview of Speech Preparation

Listen to **Chapter 3** at **MyCommunicationLab**

James was having a hard time getting started on his first speech. He had been asked to introduce himself by explaining and exploring one thing that meant a lot to him and that helped define who he was. James was pretty sure he wanted to talk about his dream of becoming a chef and of opening his own restaurant. That much was no problem. But how was he supposed to talk about himself without coming across as self-indulgent? And how was he supposed to already know how to put together and deliver a whole speech when the class had just begun? Where was he to start?

Then he began to reflect on the reasons he wanted to become a chef: his memories of helping his grandmother prepare holiday meals, his gratitude to the local chef who gave him his first job prepping vegetables in a professional kitchen, and his personal desire to develop healthier variations of the regional dishes he loved. James may not have realized it yet, but as he reflected on the details of his personal story, he was already well on the way to preparing an excellent first presentation. He was beginning to find his voice.

If, like James, you are having a hard time getting started on your first speech, you are certainly not alone. Over the years, we've found that it helps to provide a "step-by-step" overview for preparing and presenting first speeches—a summary of principles and skills that will be covered in more depth as our book develops. This overview becomes the first section of this chapter. We then discuss the art of managing the impressions we make on others, which is important to all public speaking but especially when addressing an audience for the first time. We close this chapter by discussing the speech of self-introduction, often the theme of the first speaking assignment.

Preparing and Presenting Your First Speech

Whatever your first speaking assignment, it helps to work systematically through a series of steps that takes you from choosing and focusing your topic through making the actual presentation. Figure 3.1, Major Steps in Speech Preparation and Presentation, illustrates this process.

As you proceed, keep in mind that speech preparation is rarely a perfect linear process. You may well find yourself working back and forth from step to step as you proceed. For instance, you might need to return to step 1 and refocus your topic after conducting your research. Even veteran speakers often work through several rough outlines of a speech before getting everything into focus for the actual presentation. *This makes it vitally important to get started as soon as possible and not to procrastinate until the night before you are scheduled to speak.* A good speech needs time to jell, and you need time to reflect on what you want to say.

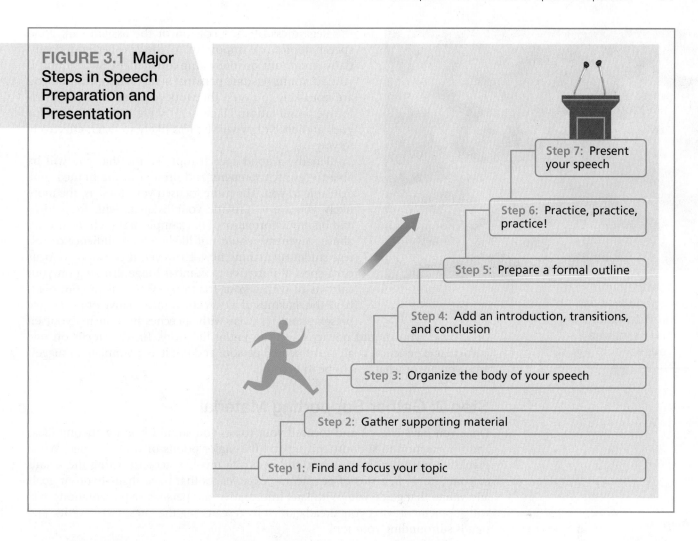

FIGURE 3.1 Major Steps in Speech Preparation and Presentation

Step 7: Present your speech

Step 6: Practice, practice, practice!

Step 5: Prepare a formal outline

Step 4: Add an introduction, transitions, and conclusion

Step 3: Organize the body of your speech

Step 2: Gather supporting material

Step 1: Find and focus your topic

Step 1: Find and Focus Your Topic

Your first step —discussed in more detail in Chapter 6—is to search for a topic that will be appropriate to the assignment, the occasion, audience needs and interests, and your own preferences. When speaking outside the classroom, both the occasion and audience expectations will often determine your choice of topic and purpose. For instance, if asked to present a "briefing" to fellow employees on how to use a new software package, you pretty much know what you'll be talking about and why you'll be talking.

With classroom assignments, you may have more freedom to choose your own topics and explore your own voice. But your choices will still be limited to some extent by the nature of your speaking assignments. For example, with informative speeches you might select topics on which you can find new and important ideas and information to convey. With persuasive speeches, you may pick topics that are controversial or that ask listeners for commitment. With ceremonial speeches, you will probably celebrate the meaning of a special moment. And with introductory speeches, you often will tell stories that will help listeners gain a better idea of who you are.

Your personal experiences can provide examples and narratives for your speech.

Regardless of the occasion or the assignment, good speech topics are important to the speaker and potentially important or interesting to listeners. Simply put, if you do not have some personal stake in a topic, then you are not likely to invest the work required to make an effective presentation. Likewise, if there is nothing in it for your audience, they will be less likely to listen effectively to you.

Finally, a good speech topic is one that you will be able to research, prepare, and present in the limited time available to you. The more focused your topic is, the more likely you are to provide your listeners with fresh ideas and quality information. For example, a speech on alcohol abuse in general would not likely tell an audience of college students anything new. However, if you were to focus on a specific initiative to combat binge drinking on your campus or within your fraternity system, then you might have the makings of an excellent informative or persuasive presentation. Likewise with speeches introducing yourself or another, you should not try to tell an entire life story. Instead, focus on one particular experience, goal, or influential person, and use it as a template to suggest who you are or what you hope to become.

Step 2: Gather Supporting Material

Once you have chosen and focused your topic, you should begin gathering ideas and information to support and expand the major points of your message. When preparing introductory speeches, this typically involves reconstructing the details of your "story" in terms of people and experiences that have shaped you or goals and values that guide you. With later informative and persuasive presentations, you will supplement what you already know by researching the latest facts, events, and trends surrounding your topic.

In Chapter 7, we discuss the process of acquiring material to support your points. You can acquire responsible knowledge by conducting online searches, using your school library, and reaching out to available experts and other local resources. We emphasize the importance of satisfying the "four R's" of good research: finding information that is relevant, representative, recent, and reliable. When researching complex scientific or technical topics, you should always establish the expert credentials of your sources as you speak. With controversial or disputed issues, make it a conscious point to explore contending positions on the topic, to sort fact from opinion, and to distinguish between reputable journalism and partisan pseudo-news. When searching the Web, which is an incredibly valuable resource but has few gatekeepers, watch out for blatant disinformation, and always look for respected backup sources to confirm information that you find posted to obscure websites.

The four most common forms of supporting information—as developed in Chapter 8—are facts and statistics, testimony, examples, and narratives.

Facts and Statistics. Because their truthfulness can be verified by independent observers, **facts** are one of the most important and powerful forms of supporting information. When speakers address unfamiliar topics, a striking fact can engage

▶ **facts** Descriptive statements that can be verified as true by observation.

audience attention from the outset. Persuasive speakers try to convince listeners that "the facts are on their side."

Statistics are facts that can be measured mathematically. Often presented in the form of percentages or contrasting fractions, statistics can be especially effective for tracing the growth or decline of trends such as unemployment or crime rates or for expressing public opinion on issues such as global warming. As discussed in Chapter 10, graphs and other presentation aids can be particularly effective for emphasizing key facts and presenting large amounts of statistical information.

As you weave factual information into your speeches, keep in mind that even the facts never speak for themselves. You must interpret their meaning artfully to support your assertions, and they are almost always more effective when you provide specific details and cite highly credible sources. Consider the following passage from a speech by Ashley Roberson documenting the challenges facing Native Americans:

> Did you know that native people have one of the lowest life expectancies of any population living in this hemisphere, second only to those living in Haiti? According to the Centers for Disease Control, the suicide rate among Native Americans is one and a half times higher than that of the general U.S. population. The homicide rate is twice as high. And according to the FBI, things are actually getting worse! Between 2000 and 2010, the murder rate on tribal lands rose 41%, reports of rape rose 55%, and arson and robbery more than doubled.

Shooting survivor and former Congresswoman Gabby Giffords used personal experience to speak about gun control.

These ominous comparisons and trends gave dramatic strength to Ashley's argument. You should certainly consider how *the power of the facts* might serve you as well.

Testimony.   Speakers use **testimony** when they cite the words or ideas of others. When you quote experts or widely respected people in support of your points, you strengthen your credibility. Testimony can also be effective for explaining the meaning of complicated subjects. Eyewitness accounts of events and statements by those whose lives have been impacted by your subject can make your speech more authentic and engaging. Finally, quotations from revered documents and respected figures can add eloquence to your speech and can invoke shared values and aspirations. As he presented his inaugural address, President John F. Kennedy said, "Ask not what your country can do for you, but what you can do for your country." Many speakers since have quoted those eloquent words to lend dignity and importance to their own messages.

When weaving testimony into your speeches, establish your source's credentials and when the words were spoken. Keep in mind that expertise is subject-specific: Being a brilliant biologist, for example, does not make someone an expert on the economy. Be careful to present the ideas and words of others as they would have you present them; do not twist their intended meaning to support your own conclusions. Finally, remember that "experts" will sometimes disagree, especially on controversial issues. At such moments, you may have to line up a number of experts to support your position.

Examples.   **Examples** provide concrete illustrations that help clarify your ideas and ground your speech in reality. Examples say, in effect, "This really happened." They can arouse emotion and move audiences to action.

▶ **statistics**   Facts that can be measured mathematically.

▶ **testimony**   Citing the words and ideas of others to support a point.

▶ **examples**   Incidents that illustrate a speaker's points.

You can use an extended example that is developed in detail or a series of brief examples. Consider how Jeff Shannon used an extended example to introduce his persuasive speech favoring comprehensive sex education:

Carla is an attractive and intelligent 15-year-old. Like most young teenagers, she has dreams and aspirations for her future—an education, a career, and maybe someday a husband and family. But, for Carla, realizing those dreams has just become a lot more complicated. She has just joined the growing ranks of single pregnant teenagers.

Whenever you doubt that your listeners may grasp your point or see its relevance to their lives, that is the moment for an example.

Narratives.   **Narratives** are stories that illustrate the ideas or theme of a speech. Like examples, stories within your speech can help to engage listeners. Effective narratives call for a lively presentation style and language that is colorful, concrete, and active. They are usually more fully developed than examples in terms of character, scene, and plot, and they move toward some sort of climax that conveys a clear point or moral. Simply put, we humans love a good story, and it is hard not to be drawn into them when we hear them. Beth Tidmore's self-introductory speech, reprinted in Appendix B and shown in MyCommunicationLab, opens with a compelling narrative that documents her mother's contribution to her dream of becoming a world-class athlete in the sport of competitive shooting:

Watch at
MyCommunicationLab
Video: "Lady with a Gun"

On April 1st, my mother said three words that weren't an April Fool's joke. She said, "We'll take it." The "it" she was referring to was a brand-new Anschutz 2002 Air Rifle. Now, this is $2,000 worth of equipment for a sport that I'd been in for maybe three months. That was a big deal! It meant that I would be going from a junior-level to an Olympic-grade rifle.

Someone outside the sport might think, "Eh, minor upgrade. A gun is a gun, right?" No! Imagine a fifteen-year-old who has been driving a used Toyota and who suddenly gets a brand new Mercedes for her sixteenth birthday. That's how I felt. But as she was writing the check, I completely panicked. I thought, "What if I'm not good enough to justify this rifle? What if I decide to quit and we have to sell it, or we can't sell it? What if I let my parents down and I waste their money?" So later in the car, I said, "Momma, what if I'm not good enough?" She said, "Don't worry about it—it's my money."

Beth Tidmore's narratives helped listeners relate to her topic.

Beth's story illustrates the use of **dialogue,** making listeners witnesses to a conversation. We feel drawn close to the action, as though we are riding in the back seat. She also illustrates the use of analogy as she invites listeners to compare her feelings with those of someone who just received a Mercedes. The analogy highlights the significance of the gift to her. Finally, notice how Beth builds suspense: Was she able to justify the purchase of such an expensive gift? After

▶ **narratives**   Stories that illustrate the ideas or theme of a speech.

▶ **dialogue**   Having the characters in a narrative speak for themselves rather than paraphrasing what they say.

mentioning that she was successful in national and international competitions, was named to the All-America shooting team, and competed in the World Cup, Beth answers that question with a concluding narrative:

> So not long ago, I asked my mother, "How did you know?" She said, "Ah, I just knew." I said, "No, Mom—really. How did you know that you weren't going to waste your money?" She got very serious and she took me by the shoulders and squared me up. She said, "When you picked up that gun, you just looked like you belonged together. I knew there was a sparkle in your eye, and I knew that you were meant to do great things with that rifle."

Taken together, facts, statistics, testimony, examples, and narratives provide the substance of your speeches. While they serve their own unique functions, they are usually more effective when used in combination.

Step 3: Organize the Body of Your Speech

Once you've chosen, focused, and researched your topic, you can develop and arrange the **body** of your speech. The body contains the major ideas you wish to develop and their supporting materials. The first step, as discussed in Chapter 6, is to formulate your **thesis statement** or central idea. This statement, expressed in a simple declarative sentence, should reflect a clear sense of what you want to accomplish. For instance, if you were making an informative presentation explaining important recent changes in the federal student aid program, your thesis statement might be: "Recent changes in the federal student aid program might make a big difference to you." If you were preparing a persuasive speech exhorting your fellow students to "get involved" in efforts to combat campus crime, your thesis might be: "We must help stop campus crime."

The next step, as addressed in Chapter 9, is to generate the **main points** that will elaborate, explain, and defend your thesis statement. To find these points, look for the ideas that emerge repeatedly in your research and ask questions suggested by your topic. For instance, if you were developing main points related to the student aid program, you might ask, "What are these changes?" and "How might they impact the lives of my listeners?" If there were two or three major changes, these might well become the main points of your speech. With the speech urging efforts to combat campus crime, you might consider why listeners should get involved. Is crime a serious problem on campus? How might students make a difference? Select no more than three main points that you can develop in your speech.

At this point, you should choose a **design** for arranging your main points in a manner appropriate to your topic and purpose. For instance, our sample speech on changes to the student aid program might well follow a *categorical design* that arranges the main points according to categories. You might discover, for example, that these changes fall into two major categories—limitations on the amount of aid available and eligibility requirements. Our speech urging student involvement with campus crime would probably follow a *problem-solution design* that focuses attention on a problem and then proceeds to offer solutions for it. Other common design patterns include

- the *causation design,* which addresses events or situations in terms of cause and effect;

- the *chronological design,* which describes events or historical developments in the order they occurred;

▶ **body**   The section of a speech that contains your main ideas and the materials that support them.

▶ **thesis statement**   The central idea of a speech stated as a simple declarative sentence.

▶ **main points**   The most important ideas developed in support of the thesis statement.

▶ **design**   Standard way to arrange the main points of a speech.

- the *sequential design,* which explains the steps of a process and is good for "how to"–type presentations; and

- the *refutative design,* which shows why an opposing argument is not valid; essentially, you first summarize the claim you wish to refute and then present evidence that contradicts it.

We discuss these and other design options in Chapter 9 and in our chapters on informative, persuasive, and ceremonial speaking.

Of special interest for speeches of self-introduction is the **narrative design**. This pattern organizes speech materials in the form of a story. Instead of the standard introduction-body-conclusion format, a speech using a narrative design follows this pattern:

- a **prologue**, which sets the scene, introduces the main characters, and foreshadows the story to come;

- a **plot**, which develops the story from scene to scene and typically builds to some sort of climax; and

- an **epilogue**, which reflects on the meaning of the story.

We develop the narrative design more fully in Chapter 16 on ceremonial speaking. Speeches of introduction often use a narrative design because it is ideal for dramatizing your experiences and reflecting on the lessons you learned from them. Sabrina Karic developed a narrative for her introductory speech (reprinted at the end of this chapter) on growing up in war-torn Bosnia and Herzegovina. Her prologue illustrates the power of narrative to involve listeners as vicarious participants in her story:

> I want you to think back to when you were six years old. Then, imagine living in a time, a place, a country, where you constantly heard the noises [gunfire] I just played. I am from the small and tragic country of Bosnia and Herzegovina. While many of you were playing with toys and learning to ride a bike, I was living through a nightmare. I was six years old, certainly not ready to experience war. But one day, I heard my first gun shots and my innocent childhood ended. Almost overnight, my family was plunged into homelessness and poverty.

When you read Sabrina's speech, you will find that the plot unfolds through three major scenes: (1) her wealthy family reduced to homeless refugees under siege in Gorazde, (2) Sabrina worrying about her parents who braved enemy lines to seek food for her family, and (3) a joyous reunion tempered by the ongoing horror of the situation. The opening of her epilogue exemplifies the value of narrative for reflecting on who you are or have become in light of a life-changing experience:

> I can't remember how this nightmare ended, but somehow it did. To this day, I vividly remember these moments, and the experience has marked me for life. Now, I appreciate small things. I find satisfaction just taking a walk in the park, thanking God I survived. The experience also made me a fighter, and gave me strength and a will to live that has carried me to this point, and brought me here to share my story with you.

▶ **narrative design**   A speech structure that develops from beginning to end through a prologue, a plot, and an epilogue.

▶ **prologue**   The opening of a narrative that establishes the context and setting, foreshadows the meaning, and introduces major characters.

▶ **plot**   The body of a narrative that unfolds in a sequence of scenes designed to build suspense.

▶ **epilogue**   The final part of a narrative, reflecting upon its meaning.

FIGURE 3.2
Outline Format for a Narrative Design

I. Prologue
 A. Describe the setting and background of the story
 B. Introduce the characters
 C. Foreshadow the meaning

II. Plot
 A. Scene 1
 B. Scene 2
 C. Scene 3

III. Epilogue
 A. Show how the story ends
 B. Present the meaning of the story

Figure 3.2 illustrates the outline for a narrative design.

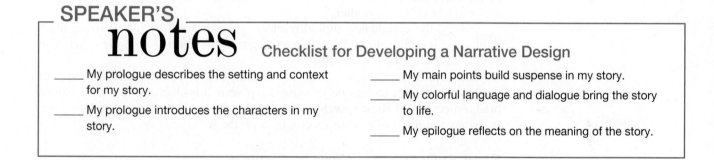

SPEAKER'S notes
Checklist for Developing a Narrative Design

_____ My prologue describes the setting and context for my story.

_____ My prologue introduces the characters in my story.

_____ My main points build suspense in my story.

_____ My colorful language and dialogue bring the story to life.

_____ My epilogue reflects on the meaning of the story.

The final step in developing the body of your speech is to prepare a **working outline** that will allow you to see the structure of your message. You should support each of your main points with subpoints and information that substantiates what you have to say. For instance, if you were to outline a speech encouraging classmates to fight campus crime, you might develop your first main point with information establishing that there is indeed a problem with crime on your campus. This might include information regarding the kinds of crime that are most common, statistics to document the assertion, and testimony from victims and campus security officers.

You would probably flesh out your second main point by providing practical steps your classmates can take. Are there any student groups or initiatives they can join or support? What personal measures can they take to better ensure their own safety?

As you proceed, keep in mind that outlining is a tentative process. You may work through several rough drafts before you settle on the final product.

▶ **working outline** A tentative plan that allows you to see the structure of your message as you develop it.

Step 4: Add an Introduction, Transitions, and a Conclusion

Once you've developed the body of your speech, it's time to add an introduction, transitions, and a conclusion. A good **introduction** should arouse the interest of your listeners and prepare them for the message to follow. Often it will establish your credibility by explaining your personal connection to the topic. It should also point out what listeners may have at stake.

One student speaker offered an effective introduction when she looked up at her listeners after arranging her notes and said: "My message today is very simple: Get off your butts." While her startled listeners watched, she reached under the lectern and produced a large jar of cigarette butts. "This," she said, "is what they call 'butt-ugly.' I gathered these beauties after lunch last Friday in front of the Student Union. That was right after I smoked my last cigarette. Today I want you to join me. Let's get off our butts together." Her introduction aroused interest and established her credibility to speak on the subject of smoking cessation.

You should also give careful consideration to **transitions**, how you will move from one point to another and connect them. Good transitions let your listeners know when you've finished one idea and are moving to the next. They often remind listeners of the ideas you have covered up to that point in the speech. You might use short bridging phrases such as "For my next point …," "Having said that …," or "In conclusion …," although sometimes a simple pause or change in vocal inflection can signal listeners that you are ready to move to the next idea. Without carefully planned transitions, you may find yourself resorting to "uhs" and "ers" as you struggle from one point to another.

Finally, the **conclusion** should reinforce your message by summarizing main points and leaving your audience something to think about. Often the conclusion will tie back in to the introduction.

In Chapter 9, we discuss a number of strategies for opening and closing your speeches. Whatever technique you use, keep your introductions and conclusions brief, especially for short speeches. Because they are vital in shaping audience impressions and the flow of your speech, commit them to memory.

Step 5: Prepare a Formal Outline

As discussed in step 3, it is a good idea to create a working outline as you develop your speech. With informative and persuasive presentations, your instructor may ask you to go one step further to submit a **formal outline** and bibliography. The formal outline represents the final, complete, polished plan of your speech. If you are not given specific instructions, ask if you may follow the discussion and models offered in Chapter 9. Most formal outlines include a title as well as a separately developed introduction, body, and conclusion. All your main and supporting points should be written as complete sentences, and you should include abbreviated source citations that support your points. You should write out the transitions that tie together the main points of your speech.

As for the bibliography, find out whether your instructor has a preferred citation style for listing your sources. We provide samples in Chapter 7, pages 145–146, that illustrate the Modern Language Association (MLA) and the American Psychological Association (APA) citation styles. Your instructor may take a close look at your bibliography when assessing the quality of your research, so be sure to provide all the information that might be needed to check your sources.

▶ **introduction** The opening to your speech that gains attention, previews your message, and establishes a favorable connection with your listeners.

▶ **transitions** Connecting elements that cue listeners that you are finished making one point and are moving on to the next.

▶ **conclusion** The ending for your speech that reinforces your main ideas and provides your audience with something to remember.

A closing note: Preparing the formal outline and bibliography imposes a discipline on the preparation process that almost always results in a better presentation. Also, with most classroom presentations it represents the one tangible item your instructor has to evaluate your work after viewing your presentation. Make sure your formal outline and bibliography are computer-generated, neat, and carefully proofed for typos, spelling, and grammar.

Step 6: Practice, Practice, Practice!

Once you have polished and outlined your speech, you should be ready to practice the actual presentation. **Extemporaneous speaking**—which is generally preferred for brief presentations—emphasizes audience interaction and eye contact more than exact wording. You should be thoroughly prepared, and you should know your ideas and materials in the order to be presented. But instead of speaking verbatim from memory or reading from a manuscript, you should speak from the general pattern of ideas imprinted in your memory during practice.

Under no circumstance should you read from your formal outline! Except for the introduction and conclusion, which should be committed to memory so that you can get into and out of the speech smoothly, the exact wording of your speech will occur as you interact directly with listeners. This will give your speech a freshness and naturalness required for effective communication.

Here's an example. The student had planned to say:

So now we see what the problem is. We know the costs in human suffering, the terrible political consequences, and the enormous economic burden. The question is: what are we going to do about it?

Here's what came out during the actual presentation:

So now you see the problem. I can see some of you nodding in agreement: you know the costs, the suffering, the terrible burden people must carry. Some of them may be people you love, may be you! So here's the question: what are you going to do about it? What are *we* going to do about it?

The second, extemporaneous version seems more natural, more direct, more interactive, and probably more effective. If the student gave the same speech a hundred times, each would be a little different, in response to the particular audience and situation.

If you need the reassurance of a safety net during presentations, use a **key-word outline,** a brief listing of words and phrases that will cue you to the flow of ideas and major points of emphasis in your speech. Should your mind go blank, you need only glance at the key-word outline to get yourself back on track.

Again, while you are speaking, focus on your ideas and your listeners. The goal is to develop a conversational speaking style so that everyone feels genuinely spoken to. Learn to adjust to audience feedback as you speak.

As you practice for your presentation, leave yourself an uninterrupted afternoon or evening. If you can, rehearse in the same room where you will be speaking. Read over your outline several times until you feel familiar with it. Then develop your key-word outline: We suggest that you put it on three-by-five note cards, which are easy to handle. You can either hold these in your hand or place them on the lectern. If you use the lectern, position them as high as possible so that you reduce the loss

---

▶ **formal outline** Represents the final, complete, polished plan of your speech.

▶ **extemporaneous speaking** A form of presentation in which a speech is carefully prepared and practiced but not written out, memorized, or read.

▶ **key-word outline** Abbreviated version of a formal outline used in presenting a speech. Focuses on cues and points of emphasis.

It helps to rehearse your speech where you will present it.

of eye contact with listeners as you refer to them. However, if you are a very short or tall person, consider not using the lectern at all. Short students can seem hidden behind it, reducing the effectiveness of gestures. Tall students can end up stooped over it when they refer to notes. Either way, the lectern can become a barrier to audience interaction.

As you prepare your key-word outline, use large lettering that you can read at a glance. If there are quotations you must read, place them on separate cards. Keep them as brief as possible, and look up frequently as you read to renew eye contact.

Beyond that, *do not read your speech!* Remember, the assignment is to speak, not read. By all means do not try to speak from a mini-manuscript written on twenty-something note cards!

As you practice, wean yourself away from the full outline until you are comfortable speaking from the key-word outline and can follow the planned pattern of ideas. Be patient with this process, and expect many starts and stops. Your goal is not to be perfect, and a few bobbles will just add to the naturalness of the communication.

During rehearsal, imagine your listeners sitting before you. Speak up and animate your voice to bring your ideas to life, work in pauses and nonverbal gestures that seem natural and prompted by the ideas, and pan the room as you maintain eye contact with your imaginary audience. Glance at your notes as you need to. If you plan to use presentation aids, practice how you will integrate them into your presentation. Time your presentation to make sure it fits within the assignment requirements. When you begin to feel as though you could present the entire speech without notes, try it. If you succeed, you're ready. Put the notes away, get some sleep, and practice a few more times the morning before your presentation.

Finally, should you find yourself experiencing a last-minute case of the jitters, know that you are in good company. Indeed, communication apprehension is so widespread that we included an entire chapter, Chapter 2, to help you deal with it. For now, keep reminding yourself that this is the first assignment of an introductory course. Again, focus on your message and not yourself. Speak loudly and clearly, and discipline yourself to maintain eye contact with your audience. Take comfort in knowing that you will improve substantially during the course of your class. You have so much to gain by finding your voice!

SPEAKER'S notes   Practicing Your Presentation

Keep these suggestions in mind as you practice your speech.

1. Visualize yourself making an effective presentation.
2. Focus on your ideas.
3. Speak naturally.
4. Present extemporaneously.

5. Maintain eye contact with your imagined listeners.
6. Practice from your key-word outline.
7. Rehearse until your speech flows smoothly.

voice   Learning from Your Classmates

As the first speeches are presented in class, build a collection of "word portraits" of your classmates. At the end of this round of speeches, analyze this material to see what you have learned about the class as a whole. What do your classmates seem most interested in? What kind of topics might they prefer to hear speeches on? Can you detect any strong political or social attitudes you might have to adjust to? Submit a report of your analysis to your instructor, and keep a copy for your own use in preparing later speeches.

Step 7: Present Your Speech

It's your time to speak. You've earned it. Now enjoy the moment with your listeners.

Managing the Impressions You Make

As you stand to speak, listeners will begin to form impressions of you that will influence how they respond to your messages. Aristotle called these impressions **ethos.** You can enhance your ethos by cultivating favorable impressions of your competence, integrity, goodwill, and dynamism. Figure 3.3 illustrates the components of ethos.

Competence

Competent speakers come across as well informed, intelligent, and well prepared. You can build **competence** by selecting topics on which you have personal experience and by strengthening your knowledge through research. You can further build competence by putting together speeches that are well organized and effectively worded and by quoting experts and citing authorities who support your position.

For example, if you are speaking on the relationship between nutrition and heart disease, you might quote a medical specialist or a publication of the American Heart Association. Melissa Anderton introduced testimony into her speech in this way: "Dr. Milas Peterson heads the Heart Institute at Harvard University. During his visit to our campus last week, I spoke with him about this idea. He told me ...." Note the competence-related elements in this example:

- She points out the qualifications of her expert.

- The testimony she uses is recent.

- She made a personal contact with her expert.

- She prepared carefully for her speech.

Explore at
MyCommunicationLab
Activity: Self-Perceived
Communication
Competence"

▶ **ethos**   Audience impressions of a speaker's competence, integrity, goodwill, and dynamism.

▶ **competence**   The perception of a speaker as being well informed, intelligent, and well prepared.

When you cite authorities in this way, you are "borrowing" their credibility to enhance your own. Competence is also enhanced if you have practiced your presentation so that you can seem in command as you speak.

Integrity

Speakers cultivate positive impressions of **integrity** by being honest, ethical, and dependable. Listeners will be more receptive to your messages if you are straightforward, personally committed to your message, and genuinely concerned with the consequences of your speaking. The more you ask of your listeners, the more important your integrity becomes. When asking audiences to commit to a course of action, you should make clear your own involvement and willingness to follow your own advice. When addressing skeptical audiences on controversial issues such as reforming health care or increasing restrictions on gun purchases, acknowledge opposing positions before explaining and defending your own.

One of our students, a former gang member named Antonio Lopez, enhanced perceptions of his integrity by citing his own involvement with the gang lifestyle. "I know how this hurt my parents," he recalled. "They didn't want to see video of me shot or arrested on the evening news. I knew I had to change." His openness showed his willingness to trust the members of his audience with sensitive information, and they responded in kind by trusting him.

Goodwill

Goodwill means that speakers have the best interests of listeners at heart.[1] Such speakers appear to value the community over their own personal agendas. Goodwill is crucial to establishing identification, those feelings of shared values, background,

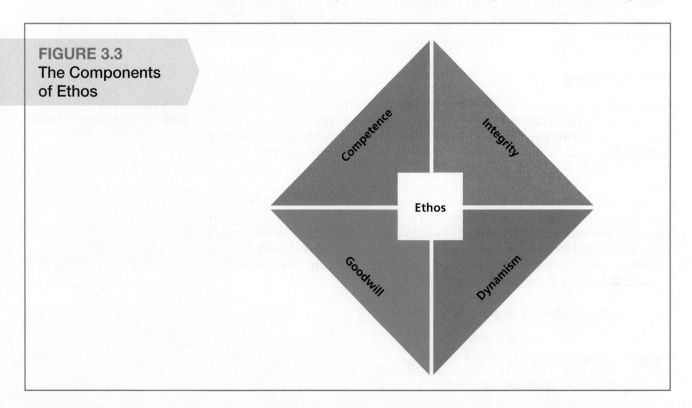

FIGURE 3.3
The Components of Ethos

▶ **integrity**   The quality of being honest, ethical, and dependable.

▶ **goodwill**   The impression that speakers have their listeners' best interests at heart.

and interest that can unite speakers and audiences.[2] As with integrity, goodwill is hard to repair once it has been violated.

There are many ways to enhance perceptions of goodwill. An engaging smile and direct eye contact can help. So can the appropriate use of humor, self-disclosure, and inclusive terms such as "we" and "us" to build symbolic bridges. Perhaps the most effective strategy for promoting goodwill is to emphasize shared values and shared experiences. The student speaker who urged her listeners to join her "stop smoking" support group expressed her keen concern for their well-being and identified closely with them. She knew how hard it would be to stop smoking, she said, but "together they would be stronger."

Smiling and engaging the audience help speakers demonstrate goodwill.

Dynamism

Finally, speakers who convey **dynamism** impress their listeners as confident, decisive, and enthusiastic. A dynamic speaking style also reinforces perceptions of competence and leadership potential. Even if you don't feel overly confident about making your first speech, try to act as though you are If you appear self-assured, listeners will respond as though you are, and you may find yourself becoming what you seem to be. In other words, you can trick yourself into developing a very desirable trait! When you appear to be in control, you also put listeners at ease. This feeling comes back to you as positive feedback and further reinforces your confidence.

You can enhance dynamism by choosing a topic that you care about. Your enthusiasm endorses your message. We discuss other ways of projecting confidence, decisiveness, and enthusiasm in Chapter 12.

YOUR ethical VOICE   The Ethics of Ethos

To build your ethos in ethical ways, follow these guidelines.

- Do enough research so that you can speak with true competence.
- Cite respected authorities in support of your ideas.
- Interpret information fairly.

- Be honest about where you stand on your topic.
- Have your listeners' best interests at heart.
- Don't feign enthusiasm.

Speeches of Introduction

Many public speaking classes open with speeches that ask you to introduce yourself or a classmate. Such speeches can help break down the initial barriers that separate classmates: Strangers can begin the process of warming to each other.

Watch at **MyCommunicationLab**
Video: Self Introduction: Bimal"

▶ **dynamism** The perception of a speaker as confident, decisive, and enthusiastic.

Watch at
MyCommunicationLab
Video: "Informative
Speech: Donald"

As a consequence, the speeches can create a receptive atmosphere in which students can grow as communicators and discover their voices. These first efforts can also create favorable ethos for later speeches.

In the advice that follows, we shall assume that the assignment asks you to introduce yourself. With only minor adjustments, you can adapt this advice for the purpose of introducing a classmate.

The self-introductory assignment has practical value beyond the classroom. In your later life, you may be called on to "say a few words about yourself" in the course of formal job interviews, when first joining new groups, in the introduction to longer formal presentations, or in running for public office. Regardless of the occasion, your ability to "tell your story" and pursue a meaningful point about who you are and what you believe is an invaluable "people skill." It certainly didn't hurt Barack Obama when he introduced himself at the Democratic National Convention in 2004 as "a skinny kid with a funny name who believes that America has a place for him, too."[3]

As you prepare your speech of introduction, ask yourself how listeners might gain a better sense of who you are as a unique individual. Don't try to tell your entire life story in the few brief minutes that are usually allotted for such speeches. Instead, focus on what really defines you. If you have any doubts about the appropriateness of prospective topic ideas, check with your instructor.

To help you explore possibilities for your speech, complete a **self-awareness inventory.** Ask yourself the following questions:

1. *Is your cultural background the most important thing about you?* How has it shaped you? How can you explain this influence to others? In her self-introductory speech, Sandra Baltz described herself as a unique product of three cultures. She felt that this rich cultural background had widened her horizons. Note how she focused on food to represent the convergence of these different ways of life:

   In all, I must say that being exposed to three very different cultures—Latin, Arabic, American—has been rewarding for me and has made a difference even in the music I enjoy and the food I eat. It is not unusual in my house to sit down to a meal made up of stuffed grape leaves and refried beans and all topped off with apple pie for dessert.

   The text of Sandra's speech may be found in Appendix B.

2. *Is the most important thing about you your hometown or the environment in which you grew up?* How were you shaped by it? What stories or examples illustrate this influence? What images of your childhood come to mind? Jimmy Green provided a vivid word-picture to help his audience envision his life growing up in rural Tennessee:

   To share my world, come up with me to the Tennessee River. We'll take a boat ride to New Johnsonville, where Civil War gunboats still lie on the bottom of the river. You'll see how the sun makes the water sparkle. You'll see the green hills sloping down to the river and the rocky cliffs. If we're lucky, we might see a doe and her fawn along the shoreline, or perhaps some great blue herons or a bald eagle overhead.

▶ **self-awareness inventory** A series of questions that allow speakers to explore their individuality so they can prepare a speech of self-introduction.

SPEAKER'S notes   Self-Awareness Inventory

1. Was your *cultural background* important in shaping you?

2. Did your hometown or *childhood environment* help shape who you are?

3. Did a *special person* or hero have a lasting impact on your life?

4. Were you shaped by an unusual accomplishment or *experience*?

5. Does a favorite *activity* or hobby add meaning to your life?

6. Does your *work* help define you as an individual?

7. Were you shaped by a special *goal* or *purpose* in life?

8. Do your *values* help define who you are?

3. *Was there some particular person—a friend, relative, or childhood hero—who had a major impact on your life?* Why do you think this person had such influence? Was it a heroic deed or accomplishment that inspired you? Was it a particular experience you shared together? In her self-introductory speech, which you can see in MyCommunicationLab, Marty Gaines explained how she had benefitted from the contrasting influences of her two grandmothers:

Watch at **MyCommunicationLab**
Video: "Martha Margaret Clark Cherry Gaines"

> Margaret Hasty was my "Memma," the kind of grandmother that always embraced me with a big hug, and always seemed to have a stash of my favorite cookies nearby. Martha Clark Akers was "Grandmother"—very strict, very formal, and always concerned with my progress in school and whether I was making the "right decisions."
>
> I guess I preferred Memma's company as a child, but in time I came to realize that I was loved and blessed by both of my grandmothers in equal if different ways. Now, there are days when I just grab my children up and tell them I love them. And I think to myself, "Thank you, Memma." And then there are days when I know that I have to be strong and strict. And I say to myself, "Give me strength, Grandmother."

4. *Have you been marked by some unusual accomplishment or experience?* What was it, and how did it affect you? What were the most dramatic moments associated with your experience? In her self-introductory speech reprinted at the end of this chapter, Sabrina Karic tells her story of surviving war and ethnic cleansing as a child and reflects on how she learned to appreciate the small things that so many of us take for granted—such as chocolate!

5. *Are you best characterized by an activity that brings meaning to your life?* Remember, what is important is not the activity itself but how it defines you. When he conducted his self-awareness inventory, David Smart decided that playing golf had taught him useful lessons:

> I don't let the little frustrations bother me and I keep going, no matter what happens. In golf, even though you hit a bad shot, you still have to go on and hit the next one. You can't walk off the course just because things aren't going your way. College life is the same way. If you have a bad day or do poorly on a test, you can't just give up and go home. You have to move up to the next tee and keep swinging.

6. *Is the work you do a major factor in making you who you are?* If you select this approach, focus on how your job has shaped you rather than simply describing what you do. Richard Bushart was quite a spectacle as he stood to present his self-introductory

Your early environment, childhood activities, and favorite hobbies can be rich sources of ideas for speeches.

speech wearing makeup and a clown suit. But those who were expecting a trivial speech were in for a surprise:

> An adult will think I'm foolish, weird, or just insane. But to a child I'm funny, caring, and a friend. Children have taught me so much.... They have inspired me to dream again and be creative. A child playing in the backyard can take a broom and turn it one way and it's a horse waiting to ride. Turn it another, and it's a hockey stick. Turn it still another, and it becomes a telescope through which she can see the universe.

7. *Are you best characterized by your goals or purpose in life?* Listeners are usually fascinated by those whose lives are dedicated to some purpose. If you choose to describe some personal goal, be sure to emphasize why you have the goal and how it affects you. Tom McDonald had returned to school after dropping out for eleven years. In his self-introductory speech, he described his goal:

> Finishing college means a lot to me now, even if that means working by day and attending school by night. The first time I enrolled, right out of high school, I "blew it." All I cared about was sports, girls, and partying. Even though I have a respectable job that pays well, I feel bad about not finishing a degree. My wife's diploma hangs on our den wall. All I have there is a stuffed duck!

8. *Are you best described by a value or a larger cause that you hold dear?* How did it come to have such importance for you? What experiences have helped teach that value to you? What have you done personally or what groups have you worked with to advance your cause? Remember that values are abstract, and you must provide concrete illustrations to help them come alive for others. As she described her commitment to family values, Velma Black discussed her experiences growing up in a large family in rural Missouri:

> When you are one of thirteen, you learn to get along with others. You have no choice. You learn to work together without whining and complaining. And you learn to love—not noisy shows of affection—just quiet caring that fills the house with warmth and strength.

FINDING YOUR
voice
The Adventure of Preparing Your First Speech

Describe your personal adventure of preparing your first speech. Which steps identified in this chapter were most difficult for you? Why? What mistakes did you make? What could you have done to avoid such problems? What have you learned about speech preparation that might be useful for your next speech? Submit your report and analysis to your instructor. Keep a copy for yourself so you can review it as you prepare later speeches.

FINAL reflections   TAKING THE FIRST STEPS

The ancient Chinese philosopher Lao-tzu once said that "a journey of a thousand miles begins with a single step." That may be true, but in the journey to find your voice, your first steps may be the hardest. The purpose of this chapter has been to help you take these initial steps as easily and as successfully as possible.

In the process, we have described not one step but seven. The first is to find a topic that really engages you, that makes you want to learn more and share your knowledge with others. The second is to make you at home in the world of research. You learn how to make contact with treasures of learning that await you and how to avoid traps of deception that may have been set by unscrupulous others. The third, fourth, and fifth steps lead you to develop artfully arranged messages that share the power of your new knowledge with others. The sixth step prepares you to present yourself and your ideas in the most favorable light, so that people will want to hear you and learn from you. The final step concerns that exhilarating moment when you actually step before an audience to bring them your message.

All these steps—quite tentative and basic at this point of development—help accelerate the process of finding your voice before a group of fellow travelers, who themselves are taking the first steps toward the ultimate destination of effective communication.

After Reading This Chapter, You Should Be Able To Answer These Questions

1 How can you go about finding a topic that will bring out the best in you?

2 How can you develop interesting and responsible content for your message?

3 What different design options can help you structure your message?

4 What are the components of ethos?

5 How can you develop favorable ethos? How can you manage listeners' impressions of you?

6 What is a self-analysis inventory?

7 How can it help you develop a speech introducing yourself or others?

Study and **Review** at **MyCommunicationLab**

For Discussion and Further Exploration

1 Create a list of topics for speeches you might develop during the course of the class term. Can you connect them in some way so that you might learn more and more about the related, larger topic area as you proceed? How might you build ethos on this larger topic area during your first speech? Discuss your idea in class to gauge audience interest and to benefit from suggestions.

2   Submit a time line for the preparation of your first speech, ending with the day you will make your presentation. How much time do you plan to spend on each step in the preparation process?

3   Write a character sketch of someone you believe exemplifies integrity. Support and develop this sketch with examples and evidence. Present your character sketch in class, and explore with others the basis of integrity revealed by these sketches.

4   Watch a contemporary political speech on YouTube. Evaluate the ethos of the speaker. Did she seem to know what she was talking about? Did he present credible evidence to validate his points [demonstrating competence]? Did the speaker seem honest and open [demonstrating integrity]? Did she seem to have your best interests at heart? Was he pleasant and likable [demonstrating good-will]? Was the speaker enthusiastic about the topic of the speech? Did she seem energetic and forceful [demonstrating dynamism]? Be prepared to explain how the speaker demonstrates each of the dimensions of ethos and how you think this impacts the effectiveness of the speech. Report what you find in class.

5   Find examples in contemporary advertising emphasizing the testimony of experts or widely respected persons. Discuss the differences between these types of testimony and when and why each might be more effective.

6   You have been chosen to present the nominating speech for the presidential candidate of your choice at the next national convention of your party. How would you go about building a favorable picture of your candidate on each of the dimensions of ethos. Describe your strategy in class.

7   How would you evaluate the effectiveness of a recent local political campaign in building the ethos of its candidate and damaging the ethos of its opponent? Consider the role of political advertising and the candidate's own statements in advancing or retarding these efforts. What part did these efforts play in the results of the campaign? Discuss in class.

Sabrina Karic gave this self-introductory speech to her class at the University of Nevada–Las Vegas. Her speech is built around a narrative that features a personal experience as the shaping force in her life. She tells about surviving the ethnic cleansing that took place in Bosnia and Herzegovina during the early 1990s when she was a child. As she described this situation, her listeners were intrigued by her power and passion.

A Little Chocolate

SABRINA KARIC

I want you to think back to when you were six years old. Then, imagine living in a time, a place, a country, where you constantly heard the noises [gunfire] I just played. I am from the small and tragic country of Bosnia and Herzegovina. While many of you were playing with toys and learning to ride a bike, I was living through a nightmare. I was six years old, certainly not ready to experience war. But one day, I heard my first gun shots and my innocent childhood ended. Almost overnight, my family was plunged into homelessness and poverty.

After the Serbs forced us out of our home, we had to endure endless nights sleeping under trees while rain poured down on us and mice crawled over our bodies. We finally made our way to Gorazde, a city that was surrounded by the Serbians and held under siege for months. The local authorities kept us all barely alive by distributing food among the families. Typically each week we would receive thirty pounds of flour, three pounds of beans, one pound of sugar, and two liters of oil. Every day, my mom made bread that was one inch thick. She divided it in half; one half for breakfast and the other for dinner. Then each half was divided in five even pieces, one piece for me, my mom, my dad, my sister, and my cousin, who lived with us.

This was incredibly hard for us. We often ran out of food before the next week's food distribution. Sometimes the supplies were delayed or not available. I can tell you that nothing etches itself more in a child's memory than the pain of hunger. During those days, I never dreamed of living in a big house, or having a pool, or even a doll to play with. I simply prayed to God for chocolate.

On January 31st of 1993, my parents decided to leave for Grebak, where the Bosnian army was situated. They would have to sneak through enemy lines to get there. If they made it, the Bosnian army would give them food to bring back to us. If they didn't make it—well, we didn't talk about that. If they didn't try, we were all going to starve anyway.

When my parents departed, they had to leave my sister and me on our own. Luckily, we had cousins who lived in Gorazde long before the war began. They took us in, and I can tell you that if it hadn't been for them, we would have starved to death. Days passed, and each day we waited for our parents. And our fears began to grow. We heard rumors that they had run into mine fields and been killed. We felt very much alone and scared.

Then on February 7th, a miracle happened. The door opened, and there were our parents! I remember the crying and hugging and kissing. And I remember hope flooding back into our hearts. Our parents explained that although many people had died, God had spared them.

That day I learned the meaning of gratitude, as well as sorrow for those whose parents would not return. But then our thoughts turned to food. My parents had brought so much of it to us! For those of you who celebrate Christmas, I'm sure I can compare my happiness on that one day to all of your holidays, added together. My parents had brought us one unforgettable treasure: Can you guess what it was?

Yes, it was chocolate, a small chocolate bar, broken into pieces during the trip. But my sister and I treasured each tiny piece, and ate it very slowly.

After the joy of that reunion, we returned to the reality of life around us. It seemed that every day, the explosions were getting closer, louder, and more frequent. I remember one particular day when I was playing with my friends outside our building. Suddenly we heard a nearby explosion, and all of us dashed for the building. We knew that we had only a few seconds at best. I just got inside the door and closed it, when a grenade exploded right where we had been playing. I fell to the floor and put my hands over my ears, waiting for the ringing to go away. After a few minutes, I peeked outside to see if any of my friends had been hurt. Thank God, all of us had been spared.

◄ In her prologue, Sabrina ducked beneath the table as she played the sounds of an explosion and gunfire, which startle the audience; then she establishes her credibility to speak from personal experience.

◄ In the first major scene of her story, as her family begins to starve in Gorazde, Sabrina uses concrete detail to help her listeners visualize and share the horror of her experience.

◄ In the second major scene, waiting for the return of her parents, Sabrina describes her growing despair. This dark feeling sets up the happiness she feels over their safe return. She uses an analogy to Christmas to help her listeners appreciate her joy. In this scene, chocolate begins to develop its larger symbolic meaning.

◄ In the third scene of her plot, Sabrina jerks listeners back into the daily horror of her situation. The image of a hand grenade interrupting the play of children is especially graphic and memorable.

In her epilogue, Sabrina ▶
reflects on the meaning
of her ordeal and invites
listeners to look for ways
to counter such inhuman-
ity. Note how she applies
her experience in global,
contemporary ways. At this
final point in the speech,
chocolate has become a
universal symbol for hope.

I can't remember how this nightmare ended, but somehow it did. To this day, I vividly remember these moments, and the experience has marked me for life. Now, I appreciate small things. I find satisfaction just taking a walk in the park, thanking God I survived. The experience also made me a fighter, and gave me strength and a will to live that has carried me to this point, and brought me here to share my story with you.

And even today, my experience makes me weep for all the children everywhere—Muslim, Jewish, and Christian—in Africa, the Middle East, and elsewhere—all the six-year-olds who experience prejudice and hatred and violence they can't understand. I weep for the loss of their innocence, for the loss of their happiness, for the loss of their lives. Can't we reach out to them and make their world a little more liveable? Can't we bring them a little chocolate?

4 Becoming a Better Listener

((· **Listen** to **Chapter 4** at **MyCommunicationLab**

Know how to listen, and you will profit even from those who talk badly.

—PLUTARCH

You're making a presentation in your psychology lab. As you stand before the class, you observe the following:

A young woman in the front row is texting on her cell phone.

A student in the back seems to be sleeping off the effects of an all-night party.

Another student seems to be working on a lab report, typing furiously on her laptop.

Oh, wait a minute—here is a student who seems ready to listen. His desk is clear of everything except a pen and notebook. He has a supportive look on his face as though actually waiting for you to make your presentation.

As you may have surmised from this opening example, a good listener is sometimes hard to find. Legend has it that President Franklin Delano Roosevelt was bemused by the poor listening behavior of people who visited the White House. To test his notion that people didn't really listen, he once greeted guests in a receiving line by murmuring, "I murdered my grandmother this morning." Typical responses ran along the lines of, "Thank you," "How good of you," and other platitudes of polite approval. Finally he met someone who had actually listened and who responded, "I'm sure she had it coming to her."[1]

Poor listening can exact a large price. Political leaders may make up their minds about the intentions of other nations and ignore information that does not support their position. Groups may be swayed by one member's personality and make poor decisions because they don't adequately process what they are hearing. Juries may not render fair verdicts because they have not listened critically. If you are not listening effectively in a classroom, you may find it hard to do well in the course.[2]

Fortunately, listening skills can be learned. In this chapter, we discuss the benefits of developing such skills and describe the major types of listening. To become an effective listener, you also must understand some of the causes of poor listening. Our major focus is on developing better listener skills and the ethical responsibilities of listeners. Finally, we consider how to use your improved listening skills to evaluate speeches.

The Benefits of Effective Listening

Why should you want to become a better listener? Most of your time in classrooms or on a job is spent listening. Developing effective listening skills can help you improve your work in other classes. It can help you as you move into the workforce. And it can help you become a better speaker.

Listening in the Classroom

It's a warm spring day. Carla's body is in her management class, but her mind is somewhere else. Her instructor's voice drones on, but the words don't register until he says, "Carla, I know you've worked in this kind of environment. Tell us what it was like."

If you have ever lived through this kind of nightmare, you already know how important listening is in the classroom. In addition to concentrating and blocking out distractions, effective listeners read assignments ahead of time to familiarize themselves with new words and to build a basis for understanding. They also take careful notes that help them to review effectively for tests.[3]

SPEAKER'S notes
Guidelines to Improve Your Note Taking

Following these guidelines will help you listen more effectively both to instructors and to classroom speeches:

1. Familiarize yourself with assigned readings ahead of time, especially for complex subjects

2. Draw a vertical line on your note paper, leaving a three-inch-wide margin on the right side.

3. Take your notes in outline form on the left side, leaving space between main points.

4. Don't try to write down everything you hear.

5. Be alert for signal words:

   a. *For example* suggests that supporting material will follow.

   b. *The three steps* suggests a list you should number.

   c. *Therefore* suggests a causal relationship.

   d. *Keep in mind* suggests this is an important idea.

6. Summarize what you hear, and jot down questions in the right margin as they come to mind.

7. Review your notes the same day that you take them.

Effective listening is particularly important in the public speaking class. Good listeners provide feedback that helps speakers adjust their messages. An attentive audience can help ease a speaker's anxiety by creating a supportive environment. Give speakers your undivided attention, and show respect for them as people, even if you disagree with their ideas.

In the public speaking classroom, effective listening can help you become a more effective speaker in at least four ways:

1. You will be better able to adapt to your audience. As you listen to their speeches, you will get a feel for what types of topics and examples might interest them, what authorities they will respect, and how they feel about important issues. Effective listening tunes you in to such factors.

2. You will become sensitive to speech techniques that work and those that don't work in different situations. Not all speaking techniques work well all the time. Some that you hear will seem brilliant, while others will fall flat. You will develop a sense of which techniques work best with your audience in various situations.

3. You will learn how to evaluate what you hear, what constitutes a credible source of information, and whether appropriate types of supporting materials are used.

4. You can use what you learn from listening to others to help you find your voice. You may hear speeches on topics you never thought you would find interesting, thus expanding your horizons. And you can learn to evaluate your personal positions on issues to see if they will stand up to critical scrutiny.

All of these skills can help you develop and present more effective speeches.

Listening at Work

At work, listening skills may mean the difference between success and failure—both for individuals and for companies. Monster.com recently suggested that 73 percent of employers considered listening skills an extremely important hiring criterion.[4] While you may not listen to many formal speeches as part of your job, you will often hear many "mini-speeches," such as instructions on how something should be done or briefings on how projects are progressing or proposals for changes in procedures or policies. Consider the following example:

John was a truck driver hauling a load of lettuce. He called his dispatcher early in the morning. "Where do you want me to take the load?"

"Jackson," she answered, and gave him the street address.

Around lunchtime, John called her back, "Well, I'm in Jackson, and I can't find the address."

"I've got it here, just as clear as can be. It says, get off I-40 at exit 82 and . . . ."

"Wait a minute," John interrupts. "I came down on I-55."

"I-55? In Jackson, Tennessee?"

"Hold it. You didn't tell me that. I'm in Jackson, Mississippi."

"Well, why didn't you ask me?" she countered.

And while they argued over who was more to blame, the poor speaker or the poor listener, a load of lettuce wilted under the Mississippi sun.

As a representative of a company, if you do not listen effectively to customers, you may damage the credibility of your organization by creating an impression of incompetence. One of your authors recalls talking to customer service representatives on the phone when she was single. After listening to a problem, the representative said, "Would you please spell that last name for me?" I typically replied, "S-M-I-T-H," but always wondered, "If they can't remember my name or can't spell Smith, how can they help me with my problem?"

Variations on these problems are played out at work every day. They cost a company both money and goodwill. For this reason, effective listening skills are valued in almost all jobs in an organization. There is also a correlation between ineffective listening and ineffective performance. If you listen effectively on the job, you will improve your chances of having a successful career

Effective listening skills are highly valued in the workplace, including listening attentively to briefings or instructions on a job site.

Understanding Listening

Listening is not the same as hearing. Hearing is an involuntary, automatic process in which sound waves stimulate nerve impulses to the brain. Listening is a voluntary process that goes beyond physical reactions to sound. It involves hearing, paying attention, comprehending, interpreting, analyzing, and evaluating.[5]

Although we spend most of our communication time listening to others speak, we receive far less formal training in listening than we do in speaking, writing, or reading. Perhaps educators assume that we are born knowing how to listen. Also, listening may be undervalued in the mainstream U.S. culture because it is typically associated with following rather than leading. Leadership is typically more admired than "followership." But being able to listen effectively increases one's ability to understand and solve problems, key ingredients of leadership.

Fortunately, this vital but sometimes neglected skill can be improved. Hearing problems can be remedied by medical or technical intervention. Listening efficiency can be increased through training.

Improved listening begins with understanding the different types of listening that are engaged in different situations. The major types of listening important in public communication include the following:

- *Comprehensive listening* involves being able to distinguish and interpret the words in a message and to pick up on nonverbal cues that affect the meaning.

- *Critical listening* adds an evaluative dimension to the comprehension of a message. It involves many of the same skills used in critical thinking, centering on whether statements are justified by adequate evidence.

- *Empathic listening* moves beyond recognizing the rationality of a speech to consider the human and humane aspects of a message.

Watch at **MyCommunicationLab** **Video:** "Difference between Listening and Hearing"

Comprehensive Listening

Comprehensive listening involves finding meaning in the sounds you hear. This includes not only the words in a message but also the way the words are spoken and the nonverbal messages that accompany them. Because we listen not only with our ears but with our eyes as well, comprehensive listening also includes being able to interpret a speaker's body language.[6] If we detect a message in body language that is at variance with the meaning of the speaker's words, we are apt to switch to the next mode of listening, critical listening. If I hear you say, "That was a delightful evening," with heavy sarcasm, you will trigger my conclusion that the words are quite wrong and that the evening was hardly delightful at all.

Explore at **MyCommunicationLab** **Activity:** "Active Listening"

Critical Listening

Critical listeners are skeptical listeners. They accept nothing at face value. The major function of **critical listening** is to enable us to detect problems in the messages or intentions of the speaker. Developing critical listening skills helps protect us from manipulative persuasion. To listen critically you must be able to evaluate supporting materials for statements or claims, determine the credibility of sources of information, detect logical fallacies, and sort through emotional appeals for their authenticity (see Chapters 14 and 15 for more on this topic).

▶ **comprehensive listening**   Listening that focuses on understanding and interpreting the verbal and nonverbal aspects of a message.

▶ **critical listening**   Listening that carefully evaluates a message.

A second function of critical listening involves understanding the ways in which pleasing language or a charismatic speaker can beguile us into accepting messages without actually evaluating them. For example, we may get so caught up in the beauty of the language, the grace of the delivery, or the personality of the speaker that we are lulled into not thinking about what we hear and possibly into ignoring flaws in a speaker's arguments or information (see Chapters 11 and 12).

Empathic Listening

Explore at **MyCommunicationLab** Activity: "Listening with Empathy"

Empathic listening is based on listening with your heart and soul. It promotes trying to see things from the speaker's perspective. Empathic listening creates a supportive environment for speaker development. It searches for the humanity in a message. As you practice empathic listening, you often access the deeper meaning of a speech.

Overcoming Barriers to Effective Listening

Explore at **MyCommunicationLab** Activity: "Effective Listening"

Even those of us who think we listen well often succumb to one or more of the barriers to effective listening. A noisy environment can disrupt effective listening. We may tune out a message and let our minds wander or get sidetracked thinking about personal matters. Sometimes we may make up our mind about what is being said before we have heard all the speaker has to say. We also may let our own emotions and biases interfere with the reception of a message.

Figure 4.1 can help you identify some of the problems that act as barriers to effective listening for you. The more items you check on this list, the more you need to work on improving your listening skills. This list will also help you pinpoint which specific areas you should concentrate on.

FIGURE 4.1
Listening Problems Checklist. Check all items that apply to you.

_____ I find it hard to listen to uninteresting material

_____ I find it difficult to listen to speeches on issues that I feel strongly about.

_____ I have strong emotional reactions to certain words.

_____ I am easily distracted by noises around me.

_____ I am easily dazzled by a glib presentation.

_____ I find myself thinking up counter arguments when I disagree with a speaker.

_____ I have trouble listening when I have a lot on my mind.

_____ I stop listening when a topic is difficult.

_____ I listen mainly for facts and ignore the rest of a message.

_____ I often jump to conclusions before I have heard a speaker out.

_____ I sometimes text friends or surf the Web when I should be listening.

▶ **empathic listening** Listening that goes beyond rationality to consider the human and humane aspects of a message.

Noise

Noise is a barrier that mainly affects comprehensive listening. When you can't hear a speaker clearly, you will have problems understanding what he or she says. For example, you really are trying to listen attentively as your comparative literature professor describes the contrasting rhyme schemes in English and Italian sonnets. Suddenly, his words are lost in the noise of students horsing around in the hall outside your classroom. "Oh, no," you think. "I can't hear with all this racket!" While you are fuming about that and the professor talks on, you may lose track of the message entirely and abandon your attempt to listen.

Speakers and listeners should work together to solve noise problems. Listeners can provide feedback to let the speaker know there is a problem. Cup your hand by your ear, or lean forward, obviously straining to hear. The speaker should pick up on that cue and talk louder in order to be heard. If the speaker doesn't respond and you still can't hear, move to a seat closer to the front of the room. If the noise comes from outside, get up and close the window or door.

Watch at **MyCommunicationLab**
Video: "Fast Food"

SPEAKER'S notes   Improving Your Listening Skills

Use these suggestions to help improve your listening skills.

1. Identify your listening problems so that you can correct them.
2. Look for something of value in every speech.
3. Put biases and problems aside when listening.
4. Control your emotional reactions to what you hear.
5. Ignore general distractions in your environment.
6. Reserve judgment until you have heard a speech all the way through.
7. Don't try to write down everything a speaker says.
8. Listen for main ideas.

Inattention

One of the most common barriers affecting listening is simply not paying attention. One cause of this problem is that our minds can process information faster than people speak. Most people talk at about 125 words per minute in public, but listeners can process information at about 500 words per minute. This "communication gap" provides an opportunity for listeners to drift away to more interesting concerns or personal problems.[7]

Chance associations with words may also cause your mind to wander. For example, a speaker mentions the word *arena*, which reminds you that there is a basketball game tomorrow night, which starts you thinking about whether you should get a date, which leads you to lascivious thoughts about the person sitting next to you. By the time your attention drifts back to the speaker, it's too late to catch up with what he or she is talking about.

Personal concerns are a third cause of inattention. When you are tired, hungry, angry, worried, or pressed for time, you may find it difficult to concentrate. Your personal problems may take precedence over listening to a speaker. Or you simply may have "listening burnout" from too much concentrated exposure to someone speaking. If you've ever attended three lecture classes in a row, you will know what this means.

FIGURE 4.2
Differences Between Good and Poor Listeners

Good Listeners	Poor Listeners
1. Focus on the message	1. Let their minds wander
2. Control emotional reactions	2. Respond emotionally
3. Set aside personal problems	3. Get sidetracked by personal problems
4. Listen despite distractions	4. Succumb to distractions
5. Ignore speaker's mannerisms	5. Get distracted by speaker's mannerisms
6. Listen for things they can use	6. Tune out dry material
7. Reserve judgment	7. Jump to conclusions
8. Consider ideas and feelings	8. Listen only for facts
9. Hold biases in check	9. Allow biases to interfere
10. Realize listening is hard work	10. Confuse listening with hearing

Overcoming inattention requires some work. Bridge the speaking/listening gap by paraphrasing to yourself what the speaker has just said. When your mind starts to drift, consciously jolt yourself to attention. Leave your personal worries at the door. Tell yourself, "This is a worry-free zone." Maintain eye contact with the speaker, and consciously commit to listening.

Figure 4.2 highlights the differences between good and poor listeners.

To become effective listeners, we may have to work to overcome boredom, fatigue, and other distractions.

Bad Listening Habits

It is all too easy to acquire bad listening habits. You probably have faked attention while tuning out a speaker. You may listen just for facts and ignore the major point of a speech.[8] Too much television viewing may lead you into the "entertainment syndrome," in which you want speakers to be lively, funny, and engaging at all times. Unfortunately, not all subjects lend themselves to entertainment. You may try to multitask by texting or checking social media on your phone and lose your concentration.[9]

Overcoming bad habits requires effort. Turn off your cell phone before entering your class. Turn it completely off, not just on vibrate. If you find yourself faking attention, remember that honest feedback helps speakers, while faking misleads them. Identify main ideas and supporting materials. Pay attention to nonverbal cues. Does the speaker's tone of voice change the meaning of the words? Are the speaker's gestures and facial expressions consistent with his or her words? If not, what does this tell you? Keep in mind that not all messages will or should be fun. Focus on what you can get out of a speech beyond enjoyment.

FINDING YOUR

voice   Identify Your Trigger Words

List three positive and three negative trigger words that provoke a strong emotional reaction when you hear them, including ideals, political terms, and sexist or ethnic slurs. Consider why these words have such a strong impact and how you might control your reactions to them. Share your insights with your classmates.

Emotional Reactions

Certain words may set off such strong emotional reactions that they become a barrier to effective listening. These **trigger words** can evoke either positive or negative reactions. Positive trigger words generally relate to values and traditions that we hold dear. Negative trigger words often relate to racial, ethnic, sexist, or religious slurs.

Positive trigger words can blind us to flawed or dangerous messages. Our reactions to them are usually subtle, and we may not realize that we are being influenced. How many times have people been deceived by such trigger words as *freedom, democracy,* and *progress* to justify certain courses of action? Negative trigger words may invoke extreme emotional reactions in us, thus lowering our estimation of a speaker's ethos and making us less likely to give his or her message a fair hearing.

How can you lessen the power of trigger words? To help you gain control over them, Professor Richard Halley of Weber State University, past president of the International Listening Association, suggests that you observe your own behavior over a period of time and make a list of words that cause you to react emotionally.[10] Then ask yourself the following questions:

- Do I let these words affect the way I respond to messages?

- Could the speaker be using these words to test or manipulate me?

- What can I do to control my reactions?

Train yourself to listen to the entire message before allowing yourself to react. By listening before reacting, you can avoid jumping to conclusions that may not be grounded in what is being said.

Biases

Your personal biases may also set off emotional reactions. All of us have biases of one kind or another. Unfortunately, they can sidetrack effective listening. Like trigger words, biases may be difficult to control. You may have biases about the topic or about the speaker. The first step in controlling biases is to recognize that you have them. Next, decide to listen as objectively as you can. Being objective does not mean that you must agree with a message, only that you will reserve judgment until you have heard the entire speech. Decide that you will look for something of value in every speech that you hear.

▶ **trigger words**   Words that arouse such powerful feelings that they interfere with the ability to listen effectively.

Problem	Try this
Noise	Alert speaker, move closer, shut door or window
Inattention	Concentrate by paraphrasing what you hear
Bad habits	Don't fake attention, don't expect to be entertained, don't try to multi-task
Trigger words	Identify them, don't jump to conclusions
Biases	Delay judgment, look for value in speech

FIGURE 4.3
Overcoming Barriers to Effective Listening

Figure 4.3 describes some techniques you can use to overcome barriers to effective listening.

Becoming a Critical Listener

Explore at **MyCommunicationLab**
Activity: "Listening"

Critical listening involves developing a healthy skepticism about what you hear. It can protect you from manipulative messages, but it requires you to give a fair hearing to ideas you disagree with. Critical listening can be learned. It uses many of the same skills involved in critical thinking: evaluating evidence, assessing credibility of the source, and considering language usage. To develop this important ability, you must learn to apply certain vital questions to what you hear:

- Do speakers provide supporting material for statements or claims?

- Are the sources of their information credible?

- Do they use language to clarify and aid understanding, or does it function more to obscure ideas or intimidate listeners?

- Are speakers using questionable strategies to make listeners more vulnerable to their messages?

Do Speakers Support Their Claims?

The claims and proposals within a speech should be justified by facts and statistics, testimony, examples, or narratives. To measure the adequacy of this justification, remember the four R's: Supporting material should be *relevant*, *representative*, *recent*, and *reliable*.

Evidence is *relevant* when it applies directly to the issue at hand. The speaker who exclaims, "The Internet is destroying family values!" and then offers statistics that demonstrate a rising national divorce rate has not established the vital connection between the Internet and family values. The information is not relevant to the claim.

Supporting materials should also be *representative* of a situation rather than an exception to the rule. For example, a speaker who insists, "Young people have no sense of values," based on a study of juvenile delinquents in London slums, has violated this particular "R."

Information should be the most *recent* available. This is especially important when knowledge about a topic is changing rapidly.

Information should also be *reliable*—we must be able to depend on it. Reliability means that the claims must be confirmed by more than one source, that the sources of information must be independent of each other, and that the sources must possess appropriate credentials. The more significant and controversial the claim is, the more reliable the evidence must be.

When evaluating supporting materials, be sure the speaker doesn't confuse facts, inferences, and opinions. **Facts** are verifiable units of information that can be confirmed by independent observation. **Inferences** are assumptions or projections based on incomplete data. **Opinions** add judgments to facts and inferences. For example, "Lee was late for class today" is a fact. "Lee will probably be late for class again tomorrow" is an inference. "Lee is an irresponsible student" is an opinion. Be alert to possible confusion among facts, inferences, and opinions as you listen to messages.

Do Speakers Cite Credible Sources?

Supporting material should come from sources that are trustworthy and competent in the topic area. Speakers should document their sources carefully, showing why they are experts on the topic. If credentials are left out or described only in vague terms, a red flag should go up in your mind. We recently found a print advertisement for a health food product that unfortunately reminded us of speaking we have seen too often on television and the Internet. The ad contained "statements by doctors." A quick check of the current directory of the American Medical Association (AMA) revealed that only one of the six "doctors" cited was a member of AMA and that his credentials were misrepresented. Always ask yourself, *Where does this information come from?* and *Are these sources really qualified to speak on the topic?*

Do Speakers Use Words to Clarify or Obscure?

When speakers want to hide something, they often use incomprehensible or vague language. Introducing people who are not physicians as "doctors" to enhance their testimony on health subjects is one form of vagueness. Another ruse is using pseudo-scientific jargon, such as, "This supplement contains a gonadotropic hormone similar to pituitary extract in terms of its complex B vitamin methionine ratio." Huh? If it sounds impressive but you don't know what it means, be careful. Also, if speakers use trigger words or inflammatory language, be careful about accepting their ideas.

SPEAKER'S
notes   Critical Thinking Red Flags

These red flags should alert you to potential problems in a message.

1. No objective evidence provided
2. Sources of information not identified
3. Questionable sources of information
4. Information inconsistent with what you know
5. Claims of exclusive knowledge

6. Opinions or inferences passed off as facts
7 Vague or incomprehensible language
8. Overdone emotional appeals
9. Outlandish promises or guarantees

▶ **facts** Information that can be verified as true by independent observation.

▶ **inferences** Assumptions based on incomplete information.

▶ **opinions** Expressions of personal feeling or belief offered without supporting material.

Critical listeners take into account the emotional aspects of a message, as well as the evidence and reasoning, to understand how a situation has colored the speaker's view of the world.

You can assume that skillful speakers will paint their positions in the best possible light. There really is nothing wrong with that, but as a critical listener, you should take it into account when you assess the merits of a message.

Emotional appeals are useful for moving people to action, but they can easily be misused. Vivid examples and compelling stories demonstrate the speaker's passion for a subject and invite the listener to share these feelings. However, if speakers do not justify such feelings with good reasons and sound evidence, you should be careful about accepting what they have to say.

You should be equally skeptical of speakers who ignore the emotional aspects of a situation. You cannot fully understand an issue until you know how it affects others, how it makes them feel, how it colors their view of the world. Suppose you were listening to a speech on global warming that contained the following statement: "The United States has 5 percent of the world's population but produces 25 percent of the world's carbon dioxide emissions." Although these numbers are impressive, what do they tell you about the human problems of global warming? Consider how much more meaningful this material might be if accompanied by stories of how people's lives have been affected by rising seas and severe weather events.

The reasoning used in a speech should also make good sense. Conclusions should follow from the points and evidence that precede them. The basic assumptions that support arguments should be those that most rational, unbiased people would accept. If the reasoning doesn't seem plausible, check out independent authorities before you commit yourself to doing what the speaker wants or asks you to do.

Speakers who try to rush you into accepting their position or to sell you something you don't need often use exaggeration. If an offer sounds too good to be true, it probably is. The health food advertisement previously described contained the following claims:

> The healing, rejuvenating and disease-fighting effects of this total nutrient are hard to believe, yet are fully documented. Aging, digestive upsets, prostrate [sic] diseases, sore throats, acne, fatigue, sexual problems, allergies, and a host of other problems have been successfully treated . . . . [It] is the only super perfect food on this earth. This statement has been proven so many times in the laboratories around the world by a chemical analyst that it is not subject to debate nor challenge.

How many times have you heard speakers make such outlandish claims? Maybe the product is also useful as a paint remover and gasoline additive! As you build your critical listening skills, you develop resistance to such persuasion from charlatans who try to mask a lack of substance or faulty reasoning with a glib presentation and irrelevant emotional appeals.

Finally, you should consider whether a speaker acknowledges alternative perspectives on issues. Ask yourself, *How might people from a different cultural background see the problem? How might gender differences affect these perspectives? Would solutions or suggestions differ as well?* Whenever a message addresses a serious topic, try to consider the issue from various points of view. New and better ideas often emerge when we look at the world through a new lens.

FINDING YOUR

voice   Listening in Challenging Situations

Find speeches outside your class—on YouTube, on TED, or elsewhere on the Internet
or on television—that challenge you as a critical and constructive listener. What external
or internal barriers in the speaker, the situation, or yourself make it hard for you to listen
effectively? What might you miss as the result of impaired listening? How might you overcome this problem? Be prepared to share your thoughts in classroom discussion.

Becoming an Empathic Listener

Listening is never truly effective unless you become an empathic listener. Empathic
listening asks you to enter the world of the speaker, to put yourself in the speaker's
shoes, to understand things from the speaker's perspective.[11] It helps you to grow
as a person and to find your own voice by comparing it with the voices of others.

Empathic listening helps speakers as well because they sense that they are
reaching their audience. They believe that their listeners are supportive, that they
are connecting on some deeper level than the mere comprehension of words, and
that there is a mutual understanding that is essential to communication.

Your Ethical Responsibilities as a Listener

The ideal of effective listening is incomplete without considering the importance of
listening ethics. Ethical listeners do not prejudge a speech but keep an open mind.
John Milton, a great seventeenth-century English intellectual and poet, argued in
his *Areopagitica* that listening to opposing ideas can be beneficial. We may learn
from them, thus gaining a new perspective on an issue. Or, as we argue with them,

Explore at
MyCommunicationLab
Profile: "Talkaholic
Scale"

YOUR

ethical VOICE   Guidelines for Ethical Listening

*The ethical behavior of listeners is often a neglected subject. Keep these guidelines in
mind to help you become an ethical listener.*

1. Turn off all electronic devices when listening to
   a speaker.
2. Give the speaker your undivided attention.
3. Open your mind to new information and ideas.
4. Park your biases outside the door.

5. Provide honest feedback to listeners.
6. Look for what is useful in a message.
7. Consider how the speech might affect others.
8. Listen to others as you would have them listen to you.

we may discover *why* we believe as we do. Open-minded listening can help us find our voice by broadening and deepening our perspectives.

Just as we should be open to new ideas, we should also be open to speakers who represent different lifestyles or cultural backgrounds. We should not deprive ourselves of the chance to explore other worlds. In comparing and contrasting our ways with those of others, we learn more about ourselves.

Finally, keep in mind the impact of your listening on others. Good listeners help develop good speakers. Good listeners are also concerned about the ethical impact of messages on others. Such listeners practice their own version of the Golden Rule: "Listen to others as you would have them listen to you." All sides benefit when speakers and listeners take their ethical roles seriously.

Evaluating Speeches

Watch at
MyCommunicationLab
Video: "Speech Critique"

Listening to speeches in the classroom offers you a controlled situation in which to develop listening skills that are comprehensive, critical, and empathic. To guide your development, you need a set of standards that answer this question: *What makes a good speech?* These standards center on general considerations, substance, structure, and presentation skills.

General Considerations

General considerations include issues that apply to the speech as a whole: commitment, adaptation, purpose, freshness, and ethics.

Commitment.   Commitment means caring. You must sense that the speaker truly cares about the subject and about listeners. Committed speakers invest the time and effort needed to gain responsible knowledge of their subject. Commitment also shows up in how well a speech is organized and whether it has been carefully rehearsed. If the speaker reads from a manuscript or constantly refers to notes, it suggests a lack of adequate preparation. Last, but not least, commitment reveals itself in the energy, enthusiasm, and sincerity the speaker projects. Commitment is the spark in the speaker that can touch off fire in the audience.

Adaptation.   The speaker must adapt the speech to the audience and to the requirements of the situation. The speaker must be tuned to the needs and interests of listeners. This audience sensitivity will be reflected in the topic that is chosen, the motivational appeals that are selected, and even the language that is chosen. For example, a speech filled with technical terms may not be understandable to many lay listeners. For such listeners, the speaker is constantly challenged to translate the world of the subject matter into the world in which listeners live. Look for many analogical expressions such as "It's like . . . " and "This resembles . . . ."

The speaker must also adapt to the requirements of the situation. Speeches outside the classroom must address the topic that has been requested and announced. Classroom speeches must fulfill the assignment. An informative speech should extend understanding of a topic, a persuasive speech should influence attitudes or actions, and a ceremonial speech should celebrate shared values on special occasions. A classroom speech should also conform to specified time limits, have at least the minimum number of references specified for the assignment, and meet the specific requirements of the assignment, such as using a presentation aid or making an extemporaneous presentation.

Purpose.

All speeches should have a clear purpose, such as informing listeners of the actions to take when a tornado warning is issued. A speech that lacks a clear purpose will drift and wander like a boat without a rudder, blown this way and that by whatever random thoughts occur to the speaker. Developing a clear purpose requires speakers to determine what they want to accomplish: what they want listeners to learn, think, or do as a result of their speeches.

Freshness.

Any speech worth listening to brings something new to listeners. The topic should be fresh, or the approach to it should be innovative. When speakers rise to the challenge of overused topics such as texting and driving, they can't simply reiterate the common advice "Don't text and drive" and expect it to be effective. The audience will have heard that hundreds of times. To get through to listeners on such a subject, speakers must find a new way to present the material or a way to provide a new perspective on a familiar problem.

Ethics.

Perhaps the most important measure of a speech is whether it is good or bad for listeners. As we noted in Chapter 1, *an ethical speech demonstrates respect for listeners, responsible knowledge, and concern for the consequences of exposure to the message.*

Respect for listeners means that speakers are sensitive to the cultural diversity of their audience. Ethical speakers accept the idea that well-meaning people may hold different positions on an issue and are considerate even as they refute the arguments of others.

Ethical speakers also ground their messages in responsible knowledge. They provide oral documentation for the vital information in their speeches and establish the qualifications of the experts they cite. Ethical speakers do not pass off opinions and inferences as facts, nor do they make up data or present the ideas or words of others without acknowledging those contributions. They are alert to potential biases in their own perspectives.

Finally, ethical speakers are aware that words have consequences. Inflammatory language can arouse strong feelings that discourage critical listening. Ethical speakers think through the potential effects of their messages before they present them.

YOUR ethical VOICE   Evaluating the Ethical Dimensions of a Speech

Public speeches can give rise to a host of ethical problems. To test the ethical dimensions of speech, ask yourself these questions:

1. Does the speaker demonstrate responsible knowledge of the topic?

2. Does the speaker show respect for the audience?

3. Does the speaker seem concerned about the impact of the speech?

4. Does the speaker orally document sources of information?

5. Does the speaker avoid inflammatory language?

6. Does the speaker avoid exaggerating claims?

The greater the possible consequences are, the more carefully these speakers support what they say with credible evidence and temper their conclusions in keeping with listener sensitivities.

Evaluating Substance

A speech is substantive when it has a worthwhile message that is supported by facts and figures, testimony, examples, and/or narratives. Skillful speakers combine different types of supporting material to demonstrate their points. Combining statistics with an example will make ideas clearer. For instance, a speaker might say, "The base of the Great Pyramid at Giza measures 756 feet on each side." Although precise, this information may be difficult for listeners to visualize. But by adding, "More than eleven football fields could fit in its base," the speaker has made the material more understandable by providing an illustration that most listeners would be familiar with.

Evaluating Structure

A good speech carries listeners through an orderly progression of ideas that makes it easy to follow. It should start with an introduction, have clearly identifiable main points, and end with a conclusion. Without a clear design, a speech may seem to be a random collection of thoughts, and the message can get lost in the confusion.

The introduction may begin with an example, a quotation, or a challenging question that draws listeners into the topic: "So you think there's no need in Montana to worry about climate change? After all, you're not subject to hurricanes like those that hit the Gulf and East Coasts. But what about forest fires? And what about the overall impact of global warming on our world?" Once speakers gain attention, they can prepare listeners for what will come by previewing the main points.

The way the body of a speech is organized will vary with its subject and purpose. A speech that tells you how to do something—such as how to plan a budget— should follow the order of the steps in the process it describes. If the subject breaks naturally into parts, such as the three major types of wine (red, white, and blended), speakers might use a categorical design.

The conclusion of a speech should summarize the points that have been made and offer a final statement that helps listeners remember the essence of the message.

Effective speeches also contain transitions that link together the various parts. Transitions bridge ideas and aid understanding. During the speech, they signal listeners when one thought is ending and a new one is beginning. They help a speech flow better and help listeners focus on the major points. Transitions are especially vital between the introduction and body of a speech, between the body and conclusion, and among main points within the body.

Evaluating Presentation Skills

No speech can be effective unless it is presented well. Both the actual words speakers use and the way they use these words are important factors in presentation.

The Language of Speaking.   The language of speeches must be instantly intelligible. This means that speakers' sentences should be simple and direct. Compare the following examples:

Working for a temporary employment service is a good way to put yourself through school because there are always jobs to be found and the places you get to work are interesting—besides, the people you work for treat you well, and you don't have to do the same thing day after day—plus, you usually can tailor the hours to fit your free time.

or

Working for a temporary employment service is a good way to put yourself through school. Jobs are readily available. You can schedule your work to fit in with your classes. You don't stay at any one place long enough to get bored. And you meet a lot of interesting people who are glad to have your services.

Which is easier to follow? The first example rambles, with the speaker pausing only to catch a breath. The second example uses short sentences, inviting the use of pauses to separate ideas. As a result, the meaning is clearer.

Concrete words are generally preferable to abstract ones because they create vivid pictures for listeners and clarify meaning. Consider the following levels of abstraction:

most abstract	my pet
	my cat
	my kitten
	my eight-week-old kitten
	my eight-week-old white kitten
most concrete	my eight-week-old white Angora kitten

As the language becomes more concrete, it is easier to visualize what is being said, and there is less chance of misunderstanding.

Presentation Skills.   An effective presentation sounds natural and enthusiastic. It is free from distracting mannerisms. Most classroom assignments call for an extemporaneous presentation in which the speech is carefully prepared and practiced but not written out or memorized. Extemporaneous speakers do not read from a script; they focus on the flow of ideas, which they can adapt according to audience comprehension and interest. If listeners look confused, extemporaneous speakers can rephrase what they have just said or provide an additional example. A speech that flows smoothly indicates that the speaker has rehearsed it well.

SPEAKER'S notes   Guidelines for Oral Critiques

1. Be supportive of the speaker's efforts.

2. Begin with a positive statement.

3. Avoid vague comments such as, "I didn't like it."

4. When you point out a problem, offer a suggestion for improvement.

5. Word suggestions tactfully, such as, "Did you consider . . . ?"

6. End with a positive statement.

Strong presentation skills encourage listeners to be attentive.

Speakers should talk loudly enough to be heard easily in the back of the room. Their posture should be relaxed but not sloppy. Movements should seem natural and spontaneous as speakers gesture in response to their own ideas and in order to emphasize the points they are making.

Critiquing a Speech. A written or oral critique of a speech should provide the speaker with honest but tactful feedback on a presentation. There is an important difference between criticizing a speaker and offering a critique of a speech. Criticism too often focuses on what someone did that was wrong. A critique should be helpful and supportive, emphasizing strengths as well as weaknesses, showing consideration for the speaker's feelings, and focusing on how a speaker might improve. The Guidelines for oral critiques are summarized in the Speaker's Notes box.

FINAL
reflections   The Golden Rule of Listening

If we practice the art of effective listening, we are putting into effect the Golden Rule of Listening: *Listen to others as we would have them listen to us.* In the workplace, you will discover that your improved listening skills may be vital to your getting a job, holding the job, and earning the promotion that turns the job into a career.

As you learn to become a better listener, you will also learn to become a better speaker. Listening to your classmates make presentations, you will learn what things interest them, how they feel about certain issues, and what techniques might work best when you are speaking. The free flow of ideas in the classroom can also give rise to novel topics and issues you may want to explore in the process of finding your voice.

In the end, there is a circularity in the relationship between speaker and listener. When we listen effectively to others, we help them become better communicators. As they become better communicators, they make it easier for us to listen. As we experience this phenomenon, we also discover that finding your voice can be contagious: In a positive classroom setting, students may find their voices together.

After Reading This Chapter, You Should Be Able To Answer These Questions

1 How can becoming a more effective listener benefit you?

2 What are the major types of listening used when listening to speeches?

3 How you can overcome common barriers to effective listening?

4 What are the most important skills needed for critical listening?

5 What must you do to become an ethical listener?

6 How should you evaluate the speeches you hear?

7 How can you provide a helpful yet supportive critique of a speech?

For Discussion and Further Exploration

1 Complete the listening problems checklist in Figure 4.1. Working in small groups, discuss your listening problems with your classmates. Develop a listening improvement plan for the three most common listening problems in your group. Report your findings to the rest of the class.

2 Review your class notes from one of your lecture courses. Were your notes coherent? Were you able to identify the main points, or did you try to write down everything that was said? Was the material easy to follow and understand? How might you change your note-taking behavior?

3 One way to improve your concentration is to keep a listening log in one of your other classes. As you take class notes, put an X in the margin each time you notice your attention wandering. By each X, jot down a few words pinpointing the cause: for example, "used *men* as generic signifier." After class, count the number of times your mind drifted, and note the causes. Can you identify a pattern of reactions? This exercise will help you identify the conditions that bring on inattention and will make you more aware of your tendency to daydream. Once you realize how often and why you are drifting away, you can more easily guard against this.

4 Think of a time when not listening effectively put you in a difficult situation. What problems did this cause you? What could you have done differently? Share your insights with a classmate, and discuss the similarities and differences in your experiences.

5 Think of a person you like to listen to (speaker, teacher, etc.). List all the adjectives you can that describe this person. Think of another person you do not like to listen to. List the adjectives that describe this person. Compare the two lists, and share your conclusions with your classmates.

6 Evaluate a contemporary political speaker on ethical grounds using the questions on page 73. Be sure to differentiate between the ethical uses of speech techniques and the moral consequences of the message. Be prepared to defend your judgments in class.

Objectives

This chapter will help you

1 Adjust your message to the age, gender, education, and sociocultural characteristics of listeners

2 Understand how group affiliations might influence listeners

3 Analyze the beliefs and attitudes held by listeners

4 Understand the motives and values that drive listeners

5 Understand the rewards and challenges of audience diversity

6 Adjust your message to the speaking situation

5 Adapting to Your Audience and Situation

((**Listen** to **Chapter 5** at **MyCommunicationLab**

After another round of proposed tuition hikes, you've decided to run for the student senate. You feel the hikes will be especially hard on students who, like you, are working their way through college. You also think the raises will result in less minority representation on campus. You are convinced that the administration has not done enough to trim spending, and that the existing student government has not been outspoken enough on this issue.

During the course of your campaign, you are invited to speak at an outdoor rally sponsored by the Black Student Association (BSA), as part of a larger program with other candidates before the Student Government Association, and to your public speaking class as your persuasive speech.

Your general message and purpose for speaking will remain the same, but the different audiences and situations will suggest different strategies and points of emphasis. The BSA is committed to promoting and retaining minority enrollment, so you should probably focus on that aspect of the issue when speaking at their rally. And because you'll be speaking outside to a large audience, you should find out if some sort of amplification will be available. When speaking to your classmates, remember that public speaking assignments are usually brief, so you should streamline your presentation by focusing on your most important ideas and information. Of course, you should make sure your speech meets the requirements of the assignment!

The adjustments you make when speaking to different audiences on different occasions are crucial to finding your voice. Compared to other forms of human communication, *public speaking is audience- and situation-centered.* Every aspect of preparing and presenting your speeches—from choosing your topic to making the actual presentation—should be tailored with your audience and situation in mind. This raises important ethical questions. We've all heard "waffling" politicians who reverse their positions from audience to audience, which is unethical. But so long as your purpose and moral compass remain constant, there is nothing unethical about adapting your message to your listeners or to the needs of a given moment. Indeed, it is absolutely necessary. You simply cannot find your voice until you learn to adapt and share your thoughts with others, and understanding your audience is a key part of that process.

You've probably already begun to develop a "feel" for your classmates and the setting in which you'll be speaking, but be cautious about putting too much

YOUR ethical VOICE   Adaptation or Pandering?

You have been asked to speak to the Community Club at your old high school about immigration problems in your area. You believe that most of the students you will address have strong negative feelings about immigrants coming into the area. Your own feelings on the topic are more complex. You recognize the economic problems that might result from a large influx of immigrants, but at the same time you understand that our country is a nation of immigrants who came to our shores searching for

opportunity. In addition, while in college you have become involved with your campus ministry's work in helping immigrants find housing and jobs. While teaching English as a second language, you have come to know many of these newcomers and to both like and respect them. What could you do to prepare a speech that would both reach your audience and stay true to your own feelings on the subject? What resources might you call on? How can you communicate your voice to your listeners?

emphasis on superficial cues such as dress or personal mannerisms. Try to develop a systematic analysis to discover

1. how much your listeners know about your topic,

2. how interested they are in the subject,

3. how they feel about your topic,

4. what appeals might be best to reach them, and

5. what challenges the speaking situation might pose.

In this chapter, we first consider getting to know your audience by analyzing their demographics and by assessing their relevant beliefs, attitudes, values, and motives. We then discuss the rewards and challenges of addressing today's diverse audiences and close by considering the public speaking situation as you prepare speeches.

Understanding Audience Demographics

The first step in getting to know the members of your audience is to consider their demographic characteristics. **Audience demographics** include their age, gender, education, sociocultural background, and group affiliations. With classroom audiences, some demographic information can usually be obtained through observation. Simply look around and soak in the diversity. Listen carefully during the first round of speeches for statements that might reveal occupational interests or cultural and group affiliations. General surveys can be useful for gathering more detailed information on less visible characteristics (see Figure 5.1 for a sample general audience survey). When preparing for unfamiliar audiences outside the classroom, you may have to obtain such information on your own. Sometimes the person or group that invites you to speak can be helpful in describing your potential listeners.

Knowledge of your audience members' demographic characteristics can provide valuable insights into how they feel about your topic. It can also suggest appeals for reaching and involving them. Politicians and advertisers spend a lot of money

Explore at
MyCommunicationLab
Activity: "Audience Analysis"

▶ **audience demographics** General characteristics of listeners, including age, gender, education, sociocultural background, and group affiliations.

FIGURE 5.1
General Audience Survey

General Audience Survey

Age: _____

Gender: _____

Religious Preference: _____

Race/Ethnicity/Cultural Background: _____

Political Preference: _____

Field of Study: _____

Career Ambitions: _____

Hobbies: _____

Recreational Preferences: _____

What I believe is the most important public issue facing us today:

_____

studying the interests and concerns of targeted groups to more effectively tailor their messages. You can find information on demographic factors from a variety of sources. Beyond the familiarity most of us already have with various demographic groups, websites and specialized publications can be helpful, as can public opinion polls posted by reputable sources such as the Gallup Organization, the National Opinion Research Center, and the Roper Center for Public Opinion Research. Be wary of surveys conducted by advocacy groups that may have a hidden agenda.

As you begin your audience analysis, consider how the following demographic variables might influence the way your audience receives your message.

Age

Since the days of Aristotle, speech teachers have taught that younger audiences are more pleasure-loving, more idealistic, and more willing to consider new ideas for

FINDING YOUR

voice Where Do Your Listeners Fit In?

Look up polling information on today's college students online at any of the major polling sites. Some helpful resources include the Pew Research Center and the Education Research Institute. From what you have observed in your classroom, consider how your audience compares with the demographic and attitude information that you find in national polls. Which demographic factors in your audience are similar to those in the polls? Which factors differ?

changing the world. Older listeners are generally more "set in their ways," more concerned with maintaining the social order and a comfortable existence. Those in the prime of life, Aristotle argued, present a balance between youth and age, being confident yet cautious, judging cases by the facts, and being willing to consider new ideas in a critical yet constructive frame of mind.[1] Contemporary research supports the relationship between age and susceptibility to persuasion that Aristotle identified.[2] The presidential elections of Bill Clinton in 1992 and Barack Obama in 2008—both of which were orchestrated around the message of change and faith in a better future—were both anchored by the overwhelming support of young first-time voters.[3]

More recently, scholars and advertisers have focused on age in terms of generational identification. The idea is that people who come of age during the same period of time tend to share experiences, worldviews, lifestyles, and dispositions that distinguish them from other generations. For instance, much has been written about the "Baby Boomers," who came of age during the 1960s and are generally characterized as more idealistic and progressive than their parents' generation, which had been hardened by the Great Depression and World War II.[4]

Younger generations are often described in less flattering terms as self-absorbed, less hard-working, and less interested in social and political issues. Some studies suggest that the current generation of "millennials" (born between 1980 and 2000) represents a resurgent idealism or optimism tempered by an emphasis on individual responsibility. They are more comfortable with new technologies, more tolerant of diversity, and more willing to adapt to a constantly changing world.[5] You can learn more about the latest generation of young college students by reading the annual report of UCLA's Higher Education Research Institute on first-year college students.

Gender

Over the past few decades, scholars have devoted considerable attention to the apparent differences between the communication styles of men and women. Although the theories remain controversial, men are often said to be more competitive in their communicative behaviors and more concerned with "winning arguments" and exerting control over the situation. Women, on the other hand, are said to focus more on maintaining social connections, nurturing mutual growth and self-discovery and are more willing to accommodate contrasting positions.[6] Women are typically pictured as more liberal than men, more likely to support spending increases on education, more concerned about environmental protections and gay rights, and more accepting of government providing for needy children and the elderly.[7] Women have been more prone to vote for Democrats than for Republicans for over thirty years and have cast a clear majority of their votes for the Democratic candidate in the past five presidential elections.[8]

We live in an age of revolutionary change with respect to gender norms and the role of women in society. For that reason, you should be careful that any demographic information you use is as current as possible. In 1968, just 37 percent of American women held full-time jobs outside of the home, and the jobs they held typically offered little pay and less power. Today, women make up 47 percent of graduates from American law schools and they are the primary breadwinners in 40 percent of American households.[9] Women are more likely to vote than men and have consistently outvoted men in recent presidential elections by margins ranging from 4 to nearly 8 million votes.[10]

Knowledge of your audience, such as the younger generation's comfort with and interest in new technologies and social media, will help you adapt your message to meet their needs and expectations.

Finally, keep in mind that there are exceptions to every demographic tendency. Married women are decidedly more conservative than single women,[11] and women leaders are playing a prominent role in reshaping the activist base of the conservative movement. Therefore, use caution in making adjustments based solely on the gender of your listeners.

Education

The educational focus and level of your listeners can be valuable indicators of their knowledge of and interest in a topic area. They can help you determine the level at which you should address your topic and whether you need to explain basic ideas or define jargon that is specific to your topic area. For instance, if you are addressing a group of advanced accounting majors, you can probably assume that they already know what a Roth IRA is, whereas with more general audiences you should probably offer a brief definition and explanation before proceeding with the rest of your speech.

Education is generally a poor indicator of political preference, and you should be cautious of the common stereotype of universities as bastions of liberal indoctrination. That said, you can expect educated listeners to be generally more informed on and more interested in current affairs, more tolerant of differing cultures and lifestyles, and more willing to listen to new ideas and fresh perspectives with an open mind. You can also expect them to be more critical and demanding consumers of messages. Educated listeners are more likely to expect you to engage opposing views when arguing disputed positions and to expect you to use knowledge as responsible evidence. If you are not well prepared, educated listeners are more likely to question your credibility for future presentations.[12]

Sociocultural Background

Watch at **MyCommunicationLab** **Video:** "Same Holiday, Different Customs"

Sociocultural background represents a broad category that can include everything from the region of the country or world your listeners are from, to racial, ethnic, or national identity, to their economic status or "class." People from different sociocultural backgrounds often have different experiences, interests, and viewpoints that can pose a challenge to meaningful communication—especially with listeners that speak English as a second language. These differences can also be a source of misunderstanding between members of various American co-cultures. Consider, for example, the different perspectives that urban and rural audiences may have on the issue of gun control. Urban listeners may be more prone to associate guns with crime and violence, whereas rural audiences may associate guns with hunting, recreation, or symbols of freedom. A white, middle-class person might have difficulty understanding what it means to grow up as a member of a minority. Northerners and southerners often have misconceptions about each other.

As you consider the sociocultural backgrounds of your listeners, be wary of overly simplistic stereotypes, and remember it is *your* audience for *your* speech that is important. Keep in mind that most Americans come from a variety of sociocultural backgrounds, and that for many people categories such as "race" are becoming increasingly less relevant. With diverse audiences, your appeals and examples

voice
The Importance of Groups

Of the groups you belong to, consider the one that means the most to you. What is it about being a part of this group that brings you the greatest satisfaction? Is it the social interaction? The opportunity to do something of value for society? The prestige it confers on you? Share this information with your classmates. What does your membership say about you as a person? What do your classmates' memberships say about them? As a class, make a list of all of your group affiliations. Are there more similarities than differences? How might this information be useful to you as you choose speech topics and prepare your speeches?

should relate to those experiences, feelings, values, and motivations that you and your listeners hold in common. We will return to the subject of addressing culturally diverse audiences later in this chapter.

Group Affiliations

The groups people belong to often reflect their interests, attitudes, and values. Knowing the occupational, political, religious, and social group memberships of your audience members can help you design a speech that better fits their interests and needs.

Occupational Groups. Your listeners' occupational affiliations or career aspirations can provide insight into how much they know about a topic, the vocabulary you should use, and which aspects of a topic should be most interesting to them. Obviously, an audience of health care providers can be expected to already know about the latest strains of flu viruses. Knowledge of occupational interests also suggests the kinds of authorities that listeners will find most credible. If many of your classmates are business majors, for instance, they may find information from the *Wall Street Journal* more convincing than information from *USA Today*. You can gather information on various occupational groups by consulting specialized publications and websites. For instance, *Spectra*—a publication of the National Communication Association—features brief articles and commentaries regarding the concerns and interests of public speaking teachers and communication professors.

Political Groups.   Knowledge of your listeners' political affiliations can provide valuable insights into strongly held moral and ideological convictions and is especially important for developing speeches on controversial issues such as gun control and health care reform. Consider Amanda Miller's speech criticizing the U.S.-sponsored "School of the Americas" as a source of right-wing terrorism in Latin America. From her audience analysis, Amanda knew that many of her listeners were conservative Republicans, and she feared that some of them might dismiss her message as a left-wing "apology for America." So she decided to open her speech by citing a prominent conservative, well known for his patriotism and willingness to use American military power and influence abroad:

> "If any government sponsors the outlaws and killers of innocents, they have become outlaws and murderers themselves, and they will take that lonely path at their own peril." President Bush spoke these words to the world shortly after the attacks on the World Trade Towers.

By citing a person held in such high regard by her listeners, Amanda invited them to look at her issue through an ironic lens: Once they knew what many graduates of the School of the Americas had actually done, they could only conclude that the United States had acted in a manner that was contradictory to our own national values and interests. The rest of her speech was well received because of the way she had adapted her message to the political leanings of her audience.

Information regarding the political affiliations of unfamiliar listeners can be tricky to ascertain. Sometimes the nature of the speaking occasion and sponsoring group can provide helpful clues. For example, a banquet hosted by your local chamber of commerce will likely attract a mostly conservative or "pro-business" audience. General surveys (see Figure 5.1) can be useful for analyzing the dynamics of smaller classroom audiences, and students with strong political ties will often make them known in the course of class discussions and their own speeches.

Keep in mind that we live in an age of declining party loyalty and adherence to party doctrines. Some Democratic and Republican politicians take positions on issues that are at odds with those of their own party. Growing numbers of young Americans now define themselves as "Independents" that evaluate issues and candidates on an individual basis.[13] We encourage you to be cautious about attributing too much to political affiliation and to supplement what you learn with more specific information regarding your audience and intended message.

Religious Groups.   Knowing the religious affiliations of listeners can provide useful information because religious training often underlies many of our social and cultural attitudes and values. Members of fundamentalist religious groups are likely to have conservative social and political attitudes. Baptists tend to be more conservative than Episcopalians, who in turn are often more conservative than Unitarians. In addition, a denomination may advocate specific beliefs that many of its members accept as a part of their religious heritage.

Another word of caution: You can't always assume that because an individual is a member of a particular religious group, he or she will embrace all of the teachings of that group. One thing you can count on, however, is that audiences are usually sensitive about topics related to their religious convictions. As a speaker, you should be aware of this sensitivity and be attuned to the religious makeup of your audience. Appealing exclusively to "Christian" values before an audience that includes members of other religious groups may diminish the effectiveness of your message with your total audience.

Social Groups.   Typically, we are born into a religious group, raised in a certain political environment, and end up in an occupation as much by chance as by design. But we choose our social groups on the basis of our interests. Membership in social groups can be as important to people as any other kind of affiliation.

Photographers may join the campus Film Club, businesspeople may become involved with the local chamber of commerce, and environmentalists may be members of the Sierra Club.

Knowing which social groups are represented in your audience and what they stand for is important for effective audience adaptation. A speech favoring pollution control measures might take a different focus depending on whether it is presented to the chamber of commerce or to the Audubon Society. With the chamber of commerce, you might stress the importance of a clean environment in persuading businesses to relocate to your community; with the Audubon Society, you might emphasize the effects of pollution on wildlife. As with political affiliations, people tend to make their important group memberships known to others around them. Be alert to such information from your classmates, and consider it while planning and preparing your speeches.

Knowing the group affiliations of your listeners can help you design a speech that fits their interests, concerns, and needs.

Some Words of Caution

Becoming aware of demographic factors is an important first step in getting to know your audience. Such knowledge might be useful for identifying points of shared interest, for framing appeals, and for avoiding sources of misunderstanding. You should be cautious about relying too heavily on any one demographic factor when analyzing your audience. Most audiences are more diverse than you might realize. Today's college classrooms are generally much more diverse in terms of minorities, economic levels, and nontraditional students than those of just a generation ago. And even if your fellow students all *look* the same, you can safely assume that most class audiences represent a healthy mix of political, religious, and other demographic categories. Finally, most people have multiple affiliations that often work together but sometimes may compete with each other to shape how they might receive your message. For instance, a listener might be a liberal Democrat on most issues, while staunchly opposed to abortion because of his religious convictions.

Perhaps more important, there is a very fine line between demographic sensitivity and stereotyping. Most public speaking audiences are relatively small, and what tends to be true for larger sections of society is often wrong when applied to specific individuals or smaller groups. Some of the most ardent critics of affirmative action are prominent African Americans. Some of the harshest critics of the Catholic Church's opposition to birth control are themselves devout Catholics. Even when your demographic presumptions are accurate, most people become uncomfortable when they feel they are being spoken to as members of groups rather than as individuals. This is especially true when speakers do not share these affiliations. The lesson should be clear: Be mindful and respectful of your audience members' demographic characteristics, but supplement that knowledge by learning about their particular beliefs, attitudes, values, and relevant motives.

Understanding Audience Dynamics

Audience dynamics refers to the beliefs, attitudes, values, and motives that shape listener behavior. A better feel for the dynamics of your particular audience can help you focus your specific purpose and message, choose the most effective appeals, decide which authorities to cite, and determine which examples and stories might work best in your speeches.

Beliefs

Beliefs express what we know or think we know about subjects and are typically acquired directly through experience and education or indirectly from friends, family members, and trusted authority figures. They may be based on verifiable facts, such as, "The price of digital cameras has dropped dramatically over the past five years." Or they may reflect subjective opinions, such as, "Democrats are soft on crime," or even popular lore, such as, "Southerners make the best chefs." At their worst, beliefs may express demeaning stereotypes about races, religions, or cultures.

Information about your listeners' beliefs can suggest what additional information you need to provide or what misinformation you may need to correct. For instance, if you are presenting a speech arguing for caps on greenhouse gas emissions to curb global warming, you will probably want to find out if your audience members believe that global warming is occurring and if they think human activity is a major cause of it. To establish the first claim, you could cite the consensus of scientific evidence and expert testimony that demonstrates that global warming is occurring. The second proposition might be trickier because the assertion that human activity is a major cause of global warming is subject to debate with some people. Your listeners may have already developed strong feelings or "attitudes" on the issue.

Attitudes

Attitudes are our feelings and disposition toward a given subject—whether we like or dislike, approve or disapprove of people, places, events, or ideas. Because they are more strongly held and more developed than beliefs, they are typically a better indicator of your listeners' willingness to consider and act upon your message. They are also harder to change and influence and may require your best use of evidence and reasoning. As we will discuss further in Chapter 14, with skeptical audiences, it is usually a good idea to establish common ground before addressing differences. You should also emphasize facts and expert opinions more than emotional appeals. On some occasions, you might even consider adjusting your specific purpose to give your speech a better chance for a favorable reception.

Consider our example above. Many ardent "greenhouse skeptics" now concede, however grudgingly, that global warming is occurring. But they also feel that cycles of nature are the major cause, and that drastic efforts to cap greenhouse emissions will be devastating to the economy. Speaking before a skeptical audience, you must provide an especially strong case. But you might also consider limiting your objective to establishing that human pollution is an important contributing factor. Figure 5.2 shows a topic-oriented attitude questionnaire that you might adapt for information that will help you plan your next speech.

Watch at **MyCommunicationLab** **Video:** "Jail Reform and Drug Rehabilitation"

▶ **audience dynamics** The beliefs, attitudes, values, and motives that influence the behavior of listeners.

▶ **beliefs** What we know or think we know about subjects.

▶ **attitudes** Feelings we have developed toward specific kinds of subjects.

Topic-Oriented Attitude Survey

Please circle the number that best represents your position for each question.

How interested are you in _____ ? [add issue]

Very interested		Unconcerned		Not interested
5	4	3	2	1

How important do you think this issue is?

Very important		No opinion		Not important
5	4	3	2	1

How much do you know about this issue?

Very much		Average knowledge		Very little
5	4	3	2	1

How would you describe your attitude toward the issue?

Strongly in favor		On the Fence		Strongly opposed
5	4	3	2	1

Please place a check beside the sources of information on this issue that you would find the most acceptable.

_____ Fox News

_____ CNN

_____ Wall Street Journal

_____ MSNBC

_____ The Huffington Post

_____ Bill O'Reilly

_____ Rachel Maddow

_____ Stephen Colbert

_____ Hillary Clinton

_____ Chris Christie

_____ Other (please specify)

Comments:

FIGURE 5.2
Topic-Oriented Attitude Survey

Values

Our most important beliefs and attitudes are often anchored by our personal, social, religious, and political **values**—the moral *principles* we live by that suggest how we should behave. Values provide us with standards for evaluating the

▶ **values**   The moral principles that suggest how we should behave or what we should believe.

rightness or wrongness of ideas and behaviors and may include such ideals as honesty, fairness, individual responsibility, and patriotism.

Values are at the core of our identity. As principles that govern our behavior and our way of seeing the world, they are even more resistant to change than strongly held attitudes. For that reason, effective speakers rarely try to challenge or change the core values of their listeners. Again as discussed in Chapter 14, it is better to invoke and reason from values the audience shares with the speaker. If you are arguing for measures to cut greenhouse gas emissions before a skeptical audience, you might do well to open by invoking the principle that humans have a shared obligation to be responsible stewards of the land and to leave future generations with a planet worth inhabiting. Such references to shared values can increase identification with your audience as well as justifying your argument.

Motives

Motives are psychological needs, desires, and impulses. Appeals to motives can be quite effective for reaching audiences. Advertisers use such appeals to sell us everything from home security systems to luxury vacations. And because motives are widely shared, such appeals may transcend barriers in today's diverse audiences.

Motivational appeals work by creating a sense of need in the minds of listeners and then associating your message with fulfilling that need. They are sometimes explicit in public speaking, as when a financial adviser opens her presentation by saying "Everyone dreams of a secure retirement, but too many of us fail to plan for it until it is too late." On other occasions, motivational appeals are implied in a good speech. For instance, a presentation that raises consciousness of a spike of violent crime in the vicinity of your college will engage your classmates' need to feel safe on campus.

Psychologists have been studying motivational appeals since the early twentieth century. In a pioneering study published during the 1930s, Henry A. Murray and his associates at Harvard University identified more than twenty-five human needs.[14] Perhaps the most influential contribution to this discussion is Abraham Maslow's five-tiered hierarchy of needs; Maslow argued that lower-level physical and security needs must be satisfied before our higher-level needs for belonging, esteem, and self-actualization come into play.[15]

Consider whether and how your speeches might invoke the following widely shared motivations.

Physical Well-Being.   As Maslow argued, all of us have physical needs for things like food, water, clean air, and sleep. We also have a basic need to feel reasonably comfortable: to keep our bodies cool when it's hot and warm when it's cold. Commercials for fitness and weight-loss products often play to this need. One student speaker caught the attention of his classmates as he appealed to this need in the introduction of his speech on the benefits of yoga:

> No pain, no gain! Right? No, wrong. If workout routines leave you heading
> for the medicine cabinet, look for another way to get your body and heart in
> shape. An exercise program that combines yoga and power walking improves
> both your body tone and your cardiovascular system.

Safety and Security.   We all need to feel free from threats such as terrorist attacks, high crime rates, and natural disasters. Appeals to the need for safety are usually based on arousing a sense of fear. You should be cautious when using fear appeals in speeches. When they are too obvious or seem outlandish, your listeners may feel manipulated and react negatively to your message. Fear appeals are especially problematic when they stereotype groups of people and depict them as a threat to our security. Should you decide to use safety appeals in your speech, be sure to avoid this danger. Revisiting an earlier example, a speech documenting a spike in violent assaults on or around your campus would be more effective if you provide your listeners with advice on how to keep themselves safe or even how to get involved and become part of a proposed solution.

Understanding.   People are naturally curious and have a deep-seated need to understand the world. We want to know what things are, why they are happening, how they work, and what we can do to make them work better. In today's rapidly changing world, speeches that explain and describe the use of new technologies in the workplace might fulfill this need. Joseph Van Matre's student speech on the use of videogame simulations in medical fields, education, the business world, and the military was well received by his classmates, who were not familiar with these applications (see this speech in Appendix B).

Relational Needs.   Human beings are social creatures, and we all have a need for the affection, companionship, acceptance, and support of others. Our friends and families help define who we are and make the world a less lonely place. The need for social bonds is often used in advertising. How many commercials have you seen suggesting that you risk losing friends if you don't use the right deodorant? Speeches that encourage listeners to join clubs typically play to our relational needs.

Achievement and Recognition.   Most people like to feel they are successful. Similarly, they want recognition for their accomplishments. Appeals to our need for achievement are commonly used by motivational speakers, as they encourage us to "take charge of our lives." Recognition appeals are often used in commercials advertising expensive new cars as a way to tell others that we've arrived. Speakers may arouse the need for recognition when they compliment their audiences in their introductory remarks. Compliments can put listeners in a positive frame of mind, making them more receptive to your message.

Personal Growth and Satisfaction.   Beyond material success and achievement, most people like to feel as if they are developing their inner potential—that they are growing in a meaningful way. Definitions of personal growth may vary from person to person and culture to culture. People may derive their sense of satisfaction from having a job they love, becoming independent, developing artistic talents, or even participating in a recreational activity such as jogging. Appeals to this need are sometimes subtle but are common in advertising, as in commercials for investment firms showing an older person who knows that her retirement will be secure. As with achievement and recognition appeals, they are also commonly used by motivational speakers.

Pleasure and Recreation.   All of us need to have fun from time to time—especially college students, who often find themselves overwhelmed with assignments, tests, and speeches to give, not to mention full- or part-time work. Appeals to our need for "R and R" (rest and recreation) are a staple of advertising, which often associates drinking alcoholic beverages with hip social gatherings and outdoor recreational activities. Student speeches can engage this need by introducing their listeners to new activities or affordable nearby places for weekend getaways.

Tradition.   Most people identify with traditions such as holidays and patriotic celebrations that give them a sense of roots. Many of our core values are steeped in traditions: appeals to tradition are so common in public speaking that we treat them as a source of persuasive argument in Chapter 15 and of ceremonial identification in Chapter 16. People feel a strong desire to reaffirm traditions in times of crisis, such as natural disasters.

Appeals to tradition may help establish identification that bridges cultural barriers. Consider the following passage, in which student speaker Stephanie Herrera describes the celebration of Christmas in Mexico:

> People walk through the neighborhood in a *posada*. This means "where they stop." The stops along the way are beautifully decorated homes where the walkers sing carols and are given gifts of food—like cookies and candies. The *posada* is a parade to honor Niño Dios, which means "baby God" in English.

Stephanie's reminder that Christmas is celebrated across cultures helped bring her listeners together during a time in which much of the public rhetoric they were hearing on immigration was driving them apart.

Altruism.   The decision to volunteer at a soup kitchen or contribute to a charity expresses this value. [16] People derive inner satisfaction from feeling they are helping others and making the world a better place. Commercials urging us to feed children in underdeveloped countries draw on this need, as do speakers encouraging us to volunteer in our communities. Beth Tidmore used this appeal when she described the benefits children with disabilities receive from the Special Olympics:

> They experience courage and victory—and, yes, they also experience defeat. They get to interact with others with disabilities and with people without disabilities. And their mental disability is not a problem. It's not weird. Their biggest achievements aren't recognized with a medal. Their biggest achievements take place over time in the growth they make through being a part of the Special Olympics.

We all experience the psychological motives discussed here in varying degrees, and we all respond to them differently. For example, while most older people place a higher value on personal safety than they do on recreation, former President George H. W. Bush celebrated his eightieth birthday by going skydiving! If you've ever moved alone to a new town, then you've probably experienced a heightened need to make friends. Finally, members of different cultures may define and prioritize these needs in differing ways. Some cultures may favor traditional ways over innovation and individual achievement. Americans may be praised for valuing achievement through hard work but criticized for their excessive comfort needs.

Appeals to traditions with which listeners identify help bridge cultural differences.

┌───┐

YOUR ethical VOICE   Putting Motives in Action

You are working on a speech urging your classmates to vote in the upcoming election. Which of the motives we have discussed might you appeal to? How would you use these appeals? What ethical issues should you be consider as you make such appeals?

└───┘

The use of psychological appeals is sometimes controversial. For example, advertisers are sometimes criticized for advocating consumerism or for inundating us with images of idealized beauty that are unrealistic or unhealthy. Politicians may be criticized for exploiting our fears. Exaggerated motivational appeals can cause listeners to react negatively both to you and to your message. Appeals to motives must stand on a foundation of strong evidence. Then they can ethically be used to gain attention and move people to action.

Gathering Information About Audience Dynamics

How can you gather information about audience beliefs, attitudes, values, and motives? In speech classes, this is usually not difficult because people often reveal this kind of information as they take part in class discussions and activities.

For speeches outside the classroom, as well as your classroom speeches, you can gather more precise information on audience dynamics by conducting a customized survey that explores what your listeners know about your topic, how they feel about it, and how they might respond to different sources of information about it. Figure 5.2 (see p. 89) is an example of the kind of audience survey questionnaire that you can use as a guide.

When preparing your survey, follow these guidelines:

- Use simple sentences with a single idea.

- Use clear, concrete language.

- Keep questions short.

- Avoid words such as *all, always, none,* and *never.*

- Keep your personal biases out of the questions.

- Keep the questionnaire short.

- Provide room for additional comments.

While administering the survey, make it a point not to sway the responses by revealing your position on your topic. Encourage respondents to provide additional comments, using the back of the sheet if necessary. Such open-ended feedback often provides valuable insights. Finally, keep in mind that any survey provides only a general snapshot of where your audience stands. Compare what you learn from a questionnaire with what you hear as you listen to others talking about the issue in question.

**FIGURE 5.3
Motives in
Speeches**

Motives in Speeches	
Physical Well-Being	Having enough to eat and drink, enjoying a comfortable temperature, being free from pain
Safety and Security	Feeling safe and secure, being free from fear
Understanding	Satisfying curiosity, answering questions about how things work in the world
Relational Needs	Satisfying desires for affection, companionship, acceptance, and support
Achievement and Recognition	Accomplishing goals, overcoming obstacles, winning awards and honors
Personal Growth and Satisfaction	Developing your potential, improving your performance, doing your job well
Pleasure and Recreation	Having a good time, going on vacation, having fun for its own sake
Tradition	Having a sense of roots, doing things as they have always been done, honoring ancestors, appreciating your history
Altruism	Taking care of others, providing comfort and aid, giving to charities, volunteering service, promoting the general well-being

Rewards and Challenges of Audience Diversity

Chances are the audiences you will address in class, at work, or in your community will be diverse in terms of age, gender, ethnicity, and sociocultural background. Learning to appreciate and interact with a diverse audience can be quite rewarding. It can help you become a more effective and ethical speaker, and it can enrich your thinking and expand your horizons.

However, with a diverse audience you can also face barriers to meaningful communication. You can give more effective speeches if you learn more about the cultural backgrounds of your listeners, invoke shared values, choose your words carefully, and avoid stereotypes and other rhetorical land mines that can destroy meaningful communication.

Become Familiar with Audience Cultures

The best way to learn about different cultures is to reach out to those who represent them. Consider attending "mixers" or social events hosted by organizations representing different minority, international, or religious groups on your campus. Such contacts

voice

Sampling Audience Diversity

With your instructor's permission, form small groups of class members who differ in age, gender, ethnicity, or other demographic features. Have them write down their five most important needs, wants, and wishes. Ask them to compare the lists and make note of their similarities and differences. Use this information to learn about each other. Consider how this information might be helpful in planning speeches.

will often acquaint you with people who can offer advice for adapting your ideas, selecting supporting materials, and avoiding language that might be offensive. Such contacts may also help you grow and find your voice as you address diverse audiences.

Use Supporting Materials Skillfully

As we will discuss in Chapter 8, facts and statistics, testimony, examples, and narratives provide support for your presentations. Different cultural groups may find different types of support important. Some groups may be persuaded by facts and expert testimony. Others might value the voices of elders or religious leaders. Still others might be engaged more by stories and dramatic examples. Try to determine what kinds of supporting materials your specific audience will find most convincing. If you are uncertain concerning audience preferences, use a variety of supporting materials. Provide facts and expert opinions to validate your main ideas, look for quotations by authorities your listeners would respect, and engage your listeners with stories and examples.

When cultural differences exist in your audience, *emphasize the use of narratives*. All people tell stories, and nothing can bring diverse groups together more effectively than narratives that help them discover their shared humanity. Former Vice President Al Gore reflected on this power of narrative in his attempts to promote peace talks between the Israelis and their Palestinian neighbors. The situation looked hopeless, he remembered, when a "miracle" occurred. In Gore's words, "The breakthroughs came when they told stories about their families. I have seen time and time again how storytelling brings people together."[17]

Speak from Shared Values

While values and the way we prioritize them may vary across cultures, most Americans share such values as faith, hard work, and individual responsibility. Focus on shared values rather than differences. In his keynote address before the Democratic National Convention in 2004—a speech largely credited with catapulting him to national prominence—then Senator Barack Obama transcended the potential barriers of politics, race, and culture by emphasizing a shared patriotism. "[T]here is not a liberal America and conservative America," he insisted, "there is only the United States of America. There is not a Black America and a White America and a Latino America and Asian America—there's the United States of America."[18]

Finally, try to invoke values that appeal to all cultures. People the world over share such values as honesty, fairness, justice, charity, freedom, self-determination, and respect for tradition.

Choose Your Words Carefully

Speakers who bridge cultural diversity use the language of inclusion. The use of pronouns such as *we* and *our* instead of *them* and *their* can enhance your chances for establishing common ground. Avoid language that calls attention to differences between yourself and listeners.

Be careful that your words do not confuse listeners. When audience members are unfamiliar with your topic, use lay language, and define terms that might be misunderstood. Consider using presentation aids to clarify and amplify your most important ideas and information. If your audience includes listeners for whom English is a second language, avoid slang terms and colloquialisms such as "he left it all out on the floor" or "she hit the wall." These and similar expressions can bring utter confusion to those who are new to our language and its idiosyncrasies.

Finally, do not try to copy the communication style of other cultures; this almost always comes across as inappropriate, if not offensive. If you try speak a language that is not your native tongue, be sure you get the pronunciation right. In a recent political race, a candidate offered a speech that he hoped would win the support of the Cuban expatriate community in Florida. As he concluded, he shouted: *"Patria o muerte, venceremos!"* ("Fatherland or death, we shall overcome"). He did not understand the icy reaction he got until someone explained that those words were the trademark sign-off of Fidel Castro.[19]

Avoid Rhetorical Land Mines

Finally, avoid stepping on land mines that can explode your efforts to communicate with diverse audiences. These land mines include stereotypes, ethnocentrism, sexism, and racism.

Invoking shared values and choosing your words carefully can bring listeners together even when issues threaten to drive them apart.

Stereotypes.   All of us categorize our experiences to help us make sense of new situations and guide our interactions with others. However, problems arise when we group people into categories that harden into **stereotypes**, or rigid beliefs, attitudes, and expectations that reflect our attitudes toward these groups. Some of the most problematic stereotypes include disparaging references to ethnicity, nationality, religion, gender, and sexual orientation. Even seemingly benign stereotypes such as "Mexican Americans are hard workers" can be hurtful and damaging. They can make people feel as though they are being addressed as members of a group rather than as individuals. Remember that your listeners do not conform to stereotypes. Respect their individuality. Critical listeners will detect stereotypes in your presentation and may reject both you and your message.

Ethnocentrism.   **Ethnocentrism** is the belief that our way of life is the "right" and superior way. In its mildest form, ethnocentrism reveals itself as patriotism or national pride. But ethnocentrism becomes problematic when it goes beyond pride

▶ **stereotypes**   Generalized pictures of a race, gender, or group that supposedly represent its essential characteristics.

▶ **ethnocentrism**   The tendency of any nation, race, religion, or group to believe that its way of looking at and doing things is right and that other perspectives have less value.

in one's own group to the derogation of others. In such cases, ethnocentrism can be an almost insurmountable barrier to communication.

The first step in controlling ethnocentrism is to recognize your own tendencies to overestimate your culture and underestimate those of others. For example, most Americans believe that over half the world's population speaks English, when actually only about 20 percent do.[20] To avoid the impression of ethnocentrism in your speeches, *show respect for the humanity of all people, and recognize that this common humanity transcends both race and culture.*

Sexism.   **Sexism** occurs when we allow gender stereotypes to control our interactions with members of the opposite sex. **Gender stereotyping** involves making broad generalizations about men or women based on outmoded assumptions, such as "men should be the head of the household" and "women don't know anything about sports." Gender stereotyping becomes problematic when it implies that the differences between genders suggest that one gender is superior to the other or when it is used to justify discrimination.

As discussed earlier in this chapter, we live in a time when gender roles are changing rapidly, and you should be sensitive to any assumptions you may have made about your listeners as you plan and prepare your speeches. Be especially cautious of **sexist language**, which, in addition to obviously disparaging labels, might include irrelevant references to gender such as "male nurse" or "female game warden." You can avoid this problem simply by saying "she" or "he" or by using the plural "they."

Racism.   Finally, be on the lookout for racial stereotypes, racially charged humor, and **racist language** that might suggest negative assumptions about racial groups. Examine your own thinking for any lurking bias. As with sexist language, racist language may include irrelevant references to race such as "Hispanic police officer" or "black mayor."

While blatant racism and discrimination are no longer acceptable in most circles, a more subtle form of **symbolic racism** still poisons popular thinking and public discourse from time to time. Symbolic racism is expressed in covert or coded fashion, as when people speak of "protecting the integrity of our neighborhoods" to convey an obvious discomfort with the prospect of having members of minority groups for neighbors. A few of President Obama's harshest critics have resorted to the language of symbolic racism, as reflected by the repeated questions raised about his identity as an American and the repeated exhortations to "take back *our* America."

SPEAKER'S notes   Avoiding Racist and Sexist Language

To avoid racist and sexist innuendos in your speeches keep these guidelines in mind.

1. Do not use slang terms to refer to racial, ethnic, religious, or gender groups.

2. Avoid using the generic *he* and gender-specific titles such as *meter maid*.

3. Avoid stereotypic references that might imply inferiority or superiority.

4. Stay away from sexist, racist, ethnic, or religious humor.

▶ **sexism** Allowing gender stereotypes to control interactions with members of the opposite sex.

▶ **gender stereotyping** Generalizations based on oversimplified or outmoded assumptions about gender roles.

▶ **sexist language** Using disparaging labels and references to gender, making irrelevant references to gender, or using masculine nouns or pronouns when the intended reference is to both sexes.

Adjusting to the Speaking Situation

Finally, you need to consider the **speaking situation** in which you will make your presentation. The situation includes the occasion for speaking as well as the physical and psychological settings.

The Occasion

Watch at
MyCommunicationLab
Video: "Truman's Decision
to Drop the Bomb"

As you prepare your speeches, consider the reasons people will gather to hear you. Listeners will have expectations about what type of presentation they will hear. When attendance is mandatory, as in work-related or classroom presentations, you need to give extra thought to attracting and sustaining attention. Your task will be to transform a captive audience into an enthusiastic one.

As we noted in Chapter 6, expectations surrounding the occasion will often dictate your choice of topic and purpose for speaking. For instance, if you are making an award presentation at a church banquet, then you should focus primarily on the nature of the award and the worthiness of the recipient. The expectations of the occasion can influence how we dress and our style of presentation. Obviously, formal occasions require formal attire but also dictate your manner of presentation and your language choices.

Audience members may become irritated when speakers violate their expectations about what is appropriate. For example, if listeners expect an informative presentation on investment strategies and your speech quickly morphs into a thinly veiled sales pitch for a mutual fund, they may question your trustworthiness. They may be more irritated than persuaded.

The Physical Setting

The physical setting includes the place where you will be speaking, the time of your presentation, and the size of your audience. Like the occasion, these factors can affect how you speak.

Place.   The place where you will speak can pose several challenges. For example, will a lectern be provided? The answer to that question might influence your planning and practice for the presentation. If you plan to use an electronic presentation aid, make sure you have an electrical outlet. When speaking outdoors or in a really large room, you might need to use a microphone to project your voice. Classroom settings are usually small and speaker friendly, but you can never be sure. We recently taught a course at a major university that was undergoing renovations. We never knew when we were going to have to suddenly project our voices loudly enough to compete with a rumbling jackhammer!

Regardless of where you will speak, familiarize yourself with the place. If possible, practice your presentation there. Such preparation usually makes you more comfortable and can help novice speakers cope with communication anxiety.

Time.   The amount of time you are allotted to speak, the time of day, the day of the week, and even the time of the year can affect the way listeners receive your message. When speaking early in the morning, at the end of a long workday, or on Mondays (when listeners are still adjusting to the weekend being over), you may need to be dynamic and use supporting materials and presentation aids that are quite interesting. Even snowy winter days or sunny spring days can sometimes put listeners in a distracted state of mind.

▶ **racist language**   Using disparaging labels and references to race or making irrelevant references to race such as "black doctor."

▶ **symbolic racism**   Indirect racism that uses code words or subtle contrasts to suggest that one race is superior to another.

▶ **speaking situation**   The occasion for speaking as well as the physical and psychological settings.

With shorter presentations, the limited amount of time you have increases the importance of focusing and streamlining your message. You must focus quickly on your most important ideas and choose your most relevant and impressive supporting materials. You should also plan introductions and conclusions that give your message punch and power.

Audience Size.   Finally, the size of your audience can affect how you should speak. With smaller audiences, you can have more audience interaction. This invites a more casual presentation. On the other hand, larger audiences may call for a more formal manner of speaking. Since you cannot make or sustain eye contact with everyone, you should choose representative listeners in various sections of the audience and pan back and forth so that everyone feels included. Your voice should be animated and your gestures more emphatic so that you can easily be heard and seen by everyone in the audience. Presentation aids and lettering should be large and bold enough to be intelligible to your most distant listeners.

Speaking before a large audience or in a vast space requires adjustments in presentation style.

SPEAKER'S notes   Checklist for Analyzing the Speaking Situation

Use this checklist to be sure you don't overlook anything important when analyzing the speaking situation.

1. Will the time or timing of my speech pose any problems?

2. How might audience expectations affect my speech preparation?

3. Is there any late-breaking news relevant to my topic?

4. How large will my audience be?

5. Does the place where I will speak call for any adjustments?

The Psychological Setting

The psychological setting for your speeches may be influenced by the context of recent events or by speeches that are presented before yours.

Recent Events.   When listeners enter the room the day of your speech, they bring with them information about recent events. This information may affect the way listeners receive and evaluate your message. Citing recent developments early on in your speech can help you establish the importance and timeliness of your topic. On the other hand, failing to acknowledge or account for recent events can damage both the effectiveness of your speech and your ethos. For instance, we once had a student present a speech that was highly critical of the "war on terror" right after a major and well-publicized attack on American soil. The speech was otherwise very thoughtful, well supported, and well put together. The fact that the speaker failed to even acknowledge the attack and was obviously not prepared for subsequent questions about it left a negative impression on his listeners.

Recent Speeches.   Many speaking occasions—such as award dinners, political rallies, and class presentations—feature a number of speeches presented in succession. The speeches presented before your presentation can have a **preliminary tuning effect** on the thinking, mood, and receptivity of your audience. This effect sometimes requires last-minute "impromptu" adjustments—usually in the introduction to your speech. For instance, if the speaker before you makes a truly outstanding presentation, you might do well to acknowledge that before launching into your own presentation. If your speech follows an effective presentation on a depressing subject such as human slavery, you might want to rethink the humor you had planned to open your speech.

The preliminary tuning effect can be quite challenging when a previous speaker makes a compelling argument against the position you intend to take in your speech. This sometimes happens in public speaking classes. For example, suppose you are going to present a speech supporting legislation to protect the habitat of an endangered species. The speaker before you has made a powerful and well-supported argument that passing the law would do incredible damage to the local economy. Do not open your speech by criticizing the speaker unless you find his or her arguments to be "over the top," reprehensible, or misleading. On such occasions, it is usually better to gracefully acknowledge the speaker and perhaps even thank him or her for raising an important issue. You might then transition into your presentation with something like, "Now let me tell you the other side of the story."

Bringing It All Together.   The audience analysis worksheet in Figure 5.4 will help you consider all the factors we have discussed in the chapter as you plan for the audience and situation of your speech. When you have sized up the situation, adding this knowledge to your analysis of audience demographics, dynamics, and diversity, you will be ready for the next challenge—choosing a suitable topic for speaking.

YOUR ethical VOICE   Guidelines for Ethical Audience Adaptation

Keep the following guidelines in mind as you consider adapting your message to your audience.

1. Change your strategies, not your convictions.
2. Appeal to shared needs and values to bridge cultural differences.
3. Resist stereotypes and biases that may lead you to misjudge others.

4. Suppress any impulses toward ethnocentrism.
5. Avoid sexist, racist, ethnic, or religious humor.
6. Show respect for the common humanity of your listeners.

▶ **preliminary tuning effect**   The effect of previous speeches or other situational factors in predisposing an audience to respond positively or negatively to a speech.

Audience Analysis Worksheet

FIGURE 5.4
Audience Analysis
Worksheet

Factor Description	Adaptations Needed

Audience Demographics

Age: _____   _____
Gender: _____   _____
Education: _____   _____
Sociocultural Background: _____   _____
_____   _____
Group Affiliations: _____   _____
_____   _____
Interest in Topic: _____   _____
_____   _____
Knowledge of Topic: _____   _____
_____   _____

Audience Dynamics

Audience Beliefs: _____   _____
_____   _____
Audience Attitudes: _____   _____
_____   _____
Relevant Values: _____   _____
_____   _____
Motivational Appeals: _____   _____
_____   _____

Speaking Situation

Time: _____   _____
Place: _____   _____
Occasion: _____   _____
Audience Size: _____   _____
Context: _____   _____

FINAL
reflections   Looking Beyond the Self

It is a natural thing for beginning speakers to be preoccupied with the first person pronouns *I*, *me*, and *my*, especially when they know their performances will be graded. "How will I do?" "Will my grade be okay?" "What will others think of me?"

These are all common, understandable concerns. Often communication anxiety underlies this concern for the self because of the discomfort it causes.

This chapter turns your attention beyond the self to those whose lives can be touched by the messages you present. Who are they, and what kind of background experiences, biases, and attitudes do they bring with them? What can you say that might be useful to them, perhaps that might even expand the horizons of their lives?

We have looked at your listeners in depth. What beliefs, attitudes, values, and motives do they have? What appeals will move them to adopt a new course of action? As audiences become culturally diverse, how can you speak across these differences to draw listeners together? And how might the speaking situation complicate your efforts?

These are all questions prompted by this chapter, and they all point you outward beyond the self. To answer them successfully is to increase your control of the power of the spoken word, and that raises a final ethical question: How will you use this new power? Will you exploit or manipulate others to serve your own purposes? The ancient philosopher Plato wrote that public speaking becomes suspect when we tell our listeners what they *want* to hear—or what we want them to hear—instead of what they *should* hear. However, there is nothing inherently wrong with adapting your messages to the humanity of your listeners or to the demands of a given moment. The Guidelines for Ethical Audience Adaptation developed here can help you maintain your moral bearings as you seek, discover, develop, adapt, and ultimately find your voice.

After Reading This Chapter, You Should Be Able To Answer These Questions

Study and **Review** at **MyCommunicationLab**

1 How can you adjust your message to age, gender, educational, and sociocultural characteristics of listeners?

2 In what ways can group affiliations influence listeners?

3 What is the difference between beliefs and attitudes and how might these affect the fate of a message?

4 How can you put values and motives to work for you in messages?

5 How can you meet the challenges of audience diversity?

6 What constraints can the physical speaking situation impose, and how can you cope with them?

7 What challenges does the psychological setting for a speech raise, and how can you adjust to make your message more effective?

For Discussion and Further Exploration

1 Before your next speech, develop a topic-oriented audience survey based on Figure 5.2. Ask permission from your instructor to distribute it to the class to complete. Adapt your speech according to what you discover.

2 Choose a controversial issue, and explore at least two public opinion polls that offer findings relevant to this issue. Are there any differences among the findings? If you used one of these polls in a speech, should you feel an ethical obligation to acknowledge the other polls as well, especially if they differ?

3 Study a recent issue of a popular magazine, record a popular television show, or check out social media to explore the range of motives engaged by their advertisements. How do these ads use the motivational appeals found in speeches?

4 Watch a persuasive speech on YouTube, and identify the motivational appeals used in it. How skillfully does the speaker use these appeals? What other motives might the speaker have used?

5 Have you ever heard speeches that were not adapted to the situation? Did they go on too long? Was the delivery adjusted to the size of the room and audience? Did they speak on a subject that was inappropriate for the occasion?

6 Investigate a cultural group different from your own. Identify the pattern of values that you think are particular to the group, as revealed in their writings and speeches. If you were to prepare a speech for an audience of members from that group, what kinds of appeals might you use? What might you have to be wary of in your speech?

7 You have been invited to present a speech on "How our government spies on us" to
   a. a class at a local high school.
   b. a meeting of the Rotary Club.
   c. a gathering at the Senior Citizens Center.
   d. your class.

How might you adapt the speech to these various audiences? Explain and defend your approach in class.

6 Finding Your Topic

Listen to **Chapter 6** at **MyCommunicationLab**

> *The life of our city is rich in poetic and marvelous subjects ...but we do not notice it.*
>
> —BAUDELAIRE

Lindsey Yoder won the first Michael Osborn Public Speaking Contest at the University of Memphis with the powerful speech that appears at the end of Chapter 14 and in MyCommunicationLab. Lindsey was then invited to present her speech on human trafficking to a community rally that involved hundreds of activists, church members, police officials, and city leaders. We asked Lindsey how she had selected the topic for her speech.

"I did not choose my topic," she said. "It chose me."

If this were the way classroom speeches were usually generated, there would be no need for this chapter. Unfortunately, Lindsey's experience is the exception rather than the rule. Most of us need help finding, refining, and adapting the topics of our speeches so that they fit assignments and the needs of our listeners. We have to follow a search process to generate the best of these topics. This chapter will describe this process and how you can conduct it successfully.

In the communication world that awaits you beyond the class, topics impose themselves upon you: Work concerns, community concerns, and political issues of the moment may all provide the impetus for your speaking. But the public speaking classroom typically offers one great advantage: It allows you to explore the universe of topic possibilities to find just those best suited to help you find your voice. This freedom of topic selection helps you exercise your creativity and realize your potential.

What Is a Good Topic?

Watch at **MyCommunicationLab**
Video: "Tips on Developing a Topic for a Speech"

A good topic must, of course, fit your assignment. Your instructor may ask you to prepare an informative, persuasive, or special occasions speech and may require that you develop a presentation aid. On the job or in the community, you may be invited to speak on a specific subject or problem area. In your role as citizen, you may have to express your views on a pressing issue of the moment, such as funding for special education needs or proposed requirements for tornado shelters.

In the greater freedom of the public speaking class, a good topic is one that involves you and that ought to involve your listeners. It allows you to express convictions that are important to you or to explore something you find fascinating. A good topic invites you to find your voice and, in the process, enrich the lives of your listeners by sharing new information or a new perspective. Finally, a good topic is one that you can speak about responsibly, given the time allotted for the preparation and presentation of your speech.

A Good Topic Involves You

Watch at **MyCommunicationLab**
Video: "Tall Girls"

Imagine yourself speaking successfully:

> You're enthusiastic about what you're saying. Your face shows your involvement in your topic. Your voice expresses your feelings. Your gestures reinforce your meaning. Everything about you says, "This is important!" or "This is interesting!" or "This will make a difference in your lives!"

Once you can identify a subject that makes you feel this way, you may well have found your topic, or your topic may have found you.

Your topic does not have to be an earthshaking issue, but it should be something your listeners ought to know more about. Trivial topics, such as "how to twirl a baton" and "how to kick a football," waste the time of both the speaker and the listeners. Overworked topics such as "don't drink and drive" also waste time unless they offer listeners a new and fresh slant.

Above all, your topic should be important to you personally and should help you develop as a speaker. It takes time to think through your ideas, research them, organize what you discover, and practice your presentation. If your topic is not important to you, you will find it hard to invest the time and effort required to speak responsibly.

A Good Topic Involves Your Listeners

Picture an audience of ideal listeners:

> Their faces are alive with interest. They lean forward in their seats, intent on what you are saying. They nod or smile appropriately. At the end of your speech, they want to ask you questions about your ideas or voice their reactions. Long after your speech, they are still thinking about what you said.

What topic will help you create this kind of audience response? By now, you probably have heard the first speeches in your class, and you know something about your listeners. Ask yourself, What are my audience's interests? What do they care about? What do they need to know more about?

A Good Topic Is One You Can Manage

The final test of a good topic is whether you can acquire the knowledge you will need to speak responsibly upon it. The time you have for the preparation and presentation of your speech is limited, and some topics are incredibly complicated.

A passion for sports can prompt ideas for speech topics.

Consequently, you should select a *manageable part* of your topic area to develop for your presentation. For example, instead of trying to cover the entire subject of terrorism—its causes, sources, kinds, purposes, leaders, and so on—it would be much better to focus on one aspect, such as your community's plan in case of terrorist attacks. This more limited topic would focus more closely on your audience's particular interests and should help you prepare a responsible presentation.

Think of your search for the right topic as a process that goes through phases of discovery, exploration, and refinement.

- In the **discovery phase**, you uncover promising topic areas.

- In the **exploration phase**, you focus on specific speech topics within these areas.

- In the **refinement phase**, you identify the general and specific purposes of speeches you might give on these topics and write out your thesis statements.

▶ **discovery phase** Identifying large topic areas that might generate successful speeches.

▶ **exploration phase** Examining large topic areas to pinpoint more-precise speech topics.

▶ **refinement phase** Framing the general and specific purposes of a speech topic and a thesis statement.

It is important to realize that *this process takes time*. Give yourself at least a week to select your topic, do your research, outline your speech, and practice your presentation. You will find that this time is well invested. Nothing comforts you more on the eve of a presentation than knowing you are well prepared.

Discovering Your Topic Area

Three techniques—brainstorming, interest charts, and media and Internet prompts—can help you discover promising speech topics.

Explore at
MyCommunicationLab
Activity: "Topic"

Brainstorming

Brainstorming is a technique that encourages free associations in the search for a topic area. Ask yourself, *If I had to pick one topic area to explore for my next speech, what would it be?* At the top of a legal pad, write down the first idea that occurs to you. Below this idea, write down at least five more ideas that occur to you in association with this topic. Do not try to think critically about these ideas until you have a sizable list. Let your mind wander. You may discover, as did a student of ours, that such "daydreaming" can be productive and creative.

Zachary came to our office one day early in the term with a serious case of topic anxiety. After we convinced him that his symptoms were not terminal, he accepted our invitation to participate in brainstorming. Zachary wrote down "Wyoming" at the top of his legal pad. He then wrote down the following associations: trout, Yellowstone, fire, drought, George Anderson (a well-known fly fisherman), catch and release, and wolves. He studied this list closely. "You know," he said, "I could speak on 'Fire and Water in Yellowstone: Too Much of One, Too Little of the Other.'" And eventually he did.

Interest Charts

Interest charts are systematic projections of your own and audience interests. Such projections may reveal themselves naturally in the social media. The subjects discussed and "liked" on Facebook and featured on the electronic posterboards provided by Pinterest can suggest promising topic areas for speeches.

Beyond these natural projections of interests, you can also probe to discover promising topic areas. The classical writers on rhetoric were the first to discover that the mind follows certain habitual paths that are productive in creative thinking. You may have already followed such paths if you developed the self-awareness inventory suggested in Chapter 3. The productive possibilities you explored in that chapter can be easily adapted and enlarged here. They appear in the form of questions that guide the mind:

1. What *places* do you find interesting?

2. What *people* do you find fascinating?

3. What *activities* do you enjoy?

4. What *things* do you find interesting?

5. What *events* stand out in your mind?

6. Which *ideas* do you find intriguing?

▶ **brainstorming** Technique that encourages the free play of the mind to generate a list of ideas for later careful consideration.

▶ **interest charts** Visual displays of speaker or audience interests, as prompted by probe questions.

7. What *values* are important to you?

8. What *problems* concern you most?

9. What *campus concerns* do you have?

You can use your responses to these queries, supplemented by what you learn about yourself and others from the social media, to develop an interest chart that projects a comprehensive visual display of your interests. To create such a chart, write out brief responses to the probe questions. Try to come up with at least five responses for each question. Your interest chart might then look like that in Figure 6.1.

Once you have completed your personal interest chart, make a similar chart of audience interests. What places, people, events, activities, things, ideas, values, problems, and campus concerns seem to spark discussions in class or in the social media? Study the two charts together, looking for shared interests. To do this systematically, make a three-column **topic area inventory chart**. In the first column (your interests), list the subjects you find most appealing. In the second column (audience interests), list the subjects that seem most interesting to your listeners. In the third column, match columns 1 and 2 to find the most promising areas of speech topics. Figure 6.2 shows a sample topic area inventory chart.

In this example, your interests in cycling and hiking coincide with the audience's interest in unusual places and suggest a possible topic area: "weekend adventures close to campus." Similarly, your concern for physical fitness pairs with the audience's interest in deceptive advertising to generate another possibility: "exercise spa rip-offs." Your concern over tuition costs intersects with audience interests in economic problems, leading to "keeping college affordable." Finally, your interest in gourmet cooking resonates with audience concerns over good health to suggest the topic area "eating well and living healthy."

FIGURE 6.1
Your Interest Chart

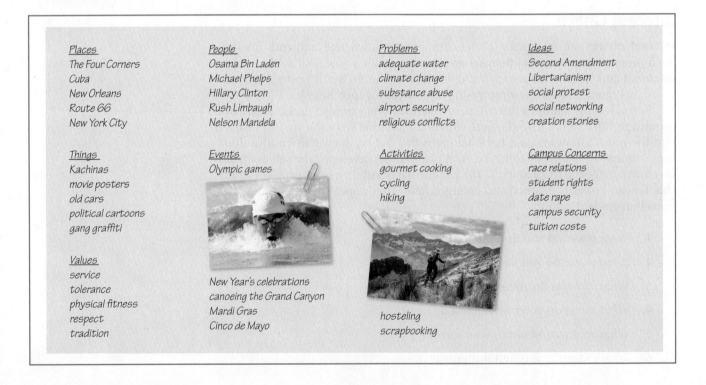

<u>Places</u>
The Four Corners
Cuba
New Orleans
Route 66
New York City

<u>People</u>
Osama Bin Laden
Michael Phelps
Hillary Clinton
Rush Limbaugh
Nelson Mandela

<u>Problems</u>
adequate water
climate change
substance abuse
airport security
religious conflicts

<u>Ideas</u>
Second Amendment
Libertarianism
social protest
social networking
creation stories

<u>Things</u>
Kachinas
movie posters
old cars
political cartoons
gang graffiti

<u>Events</u>
Olympic games

<u>Activities</u>
gourmet cooking
cycling
hiking

<u>Campus Concerns</u>
race relations
student rights
date rape
campus security
tuition costs

<u>Values</u>
service
tolerance
physical fitness
respect
tradition

New Year's celebrations
canoeing the Grand Canyon
Mardi Gras
Cinco de Mayo

hosteling
scrapbooking

▶ **topic area inventory chart**   A means of determining possible speech topics by listing topics you and your listeners find interesting and matching them.

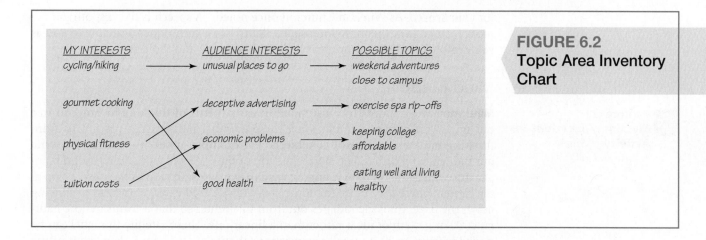

FIGURE 6.2
Topic Area Inventory Chart

Media and Internet Prompts

If brainstorming and interest charts don't produce enough promising topic discoveries, **media and Internet prompts** provide another excellent source. When using such prompts, you jump-start the creative process by scanning newspapers, magazines, and the electronic media for ideas. Go through the Sunday paper, scan *Time* and *Newsweek* or quality periodicals such as *The Atlantic* or *Smithsonian*, or read the daily headlines of the *New York Times* or *Wall Street Journal* online.

The Internet also offers some special resources if you are selective. For example, if you type in the words "speech topics" on a search engine, you may find a few gems among the garbage. Again, check the postings on Pinterest. In addition, some sites are especially helpful. See, for example, the "Topic Selection Helper" developed by Ron St. John of the University of Hawaii's Maui Community College Speech Department (see the Public Speaking Web Guide website).

As you scan media resources, consider the headlines, advertisements, and pictures. What catches your attention? The headline "Travel Money Tips Offered" might inspire you to speak on "champagne travel on a beer budget." Or the personals section in the classified ads might prompt a speech on "the dangers of Internet dating services."

The media-prompts technique has one great advantage: The topics it generates are timely. But be careful not to misuse this technique. The media and Internet can suggest ideas for speeches, but you can't simply summarize an article and use it as a speech. The article should be only a starting point for your thinking and further research. *Your* speech must be *your* message, designed to appeal to *your* specific audience. You should always bring something new to your topic—a fresh insight or a special application for your listeners.

Exploring Your Topic Area

What you typically discover as you brainstorm, develop interest charts, and employ media and Internet prompts are not actual topics for speeches, but topic *areas*. Topic areas are promising but broad subjects that often cover too much ground for typical classroom speeches. You must explore topic areas carefully and then narrow and focus them until they become specific enough to handle in the time allotted

▶ **media and Internet prompts**
Sources such as newspapers, magazines, and the electronic media that can suggest ideas for speech topics.

for your speech. As Winston Churchill once noted, "A speech is like a spotlight; the more focused it is, the more intense the light."[1] Two techniques available to you as you explore promising topic areas are mind mapping and topic analysis.

Mind Mapping

Mind mapping disrupts the customary linear patterns of thinking in order to free our minds for creative exploration.[2] These habitual patterns can prevent us from thinking fully and freely about subjects. For example, most of us, when we write our thoughts out on a tablet, start at the top of the page and work down. Mind mappers turn the tablet on its side and, instead of starting at the top of the page, begin at the center, where they place the topic area they wish to explore. Instead of flowing down the page, thinking radiates out from this center so that it forms a more natural circular pattern of ideas rather than a linear one. These satellite thoughts can be ringed by even more particular associations that relate to them.[3] Using contrasting colors can further stimulate creativity.

To see how mind mapping works, let's assume that you have carefully completed the interest charts. You have discovered that your strongest interest is in American popular music. You think this interest will be shared by many of your listeners. This convergence of interests has produced a promising topic area, the innovative music that flowed out of Sun Studio in Memphis, Tennessee, during the last half of the twentieth century. You have already begun to read about this subject and have started to accumulate information. To explore this topic area using mind mapping place it at the center of your page, as indicated in Figure 6.3.

As your mind roams freely around this central idea, you come up with five major satellite ideas: "Early Artists," "Later Artists," "Business Practices," "Musical Significance and Birth of Rock-and-Roll," and "Cultural Significance." As you reflect on each of these satellite ideas, you develop even more specific associations that radiate from each.

Looking at these ideas as they form a spatial pattern, you can see any number of speech topic possibilities. One of these might connect three of the major satellite ideas. You could focus on the early artists who performed the first significant rock-and-roll hits and show how they blended elements of blues, country, and gospel music into rock-and-roll. You might title this speech "Sun Studio: Birthplace of an American Musical Form." You could develop presentation aids using photographs and selections from the music to make the speech truly colorful, enjoyable, and informative.

Mind mapping is a free-form exploratory technique that can be highly creative. The next technique we discuss offers a more systematic, disciplined way to explore topic areas.

FINDING YOUR
voice   Discovering Your Topic Area

Use brainstorming, an interest chart, and media and Internet prompts to discover at least three promising topic areas on which you might speak. Rank these in order of preference, and explain either in class or in a written report how you discovered these areas and why you ranked them this way.

▶ **mind mapping**   Changes customary patterns of thinking to encourage creative exploration.

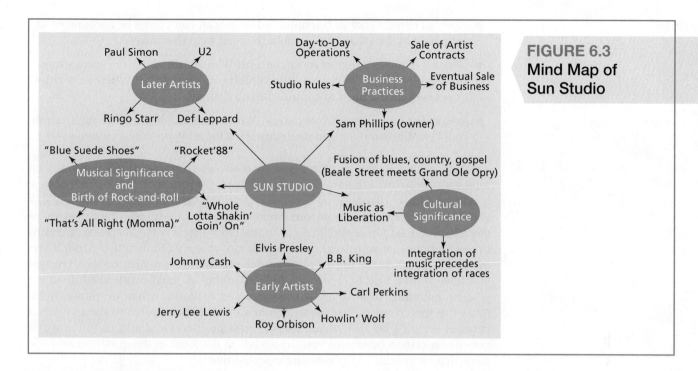

FIGURE 6.3
Mind Map of Sun Studio

Topic Analysis

The beginning college course in journalism introduces fledgling reporters to the basic questions they need to ask as they investigate a story: *Who? What? Why? When? Where? How?* Rudyard Kipling once described these questions as follows:

> I keep six honest serving-men
> (They taught me all I knew):
> Their names **are** What and Why and When
> And How and Where and Who.[4]

The idea is that if reporters ask these questions as they explore a story, the odds increase that they will not neglect anything important.

The noted scholar Wayne Booth has endorsed these questions as a more general method of exploring the value of topics: "Decide which questions stop you for a moment, challenge you, spark some special interest."[5] For the public speaker who is exploring the possibilities of a topic area, these "honest serving-men" constitute the technique we call **topic analysis**. Let's consider climate change as a topic area and see how these questions might prompt inquiry:

- *What* is climate change? What are the major causes of it? What are the contributing causes in our community? What part can individuals play in reducing it? What can government do to control it? What is the role of international organizations?

- *Why* do we have climate change? Why do some countries and some companies resist reducing greenhouse emissions?

- *When* did climate change first become an issue? When was the first important book about climate change published? When were the first U.S. laws relating to climate change passed?

▶ **topic analysis** Using questions often employed by journalists to explore topic possibilities for speeches (who, what, why, when, where, and how).

- *How* can climate change be controlled? How can companies be encouraged to cooperate in this effort? How can individuals help the cause?

- *Where* is climate change of most concern? Where are endangered species most susceptible? Where are human health problems most acute? Where have cities or states done the most to control climate change?

- *Who* suffers most from climate change? Who is responsible for enforcing emission controls? Who brought climate change most forcefully to public awareness?

As you consider the six prompts, write down as many specific ideas about your topic area as you can. What would be the best topic for your speech if you indeed were to address climate change? That depends a great deal on your audience and locale. If you live in an area with an obvious emissions problem, a speech that zeroes in on that situation might have specific local appeal. Your listeners might also be interested in the history of relevant legislation in your city or state. On the other hand, if you live in an area where the impact of climate change is not immediate or apparent, you may have to work hard to convince listeners that they should be concerned about it.

The preceding topic analysis was geared to exploring what are primarily informative speech topics, but the technique can easily be adapted to the analysis of persuasive topics. Because persuasion concerns problems and asks us to change or not change certain behaviors, you simply adjust the focus of the questions and add a few that are specific to the persuasive perspective:

Who is affected by this problem?
What are the most important issues?
Why did the problem arise?
Where is this problem happening?
When did the problem begin?
How is this problem like or unlike previous problems?
How extensive is the problem?
What options are available for dealing with the problem?

After you have discovered and explored topic areas, one or several topics should emerge as promising possibilities for your speech. As you ponder these options, keep in mind how well they fit the assignment, whether you could speak on them in the time available, whether you will be able to research them responsibly, and how useful they might be for listeners.

FINDING YOUR

voice   Exploring Your Topic Area

Use mind mapping and topic analysis to explore the preferred topic area you identified in "Finding Your Voice: Discovering Your Topic Area." List in order of preference three promising speech topics that emerge from this exploration. Explain in class or in a written report how and why these topics emerged and why you ranked them in the order selected.

Refining Your Topic

Having discovered and explored topic areas, let us assume you have decided on a promising topic. Now you move to the final phase of topic selection: refining and focusing the topic in preparation for speaking. To complete this phase, you must consider the general purpose of your speech, determine your specific purpose, and prepare a thesis statement.

General Purpose

Invitations to speak outside class will usually specify the **general purpose** of your speech: "Could you help us understand changes in the tax code?" or "Would you tell us why you are opposed to changes in the tax code?" or "Will you help us thank the senator for her leadership in changing the tax code?" Speeches that would address such questions seek understanding, offer a position on a controversial issue, and express appreciation, respectively. They correspond to the general purposes of *informing, persuading,* and *celebrating:*

Watch at **MyCommunicationLab** **Video:** "Tips on Developing a Purpose of a Speech"

- *The general purpose of a speech to inform is to share knowledge with listeners.*

- *If your general purpose is to persuade, you will advise listeners how to believe or act and offer them reasons to follow such advice.*

- *A speech of celebration emphasizes the importance of an occasion, event, or person, often with the intention of amusing or inspiring listeners.* Speeches of celebration include eulogies, toasts, after-dinner speeches, and tributes.

Your instructor may specify the general purpose of your speech as part of your assignment.

Specific Purpose

Determining your **specific purpose** helps you narrow your topic until it comes into sharp focus. It states precisely what you want your listeners to understand, believe, feel, or do. Having your specific purpose clearly in mind helps direct your research so that you don't waste valuable time wandering around the library or surfing the Internet for irrelevant material. You should be able to state your specific purpose clearly in a single phrase.

Let's look at how a specific purpose statement can give focus to a speech:

Effective speeches develop a central idea, allow speakers to speak with conviction and passion, and promise listeners important information and insights.

| Topic area: | The Artistry of Dr. Seuss |
| General purpose: | To inform |

Jessica Bradshaw had been entertained by the books of Dr. Seuss when she was a child. Now as an undergraduate student, she remained fascinated with his books, suspecting that their simplicity might result from a quite sophisticated creative process. However, her topic area, as stated here, would be much too vast and general to cover in a five- to six-minute speech. She would never be able to consider the entire range of ideas that might be associated with it, much less provide examples

▶ **general purpose** The speaker's intention to inform or persuade listeners or to celebrate some person or occasion.

▶ **specific purpose** The speaker's particular goal or the response that the speaker wishes to evoke.

and supporting content. After all, Dr. Seuss wrote many books, any number of which might well be mentioned in developing such a topic. And "Artistry"? That's certainly a vague and probably extensive subject. If there was ever a topic area that needed to be refined, narrowed, and focused in a specific purpose statement, this was surely it!

As Jess read more about Dr. Seuss, she found a really interesting interview with him that spelled out how he had created *The Cat in the Hat*. This book, she decided, would provide her point of focus. And the incredible story of how he labored to create such a simple-seeming text would be a further point of refinement. Jess came up with the following:

> Specific purpose: To inform my audience of Dr. Seuss's creative persistence as he composed *The Cat in the Hat*.

Jess had just made a major move in refining her topic. Now she was ready to test and possibly improve this specific purpose statement.

Testing Your Specific Purpose Statement.   Developing a successful specific purpose statement is one of the most important steps in topic refinement. The following tests should help you:

1. *Does the specific purpose promise new information or fresh advice?* You may be greeted with yawns if you propose "to inform listeners that drunk driving is dangerous." You will have tied yourself to a tired topic. When you tell listeners something they have already heard many times, you simply waste their time and yours.

2. *Can you accomplish your specific purpose in the allotted time?* If you propose "to persuade listeners that health care in the United States is too costly and inefficient," you will have bitten off far more than you can chew. Remember, in a five-minute speech you have only about 700 words to get your message across. You may need to limit your remarks to the health care crisis in your community in order to meet time restrictions. That strategy might also be more interesting to your listeners.

3. *Have you avoided the double-focus trap?* It is sometimes difficult to make that final decision to narrow your topic to a single focal point. It may be tempting to fall into the trap of double focus: "to inform my listeners of hiking *and* camping opportunities in Shenandoah National Park." If you attempt to address both these subjects in any meaningful way, you may go beyond your time limit. The "and" in such statements is often a red flag that signals a double-focus problem.

4. *Have you avoided the triviality trap?* When you speak to twenty-four people for five minutes, you will be taking up two hours of their collective time. What are you offering them in return? If you promise to inform them about "how to mix a martini" or "how to punt a football," you may well leave your listeners feeling shortchanged. They may react with a blunt, "So what?" You must convince listeners that you have a specific purpose that promises them important information, insights, or advice, so that by the end of the speech they feel they have invested their time wisely.

5. *Have you met the test of relevancy?* Jess Bradshaw's assumption in selecting her topic was that many listeners shared her background as early fans of the Dr. Seuss books. She thought she could convince them of the relevancy of her topic

to their interests. However, what might be a good topic for one audience might not be so relevant to another. If your specific purpose is to advocate your proposal to raise the eligibility age for Social Security benefits, you might struggle to close the relevancy gap between your topic and your youthful audience. You might be on better ground if you instead discussed ways students can reduce the debt burden many of them acquire during the college years.

6. *Have you avoided the technicality trap?* Sometimes speakers forget that listeners may not share their technical vocabulary. They are puzzled when listeners respond with dazed, bewildered looks and the question, "Huh?" Speakers who promise "to inform listeners of the principles of thermonuclear energy" or "to inform my audience about the intellectual evolution of Kant's meta-ethics" are stepping directly into this trap. They have not factored audience background into their topic selection. This failure becomes evident when they write out their specific purpose statements.

7. *Have you avoided signs of bias?* If you offer as your specific purpose "To explain why we should fire our *dumb* football coach," judicious listeners could well conclude that your mind is so closed on this subject that you have not been able to judge evidence fairly and dispassionately. Your obvious bias would prevent you from being a trustworthy speaker on this topic.

SPEAKER'S notes   Testing Your Specific Purpose Statement

Your specific purpose statement must pass all the following tests:

1. Does it project a speech that will offer new information and/or fresh advice?

2. Can you accomplish your purpose in the time allotted for the speech?

3. Do you focus on a single topic, that is, do you avoid double focus?

4. Do you focus on an important topic, avoiding triviality?

5. Would your speech be relevant to your particular audience's interests and needs?

6. Is your speech geared to a general audience, avoiding overly technical language and subject matter?

7. Are you free from bias?

Improving Your Specific Purpose Statement.   Let's look at several examples of flawed specific purpose statements and see how they might be improved:

Flawed:	To persuade my audience that driving while distracted is dangerous
Improved:	To persuade my audience not to text while driving

The flawed specific purpose is vague, and it tells the audience nothing new. Who would argue that driving while distracted is not dangerous? The improved version focuses more precisely on a contemporary problem.

Flawed:	To inform listeners of major attractions at Yellowstone and Glacier National Parks
Improved:	To inform listeners of exciting destinations in Yellowstone Park

The flawed specific purpose here presents a classic double-focus problem. Choose one or the other, as in the improved version, so that you can develop its appeal in greater detail.

Flawed:	To convince listeners to take their "meds" on a regular basis
Improved:	To convince listeners of immediate and long-term health benefits of sustained exercise programs

In addition to being vague, the flawed specific purpose could present a major relevancy problem, as most college-age students are not confronted (yet!) with long lists of daily required medicines. Ongoing exercise programs, on the other hand, are desirable throughout a lifetime.

Thesis Statement

Writing your **thesis statement** or central idea is the final refinement in preparing a topic for a speech. The thesis statement summarizes in a single sentence the message of your speech. For example, Jess Bradshaw's speech began with this thesis statement: *"The Cat in the Hat* is the incredibly simple product of an incredibly complicated creative process." B. J. Youngerman focused his persuasive speech in defense of Walmart on the following thesis statement: "Walmart is a positive force in American public life." Such sentences, notes scholar Wayne Booth, "state a potential claim" that the speeches themselves must demonstrate or prove.[6]

In most cases, speakers should integrate the thesis statement into the introduction of their speech so that listeners will know their intentions from the outset. Although you should integrate your thesis statement, you should not boldly proclaim, "My thesis statement is…". The thesis statement should arouse interest and should provide sharp focus for the speech. Effective speeches are structured to develop a central idea. When that idea is obscure, there is no central focus to hold the structure of thoughts together. The speech then rambles about in a disorganized way and leaves no lasting impression on the audience. When listeners ask, "What exactly are you trying to say?" or "What would you like us to do?" chances are the thesis statement has not been clearly realized or well stated.

At times, however, ethical speakers may omit the thesis statement from their presentations, leaving it to be constructed by listeners from cues within the speech. Cecile Larson left the thesis statement implicit in her speech "The 'Monument' at Wounded Knee," which appears in Appendix B. Her intent was to create a dramatic effect as listeners discovered her thesis statement for themselves. But this technique also entails considerable risk. Listeners may miss the point!

Most of the time your specific purpose will be revealed in your thesis statement, but the two are not identical. *The specific purpose expresses what you want to accomplish; the thesis statement summarizes what you intend to say.* One student developed a relationship between the specific purpose and thesis statements of a speech as follows:

Specific purpose:	To persuade listeners that binge drinking is a serious problem on our campus
Thesis statement:	Today I want to discuss a major problem on campus—binge drinking—and what we can do about it.

In ethical speaking, the thesis statement will usually reveal the speaker's specific purpose; at the very least, it will not disguise it. *But let the listener beware!* Speakers

▶ **thesis statement**　Summarizes in a single sentence the central idea of your speech.

YOUR *ethical* VOICE   The Ethics of Topic Selection

Ethical problems can infiltrate the process of topic selection for speeches. To avoid many of these problems follow these guidelines:

1. Do not select a topic that could be hurtful, such as "how to make a pipe bomb."

2. Do not select a topic that potentially invites illegal activity, such as "growing marijuana in your dorm room."

3. Do not select a topic on which you cannot obtain responsible knowledge.

4. Do not purposely obscure your thesis statement in order to hide your specific purpose.

sometimes hide their actual intentions. If you consider the hidden agendas of cult leaders or sometimes even leaders of nations, you can see how serious this problem can become. *The greater the distance between the hidden specific purpose and the thesis statement disclosed in the speech, the larger the ethical issue.*

An Overview of the Topic Selection Process

Let us now look at the entire process of moving from general topic area to thesis statement to see how these steps can evolve in actual speech preparation. Jess Bradshaw's experience provides a good example.

Topic area:	The Artistry of Dr. Seuss
General purpose:	To inform
Specific purpose:	To inform my audience of Dr. Seuss's creative persistence as he composed *The Cat in the Hat*
Thesis statement:	*The Cat in the Hat* is the incredibly simple product of an incredibly complicated creative process.

FINDING YOUR *voice*   Refining Your Topic

Refine the preferred topic identified in "Finding Your Voice: Exploring Your Topic Area" until you have determined its general purpose, specific purpose, and thesis statement. What are the strengths and limitations of the speech you might give on this topic? As you answer this question, be sure to consider the assignment, the time limits, and audience needs and interests as well as the intrinsic value of the topic.

The refinement phase of topic selection is like looking at a topic successively through the lenses of a microscope. When you identify the general purpose, specific purpose, and thesis statement of a speech topic, you bring the topic into sharper and sharper focus. At the end of the process, what was at first vague should now have become precise. You should be ready to conduct the research and planning that will develop the topic into a successful speech.

FINAL reflections   The Great Chain of Communication

Cicero, the renowned Roman orator and communication theorist, once wrote that public speaking is an art made up of five great arts: creating the content of a speech, organizing its ideas, expressing them in effective language, committing the speech to memory, and presenting the speech powerfully. These arts are obviously all connected and form the great chain of the communication process.

This chapter helps you forge the first link in Cicero's chain, developing something worthwhile to say. Until you have a clear, compelling idea of what you want to talk about, it is useless to discuss any of the other arts.

There are moments when we have little choice in selecting speech topics: Problems arise in the workplace, and we must address them. Or we may be invited to speak at public meetings as experts or concerned citizens on issues of immediate concern. On such occasions, we are constrained by the urgencies of the moment and by our own background of competence.

But the public speaking classroom typically offers freedom to explore a wide range of issues and interests before we speak. The topic we finally select may come to us in a flash of intuition. But there are systematic ways to assure that we are on the right track before we commit to a speech. As we have seen, these systems involve discovering potential topic areas, exploring them for possible topics, and refining these topics until they focus precisely on whom we wish to serve and what we wish to accomplish as we speak.

Finding your topic—one that fascinates and excites you, that you can commit to and become passionate about, that justifies your investment of time and energy— is also an essential step in finding your voice.

After Reading This Chapter, You Should Be Able To Answer These Questions

Study and
Review at
MyCommunicationLab

1 What is a good speech topic?

2 How can you find promising topic areas?

3 How can you develop effective interest charts?

4 How can you explore fertile topic areas to focus on the best topics?

5 Why can mind mapping be an effective tool for exploration?

6 How can you refine your chosen topic in preparation for speaking?

7 How are the specific purpose and thesis statements related, and how can they differ?

For Discussion and Further Exploration

1 Complete a chart of your interests, including at least three entries in each of the suggested categories. Report on these, and with the help of classmates, complete a topic area inventory chart that lists audience interests as well. Based on the interaction of your interests and theirs, rank the most promising topic areas.

2 In connection with the interest chart exercise just discussed, develop a mind map around the most promising topic area. Does this exercise produce any specific ideas for speech topics?

3 Follow up the mind map just discussed by using the topic analysis method to explore the most promising topic areas. Does the application of the *who, what, why, where, when,* and *how* questions help clarify and develop the topic options?

4 Choose the best topic ideas that emerge from the previous topic analysis exercise, and proceed in class discussion to frame possible specific purpose and thesis statements for them. Keep in mind the virtues of simplicity, clarity, specificity, ethicality, and appeal to your anticipated audience. Are the specific purpose and thesis statements in close relationship? Would you have time enough in your speech to cover the content suggested by these statements?

5 Develop a topic briefing, in which you propose a topic or series of topics you would like to explore in classroom speeches. At the discretion of your instructor, present your topic briefing either as a written proposal or as an oral presentation to a small group or to the class as a whole. Explain why you want to give these speeches and how listeners might benefit from them. Identify any communication problems you might have and how you plan to deal with them. List the major sources of information you plan to draw upon in preparing your speeches.

   If presented orally, your presentation should invite questions and suggestions. For more on topic briefings, read the supplementary material offered in MyCommLab.

6 Discuss the defects in the following specific purpose statements:
   a. To explain how to swing a golf club
   b. To inform the audience about nuclear physics
   c. To inform the audience about indoor and outdoor gardening
   d. To persuade the audience to boycott our stupid commencement ceremonies
   e. To persuade listeners to support our foreign policy in the Middle East
   f. To inform listeners how to reduce their tax burdens
   g. To help listeners understand the theory of electricity

7 Identify three topics you believe would be unethical to develop for classroom speeches. Explain and defend your position in class.

"PULLING A CAT OUT OF A HAT"

At various moments in this chapter, we have referenced the experience of Jess Bradshaw in developing her topic concerning the artistry of Dr. Seuss. What follows is the final product of her careful preparation, as the speech was presented to her Davidson College class. Concerning how she came up with her topic, Jess reports that she had loved the Seuss books since childhood and suspected that many in her audience would share her fond memories of them. Her biggest problem in topic development, she says, was narrowing the topic, making the hard decision to get rid of interesting but irrelevant information.

Jessica Bradshaw

Have you read *The Cat in the Hat*?

Of course you have. I'm sure of that!

And how about *Green Eggs and Ham*? Did you dig that Sam-I-Am?

Or *Yertle, the Turtle* you got from Aunt Myrtle?

And, did you enjoy the grouchy Grinch?

Of course you did—that was a cinch!

▶ The speech follows a narrative pattern, telling the story of how a classic work was composed. In developing the story, Jess makes effective use of expert testimony. This paints a favorable impression of her ethos as a competent, responsible person whose information can be relied on. This impression would create a positive presumption in favor of speeches she would later give on other topics.

What Dr. Seuss gave you, as he proclaims in his opening of *The Cat in the Hat*, was good fun that is funny. His books may not seem all that complex, realistic, or even deep, but it was not without much work that Theodore Seuss Geisel, otherwise known as Dr. Seuss, was able to make you laugh and smile. Indeed, *The Cat in the Hat* is the incredibly simple product of an incredibly complex creative process. Geisel was amazingly persistent in developing, writing, and editing what would become a classic in children's literature.

The idea behind *The Cat in the Hat* did not come in one great moment of inspiration; instead, it was the result of over four months of brainstorming, drafting, rejecting, and brainstorming again. As told by Philip Nel, in *Dr. Seuss: American Icon*, William Spaulding, the educational director of Houghton Mifflin publishing company, challenged Geisel to write a story using only 225 words from a list of 348 words that first graders were able to recognize by sight or phonics. Geisel accepted the challenge, expecting to spend a few weeks on the project, according to Ruth MacDonald, author of the book *Dr. Seuss*.

Geisel, writing in the *New York Times Book Review*, reported searching for weeks for a topic before finally receiving his answer in a dream. Rushing off to his typewriter, he wrote thirty-two pages of *The Queen Zebra* before realizing that the words "queen" and "zebra" were not on the list. Four months later, Geisel was still working on the assignment, this time attempting to write a story about a bird without using the word "bird"—because it too wasn't on the list! But without the word, he was unable to get the project off the ground. Sorry. Bad pun!

By then, according to *The New Yorker* article "Cat People: What Dr. Seuss Really Taught Us," Geisel had reached a moment of crisis:

I thought it was impossible and ridiculous and I was about to get out of the whole thing; then I decided to look at the list one more time and to use the first two words that rhymed as the title of the book—cat and hat were the ones my eyes lighted on.

But writing *The Cat in the Hat* took as much persistence as the brainstorming for it required. "You got an idea and then found out you had no way to express yourself," Geisel states in *American Icon*. But Geisel worked through the difficulties in a complex process that he described in the *New York Times Book Review*:

> The method I used is the same method you see when you sit down to make apple strudel without the strudel… . You take your limited, uninteresting ingredients and day and night, month after month, you mix them up into thousands of combinations. You make a batch. You taste it. Then you hurl it out the window. Until finally one night, when it is darkest just before dawn, a plausible strudel-less strudel begins to take shape before your eyes!

And for nine months, Geisel worked at editing the strudel-less strudel that is the beloved *The Cat in the Hat*. Later in *American Icon* he described the process: "To produce a 60-page book, I may easily write more than 1,000 pages before I'm satisfied. The most important thing about me, I feel, is that I work like hell—write, rewrite, reject, re-reject, and polish incessantly." According to Seussentennial, the official website for the Dr. Seuss Enterprises, Geisel purchased an old observation tower in La Jolla, California, where he worked eight hours a day for nine months manipulating the 225 words he used in *The Cat in the Hat*. That amounts to 67 hours per word!

To reports of his genius, Geisel retorted, "If I'm a genius, why do I have to work so hard? I know my stuff looks like it was all rattled off in 28 seconds, but every word is a struggle and every sentence is like the pangs of birth."

But eventually his persistence paid off. According to *Publisher's Weekly*, *The Cat in the Hat* is the sixth best-selling children's book of all time. So the next time you're sitting in your tower, on the third floor of the library, working on that paper idea, remember the persistence of Theodore Seuss Geisel in developing, writing, and editing *The Cat in the Hat*. And even in your gloom, maybe you will smile, remembering what Dr. Seuss himself went through.

◄ The use of direct quotations from Geisel is much more striking and colorful than if Jess had used paraphrase to summarize his thoughts. The exact, colloquial words give the speech an air of freshness and authenticity it otherwise would have lacked.

◄ Having completed the remarkable narrative of how Dr. Seuss pulled a cat out of a hat, Jess ties her speech directly to the experience of her listeners. A little Seuss-like persistence might help them develop their assigned papers, she suggests. This lighthearted turn in the speech brings it to a graceful close.

7 Building Responsible Knowledge

((⊱ Listen to **Chapter 7** at **MyCommunicationLab**

> *Learn, compare, collect the facts! Always have the courage to say to yourself, "I am ignorant."*
>
> —IVAN PETROVICH PAVLOV

As a student, Marisol lived on a tight budget. In choosing her groceries though, she had always felt that it was best to buy "green" products whenever she could afford it, even if it cost a bit more. She believed these products came from companies that respected the earth as much as she did. Marisol especially thought it was important to buy "sustainably harvested" fish because she loved the ocean and wanted to do all she could to protect marine ecosystems.

Marisol felt that this would make a good topic for her persuasive speech. She could educate her classmates on the virtues of spending the extra money for sustainably harvested fish and raise awareness among her peers about vital marine ecology issues. She was excited about her topic and ready to begin her research.

Marisol began her research by checking to see what was available in the seafood department at Whole Foods and making note of the price differences between regular and "sustainably caught" fish. Her next step was to search the Internet. The amount of information she found was overwhelming and sometimes contradictory. Some sites even suggested that these "sustainably caught" claims were no more than a marketing ploy. Consumers, they said, were being "greenwashed," duped into paying more for products by labeling them as "sustainable." Actually, they contended, the populations from which these fish were harvested could not possibly survive in the long term with the pressures that commercial fishing was imposing on them.

Which sources were telling the truth? Was Marisol herself a victim of "greenwashing"? How could she ensure that she had the most accurate and unbiased information possible? Marisol realized that it would take careful research and critical thinking skills to develop an ethical and unbiased speech on this topic and that she might even have to change her own point of view.

Careful research: That is the business of this chapter. We want to help you discover what we call responsible knowledge on your topics. We shall examine the meaning of that concept, tell you how to pursue it, explore its sources, evaluate what you discover, and record it for use in your speeches.

The Quest for Responsible Knowledge

Acquiring **responsible knowledge** means that you have gained a comprehensive understanding of your topic that includes

- *understanding the main issues or features of your topic.*
- *knowing who the respected authorities on your topic are and what they say about it.*
- *being aware of the latest developments concerning it.*
- *knowing how your topic might impact the lives of listeners.*

Having responsible knowledge earns you the right to speak. It allows you to present good information or advice to your audience. It also conveys a favorable impression of your mind and character, placing these on display. For this reason, acquiring responsible knowledge is a vital part of finding your voice. It allows you to speak ethically, credibly, confidently, and effectively. Finally, acquiring responsible knowledge helps satisfy one of the demands of ethical communication mentioned in Chapter 1: respect for the integrity of ideas and information.

Preparing for Research

How does one acquire responsible knowledge? This may seem like a lofty goal, but you already have many of the skills needed to get started. When you want to find out about the latest movies to be released, the best places to get pizza in your town, or the way to get to the next level in your favorite computer game, what do you do? You go online and find the information. That is research, and you already know how to do that—or at least how to get started. You have been doing research for years! You will follow much the same process as you do the preliminary work for researching your speech topic.

Planning Your Time

Time is a major consideration. Although you cannot become an authority on most topics with ten hours or even ten days of research, you can certainly learn enough to speak responsibly. Leave yourself enough time to satisfy the four requirements above as you seek to identify the main issues, authorities, latest developments, and possible impact on listeners.

Developing the Right Research Attitude

Attitude is another key consideration. Your speech should convince listeners that you are a seeker after truth, wherever that path to truth happens to take you. You are open-minded, willing to learn and change your position when you uncover the facts of a situation. Even if you are convinced that one side of a controversial issue is correct, you are willing to give the other side a fair hearing. You should also come across as a sympathetic person, in tune with how your topic might intersect the lives of listeners in personal ways.

▶ **responsible knowledge** An advanced state of awareness concerning a topic, understanding its major features, issues, latest developments, and local applications.

Setting Your Research Priorities

As you initiate research, what especially should you be looking for? The qualities of responsible knowledge suggest the following priorities:

- *What are the issues or features of your subject that might have the most significant impact on the lives of your listeners?*

- *Who are the major players—the leaders, activists, and experts—who are prominent in connection with your subject?*

- *What information, statements, examples, and stories should especially concern and engage your listeners?* These will constitute the resources you will use to strengthen, verify, clarify, and illuminate the points you develop in your speech.

- *What is the most timely information available?* The latest is almost always the best and, in some rapidly changing situations, absolutely essential.

- *What key words might expand your knowledge when you insert them into search engines?*

- *What books and articles must you read to expand your understanding?*

These priorities become points of focus as you start the research process.

Recording What You Discover

Having her subject in mind, Marisol plunged on into her research. Soon she was reading articles and books, expanding her knowledge of the wild fish controversy. It was so interesting that she moved hastily from one reading to another, confident that she would remember the source particulars later.

Finally, she was ready to begin designing and planning her speech. For her opening, she would use that fascinating quotation on greenwashing. Now, *who* said it? And *where* was it said? Marisol was stumped. Several precious lost hours later, as she backtracked through these readings, Marisol finally found the quotation—and discovered that it was not quite what she had remembered!

Marisol's experience makes our case. You need a system for recording *what* you discover *at the time* you discover it. All your authors can testify ruefully to this truth—don't trust your memory!

There is no magic formula for recording research. What follows is a system that may work for you or that you can adapt for your particular needs. We will assume for the moment that you will be working on a computer. Develop a folder on your desktop devoted to research on your topic. Within this folder, develop a **source file**, which contains complete information on every source of information you find helpful, whether on the Internet, in the library, on television or radio, or in a personal interview. Especially vital will be *who* is speaking or writing and *when* and *where* their views are presented. You will offer this information when you introduce relevant material in your speeches: This is called "citing your sources."

Other data, such as the complete source title, editor, publication place, exact pages, and URL (universal resource locator) address, may prove necessary should your instructor ask you to submit a formal outline and bibliography (the Modern Language Association [MLA] format no longer requires the use of URLs in citations). Because websites and news stories are routinely removed or revised or reposted with

▶ **source file** Contains complete information on every source you find helpful.

FIGURE 7.1
Sample Source
File Entry

[*Source data*] Zwerdling, Daniel and Margot Williams, "Is Sustainable-Labeled Seafood Really Sustainable?" NPR 11 (2013). Web. 4 Apr. 2013

[*Explanation*] In-depth investigation of the practice of "greenwashing."

new addresses, record the date you accessed a site from the Web as well as the date the information was posted or last revised.

You also may wish to add to your source file a short explanation of the material, information about the author's credentials, and your own reactions. See the sample source file entry in Figure 7.1.

Find out if your instructor prefers the American Psychological Association (APA) or the MLA format, and record your source data in that format. Figure 7.5, Citation Guide, at the end of this chapter (pp. 145–146), illustrates some of the major differences between these formats and offers models that you can follow. For a more complete summary of these styles, see the Purdue Online Writing Lab for samples of both the MLA and APA styles.

Second, you should develop **subject files**, which identify main divisions in the information that you encounter as you do research. The subject files contain exact quotations, statistics, data, examples, and stories found in the sources fully identified in the source file. For example, Marisol soon discovered that much of the information she was collecting on the sustainable seafood issue divided along the lines of cost, availability, and environmental impact. Each of these topics became a subject file in her folder. Note in Figure 7.2 that Marisol included an abbreviated source citation ("NPR 2"). This served as a cue to the full citation that she had listed in her source file.

FIGURE 7.2
Sample Subject
File

[*Subject heading*] Environmental Impact

[*Subject entry*] "Seafood is the last major food that people catch in the wild, and 'we can't just go out and find more fish to catch,' says Carrie Brownstein, global seafood quality standards coordinator for Whole Foods.

Brownstein cites a 2012 United Nations report that warned that almost 30 percent of the world's wild fisheries are 'overexploited,' and more than 57 percent of wild fisheries are 'at or very close' to the limit." (NPR 2)

▶ **subject files** Main divisions in the information you encounter as you research your topic.

Third, build a **documents file**, in which you place articles you have down-loaded from search engines or pages you have scanned into your computer. Be sure to identify the source of such selections on the document itself.

Finally, you should create a **research log**, a computer file in which you can jot down ideas as they occur to you during your research adventure. Your log is also a place to develop a list of key terms as you uncover them and to pinpoint the read-ings you wish to pursue. Your research log can trace the evolution of your think-ing. You might even find that you must modify your specific purpose and thesis statement in light of your discoveries. The research log becomes the story of your research voyage, from embarkation to final destination.

This kind of orderly recording of information and ideas helps you keep track of all you accumulate so that it is readily accessible when you are designing and build-ing your speech. You are now prepared to pursue responsible knowledge.

Avoiding Chance Plagiarism

Our final admonition as you begin the research process is to avoid blundering into chance plagiarism. As we discussed in Chapter 1, many students commit unintentional plagiarism, either because they do not understand what plagiarism encompasses or because they keep poor records during the research process. Plagiarism.org offers the following tips for avoiding plagiarism:

- Consult with your instructor or reference librarian when you are in doubt about citation issues.

- Know what you're looking for. Having a clear, specific purpose in mind and a clearly formulated thesis statement will help you to keep straight which ideas are yours and which are the intellectual property of someone else.

- Take thorough notes during the research process, noting direct quotes and distinguishing the ideas of others from your own thoughts. It may be helpful to highlight direct quotes in yellow so that you don't confuse them with your personal summaries or reactions.

- When in doubt, cite your sources. Properly cited use of others' ideas will *not* weaken your speech.

- Learn to paraphrase properly. This means that you put another's ideas into your own words and then cite the source. Do *not* just change a few words.

- Run your completed work through an online plagiarism checker such as Turnitin. You can probably do this free of charge through your school. You will receive an originality score along with a report showing where you need to make changes to avoid committing plagiarism. *Hint:* Your instructors may well use a plagiarism checker anyway, so beat them to the punch and check your own work before turning it in.

Explore at **MyCommunicationLab** Activity: "Avoid Plagiarism"

Your Quest for General Knowledge

You should start your research adventure guided by this principle: *Work from the general to the specific.* Begin by acquiring a good general knowledge of your topic area; then focus on acquiring the specific, more in-depth knowledge that will qual-ify you to speak responsibly.

▶ **documents file**   Contains articles downloaded from search engines or pages you have scanned into your computer.

▶ **research log**   Computer file in which you jot down ideas, list key terms, and prioritize readings.

During the general phase, you will become acquainted with the overall features of your topic and begin to develop your subject files. This implies that you will be learning the major issues and questions relevant to your topic. These points of focus will evolve into the main points that you will develop in your speech. Acquiring the information needed to support and develop these points—the facts, statistics, testimony, examples, and stories—is the business of the in-depth phase of research that will follow.

How can you acquire the kind of general knowledge on which you can build confidently? Good places to start might be your own personal experience, certain sites on the Internet, certain sources in the library, and the social media.

Drawing on Personal Experience

Watch at **MyCommunicationLab** Video: "How to Survive Winter Break"

Personal experience can add credibility, authenticity, and interest to your speech. Such experience can be an especially rich source of stories and examples. Although you may not be an acknowledged authority on a subject, your personal experience can suggest that you have unique insights and can make it easier for your listeners to identify with you and your topic.

If you lack direct experience with a topic, you can arrange to acquire some. Suppose you are planning a speech on how local television stations prepare newscasts. You are gathering information from books and periodicals, but it seems rather dry and lifeless. How can you enliven this information? Call a local television station and ask the news director if you might visit the newsroom so that you can get a feel for what goes on during that hectic time right before a newscast. Take in the noise, the action, and the excitement before and during a show. This experience can help enrich your speech. You might also schedule an interview with the news director while you are at the station.

As valuable as it is, personal experience is seldom sufficient to provide all the information that you will need for your speech. Your personal knowledge may be limited, the sources from which you learned may have been biased, or your experiences may not have been typical. Even people who are acknowledged authorities on a subject look to other experts to give added authority to their messages. Use your personal knowledge as a starting point, and expand it through other sources.

Personal experience, such as surviving breast cancer, can be a rich source of stories and examples, adding credibility and interest to a speech.

Certain Sites on the Internet

The Internet could jump-start your search for general knowledge with review articles found in online reference sources. Go to the Library Spot for links to online dictionaries and encyclopedias and a wealth of other free online research tools. Use the online dictionaries to look up any terms associated with your topic that you do not understand. Read encyclopedia articles to gain a general understanding of your topic and to identify keywords to search. You will also find links to an online thesaurus. Find synonyms there that provide other keywords to explore.

Wikipedia is a free, collaboratively edited online encyclopedia that contains over 25 million articles (in 285 languages) on a wide variety of topics. Because the public is allowed to make changes or contributions, there have been concerns about the accuracy of the information. But when this is an issue, you will get a warning on the webpage. Moreover, a 2005 study published in the journal *Nature* found that even at that time Wikipedia was close to other major encyclopedias in terms of the accuracy of its scientific information.[1] So the general rule is this: *Be cautious using Wikipedia for specialized research, but as a place to get started, it is hard to beat.* Among Wikipedia's best features are the references found at the ends of most articles. Many even provide direct links to other websites referenced in the article, so you can go right to these other sources of information with a simple click of the mouse. Because some people remain wary of it, however, you should not cite Wikipedia as a major source as you present your speech.

Certain Places in the Library

In the library, a convenient place to start your quest for general knowledge could be the periodical indexes, such as the *Reader's Guide to Periodical Literature.* The *Reader's Guide* covers journals of general interest that often offer comprehensive views of subject matter.

Exploring the Social Media

Social media sites allow individual users to create and share content, including lists of "likes," on everything from sports teams and music to retailers and non-profit groups or causes. There may be several organizations involved with your topic—businesses, advocacy groups, or individuals—who have Facebook pages or Twitter accounts and who are posting the most recent happenings in the field on a daily basis. While these posts are usually not edited for accuracy, quality, or bias, they can be useful tools during the preliminary research phase. Try plugging your keyword search terms into Facebook, Twitter, Pinterest, or YouTube and see what pops up.

When Marisol did just that in the early phases of preparing her speech on sustainable seafood, she found a Facebook page sponsored by the San Diego Oceans Foundation promoting what they called Sustainable Seafood Week. She "liked" the page and received daily posts in her newsfeed rich with ideas and examples relevant to her topic. Through searching the archived Twitter tweets of a group called Fish Sustainably, Marisol was also able to find numerous news articles on her topic that she may have otherwise overlooked. Still other ideas for utilizing social media in research include blogging about your topic to find others with similar interests and searching YouTube for relevant video clips.

Seeking In-Depth Knowledge

You should now have a good overall understanding of the issues and questions surrounding your topic as well as an idea of the main points you will develop in your speech. But before you can answer these questions and build the supporting superstructure of subpoints and sub-subpoints that we discuss in Chapter 9, you will have to acquire in-depth knowledge. You will need to find facts and statistics, expert testimony, and illustrative examples and stories. To discover this deeper knowledge, you must return to the Internet and the library and often arrange personal interviews with experts who can speak with authority on the issues.

Going Deeper on the Internet

The Internet is an increasingly valuable resource for accessing the latest information in local news and government documents. You will also find a growing number of databases for searching both popular and scholarly sources of information. The most basic tools for researching the Internet are search engines and subject directories.

Search Engines.   A **general search engine** such as Google or Bing allows you to search the World Wide Web for sites containing a given keyword or phrase. The results are typically organized in terms of relevance, popularity, or date of placement on the Web. We encourage you to use a variety of search engines, as they will differ in terms of what they find. Using more than one search engine will yield a broader variety of responses. Always make sure your antivirus and spyware programs are up to date and running whenever you explore new websites and services.

A note of caution: Both Google and Bing are commercial enterprises that sell advertisements. As a result, the first few sites that are listed in your results may be there only because they paid for that privilege and not because the information contained is especially useful. Check to see whether these initial sites are marked as advertisements, and if they are, skip them as you do your research. For example, British Petroleum created quite a stir at the height of the Gulf oil crisis when it purchased the right to preferentially place its material in search results for "oil spill" and similar terms. To see this premium placement as anything other than a commercial enterprise can lead your carefully planned research astray.

Perhaps the greatest challenge in conducting responsible research on the Internet is the sheer amount of posted materials and the lack of editorial oversight and quality control. Indeed, searching topics by keyword alone on the Web is a bit like shopping thrift stores. There are plenty of gems out there, but you usually end up sifting through a lot of garbage to find them, and you don't always find what you're looking for. You can either expand or focus your searches on both Bing and Google by using their advanced search options and by consulting the advice we outline in "Speaker's Notes: Tips for Refining Internet Searches."

Another useful feature found on most search engines is the option to choose the kind of source that best suits your purpose. Once you have your search results, you can narrow your results by type of source. For example, when Marisol Googled "sustainable seafood," she got 974,000 results. She clicked the "Images" option on the results pages and got photos, logos for organizations, and a Seafood Watch ratings illustration that proved to be very useful as a visual aid for her speech. She then went back to her initial results page and clicked the "News" link to narrow her results to news articles pertaining to her topic.

Subject Directories.   You can also focus your searches by using free online subject directories. A **subject directory** organizes links on topic-specific materials such as the humanities, the natural sciences, politics, technology, entertainment, or sports. Because they are compiled and screened by humans, they tend to yield more selective and often higher-quality results than general search engines. The Open Directory Project and Yahoo! Directory are both useful for searching popular topics and for searching by category. Infomine, Internet Public Library, Academic Index, and Google Scholar can help you locate a wealth of high-quality materials and publications that general search engines will usually not uncover.

▶ **general search engine** An Internet search engine that allows you to enter a keyword and find related websites.

▶ **subject directory** An organized list of links to websites on specific topics.

Perhaps the greatest barrier to conducting research on the Internet is that many of the most authoritative magazines, journals, reference materials, and newspapers are no longer available free of charge. However, you should be able to access most of them through your school library's electronic databases. We will discuss this further in the next section on doing library research. You might find these additional Web resources particularly valuable:

- *Science Daily*: Provides news on the latest scientific discoveries, including research articles, images, encyclopedia entries, videos, and book reviews.

- *Procon*: Offers analyses of controversial topics, including a synopsis of both sides, pro and con, for each issue.

- *Google News*: Offers an archive of news stories that can be searched by topic, date, source, and location.

- *Merriam-Webster Online*: Provides a highly credible online dictionary with links to a thesaurus, Spanish–English translations, medical terms, and even audio pronunciations.

- *About.com:* Provides a database with over 2 million entries written by experts on a wide variety of topics ranging from travel and product reviews to science, philosophy, and history.

- *Hulu*: Offers an impressive archive of informative documentaries that might help you to gain a broader appreciation for your topic area.

- *YouTube*: Provides a source of visual aids, but be aware that this is a very unstable medium; what was there one night may not be there the next morning. Try to download the material to your personal computer so that you can access it when you need it.

- *SearchGov.com:* Can help you navigate and access the millions of free federal, state, and local government documents that are posted online.

- *American Fact Finder*: Provides a wealth of information gathered by the U.S. Census Bureau regarding the demographic, social, and economic makeup of your community.

- *FedStats.gov*: Allows access to statistics developed by various agencies of the federal government on just about every subject.

- *WhiteHouse.gov*: Provides access to all major speeches, press releases, and position statements by the president. Websites hosted by both the U.S. House of Representatives and the Senate provide information on their proceedings as well as links to their respective members.

- *American Rhetoric*: Provides access to advanced materials and readings on public speaking and the most thorough and authoritative online anthology of historical and current American speeches available.

For more information on researching your topics online, we recommend that you visit "Finding Information on the Internet: A Tutorial," posted by the University of California, Berkeley, Library.

The Internet is an increasingly valuable resource for speech ideas and responsible knowledge, but materials should always be evaluated carefully.

SPEAKER'S notes
Tips for Refining Internet Searches

The following tips can help you expand or focus your searches:

1. Use AND to limit your search to sites that include both terms or phrases: mammogram AND ultrasound.

2. Use OR to broaden your search to sites that include either term: Memphis OR barbecue.

3. Use a minus sign (a space followed by a hyphen) to restrict your search by excluding sites containing the term or phrase following the sign: Lions -Detroit.

4. Use NEAR when words should be close to each other in the document: pollution NEAR global warming.

5. Use quotation marks to restrict your searches to a given phrase: Baltimore Preparatory School gives

2,765 hits, whereas "Baltimore Preparatory School" gives 275 hits.

6. Use "site:" following a term or phrase to restrict your search to a given site or domain. For example, typing "oil spill site:whitehouse.gov" will limit your search results to presidential statements on the topic; "Afghanistan site:edu" will limit your search results to articles posted on educational websites.

7. When all else fails, read the instructions under "Advanced Search Tips" on your search engine home page.

Going Deeper in the Library

In this age of the Internet, we sometimes forget the tremendous resources libraries can provide for in-depth research. Most college and large municipal libraries offer the following advantages:

- *Reference or Research Librarian:* This person is the most valuable resource in the library. Some libraries even offer "research consultations" with the reference librarian that you can schedule from your computer. This person can help steer you to the most useful materials for researching your topics.

- *Online Catalog:* The online catalog lists the books and periodicals available in the library, tells you where the items are located, and also indicates whether the items are available, have been checked out, or have been placed on reserve.

FINDING YOUR voice
Expanding Your Sources of Information

Go to Procon.org, and choose a controversial topic on which you already have a strong opinion. Read the arguments, both pro and con, for this topic. Do those posting the arguments seem credible? How can you tell? Do you find that you are open to both sides of the argument, or do you evaluate the postings based on your original opinion? After reading both sides of the issue, reevaluate your feelings about this topic. Has your opinion changed, or do you feel stronger in your convictions? Report your findings to the class.

You can search for books by author, title, subject, or keyword. When you find a book that looks interesting to you, look for the call number on the catalog entry. With that in hand, you can go directly to the holdings area and find your book.

■ *e-Books:* Most libraries subscribe to hundreds of thousands of electronic books and e-texts on a variety of topics. You can usually find these through your library's online catalog or through a listing on the library's website.

■ *Reference Area:* This area contains encyclopedias, yearbooks, dictionaries, almanacs, and atlases. Specialized encyclopedias, such as *the International Encyclopedia of the Social and Behavioral Sciences,* cover specific topics in greater detail, while specialized dictionaries are available on all sorts of topics from American slang to zoology.

Libraries are an excellent resource for in-depth research on a speech topic.

When you need facts and figures, consult an almanac, yearbook, or atlas. Almanacs and yearbooks provide accurate, up-to-date compilations of information on a wide range of topics. For example, they may include data on such things as population density or industrial production. Such materials go beyond simple lists and often include graphics that you can adapt for presentation aids. Two especially useful yearbooks are *Facts on File* and *World Almanac and Book of Facts.*

Biographical resources, such as *International Who's Who* and *Who's Who in America,* can provide information about the qualifications of experts on your topic. Books of quotations, such as *Bartlett's Familiar Quotations,* can provide valuable material for the introductions and conclusions of speeches.

■ *Electronic Databases:* Most universities provide free access to a variety of paid databases that allow you to search and download full-text versions of popular, scholarly, and government publications. Often you can access these materials from your personal computer at home. You should check to see which of the following your library offers.

○ Periodical and newspaper databases: These databases allow you to locate timely articles relevant to your topic in leading newspapers such as the *Wall Street Journal* and *New York Times* and in popular periodicals such as *Time* and *The Atlantic.* One such database is LexisNexis Academic, which provides full-text access to over 45,000 information sources, including articles from over 500 leading newspapers around the world. Others are ProQuest and Ethnic Newswatch. Some popular periodicals, such as *Scientific American,* are perceived as highly credible and objective, whereas others may be less acceptable to a critical audience.

○ Scholarly databases: In contrast to even the finest journalism, which reports the trajectory of human experience, scholarship seeks to discover what makes the world and all those who live upon it tick. Journalists follow a story for a limited period of time before reporting and moving on to another story; scholars often devote their lives to a specific quest for knowledge. Scholarly journals contain articles that have been through a process called

peer review. This means that the article has been checked by several experts in the field for quality and accuracy before being approved for publication. The following databases cross various disciplines and fields of knowledge to provide a comprehensive picture of scholarship up to the present:

> JSTOR catalogues over 1,000 academic journals in various disciplines.
>
> EBSCOhost provides links to special databases covering scholarly journals and publications. Among these databases are Academic Search Premier, Humanities Abstracts, and Communication and Mass Media Complete.
>
> InfoTrac OneFile accesses over 100 million articles in areas from economics and sociology to science and medicine.

As you read various popular and scholarly articles, you may discover that one or several books are frequently mentioned. Check the *Book Review Index* for summaries of reviews to help you decide how much research time to spend on them.

- *Government Documents Area:* Most libraries still maintain collections of federal, state, and local government publications in hard copy, although most current documents are now available and more readily accessible in electronic form.

- *Nonprint Media Archives:* Collections of films, videos, DVDs, CDs, recordings, and microfilms can be found in the media archives.

- *Special Collections Area:* Many libraries have areas that provide access to local publications, resources, and unique archives that can help you adapt your speeches to the needs and interests of your surrounding community. For example, the University of Memphis in its Mississippi Valley collection houses a world-famous archive of materials relating to the Memphis Sanitation Strike of 1968, during which Dr. Martin Luther King, Jr., was assassinated.

Before you go to the library, take some time to explore your school library's website. Follow the links on the home page to familiarize yourself with the wealth of information and services provided. Look for an online "virtual tour" and for a floor plan showing where the various materials are kept. Additionally, many libraries have subject-specific "research guides" available on their website with tabs for suggested reference materials, books, journal articles, and databases. You will likely be amazed to find that your library is much more than just a warehouse for books and magazines.

Conducting Personal Interviews

Personal interviews can provide special information, stories, and opinions that are not available through Internet or library research. An interview of a local expert or of a community member who is directly affected by your topic can clearly demonstrate to your listeners how your topic may impact their lives or the lives of those in their communities. For example, if you have decided on sustainably harvested seafood as your topic, you might interview the manager of the seafood department at your local supermarket. You can discuss how this issue affects cost, quality, and availability of seafood for your listeners and their families. Such interviews add credibility to your speech, and your audience will appreciate the special effort you have made to enhance their listening experience by making the material directly *relevant* to their lives.

▶ **peer review** Process by which articles in scholarly journals are checked by experts in the field for quality and accuracy before being approved for publication.

As valuable as they can be, interviews also pose some challenges. Finding the right person to interview can be difficult. You must make sure your expert has the appropriate qualifications to offer opinions you can use confidently. Also, personal interviews should be the last stage of your research strategy. Before asking a person for his or her valuable time, you must make sure that your questions cannot be easily answered online or through library research. You need sufficient knowledge of your subject before you can ask intelligent questions or be able to listen critically to the answers. However, the potential benefits of a good interview far outweigh any possible shortcomings. To minimize problems, use these strategies:

- Make interviews the final phase of your research process.

- Check local news sources to help you identify qualified prospects for interviews.

- Although it is generally preferable to conduct an interview face to face, you can identify widely recognized experts for possible telephone or e-mail interviews through your initial online and library research.

- Survey the research interests of your school's faculty members to identify additional interview possibilities.

Once you have identified prospects for interviews, you must schedule the interviews, prepare your questions, conduct the interviews, and record what you learn. Don't trust yourself not to forget that vital quotation!

Schedule the Interview.   The best way to ask for an interview is to telephone the prospect directly. Express your sincere interest in the subject, and explain that you are preparing a public speech on a topic that is important to you both. Most people will be flattered that you recognize their expertise and value their opinion and will likely grant you the interview if they can. Discuss the kind of questions you wish to ask and how much time you will need. Schedule a specific date and time for the interview, and follow up with a confirmation e-mail. It may be helpful to record the interview, but you must ask permission to do so. *Never record an interview without permission.*

Prepare for the Interview.   Complete most of your library and Internet research before you conduct the interview so that you know what questions to ask and can converse intelligently on the subject. You should also have a clear idea of the purpose of your interview. What do you hope to learn from this person? Write out interview questions that are relevant to your specific purpose.

Plan open questions that invite discussion. If you ask questions that invite a yes or no answer, that is likely all you will get. Do not ask questions that are leading or that sound abrasive, and save any controversial questions for late in the interview, after you have established rapport. Then ask touchy questions tactfully: "The sustainable seafood movement has been criticized by some who claim that there really is no difference between wild-caught fish and wild-caught fish labeled as sustainable. They claim that this is simply a marketing gimmick, a way to charge more for essentially the same product. Can you comment on that?" If asked with sincerity rather than hostility, this type of question can produce the most interesting part of your interview.

Order your questions in a logical sequence so that one question flows into the next. Consider your time limitations and plan your questions accordingly.

Conduct the Interview.   Dress appropriately to show that you take the interview seriously. By appropriately, we mean that you should dress as if you work with the

Personal interviews can provide special information, stories, and opinions, and can add credibility to your speech.

person you are interviewing—that is, in a manner appropriate to the setting of her work. In one setting, such as the San Francisco wharf, blue jeans might be appropriate; in another, perhaps the interviewee's office, nicer attire might better suit the surroundings.

Arrive a few minutes early. Bring along a notepad for taking notes, extra pencils, your list of questions, and your recording device if you have permission to record the interview. Make sure that your device works properly and that you know how to use it.

Introduce yourself and remind your subject of the purpose for the interview. You might break the ice by discussing something you admire about the person's work and telling her why you wished to interview her. Begin on your list of prepared questions, but use these only as a guide. Be open to asking questions that you had not planned but that come up in the course of the interview. Let the expert do most of the talking while you do the listening. Allow the person you are interviewing to complete the answer to one question before you ask another, Adapt to the flow of conversation.

Be alert for opportunities to follow up on answers by using probes, mirror questions, or reinforcers. **Probes** are questions that ask a person to elaborate on a response: "Could you tell me more about …?" **Mirror questions** reflect part of a response to encourage additional discussion: "So you're saying that…." A **reinforcer** provides encouragement for the person to communicate further. Smiles, nods, and comments such as "I see" are reinforcers that can keep the interview moving.

If you feel the interview beginning to drift off course, you can often steer it back with a transition. As your expert pauses, you can say, "I believe I understand now the marketing side of the sustainable seafood issue, but is the future availability of seafood likely to be affected without protections?"

As the interview draws to a close, summarize the main points you heard and how you think they may be useful in your speech. A summary allows you to verify what you have heard and reassures the expert that you intend to use the information fairly and accurately. Thank your expert for her time, and follow up with a thank-you note in which you report the successful results of your speech.

SPEAKER'S
notes   Guidelines for Interviewing for Information

To conduct an effective information interview, follow these guidelines:

1. During your preliminary research, identify possible interview prospects.

2. Make contact with the person you wish to interview.

3. Research your topic thoroughly before the interview.

4. Plan a series of questions that relate to your specific topic.

5. Act professional: Be on time, dress appropriately, and be courteous.

6. Ask positive, open-ended questions that encourage discussion.

7. Let the expert do most of the talking, but don't hesitate to ask for clarification or additional information.

8. Summarize the main points of the interview, and thank the person for her time.

▶ **probe**   A question that asks a person to elaborate on an answer.

▶ **mirror question**   A question that repeats part of a previous response to encourage further discussion.

▶ **reinforcer**   A comment or action that encourages further communication from someone being interviewed.

Record What You Learn.   You should take notes during the interview even if you are recording; technology sometimes fails. Just note the highlights of your subject's answers. Trying to write everything will slow the interview down and may have a negative impact on the interview. After you have completed the interview, go over your notes, and write out the answers to important questions while your expert's wording is still fresh in your mind.

Evaluating What You Discover

You should evaluate all information carefully before using it in your speeches. As you research sources of information—including Internet sites, books, periodicals, and even personal interview subjects—ask yourself the following questions:

- Does this source provide relevant factual and statistical information?

- Does this source cite experts I can quote or paraphrase in my speech?

- Does this source provide interesting examples that can help illustrate my main ideas?

- Does this source provide narratives that can bring my topic to life?

Beyond determining what an individual source has to offer, you should consider all researched information in terms of the four R's previously discussed in Chapter 4: relevance, representativeness, recency, and reliability:

- *Relevance* concerns the extent to which supporting materials apply directly to your topic and purpose for speaking.

- *Representativeness* means the extent to which supporting materials depict a situation or reality as it typically exists.

- *Recency* refers to the timeliness or currency of supporting materials.

- *Reliability* concerns the overall credibility of supporting materials.

The challenge of evaluating what you discover differs depending on whether the source is the Internet, the library, or a personal interview.

Information from the Internet

You must be especially careful while evaluating information you find on the Internet. Remember that virtually anyone can put anything on the Internet. Sometimes sites are taken down for various reasons (copyright infringements, repugnant content, etc.), but Internet materials are generally subject to few, if any, editorial constraints. This makes it especially important to use your critical thinking skills. Start by determining what kind of site you are looking at. As you "surf" in search of information, consciously distinguish among advocacy, information, commercial, and personal websites. Advocacy and information sites can be valuable tools for preparing speeches, but commercial and personal websites are usually not good sources for responsible research

Watch at **MyCommunicationLab Video:** "Credibility of Online Sources"

Advocacy Websites.   The purpose of an **advocacy website** is to raise consciousness and influence attitudes or behaviors on a given issue or to promote a

▶ **advocacy website**   A website whose major purpose is to change attitudes or behaviors.

FINDING YOUR

voice Discovering Advocacy Websites

Use the World Advocacy website to locate a specific website for a cause or controversial issue that interests you, such as immigration laws, health care reform, gun control, or clean energy alternatives. Locate an information website on the same topic, and describe the differences between the two sites. Do you detect an agenda beyond being informative in either or both sites? What tips you off?

special agenda. An advocacy site might ask for contributions, try to influence voting, or simply strive to promote a cause. The URL of a nonprofit advocacy site often ends with .org. Some examples of advocacy sites include the Sierra Club, Citizens Against Government Waste, and the Southern Poverty Law Center.

The Sierra Club home page, shown in Figure 7.3, illustrates the features of an advocacy website. The top ribbon bears a truncated mission statement: "Explore, Enjoy and Protect the Planet." Windows across the top menu document the organization's

FIGURE 7.3
Advocacy Website Home Page

Reprinted by permission of the Sierra Club.

past and continuing work promoting environmental causes. The "News" window provides links to news stories and other sources of information, and the "Donate," "Take Action," and "Join/Renew" sidebars promote the group's agenda and beat the drums for donations.

Like the Sierra Club home page, many advocacy websites contain good information and links to other credible sources of information, although such sources typically present only one side of an issue. Therefore, you should carefully evaluate what you read, strive for balance by finding out what opposing groups and advocates have to say, and corroborate any information that is especially compelling or important by cross-referencing it with other, less partisan sources.

Information Websites. The purpose of an **information website** is to provide factual information on a specific topic. Information websites may include research reports; current world, national, or local news; government statistics; or simply general information such as you might find in an encyclopedia or almanac. The URLs of information websites may have a variety of suffixes, such as .edu, .gov, or .com. For example, both Mayo Clinic and MEDLINEplus are excellent sources of information about health issues. The material on the Mayo Clinic website has been prepared by physicians and editors associated with the site; the material on the MEDLINEplus website comes from the government-sponsored National Library of Medicine.

Figure 7.4 shows the Mayo Clinic home page. Even though this website is registered in the commercial domain (.com), the focus is primarily on providing health-related

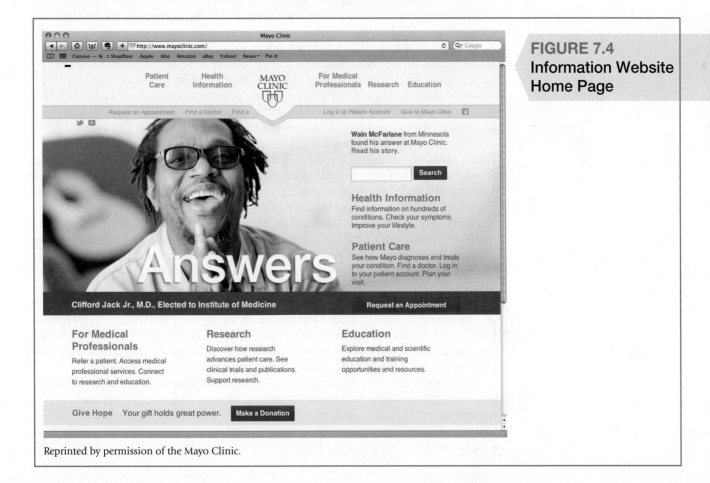

Reprinted by permission of the Mayo Clinic.

FIGURE 7.4
Information Website Home Page

▶ **information website** A website designed to provide factual information on a subject.

information. Note some of the differences between this information home page and the advocacy home page shown in Figure 7.3. While you are subjected to the occasional advertisement, you are not asked for a donation, and the website is not trying to sell you any products.

It is not always easy to differentiate between advocacy and information websites. Some nonprofit sites walk a fine line between informing and advocating without damaging their credibility. For instance, the home page of the American Red Cross (www.redcross.org) offers links to a wealth of highly credible information on disaster relief efforts, but it is presented in a manner that is obviously calculated to arouse your sympathies and financial generosity. Some advocacy sites seek to mask their persuasive agendas behind the appearance of informative expertise and objectivity. Be especially wary of anonymous studies, "fact sheets," and news stories posted by partisan activist groups, and watch out for blatant disinformation that fabricates or distorts information beyond reason to advance a hidden agenda.

No single article or website can provide all the information you need on a topic. Reputable websites will contain links to additional information or research that should be useful. When you are visiting an advocacy website, remember that you are reading one side of an issue, so you should visit another that provides balance. In general, you should assume that any single source offers only a partial view.

Again, recency is crucial when addressing current events, disputed issues, and topics relating to science and technology. With such topics, most of your online information will likely come from news sources and popular periodicals, information and advocacy websites, and government documents. Most reputable sites will date archived information. When they don't, you must rely on the date the site was last updated or depend on the credibility of the host site or sponsoring agency.

Reliability is especially important when evaluating information retrieved from Internet sources. The reliability of a source usually boils down to its authority, accuracy, and objectivity. **Authority** refers to the credibility and expertise of a given source of information with respect to a given issue or subject area. As noted earlier, you should be wary of anonymous studies, news reports, and "fact sheets" posted by activist groups. As a general rule, websites posted by credible organizations cite their sources and make it easy for you to identify their sponsoring agencies. You can search most organizations by their URL addresses. If it is hard to determine who is sponsoring a website, you should probably not use it. Again, you can assess the "recognized" authority of most experts and organizations by simply searching their names and/or titles, enclosed in quotation marks, in a search engine.

Accuracy refers to the precision or truthfulness of information. The best way to ensure the accuracy of the information you locate during your research is to use sites hosted or sponsored by credible sources such as recognized experts, compilers of reference materials, and "mainstream" news organizations. Again, credible sites usually document sources and provide links to other credible information. Watch out for statistical information and studies generated by advocacy organizations and commercially funded "think tanks" with an obvious interest in the outcome. Be wary of information that seems purposefully obscure and inaccessible to the average reader. As always, check any information on advocacy sites that seems "too good to be true" by consulting other, less partisan sources of information.

Objectivity concerns the extent to which information on websites is free from personal feelings, bias, and hidden agendas. Most recognized experts and "mainstream" news organizations have a vested interest in maintaining their ethos as objective sources of ideas and information. Most reputable advocacy and commercial websites are honest about their biases and strive to present information reliably and

▶ **authority** Criterion for evaluating the credentials of the author.

▶ **accuracy** Criterion for evaluating the correctness of information by checking it against other information.

▶ **objectivity** Criterion for evaluating whether or not a source is free from bias.

accurately. However, knowing that a source has an agenda should cue you to look for additional information from differing perspectives. As mentioned earlier, the advocacy sites that try to hide their objectives are the ones you really must watch out for. The lack of an "About Us" or "Mission Statement" link on the site should be a clear indication that it may be peddling disinformation. For example, there are racist and anti-Semitic groups that have been known to disguise their messages of hatred by developing what at first glance look like benign informative websites.

We close with a caveat that bears repeating. *Because literally anyone can put anything on the Internet, it is very important for you to be a thoughtful and critical consumer of online ideas and information.* For an excellent tutorial on assessing the quality of websites, we recommend "Evaluate Web Sources" which is posted by the Widener University Library. The Annenberg Center for Public Policy offers a site titled "FactCheckEd.Org" which lists and assesses informative and advocacy websites dealing with public issues.

SPEAKER'S notes — Checklist for Evaluating Internet Materials

When using the Internet to do research, use the following checklist to evaluate the information you find.

1. What type of website have I accessed? Advocacy? Information?

2. Is the author or sponsoring agency identified?

3. Does the author or sponsoring agency have appropriate credentials to address the issue?

4. Does the material contain links to other information on the subject or citations of available print resources?

5. Is the material objective, or does it seem biased?

6. Do other authorities confirm the information on the website?

7. Is the material up to date on time-sensitive topics?

8. Is the material covered with enough breadth and depth?

Information from the Library

We may be inclined to place more trust in information found in the library than on the Internet. After all, the printed word seems less elusive, subject to more controls. Material that is submitted for publication usually must pass rigorous tests for quality: Tough-minded editors often play a "gatekeeper" role in protecting a book company or a professional discipline from shoddy publication. Peer reviews conducted by "blind reviewers" (reviewers not revealed to the authors) subject submitted manuscripts to stringent tests. We may place trust in publications that have passed such texts, and we may think that just being in the library somehow endows the printed word with the presumption of credibility.

And that is where we can go wrong. Quality advocacy is still advocacy, perhaps all the more dangerous and seductive because of its quality. The mere fact of being in print does not confer trustworthiness. For this reason, you should not let your guard down when evaluating information from library research.

As you do such research, consider the credibility of your sources, an important part of that reliability test we have mentioned previously. Also remember that the timeliness of information is critical for topics addressing current events, disputed issues, and the latest developments in science and technology. The printed word can grow stale and dated, so seek out the most up-to-date information available.

As you assess the credibility of an author, ask yourself, *Is this person an expert on my topic?* Remember that scientists and college professors are not necessarily experts on every subject. You should be able to assess the credentials of most experts (such as their professional associations) and determine what other experts have to say about them by searching their names in a general search engine (enclosed in quotation marks). When assessing authors who are journalists, evaluate the credibility of the "experts" cited in their articles.

You should also consider the publication in which the material appears. Professional journals are generally seen as more credible than popular periodicals such as magazines and newspapers. In turn, popular periodicals themselves vary in terms of their credibility. For most audiences, mainline newspapers are considered more credible than tabloids, and upscale magazines such as *The Atlantic* are more credible than *Reader's Digest*. Popular periodicals may also reflect political or social biases. For example, *The Nation* offers a liberal perspective on contemporary issues, and the *National Review* presents a conservative outlook. Consequently, as you select authors and publications to cite in your speeches, you should consider how their reputations might affect the way your listeners respond to your message.

Information from Personal Interviews

From one point of view, you should be less vulnerable to bad information gained from personal interviews. By the time of the interview, you should have done a good deal of library and Internet research: You should know the general features and issues surrounding your subject and should have acquired some in-depth knowledge about them. Therefore, if the interviewee should make really partisan or outlandish statements, you should be able to detect such claims for what they are.

But on the other hand, you should approach the interview with some gratitude to the interviewee for consenting to talk with you. If the person is charming, affable, and flattering, you may find yourself *wanting* to agree with what he says, no questions asked. Be aware of this personal tendency, and be cautious: You can be grateful to a person without endorsing what he has to say, especially if other respected sources of knowledge you have consulted hold different views.

YOUR ethical VOICE   Guidelines for Ethical Research

To be sure your research meets the ethical standard of respect for the integrity of ideas and information, apply the following guidelines:

1. Allow sufficient time for research.
2. Investigate differing perspectives on your topic.
3. Access credible sources of information.
4. Never fabricate or distort information.

5. Take careful notes on what you read.
6. Avoid plagiarism by indicating in your notes which ideas are yours and which derive from other sources.
7. Cite your sources in your presentation.

SPEAKER'S notes   Checklist for Acquiring Responsible Knowledge

Use this checklist to assure that you have covered all the bases in your research.

1. ____ I have cultivated a general knowledge of my topic, including its major features and surounding issues.

2. ____ I have sought in-depth knowledge on the points and issues I wish to explore in my speech.

3. ____ I have explored a variety of knowledge sources, including the Internet, the library, and personal interviews with experts.

4. ____ I have sought information that is timely and relevant.

5. ____ I have sought the judgments and opinions of experts on my topic.

6. ____ I have sought information that would be most useful to my listeners.

7. ____ I have sought examples and stories that will bring my subject to life and illustrate its relevance.

8. ____ I have tested my research findings in terms of relevance, representativeness, recency, and reliability.

FINAL reflections   Empowering Your Voice

Not long ago, we asked some of our colleagues and advanced students to describe the meaning of research to them, using whatever comparisons came to mind. One described research as a treasure hunt, in which one seeks those gems of knowledge that will enrich a message. Another described it similarly as an archaeological dig, in which one sifts through the writings of others in search of valued discoveries.

For yet another, research is a voyage of discovery, in which one sets out in a general direction not really knowing what one might encounter along the way. Another described research as opening a succession of doors, which lead into larger and larger banquet halls. And for yet another, the process of research was like building a foundation of knowledge, first framing the general outlines and then pouring in the particulars.

For Marisol, research was a time for self-correction and redirection. First, she discovered that she had indeed been "greenwashed" by unscrupulous marketers, who promised to protect wild fish populations but were actually endangering them by hoodwinking the buying public. Second, she refocused her environmental concerns on how to protect these endangered fish.

Who can say what your research adventure might mean to you? The end result should be to find and empower your voice and to justify your speaking on your topic. Beyond any particular discoveries, you will be acquiring a set of skills that you can use throughout your life to help you understand and verify what is going on in your world.

After Reading This Chapter, You Should Be Able To Answer These Questions

1 What are the four dimensions of responsible knowledge that must be developed in the course of your research?

Study and **Review** at **MyCommunicationLab**

2 What research priorities are appropriate to the pursuit of responsible knowledge?

3 How can you organize and store information uncovered in your research?

4 What are the strengths and limitations of personal experience as a source of responsible knowledge?

5 How can you evaluate a website for credibility?

6 What special problems does the Internet present in terms of credibility of sources?

7 What special advantages can the library offer as a source of responsible knowledge?

8 How can personal interviews be used to strengthen your speech?

For Discussion and Further Exploration

1 As you watch television news or read the morning newspaper, be alert for stories that contain opinions disguised as information. What clues you to the deception? Bring your examples to class for further discussion.

2 Find an advocacy website and an information website for a topic that interests you. Compare the two sites. How do they differ? Which would make a better source for your speech, and why?

3 You are preparing an informative speech on the latest research technology available through your school's library, and the research librarian has graciously agreed to an interview. Prepare a list of five questions that you will ask in the interview.

4 For your speech topic, find three websites with URLs that end in .com, three that end in .org, and three that end in .edu. Evaluate each in terms of the four R's: relevance, representativeness, recency, and reliability.

5 Surf the Internet, seeking answers to the following questions. Keep a record of how long it takes you, what resources you use, and the results of your search. Report this information in class.
   a. What was the population of the city in which you were born in the year of your birth?
   b. What television show had the highest Nielsen rating when you were six years old?
   c. Select the contemporary figure that you admire most. When was he or she born? What awards has he or she received?
   d. Who won the Pulitzer Prize for literature in the year you were born? For what work was this awarded? For what other works is the author noted?
   e. What actress won the Academy Award for best supporting actress in the year of your birth? What movie was she in?
   f. What noteworthy event took place during the month and year of your birth? When and where did this happen?

6 In question 5 above, substitute a parent or guardian for yourself. Then use the library instead of the Internet to locate the answers to these questions. Keep track of how long it takes you to find the information, where you find it, and the results. Compare the two sources in terms of efficiency and quality of information, and report in class.

7 Prepare a formal bibliography of the readings you consult as you develop your next speech. Follow either the APA or the MLA style format illustrated in Figure 7.5 depending on your instructor's preference.

Book, Print

MLA: Blackford, Mansel. *Making Seafood Sustainable: American Experiences in Global Perspective.* Philadelphia: University of Pennsylvania Press, 2012. Print.

APA: Blackford, M. G. (2012). *Making seafood sustainable: American experiences in global perspective.* Philadelphia: University of Pennsylvania Press.

Scholarly Journal Article with One Author, Print

MLA: Iles, Alastair. "Making Seafood Sustainable: Merging Consumption and Citizenship in the United States." *Science and Public Policy* 31.2 (2004): 127-138. Print.

APA: Iles, A. (2004). Making seafood sustainable: Merging consumption and citizenship in the United States. *Science and Public Policy,* 31(2), 127-138.

Scholarly Journal Article with Two Authors, Print

MLA: Klinger, Dane, and Rosamond Naylor. "Searching for Solutions in Aquaculture: Charting a Sustainable Course." *Annual Review of Environment and Resources* 37 (2012): 247-276. Print.

APA: Klinger, D., & Naylor, R. (2012). Searching for solutions in aquaculture: Charting a sustainable course. *Annual Review of Environment and Resources,* 37, 247-276.

Magazine Article, Print

MLA: Oz, Mehmet. "What to Eat Now: The Anti-Food-Snob Diet." *Time 3* Dec. 2012: 38-46. Print.

APA: Oz, M. (2012, December 3). What to eat now: The anti-food-snob diet. *Time,* 180(23), 38-46.

Newspaper Article, Print

MLA: Osborn, Claire. "Legendary Chimp Expert Goodall Draws Thousands." *Austin-American-Statesman* 4 Apr. 2013, B2. Print.

APA: Osborn, C. (2013, April 4). Legendary chimp expert Goodall draws thousands. *Austin American-Statesman,* p. B2.

Article in an Edited Collection or Essay or Chapter of a Book in an Anthology, Print

MLA: Pawley, Thomas. "The Black Theatre Audience." *The Theatre of Black Americans: A Collection of Critical Essays.* Ed. Errol Hill. New York: Applause Theatre & Cinema Books, 1987. 307-317. Print.

APA: Pawley, T. D. (1987). The black theatre audience. In E. Hill (Ed.), *The theatre of black Americans: A collection of critical essays* (pp. 307-317). New York, NY: Applause Theatre & Cinema Books.

FIGURE 7.5
Citation Guide

FIGURE 7.5 (continued)

Speech

MLA: Johnson, Lyndon Baines. "The Great Society." University of Michigan Commencement Ceremony. University of Michigan, Ann Arbor, MI. 22 May 1964. Commencement Address.

APA: Johnson, L. B. (1964, May). *The great society.* Speech presented at the commencement ceremony, University of Michigan, Ann Arbor, MI.

Personal Interview

MLA: Sanchez, Mario. Personal interview. 13 Feb. 2013.

APA: Because personal interviews do not provide recoverable data, they are not included in the reference list according to APA style guidelines. They should, of course, be cited in your speech and listed in your bibliography as follows: M. Sanchez (personal communication, February 13, 2013).

Website with an Organizational Author

MLA: National Down Syndrome Society. "Down Syndrome Facts." *National Down Syndrome Society: The National Advocate for People with Down Syndrome Since 1979.* 2012. Web. 6 Apr. 2013.

APA: National Down Syndrome Society. (2012). Down syndrome facts. Retrieved from http://www.ndss.org/Down-Syndrome/Down-Syndrome-Facts/

Online Newspaper Article

MLA: Jolly, David. "McDonald's to Serve Sustainable Fish in Europe." *New York Times.* New York Times Company, 8 June 2011. Web. 4 Apr. 2013.

APA: Jolly, D. (2011, June 8). McDonald's to serve sustainable fish in Europe. *The New York Times.* Retrieved from http://www.nytimes.com

Online Magazine Article

MLA: Gounder, Celine. "Medical Emergencies at 40,000 Feet." *The Atlantic.com,* Atlantic Monthly Group, Apr. 2013. Web. 6 Apr. 2013.

APA: Gounder, C. (2013, April). Medical emergencies at 40,000 feet. *The Atlantic.com.* Retrieved from http://www.theatlantic.com

Sources:

MLA Handbook for Writers of Research Papers, Seventh Edition, 2009; Publication Manual of the American Psychological Association, Sixth Edition, 2010; http://owl.english.purdue.edu/owl/resource/747/1/ (MLA); http://owl.english.purdue.edu/owl/resource/560/01/ (APA)

8 Supporting Your Ideas

((· **Listen** to **Chapter 8** at **MyCommunicationLab**

The Golden Gate Bridge has occupied a prominent place in the American imagination since it opened in 1937. Its architects, engineers, and construction workers had to triumph over fierce winds, dense fogs, swirling tides, a channel nearly 400 feet deep, and a span of water over two miles wide. Thus, it stands as a monument to the human power to tame and overcome vast forces of nature. Today, at a time of deep political and religious divisions between vast populations, the bridge (like so many such bridges around the world) may promise that we can build connections between separated people, even when the task of doing so seems formidable.

Think of speeches as bridges that carry messages that can connect speakers and audiences. And think of yourself as a builder of these symbolic bridges. To be successful, you must learn how to construct thought structures that rest on solid pillars of supporting materials. To be a good builder, you must know your materials and what they can support. You need to know how to select and use them wisely. Just as a bridge must carry heavy weights and withstand storms and high winds, your speech must withstand doubt and controversy. When you rise to speak, you must be confident of its structural integrity.

Supporting materials—facts and statistics, testimony, examples, and narratives—are the pillars, braces, and cross-braces of serious speech-making. The effective and ethical use of supporting materials encourages others to take your ideas seriously. Such materials give strength and human appeal to the voice you are discovering and developing.

At this point, you should have gathered a wealth of information and begun to generate your main ideas, as discussed in the previous two chapters. In this chapter, we discuss the four forms of supporting materials that make use of this information, point out how to put them to work in your speeches, and discuss how to combine them to maximum advantage.

Facts and Statistics

As discussed in the previous chapter, your first objective when researching any topic is to get your facts straight. Facts and statistics are indispensable to responsible speaking—especially when addressing informative or persuasive topics. When audience members get the impression that "the facts are in your favor," they are likely to give you attention and respect.

Facts are statements that can be verified as true or false. On April 15, 2013, three people died near the finish line of the Boston marathon as a result of a terrorist attack. On November 6, 2012, Barack Obama was reelected president of the United States. As of March 2013, approximately 8 percent of the American labor force remained out of work.

Very few people would question that these statements are factual. What they "mean," however, and what we should do about them are often vigorously debated. With terms such as *terrorist*, how they should be defined and whether they are rightfully applied in a particular case can be especially controversial.

▶ **supporting materials** The facts and statistics, testimony, examples, and narratives that are the building blocks of substantive speech-making.

▶ **facts** Descriptive statements that can be verified as true by independent observation.

Statistics are facts measured mathematically. In our "show me the numbers" culture, statistics are useful for describing size precisely, making predictions, illustrating trends, and demonstrating important comparisons. The following is an illustration:

> According to the Centers for Disease Control and Prevention, the percentage of children aged six to eleven years in the United States who were obese increased from 7 percent in 1980 to nearly 18 percent in 2010. Similarly, the percentage of adolescents aged twelve to nineteen years who were obese increased from 5 percent to 18 percent over the same period. These are ominous trends for the health of this country.

We typically listen carefully and respectfully to such statistical claims. In democratic societies, public opinion polls that demonstrate "the will of the people" can strongly influence policy decisions.

Constructing Facts and Figures

"The art of the fact" may seem a strange expression. Don't facts stand alone, without need for further help from the speaker? Despite that commonplace assumption, the truth is that facts don't speak for themselves. *You* must explain what they mean. You select them to make some point and then interpret them. Developing the ability to frame facts effectively is vital to finding your voice.

Consider this statement: "According to a U.S. Department of Labor report issued on March 1, 2013, the unemployment rate in this country was 8.1%."[1] That is certainly a factual statement, but what point is it trying to make? One person might argue, "That's an alarming number of people who remain out of work. The president's policies are a failure." Another might answer, "That represents a huge drop from 9.7 percent in 2010. The president's policies are working."

These dramatically different claims interpret the meaning of the fact. Which one is correct? Ironically, both could be, based on these statements alone. Effective speakers should introduce additional evidence to strengthen their cases. Our point, however, is that facts and figures can't just stand alone. *You must explain to listeners how the facts relate to your message and what it is that they demonstrate.*

The preceding example illustrates another important decision you must make as you practice the art of the fact: whether to state your fact in general or precise terms. One often hears statements such as the following: "As of March 2013, almost one out of twelve Americans looking for work could not find it." Presenting statistics in such a "rounded off" manner can have more impact and be more easily remembered. On the other hand, there are some audiences and situations for which the exact numbers and sources of data could be critical issues. Your college audience of critical listeners might be such an audience. You must decide whether the general or the precise way of expressing facts will work best for you. If you are uncertain on this point, our advice is to err on the side of precision.

Because facts and figures are so vital to responsible knowledge and to ethical speaking, we may have a tendency to overemphasize them. Remember to use a variety of supporting materials and pick the spots in your speech at which the use of facts and figures will be most effective. Don't drown your listeners in a sea of numbers that will numb them to your underlying ideas. Again, be selective.

Remember also the possible use of presentation aids. As we discuss in Chapter 10, presentation aids can be very effective for communicating factual and statistical information. Simple bulleted textual graphics can help to emphasize the importance

▶ **statistics** Facts that can be measured mathematically.

of one or a few particularly compelling facts. For instance, if you really want your audience to know and remember that in 2010 nearly 10 percent of Americans were unemployed, simply displaying the latter number in a chart or graph could be very effective.

Journalists are taught to seek more than one source for information before rushing into print with a story. This search for additional supporting sources is the key to responsible reporting. It is also the way to satisfy critical listeners when statements are controversial and important to the well-being of the audience. Before an audience of critical listeners, cite several credible sources to establish the validity of your points. As Austin Wright built his case against the government's use of faulty databases in the War on Terror, he carefully supported each of his vital points with at least two credible sources of information.

It becomes increasingly clear that to practice "the art of the fact" skillfully, you must become a critic of your own work. It is to this part of finding your voice that we now turn our attention.

Testing Facts and Figures

Explore at **MyCommunicationLab** **Activity:** "Testing for Relevance of Supporting Ideas"

For most speech topics, your research should yield an array of facts and statistics. To test them for their usefulness in your speech, you must subject them to the four R's, learn how to assess the value of sources, and develop the ability to distinguish fact-based interpretations from opinions.

The Four R's.   In Chapter 7, we mentioned the importance of evaluating information in terms of *r*elevance, *r*epresentativeness, *r*ecency, and *r*eliability. The factual information you present in your speeches should relate to the point you are making, should be representative of the reality or situation you are discussing, should be fresh and timely, and should come from sources that are highly credible.

Sometimes facts about a subject may seem so fascinating that you are tempted to mention them even though they don't really advance your particular purpose. Whenever you are tempted to say, "By the way, did you know that …," avoid going down that path. It only leads your listeners away from your topic and risks confusing or distracting them.

You should also resist the temptation to describe some event or accomplishment as representative of reality when actually it is an exception to the rule. Be wary as well of whether a general conclusion actually applies to the situation you are describing. Assume for a moment that you are in Nebraska and you want to talk about the "crisis of unemployment" in that area, basing your claim on the previously mentioned national average of 8.1 percent. You would have a real credibility problem if someone in the back of the room should stand and say, "Pardon me, but according to the Department of Labor, Nebraska in 2012 had an unemployment rate of 3.9 percent, less than half of what you claim."

Also remember that change is constant. Yesterday's fact may be today's illusion. For example, a perception that the economy is rebounding based on last month's statistics might be dispelled when the latest jobs report is released. Be sure to cite the most recent data, especially when situations are fluid.

Finally, be mindful that statistical predictions represent probability, not certainty, and that even credible statistics can be distorted by partisan interest groups. Speakers for both major political parties often "spin" the same or similar polls to reach opposing conclusions. Be wary as well of *who* "the people" are and *what* "the people" want, based on such conflicting claims.

FINDING YOUR

voice   Detecting Disinformation

Look in newspapers or magazines for "news" stories or statements by public officials that claim to be factual but that may actually contain distortions or fabrications. What tips you off to the disinformation? In your judgment, would most readers be likely to detect this bias? How do these "news" sources differ from online news, including social media? For example, consider how quickly disinformation about the April 2013 Boston bombings got circulated and even picked up by reputable TV and cable news outlets. Reporters and commentators, as well as those on Twitter and other social media, tried to reconstruct events and analyze leads in the chaotic days following the tragic bombings, resulting in some wild speculation and spin on threads of information as well as the garbling of true stories. How can you judge the accuracy of such news stories, even in the heat of "breaking news," especially when some of the information (such as the "Captured" tweet or the lockdown situation in Boston) *is* accurate and also provides vital communication?

The Sources of Your Data.   The facts and statistics you use in your speeches should come from recognized experts, respected research institutions, and news outlets that have a reputation for balance and objectivity. More liberal listeners might be suspicious of information that flows from Fox News, whereas conservative listeners might have issues with MSNBC. Citing such sources might divide your audience if many listeners discredit your argument because of the source of the information.

Remember also that there are many pseudo-news sources, especially on the Internet. Don't use them until you have checked out their credentials and are convinced of their reliability. Finally, be alert for **disinformation**, sometimes sensational pseudo-discoveries that have been willfully fabricated and packaged as "news" to advance a hidden agenda.[2] The Internet especially is rife with disinformation: At any given moment, you might "discover" that "aliens from outer space have just landed in California" and that "Big Foot has been spotted in Canada."

Interpretation Versus Opinion.   There is a real difference between **opinions**, which are expressions of personal feeling and conviction, and fact-centered interpretations. As careful speakers and critical listeners, we learn to value interpretations over opinions when these are used as supporting materials.

Consider, for example, this claim: "The Scion FR-S is the best affordable sports car on the market." Offered without any factual or statistical support or expert testimony, the statement is an opinion. It may or may not be true. But contrast its usefulness with the following statement: "According to the 2013 *U.S. News* analysis of six published reviews and test drives, the Scion FR-S ranks number one in quality among affordable sports cars. The analysis concludes, 'The FR-S proves that thrilling performance doesn't have to cost a fortune.'" This is a fact-based interpretation. You could argue with it, but its value far exceeds mere opinion.

▶ **disinformation** Information that has been fabricated or distorted in order to advance a hidden agenda.

▶ **opinions** Expressions of personal feeling and conviction that may lack supporting material.

SPEAKER'S notes — Constructing Facts and Statistics

Follow these guidelines for using facts and figures in your speeches.

1. Demonstrate how a fact fits the points you are making.
2. Decide whether to present your facts in general or precise terms.
3. Don't overwhelm your listeners with too many facts.
4. Support controversial claims with facts from more than one source.
5. Test facts for relevance, representativeness, recency, and reliability.
6. Avoid using sources that are obviously biased.
7. Carefully distinguish between fact-based interpretations and opinions.

Of course, there is nothing inherently wrong with expressing honest convictions and feelings in a speech. Freedom of speech assures us of the right to do just that. But if we wish to influence others, our expressions should be justified by facts and statistics—they should be anchored in reality.

For more on the uses and misuses of statistics, see the brief but excellent online primer compiled and maintained by Robert Niles, "Statistics Every Writer Should Know." See also our discussion of fallacies in Chapter 15.

Testimony

You use **testimony** when you quote the words or summarize the ideas of others to support and illustrate your points. Using testimony is like calling witnesses to speak on your behalf. You add their ethos to yours. The three forms of testimony are expert, lay, and prestige.

Using Expert Testimony

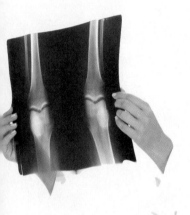

Expert testimony comes from people who are qualified by training or experience to speak as authorities on a subject. Such support can be especially useful when you are not a recognized expert and when your topic is complicated, unfamiliar, or controversial.

When you use expert testimony, remember that competence is area specific: Your experts can speak as authorities only within their area of expertise. As you introduce such experts in your speech, stress their credentials. If their testimony is recent, mention that as well. If the testimony appears in a prestigious journal, book, or newspaper, let listeners know where you found it. Note how Gabrielle Wallace, whose speech appears in Appendix B, wove the testimony of *three* expert sources together to support her speech comparing French and American eating customs:

> According to Paul Rozin, a nutritionist at the University of Pennsylvania, French portion sizes on average are about 25% smaller than American portions—which might explain why Americans are roughly three times more likely to become obese than French people.
>
> A factor that might account for this is the French upbringing. Mireille Guiliano, author of *French Women Don't Get Fat*, says that the French are not

Citing expert testimony adds substance to your speech.

▶ **testimony**   Citing the words and ideas of others to support a point.

▶ **expert testimony**   Citing the words of people (or institutions) qualified by training or experience to speak as authorities on a subject.

conditioned to overeat. Instead, they are taught to eat only until they are full, and then stop! A recent University of Pennsylvania study confirmed this tendency. The study compared the eating habits of students from Paris and Chicago. It found that French students stopped eating in response to internal cues, like when they first started feeling full or when they wanted to leave room for dessert. The American students, on the other hand, relied more on external cues. They would, for example, eat until the TV show they were watching ended, or until they ran out of a beverage. There's no question that eating habits are a vital point of difference between the French and American cultures.

This was powerful testimony, enhancing the credibility of both the speaker and the speech. Just think of how much weaker the speech would have been had Gabrielle *not* cited these authorities, relying simply on her own assertions. Much of its power lay in how Gabrielle established the credentials of her experts.

It's important that you guard against bias as you select expert testimony. Also be aware, however, that on some occasions, the perception of bias can actually enhance the usefulness of a source. One of the most powerful forms of testimony, **reluctant testimony**, occurs when experts testify *against* and *despite* their apparent self-interest.[3]

One of the most dramatic examples of such testimony in recent memory occurred in 2013 when President Obama admitted that some IRS agents had shown bias in determining the tax-exempt status of some conservative political groups. In effect, the president admitted that this misuse of power had happened on his watch.

Developing Lay Testimony

Lay testimony represents the wisdom of ordinary people. It may come from people who have firsthand experience with a topic or issue or who simply have strong feelings about it. While not appropriate for validating complex or disputed ideas, lay testimony helps illustrate real-life consequences and adds authenticity to your speech. It is highly regarded in democratic societies, in which the experiences and opinions of everyday folk are highly valued.

As he addressed the annual meeting of the Public Broadcasting System, Bill Moyers used lay testimony to emphasize the value of public radio and television:

> There was a cabbie [in New York City] named Youssef Jada. He came here from Morocco six years ago. . . . Youssef kept his car radio tuned to National Public Radio all day and his television set at home on Channel Thirteen. He said—and this is a direct quote—"I am blessed by these stations." He pointed me to a picture on the dashboard of his 13-month-old son, and he said: "My son was born in this country. I will let him watch Channel Thirteen so he can learn how to be an American."
>
> Think about that. . . . Why shouldn't public television be the core curriculum of the American experience?[4]

Stories featuring lay testimony are a common staple of both television and print journalism. The "letters to the editor" section of most newspapers and even the blogs and opinion threads that follow many online news stories can be colorful, if somewhat dubious, sources of popular opinion. Opinion polls can serve as a powerful form of collective lay testimony by representing the voice of the people, especially in societies in which "the people" is a positive symbol that represents the final repository of political power.[5] See, for example, Gallup International's "The Voice of

---

▶ **reluctant testimony** Invoking the words of sources who appear to speak against their own interests.

▶ **lay testimony** Citing the words or views of ordinary people on a subject.

Bill Moyers used testimony to illustrate the importance of public radio.

Watch at **MyCommunicationLab**
Video: "Hillary Clinton: Immigration"

the People." If you decide to use testimony from survey data, be sure that it is from a reputable polling organization and that it meets the recency criterion.

Also, be aware that polls measure the popularity of a subject but not necessarily its rightness or wrongness. Don't assume that a majority opinion at a given moment equates with ethical correctness. John Stuart Mill, in his classic treatise *On Liberty*, warned of what he called "the tyranny" of majority opinion.

Finally, if you wish to use lay testimony, look in your own backyard: Conduct your own informal interviews among audience members. You can create special bonds of identification with your listeners when you quote them in your speech.

Constructing Prestige Testimony

Prestige testimony associates your message with the words of an admired figure—for example, Thomas Jefferson—or text—such as the Declaration of Independence. While such sources do not typically provide expertise with respect to your particular topic, their words can lend a heightened elegance and wisdom to your speeches. Because of this quality, prestige testimony is often used as a source of inspiration in ceremonial speaking.

Barack Obama, in his "Speech on Race" delivered during his first campaign for the presidency, relied heavily on prestige testimony. He cited the Constitution of the United States ("We the people, in order to form a more perfect union"), William Faulkner ("The past isn't dead and buried. In fact, it isn't even past"), and the Bible ("We are commanded to do unto others as we would have them do unto us. Let us be our brother's keeper, Scripture tells us. Let us be our sister's keeper.").[6] This combined prestige testimony from an iconic political document, a noted author, and a sacred text lent considerable eloquence to Obama's argument. Figure 8.1 provides some guidelines for evaluating testimony.

If you are using prestige testimony, think about how your listeners might feel about the person you are citing. You should also consider whether associating with this person will increase your credibility as a speaker and the credibility of your message. As with lay testimony, prestige testimony should not be used to verify facts.

Designing Testimony: Other Considerations

As you frame testimony for use in your speech, decide whether to quote or to summarize what others say. When you repeat the exact words of others, you are using a **direct quotation**. Generally speaking, direct quotations are the more powerful form of citation. They are useful when statements are brief and eloquent or when the exact wording is important for the point you are making. They are also effective for supporting complex or controversial assertions before skeptical audiences.

Write out quotations on separate note cards to preserve the exact wording. Give some thought to how you will blend them into your speech: for example, "According to . . ." or "In the words of. . . ." Pause as you read the words to increase their impressiveness, and maintain eye contact with listeners during the pauses.

When quotes are too long or complex to present word for word, you may **paraphrase**, or restate what others have said in your own words. If your sources are experts on current topics or issues, stress their credentials and the timing of their testimony.

As you use testimony, be sure that the quotation you select reflects the overall meaning and intent of its author. Never twist the meaning of testimony to make it

---

▶ **prestige testimony**   Citing the words of a person who is highly admired or respected but not necessarily an expert on your topic; similarly, citing a text in this way.

▶ **direct quotation**   Repeating the exact words of others to support a point.

▶ **paraphrase**   Rephrasing or summarizing the words of others to support a point.

General

_____ Is this testimony relevant to my purpose?

_____ Am I quoting or paraphrasing accurately?

_____ Am I using the appropriate type of testimony for my purpose?

Expert Testimony

_____ Have I verified the credentials of my source?

_____ Are my expert's credentials appropriate for my topic?

_____ Will this expert be acceptable to my listeners?

_____ Is my expert free from vested interest?

_____ Is this testimony consistent with that of other authorities?

_____ Does this testimony reflect the latest knowledge on my topic?

Lay Testimony

_____ Does this testimony demonstrate the human applications of my topic?

_____ Does this testimony enhance identification with my topic?

_____ Are the people cited likable?

_____ Is polling data from a reputable organization?

_____ Is polling data recent?

Prestige Testimony

_____ Do my listeners believe this person is prestigious?

_____ Does this testimony add grace and dignity to my speech?

_____ Does associating with this person enhance my credibility as a speaker?

_____ Does associating with this person enhance the credibility of my speech?

FIGURE 8.1
Checklist for Evaluating Testimony

fit your purposes—this unethical practice is called **quoting out of context**. Political campaign advertising is often rife with this abuse. For example, during a political campaign in Illinois, one state representative sent out a fund-raising letter that claimed he'd been singled out for "special recognition" by *Chicago* magazine—and indeed he had. He had been cited as "one of the state's ten worst legislators."[7]

Watch at **MyCommunicationLab Video:** "In Defense of Lawyers"

SPEAKER'S notes   Using Testimony

Keep these guidelines in mind as you plan the use of testimony in your speeches.

1. Use *expert testimony* to validate information.

2. Use *lay testimony* to build identification and add authenticity.

3. Use *prestige testimony* to enhance the stature of your message.

4. Select sources your audience will respect.

5. Quote or paraphrase materials accurately.

6. Point out the qualifications of experts as you cite them.

▶ **quoting out of context**   An unethical use of a quotation that changes or distorts its original meaning.

Examples

Examples bring a speech to life. Just as pictures serve as graphic illustrations for a printed text, **examples** serve as verbal illustrations in a speech. Listeners reveal their importance when they ask, "Can you give me an example?"

Examples involving people help listeners relate to your message by showing the human side of situations. It's one thing to talk in general terms about the growing problem of students who have to borrow huge sums to finish college. It's quite another when you can say, "It's tough to start out in life $60,000 in the hole. That's what happened to Clarissa Mayhew, who graduated from here last May."

When examples are drawn from your personal experience, they help establish your credibility to speak on the topic. When listeners have had similar experiences, a bond is created between you and them. You share understanding, which can lead in turn to identification.

Because of the power of examples in oral communication, speakers often use them to open speeches. Austin Wright began his persuasive speech on government abuse of individual rights with the following example:

> On September 26, 2002, Canadian citizen Maher Arar boarded a flight home from a family vacation in Tunisia. During a layover in New York City, American authorities detained Arar, interrogating him for the next twelve days. After repeatedly denying any connection to Al Qaeda, Arar was shackled and loaded onto a private, unmarked jet headed for Syria, where he was tortured for the next ten months.

Because they are more concrete and colorful than abstract words, examples can more easily arouse emotions. They can touch people with the humanity of situations, even though listeners may come from different cultural backgrounds. When Dolapo Olushora wanted to reach out to her American listeners concerning the plight of AIDS orphans in her native sub-Saharan Africa, she talked about one representative child, whom she had worked with as a volunteer. To magnify the poignancy of the example, she showed photos, which touched the heartstrings of listeners. Several responded by volunteering to help her raise money.

Finally, examples provide emphasis. When you make a statement and follow it with an example, you are pointing out that what you have just said is *important*. Examples amplify your ideas. They say to the audience, "This deserves your attention." Examples are especially helpful when you introduce new, complex, or abstract material. Not only can they make such information clearer, but also they allow time for the audience to process what you have said before you move on to your next point.

Types of Examples

The most commonly recognized types of examples for use in public speaking are brief, extended, factual, and hypothetical examples. A **brief example** mentions a specific instance to demonstrate a more general statement. Brief examples are concise and to the point. Sometimes a series of brief examples can help to drive home an idea. In a speech to the National Prayer Breakfast, rock star and social activist Bono used a series of brief examples while exhorting American leaders to set aside 1 percent of the federal budget for African relief programs:

> One percent is not merely a number on a balance sheet. One percent is the girl in Africa who gets to go to school, thanks to you. One percent is the AIDS

▶ **examples** Incidents that illustrate a speaker's points.

▶ **brief example** A concise reference to an example to illustrate or develop a point.

patient who gets her medicine, thanks to you. One percent is the African entrepreneur who can start a small family business, thanks to you. One percent is not redecorating presidential palaces or money flowing down a rat hole. This one percent is digging waterholes to provide clean water.[8]

An **extended example** provides more detail, which allows the speaker to more fully develop the example. Chris Christie, governor of New Jersey, used this technique when he described how one child responded to Hurricane Sandy in his 2013 State of the State Address:

Chris Christie, governor of New Jersey.

I met nine-year-old Ginjer. Having a 9-year-old girl myself, her height and manner of speaking was immediately familiar and evocative. Having confronted so many crying adults at that point I felt ready to deal with anything. Then Ginjer looked at me, began to cry and told me she was scared. She told me she had lost everything; she had lost her home and her belongings. She asked me to help her.

As my eyes filled with tears, I took a deep breath and thought about what I would say to my Bridget if she said the same thing to me. If she had the same look on her face. If she had the same tears in her eyes. I asked her where her mom was and she pointed right behind her. I asked her if her dad was okay. She told me he was. So I told Ginjer, you haven't lost your home; you've just lost a house. A house we can replace, your home is with your mom and dad. I hugged her and told her not to cry—that the adults are in charge now and there was nothing to be afraid of anymore. Ginjer is here today—we've kept in touch—and I want to thank her for giving voice to New Jersey's children during Sandy and helping to create a memory of humanity in a sea of despair.[9]

A **factual example** is based on an actual event or the experiences of a real person. Factual examples provide strong support for your ideas because they actually did happen: They authenticate the point you are trying to make. Joseph Jimenez, CEO of Novartis, used the following factual example to support a more positive view of his pharmaceutical company:

We believe . . . it is our obligation to offer low-cost generics to lower health-care costs around the world.

Here's just one example. We introduced generic enoxaparin in this country last year. This is a medicine that helps prevent blood clots. It matters because clots can break free, and cause a deadly blockage in the lung. When we introduced a generic version, it saved the U.S. government $700 million. That's a big deal.[10]

A **hypothetical example** is not offered as "real" so much as representative of actual people, situations, or events. This kind of example can be useful when factual examples are not available or when their use would not be appropriate. While generally not as authoritative as their factual counterparts, hypothetical examples can still be very effective. They can be the fiction that reveals reality. Consider the following hypothetical example, which illustrates the growing problem of childhood obesity:

▶ **extended example** A more detailed example that speakers use to illustrate or develop a point.

▶ **factual example** An example based on something that actually happened or really exists.

▶ **hypothetical example** An example offered not as real but as representative of actual people, situations, or events.

Let me introduce you to Madison Cartwright. Madison is twelve years old. She's four feet eleven inches tall. She weighs 155 pounds. Her body mass index is over 29. This means that Madison is one of the more than nine million children and teenagers in this country who can be classified as obese.

How does this affect her? Not only is she a prime candidate for health problems such as childhood diabetes, but she also has other problems. She loves softball, but has difficulty playing because she gets short of breath. So she sits in the bleachers and watches her classmates. Madison is very smart, but she hates school. She is often the butt of "fat" jokes and teasing by her classmates. Instead of playing outside or socializing with friends after school, Madison goes home and watches TV by herself. Her self-esteem is very low.

Is Madison a real person? Well, yes and no. You may not find someone with her name at the middle school you attended, but you will find many Madisons in the seventh grade there. Childhood obesity in the United States has reached epidemic proportions.

Be careful that your hypothetical examples are representative of the issue or situation you are addressing. Don't distort the truth just to make your point. Always alert your listeners to the hypothetical nature of your example. You can do this by beginning your example with an introductory phrase such as "Imagine yourself . . ." or "Picture the following. . . ." Or, as in the preceding example, you can let listeners know near the end.

Fashioning Powerful Examples

The first thing you must do in fashioning powerful examples is to accept the need for them. Rare is the speech that cannot be improved by examples. Then you must decide which kind of example will best serve the needs of your speech—brief example, extended example, factual example, or hypothetical example.

Once you choose the kind of examples you will use, you can begin their actual construction. Examples should be colorful and lively, so select details that will make them come to life. Keep them concise and to the point, even when you are using extended examples. When Joseph Jimenez wished to emphasize that "caring and curing" is the theme of his pharmaceutical company, he chose the following example:

> . . . We're joining the WHO [World Health Organization], the Gates Foundation and others to work to end leprosy, a disease that goes all the way back to the Bible.
>
> It's a terrible disease with an intense social stigma. In ancient times, people with it were forced to wear cowbells, so everyone else could hear them coming and get away.
>
> . . . But we make a therapy to treat leprosy and cure it. And with it, people can live a normal life. That's why we're committed over the next 10 years to providing the therapy free to everyone who needs it.[11]

When you keep examples concise but striking in this way, listeners are stimulated to provide details on their own, and their imaginations fill out the example.

Emphasize concrete details. Name the people, times, places, and groups in your examples. Listeners will relate more to Luis Francesco with the United States Postal Service than they will to some unnamed delivery person.

Pick your spots. Examples can work well to open and close speeches, to clarify your main ideas, and to ground your speech in reality. But don't make your speech a running series of examples when what you really need is a combination of facts, statistics, and testimony affirming that your examples are valid and representative of situations.

Finally, use transitions to move smoothly from statement to example and from example to statement. Phrases such as "For instance . . ." and "As you can see . . ." work nicely.

SPEAKER'S
notes   Using Examples

Let the following suggestions guide your use of examples in speeches.

1. Use examples to emphasize major points.
2. Use examples to attract and hold attention.
3. Use examples to clarify abstract ideas.

4. Name the people and places in your examples.
5. Use factual examples whenever possible.
6. Keep examples concise and to the point.

Testing Your Examples

Test the examples you are constructing to determine whether they fit your point, are representative, and will be believable (see Figure 8.2). If an example does not fit your specific purpose or help clarify the point you wish to make, it will more likely distract and confuse listeners. Avoid examples that are actually exceptions to the rule. If your examples seem far-fetched, listeners will grow suspicious of both you and your speech. You may have to use other supporting materials to prove the legitimacy of your examples.

Keep in mind that what works well with one audience may not click with another. Ask yourself if the example will fit well with the experiences, motivations, and interests of your listeners. Examples should meet the tests of good taste and propriety. You should risk offending listeners only when they must be shocked into attention before they can be informed or persuaded.

Last, but certainly not least, be sure any example you use is interesting. Dull examples never help a speech.

_____ Is this example relevant to my topic and purpose?

_____ Does this example fairly represent the reality of a situation?

_____ Will this example make my ideas more understandable?

_____ Will this example make my point more memorable?

_____ Will my listeners find this example believable?

_____ Is this example appropriate for this audience?

_____ Is this example in good taste?

_____ Is this example interesting?

FIGURE 8.2
Checklist for Testing Examples

Narratives

Watch at
MyCommunicationLab
Video: "Martha Margaret
Clark Cherry Gaines"

We humans are storytellers.[12] Since the dawn of time—probably before we started putting together abstract arguments and chains of thought—we've used stories to entertain each other, celebrate heroic deeds, teach and reaffirm values, and interpret the often chaotic ebb and flow of human experience. In the words of noted author and storyteller Norman Mailer:

> We tell stories in order to make sense of life. Narrative is reassuring. There are days when life is so absurd, it's crippling—nothing makes sense, but stories bring order to the absurdity.[13]

A **narrative** is a story that conveys an idea or establishes a mood. Like examples, narratives provide concrete illustrations of abstract ideas and issues, engage listeners in the speech, and help to cross the barriers that often separate people. But more than examples, they describe a sequence of actions that unfolds over time. We use narratives to remember the past, illustrate our ideals, and transmit our cultural traditions from one generation to another. Americans, for instance, have long been fond of "rags to riches" stories celebrating our commitment to hard work and individual responsibility—not to mention riches! Stories such as these help to define who we are and what we're about.

Maya Angelou often uses narrative to illustrate ideas in her speeches.

You can draw narratives from many sources. You might tell stories you have made up or that re-create "real-life" experiences. The incredible story of how Dr. Seuss wrote *The Cat in the Hat* is central to Jessica Bradshaw's "Pulling a Cat out of a Hat," the speech that concludes Chapter 6. You also might adapt well-known stories from history, folklore, literature, and even popular television shows. As discussed in Chapter 3, narratives documenting personal experiences are common in self-introductions, but they also can be useful in all forms of public speaking to establish identification and credibility. In any case, your narratives should be fresh and directly relevant to your topic and purpose for speaking.

Types of Narratives

The forms of narrative often found in speeches are embedded, vicarious experience, and master narratives. **Embedded narratives**—which occur at specific points within the overall structure of a speech—are the most commonly used form. Such narratives are often included as part of the introduction or conclusion of a speech. You should use pauses and transitions to signal listeners that you are beginning or ending the story. Your narrative might be solemn and serious or humorous and lighthearted, but it should make a point that supports your speech.

Student speaker Brandon Marshall concluded his inspirational speech by telling a story:

> You would be amazed at how many people I hear complain about the "obstacles" in their lives. So often, whenever we face obstacles, we just put our heads down and

---

▶ **narratives** Stories that illustrate the ideas or theme of a speech.

▶ **embedded narratives** Stories inserted within speeches that illustrate the speaker's points.

quit. The Native Americans used to say that when you prayed for strength, the gods would often send you some sort of tribulation, so that you could overcome it.

I was driving with my friend the other day down Poplar Avenue when I saw a homeless man, fighting his way up the sidewalk in his second hand wheelchair. I had seen him before, digging through trash at Overton Park, pulling out half eaten bananas and old sandwiches. This particular day, he was stuck at a small section of concrete that had been worn away to rocky gravel. The whole way down the street until I couldn't see him anymore, I watched him push and push, only to move maybe a foot. Now that's an obstacle.

So the next time you're in the midst of a struggle, don't focus on yourself. Look at the situation as an opportunity to become a stronger individual, and ask yourself what you can do for someone else.

This concluding embedded narrative ensured that those in the audience had something to take with them.

Speakers who want to involve the audience often use a **vicarious experience narrative**. Such a narrative invites listeners into the action so that they imagine themselves participating in the story. A vicarious narrative will often begin with a statement such as "Come along with me . . ." or "Picture yourself. . . ."

Finally, sometimes a speech will develop a single **master narrative**. In this case, the use of narrative does not support your speech—it *is* your speech. Your entire speech is told in the form of a story. Master narratives are common with testimonials and introductory speaking, as we saw illustrated in Sabrina Karic's "A Little Chocolate." This speech, which narrates Sabrina's experiences as a child in war-torn Bosnia, may be found at the end of Chapter 3. Review that chapter for its discussion of how to design your presentation around a master narrative.

Building Narratives

Even though storytelling may come naturally to us as humans, there is an art to presenting stories orally. They should be carefully planned and carefully rehearsed. We recently had a student who "teased" his listeners with vague promises of stories that never materialized in his speech. He would say, "This one was really funny," and then ramble on without telling us the story. At best, he would simply paraphrase the story or present a punch line without any preparation. Listening to him was a frustrating experience.

In Chapter 3, we described how to develop the prologue, plot, and epilogue in longer narratives. But these elements occur as well in miniature in embedded narratives. Note how vividly—even though briefly—Sandra Baltz described the setting in her prologue for the story opening her speech on scarce medical resources:

On a cold and stormy night in 1841, the ship William Brown struck an iceberg in the North Atlantic.

Her plot continued Sandra's vivid account of what happened:

Passengers and crew members frantically scrambled into the lifeboats. To make a bad disaster even worse, one of the lifeboats began to sink because it was overcrowded. Fourteen men were thrown overboard that horrible night. After the survivors were rescued, a crew member was tried for the murders of those thrown overboard.

▶ **vicarious experience narrative**
Speech strategy in which the speaker invites listeners to imagine themselves enacting a story.

▶ **master narrative** A speech that is structured around a story that reveals some important truth.

In her epilogue, Sandra reflected on the meaning of this action, relating it to her speech:

> Fortunately, situations like this have been rare in history, but today we face a similar problem in the medical establishment: deciding who will live as we allocate scarce medical resources for transplants. Someday, your fate—or the fate of someone you love—could depend on how we resolve this dilemma.

The art of the story boils down to how you use language and how you present the story. The characters and action must come alive through your words. Let listeners see things by using colorful language that is pictorial. Use voice and dialect changes to signal that a "character" is speaking.

As you tell a story, let yourself get caught up in it. The more "into it" you seem, the more likely your audience will experience your narrative with you. Pause to increase the impact of important moments in your story, especially when something you say evokes astonishment or laughter.

Because storytelling is a more intimate form of communication, you should move out from behind the lectern and closer to your listeners. Stories invite informality. If your story evokes laughter, wait for it to die down before going on. Practice telling your story so that you get the wording and timing just right. Polish and memorize the punch lines of humorous tales: The story exists for them. They are the gem at the center, the capstone at the top.

Use dialogue rather than paraphrasing what someone says. Paraphrasing can save time, but it robs a story of power. Let your characters speak for themselves!

Finally, a well-told narrative can add much to a speech, but too many stories can turn a speech into a rambling string of tales without a clear focus. Save narratives for special moments. For more on the art of storytelling, see the online tutorial "Effective Storytelling," developed by Barry McWilliams

Testing Your Story

Narratives should not exist for themselves, but rather they should serve a real purpose in your speech. Some speakers have the mistaken notion that they should start with a joke, whether relevant or not. It's a rather cheap trick, and most listeners see through it. As a result, they usually don't take such speakers or their messages very seriously. Other speakers betray their own ethos by using offensive language in stories that foster and reinforce negative stereotypes about their subjects and themselves. Don't make their mistake.

FINDING YOUR

voice Your Favorite Story

Think back to your childhood, and remember your favorite story. Prepare a brief presentation (less than three minutes) of this story. Practice presenting it as if you were telling it to a group of first graders. Working in small groups, share your story with other group members. Listen to their stories. What storytelling techniques seemed most effective? What made some of the stories less effective?

SPEAKER'S notes   Using Narratives

Keep the following suggestions in mind as you plan narratives to use in a speech.

1. Use stories to involve the audience with your topic.
2. Practice telling your stories so that they flow smoothly.
3. Make the characters in your stories come to life.

4. Use voice and dialect changes for different characters.
5. Use dialogue rather than paraphrase.
6. Use colorful, vivid language.

According to Walter Fisher, stories should be evaluated in terms of narrative probability and fidelity. By **narrative probability**, he means how well a story hangs together.[14] A good story offers a vividly described scene, character development and interaction, and a plot that moves toward some sort of climax or—in the case of humorous narratives—a punch line. All of these elements—scene, action, characters—must be consistent with each other to satisfy the requirement of narrative probability.

By **narrative fidelity**, Fisher means whether your story rings true for listeners, whether it fits the world they have experienced and whether its characters act in ways that seem believable. When the story passes the test of likelihood and authenticity, it helps listeners make sense of problems and situations to which it is applied. It helps illuminate the past and options for the future. Figure 8.3 provides some guidelines for evaluating narratives used in speeches.

_____ Is the narrative relevant to my topic and purpose?

_____ Does the narrative fairly represent the situation?

_____ Will the story help listeners make sense of things?

_____ Will the narrative draw listeners into the action?

_____ Is the narrative appropriate for this audience?

_____ Will the story provide appropriate role models?

_____ Will the story enhance identification among listeners, topic, and speaker?

_____ Will the narrative make my speech more memorable?

_____ Does the story set an appropriate mood for my message?

_____ Is the narrative fresh and interesting?

_____ Does the story flow well?

_____ Is the narrative believable?

_____ Is the narrative in good taste?

FIGURE 8.3
Evaluating Narratives

▶ **narrative probability** Measures the *skill* of the speaker in blending scene, characters, and action into a compelling story.

▶ **narrative fidelity** Measures the authenticity of the story, the likelihood that it happened or might happen.

Selecting and Combining Supporting Materials

In responsible speaking, the four forms of supporting materials—facts and statistics, testimony, examples, and narratives— rarely stand alone and apart from each other. If you combine them, they lend great strength to your speech. Facts and figures ground your message in reality, while expert testimony provides credibility to your claims. Lay testimony brings your message home to ordinary folks and adds the wisdom of the streets, while prestige testimony aligns you with respected authority figures. Examples reinforce facts and figures by focusing on the experiences of representative individuals and situations. Narratives tell stories that add drama and sometimes humor to your message. Examples and narratives can also engage audience feelings in support of your position.

How you combine these forms of supporting materials leaves room for individual artistry. Sandra Baltz began her speech on scarce medical resources by telling the dramatic story we quoted earlier in this chapter. Having aroused audience interest, she went on to introduce facts and figures that established the real dimensions of the problem she was discussing. She followed this by telling the moving story of an individual whose fate was very much affected by the medical resources problem. She concluded by offering a solution proposed by experts in the medical resources field. This particular combination of supporting materials strengthened her message and gave resonance to her voice.

Different situations will call for different emphases as you combine supporting materials. Your choice of materials should reflect careful consideration of the challenges posed by your particular speech.

- If your topic is *controversial,* rely primarily on facts, statistics, factual examples, or expert testimony.

- If your ideas seem *abstract,* bring them to life with examples and narratives.

- If a point is highly *technical,* define key terms and supplement facts and statistics with expert testimony.

- If you need to *arouse emotions,* use lay testimony and vivid examples or narratives.

- If you need to *defuse emotions,* emphasize facts, statistics, and expert testimony.

- If your ideas are *novel or unfamiliar,* provide key facts and illustrative examples, define and explain basic terms and concepts, or provide analogies based on the experience of your listeners.

Above all, keep your audience at the center of your thinking, and ask yourself these critical questions: Which of these materials will make the biggest impression on my listeners? Which of these materials will listeners be most likely to remember? Which of these materials will listeners find most credible? Which materials will most likely make listeners want to act?

Lastly, the use of supporting materials can sometimes raise ethical questions, as we see in "Your Ethical Voice: The Ethical Use of Supporting Materials." Keep the guidelines discussed here in the forefront of your thinking.

YOUR ethical VOICE The Ethical Use of Supporting Materials

To be certain that you are using supporting materials in ethical ways, follow these guidelines.

1. Provide the date, source, and context of information cited in your speech.

2. Don't present a claim or opinion as though it were a fact.

3. Remember that statistics are open to differing interpretations.

4. Protect your listeners from biased information.

5. Don't quote out of context to misrepresent a person's position.

6. Be sure examples are representative of the reality you are addressing.

7. Don't present hypothetical examples as though they were factual.

FINAL reflections Developing a Well-Supported Voice

At the beginning of this chapter, we likened the structure of a well-supported speech to that of the Golden Gate Bridge. That beloved bridge joins Marin County with San Francisco. It is as impressive now as it was when it opened more than seventy-five years ago. But the great speeches of our time may attempt even more spectacular feats, as they strive to connect distant cultures and audiences that may be deeply suspicious of each other. At the rare moments when they are successful, these speeches stand at the pinnacle of human achievement.

Your challenge in constructing a message to deliver to your listeners may seem far less daunting, but nevertheless it is considerable. Like those who build the great bridges that bear many times their own weight, you must make, choose and use supporting materials in the right way. You must combine facts and statistics, testimony, examples, and narratives to build a message that is considerably stronger than the sum of its parts. And if you've ever watched somebody present an obviously suspect piece of information to support an important or disputed claim, you also know that, like a bridge, a speech is only as strong as its weakest support.

This quality of strength is certainly one that you want associated with the voice you are discovering. Think of other desirable qualities you might like to add as well to that emerging voice. Would "credible," "colorful," "appealing," "moving," and "interesting" be among them? You can create all of these impressions by selecting and using effective supporting materials. Develop these materials, and you can add these qualities to your voice.

Study and
Review at
MyCommunicationLab

After Reading This Chapter, You Should Be Able To Answer These Questions

1 How do facts and statistics strengthen your speech?

2 How do expert, lay, and prestige testimony differ?

3 What special strength can examples bring to your speech?

4 How can narratives make a speech more effective?

5 How can you determine which kind of supporting material to use in your speech?

6 Why does a combination of supporting materials usually work best?

7 What ethical standards should guide your selection and use of supporting materials?

For Discussion and Further Exploration

1 Evaluate the use of testimony in two of the student speeches in Appendix B. Is there sufficient use of testimony? What types are used? Are they appropriate to the purpose? Do the speakers introduce source qualifications?

2 Which types of supporting materials in what combinations might help you use to build a case for or against the following claims?
   a. We should increase spending on preschool education.
   b. We should cut taxes paid by small business owners.
   c. Security measures on campus are inadequate.
   d. We should emphasize restoring the environment over creating jobs and providing health care.
   e. The use of drones in modern warfare is permissible.
   Explain and defend your choices.

3 Report to your class on a television ad that tells a story in order to sell a product. What narrative qualities make these ads effective or ineffective?

4 Google *Vital Speeches of the Day,* and access the free sample issue. Look for a speech that contains statistical information. Were the statistics convincing? Were sources clearly identified? Did the speaker make the information come alive? What advice would you give the speaker on how to make more effective use of statistics? Report your findings in class.

5 Develop an example or narrative to illustrate one of the following abstract concepts:
   love
   compassion
   dedication
   courage
   justice
   If you used it in a speech, how might this narrative or example help you?

6 Share your reactions to a current television ad based on prestige or celebrity testimony. How relevant is the celebrity to the product being sold? How effective do you think the ad is? What drawbacks might there be to this type of advertising?

Objectives

This chapter will help you

1 Develop speeches that are simple, well ordered, and balanced

2 Understand the design options as you arrange the main points of your speech

3 Learn how to develop and support your main points

4 Plan transitions to make your speeches flow smoothly

5 Create an effective working outline

6 Prepare introductions and conclusions

7 Complete a formal outline

9 Structuring and Outlining Your Speech

Listen to **Chapter 9** at **MyCommunicationLab**

> *Every discourse ought to be a living creature; having a body of its own and head and feet; there should be a middle, beginning, and end, adapted to one another and to the whole.*
>
> —PLATO

Overheard at the Student Union:

" I've got to take Intro Biology this semester. I can take Forsyth or Bennett. Have you had either of them?"

"Yes, both. Forsyth is a really funny guy. Keeps you laughing."

"Sounds like my kind of guy."

"Well, there is one small problem: Dude is totally disorganized. Jumps all around in his lectures. Hard to take notes."

"Hmmm. How about Bennett?"

"Not so funny. But she knows her stuff. She's easy to follow and makes it easy to learn."

"Okay. I think I know my choice."

Any real doubt who this student selected? Everyone likes to be entertained, but most people prefer well-organized speakers, especially when the message is important. Indeed, studies suggest that students learn more from teachers who are well focused and that they are annoyed by instructors who ramble and jump from one idea to another.[1]

Well-organized speeches are easier to follow, understand, and remember.[2] Being well organized will enhance audience perceptions of your competence and will help you be more confident.[3] Clearly, developing a well-organized speech is an important phase in the process of finding your voice.

Recent research confirms that students learn how to structure messages more effectively in public speaking classes, and that these skills transfer to improved writing as well.[4] Developing organizational skills is also important to finding your voice as an ethical speaker. As we noted in Chapter 1, ethical speaking encourages responsible listening. You have invested much time in finding a good topic, refining and researching it, and gathering vital information about it. But until you can focus all these discoveries in a well-structured speech that listeners will find valuable and easy to grasp, you will not have found your voice. Worse still, the cause that calls you to speak will not have been served well.

In this chapter, we discuss some basic principles of a well-structured speech. We then take you step by step through the process of constructing such a speech from generating, arranging, and outlining main ideas to adding transitions, writing effective introductions and conclusions, and developing formal outlines.

Principles of a Well-Structured Speech

The principles of a well-structured speech reflect the importance of simplicity, order, and balance.

Simplicity

A simple speech is easier for listeners to grasp and remember and for speakers to present effectively. To achieve **simplicity** in your speeches, you should limit the

▶ **simplicity** Suggests that a speech has a limited number of main points and that they are short and direct.

number of main ideas, repeat them for emphasis, and keep your wording direct and to the point.

Limiting the Number of Main Points.

As a general rule, the fewer the main points in a speech, the better. It takes time to develop each point with supporting ideas and materials, and audience members can only absorb so much. Short classroom speeches should usually develop no more than three main points.

These considerations encourage a disciplined process of thinking that prioritizes and subordinates main and supporting ideas and materials. This process further emphasizes the importance of focus and depth over breadth of coverage. For instance, if you were researching and developing a speech in favor of welfare reform, you might initially come up with several ideas and impressions:

- We have too many welfare programs.

- Most of our programs are underfunded.

- Some programs spend money wastefully.

- Some programs duplicate coverage.

- People who genuinely need assistance are sometimes denied.

- Recipients have little input as to what is needed.

- Traditional welfare programs can create a culture of dependence that stifles initiative and fosters a lack of self-respect.

Each of these points may be important. However, presented in such random fashion, they may confuse and overwhelm your listeners. As you engage in the process of prioritizing and subordinating ideas and information, you might begin to hammer out the following simpler and more coherent train of thought:

Thesis statement:	Our approach to welfare doesn't work.
First main point:	I. It doesn't work because it's inadequate.
Subpoints:	A. Existing programs are not sufficiently funded.
	B. People who genuinely need help are left out.
Second main point:	II. It doesn't work because it's inefficient.
Subpoints:	A. There are too many duplicate programs.
	B. There is too much waste of money.
Third main point:	III. It doesn't work because it's insensitive.
Subpoints:	A. It creates dependence that stifles initiative.
	B. It robs recipients of self-respect.
	C. Recipients have little input.

This simpler structure makes the message easier to follow. The thesis statement offers an overview of the message. Each main point elaborates and develops the thesis statement. The subpoints organize and focus the secondary ideas so that they support the main points. Important but overlapping ideas might be combined, while interesting but irrelevant ideas and materials might be discarded. In the process of simplifying your ideas and information, you have already begun developing a structurally coherent answer to the question of why approaches to welfare are not working.

A well-organized speech, including well-planned and designed presentation aids, is easy to follow.

Repeating Key Points for Emphasis.   Repeating key ideas and information helps simplify the structure of a speech and reinforce its central ideas and information. Consider our preceding revised example. The central message, "Our approach to welfare doesn't work," is reinforced by repeating the point "It doesn't work because … " while introducing each of the system's three main shortcomings. This method of repeating much of the wording of main points while emphasizing their different points of focus is called **parallel construction.**

Repetition is literally built into the standard format of well-organized speeches. Speakers preview their messages in the introduction, repeat these messages as they develop them in the body, and repeat these messages again as they review them in the conclusions of their speeches.

Phrasing Main Points.   Learning to express your ideas and information as simple, direct statements is crucial to developing your communication skills. Again, consider our revised example. Not only has the wording been simplified, but also the use of the same word pattern to introduce each main point creates a message that is easy to understand. The repeated phrase, "It doesn't work because," suggests that these are the main points and makes them easy to remember.

Order

Order in a speech requires a consistent pattern of development from beginning to end. A well-ordered speech opens by introducing the message and orienting the audience, continues by developing the main ideas in the body of the speech, and ends by summarizing and reflecting upon the meaning of what has been said. In addition, the main points within the speech body should be developed and organized within a design scheme (categorical, problem-solution, narrative, etc.), as discussed later in this chapter. To build an orderly speech, you should design and construct the body of your speech first because that is where you will present, illustrate, and substantiate your message. Once you have structured the body, you can prepare an introduction and a conclusion that are custom-tailored for your message.

Balance

Balance means that the major parts of your speech—the introduction, the body, and the conclusion—should receive appropriate development. For most speaking occasions, and certainly for classroom speeches, you will be given specific time requirements, which you should keep in mind as you plan your message. It can be very upsetting to finish your first main point only to find out that you have one minute left to finish two other main points and the conclusion. The following suggestions can help you plan a balanced presentation:

1. *The body should be the longest part of your speech.* This is where you develop your main ideas in full. If you spend two minutes introducing your speech and then a minute and a half on the body, your speech will come across as unbalanced and underdeveloped. Again, since this is the most important part of your speech, we suggest you construct it before developing your introduction and conclusion.

▶ **parallel construction** Wording points in a repeated pattern to emphasize their importance and to show how they are both related and contrasted.

▶ **order** A consistent pattern used to develop a speech.

▶ **balance** Suggests that the introduction, body, and conclusion receive appropriate development.

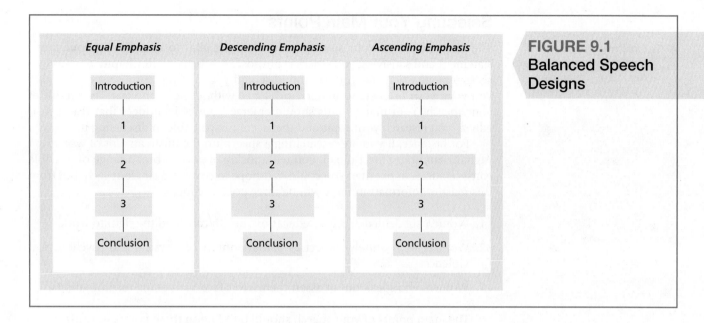

FIGURE 9.1
Balanced Speech Designs

2. *Balance the development of each main point in your speech.* If your main points seem equally important, strive to give each point *equal emphasis.* This strategy would seem appropriate for the message outlined earlier on the three I's of welfare—inadequate, insufficient, insensitive—in which each point seems to merit equal attention. If your points differ in importance, you might start with the most important point, spending the most time on it, and then present the other points with a *descending emphasis,* according to their importance. For example, if you are presenting a problem-solution speech in favor of health care reform before an audience of listeners who do not believe we need health care reform, you should probably spend most of your time establishing the existence of a problem and then just touch upon prospective solutions. However, to the extent your audience already agrees that we need health care reform, you might use an *ascending emphasis* that touches briefly on the problem and focuses primarily on prospective solutions and how audience members might become actively involved in promoting them.

3. *With short presentations, your introduction and conclusion should be brief and approximately equal in length.* Introductions often run slightly longer, but the combined length of both should be less than the body of your speech.

Structuring the Body of Your Speech

The **body** of your speech should develop your main ideas and materials that support them. The process of structuring the body involves

- selecting, arranging, and developing your main and supporting points and materials.

- developing a working outline.

- adding transitions that connect the various points of your speech.

▶ **body**   The section of a speech that contains your main ideas and the materials that support them.

Selecting Your Main Points

Explore at
MyCommunicationLab
Activity: "Scrambled
Speech: Grant Proposal"

The **main points** of your speech are those most vital to establishing your thesis statement and satisfying your specific purpose. As discussed in Chapter 6, your thesis statement articulates your central idea, and your specific purpose specifies what you want your listeners to understand, agree with, do, or appreciate as a result of your speech. Your main points should emerge from general ideas that rise repeatedly as you research your topic and that seem unavoidable in discussing it.

For instance, if you are researching a speech on the mistreatment of women in Afghanistan under the Taliban, you will quickly discover a broad range of possible considerations, more than you could ever hope to cover in a single speech. But from this mass of information there will be three points of focus:

1. Women are denied access to education, health care, and the right to work.

2. Women are routinely subject to barbaric forms of physical and psychological violence.

3. Women who speak out or assert themselves face frightening recriminations.

The main points of your speech should build upon these points of emphasis.

Arranging Your Main Points

Explore at
MyCommunicationLab
Activity: "Organization"

Once you have chosen your main points, you should arrange them using a design that fits your material, your purpose, and your audience. There are many patterns available to you: categorical, comparative, spatial, sequential, chronological, causation, problem-solution, refutative, and narrative. All of these patterns reflect the different ways we think about subjects as well as what we discover in them during research. We will introduce them here and develop them in later chapters in connection with speech types that typically use them. We will provide a more detailed discussion of categorical, comparative, spatial, sequential, chronological, and causation designs in our chapter on informative speaking (Chapter 13). We will develop problem-solution and refutative designs in further detail in our chapter on persuasive speaking (Chapter 14). In our chapters on speeches for special occasions (Chapters 3 and 16), we further consider the narrative design.

All of these patterns reflect the different ways we think about subjects as well as what we discover in them during research.

Watch at
MyCommunicationLab
Video: "Intercultural
Communication in Italy"

Categorical.   The **categorical design,** sometimes called topical design, arranges the main ideas of a speech so that they reflect major points of emphasis uncovered during research. In the speech outlined above, the main points express three categories of abuse discovered in the Afghan treatment of women.

Specific Purpose:	To inform listeners how the Taliban routinely abuse women in Afghanistan
Thesis Statement:	The fate of women under Taliban rule is dark and hopeless.
Main Points:	I. Women are denied access to education, health care, and the right to work.
	II. Women routinely suffer physical and psychological abuse.
	III. Women are punished in frightening ways if they speak out in protest of their treatment.

▶ **main points**   The most important ideas developed in support of the thesis statement.

▶ **categorical design**   Arranges the main ideas of a speech by natural or customary divisions.

Comparative. A **comparative design** explores the similarities and differences among things. For example, a speaker might develop a speech comparing three major features between the cities of New York and London, emphasizing them perhaps as centers of arts and entertainment, business, and politics. This kind of comparison would be *literal*, based on comparing the same kinds of things. Another, often more creative kind of comparative design is *figurative*, relating two subjects that belong to different worlds of experience. In her informative speech on nutrition, Thressia Taylor made that often boring subject come alive by comparing it to taking care of a car.

Specific Purpose:	To inform listeners of the importance of good nutrition
Thesis statement:	Feed your body the same way you would care for a classic car.
Main Points:	I. Proteins provide the octane in your gasoline.
	II. Carbohydrates give you energy and fast acceleration.
	III. Good fats keep you well lubricated and running smoothly.

Good comparative designs spark interest and often appreciation for the speaker's creativity. They can also relate the unknown to the known, making subjects easier to understand.

Spatial. A **spatial design** arranges the main points of a subject as they occur in actual space, often taking listeners on an imaginary tour. For example, if you are asked to address a group of incoming freshmen on the resources available to them in the library, you might use a floor plan as a presentation aid as you point out where different departments are located. An effective spatial design provides your listeners with a verbal map. Just be sure to select points of emphasis carefully to help your listeners retain this map, and don't overburden them with excessive detail.

In contrast, if you were to use a categorical design in such a speech, you might ask this question: "Where in the library might you find major resources for your speeches?" You might then focus on current periodicals, book holdings, and government documents as the main points for developing your speech. Either design would offer advantages and disadvantages, and your choice between them would again be determined by your purpose and audience needs.

Sequential. A **sequential design** explains the steps of a process in the order in which they should be taken. Most "how to" speeches use a sequential design scheme. For instance, if you were to give a speech on how to administer CPR or (as in Chapter 3) how to take in order the seven steps to planning a successful speech, you would use a sequential design. Speeches following the sequential design often make use of presentation aids, such as models of human figures to illustrate the process of CPR or charts showing how to brew your own beer.

Chronological. A **chronological design** explains events or historical developments in the order in which they occurred. Chronological designs often survey the pattern of events that led up to a present-day situation. D'Angelo Crawford described such a pattern as he explored the history of the T-shirt.

▶ **comparative design** Explores the similarities and differences among things.

▶ **sequential design** Explains the steps of a process in the order in which they should be taken.

▶ **spatial design** Arranges the main points of a speech as they occur in actual space, creating an oral map.

▶ **chronological design** Explains events or historical developments in the order in which they occurred.

Specific purpose: To inform listeners how the T-shirt has become an important item of clothing

Thesis statement: The T-shirt began a century ago as an undergarment, became outerwear in the mid-twentieth century, and has now become a personal billboard.

Main Points: I. They were first designed for sailors to spare sensitive persons the sight of hairy armpits.

II. In World War II they were used as outerwear in the tropics.

III. They now often carry pictures or personal or political messages.

Chronological presentations are effective when speakers keep their presentation of events simple, in the order in which they occurred, and related to the message of the speech.

Causation.

A **causation design** traces the origins or consequences of a situation or event, proceeding from cause to effect or from effect to cause. Causation designs are often used to explain current developments and forecast future events. Alexandra McArthur used a causation design to show how tourism can have a negative impact on developing nations.

Specific Purpose: To persuade listeners that tourism can harm developing nations

Thesis Statement: Tourism can cause economic, sociological, and political problems for developing nations.

Main Points: I. Tourism can encourage the unequal distribution of wealth and the loss of capital to foreign investors.

II. Native workers resent exploitation and abuse.

III. Tourism reinforces class inequities and dislike of foreign nations.

The causation design can provide the framework for both informative and persuasive speeches.

Problem-Solution.

The **problem-solution design** focuses attention on a problem and then provides an answer to it. Because life constantly confronts us with difficulties, the problem-solution pattern is one of the most frequently used speech designs, especially in persuasive speeches. To make it work, you must first convince listeners that they do have a problem that they must deal with. Then you must show them that you have a solution that makes sense, that is practical and affordable, and that will very much improve their lives.

The **motivated sequence** offers an elaborate version of the problem-solution pattern. This popular design, first developed years ago by Professor Alan Monroe, follows five steps: (1) drawing *attention* to a situation, (2) demonstrating a *need* to change it, (3) explaining how a plan might *satisfy* this problem, (4) *visualizing* the results of following or not following the speaker's advice, and (5) issuing a call for *action*.[5] Several generations of student speakers have used the motivated sequence variation to great advantage.

▶ **causation design** Considers the origins or consequences of a situation or event.

▶ **problem-solution design** Focuses attention on a problem and offers a solution for it.

▶ **motivated sequence** Expanded version of the problem-solution design that emphasizes attention, need, satisfaction, visualization, and action steps.

Refutative.   The **refutative design** proceeds by defending a disputed thesis and confronting opposing views with reasoning and evidence. Found in debates over public policy, this pattern of thought proceeds by identifying a key opposing argument and then showing why it is mistaken or logically flawed. Nick McDonald demonstrated this pattern as he defended birth control education programs in public education.

Specific Purpose:	To persuade listeners that attacks on birth control education in the public school system are not justified
Thesis Statement:	The key argument against such education, that it merely increases sexual activity, is not borne out by the facts.
Main Points:	I. The latest published research does not support this contention.
	II. Instead, the evidence shows a striking reduction in teen pregnancies in schools that offered such education.
	III. Therefore, birth control education programs offer hope for one of our largest social problems—that of children having children.

Those who follow this design should be careful not to let their refutations degenerate into personal attacks. Respect your opponents by refuting them tactfully.

Narrative.   The speech that follows a **narrative design** tells a story. In contrast with designs that follow a linear, logical pattern, a narrative design follows a dramatic pattern that proceeds from *prologue* to *plot* to *epilogue,* as we discussed in Chapter 3. The prologue introduces the story by setting the scene for action. It foreshadows the meaning of the speech and introduces the main characters. The plot is the body of the narrative, in which the story unfolds through a scene or series of scenes that build to a climax. The epilogue reflects on the meaning of the story by drawing a lesson from it that audience members can apply. Narratives help illustrate and add human interest to a speech.

The preceding designs are often used in combination. For example, our earlier discussion of three forms of oppression suffered by Afghan women suggests a categorical design. But such a speech might also incorporate a cause-effect pattern to explain how such oppression originated or combine with a problem-solution design to encourage support for changes in policy. Again, we discuss these designs in more detail as they become particularly relevant to informative, persuasive, and ceremonial speaking, as indicated in Figure 9.2.

Developing Your Main Points

Once you have selected and arranged your main points, you need to develop the subpoints and sub-subpoints that will support them. Main points are general statements, while **subpoints** supply more specific materials that flesh them out, make them credible, and bring them to life. In complex units of thought, **sub-subpoints** perform the same kind of service for subpoints. In effect, subpoints and sub-subpoints answer basic questions any critical listener might ask, such as the following: How do I know this is true? What does it mean? Why should I care?

To illustrate these thoughts, imagine that you are developing one of the earlier main points concerning the mistreatment of Afghan women. To support the

---

▶ **refutative design**   A persuasive design in which the speaker challenges other views.

▶ **subpoints**   The major divisions of a speech's main points.

▶ **narrative design**   Speech structure that develops a story from beginning to end through a prologue, plot, and epilogue.

▶ **sub-subpoints**   Strengthen subpoints by supplying relevant supporting materials.

FIGURE 9.2
Design Options

Categorical	Arranges points by their natural or customary divisions (Chapter 13).
Comparative	Compares different ideas to reveal their similarities and differences (Chapter 13).
Spatial	Arranges points as they occur in physical space, taking listeners on an imaginary tour (Chapter 13).
Sequential	Arranges points in order of their occurrence, as in the steps of a process (Chapter 13).
Chronological	Arranges points in terms of their historical development in time (Chapter 13).
Causation	Presents the causes and/or effects of a problem (Chapter 13).
Problem-Solution	Discusses a problem, then offers a solution (Chapter 14).
Refutative	Persuades listeners by answering opposing arguments (Chapter 14).
Narrative	Follows the form of a story with a prologue, plot, and epilogue (Chapters 3, 16).

general claim that Afghan women under the Taliban are routinely subjected to barbaric forms of physical and psychological violence, you should cite the most widely reported specific forms of violence, such as domestic abuse with impunity, gang and honor rapes, and horrific forms of public punishment. Even more specific facts, examples, and quotations from survivors and perpetrators might well become sub-subpoints. Figure 9.3 provides a format for supporting a point.

In short, to strengthen both main points and subpoints you must use supporting materials. As we discussed in Chapter 8, *facts*, *figures*, and *expert testimony* help to support ideas that are disputed, complicated, or new to your audience. *Examples* and *narratives* engage listeners by showing how your ideas apply to specific situations.

The different forms of supporting information are usually most effective when used in combination. An ideal model of support includes the most relevant facts and statistics, the most authoritative testimony, and at least one story or example that clarifies your ideas and brings them to life. Again, if you were supporting our point about violence against women under the Taliban, you might look for credible statistics and expert testimony to document the extent of the violence and for real-life examples and narratives to put a human face on the women's oppression.

Developing a Working Outline

At this point, you should begin developing a rough or **working outline**—a *tentative* plan illustrating the pattern of your main and supporting points and how they fit together. Outlining is a process that allows you to see the structure and interrelation of your ideas and materials as you develop them. It is a tool for untangling your thoughts and information, getting them down on paper where you can work with them, and shaping them into a coherent pattern.

The two most basic and interrelated principles of outlining are coordination and subordination. The principle of **coordination** suggests that all statements at a given

▶ **working outline**   A tentative plan showing the pattern of a speech's major parts, their relative importance, and the way they fit together.

▶ **coordination**   The requirement that statements equal in importance be placed on the same level in an outline.

Statement: _____
_____

(Transition)

1. Factual information or statistics that support statement:
_____
_____

(Transition)

2. Testimony that affirms statement:
_____
_____

(Transition)

3. Example or narrative that illustrates statement:
_____

(Transition)

Restatement: _____
_____

FIGURE 9.3
Format for Supporting a Point

level of your outline should be of similar importance; thus, the three main points concerning the mistreatment of women in Afghanistan appear to share the same approximate significance. The principle of **subordination** requires that supporting ideas and materials descend in importance from the general to the specific as the outline moves from main points to sub-subpoints. Use indentation to show in your outline that subpoints are subordinate to main points, and indent again to show the subordinate status of sub-subpoints. Note how this process of indentation is indicated in the Figure 9.4, Format for a Working Outline.

An outline of our main points describing the various forms of violence against women under the Taliban might take the following form:

Main point: Afghan women were subject to various forms of violence under the Taliban.

Subpoint A: Women were subject to high rates of domestic abuse.

Sub-subpoint 1: Wives and daughters were generally regarded as the property of their husbands and fathers.

Sub-subpoint 2: Taliban officials routinely ignored attempts to report abuse.

Subpoint B: Women were subject to high rates of sexual assault.

Sub-subpoint 1: Young girls were forced into arranged marriages with older men.

Sub-subpoint 2: Gang and honor rapes were perpetuated by rival factions.

Sub-subpoint 3: Victims who reported assaults were branded social outcasts.

▶ **subordination** The requirement that material in an outline descend in importance from the general to the specific — from main points to subpoints to sub-subpoints and so on.

FIGURE 9.4
Format for a Working Outline

Topic: _____

Specific purpose: _____

INTRODUCTION

Attention material: _____

Thesis statement: _____

Preview: _____

(Transition to body of speech)

BODY

First main point: _____

    Subpoint: _____

        Sub-subpoint: _____

        Sub-subpoint: _____

    Subpoint: _____

(Transition to second main point)

Second main point: _____

    Subpoint: _____

    Subpoint: _____

        Sub-subpoint: _____

        Sub-subpoint: _____

(Transition to third main point)

Third main point: _____

    Subpoint: _____

    Subpoint: _____

(Transition to conclusion)

CONCLUSION

Summary statement: _____

Concluding remarks: _____

Subpoint C: Women who resisted or asserted themselves faced frightening recriminations.

    Sub-subpoint 1: Arbitrary humiliation and flogging by Taliban officials.

    Sub-subpoint 2: Macabre forms of public punishment.

As you zero in on a working outline of the body of your presentation, consider whether you've adequately supported your thesis statement and satisfied your purpose for speaking, whether your main ideas are arranged in a sensible design scheme, and whether the overall structure of your body is balanced and appropriately developed. Be honest with yourself. It's better to be frustrated and revising now than regretful later. Outlining is a corrective as well as creative process, and you may go through several drafts as you polish and develop your speeches.

Adding Transitions

Explore at
MyCommunicationLab
Activity: "Better
Transitions"

Once you have identified, developed, and outlined your main ideas, you should plan transitions. **Transitions** are verbal and nonverbal cues that let your audience know you are finished making one point and are moving on to the next. Effectively

▶ **transitions** Connecting elements that cue listeners that you are finished making one point and are moving on to the next.

planned transitions connect the main points of the body of your speech and tie the body to the introduction and conclusion. They help your audience follow the overall structure and direction of your message.

For example, after you voice your thesis statement, you might say something of this sort: "How do we know this is true? Let's consider the evidence." This transition would move you effectively into the body of your speech.

After developing your first main point, you might say: "So now we see that the latest facts support what I'm saying. What about the experts? How do they feel about this situation?" This transition would help listeners interpret the significance of what you have just established. The two rhetorical questions would then move you on to your next point.

When you complete that demonstration, you might say: "So both the experts and the facts support what I'm saying. But how does that affect people's lives? How might it affect you?" This transition would help listeners remember what you have demonstrated. Again, the rhetorical questions would point you toward your next point, involving stories and examples.

You might then move into your conclusion: "So the facts favor my position. The experts agree. And the impact on your life and the lives of those you care about could be vital. So what should you do about it?" Now you would be ready in this imagined persuasive speech to point listeners towards the action you would have them take.

Some transitions are quite subtle. A brief pause coupled with a change in vocal inflection can effectively cue your audience that you are moving on to the next point or part of your speech. Short, simple phrases such as *for my next point* and *having said that, consider this* can help your audience see the connections between your ideas. Phrases such as *until now* and *just last week* point out time changes. Transitions such as *in addition* show that you are expanding on what you have already said. The use of the word *similarly* indicates that a comparison follows. Phrases such as *on the other hand* cue listeners to a contrast. Cause-and-effect relationships can be suggested with *as a result, consequently*, and similar phrases. Introductory phrases such as *traveling north* can indicate spatial relationships. Phrases or words such as *in short, finally*, and *in conclusion* signal that the speech is coming to an end.

Preview and summary statements can also serve as effective transitions connecting the major parts of a speech—previews leading into the body; summaries leading into the concluding remarks. Especially with longer, complicated presentations, an **internal summary** within the body of a speech can help remind listeners of the points you have already covered before you move on. Internal summaries are especially useful in problem-solution speeches, where they signal that you have finished your discussion of the causes or problem and are now moving on to solutions. They should be brief and to the point so that they highlight only major ideas. Consider the following example from a speech supporting caps on greenhouse gas emissions:

> So now we know that global warming is real and getting worse. We know it exacts a frightening economic and environmental toll. And we know that human pollution and greenhouse gas emissions are a major contributing cause of global warming. The only question is, What are we going to do about it? Experts agree that the following measures could help make a real difference.

News accounts of Afghan mistreatment of women prompted an interesting speech.

Explore at
MyCommunicationLab
Activity: "Connecting to Key Ideas"

▶ **internal summary**   A transition that reminds listeners of major points already presented in a speech before proceeding to new ideas.

FINDING YOUR

voice   Structuring Your Speech

Ask your instructor to help you set up a self-help group of three to five classmates to work on the next speech assignment. Share working outlines with each other, explaining what the strategy is behind your proposed structure and how your outline satisfies the principles of coordination and subordination. Demonstrate that you have adequate supporting material for each main point. Revise your working outline in light of the suggestions you receive.

Whatever techniques you use, plan your transitions carefully. Otherwise, you may ramble or lapse into vocalized pauses such as "uh" and "you know." Figure 9.5 lists some common transitions used in speeches.

FIGURE 9.5
Common Transitions

To Indicate	Use
Time Changes	until, now, since, previously, later, earlier, in the past, in the future, meanwhile, five years ago, just last month, tomorrow, following, before, at present, eventually
Additions	moreover, in addition, furthermore, besides
Comparison	compared with, both are, likewise, in comparison, similarly, of equal importance, another type of, like, alike, just as
Contrast	but, yet, however, on the other hand, conversely, still, otherwise, in contrast, unfortunately, despite, rather than, on the contrary
Cause-Effect	therefore, consequently, thus, accordingly, so, as a result, hence, since, because of, due to, for this reason
Numerical Order	first, second, third, in the first place, to begin with, initially, next, eventually, finally
Spatial Relations	to the north, alongside, to the left, above, moving eastward, in front of, in back of, behind, next to, below, nearby, in the distance
Explanation	to illustrate, for example, for instance, case in point, in other words, to simplify, to clarify
Importance	most importantly, above all, keep this in mind, remember, listen carefully, take note of, indeed
The Speech Is Ending	in short, finally, in conclusion, to summarize

Introducing and Concluding Your Speech

Once you have structured the body of your speech, you should prepare an introduction and a conclusion. Listeners tend to be most affected by what they hear at the beginning and end of a speech. Introductions and conclusions set the tone of the entire message and often contain its richest language and clearest statement of the speaker's main ideas and purpose. In this section, we identify some basic functions and techniques and offer advice for effectively introducing and concluding your speeches.

Introducing Your Speech

The **introduction** to your speech should capture your audience's attention, establish your ethos as a credible speaker, and preview your message to make it easier for your audience to follow.

Capturing Attention.   All too often, speakers open their presentations with something like "Good morning, my speech is on … ," which actually has the effect of turning listeners off. The opening lines of a speech should arouse attention and curiosity, convincing listeners that they have something to gain from the speaker's message.

Among the most commonly used strategies for capturing attention are acknowledging the audience, location, or occasion; invoking shared interests and values; urging audience participation; using appropriate humor; opening with a narrative; opening with a quotation; and startling the audience.

Acknowledging the audience, location, or occasion.   In speeches given outside the classroom, speakers often begin with a few remarks acknowledging the audience, the location, or the purpose or meaning of the occasion. Such references are usually brief and should convey a touch of eloquence. Consider the following words from the introduction of a speech by President John F. Kennedy at a White House dinner honoring Nobel Prize winners:

> I think this is the most extraordinary collection of talent, of human knowledge, that has ever been gathered together at the White House, with the possible exception of when Thomas Jefferson dined alone.[6]

Invoking shared interests and values.   Speakers who seem to differ from listeners in race, religion, political affiliation, and so on will often begin their speeches by appealing to shared interests and values. They create a platform of identification on which they can build the remainder of their speech. An example of this kind of opening occurred when Pope Francis addressed an ecumenical meeting at the Vatican at which churches of various Christian denominations were represented. The Pope used the metaphor of a shared journey and pilgrimage toward the unifying vision of Christian faith. On this platform, he would erect not just a speech but also an ongoing relationship with his listeners:

> I begin my Apostolic Ministry in this year during which my venerable Predecessor, Benedict XVI, with true inspiration, proclaimed the Year of Faith

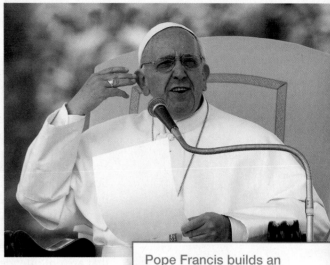

Pope Francis builds an ongoing relationship with listeners by appealing to shared interests and values, including their shared journey in faith.

Watch at **MyCommunicationLab** **Video:** "I Have a Dream"

Watch at **MyCommunicationLab** **Video:** "Investing in Our Future"

▶ **introduction**   That part of your speech that should capture listeners' attention, establish your ethos, and preview your message.

for the Catholic Church. With this initiative, that I wish to continue and which I hope will be an inspiration for everyone's journey of faith, he wished to mark the 50th anniversary of the Second Vatican Council, thus proposing a sort of pilgrimage towards what for every Christian represents the essential: the personal and transforming relationship with Jesus Christ, Son of God, who died and rose for our salvation.[7]

In an increasingly divided world, this kind of unity quest seems a more and more common way for speakers to begin their speeches.

Urging audience participation.   Another common technique is to solicit the participation of audience members. Posing a well-worded series of questions, requesting a "show of hands," or getting your audience to repeat a catchphrase aloud can be very effective. However, not all such strategies require a direct response. The simple use of inclusive pronouns such as *we* and *our* can help to promote identification and involvement. Another technique is the use of **rhetorical questions** that are not intended to provoke a response so much as to engage curiosity. For instance, knowing that most of his classmates were familiar with popular video games, University of Arkansas student Joseph Van Matre opened his speech on their constructive applications with the following rhetorical questions:

> If I say the word *gamer*, what words come to mind? Antisocial? Geek? Dropout? Well, how about fighter pilot? Fitness guru? Or intelligence analyst? I'm not a hard-core gamer, but I do enjoy the company of my Wii from time to time, as well as an occasional round of Madden football with my friends. So when I heard in a radio interview that video games actually have many constructive educational and professional applications, I was intrigued and decided to do some reading. What I learned was highly surprising.

Using appropriate humor.   Appropriate humor, especially at the beginning of a speech, offers some real advantages. Listeners are usually grateful to speakers for the pleasure of laughter. Because laughter is shared, it can also function to promote identification, drawing speakers and listeners together. As Henri Bergson, the French philosopher, once noted, "Laughter appears to stand in need of an echo…. Our laughter is always the laughter of a group."[8] Another advantage is that successful humor at the beginning of a speech can put both listeners and speakers at ease with the speaking situation and can sometimes make it easier for speakers to tackle difficult or obscure topics.

The use of humor in an introduction gains audience attention and draws listeners and speakers together.

Unfortunately, humor can also be one of the most abused techniques for opening a speech. Some speakers have the mistaken notion that, if they will just tell a joke at the beginning of their speeches—any joke—listeners will like them and listen to their message. There's no way of knowing how many listeners have suffered, and how many speakers have bombed, over this misapprehension!

The truth is that humor may not work well for everyone and it can be grossly inappropriate for some topics on some occasions. Keep in mind that audience members tend to be especially sensitive to "politically incorrect" humor. Avoid any kind of humor based on ethnicity, gender, religion, or sexual orientation.

▶ **rhetorical questions** Questions that have a self-evident answer or that provoke curiosity, which the speech then proceeds to satisfy.

Should you decide to open your speech with humor, keep it fresh, relevant, and brief so that it does not upstage your message. Be cautious about relying on humor to cope with communication anxiety. While effective humor can put both speaker and audience at ease, humor that falls flat can have just the opposite effect. Remember that there are other good ways to come across as likable and to capture audience attention. Explore your strengths as a speaker and play to them—this is a vital part of finding your voice and gaining confidence as a speaker.

SPEAKER'S notes   Using Humor

Keep the following in mind when considering the use of humor in your speeches.

1. Don't use humor just to be funny. Keep it relevant to your topic.

2. Use humor to put audience members at ease and make them receptive to your ideas.

3. Avoid religious, ethnic, racist, or sexist humor, all of which speak poorly of you.

4. If you must poke fun at someone, let it be yourself.

5. Don't use humor that might trivialize a serious topic.

6. Avoid planned humor if you are really anxious about speaking.

Opening with a narrative.   Storytelling can be a powerful means of creating identification with your audience. Narratives educate us by helping us remember the past and shared moral commitments. Effective narratives use vivid, graphic language to help us envision abstract topics and issues in concrete human terms. Stories may be imaginary or based on real-life experiences and historical events. Depending on your purpose for speaking, they can be lighthearted and humorous or somber and serious.

In either case, introductory narratives should be brief. Consider the opening narrative to Ashlie McMillan's introductory speech on scuba diving:

> Imagine you're sitting aboard a dive boat. It's rocking back and forth, you can feel the sun beating down on you. You can feel the wind blowing on you. You smell the ocean, the salt water. You can hear the waves crashing up against the boat. You put on your dive pack with your heavy oxygen tank and you walk unsteadily across the deck of the rocking boat. And all of a sudden you plunge into a completely different environment. All around you is vast blueness and infinite space, a world completely different from the one you left above. But all you have to do is turn on your back and look above and you see the sunlight streaming in through the top of the water. And you can see the world that you left behind.

Ashlie's skillful use of action words—such as *rocking, blowing, crashing*—and her vivid appeals to the senses made this scene come alive for her listeners and placed them in the middle of it. See Chapter 3 for more advice on developing narratives in your speeches.

Opening with a quotation.   Starting with a striking quotation or paraphrase from a highly respected text or figure can both arouse interest and dignify your speech.

For instance, references to revered political documents such as the Declaration of Independence or well-known authors such as George Orwell and Maya Angelou can be very effective.

However, opening quotes need not come from such elevated sources. University of Arkansas student Guy Britton introduced his speech concerning illegal immigration with the following ironic quotation: "An anonymous author once said: 'The early North American Indian made a great mistake by not having an immigration bureau.'"

Quotations should be short, to the point, and relevant to your purpose. Several excellent collections of quotations are available online, including quoteland, creative quotations, and Bartleby quotations.

Startling the audience.   Sometimes speakers open with a shocking piece of information intended to startle listeners into close attention. Landon West used this technique to introduce his informative speech:

> I want to introduce you to a person whom I have known for a very long time. He is like many of you. He knew that he could be anything that he wanted to be, given the chance. But there was something about him that his peers would never let him forget: he was fat! (Shows enlarged photo.) The more he began to accept that he was going to live life obese, the more his willingness to contribute diminished. Who is this person? Well, he doesn't really exist anymore. This is me, just a year and a half and 100 pounds ago. I was a statistic for the epidemic of obesity that plagues this country.

With this opening, Landon did more than create intense interest. He also justified himself as an authentic speaker on the obesity problem and enhanced his own ethos. By confiding in his audience, he came across as a trusting person whom they could trust in return.

As effective as this technique can be, you should use it carefully. If your opening is too sensational, you run the risk of it upstaging the rest of your speech. Keep your use of startling information within the boundaries of good taste. Remember, the point is to startle those in your audience into listening, not to traumatize and offend them.

SPEAKER'S
notes Capturing Attention

Try the following strategies to gain attention in the introduction of your speech.

1. Acknowledge the audience, location, or occasion.

2. Invoke shared interests and values.

3. Solicit audience involvement and participation.

4. Open with a narrative that relates to your topic.

5. Engage your listeners with appropriate humor.

6. Begin with a striking quotation.

7. Startle your audience with powerful information or a novel approach.

Establishing Your Credibility.   The second major function of an effective introduction is to establish you as a credible speaker. In Chapter 3, we discuss the importance of listeners forming favorable initial impressions of your ethos: your competence, integrity, goodwill, and dynamism. Outside the classroom, you enter a speaking situation with some initial ethos based on what listeners know or have heard of your reputation and experience. A good introduction before you stand and speak can further "prime" listeners to give you a favorable hearing.

In classroom situations, however, it's up to you to establish in your introduction special reasons that qualify you to speak. Have you had special personal experiences that brought home to you the importance of your topic and created your passion for it? Do you bring special work experience to bear? In your introduction, tell your story about such experiences. Your listeners will conclude that you bring authentic interest and credentials to your topic, and they will listen more respectfully to what you have to say.

When you establish favorable ethos in the introduction of your speech, you convey the impression that you have found your voice. When you seem likable, sincere, competent, and dynamic, your listeners want to identify with you. Your effectiveness as a speaker and your value as a spokesperson for your cause are magnified.

Previewing Your Message.   The final function of an introduction is to preview the body of your speech. The **preview** indicates the main points you will cover and offers your listeners an overview of the speech to come. Common to persuasive and informative presentations, preview statements are especially useful for speeches addressing unfamiliar, complicated, or technical topics. They help listeners follow what you are saying and serve as effective transitions into the body of your speech.

Preview statements need not be of the mundane "In this speech, I'm going to talk about three points" variety. For her speech informing her Davidson classmates of how French people can eat indulgent foods, while still remaining healthy, Gabrielle Wallace offered the following preview:

> To understand the French paradox, we must take a close look at how they combine food choices, their consumption of beverages, and the cultural attitude they have developed toward food.

In speeches developing a narrative design as discussed in Chapter 3, the preview may take the form of a prologue, using a foreshadowing technique: "I never expected that my life would be forever changed by what would happen that day." When speakers foreshadow their stories, they don't tell their listeners exactly what will happen, but they do alert them that something important will happen. Thus, they prepare them to listen intently to the story.

Concluding Your Speech

Just as you should not begin a speech with, "Hello, my speech is about… ," you should not end it with, "Well, that's it!" Your conclusion is your last opportunity to reinforce your central message, make a lasting impression, and when appropriate,

As the mother of a Newtown, Connecticut, shooting victim, Scarlett Lewis calls on her personal experience to enhance her credibility as she speaks at a fundraiser for the organization set up in her son's memory: The Jesse Lewis Choose Love Foundation.

▶ **preview**   The part of the introduction that identifies the main points to be developed in the body of the speech and presents an overview of the speech to follow.

move listeners to action. An effective **conclusion** should summarize your message and provide some concluding remarks.

Watch at
MyCommunicationLab
Video: "Using Recapping/
Summary"

Summarizing Your Message.

The more complicated your topic is, the more important a summary becomes. It reminds your listeners of what they have heard. A brief summary of your main points can also serve as a transition between the body of your speech and your concluding remarks. It signals the audience that you are about to finish.

A summary should not be a simple repetition of main points so much as a chance to reflect on and reinforce the central message of your speech. Consider the conclusion to Gabrielle Wallace's speech:

> For the French, eating is an important part of their lives. It is engrained in their culture and permeates their daily existence. The three factors of eating correctly, drinking wisely, and making a meal an enjoyable experience are what keep the French paradox alive.

Watch at
MyCommunicationLab
Video: "Conclusions"

Providing Concluding Remarks.

Although a summary statement can offer listeners a sense of closure, to seal that effect you need to provide concluding remarks that stay with your listeners. Many of the techniques that create effective introductions can also be used to develop memorable conclusions.

Echoing your introduction. Sometimes called a "bookend," a conclusion that applies the same technique used in the introduction can help to provide a nice sense of closure. For example, you might finish a story that you started in the introduction or refer back to your startling information, rhetorical question, or opening quotation. Referring back to the introduction can be an effective means of letting listeners know that you are bringing your message full circle. For instance, the student speaker who opened with the example of Earl Washington's wrongful conviction for murder concluded her plea for judicial reforms by stating: "There are more Earl Washingtons out there, and they're counting on us!"

Restating the relevance of your message to your audience. At the beginning of a speech, you should involve your listeners by showing them how your message relates directly to their lives. In the conclusion, you should remind them of what they personally have at stake. Consider Doneal McGee's closing plea for a speech opposing "abstinence only" sex education in American high schools:

> These kids are our future, and their problems will become ours in many ways. Babies having unplanned babies out of wedlock are more likely to end up quitting school and on welfare, producing expensive wards of the state and swelling the ranks from which a vast majority of troubled children arise. We have no choice but to support the responsible teaching of sex education in our high schools. They're our kids, and our future may well hang in the balance!

Issuing a call to action. In persuasive speeches, concluding remarks often urge listeners to take the first step to confirm their commitment to action and change. Beth Tidmore used this technique to conclude her speech urging her classmates to volunteer for the Special Olympics:

> Becoming a volunteer is the best way that you can help. If you can't give a weekend, give a couple of hours. If you can't become a leader, just become a cheerleader. Show up. Be a happy smiling face. It's the best way to give to

▶ **conclusion** The ending for your speech that reinforces your main ideas and provides your audience with something to remember.

charity, because you can see the results right in front of you. You can see the shiny medals, the triumphant finishes, the happy faces, the screaming fans. And you know that you're helping someone else and giving of yourself to them…. Can drives need cans. Blood drives need blood. And, the Special Olympics need volunteers. They need warm hearts and open minds. In Special Olympics, everyone is a winner—especially the volunteers!

Asking rhetorical questions.   When used in an introduction, rhetorical questions can help arouse attention and curiosity. When used in a conclusion, they give your listeners something to think about after you have finished. Elinor Fraser opened a speech attacking the use of cell phones while driving in the following way: "How many of you were chatting on your cell phones while driving to class this morning?" After a speech that established the danger of such behavior in graphic terms, her final words were "So, now that you know the risk you are running, are you going to use your cell phones again while you're on the way home? If so, let me know so I can drive in a different direction."

Closing with a story.   Just as stories can effectively introduce a speech, concluding narratives can help your audience experience the meaning of your message. To end her speech on dangerous off-campus housing conditions, Anna Aley told the following story about her neighbor:

> I got out of my apartment with little more than bad memories. My upstairs neighbor was not so lucky. The main problem with his apartment was that the electrical wiring was done improperly; there were too many outlets for too few circuits, so the fuses were always blowing. One day last November, Jack was at home when a fuse blew—as usual. And, as usual, he went to the fuse box to flip the switch back on. When he touched the switch, it delivered such a shock that it literally threw this guy the size of a football player backwards and down a flight of stairs. He lay there at the bottom, unable to move, for a full hour before his roommate came home and called an ambulance. Jack was lucky. His back was not broken. But he did rip many of the muscles in his back. Now he has to go to physical therapy, and he is not expected to fully recover.

Closing with a quotation.   Brief quotations that capture the essence of your message can make for effective conclusions. For example, if you open a speech with a historical quotation, another on the same theme or from the same person might provide an elegant sense of closure. Arkansas student Guy Britton, who opened his speech on illegal immigration with a humorous quotation, achieved a nice book-end effect by closing with another example of the same technique: "Jay Leno once said: 'This problem with illegal immigration is nothing new. In fact, the Indians had a special name for it. They called it white people.'" Guy's sly humor took some of the ethnocentric steam out of a hot-button issue.

Closing with a metaphor.   A memorable metaphor can end your speech effectively. As we discuss in Chapter 11, metaphors combine things that are apparently unlike so that we see unexpected relationships. In the conclusion of a speech, an effective metaphor may reveal hidden truths about the speaker's subject in a memorable way. Another University of Arkansas student, Simone Mullinax, closed

Persuasive speeches designed to recruit volunteers often end with a call to action.

her classroom tribute to her grandmother by concluding a metaphor that had run throughout her speech:

> Years from now I will be teaching my granddaughter to build the perfect key lime pie. And I will be thinking about my grandmother, whose love seeps into all the crust that holds me together. We will work the fillings together and we will know just what to top it off with to make it perfect. And we will bake pies like friends hold conversations, the intricacies hidden beneath the taste and the impressions lasting beyond the words.

Using strategic repetition. Repetition helps implant ideas in the minds of your listeners. The form of repetition discussed earlier called parallel construction—in which certain phrases are repeated in close succession for added emphasis—can make for conclusions that are both elegant and dramatic.

> So now we see why our welfare program just doesn't work. It doesn't work because it's inadequate. It doesn't work because it's inefficient. And it doesn't work because it's insensitive. It's time for a better idea.

Selecting and Using Introductory and Concluding Techniques

Watch at **MyCommunicationLab** Video: "Effective Introductions"

Watch at **MyCommunicationLab** Video: "Effective Conclusions"

Because introductions and conclusions are so crucial in shaping audience impressions and setting the tone for your speech, you should give them considerable thought. Because they are so vital, we suggest that you write them out and commit them to memory.

As you review your research notes, look for materials that might be effective openers and closers. The following guidelines may help:

- Consider relevance to your message and the mood you wish to establish. Some messages and occasions call for a light touch, while others are more serious.

- Consider the members of your audience and what techniques might best tune your message to their needs and interests. We discuss audience analysis and adaptation in Chapter 5.

FINDING YOUR

voice   Critiquing Through Outlining

Select one of the speeches from Appendix B, or a speech broadcast on CSpan, or a speech shared and viewed on YouTube, and prepare a working outline of it. Does the outline clarify the structure of the speech? Does it reveal any structural flaws? Can you see any different ways the speaker might have developed the speech? Write an alternative introduction and conclusion, using a different technique. Compare the new with the original. Which works better, and why?

- Keep it brief! Again, the combined length of your introduction and conclusion should be considerably less than the body of your speech.

- Do what you do best. Some people are natural storytellers, others are funny, still others are better with striking statistics or quotations. Play to your strengths.

SPEAKER'S notes   Checklist for a Working Outline

You can trust your working outline if the following statements accurately describe it:

1. My topic, specific purpose, and thesis statement are clearly stated.

2. My introduction contains attention-getting material, establishes my credibility, and focuses and previews my message.

3. My main points represent the most important ideas on my topic.

4. I have an appropriate number of main points for the time allotted.

5. Each subpoint supports its main point with more specific detail.

6. My conclusion contains a summary statement and concluding remarks that reinforce and reflect on the meaning of my speech.

7. I have planned transitions to use between the introduction and body, between each of my main points, and between the body and conclusion of my speech.

Preparing Your Formal Outline

Once you have developed your working outline and have a good idea of how you will introduce and conclude your speech, you can put together your **formal outline.** The formal outline represents the completed plan of your speech, offering an overview of its major components and how they fit together and listing the research sources that support it.

Most formal outlines include

- a heading with a title, topic, and specific purpose statement;

- an introduction, including attention material, thesis statement, and preview;

- the fully developed body of your speech;

- a conclusion offering a summary statement and concluding remarks; and

- a list of works consulted or cited.

Figure 9.6 offers a formal outline format. See also the sample formal outline at the end of this chapter.

Explore at **MyCommunicationLab Activity:** "Annotated Outline: Helen Keller International"

Heading

The heading offers your title, topic, and specific purpose statement. Again, your specific purpose statement should specify what you want your audience to understand, agree with, do, or appreciate after hearing your speech. Remember: Do not begin

---

▶ **formal outline**   Represents the completed plan of your speech, offering an overview of its major components and how they fit together and listing the research sources that support it.

FIGURE 9.6
Format for a Formal Outline

HEADING

Title: _____
Topic: _____
Specific Purpose: _____

INTRODUCTION

Attention material: _____
_____

Thesis statement: _____
_____

Preview: _____
_____

(**Transition** into body of speech)

BODY

I. First main point: _____
   A. Subpoint or supporting material: _____
   B. Subpoint or supporting material: _____
     1. Sub-subpoint or supporting material: _____
     2. Sub-subpoint or supporting material: _____

(**Transition** into next main point)

II. Second main point: _____
   A. Subpoint or supporting material: _____
     1. Sub-subpoint or supporting material: _____
     2. Sub-subpoint or supporting material: _____
   B. Subpoint or supporting material: _____

(**Transition** into next main point)

III. Third main point: _____
   A. Subpoint or supporting material: _____
   B. Subpoint or supporting material: _____
     1. Sub-subpoint or supporting material: _____
     2. Sub-subpoint or supporting material: _____
       a. Sub-sub-subpoint or supporting material: _____
       b. Sub-sub-subpoint or supporting material: _____

(**Transition** into conclusion)

CONCLUSION

Summary statement: _____
_____

Concluding remarks: _____
_____

WORKS CONSULTED

your actual speech with statements such as "My topic is …" or "My specific purpose is…." These are vital parts of the plan of your speech but should not appear in that form in the speech itself.

Note that in contrast with working outlines, formal outlines often offer a title for the speech. If mentioning a title helps you arouse curiosity and attention, it can also help during your presentation. Consider the way Elizabeth Lyles wove references to her title, "The Abused Women of Afghanistan," into the introduction of her speech on the continued oppression suffered by Afghan women:

> Of course, such brutalities are hardly unknown to *the abused women of Afghanistan*. But this was the Spring of 2009—nearly eight years after the so-called liberation of the Afghan people by a U.S.-led coalition of forces. *The abused women of Afghanistan* need your support now for efforts to defend their basic human rights.

A title should not promise what the speech itself can't deliver. Titles that promise everything from eternal peace of mind to the end of taxation often disappoint listeners. To frame an effective title, wait until you have finished outlining the rest of your speech.

Introduction

Your introduction performs vital work. Here is where you gain the attention you want to sustain throughout the speech. Here also is where your meaning should come into sharp focus with your thesis statement. And here is where you offer listeners a map of the territory ahead as you preview the remainder of your speech. Again, we recommend that you write out your introduction and commit it to memory. This will help you get into and out of your speech gracefully and effectively. There certainly may be moments when you wish to change your introduction slightly to take advantage of a situation (we discussed such moments in Chapter 5). But knowing exactly what you want to say and how you want to say it gets you off to a good start and helps you build confidence.

Body

The body of your outline should consist of main points, subpoints, and sub-subpoints in the order of their presentation. In contrast to working outlines, formal outlines adopt a more precise and abbreviated system for indicating coordination and subordination. Roman numerals (I, II, III) typically are used for main points, capital letters (A, B, C) for subpoints, Arabic numbers (1, 2, 3) for sub-subpoints, and—should you need them—lowercase letters (a, b, c) for sub-sub-subpoints.

The entries in a working outline are often sentence fragments, indicating their status as tentative, emerging ideas that are subject to change and revision. By the time you are ready to prepare your formal outline, these entries should have evolved into more confident and finished form. To indicate this evolution, *each main and supporting point of a formal outline should be worded as a complete, simple sentence containing only one idea*. Qualifying and dependent clauses and supporting information should be subordinated as subpoints and sub-subpoints. For example, the statement "Bad eating habits are harmful because they are unhealthy and can damage your self-image" might be outlined to read:

> I. Bad eating habits are harmful.
>   A. They are unhealthy.
>   B. They can damage your self-image.

Breaking down complex sentences into outlined format helps you to focus what you are going to say. It suggests what you should emphasize and helps clarify the structure and logic of your speech.

We also recommend that you write out your transitions between main points and commit them to memory as well. This will assure that your speech flows well. Make sure that you support every assertion in your speech that is new, complicated,

Explore at **MyCommunicationLab** **Activity:** "Video Games and Violence"

or disputed with research and illustrative examples or stories. Include abbreviated **source citations** within the formal outline for each piece of supporting information you use (you will provide full references at the end of the outline in your list of works consulted or cited).

The sample formal outline offered at the end of this chapter provides a model of these abbreviated source citations. Note that in most cases the author's last name or an abbreviated source or title will suffice, included in parentheses at the end of the point or subpoint to which it applies. List the last name of the author plus the page number when you refer to different pages in the same source. List the author's last name with an abbreviated title in quotation marks if you are citing more than one work by the same author. If the author is a group or organization, list its name in abbreviated form. If the author is not provided, provide an abbreviated title in quotation marks as the source of the information.

Placement of an abbreviated source citation at the end of a main point indicates that this source supports all claims in the subpoints and sub-subpoints below it. If the citation is placed at the end of a subpoint or sub-subpoint, it applies only to that more specific subpoint or sub-subpoint. Again, for illustrations of these points see the sample outline.

Documenting your sources in your outline does not satisfy the need for **oral citations** to support your points as you present your speech. Your listeners are not privy, of course, to your formal outline and list of works cited—they know only what you decide to tell them. Don't overwhelm them with citations, but *do* use such citations to support your most important and possibly controversial statements and claims. "Speaker's Notes: Guidelines for Oral Documentation" will help you construct effective oral citations.

SPEAKER'S
notes   Guidelines for Oral Documentation

To develop effective oral documentation, follow these guidelines:

1. Identify the publication in which the material appears.

2. Identify the time frame of the publication (usually the year is sufficient unless the material is time-sensitive).

3. Offer "highlight" credentials for the experts you cite.

4. Select direct quotations that are brief and that will have an impact.

5. Avoid presenting every detail of the written citation.

6. Controversial and time-sensitive material requires fuller oral documentation.

Conclusion

Your conclusion brings your speech to a satisfying completion. It includes a summary statement, which helps your listeners remember your major points in a final overview, and concluding remarks, which integrate your speech into larger patterns of meaning. You should end on a high note.

Works Cited or Consulted

You should conclude your formal outline with a list of works cited or consulted depending on your instructor's preference. A **works cited list** includes only those

---

▶ **source citations** Abbreviated references in a formal outline to research sources that support the points made.

▶ **oral citations** References to supporting materials during the speech that strengthen the credibility of the speech and support controversial and surprising claims.

▶ **works cited list** Supplies complete, relevant information about sources of research actually cited in the speech.

sources you actually refer to in your speech. A **works consulted list** includes all the works you used while preparing your speech, whether you cite them or not.

In either case, your list of referenced sources is crucial to documenting your research and demonstrating your acquisition of responsible knowledge in support of your claims. Provide full and proper citations so that you can refer curious listeners or your instructor to the exact sources of information. In order to list your references in proper form, refer to the sample formats provided in Chapter 7 (Figure 7.5, p. 145), illustrating the Modern Language Association (MLA) and American Psychological Association (APA) styles. Your instructor may indicate a preference between these two styles. You can also consult the tutorial posted by the University of Purdue.

Formal Outlines: A Caution

Formal outlines have one great advantage. They impose a discipline on the preparation process that can help you develop a substantive speech that rises to the high standards of responsible knowledge. They also have one great disadvantage: If used during presentation, they can suck the life right out of a speech. You can end up reading from them rather than speaking in a fresh, direct, and apparently spontaneous way to the listeners in front of you. The only time you should read during your speech is when you are quoting the words of someone else because the exact wording is dramatic, impressive, and vital. Emblazoned across the bottom of every formal outline should be, in large red letters, "WARNING: Do Not Use During Presentation!"

At this point, you should refer back to Chapter 3's advice on key-word outlines, especially as you move toward practicing your presentation, discussed in Chapter 12. These outlines, you may recall, are skeletal versions of the formal outline that you may take with you to the podium. They trace the flow of the speech through the main points and subpoints, but rather than full sentences they offer single words or at most simple phrases to highlight the essential ideas of the speech. At the point of presentation, these ideas should be in your head, not on paper. Repeated practices and rehearsals should have made the outline part of you. The key-word outline serves as a prompt, should you wander off the track of the speech during presentation. One important use of PowerPoint is that it can occasionally perform the functions of a key-word outline—IF (and that is a large IF!) it is properly designed. See Chapter 10 for additional discussion of the uses and abuses of PowerPoint.

FINAL
reflections   Deep Roots of Structuring and Outlining

The various design options we have discussed are templates that we use to understand the world and to grasp its meaning for our lives. Thus, we want to know how things come to be, so we seek causes and effects. We often divide subjects into categories that reflect our interests; for example, when we are considering a proposal, we may consider it in terms of its *cost*, *benefits*, and *likelihood of success*. This becomes one of the most popular forms of categorical order. Chronological order reflects our orientation in time, and even spatial order reflects our own deeper interests.

▶ **works consulted list** Supplies complete, relevant information about all sources of research considered in the preparation of the speech.

For example, an environmentalist may look at mountains in terms of plant and animal life at different altitudes, while mine owners might see the same mountains in terms of the seams of coal they contain. In a world of infinite possibility, difficulties are always arising that must be dealt with if we are to live successfully: thus, the persistence of the problem-solution pattern.

We are also creatures who need to see a pattern completed, once it has begun. A discussion of causes does not satisfy us when we can't see the effects. If you discuss a problem, we want to see a solution; likewise, any discussion of solutions seems senseless if we aren't given a clear understanding of the problem. In short, we must have closure to satisfy the patterns of expectation we bring to our experience.

It is now clear that to be a successful speaker, you must know how to arrange what you have learned into attractive patterns of knowledge that listeners will find easy to access and hard to forget. You must be able to build a structure of reasons so compelling that the conclusion will seem irresistible to fair-minded listeners. As you find your voice, you will come to place great value on the disciplines of structuring and outlining.

After Reading This Chapter, You Should Be Able To Answer These Questions

Study and **Review** at **MyCommunicationLab**

1 What are the three principles of a well-structured speech?

2 What design options can help you arrange the main points of your speech?

3 How can you develop and support your main points?

4 What functions do transitions serve?

5 How can you develop a working outline of your speech?

6 What are the different ways you can introduce and conclude your speech?

7 What are the major distinguishing features of a formal outline?

For Discussion and Further Exploration

1 Read and evaluate a speech from Appendix B. How well does it satisfy the principles of effective structure? What design option does the speech exemplify? How well does it develop its main points? How effective is its introduction and conclusion? Does it make good use of transitions? How might it have been improved in these respects?

2 For your next speech, develop a formal outline, following the model provided in Figure 9.6. Exchange these with several friends in class before you speak, and ask for their reactions and suggestions.

3 Find and tape two commercials you see on television, the one effective, the other ineffective. Can you identify structural reasons for the difference? Present the ads in class, along with your analysis.

4 Working in small groups, share summaries of the research you have done for your next speech. What are the main points suggested by these summaries? What would be an appropriate design for these points? Explore different options, and explain why you have made your final choice from among them.

5 Suggest an appropriate structural design for the following specific purposes:
   a. To inform listeners where they might see a grizzly bear in the wild
   b. To inform the audience about sexist advertising practices
   c. To inform listeners about the ideal way to prepare for an examination
   d. To persuade listeners to help control global warming
   e. To persuade listeners to vote Republican (or Democratic or some other choice) in the next election
   f. To inform listeners of major events in the women's suffrage movement
   g. To persuade listeners that tax cuts can stimulate the economy
   h. To inform listeners of the story behind Amelia Earhart's last flight
   i. To persuade listeners that drones are not a good answer for national security problems

6 The following list of items provides the raw materials for an informative speech on auctions. Design a working outline for them, extending from the specific purpose statement to the conclusion. Compare these outlines in class, and seek consensus on what might be the best outline and why.
   a. The right type of auction for you is not hard to find.
   b. The first principle of auctions is that merchandise always goes to the highest bidder.
   c. Set a maximum amount you are willing to pay, and do not bid beyond it.
   d. Quote National Association of Auctioneers' definition of auctions.
   e. Have you been to an antique or art store lately, only to be blown away by the astronomical prices?
   f. Today, we've considered how auctions work, how to find them, and how to make good buys at them.
   g. Choose an auction according to what you want and what's available to you.
   h. To inform my audience how to make auctions work for them
   i. Auctions are available on the Internet and in the classified section of most Sunday newspapers.
   j. Once you find your auction, consider the following four tips for making the buy.
   k. Auctions are a fun and economical way to make purchases.
   l. Be alert for when your item goes up for sale.
   m. Estate auction
   n. There are many types of auctions.
   o. Having worked around auctions for several years, I've come to know and appreciate this fascinating form of free trade.
   p. Today, I'm going to tell you how auctions work, where to find them, and some basic tips for making smart buys.
   q. There is a better way to purchase the rare, valuable, or just out-of-the-ordinary items you fancy.
   r. Art and antique auctions
   s. Auctions are a fascinating alternative for making purchases.
   t. So maybe I'll see you at an auction someday, and you, too, can learn to duck the ridiculous prices of "fine" shopping.
   u. Determine if the merchandise is in good shape.
   v. Municipal auctions
   w. Determine if the merchandise is what you really want.
   x. Arrive early to inspect the merchandise to see if it's worth buying.

SAMPLE FORMAL OUTLINE

Adapted from a speech by Elizabeth Lyles, Davidson College

HEADING

Title: The Abused Women of Afghanistan
Topic: Plight of the Women of Afghanistan
Specific Purpose: To win support for efforts to protect women in Afghanistan.

Elizabeth's introduction gains attention by combining two techniques: *opening with a narrative* and *startling the audience*. Essentially, she tells a story that shocks her listeners with its graphic detail. ▶

INTRODUCTION

Attention Materials: Orbal could hardly believe the news from her native homeland. A nineteen-year-old girl had just been executed in public for adultery. That same month, a public gathering of women had been attacked by an angry mob and pelted with stones, an outspoken advocate for women's issues had been gunned down in broad daylight, and the president had just signed a law making it illegal for women to refuse sex on demand to their husbands (Taylor). Of course, such brutalities are hardly unknown to the abused women of Afghanistan. But this was the Spring of 2009 – nearly eight years after the so-called liberation of the Afghan people by a U.S.-led coalition of forces.

Thesis Statement: The abused women of Afghanistan need your support now for efforts to defend their basic human rights.

Preview: We will consider how the U.S. invasion brought hope to Afghanistan's women, how these hopes are now being dashed, and finally, how you might help in this struggle for human dignity.

(**Transition:** "First, let's revisit the hour of their promised liberation.")

The body of the speech combines two prominent design options. First, its main points develop (1) the promise of the invasion for women's rights, (2) the disappointment over the results, and (3) the renewed hope now embodied in the RAWA organization. While it develops within this categorical design, the speech also follows the problem-solution pattern of identifying a problem (disappointed hope) followed by a solution (renewed hope as represented in the work of RAWA). ▶

BODY

I. The U.S.-led invasion in 2001 brought great promises and hopes for the women of Afghanistan.
  A. President George Bush and other Western leaders emphasized liberation in making their case for war to the Afghan people.
    1. American bombers dropped leaflets depicting the mistreatment of Afghan women ("Silent Scream").
    2. UN Secretary General Kofi Annan insisted there could be no real peace and recovery in Afghanistan without restoring basic human and civil rights for women (United Nations).
    3. First Lady Laura Bush explicitly associated the invasion with advancing their cause. "Because of our recent military gains in much of Afghanistan women are no longer imprisoned in their homes. The fight against terrorism is also a fight for the rights and dignity of women" ("An Overview").
  B. The new Afghan constitution guarantees equal rights for women ("Women in").
    1. Women are once again voting and serving in public office.
    2. In some areas women now have access to rudimentary education, health care, and a level of freedom they have not experienced in decades.

To develop the first main point, Elizabeth relies on subpoints and sub-subpoints based on testimony from world leaders. ▶

(**Transition:** "However, the reality does not always live up to the promise.")

II. Afghan women fear that their newly gained freedoms are already being rolled back.
    A. The central government under Hamid Karzai is incapable of or unwilling to protect women.
        1. Mujahideen and Taliban connected "warlords" still control most of rural Afghanistan ("Women of").
        2. "Warlords" dominate the Loya Jirga or Afghan legislative body ("An Overview").
            a. According to the warlord chair of that assembly, "God has not given you [women] equal rights because under his decision, two women are counted as equal to one man" ("Women of").
        3. Karzai has signaled his willingness to sacrifice women's rights for reconciliation.
            a. He is engaged in talks with "moderate" elements of the Taliban ("UN Head").
            b. News has recently surfaced of a secret "reconciliation law" granting amnesty for all crimes committed before 2002 ("UN Head").
            c. In 2009, he signed the infamous "rape law" that makes it illegal for women of the Shia minority to deny their husband's sexual advances on demand (Abawi).
    B. Reports of violence and oppression against women are again on the rise ("Women of").
        1. Corrupt local officials typically ignore reports of domestic abuse and sexual assault.
        2. Many schools have been shut down by a reign of terror and violence.
            a. Girls have been harassed, mutilated, and even killed for attending classes.
            b. Less than 10% of Afghan girls in rural areas have access to education.
        3. In many areas women still live in obvious fear of harsh recrimination for behaviors deemed un-Islamic.

(Transition: "There is a little light in all this darkness. I want to tell you now about a remarkable group of women who have been fighting for these rights for over thirty years.")

III. The Revolutionary Association of the Women of Afghanistan (RAWA) is the most prominent organization for women's rights and social justice in Afghanistan.
    A. RAWA sponsors a number of humanitarian projects.
        1. They create educational opportunities for women and their children.
            a. They operate fifteen primary and secondary schools in Afghan refugee camps.
            b. They provide home-based schooling for women and girls where it is still unsafe to attend school.
        2. They provide health care to abused women and children.
            a. They operate small hospitals that provide free care.
            b. They operate mobile health teams that travel throughout the troubled regions of Afghanistan and Pakistan.
        3. They provide vocational training and financial opportunities to help Afghan women support their families and become self-sufficient.

◀ To develop the second main point, Elizabeth creates a structure of sub-points and sub-subpoints built on alleged factual evidence and testimony. Any one of the sources she uses might be suspect on grounds of bias. Knowing this, she depends more on an impressive array of concurring evidence to support her claims.

◀ To establish her third main point, Elizabeth builds through her subpoints and sub-subpoints a detailed picture of the work of RAWA to support the conclusion that the group deserves audience support. This impression would be further strengthened had she presented factual evidence confirming the success of RAWA's work.

    a. They encourage chicken farms, weaving shops, and bee-fostering
       projects.
    b. They offer small loans to start small businesses.
IV. So how can you light a small candle in the Afghan darkness?
    A. Go to the RAWA website (RAWA.com) and find out how you can get involved.
    B. Demand that our President and our legislators not abandon the women of
       Afghanistan.

(Transition: "So we see that the view of Afghanistan through the eyes of women is not a happy one.")

CONCLUSION

Summary statement: It's a story that started with high hopes as the U.S. invaded Afghanistan. Then those hopes and promises began to shrivel as fundamentalist values once again spread and stained the fabric of Afghan culture. But RAWA holds high the beacon of hope for the abused and forgotten women of Afghanistan. These heroic fighters for women's rights deserve your commitment, because, as Martin Luther King Jr. said right before he died, "We are all tied together in a single garment of destiny." Go to RAWA.com and find out how you can help.

Concluding remarks: My friend Orbal, herself a RAWA activist, choked back tears as she relayed the story of an eleven-year-old neighbor that had been abducted, beaten, raped, and then traded for a dog by a local warlord. Orbal and women like her have choked back enough tears. Get involved! We must not forget the women of Afghanistan.

Elizabeth's summary statement offers a skillful review of the main points of the speech. It invokes a powerful appeal to listeners based on stirring images that contrast fundamentalist values with the hope represented by RAWA. The concluding remarks return to the opening narrative to provide a sense of closure and to make a final appeal to the feelings of listeners.

WORKS CONSULTED

Abawi, Atia. "Afghanistan 'Rape' Law Puts Women's Rights Front and Center." *CNN.com/asia*. Cable News Network, 7 April 2009. Web. 27 March 2010.
"An Overview on the Situation of Afghan Women." *Revolutionary Association of the Women of Afghanistan (RAWA)*. Revolutionary Association of the Women of Afghanistan (RAWA), n.d. Web. 2 April 2010.
"Letter to the United Nations." *Revolutionary Association of the Women of Afghanistan (RAWA)*. Revolutionary Association of the Women of Afghanistan (RAWA), 28 April 2007. Web. 2 April 2010.
"RAWA's Social Activities." *Revolutionary Association of the Women of Afghanistan (RAWA)*. Revolutionary Association of the Women of Afghanistan (RAWA), n.d. Web. 5 April 2010.
"Silent Scream." *BBC News World Edition*. BBC, 8 April 2002. Web. 27 March 2010.
Siun. "McChrystal Digs In, Afghan Women Say Get Out." *Rethink Afghanistan*. Brave New Foundation, 13 July 2009. Web. 14 Apr. 2010.
Taylor, Rupert. "Women's Rights Abused in Afghanistan: Ancient Prejudice Against Females Is Hard to Defeat." *Middle Eastern Affairs*. Suite101.com, 20 April 2009. Web. 27 March 2010.
"The Women of Afghanistan." *CBC News Online*. CBC, 1 March 2005. Web. 26 March 2010.
"UN Head in Afghanistan Meets with Militant Group." *Yahoo! News*. Yahoo Inc., 25 March 2010. Web. 26 March 2010.
United Nations. "The Situation of Women in Afghanistan." *Afghan Women Today: Realities and Opportunities*. The United Nations, 2002. Web. 26 March 2010.
"Women in Afghanistan." *Independent Lens: Afghanistan Unveiled*. Independent Television Service, 17 November 2004. Web. 26 March 2010.

Objectives

This chapter will help you

1 Appreciate how presentation aids can help—or hinder—your speech

2 Understand the functions served by different types of presentation aids

3 Select the most appropriate means of presenting your aids

4 Plan, design, and prepare presentation aids

5 Use presentation aids well

OUTLINE

The Advantages and Disadvantages of Presentation Aids

Types of Presentation Aids

Presentation Media

Preparing Presentation Aids

Using Presentation Aids

Ethical Considerations for Using Presentation Aids

Final Reflections Amplifying Your Voice

10 Presentation Aids

Listen to **Chapter 10** at **MyCommunicationLab**

Alumnus of West Point and the Naval War College, former senior fellow at the Kennedy School of Government at Harvard, veteran of thirty-five years of military service, General Stanley A. McChrystal sat stunned before a convoluted PowerPoint slide. The head of American and NATO forces in Afghanistan tried to decipher the eight colors, twelve labels, almost one hundred names, and dozens upon dozens of arrows detailing the dynamics affecting stability in that country. Finally, he wryly observed, "When we understand that slide, we'll have won the war."[1]

Although you might not have encountered a presentation aid of quite this complexity, you surely recognize the use of aids that simply perplex and overwhelm the audience. Yet when well designed and well used, *presentation aids can really help you find your voice effectively in your speeches.*

Let's say you've chosen to speak about dyslexia. You might cite the entry from *Black's Medical Dictionary*, which defines it as "difficulty in reading or learning to read, . . . always accompanied by difficulty in writing, and particularly in spelling."[2] That helps your audience understand the condition on an abstract level. Imagine then taking it a step further and *showing* your audience what a dyslexic person might see when trying to read a passage (see Figure 10.1). All of a sudden, your audience gains a better understanding of what it *feels* like to be dyslexic.

Or perhaps, after a semester studying in Australia, you want to share the finer points of a didgeridoo. You could describe this instrument as a pliable mouthpiece on a long hollow tube without holes. Think of how much more vivid it would be to show a picture of one, or to play a recording or a video clip, or to bring one to class to demonstrate. Your verbal descriptions of the didgeridoo's distinctive droning buzz could then truly come alive for your audience.

With the advent of computer technologies, the types and uses of presentation aids are multiplying rapidly. In this chapter, we describe various kinds of presentation

FIGURE 10.1
A Dyslexic Person's View of Dyslexia

"bifficulty on reading ir learniny two reed, . . .

alwags aggompanieb by bifficulty on riding,

end particulately on pseling."

aids and the media used for them, identify the ways they can be used in speeches, offer suggestions for preparing them, and present guidelines for their use.

You should use presentation aids only when they increase the clarity and effectiveness of your speech. If your assignment requires you to incorporate a presentation aid, don't try the approach of the student who showed a photograph at the beginning of the speech and set it aside, quipping, "Okay, now that's over with!" Instead, embrace the challenge to discover how you can expand the range and impact of your voice. No matter what types of aids and media you employ, make sure that you and your message are front and center.

The use of charts or models might have helped listeners better understand Dr. William Mackey's description of removing shrapnel from victims of the Boston Marathon bombings.

The Advantages and Disadvantages of Presentation Aids

Presentation aids are *supplementary materials used to enhance the effectiveness and clarity of a presentation.* Whether visual, auditory, or a combination of the two, they give your audience direct sensory contact with your message. When properly prepared and used, presentation aids can help speeches in many different ways. But if they are used improperly, they can become a liability. Figure 10.2 summarizes the major advantages and disadvantages of presentation aids.

Advantages of Presentation Aids

Presentation aids complement words as communication tools. As powerful as words can be, they are by nature abstract. Presentation aids offer concrete and immediate images that can involve and educate listeners. Imagine how hard it would be through words alone to describe the inner workings of the human hand. Even with models or charts, such a speech would still be difficult for many of us to understand. It can require both words and presentation aids, used skillfully together, to explain some topics to some audiences. The concreteness of presentation aids creates some specific advantages both for your audience and for you as a speaker.

Watch at **MyCommunicationLab** **Video:** "How to Color Eggs"

Advantages for the Audience
1. Increases understanding
2. More memorable speech
3. Adds variety and interest

Advantages for the Speaker
1. Enhances authenticity
2. Improves credibility
3. Improves delivery

Disadvantages for the Audience
1. Can be distracting
2. Can be confusing

Disadvantages for the Speaker
1. Can damage credibility
2. Can be distracting
3. Can reduce eye contact
4. Risks uncooperative equipment

FIGURE 10.2
Major Advantages and Disadvantages of Presentation Aids

▶ **presentation aids** Visual and auditory materials intended to enhance the clarity and effectiveness of a presentation.

Presentation aids can help your audience:

■ **Presentation aids increase understanding.** Words are abstractions that listeners transform into mental images. Different listeners may conjure up different mental images for the same words, which may not be consistent with what you intend. As a speaker, you have more control over these images when you present both words and visuals to augment them. It is easier to give directions to someone when there is a map that both of you can see. Similarly, it is easier to explain the steps in a process when listeners are shown each part of the sequence.

■ **Good presentation aids make your speech more memorable.** Research suggests that audiences recall an informative presentation better when visuals are used and that recall is even better when the visuals are in high-quality color.[3] Advertisers, for example, know that the combination of verbal and visual elements can "produce more mental images and lead to a more favorable attitude," which in turn aids recall of the message.[4] Presentation aids are easier to remember than words because they are concrete. A photograph of the devastation after a tornado may linger in your memory, thus increasing the influence of a speech urging you to contribute to the Red Cross.

■ **Presentation aids add variety and interest to a speech.** Too much of a good thing, even a well-fashioned fabric of words, can become numbing. Just as pictures and boxed materials may be used to break up long stretches of text in a book, presentation aids can be used to break up long stretches of words in a speech. Variety creates interest and helps sustain or recapture attention, as well as appealing to the different learning preferences of audience members— particularly in today's visually oriented society

Presentation aids can help you as the speaker:

■ **Presentation aids help establish the authenticity of your words.** When you show listeners what you are talking about, you demonstrate that it actually exists. This type of evidence is important in both informative and persuasive messages. If your audience can actually see the differences between digital cameras and film cameras, they are more likely to be convinced that one is better than the other.

■ **Neat, well-designed presentation aids enhance your credibility.** They tell listeners that you put extra effort into preparing your speech. Speakers who use presentation aids are judged to be more professional, better prepared, more credible, more interesting, more concrete, and more persuasive than speakers who do not use such aids.[5] In some organizational settings, audiences expect speakers to use presentation aids, such as PowerPoint slides. If you don't have them, the audience may be disappointed, and your credibility may suffer.

■ **Presentation aids can help improve your delivery skills.** Using a presentation aid encourages movement as you display your aid. Movement energizes a speech, getting you away from the "stand behind the lectern/talking head" mode of delivery that many audiences find boring. If you have communication apprehension, purposeful movement—such as pointing to something on an aid as you display it—provides a constructive outlet for nervous energy. It directs your attention away from yourself and toward your message.

Disadvantages of Presentation Aids

Despite these advantages, the opening story about the confusing PowerPoint slide demonstrates that sometimes, presentation aids can do your speech more harm than good. Be aware of these potential problems so that you can avoid them.

Presentation aids can be problematic for your audience:

■ **Presentation aids may distract listeners.** They can draw attention away from your message if they are not used properly. For example, if your audience has difficulty reading an aid, they will strain to see it rather than listening to you. If they are passing around your handouts, objects, or photographs during your speech, they will be distracted from what you are saying. If the images are gruesome, some may be repelled. One student who was a paramedic showed pictures of child abuse victims taken in a local emergency room. Some members of the audience became so upset that they were not able to concentrate on her message. Your aids may also be so compelling that the audience becomes engrossed in them instead of your real message.

■ **Presentation aids may confuse listeners.** As the opening example demonstrates, a complex presentation aid risks leaving the members of your audience not nodding their heads but scratching them. Blurry images, unclear graphs, and overloaded slides likely result in an audience that is more mystified than enlightened.

Presentation aids can be problematic for you as speaker:

■ **Poor presentation aids can damage your credibility.** Sloppy or inaccurate aids will harm your credibility. Listeners may think you did not care enough about your presentation to invest the time and effort needed to prepare an effective presentation aid. Even worse, they may think you are incapable of preparing one.

■ **Presentation aids can distract speakers.** If you haven't practiced your speech using your presentation aid, you may worry so much about how you are going to use it that you lose track of what you are saying. If you are not confident in your ability to use the technology, this uneasiness may show up in your presentation. If the technology goes awry, it might throw you completely off course.

■ **Presentation aids can reduce your eye contact with the audience.** If you look at your presentation aids more than your audience, you risk losing their attention as well as your ability to assess the audience's confusion or comprehension. That in turn may damage your ethos: Don't you know your material well enough to talk to the audience rather than to the aid?

■ **Presentation aids can put you at the mercy of technology.** If the site for your speech is not equipped to handle computerized presentation aids, you must use other forms. Even with the best of preparations, the techno-gremlins may play havoc with your original intentions, requiring a backup plan.

In short, presentation aids can either help or hinder your speech. An aid may be beautifully rendered, or wonderfully funny, or impressive to behold—but if it does not help you find your voice on this topic with this audience, you should not use it.

You have a multitude of presentation aids from which to choose, as the following sections suggest. Investigate the specific options you have as well as the benefits and challenges of each. In determining which types of aids and media would be the best, ask yourself these questions: *How will a presentation aid help my audience understand my thesis, main points, and supporting materials? How will a presentation aid empower my voice?*

Types of Presentation Aids

In considering potential presentation aids for your speech, you might be tempted to jump to media: Should I use PowerPoint or a handout? (Or you might just assume that, of course, you will use PowerPoint—in which case we hope you will consider the ample alternatives to this overused form.) Before determining the *medium* you will use to share your presentation aid (which we'll discuss in the next section), you first need to decide what *type* of aid best suits your speech. Of the many kinds of presentation aids, you can choose among such frequently used categories as those discussed in this section: people, objects, models, graphics, and pictures.

People

For good or bad, you are always a presentation aid for your speeches. Your body, grooming, actions, gestures, voice, facial expressions, and demeanor are important considerations. What you wear for a presentation can influence how your speech is received. If you will be speaking on camping and wilderness adventures, blue jeans and a flannel shirt might be appropriate. If you are a nurse discussing a medical topic, your uniform can enhance your credibility. If you are talking about how to dress for an employment interview, your own attire should illustrate your recommendations. We discuss the importance of personal appearance in more detail in Chapter 12.

Incorporating dance steps for a speech on African American dance can enhance the presentation and clarify complex moves.

Ben Lane, one of our students, used his body during his informative speech on competitive diving to demonstrate several different kinds of dives (stopping short of diving face-first onto the floor, of course). Another, Lazetta Crawford, incorporated a number of key dance steps to illustrate her speech on "stepping," an African American dance form that combines footsteps, the spoken word, and hand claps to produce complex rhythms and sounds. In each case, the demonstration added clarification, liveliness, and a sense of immediacy.

You can also use other people as presentation aids. John Kache was a freshman in college when he contracted meningococcal meningitis, a life-threatening disease for which immunizations are available. John survived his illness, but he lost his right leg and all of the fingers on his hands. After his recovery, he often spoke to high school students, urging them to get their shots before they went off to college. Typically, he would use a volunteer from the audience to demonstrate what life without fingers was like for him. As he put it, "I'd wrap up one of the student's hands in an Ace bandage, then throw him a bag of candy and tell him to open it and pass the candies around."[6] This demonstration dramatically illustrated the seriousness of this disease and the importance of being immunized.

Your use of people as a presentation aid does not need to be this dramatic to be effective. One of our students, Neomal Abyskera, used two of his classmates to illustrate the lineup positions in the game of rugger, as played in his native Sri Lanka. At the appropriate moment, Neomal said, "Pete and Jeff will show you how the opposing players line up." While his classmates demonstrated the shoulder grip position, Neomal explained when and why the position was assumed. The demonstration was more understandable than if he had simply tried to describe the positioning verbally or had used stick-figure drawings.

The people you ask to function as a presentation aid should be willing to do so. They should understand that their role is to illustrate your message, *not to draw attention away from it*, and should agree to meet with you to rehearse the presentation. During the presentation, they should sit in the front row so that they can quickly and easily come forward when you need them and then return to their seats after the demonstration.

Objects and Models

Displaying the actual objects you are discussing can gain attention, increase understanding, and add authenticity to your speech. If using actual objects is a problem, you might consider a model.

Objects. Specific objects may exemplify the concepts in your presentation, whether the objects are ingredients for a simple meal, your favorite fly-fishing rod, or a set of decorations used to celebrate Día de los Muertos, the Mexican holiday honoring the deceased. In talking about how her research as a neuroanatomist gave her "a stroke of insight" when she suffered a stroke, Dr. Jill Bolte-Taylor used a riveting object to describe how the two hemispheres function: an actual human brain.[7] The success of Dr. Bolte-Taylor's use of this distinctive object depended on her credibility as a scientist, her comfort in handling the brain, and her assessment of the audience as being far more fascinated than turned off by its use.

Inanimate objects work better than living things, which you can't always control. One of our students brought a small puppy to use in a speech on caring for young animals. At the beginning of her speech, she spread out some newspapers on the table and placed the puppy on them. We are sure you can imagine what happened. The first thing the puppy did was wet on the papers (including her note cards, which she had put on the table while trying to control the puppy). The first thing the audience did was giggle. From there, it was all downhill. The puppy squirmed, yipped, and tried to jump on the speaker the whole time she was talking. She was totally upstaged by her presentation aid.

Presentation aids meant to shock the audience into attention can cause serious problems. *Objects that are dangerous, illegal, or potentially offensive, such as guns, drugs, or pornography, must not be used in classroom speeches.* One speaker unwisely chose to demonstrate fire safety by setting fire to paper in a trash can, resulting in the evacuation of the building and the arrival of the fire department. Even replicas of dangerous materials can cause problems. One of our students brandished a very realistic-looking "toy" semiautomatic weapon that he pulled from beneath the lectern during the introduction of a speech on gun control. Several audience members became so upset that they could not concentrate on his message.

Using a simple object can be all the more effective in this age of electronic wizardry. When Andrew Evans brought a glass of water to the front of the room for his persuasive speech on faith and reason, we thought he just wanted it in case

Watch at **MyCommunicationLab**
Video: "Preventing Sexual Assault"

Watch at **MyCommunicationLab**
Video: "The Cocker Spaniel"

his throat got dry. Instead, in the middle of his speech he picked it up to suggest that the water represented human reason and the glass, faith. Noting that the water can be transferred from one container to another but cannot stand on its own without any support, he suggested that reason has to have some kind of faith—in God, in science, in something—to support it.

Most "how to" speeches require objects as presentation aids to demonstrate procedures. In a classroom speech on how to carve a jack-o'-lantern, the speaker showed listeners how to draw the face on a pumpkin with a felt marker and then how to make a beveled cut around the stem so that the top wouldn't fall in. As she exhibited these techniques, she told stories of the ancient myths surrounding jack-o'-lanterns. Her presentation aid and her words helped each other: The demonstration enlivened her speech, and the stories gave the demonstration depth and meaning. When she came to her closing remarks, she reached under the lectern and produced a finished jack-o'-lantern complete with a lighted candle. The effect was memorable.

Demonstrating a process becomes clearer with an object as a presentation aid.

Models. Sometimes an object is too large, too small, very rare, expensive, fragile, or simply unavailable for class use. In these cases, a replica of the object can work well as a presentation aid. George Stacey brought a slightly smaller-than-life-sized model of a person to demonstrate cardiopulmonary resuscitation (CPR). The model folded into a suitcase, so that it could be kept out of sight when not in use.

Graphics

Graphics are visual representations of information, such as sketches, maps, graphs, charts, and textual materials. Because graphics will be displayed for only a short time during your speech, they must be instantly clear. Each graphic should focus on one idea. Because the graphics will be viewed from a distance, their colors should be intense and should contrast sharply with the background. We cover such considerations more fully under "Preparing Presentation Aids" later in this chapter.

Sketches. Sketches are simplified representations of your subject. One student speaker used a sketch transferred to a transparency to illustrate the measurements one should take before buying a bicycle. While talking about how to make bar-to-pedal and seat-to-handlebar measurements, he pointed to the appropriate area of the bike on the sketch.

Maps. As a representation of physical space, a map can show listeners the locations of occurrences and put problems into perspective. Because commercially prepared maps typically contain too much detail, the best maps are those that you create specifically for your speech, making them simple, relevant to your purpose, and uncluttered. To illustrate the wide open spaces of the west, for example, you might show Figure 10.3 with its many blank areas. Another

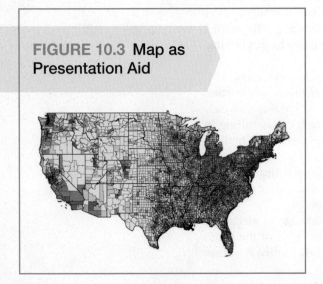

FIGURE 10.3 Map as Presentation Aid

▶ **graphics** Visual representations of information, such as sketches, maps, graphs, charts, and textual materials.

student speaker used a simplified map to help his listeners see where a series of earthquakes occurred along the New Madrid fault and understand how a recurrence of such earthquakes might endanger his mid-South classmates.

Maps are also useful for illustrating speeches based on spatial relationships. It is hard to give people instructions on how to get somewhere with words alone. In a speech on the major attractions in Yellowstone Park, Tiffany Brock used an outline map of the park to show the route from the South Visitor's Center to Old Faithful, Mammoth Hot Springs, and the Grand Canyon of the Yellowstone River. Seeing the map helped listeners put the locations and distances into perspective.

Graphs. Mrs. Robert A. Taft, wife of a prominent former senator and lioness of Washington society, once commented, "I always find that statistics are hard to swallow and impossible to digest. The only one I can ever remember is that if all the people who go to sleep in church were laid end to end, they would be a lot more comfortable."[8] Many people share her feelings about statistics. As we noted in Chapter 8, masses of numbers presented orally can be overwhelming. But a well-designed graph can make statistical information easier for listeners to understand and appreciate.

A **pie graph** shows the size of a subject's parts in relation to one another and to the whole. The "pie" represents the whole, and the "slices" represent the parts. The segments, or slices, are percentages of the whole and must add up to 100 percent. The most effective pie graphs for use as presentation aids have no more than six segments because too many slices make a graph difficult to read. The pie graph in Figure 10.4 shows Internet users' perceptions of the reliability of information from Internet websites.

A **bar graph** shows comparisons and contrasts between two or more items or groups. Bar graphs are easy to understand because each item can be readily compared with every other item on the graph. Bar graphs can also have a dramatic visual impact. Figure 10.5 is a horizontal bar graph that illustrates the relative popularity of the top six social networking sites. Figure 10.6 offers a vertical bar graph prepared by Dolapo Olushola for her speech illuminating a tragic crisis created by the HIV/AIDS epidemic in Africa. When the variables on the vertical axis need longer titles, horizontal charts often provide greater legibility.[9]

Some bar graphs make use of pictographs, or stylized drawings, in place of linear bars. One student's speech on the relationship between college students' consumption of alcohol and the grades they earned, for example, showed three and a half bottles to represent the number of drinks per week for "A" students, as compared to ten and a half bottles for "D" students. If you plan to use pictographs in place of bars, be sure they are simple depictions that do not distract from the impact of your material.[10]

FIGURE 10.4 Pie Graph

Perception of Internet's Reliability

- Small Portion Reliable
- About Half Reliable
- Most Reliable
- All Reliable

3% 7% 41% 49%

Source: UCLA Center for Communication Policy, "The UCLA Internet Report – Surveying The Digital Future."

FIGURE 10.5 Horizontal Bar Graph

Top Social Media Sites
Updated 5/1/2013

Millions

1 Facebook
2 Twitter
3 LinkedIn
4 Pinterest
5 Myspace
6 Google+

FIGURE 10.6 Vertical Bar Graph

Number of HIV/AIDS Orphans

- Sub-Saharan Africa
- Rest of the World

2000 2010

▶ **pie graph** A circle graph that shows the size of a subject's parts in relation to each other and to the whole.

▶ **bar graph** A graph that shows comparisons and contrasts between two or more items or groups.

FINDING YOUR voice Exploring Graphs

Using the same set of statistical data, prepare a pie graph, a bar graph, and a line graph. What aspects of the data does each version highlight? What aspects are less evident in each version? Which version makes the information clearest and most striking for an audience? Which version seems to best represent the data? If the version that seems best for the audience is not the version that seems most representative of the data, what ethical questions does that inconsistency raise?

FIGURE 10.7 Line Graph

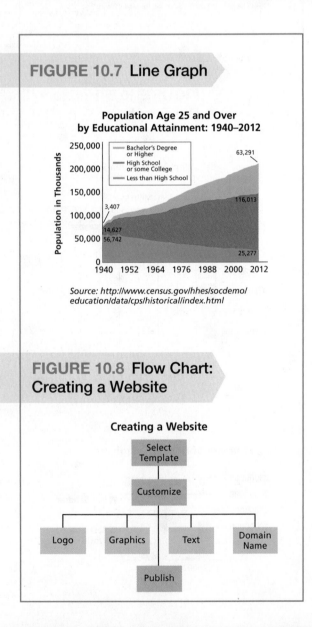

Population Age 25 and Over by Educational Attainment: 1940–2012

Legend:
- Bachelor's Degree or Higher
- High School or some College
- Less than High School

Values shown on graph: 250,000; 200,000; 150,000; 100,000; 50,000; 0 (Population in Thousands); years 1940, 1952, 1964, 1976, 1988, 2000, 2012; 63,291; 3,407; 14,627; 56,742; 116,013; 25,277

Source: http://www.census.gov/hhes/socdemo/education/data/cps/historical/index.html

FIGURE 10.8 Flow Chart: Creating a Website

Creating a Website

Select Template → Customize → (Logo, Graphics, Text, Domain Name) → Publish

---

A **line graph** demonstrates changes across time, and it is useful for showing trends in growth or decline. Figure 10.7 shows the level of education achieved by Americans from 1940 to 2012. The upward-sloping lines confirm the steady increases over time in the numbers of people earning high school and college degrees and the diminishing numbers of people with less than a high school education. When you plot more than one line on a graph, use distinct colors. Limit the number of lines to three at most so that you don't confuse your audience.

Charts. Charts provide visual summaries of relationships that are not in themselves visible. Charts can be quite complex, so the speaker's challenge is to simplify them without distorting their meaning. The listeners must be able to understand a chart instantly and to read it from a distance.

One frequently used type of chart is a flow chart. A **flow chart** can show the steps in a process, the hierarchy and accountability in an organization, or the genealogy of a family tree. In a flow chart that explains a process, the levels, lines, and arrows indicate what steps occur simultaneously and what steps occur sequentially. Figure 10.8 is a flow chart that indicates the process of developing a website.

To avoid the problem of overloading charts with too much information, consider using a series of charts, presented in succession. It is much better to have several clean, clear charts than one that tries to do too much, overloading both the audience and the speaker in the process.

Textual Graphics. **Textual graphics** are visuals that contain words, phrases, or numbers. Unfamiliar material is clearer and easier for listeners to remember when they can both hear and see the message. Presenting the key words in a message visually can help an audience follow complicated ideas more easily. For example, when one of the authors presented an informative speech on the process by which

---

▶ **line graph** A visual representation of changes across time; especially useful for indicating trends of growth or decline.

▶ **flow chart** A visual method of representing power and responsibility relationships or describing the steps in a process.

▶ **textual graphics** Visuals that contain words, phrases, or numbers.

a marketing task force approached its charge for a campus communication center, the language in Figure 10.9 previewed the process for the audience. This figure shows the most frequently used form of textual graphics, a **bulleted list** of information. When you make a bulleted list, begin with a title, and then place the material under it. Unless you are discussing all of the elements in quick succession, you should reveal each element as you talk about it.

Another frequently used type of textual graphic presents an **acronym** composed of the initial letters of words to help your audience remember your message. The transparency in Figure 10.10 used the acronym EMILY (adapted from Emily's List, a political network) in a persuasive speech urging students to start saving early for retirement. When preparing such a graphic, use the acronym as a title; then list the words under it. Use size and/or color to make the first letters of the words stand out.

Keep textual graphics simple, with colors that make ideas stand out. A single word or phrase is far more effective than a full sentence, which competes with you for attention.

Pictures

Photographs and illustrations can be powerful presentation aids. A good photograph can authenticate a point in a way that words cannot. It can make a situation seem more vivid and realistic. For instance, a speaker could talk about the devastating environmental effects of a hurricane, which might evoke a modest response from the audience. Suppose, however, the speaker also projected the photograph in Figure 10.11 on a screen in the front of the room as she said these words. Would the point have more impact with or without the picture?

When Jody Cross spoke to the Kansas City Association of Realtors, she included the group's logo and several photographs of

FIGURE 10.9 Bulleted List

Marketing Task Force
- Mission Statement
- Current Image
- Target Market
- Desired Image

FIGURE 10.10 Acronym Graphic

EMILY

EARLY
MONEY
IS
LIKE
YEAST

IT MAKES DOUGH GROW!

FIGURE 10.11 Projected Photograph

▶ **bulleted list**   A presentation aid that highlights ideas by presenting them as a list of brief statements.

▶ **acronym**   A word composed of the initial letters of a series of words.

homes from their own website. By doing so, she not only brought home her point about using visual images to connect with her audience but also earned the appreciation of her listeners for demonstrating that she understood them.[11]

Presentation Media

The many *types* of presentation aids can be shared with your audience through a variety of presentation *media*. Traditional media include flip charts, posters, handouts, chalk or marker boards, transparencies, videotapes, and audiotapes. Newer presentation media use computer programs such as PowerPoint and Prezi that can incorporate slides, films, DVDs, and sound. These newer media have become the standard for presentations in organizational and educational settings. Although you may be best acquainted with the computer versions, familiarity with other media allows you greater creativity as well as options when technology is not available.

Traditional Media

Flip Charts.   A **flip chart** is a large, unlined tablet placed on an easel so that each page can be flipped over the top when you are done with it. Most flip charts are newsprint pads that measure about 2 feet wide by 3 feet high. Flip charts are convenient, inexpensive, and adaptable to many settings. Because flip charts are meant to be used spontaneously, they are especially useful at meetings when subjects come up that should be written out so that they can be analyzed and understood.

Although flip charts can be effective in some group communication settings, they don't work as well in classroom speeches. Their use suggests that the speaker did not care enough to prepare a polished presentation aid. Writing on a flip chart also forces speakers either to stop speaking while they write or to speak while facing away from the audience, which may offset any gain from using the charts.

FINDING YOUR voice Alternative Media

Consider this scenario: Due to a complicated legal battle, all computer-generated programs have been temporarily withdrawn from the market—but you still need to give a presentation, and you need to illustrate several of your points. How could you use traditional media to give voice to your ideas in ways that would engage your audience?

Chalk and Marker Boards.   A chalk or marker board is available in almost every classroom and corporate conference room. Like flip charts, these boards are best used spontaneously. Despite careful speech preparation, you may sometimes realize that some of your listeners have not understood what you have just said. One way you can respond to their apparent confusion is by writing a few words on the board or by drawing a simple diagram. Because you inevitably lose eye contact with listeners while writing on a board, do not use this medium for anything that will take

▶ **flip chart**   A large, unlined tablet, usually a newsprint pad, that is placed on an easel so that each page can be flipped over the top when it's full.

more than a few seconds to write or draw. Never use chalk or marker boards simply because you did not want to take the time to prepare a polished presentation aid.

Posters. Posters can be used to display pictures, sketches, maps, charts, graphs, or textual graphics. In an average-size room with a small audience, posters about 14 by 17 inches may work best; they are easier to handle than larger posters. You can place the posters face down on the lectern or table and display them as you refer to them. You can also use the back of a poster to remind you of names of people or to cue you to the next point in your presentation. One student had trouble remembering the name of the president of Iran, a brief but important reference in his speech. He wrote it on the back of the large photograph of the man, so when he raised it to show the audience, he could read "Ah-ma-di-ne-jad."

Handouts. Handouts are useful when your subject is complex or your message contains a lot of statistical information, and they can extend the impact of your speech and validate the information you have presented. Pass out these handouts *after* your speech so listeners have something to remind them of what you said. If you distribute a handout before you speak, the audience will read it rather than listening to you. You should distribute handouts before your speech *only* when it is absolutely necessary for listeners to refer to them during your presentation. Never distribute handouts during your speech. This is a sure-fire way to disrupt your presentation and confuse or lose listeners. Multipaged handouts are multi-distracting.

Transparencies, Projections, and Slides. Transparencies, projections by document cameras, and slides allow audiences to see graphics or photographs more easily, especially when audiences are large or spread out in a large room. Business speakers often prefer them to posters or flip charts because they look more professional.

Transparencies are easier to use than slides because you don't have to darken the room when you show them. They are simple to make and inexpensive. You can write on a transparency while it is being shown, adding spontaneity to your presentation. You can also use a pen or pencil as a pointer to direct listeners' attention to features you want to emphasize.

Document cameras can project either transparencies or hard copy onto a large screen. To explain how to read music, for example, you might show the score of Handel's *Messiah* while playing a recorded section, pointing to the various parts in the score as the instruments and choral parts enter in the piece.

When you show slides with a carousel projector, the room usually has to be darkened. Unfortunately, this means that the illuminated screen becomes the center of attention rather than you. One major disadvantage of using transparencies, document cameras, or slides is that often you must speak from where your equipment is located. If you have to stand behind listeners or in the middle of the audience to run the projector, you will be talking to someone's back. If remote-controlled equipment is not available, your best solution may be to practice having a classmate change the projections or slides on cue.

Most transparencies and slides are now prepared on personal computers. You can purchase transparency sheets for use with most printers. You also can draw or print your material onto plain paper and convert it to a transparency on a copying machine. If you have access to only a black-and-white copier or printer, you can add color with opaque markers. Framing your transparencies will avoid glare from light showing around the outside edges of the projection.

When you arrange slides in a carousel, be sure they are in the proper order and that none of them is upside down and/or backwards. Today, most personal computers are packaged with software that allows you to prepare and present slides without a carousel projector. We discuss this in greater detail in our section on new media.

Video and Audio Resources.   Such video resources as DVDs and videotapes and such audio resources as MP3 or computer recordings and audiotapes can add variety to your presentation. Make sure in advance that the place where you will be making your presentation has the proper equipment to work with your materials.

Video resources are useful for transporting the audience to distant, dangerous, or otherwise unavailable locations. Although you could verbally describe the beauty of the Montana Rockies, your word-pictures can become more powerful if reinforced with actual scenes projected electronically.

Using video poses some special problems for speakers. Moving images attract more attention than does the spoken word, so they can easily upstage you. In a short speech, keep the focus on the speaker by limiting clips to thirty seconds or less. A videotape segment must be edited so that splices blend cleanly. Such editing takes special skill and equipment. A simpler means is to transfer this material onto a CD, which can be done on most personal computers with a DVD/CD burner. For certain topics, carefully prepared videos can be more effective than any other type of presentation aid. A student at Northwest Mississippi Community College who was a firefighter used videotape in an informative speech on fire hazards in the home. By customizing the video to fit the precise needs of his speech, he was able to show long shots of a room and then zoom in on various hazards.[12] He prepared the video without sound so that his speech provided the commentary needed to interpret and explain the pictures. Using this technique, he made his subject much more meaningful for listeners.

Audio resources may also be useful as presentation aids. Sabrina Karic started her self-introductory speech on growing up in war-torn Bosnia and Herzegovina with a recording of a loud explosion and gunfire, during which she ducked beneath the table as the audience jumped (see "A Little Chocolate" at the end of Chapter 3). When in doubt about the wisdom or practicality of using such aids, consult your instructor.

SPEAKER'S
notes   Deciding What Presentation Media to Use

Let the following suggestions guide your selection of presentation media.

When you need to . . .	try using . . .
■ adapt to audience feedback	■ flip charts or chalk or marker boards
■ display maps, charts, graphs, or textual graphics	■ posters or computerized programs
■ present complex information or statistical data	■ handouts
■ display graphics or photos to a large audience	■ slides or transparencies
■ authenticate a point	■ audio and video resources
■ make your presentation appear more professional	■ computerized programs

PowerPoint, Prezi, iPad Apps, and More

Computer-generated presentations have become ubiquitous. When properly designed and used well, they can bring together text, numbers, pictures, music, video clips, and artwork, all of which can be made into slides, videos, animations, and audio materials in a polished, compelling way. Used poorly—as with the complicated slide of Afghanistan war strategy described in our opening vignette—they will bore, confuse, and annoy your audience, and perhaps you as well. Rebecca Ganzel in *Presentations* magazine pictured the following scenario:

> It's that nightmare again—the one in which you're trapped in the Electronic Presentation from Hell. The familiar darkness presses in, periodically sliced in half by a fiendish light. Bullet points, about 18 to a slide, career in all directions. You cringe, but the slides keep coming, too fast to read, each with a new template you half-remember seeing a hundred times before: Dad's Tie! Sixties Swirls! Infinite Double-Helixes! A typewriter clatters; brakes squeal. Somewhere in the shadows, a voice drones on. Strange stick people shake hands and dance around a flow chart. Typefaces morph into Word Art.
>
> But the worst is yet to come. As though you're watching a train wreck in slow motion, you look down at your hand—and *you're holding the remote.*[13]

If swirling backgrounds and flashy transitions attract more attention than your ideas do, they will overpower your voice. Yet electronic presentation aids can provide vivid, engaging enhancements that bring your ideas alive for your audience. The major options among presentation software are summarized in Figure 10.12.

Watch at **MyCommunicationLab** Video: "Writing Position Papers"

Watch at **MyCommunicationLab** Video: "Group Presentation on Sleep"

FIGURE 10.12

Presentation Software

Software	Language	Visuals	Graphs	Animation	Sound	Video
PowerPoint	Yes	Yes	Yes	Yes	Yes	Yes
Prezi	Yes	Yes	Yes	Yes	Yes	Yes
HAIKU DECK	Yes	Yes	Yes	No	No	No
Perspective	Yes	Yes	Yes	Yes	Yes	Yes

▶ **computer-generated presentation**
The use of commercial presentation software to join audio, visual, textual, graphic, and animated components.

Moreover, in certain settings such presentation formats are simply expected. Using them well will set you apart from the countless speeches that commit "Death by PowerPoint."

PowerPoint Presentations and Their Cousins.

Undoubtedly, the most ubiquitous form of presentation software is PowerPoint. Why is PowerPoint so popular? For starters, it is the most widely available software of its type. It comes prepackaged on many computers sold to businesses and educational institutions. PowerPoint is also fairly easy to use. The software contains templates and comes with a step-by-step online tutorial. Apple's version of presentation software is Keynote. Some users—especially Mac devotees—find it more straightforward with better graphic design and multimedia interfaces than PowerPoint. However, some run into problems of incompatibility in a PowerPoint-dominated world.[14] Android users have a similar alternative in SoftMaker Presentations Mobile, an inexpensive app that can create PowerPoint-like slides on the go. As presentation software, it is a less agile cousin to PowerPoint, but it can also import PowerPoint shows from a variety of sources, including Dropbox and Google Drive. Although other programs are proliferating—for example, Apache OpenOffice, Symphony, Impress, Kingsoft Presentation Free, Google Presentation, and Zoho, to name a few—PowerPoint still dominates the market.

PowerPoint is not only the most used but also the most frequently *misused* type of presentation aid, in part *because* it is easy to use. Who has not been subjected to poor PowerPoint presentations that annoy the audience, mask the message, and harm the speaker's credibility? Peter Norvig, the director of research for Google, endured one too many of these suffocating speeches. He responded by creating a tongue-in-cheek PowerPoint version of the Gettysburg Address that "captured the main phrases of the original, while losing all the flow, eloquence, and impact."[15]

Yet used well, PowerPoint can be a powerful tool that amplifies your voice instead of masking it. Attorney Mark Lanier showed the potential of PowerPoint in a significant trial charging Merck, the company producing Vioxx, with causing the death of Bob Ernst. After addressing the jury and introducing them to Bob's widow, Carol (Lanier's client), the lawyer displayed a family photograph of the couple as he told anecdotes and family history. His next slide retained the image of the couple, but this time without the background, as he talked about what started to go wrong. The next slide showed Carol and the blank background, but now Bob's figure was replaced with a big black outline such as you see at murder scenes. Against this slide, Lanier told the jury that Bob Ernst was dead. By pairing verbal and visual storytelling, Lanier eventually won the trial for his client, even in a conservative part of the country not prone to award damages against a large company.[16]

Using PowerPoint well requires an understanding that it is fundamentally a *visual* medium. Moreover, it is a *design* medium rather than a brainstorming medium. If your first instinct is to create your speech in PowerPoint, step away from the computer, and reconsider. If your second instinct is to cut and paste what you've written, step away from the computer, and reconsider. Presentation designer Garr Reynolds observes that, if you attempt to merge a document for a written presentation into slides for an oral presentation, all you end up with is a "slideument" that doesn't serve either purpose well.[17] And if you do end up with a "slideument," your audience will read faster than you can speak, and in the process everyone—including you—will be bored. As graphic designer Robin Williams notes, "The problem is not really that you are reading the slide—*the problem is that you have put everything you're going to say on that slide.*"[18]

When Amazon CEO Jeff Bezos introduced the Kindle Fire HD, he wanted to emphasize that the new version of the e-reader had an eight-week battery life. He might have put it as one entry in a long line of bulleted points. Snooze! To pack a greater punch, Bezos showed a calendar with the months September and October. September 6, which was the day of his presentation, was highlighted in red. Bezos explained that if turned on during his presentation, the Kindle Fire's 8 week battery would last until the end of October. That's a powerful image that most likely will not be forgotten.[19]

Gabrielle Wallace used a similar approach in her informative speech on the apparent contradiction of the French eating and drinking well but rarely gaining weight. Rather than using PowerPoint to list her thesis, detail her main points, and repeat her quotations, she paired her discussion of how the French dine with photographs of red wine, fruits, vegetables, and bread. Instead of putting her pre-lunch audience to sleep, she had us drooling over her vibrant visual images and hanging on her every word.

Conceptualizing your PowerPoint as a fundamentally visual presentation aid is an important first step. In addition, other basic principles can help you find your voice:

- Follow the *basics of preparation* detailed in the next section, with particular attention to using a simple template, contrasting colors, clear images, and minimal language. Avoid the temptation of using the numerous overwrought templates available.

- *Pare your language* to the absolute minimum. The rule of thumb is no more than six lines, with no more than six words per line—but that does not mean that you should cram thirty-six words onto a slide. Focus on your key words, and determine whether, like Jeff Bezos, you would get a bigger bang from "eight weeks' worth of battery life" or a highlighted calendar.

- As you design the slides, *step back from the computer* to get a better idea of how it will look to your audience. Nancy Duarte of Duarte Designs suggests measuring your computer screen diagonally and then translating inches into feet: For a 17-inch computer screen, for example, stand 17 feet away. That will give you a better way to gauge the visibility of your slides when they are projected than you have by sitting right next to the monitor.[20]

- If one slide contains material that you will discuss sequentially, such as before-and-after pictures or the bulleted list of Figure 10.9, *use the "entrance" code* to make subsequent portions appear at the click of the mouse. Structure each slide similar to a billboard, for which you only have three seconds to process the information as you zoom by.[21]

- At the points in your presentation when you do not need an aid, *insert blank slides* so that your audience will not be distracted.

- Make sure that your slides don't overwhelm your presentation. You don't want your speech to become just a voice-over for a slide show.

- Be sure to *proofread* your slides carefully—and have others proofread for you as well. It's really embarrassing, distracting, and harmful to your ethos to have major typos projected for all to see.

- *Check your presentation in the room* where you will present. What's clear when it's right in front of you on the computer may appear murky when it's projected.

FIGURE 10.13
How *Not* to Use PowerPoint

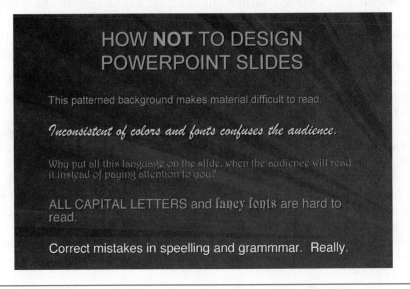

HOW **NOT** TO DESIGN POWERPOINT SLIDES

This patterned background makes material difficult to read.

Inconsistent of colors and fonts confuses the audience.

Why put all this language on the slide, when the audience will read it instead of paying attention to you?

ALL CAPITAL LETTERS and fancy fonts are hard to read.

Correct mistakes in speelling and grammmar. Really.

- After you've finalized your presentation, *save it as "PowerPoint Show"* so that you can immediately open to the first slide rather than having to click your way into it.

Slate's technology columnist Farhad Manjoo observes, "When people write annoying e-mails or make inscrutable spreadsheets, we don't blame Outlook and Excel; we blame the people. But for many of us, PowerPoint software is synonymous with the terrible output it often generates."[22] Follow the guidelines above, and you will give a good name to PowerPoint and a better name to yourself. Avoid committing "suislide" by displaying a PowerPoint slide like that in Figure 10.13.[23] The tutorials accompanying PowerPoint often encourage the use of busy templates, bullet points, animation schemes, and other distractions; choose wisely, with your audience in mind.

A Prezi presentation on the historic sites and monuments along the Boston Freedom Trail might use the trail's emblem as the primary organizing visual image.

Prezi Presentations. Whereas PowerPoint uses a linear approach with one slide appearing after another, a newer entry called Prezi enables a three-dimensional approach to explore the interconnections. Rather than one slide following another, Prezi emphasizes interconnections and relationships by using a "canvas" on which you place your concepts. You can group ideas, layer concepts, zoom in to focus in more detail on one aspect, and then zoom out to return to the big picture. As with PowerPoint, you can incorporate images, videos, sound, and language. Dr. Scott Titsworth of Ohio University explains,

> Prezi allows you to visually travel inside ideas. As a child did you ever go into your backyard and use a magnifying glass to look at things? You get a broad view and then zoom down to see very fine details to learn more about the big picture. Prezi does that for you in presentations. You create everything for your presentation on a big canvas, and can embed smaller pictures or clusters of ideas within that larger picture (this can create some very cool surprises for those in the audience). . . . Prezi allows you to think about ways in which holistic visual designs can enhance and augment a spoken narrative.[24]

Prezi offers a visually stimulating, layered, almost cinematic approach to presentation aids. Katie Lovett used Prezi to develop a powerful persuasive speech against bottled water. She took her audience inside the marketing strategies, consumer misconceptions, and environmental effects, showing relationships and consequences in a dynamic way that had us mesmerized. Although she found it relatively easy to learn, she did caution that she so enjoyed playing with the software that she had to rein herself in. Other students have found it more difficult to figure out, particularly if they are unaccustomed to visualizing their information.

Graphic design professor Shawn Apostel suggests that good Prezis start with visual metaphors.[25] Those metaphors often form the overall shape of the presentation, either used at the beginning and ending or revealed only as a zoom-out at the conclusion. Examples include the influence of jazz bass players in the shape of a guitar, an explanation of the process of designing a new public school library displayed as a tree, and budgeting for a college student conceived as income versus debts on a set of scales. In each case, the Prezi moves from the macroscopic view to more microscopic perspectives. In the Prezi on jazz bass players, for example, the overview of the guitar then moves along the guitar's neck as a timeline, with various players placed along the frets in chronological order. Short video examples are embedded along the way.

Effective Prezis do not need to be this complicated, however. Apostel advises using shapes as simple as a circle or a square to frame your presentation or a background image such as a cloud.[26] Perhaps you want to take your audience on a guided tour of the Boston Freedom Trail, from Boston Common to Faneuil Hall to the Old North Church. You could use the medallion embedded in the streets as your background and then move to each site with photographs of buildings and people, dates, quotations, and a brief song from the era.

Give your audience the overview at the outset, to serve as a visual preview, and then move through each point in turn. If you prepare your audience for movements among areas and use big jumps in perspective sparingly, they will mean more, and your audience won't suffer motion sickness.

Using Prezi does pose certain challenges. With its constant changes, Prezi does not serve longer presentations well, as it's likely to cause "Prezilepsy."[27] Like Keynote fans in a PowerPoint world, not all technology is equally receptive. Some Prezi users report that the presentations work better on Macs than on PCs; others have not been able to get the program to work with a remote control mouse. Prezi.com contains a description, tutorials, and sample presentations on a wide variety of topics. The basic format is available to the public free of charge; students and educators can receive a more advanced free version by registering. Apostel offers a useful tutorial about design for Prezi, in Prezi, that can guide your development of a presentation aid that you can find on Prezi.com. One caution about examples of Prezis online: Many are designed as self-contained messages as opposed to a presentation aid, so they include far too much text to be used for a speech.

iPad Apps.

Two applications may be especially useful for iPad aficionados: Haiku Deck and Pixxa Perspective. *Haiku Deck* draws its name from a form of Japanese poetry that is beautiful and evocative in its simplicity. That form evokes the goal of this software's developers: The three young men from Seattle wanted a format for iPads that would be clean, concise, and fun. Key to the success of Haiku Deck: the numerous ways to incorporate images—from your own iPad, from websites (including social media), or from their vast store of illustrations available through Creative Commons without copyright entanglements and with automatic attribution. Searching that store of illustrations proves as simple as typing in a key word or two—for example, "mountains" or "winter scenes"—and looking through the options.

This easy access to visual images combines with sharp constraints on the amount of language that can be included on each slide. Haiku Deck allows only two lines of language and only five items per bulleted list. Such "radical simplicity," as one user calls it, can be both an advantage and a disadvantage: Although the software emphasizes clean, clear visual storytelling, it may create challenges for those who are not comfortable working within its restrictions.[28] In addition, its current version does not allow for sound, transitions, or animations, although these capacities may be added soon.

Haiku Deck is free, with additional resources available for a small fee. Online tutorials and blogs can assist in the construction of slide decks. Currently, it can be used only on iPads and will not work even on other Apple products (although pressure is growing for its accessibility on other platforms). You can export your presentation to PowerPoint or Keynote after uploading it on the Haiku Deck site, or you can share it via Facebook, Twitter, or e-mail—a handy way to get additional guidance from your instructor before the presentation.

A second application for iPads is *Pixxa Perspective*. Unlike the predominantly free Haiku Deck, after one free story (which you can edit numerous times) Pixxa Perspective costs roughly $20 to $100. Yet for that charge, Perspective provides the capacity for not only text, images, and diagrams for each "scene" or slide but also "interactive motion charts." If you wanted to show, for instance, the relationship between tuition costs and initial salaries after graduation, you could post a graph and then put it in motion to show the changes in the correlations or to pass through the data from various years. A spreadsheet can be turned into charts quickly. Perspective has also added the capacities to incorporate both sound and video.

Like Haiku Deck, Perspective presentations are available only for iPads and can be tweeted and e-mailed. Unlike Haiku Deck, wireless connections may allow projection to a large screen, and Perspective can be used to record your presentation for playback and analysis.

As you might imagine, some users—especially those who are not familiar with the technology—may find that Perspective poses more challenges to learn than Haiku Deck, even with online assistance. In either case, adapt the guidelines for developing effective PowerPoint presentations, and prepare for the prospect that the techno-gremlins that lurk in *any* technology may wreak havoc, especially for people who are not as comfortable with the software and nervous about their presentations to boot.

What Will They Think of Next?

Although PowerPoint, its younger relative Prezi, and new iPad arrivals overshadow other presentation media, other technologies that can be incorporated into speeches spring up regularly. Clickers, for example, can be used during an informative speech to let the listeners test themselves on their knowledge of the topic or during a persuasive speech to identify how audience members react to particular ideas and proposals. PowerPoint now comes in a version for tablets, and smartphones have an app for that.

One commencement speaker made an ingenious use of modern technology. Addressing graduates at Queens University of Charlotte, Eric Newton of the non-profit Knight Foundation showed them brief videos about three nonprofit organizations and then asked them to use their cell phones to text their choice of the three. The winning organization received a $50,000 check on the spot. Newton then challenged the graduates:

> Doesn't it feel good to give? . . . Tonight, my hope is that students walk away with a clearer understanding of the incredible power of digital media. We have the ability, at our fingertips, to make an instant difference in the lives of those in need, and it is our responsibility as noble citizens to do just that.[29]

By asking the graduates to bring their cell phones (not that they needed much urging), Newton created suspense. By asking them to vote and then acting on the results, he involved the audience in an immediate way. By showing them what a difference their digital involvement made, he capitalized on the opportunity to demonstrate that small actions have big consequences and that each person can indeed make a difference.

Technological innovations proliferate at such a rapid pace that from the beginning of any given semester to its end, more presentation media will probably appear. Tried and true or new and sexy, presentation aids can help you find your voice if you prepare and use them well.

Preparing Presentation Aids

The types of aids and media you use are far less important than expressing your ideas well so that your audience understands them. And that brings us to how you prepare your presentation aids. As the discussion so far suggests, presentation aids can either make or break a speech. Thinking carefully about how they will contribute to your presentation makes the difference. Take the time to consider how particular presentation aids can enliven and enrich your presentation. This process will require time to let your ideas "incubate," grow, and develop.[30]

If your first instinct in developing a presentation aid is to plop yourself in front of a computer, *stop*. Design specialists recommend good old-fashioned pencil and paper, or the ever-handy sticky notes, for your initial ideas.[31] That way you can easily move among the possibilities, rearrange your options, and create presentation aids that will strengthen your voice. Once you have selected the appropriate types of aids and media to give voice to your ideas, create them following basic principles of design and color. "If the content . . . can't be understood because of poor design," PowerPoint consultant Dave Paradi points out, "there is no way it can be an aid to the presenter."[32]

Principles of Design

A good presentation aid is simple, easily seen, appropriately focused, and well balanced. Consider the basic principles of *simplicity*, *visibility*, *emphasis*, and *balance* as you plan and prepare your materials. Look at your aids from the perspective of an audience member, and see if they meet these criteria. As graphic designer Alex W.

White quips, "One definition of good design is the balance between monotony and the designer's self-indulgence."[33]

Simplicity.   Many speakers—novices and professionals alike—try to cram too much information into a single presentation aid. Too much information distracts listeners as they try to figure out what everything is and what it means. We had one student divide a standard 2- by 3-foot poster into twelve segments, glue samples of medicinal herbs in each box, and then print its name and use under each sample. Needless to say, only listeners in the front row could actually read any of the print, and the aid created more confusion than illumination. He would have been better served had he used a series of smaller posters, each featuring one herb, displayed as he talked about each one in turn.

Consider how much language is really necessary on your aid. Think back to the opening of this chapter: As a listener, would you be more engaged by the speaker reading a slide with the definition of dyslexia from *Black's Medical Dictionary* or by the visualization of what a dyslexic might see? You might be tempted to use moving objects, flying text, or repeated sound effects. Surveys report that these "special effects" regularly make the Top Ten list of annoying presentation features.[34]

Visibility.   The size of any presentation aid must be appropriate to the setting in which it is used. Listeners in the back of the room must be able to see your presentation aid without straining. Bringing a full-sized canoe into a small room will prove both cumbersome for you and overwhelming for your listeners. Bringing a six-inch model or photograph of a canoe may be more manageable, but those beyond the first row will be irritated that they can't see it.

Visual images cannot have a strong impact if they cannot be deciphered. That photograph of your first date might be a riot, but if most of your audience can't tell who's in it or what the setting is, you'll have to figure out a better way to share it. You may love the way a chart of the impact of a tornado ripping through Oklahoma represents its complexity and the scope of the disaster, but if your audience can't make heads or tails of the elaborate connections, it will drown out your own voice.

Make sure the words are clearly legible, or risk committing another sin from the Top Ten.[35] For slides, for example, use at least a 24 point type font for titles, 14 point for subtitles, and 12 point for other text. Use an easily read typeface that emphasizes your ideas rather than itself. Garr Reynolds points out that your audiences may not even be aware of it, but "the type face says something about your content, and even about you."[36] Examine how the different typefaces in Figure 10.14 convey different personalities and meanings. On rare occasions, you might employ one of the fancier fonts, but as a rule stick to those that are clearly legible from a distance. If you're writing or drawing on a poster, the board, or a flip chart, use wide markers in strong colors to make sure that those in the back of the room can see clearly.

Members of your audience need to be able to easily read visual materials; they

FIGURE 10.14

Empowering your voice:	Shouting over your voice:
Baskerville	**Algerian**
Bodoni	*Brush Script*
Franklin Gothic	Curlz
Garamond	Old English
Rockwell	**Snap**

need to be able to easily hear audio materials. If the sound of a recording or video is so soft that your listeners can't hear, then your point about the differences in hip-hop styles will be lost. If it's too loud, you risk blasting them out of the room.

Emphasis. Your presentation aids should emphasize what your speech emphasizes. Your listeners' eyes should be drawn immediately to what you want to illustrate. On the acronym chart (see Figure 10.10), the first letter of each word stands out. The map of Yellowstone Park mentioned earlier contained only the attractions the speaker planned to talk about and the route between them. Had she added pictures of bears to indicate grizzly habitats, drawings of fish to show trout streams, and photos of mountains to designate the terrain, the presentation aid would have seemed cluttered and distracting.

Choose only the aspects of the image, the language, or the sounds that are most directly relevant to the point you want to make, and focus on those. Full sentences and complex diagrams also make the dreaded Top Ten list.[37] As designer Robin Williams advises, you want to "get rid of superfluous stuff. You don't need all kinds of gewgaws sitting on your slide cluttering up your information."[38] Illustrating the workings of an airplane cockpit will make more sense to your audience if you highlight each control as you discuss it.[39] When in doubt, leave the details out. Let your spoken words provide the elaboration.

Balance. Presentation aids that are balanced are pleasing to the eye. You achieve balance when you position textual materials so that they form a consistent pattern. Don't overload a slide or try to use every square inch of a poster board. White space frames the material and helps focus your audience's attention. On computer-generated slides, you should leave blank space at both the top and the bottom and have equal side margins. The unbalanced and cluttered slide in Figure 10.13 violates all of the principles of design, while the slide in Figure 10.14 illustrates a balanced design.

Principles of Color

As many of the illustrations in this chapter show, color adds impact to presentation aids. Most color presentation aids attract and hold attention better than black-and-white ones. Color also can convey or enhance meaning. A speech about crop damage from a drought, for example, might use an enlarged outline map with natural colors to reinforce the message: the least affected areas in green, moderately damaged areas in orange, and severely affected areas in brown.

Color can also be used to create moods and impressions. Figure 10.15 shows some of the reactions that various groups might have toward colors. For most Americans, blue suggests power, authority, and stability (blue chip, blue ribbon, royal blue). Using blue in your graphics can evoke positive

FIGURE 10.15
Meanings of Colors

	Movie-goers	Financiers	Doctors
Blue	Tender emotions	Reliable	Cold
Green	Playful	Profitable	Infection
Yellow	Happy	Highlighted/important	Jaundice
Red	Exciting	Unprofitable	Hot/radioactive

Source: *How to Lie with Charts*, 2000

reactions toward a proposal. Red signals excitement or crisis (in the red, red ink, "I saw red"). Line graphs tracing a rise in campus crimes could be drawn in red to convey the urgency of the problem. On the other hand, you should avoid using red when presenting financial data unless you want to focus on debts or losses. In American culture, green is associated with both money (greenbacks) and environmental concerns (Greenpeace), but medical personnel associate it with infection. Cultural differences also influence how people interpret colors. In the United States, for example, white is associated with weddings, baptisms, confirmations, and other joyous rituals. In Japan, however, white is a funeral color, associated with sadness. Going online to Visually.com can enable you to explore more culturally based color associations.

The way you use colors in combination can convey subtle nuances of meaning. An **analogous color scheme** uses colors that are adjacent in the color spectrum, such as green, blue-green, and blue. This type of color scheme shows the differences among elements, while also suggesting their close connection and compatibility. For example, a pie graph could use analogous colors to represent the students, faculty, and administration of a university. The different colors suggest that, although these parts are separate, they belong together. In this subtle way, the presentation aid implies that these components of a university should work together.

A **complementary color scheme** uses colors that are opposites on the color wheel, such as red and green. Complementary color schemes suggest tension and opposition among elements in a speech. Because they heighten the sense of drama, they may enliven informative speaking and encourage change in persuasive speaking.

A **monochromatic color scheme** uses variations of a single color. The acronym graphic (Figure 10.10) uses a monochromatic color scheme. These schemes suggest variety within unity. A monochromatic color scheme would be inappropriate for bar graphs or line graphs because they require more contrast to be effective.

Figure 10.16 illustrates these three types of color schemes. Find an online tool to assist with color choices at colorschemedesigner.com.

The colors you use for text in a presentation aid should contrast with the background. As Figure 10.13 demonstrates, patterned or shaded backgrounds can make words difficult to read. Generally, light-colored backgrounds contrast clearly with strong primary colors such as blue and green. However, don't use red letters against a light background. Red tends to bleed, making the words blurry and difficult to read, and a light background can create glare. Therefore, you might want to use a strong primary color for the background and have the text or other graphic elements printed in white, especially in a bright room.

Color contrast is especially important for computer-generated slides and transparencies. Because projection creates a lower resolution, colors will appear less distinct when projected than they do when seen on a computer monitor. Such colors as pastel pink, light blue, and pale yellow or hues with a grayish tinge may not be strong enough for good graphic emphasis in any type of presentation aid. The rich burgundy background that looks so great on your computer might look more like muddy water once it is projected. Run a sample, and

FIGURE 10.16 **Types of Color Schemes**

Color Schemes

ANALOGOUS	COMPLEMENTARY	MONOCHROMATIC
students	problem	beginning
faculty	solution	middle
administration		end

▶ **analogous color scheme** Colors adjacent on the color wheel; used in a presentation aid to suggest both differences and close relationships among the components.

▶ **complementary color scheme** Colors opposite one another on the color wheel; used in a presentation aid to suggest tension and opposition.

▶ **monochromatic color scheme** Use of variations of a single color in a presentation aid to convey the idea of variety within unity.

project it to see how the final colors will actually look to an audience. If the results are not what you expected, try other colors until you are satisfied. Keep uppermost in your mind the maxim from designer Garr Reynolds: "think communication—not decoration."[40]

SPEAKER'S notes   Checklist for Preparing Presentation Aids

Each presentation aid should meet these criteria:

_____ My aid emphasizes a key point in my presentation.

_____ I have limited myself to one major idea per aid.

_____ My aid is easy to see (or hear).

_____ My presentation aid is as simple as I can make it.

_____ My images and print are large enough to be seen from the back of the room.

_____ I have good color contrast on my aid.

_____ I use colors and lettering consistently.

_____ I have ample margins at the top, bottom, and sides of my aid.

_____ I have checked for spelling errors.

_____ I have checked the room where I will give my speech and know that my presentation aid will work there.

_____ I know how I will show each aid at the appropriate point and how I will hide it before and after.

Using Presentation Aids

Even the best-designed presentation aid requires skillful use to enhance a speech. As we discussed each type of presentation aid, we made suggestions on how to use it in a speech. Here, we bring these suggestions together and extract some general guidelines.

Explore at **MyCommunicationLab** Activity: "Presentational Aids"

Watch at **MyCommunicationLab** Video: "Using Presentation Aids"

Be sure to practice using your presentation aids so that you don't end up fumbling around when you are making your presentation. Try them out as you practice your speech. Plan transitions such as, "As you can see on this chart . . ." to integrate the material into your message. Be sure that you aren't committing the number one sin on the Top Ten list of annoying presentations: reading directly from your slides.[41]

Well before your speaking time, check out the site to determine the logistics. Step back and inspect your presentation aid from the back row of your audience. Can you read it without straining? Is everything spelled correctly? Is your eye drawn to what is most important? Have you positioned your material so that it looks good? Do the images look balanced? Have you included credit for the sources of the material? Check out any electronic equipment you will use (e.g., computer, document camera, or DVD player) in advance of your presentation, and practice using it in the room in which you will speak. Do you need an extension cord or a remote mouse? Can you control the level of light in the room so your presentation aids can be seen and you can as well? What works on your personal computer, for example, might not work on the classroom computer. Be certain that any equipment in the classroom is working properly and that you can operate it. If you are using computerized materials on a CD, DVD, or jump drive, be sure that it is compatible with the

FIGURE 10.17
The Dos and Don'ts of Using Presentation Aids

Do	Don't
1. Practice using your aids.	1. Try to "wing it" using your aids.
2. Display aids only when referring to them.	2. Leave aids in view throughout speech.
3. Stand to the side of aid as you speak.	3. Stand in front of aid as you speak.
4. Point to what is important on aid.	4. Make listeners search for what's important.
5. Maintain eye contact with listeners.	5. Deliver your speech to your aid.
6. Distribute handouts after your speech.	6. Distribute handouts during speech.
7. Limit the number of aids in your speech.	7. Become a voice-over for a slide show.

equipment in the room. For objects, models, posters, flip charts, and other physical aids, determine where or how you will conceal your aid both before and after you use it and how you will display it. Do you need an easel for a poster board or flip chart? Should you bring masking tape or push pins?

As the previous paragraph indicates, it's important that you not display your presentation aid until you are ready to use it; otherwise, it will distract your audience. When you have finished using the aid, once again cover or conceal it. A blank screen will not compete with your voice; a display of what you've already covered or are about to discuss will. Don't stand directly in front of your presentation aid; rather, stand to the side of it, and maintain eye contact with listeners. You want them to see both you and your presentation aid. As you refer to something on the presentation aid, point to what you are talking about: Don't leave your audience searching for what you are describing. Never deliver your speech to your presentation aid; it doesn't care what you're saying! Instead, maintain eye contact with your listeners, who *do* care.

Do not distribute materials during your speech. If you have prepared handouts, the best time to distribute them usually comes after you speak. Don't pass around pictures or objects for listeners to examine. You want them to focus on you and your message, not on your presentation aid.

Try to anticipate what might go wrong. Before each speech, review the list of what to do and what to avoid in Figure 10.17. Consider how you will handle the situation if the techno-gremlins are at play, or the vase that is the centerpiece of your presentation breaks, or the downpour on the way to class smudges your charts. Foresight will enable you to address the situation more calmly.

Ethical Considerations for Using Presentation Aids

Presentation aids can enlighten a message, but they can also mislead listeners. As with any aspect of speaking, you make choices with your presentation aids, and you should be aware of the ethical implications of those choices. Charts and graphs, for example, can be rigged so that they misrepresent reality.[42] As Figure 10.18 shows,

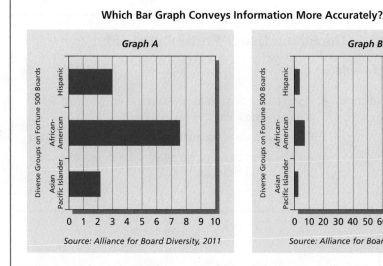
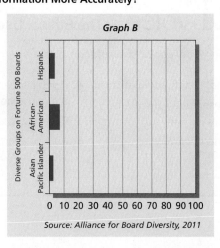

Which Bar Graph Conveys Information More Accurately?

FIGURE 10.18
Bar Graphs That Are Misleading and Not Misleading in Presenting the Same Material

one version of a graph suggests that people of color represent a significant number of board members for Fortune 500 companies, while the other stresses the minimal nature of those numbers.[43] Make sure your presentation aid presents the information in an appropriate context.

You also want to credit your sources on your presentation aids. Be sure to include this information in smaller (but still visible) letters at the bottom of any material you plan to display, as Figure 10.18 shows. Citing your source on your presentation aid verifies the information presented and reminds you to mention the source in your oral presentation.

Some of the most interesting ethical questions involve the use of film and visual materials. For example, the most famous photographer of the Civil War, Mathew Brady, rearranged bodies on the battlefield to enhance the impact of his pictures. Eighty years later, another American war photographer carefully staged the now celebrated photograph of U.S. Marines planting the flag at Iwo Jima.[44] Sixty years after that, *Newsweek* placed Martha Stewart's head on a slimmer body to imply that she had lost weight during her time in prison.[45] On one hand, these famous images are fabrications: They pretend to be what they are not. On the other hand, they bring home reality more forcefully. In other words, the form of the photos may be a lie, but the lie may reveal a deeper truth. So are these photographs unethical, or are they simply artistic?

With today's technology, the potential for abuse looms ever larger. Video and audio editing easily produces illusions of reality. Consider how moviemakers depicted Forrest Gump shaking hands with Presidents Kennedy, Johnson, and Nixon. Notice how televised political commercials often use a shot from a video that catches an opponent with eyes half shut or mouth gaping open. In movies and ads, such distortions might be easily discerned; we know the images are constructed, so they don't do as much damage. In real life, however, they can be dangerous. When doctored images are passed off as actual objects or events, as when television networks or newspapers "stage" crashes to make their stories more dramatic, they can be

YOUR ethical VOICE   The Ethical Use of Presentation Aids

Follow these guidelines to avoid unethical use of presentation aids:

1. Be certain charts or graphs do not distort information.
2. Be aware of how the visual representation of material suggests a particular perspective.
3. Never manipulate visual images to deceive your audience.
4. If you alter an image to reveal some deeper truth, let the audience know.
5. Cite the source of your information on a presentation aid.
6. As a listener, be on guard against the power of presentation aids to trick you.

quite deceptive.[46] We have been conditioned by experience and taught by tradition to trust the "reality" revealed by our eyes and ears. Blindly accepting the adage that "seeing is believing" can make us prey for unscrupulous manipulators.

To be an ethical communicator, you should alert your listeners to an illusion whenever you manipulate images so that they reveal your message more forcefully. You should also be able to defend your "creation" as a "better representation" of the truth. As a listener, you should develop a skeptical attitude about images and seek additional evidence if there is any question concerning their validity.

FINAL reflections   Amplifying Your Voice

When poorly conceived, designed, and used, presentation aids can overpower your voice. We once had a student who volunteered with the local rescue squad. He gave a persuasive speech urging his classmates to join the squad. After his introduction, he announced, "Now we are all going outside," where we found an emergency vehicle. While the speaker tried to tell listeners about the equipment, they were climbing in and out of the vehicle. He lost their attention completely and was never able to complete his speech.

When well conceived, designed, and used, presentation aids can empower your voice, giving nuance, power, and character to your speech. In her informative speech on the fashions typical of the three major tribes of her native Nigeria, Dolapo Olushola used an imaginative mix of a map, photographs, and fabrics to help her audience understand the cultural significance of clothing. Seeing the quality of the actual materials, as well as how they created distinctive styles of dress, created visual immediacy and appreciation.

Imagine yourself as a member of the audience: What kind of aid would help you as a listener? What would engage your interest, increase your understanding, and improve your retention? How could the speaker share enthusiasm for a topic in creative ways? And what would be overkill?

And always remember the bottom line: A presentation aid should *aid* the presentation, not *be* the presentation.

After Reading This Chapter, You Should Be Able To Answer These Questions

Study and
Review at
MyCommunicationLab

1 How can presentation aids help your speech? How can they be problematic?
2 How do you decide which type of presentation aid you should use?
3 What are the advantages and disadvantages of using the different kinds of media as means of producing presentation aids?
4 How do you plan and design effective presentation aids?
5 What are the guidelines for using presentation aids well?

For Discussion and Further Exploration

1 Your speech assignment includes the requirement to use a presentation aid. Consider how you will approach the assignment to maximize the effect of your presentation aid. Make some notes on what you would illustrate with which types of aids and why, and then share these with your classmates. If they disagree with your choices, what does that suggest about how you need to adapt to your audience?

2 You want to give a speech about backpacking in Colorado. For what aspects of the speech might you use a person, an object, a model, and a picture?

3 Select a speech from Appendix B, and prepare a rough draft of a presentation aid that might have been used with it. Consider how the aid might have helped the speech and what considerations of design and use would influence its effectiveness.

4 Return to the topics presented at the end of Chapter 8 on supporting materials. What types of presentation aids would effectively amplify your voice for each of these topics?
   a. We should increase spending on preschool education.
   b. We should cut taxes paid by small business owners.
   c. Security measures on campus are inadequate.
   d. We should emphasize restoring the environment over creating jobs and providing health care.
   e. The use of drones in modern warfare is permissible.

   Explain the types of aids you would use as well as the presentation media you would choose, and defend your choices.

5 Now that you've decided which types of presentation aids would be the most effective for each of the topics in question 4, explore the implications of your means of presentation. For example, what would be the advantages and disadvantages of using a poster or a transparency as opposed to a PowerPoint or Prezi?

6 Select one of the presentation aids you have developed for questions 4 and 5, and explain how you would prepare it using the principles of design and color.

7 Like an international PowerPoint version of a chess match, Pecha Kucha uses a "20×20" rule: 20 PowerPoint slides automatically shown for only 20 seconds each, requiring the presenter to hone a carefully crafted presentation to fit six minutes and forty seconds. Go to the Pecha Kucha website, select an example, and determine how well the speaker uses PowerPoint.

8 Go online to a site like TED, and find a presentation using presentation aids. How appropriate are the aids to the presentation? How well designed are they? How well does the speaker use the aids? Do the presentation aids appear to present the material ethically?

Objectives

This chapter will help you

1. Understand the differences between oral and written language

2. Understand how words can shape our perceptions and feelings

3. Grasp how words can influence how and whether we act

4. Understand how words can express our values and identity

5. Apply six standards for effective language use

6. Identify and use figurative language for special impact

7. Learn how other language techniques can magnify the power of expression

OUTLINE

11 Putting Words to Work

Listen to
Chapter 11 at
MyCommunicationLab

> *Give me the right word and the right accent, and I will move the world.*
>
> —JOSEPH CONRAD

A legislator was asked how he felt about whiskey. He replied, "If, when you say whiskey, you mean the Devil's brew, the poison scourge, the bloody monster that defiles innocence, dethrones reason, creates misery and poverty—yes, literally takes the bread from the mouths of little children; if you mean the drink that topples Christian man and woman from the pinnacle of righteous, gracious living into the bottomless pit of degradation, despair, shame and helplessness, then certainly I am against it with all my power.

"But if, when you say whiskey, you mean the oil of conversation, the philosophic wine, the ale that is consumed when good fellows get together, that puts a song in their hearts and the warm glow of contentment in their eyes; if you mean Christmas cheer; if you mean the stimulating drink that puts the spring in an old gentleman's step on a frosty morning; if you mean that drink, the sale of which pours into our treasury untold millions of dollars which are used to provide tender care for our crippled children, our blind, our deaf, our dumb, pitiful, aged and infirm, to build highways, hospitals, and schools, then certainly I am in favor of it.

"That is my stand, and I will not compromise."[1]

The "Whiskey Speech," a legend in southern politics, was originally presented some years ago by N. S. Sweat, Jr., during a heated campaign to legalize the sale of liquor-by-the-drink in Mississippi. Because about half of his constituents favored the initiative and the other half were opposed, Representative "Soggy" Sweat decided to handle the issue with humor. In the process he provided an illustration of how words can extend or transform meaning.

In this chapter, we discuss how to make language work for you. We explain six standards for the effective and ethical use of language in your speeches. We end by exploring special techniques you can use to magnify the power of your voice.

What Words Can Do

Consider Joseph Conrad's eloquent statement about the power of language at the beginning of this chapter. Until speakers find the right words, they will not find their voice. Before speakers can move the world, or anyone in it, they must first discover what they believe and the importance of their subjects. It is words that form, frame, and express these understandings.

Words can reveal the world in many ways. They can arouse or dull our feelings. They can be magnets that draw us together or drive us apart. They can goad us into action. They make up the rituals that celebrate who we are and what we believe. Clearly, words are vital not just in finding our voice but also in helping us express ourselves.

The ability to use words effectively is one of the most important skills you will ever acquire. Most of us think in words, and the words of our language shape the way we think. For example, in most parts of the United States, we have just one word for and one conception of snow. However, in the Far North, where snow is much more frequent, indigenous people have many words to describe different types of snow.

Language also is a major part of our cultural identity. This becomes most evident when a language faces the possibility of extinction. D. Y. Begay, a prominent Navajo weaver and art curator, noted, "My father says when you stop speaking the language is when you stop being Navajo."[2]

What Makes Oral Language Special

To understand the special power of oral language, we must contrast it with written language.

- **Oral language is less formal.** A journalist might write, "One thousand, two hundred fifteen students dropped out of Bay County high schools last year." A speaker, communicating the same information, would more likely say, "More than twelve hundred students dropped out of Bay County high schools last year!" It's not really important that listeners know the exact number of cases. What's important is that they grasp the magnitude of the problem. Rounding off numbers helps listeners focus on the large picture.

- **Oral language is more colorful and intense.** These qualities are vital to the effectiveness of speaking, as many studies have demonstrated.[3] Sentence fragments and slang expressions can add to color and intensity and are more acceptable in speeches than in written discourse.

- **Oral language is more personal.** For speeches to be effective, the words must engage listeners personally. Speakers use inclusive pronouns, such as "we" and "us" to promote closeness with listeners. They may evoke a "you are there" feeling that helps listeners experience the action described in the speech. Notice how Stephanie Lamb, a student at the University of Arkansas, used words to create this sense of vicarious participation at the beginning of her speech:

    We've all seen it. Driving down the road in the heat of traffic in the early morning on your way to school or in the late afternoon during rush hour. You glance at the driver in the car beside you, and you see him talking on his cell phone and gesturing. The traffic picks up, but the driver is so absorbed in his cell phone conversation that he fails to notice that traffic has come to a stop. Wham! Another fender-bender.

Speakers often use such interactive language at the beginning of their speeches. They may ask rhetorical questions that engage listeners directly. Note how Davidson student BJ Youngerman drew in his listeners at the beginning of his speech in defense of Walmart:

    What if you could save over $900 a year on your grocery bill? What if you could save at least that much more on toys, clothes, and furniture? The fact is that if you shop at Wal-Mart on a regular basis, over the course of a year you do save that much money.

■ **The spoken word has different constraints.** Speakers must be sensitive to the limitations of audiences. Communication consultant Jerry Tarver reminds us that listeners cannot "reread" words that are spoken. Consequently, oral language must be simpler, and speakers often must use repetition to be understood. Speakers also may need to use more examples or narratives to make sure listeners get the point.[4]

These examples illustrate the informal, intense, and personal qualities of oral language. And, as we shall see in Chapter 12, speakers use pauses and changes in loudness and pitch to clarify and reinforce meaning. Such oral resources are not available in written communication.

SPEAKER'S notes Features of Oral Language

1. Oral language is less formal.
2. Oral language is more colorful.
3. Oral language is more personal.
4. Oral language is more interactive.

5. Oral language contains more repetition.
6. Oral language uses simpler sentence structure.
7. Oral language uses more examples and narratives.

Shaping Perceptions

To listen to speakers is to see the world as they see it. We look at subjects through the speaker's windows. But as the Renaissance scholar Francis Bacon once suggested, the glass in these windows may be enchanted. For example, the so-called "moonlight and magnolias" orators who were popular in the South after the Civil War offered idealized pictures of plantation life before the war. These false depictions both defended the pre-war slave society and justified post-war practices of segregation that treated the freed slaves as second-class citizens.

This may seem like ancient history, but such images of the past can linger into the present and influence behavior. In the deposition she offered in a 2013 suit alleging racist and sexist practices in her business dealings, Paula Deen, former cooking show host and Emmy Award winning television personality, revealed that she accepted the "moonlight and magnolias" fantasy as an accurate reflection of an era in national life:

> When asked if she wanted black men to play the role of slaves at a wedding she explained she got the idea from a restaurant her husband and she had dined at saying, "The whole entire waiter staff was middle-aged black men, and they had on beautiful white jackets with a black bow tie. "I mean, it was really impressive. That restaurant represented a certain era in America . . . after the Civil War, during the Civil War, before the Civil War . . . . It was not only black men, it was black women . . . I would say they were slaves."[5]

Obviously, this ability of words to shape perceptions can pose serious ethical problems. But this power can also serve positive functions. Shaping perceptions can be vital, for example, when listeners have no prior experience with the subject. When astronauts first walked on the moon, they had to communicate what they saw to our earthbound understandings. They had to describe what had never before been seen. The conversations between space and mission control are filled with passages like the following:

> I'm looking out here at this mountain and it's got—it looks like somebody has been out there plowing across the side of it. It's like one sort of terrace after another, right up the side.[6]

When speakers and listeners see subjects in different ways, words can close the gap that separates them.

Arousing Feelings

The words we use can arouse strong feelings and even change attitudes. This power of words is used ethically when it *strengthens* sound reasoning and credible evidence. It is abused when it *substitutes* appeals to feelings for evidence or reasoning. To arouse emotions, language must overcome barriers of time, distance, and apathy.

Overcoming Time.   Listeners live in the present. This makes it hard to awaken feelings about events that lie in the distant past or future. Skillful speakers use words to make the past and future come alive. Stories that recapture feelings from the past are often told at company meetings to re-create the human dimension of the business and to reestablish corporate heritage and culture. In the following story, the speaker reminds listeners of the legend of Federal Express, a pioneer in overnight delivery:

> It's hard to remember that Federal Express was once just a fly-by-night dream, a crazy idea in which a few people had invested—not just their time and their money but their lives and futures. I remember one time early on when things weren't going so well. Couldn't even make the payroll that week and looked like we were going to crash. Fred [Smith, founder of the company] was in a deep funk. "What the hell," he said, and flew off to Las Vegas. The next day he flew back and his face was shining. "We're going to make it," he said. He had just won $27,000 at the blackjack table! And we made it. We met the payroll. And then things began to turn around, and Federal Express grew eventually into the giant it is today.[7]

This story brings the past to life by emphasizing the contrast of emotions—the "deep funk" versus the "shining" face. The use of lively, colloquial dialogue—"What the hell" and "We're going to make it"— creates excitement and brings those feelings into the present. It would not have been as effective had the speaker simply said, "Fred was depressed, but after he got back from Las Vegas he was confident." Such a bare summary would have distanced the listener and diminished the power of the scene.

Language can also make the future seem close to listeners. Because words can cross the barrier of time, both tradition and a vision of tomorrow can guide us through the present.

Overcoming Distance.   The closer anything is to us, the easier it is to develop feelings about it. But what if speakers must discuss faraway people, places, and

Explore at **MyCommunicationLab** **Activity:** "Verbal Communication"

objects? Words can act like the zoom on your computer to bring such subjects closer to your audience.

Beth Tidmore, our student who won the U.S. Junior Olympics air rifle event at Colorado Springs, was effective when she asked her listeners to get involved with Special Olympics.

She used the vicarious experience narrative described earlier in Chapter 8, which invited listeners to imagine themselves participating in the action:

> I've had so many great experiences that are hard to describe without overusing words like "fulfilling" and "rewarding." So I'm going to let you experience it for yourself. I want everybody to pack your bags—we're going to the Special Olympics summer games in Georgia!

Beth then became a tour guide for this imaginary trip, walking listeners through the moments that would involve them in dramatic ways. This technique effectively bridged the distance between her subject and her audience.

Overcoming Apathy.

We live in an age of information overload. We are bombarded with information from both traditional and digital media. Much of what we see and hear through the media has an emotional impact. Stories are selected on the basis of how much attention they will attract, and emotionality is one means of attracting attention. As a result, many of us become jaded and resistant to appeals to feelings.

Sally Duncan found a poignant way to overcome such apathy. She began her speech by projecting a picture of her grandmother on the screen behind the lectern. Sally described her as a cultured, elegant woman who had a master's degree, taught English for years, and took Sally to museums and theatrical productions. "Now," she said, "let me read my last letter from Nanny."

> Dear Sally. I am finally around to answer your last. You have to look over me. Ha. I am so sorry to when you called Sunday why didn't you remind me. Steph had us all so upset leaving and not telling no she was going back but we have a good snow ha and Kathy can't drive on ice so I never get a pretty card but they have a thing to see through an envelope. I haven't got any in the bank until I get my homestead check so I'm just sending this. Ha. When you was talking on the phone Cathy had Ben and got my groceries and I had to unlock the door. I forgot to say hold and I don't have Claudette's number so forgive me for being so silly. Ha. Nara said to tell you she isn't doing no good well one is doing pretty good and my eyes. Love, Nanny.

Sally paused for a long moment and then said, "My Nanny has Alzheimer's." We were riveted as she went on to describe the disease and how to cope with loved ones who have it.

The role of words in arousing feeling is also underscored by the contrast between denotative and connotative forms of meaning. The **denotative meaning** of a word is its dictionary definition. For example, the denotative definition of *alcohol* is "a colorless, volatile, flammable liquid, which is widely used as a solvent, drug base, explosive, or intoxicating beverage."[8]

How different this definition is from the two connotative definitions offered in this chapter's opening example! **Connotative meaning** invests a subject with the speaker's personal associations and emotions. Thus, the "intoxicating beverage" is no longer just a chemical substance but rather "the poison scourge" or "the oil of

---

▶ **denotative meaning**   The dictionary definition or objective meaning of a word.

▶ **connotative meaning**   The emotional, subjective, personal meaning that certain words can evoke in listeners.

conversation." Connotative language intensifies feelings; denotative language encourages detachment.

Bringing Listeners Together

In many situations, individual action is not enough. It may take many people working together to get things done, and skillfully used language can bring them together. This power of language is especially evident during times of grief when tragedy reminds people of their need for one another. During the dark days of April 2013, as the nation mourned the bombings at the Boston marathon, President Barack Obama spoke at the memorial service held for victims and used the occasion to also affirm national purpose and identity:

> I'm here today on behalf of the American people with a simple message. Every one of us has been touched by this attack on your beloved city. Every one of us stands with you.
>
> Because, after all, it's our beloved city, too. Boston may be your hometown, but we claim it too. It's one of America's iconic cities. It's one of the world's great cities. . . .
>
> Our faith in each other, our love for each other, our love for country, our common creed that cuts across whatever superficial differences there may be—that is our power. That's our strength.
>
> That's why a bomb can't beat us. That's why we don't hunker down. That's why we don't cower in fear. We carry on. We race. We strive. We build, and we work, and we love—and we raise our kids to do the same. And we come together to celebrate life, and to walk our cities, and to cheer for our teams. . . .
>
> Scripture tells us to "run with endurance the race that is set before us."[9]

Obama's use of inclusive language and appeals to our national identity brought listeners together at the interfaith prayer service for the victims of the Boston Marathon bombings.

Consider here the emphasis on "we" and "our," the great pronouns of inclusion. Other words can drive people apart: name-calling, exclusionary language (such as "them" and "us"), and unsupported accusations can be notorious dividers.

Moving Listeners to Action

Sometimes listeners are just not ready to act. What barriers to action might you need to overcome? Your listeners may not be convinced of the soundness of your proposal. They may not trust you. They may not believe they can do anything about a problem. They may not be ready to invest the energy or take the risk that action demands.

Your language must convince listeners that action is necessary, that your ideas are sound, and that success is possible. In her speech urging students to act to improve off-campus housing conditions (see Appendix B), Anna Aley painted vivid word-pictures of deplorable off-campus housing. She supported these descriptions with both factual examples and her personal experiences. She also reminded listeners that, if they acted together, they could bring about change:

Watch at **MyCommunicationLab**
Video: "Franklin D. Roosevelt's First Inaugural Address"

Explore at **MyCommunicationLab**
Activity: "Power of Words"

What can one student do to change the practices of numerous Manhattan landlords? Nothing, if that student is alone. But just think of what we could accomplish if we got all 13,600 off-campus students involved in this issue! Think what we could accomplish if we got even a fraction of those students involved!

Anna then proposed specific actions that did not demand great effort or risk. In short, she made commitment as easy as possible. She ended with an appeal to action:

> Kansas State students have been putting up with substandard living conditions for too long. It's time we finally got together to do something about this problem. Join the Off-Campus Association. Sign my petition. Let's send a message to these slumlords that we're not going to put up with this any more. We don't have to live in slums.

Anna's words expressed both her indignation and the urgency of the problem. Her references to time—"too long" and "it's time"—called for immediate action. Her final appeals to join the association and sign the petition were expressed in short sentences that packed a lot of punch. Her repetition of "slumlords" and "slums" motivated her listeners to transform their indignation into action.

Anna also illustrated another language strategy that is important when you want to move people to action: the ability to develop dramas showing what is at stake and what actions listeners should take.[10] Such depictions draw clear lines between right and wrong. Be careful, however, not to go overboard. Ethics require that you show respect for all involved in a conflict. As both a speaker and a listener, be wary of melodramas that offer stark contrasts between good and evil. Such depictions often distort reality.

Celebrating Shared Values

It is important for people to remind themselves occasionally of the values that tie them together. To celebrate these values is to strengthen them and the communities that share them. Often these celebrations take place during ceremonies such as those that celebrate Memorial Day, the Fourth of July, or presidential inaugurals.

Over two thousand years ago, Aristotle noted that celebratory speeches should emphasize imagery. Images paint vivid word-pictures that show us our values in action. They may tell stories that teach us to treasure our traditions. Such language is colorful, concrete, and graphic—it appeals to the senses. Note how the late President Reagan used such language in his second inaugural address to call up memories of heroes and to strengthen the image of the American heritage:

> Hear again the echoes of our past. A general falls to his knees in the harsh snow of Valley Forge, a lonely President paces the darkened halls and ponders his struggle to preserve the Union, the men of the Alamo call out encouragement to each other, a settler pushes West and sings a song, and the song echoes out forever and fills the unknowing air.
>
> It is the American Sound. It is hopeful, big-hearted, idealistic—daring, decent and fair. That's our heritage. That's our song.[11]

You, too, can use the power of words to evoke the past as you find your own voice. The right words and phrases, used in the right places, can create a lasting picture.

YOUR ethical VOICE   Managing Powerful Language

To use the power of words in ethical ways, follow these guidelines:

1. Let your words illuminate the subject, not blind the listener.
2. Use words to support reasoning, not substitute for it.
3. Use language to celebrate past traditions.
4. Use words to provide visions of the future.
5. Use images to strengthen shared values.
6. Use words that bring people together, not divide them.
7. Use language to move listeners to action.
8. Avoid language that degrades people.

The potential power of language is great, ranging from shaping perceptions to revitalizing group culture. How can you use words in ways that will help you both find your voice and express it in powerful ways? We turn now to the standards you must apply as you seek the answers to that question.

The Six C'S of Language Use

For words to work for you, they must meet certain standards: clarity, color, concreteness, correctness, conciseness, and cultural sensitivity. We call these the six C's of oral language usage.

Explore at **MyCommunicationLab** **Activity:** "Language"

Clarity

PLAIN, the Plain Language Action and Information Network, is an organization of federal employees "dedicated to the idea that citizens deserve clear communication from government." In effect, PLAIN recognizes that too much communication in modern life is needlessly complex and obscure. To counter these problems, the network stresses simplicity and clarity.[12]

If your words are not clear, listeners will not understand you. To be clear, you must first understand what you want to say. Then, you must find words that convey your ideas as directly and simply as possible. The standard of clarity is met when something closely approximating what you intend is implanted in the minds of listeners.

One factor that reduces clarity is the use of **jargon**, the technical language that is specific to a profession. If you use jargon before an audience that doesn't share that technical vocabulary, you may not be understood. When jargon is used, the results are often unpredictable. For example:

> Back in the 1930s, during the early years of media communication, the novice editor of a small-town newspaper in Colorado wanted to get the final results of the Indianapolis 500 race for his next edition. Unfortunately, his paper's AP wire would close before the race was over. So the editor asked the AP to send him the results by some other means.
>
> The AP immediately wired back this reply, "WILL OVERHEAD WINNER INDIANAPOLIS RACE." This meant that they would "overhead," or send the result by Western Union. The editor, however, wasn't familiar with the word

▶ **jargon**   Technical language related to a specific field that may be incomprehensible to a general audience.

"overhead" in that technical context. He assumed that the race had been completed and the results were in. His headline the next day read, "OVERHEAD WINS INDIANAPOLIS RACE."[13]

Speakers who fall into the jargon trap are so used to using technical language that they forget that others may not grasp it. It does not occur to them that they must translate the jargon into lay language for it to be understood by general audiences.

A similar problem is using words that are overblown and pretentious. A notorious example occurred when sign makers wanted to tell tourists how to leave the Barnum museum. Rather than drawing an arrow with the word "Exit" above it, they wrote, "To the Egress." There's no telling how many visitors left the museum by mistake, thinking that they were going to see that rare creature—a living, breathing "Egress."

Sometimes speakers may deliberately avoid clarity—because the truth may hurt or because they want to mislead listeners. For example, the term "corporate restructuring" masks the reality that a company has serious problems. Hunger can be masked as "food insecurity." Such efforts to soften and obscure the truth are called **euphemisms.** Some efforts are more lighthearted, as when a sports commentator, speaking of the quarterback on a football team, said, "He has ball security issues" when he really meant, "This guy fumbles a lot."

At its worst, the use of euphemism degenerates into **doublespeak**, the use of words to deliberately befuddle listeners and hide unpleasant truths. The language of doublespeak points listeners in a direction opposite from the reality of a situation. Public television commentator Bill Moyers once warned of the dangers of this misuse of language:

> If you would . . . serve democracy well, you must save the language. Save it from the jargon of insiders who talk of current budget debate in Washington as "megapolicy choices between freeze-feasible base lines." Save it from the smokescreen artists who speak of "revenue enhancement" and "tax-base erosion control" when they really mean a tax increase.[14]

Figure 11.1 provides some common examples of doublespeak.

How can you avoid such violations of clarity and ethics? One way is through **amplification**, which extends the time listeners have for thinking about an idea and helps them bring it into sharper focus. You amplify an idea by defining it, repeating

FIGURE 11.1
Doublespeak

When they say:	What they often mean is:
Marital discord	Spouse beating
Downsizing	Firing
Making a salary adjustment	Cutting your pay
Failed to fulfill wellness potential	Died
Chronologically experienced citizen	Old codger
Initial and pass on	Let's spread the blame
Friendly fire	We killed our own people
Collateral damage	We killed innocent people

▶ **euphemism** Words that soften or evade the truth of a situation.

▶ **doublespeak** Words that point in the direction opposite from the reality they supposedly describe.

▶ **amplification** The art of developing ideas by restating them in a speech.

it, rephrasing it, offering examples of it, and contrasting it with more familiar and concrete subjects. In effect, you tell listeners something and then expand what you have just said.

Color

Colorful language is vivid and animated. It often expresses the speaker's involvement and feelings by using the fragments, rhythms, and colloquialisms of everyday conversation. A popular local professional wrestler once described his role as a bad guy in colorful terms: "I was meaner than a damn rattlesnake and tougher than a two-dollar steak."[15]

Colorful words paint striking pictures for listeners that linger in the mind. In her speech urging the purchase of hybrid cars, Davidson student Alexandra McArthur framed a colorful conclusion based on a **neologism**, an invented word that combines previous words in a striking new expression. In this case, Alexandra created her new word by combining "hybrid" and "hubris":

> If you do end up buying a hybrid, as you drive around town looking trendy, cruising past the gas stations, you may start feeling pretty good about yourself and talking about your car any chance you get. This new form of pride, commonly called *hybris*, may be annoying to your friends but is nothing incurable. I'm sure they will forgive you when they get their first hybrid.

One very special type of colorful language is **slang**, the language of the street. You may have been advised not to use slang. You may have been told that slang is coarse and vulgar, and that it epitomizes "bad" English. But according to general semanticist S. I. Hayakawa, slang can also be "the poetry of everyday life." Or, as the poet Carl Sandburg noted, slang is "language that rolls up its sleeves, spits on its hands, and goes to work."

Slang has its use in speeches: It can add energy to your message and be a source of identification between you and listeners. But use it with caution. Slang is not appropriate on formal occasions when a high level of decorum is called for. Moreover, you must be certain that your audience will understand your slang expressions. You should also avoid using ethnic slang or other words that your audience might find offensive. Finally, slang should be used sparingly—to emphasize a point or add a dash of humor and color. It should supplement standard English usage in your speech, not replace it.

Concreteness

It is almost impossible to discuss any significant topic without using some abstract words. However, if you use language that is too abstract, your audience may lose interest in what you are saying. Moreover, because abstract language is more ambiguous than concrete language it invites misunderstanding. Consider Figure 11.2, which illustrates movement along a continuum from abstract to concrete terms.

The more concrete your language, the more pictorial and precise the information you convey. Consider how Olivia Jackson began her speech advocating study abroad as a part of higher education:

> A fresh coat of snow covers the peaks of the Alps. Rain pelts the window, slowly rolling down onto the windowsills. It is only October and I need a

Colorful language and a lively presentation bring speeches to life.

▶ **neologism**   An invented word that combines previous words in a striking new expression.

▶ **slang**   The language of the street.

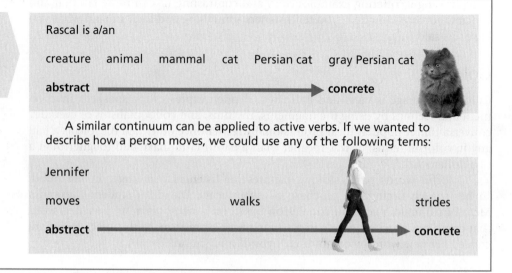

FIGURE 11.2
Abstract to Concrete Continuum

Rascal is a/an

creature   animal   mammal   cat   Persian cat   gray Persian cat

abstract ⟶ concrete

A similar continuum can be applied to active verbs. If we wanted to describe how a person moves, we could use any of the following terms:

Jennifer

moves   walks   strides

abstract ⟶ concrete

scarf, a heavy winter jacket, and boots to walk outside. The radiators on the bus are belching heat, causing the windows to fog up. Using my scarf, I rub an oval through which I gaze at the passing scenery. The bus roars down the autoroute, passing the pharmacy's flashing green cross, a Carrefour super store, and numerous small boutiques that line the narrow street. Little cars are lined up at the stoplight waiting as the tram zips by and bicyclists hurry to cross the street before the stream of cars commences. This was a typical morning for me in France during my fall term this past year. Every morning, I would see new people, notice different buildings, and watch the city of Grenoble awaken.

The attractive image Olivia creates in our minds both gains our attention and helps support her later argument that study abroad programs are desirable parts of the educational experience. Your language should be as concrete as the subject permits. Figure 11.2 illustrates this continuum of abstract to concrete language.

Correctness

Nothing can damage your credibility more than the misuse of language. Glaring mistakes in grammar can make you seem uneducated and even ignorant. While touting his education plan, one prominent politician told listeners that the most important consideration should be, "Is your children learning?" Hopefully, they would not miss the lesson on subject–verb agreement! Other common grammatical errors that make listeners cringe are listed in Figure 11.3. Figure 11.3 illustrates some common grammatical errors.

Mistakes in word selection can be as damaging as mistakes in grammar. People often err when using words that sound similar. Such confusions are called **malapropisms,** after Mrs. Malaprop, a character in an eighteenth-century play by Richard Sheridan. She would say, "He is the very *pineapple* of politeness," when she meant *pinnacle*. A sports writer noted that the players on a losing team had "digressed" (he meant "regressed") to committing earlier playing mistakes. William J. Crocker of Armidale College in New South Wales, Australia, collected the following malapropisms from his students:

▶ **malapropisms**   Language errors that occur when a word is confused with another word that sounds like it.

A speaker can add interest to his talk with an *antidote*. [anecdote]
The speaker hopes to arouse *apathy* in his audience. [empathy?]
Good language can be reinforced by good *gestation*. [gestures]
The speaker can use either an inductive or a *seductive* approach.
[deductive][16]

---

1. Using the wrong tense or verb form:
   Wrong: He *done* us a big favor.
   Right: He *did* us a big favor.

2. Lack of agreement between subject and verb:
   Wrong: *Is* your students giving speeches?
   Right: *Are* your students giving speeches?

3. Using the wrong word
   Wrong: *Caricature* is the most important factor in choosing a mate.
   Right: *Character* is the most important factor in choosing a mate.

4. Lack of agreement between a pronoun and its antecedent:
   Wrong: A hyperactive *person* will work *themselves* to death.
   Right: Hyperactive *people* will work *themselves* to death.
   or
   A hyperactive *woman* will work *herself* to death.

5. Improper type of pronoun used as subject:
   Wrong: *Him* and *me* decided to go to the library.
   Right: *He* and *I* decided to go to the library.

6. Improper type of pronoun used as object:
   Wrong: The speaker's lack of information dismayed my students and *I.*
   Right: The speaker's lack of information dismayed my students and *me.*

7. Double negative:
   Wrong: I *don't never* get bad grades on my speeches.
   Right: I *never* get bad grades on my speeches.

FIGURE 11.3
Correcting Grammatical Errors

Fictional characters, sports writers, and students are not the only ones who make such blunders. Elected officials are also not above an occasional malapropism. One former U.S. senator declared that he would oppose to his last ounce of energy any effort to build a "nuclear waste *suppository*" [repository] in his state (sounds like an incredible new cure for constipation!). The Speaker of the Texas legislature once acknowledged an award by saying, "I am filled with *humidity*" (perhaps he meant moist hot air as well as humility).

The lesson is clear. To avoid being unintentionally humorous, use a current dictionary to check the meaning of any word you feel uncertain about. For additional help, refer to the website developed by Professor Paul Brians of Washington State University to help students avoid common errors of usage.

Conciseness

In discussing clarity, we talked about the importance of amplification in speeches to expand understanding. Although it may seem contradictory, you must also be concise, even while you are amplifying your ideas. You must make your points quickly and efficiently.

Simplicity and directness help you be concise. Thomas Jefferson once said, "The most valuable of all talents is that of never using two words when one will do." Abraham Lincoln was similarly concise as he criticized the verbosity of another speaker: "He can compress the most words into the smallest idea of any man I know."

One way you can achieve conciseness is by using **maxims,** compact sayings that encapsulate beliefs. To reinforce his point that we need to actively confront the problems of racism, sexism, and homophobia, Haven Cockerham, vice president of human resources for Detroit Edison, came up with this striking maxim: "Sometimes silence isn't golden—just yellow."[17]

Maxims attract mass-media attention during demonstrations. When used on signs, they can be picked up as signature statements for movements or campaigns. Their brevity and dramatic impact make them well suited to display on television's evening news.

A caution is in order about using maxims: They should not be substituted for a carefully designed and well-supported argument. But once you have developed a responsible, substantive speech, consider whether you might use maxims to reinforce your message. Just remember that conciseness can be carried too far, as in the case of the student who was asked to write a very short story containing religion, sex, and mystery: "Dear God. I'm pregnant. I wonder who did it."

Cultural Sensitivity

Because words can either lift and unite or wound and hurt your audience, you must exercise **cultural sensitivity** in your choice of language. Looking back into the history of human communication, you will find little about cultural sensitivity. The ancient Greeks, for example, worried only about speaking to other male Athenians who were "free men" and citizens. Today, with our increasing awareness of different lifestyles, racial diversity, and the pursuit of gender equity, cultural sensitivity becomes an important ethical standard for effective language usage.

Cultural sensitivity requires adaptation and respect, as well as the careful choice of language.

As mentioned earlier in the chapter, Paula Deen, prominent author, restaurant owner, and television personality, has confirmed the importance of cultural sensitivity to her dismay. Faced with a lawsuit charging that racial slurs and jokes about women, Jews, and blacks were common in the kitchen of one of her restaurants, Ms. Deen had her popular television show dropped by Food Network and lost prominent corporate sponsors. In her apology, she said: "I want to apologize to everybody for the wrong that I've done. . . . Inappropriate, hurtful language is totally, totally unacceptable."[18]

A lack of cultural sensitivity almost always has negative consequences. At best, audience members may be mildly offended, at worst, they will be irate enough to reject both you and your message.

▶ **maxims**   Brief and particularly apt sayings.

▶ **cultural sensitivity**   The respectful appreciation of diversity within an audience.

How Language Techniques Can Magnify Your Voice

There are critical moments in a speech—often at the beginning or the ending or as arguments reach their conclusions—when you want your words to be most effective. At these moments, you can sometimes call on certain language techniques to magnify the power of your voice.

The branch of communication study that deals with identifying, understanding, and utilizing these techniques is called *rhetorical style*. Over the centuries, many such techniques have been identified; they seem to be grounded in our nature and to have evolved to meet basic needs for effective communication. Here, we discuss three broad categories of techniques that are especially useful for public speaking: *figurative language;* techniques that change the customary *order* of words; and techniques that exploit the *sounds* of words for special effects.

Using Figurative Language

Figurative language uses words in unusual ways to create fresh understandings. We focus here on seven forms that may be especially useful for public speakers: metaphor, enduring metaphor, simile, synecdoche, personification, culturetype, and ideograph.

Metaphor.

"A speech is a bridge of meaning that connects a speaker and a listener." Such expressions often help listeners understand unfamiliar ideas or gain new appreciation for familiar ones. A **metaphor** offers an implied comparison that can be startling and revealing. Good metaphors can also add color to your message. Because they can change and enrich the way we see things, metaphors can be important tools in shaping perceptions.

Metaphors are often useful in introducing and concluding a speech, in that they establish the speaker's unique perspective on a subject and give final expression to it. In his Boston bombings memorial speech, Obama both opened and closed with the same metaphor: "Scripture tells us to run with endurance the race that is set before us." The expression was particularly apt, given the setting of the Boston Marathon and the situation.

In her 2013 commencement address to Williams College graduates, tennis great and social justice advocate Billie Jean King found just the right metaphor for her unique perspective: Every second, she said, presents a new opportunity, and "If you miss, it's feedback. . . . The next time you get a similar shot, try to hit it just right. I think that's the perfect metaphor for life."[19]

Metaphors used as a conclusion can offer a final frame of understanding that interprets the speech for listeners. Student speaker Alexandra McArthur finished her speech warning listeners not to accept at face value the pictures of foreign countries painted in travel brochures: "Tourism may be an economic band-aid for the gaping wound of poverty." Because they are unusual, metaphors are easily remembered.

Because metaphors can be so powerful, you should select them carefully and use them with restraint. First, *the gravity of the metaphor must match the seriousness of your subject.* Just as you would not typically wear cut-offs to a funeral, you should not use certain metaphors to express certain subjects. We once heard a speaker who was a farmer present the welcoming speech at a banquet for new faculty. Moved by the moment and impressed by the group before him, the speaker intoned: "If

---

► **figurative language**   Words used in surprising and unusual ways that magnify the power of their meaning.

► **metaphor**   An implied comparison that connects subjects not usually related to create a surprising perspective.

you want to grow a good crop, you have to use good fertilizer." He did not seem to understand the laughter that followed. The lesson is clear: Be sure the dignity of the metaphor matches the subject to which it is applied.

Second, *mixing metaphors by combining images that don't fit together can confuse listeners and lower their estimation of your competence.* In 2013, the United States underwent *sequestration*, the indiscriminate across-the-board reduction of funds for federal programs. One commentator on the effects of sequestration noted:

> The conventional wisdom now seems to be that . . . the Obama administration cried "wolf!" unnecessarily. Sorry, but the wolf is here all right: he's just eating the seed corn stored out of sight in the warehouse, as opposed to the food on the table.

Most of those in the audience were left scratching their heads trying to figure out why wolves, who are carnivorous creatures of the forest, would be eating corn in a warehouse.

Third, *you also should avoid trite metaphors,* such as "I was on an emotional roller coaster." Overuse has turned these metaphors into clichés that no longer have any impact. Not only are they ineffective, but also using them may damage your ethos. Tired comparisons suggest a dull mind.

As useful and powerful as metaphors may be, they can also be dangerous. Certain animal metaphors, for example, can project and justify dehumanizing, scornful attitudes about groups of people. Consider this statement from a recent lieutenant governor of South Carolina about government assistance to the poor:

> My grandmother was not a highly educated woman, but she told me as a small child to quit feeding stray animals. You know why? Because they breed! You're facilitating the problem if you give an animal or a person ample food supply. They will reproduce, especially ones that don't think too much further than that.[20]

Enduring Metaphor.

One special group of metaphors taps into shared experience that persists across time and that crosses many cultural boundaries. These **enduring metaphors**—or "archetypal metaphors" as they are sometimes called—are especially popular in speeches, perhaps because they appeal to deep motives and can bring people together. They connect their subjects with timeless themes, such as light and darkness, storms, the sea, disease, and the family. A brief look at three of these metaphors demonstrates their potential power to magnify meaning.[21]

Light and darkness.

From the beginnings of civilization, people have made negative associations with darkness. The dark is cold, unfriendly, and dangerous. On the other hand, light brings warmth and safety. It restores control. When speakers use the light–darkness metaphor, they usually equate problems or bad times with darkness and solutions or recovery with light. Olivia Jackson spoke of her grandfather's experience with Alzheimer's disease as a "dark abyss of emptiness and forgetfulness" and as a "descent into darkness." Lindsey Yoder began her persuasive speech at the end of Chapter 14 by picturing African American slavery as a time of darkness. She concluded her speech by asking listeners to join the campaign against twenty-first–century sex slavery with a striking quotation: "Dare to reach out your hand into the darkness, to pull another hand into the light." Thus, she framed her appeal in terms of an enduring metaphor.

▶ **enduring metaphors** Metaphors of unusual power and popularity that are based on experience that lasts across time and crosses many cultural boundaries.

Another closely associated metaphor is "fire." In its positive sense, fire has long represented our power to light the darkness and warm ourselves against the cold.

Storms and the sea. A storm metaphor is often used to describe serious problems. Often the storm occurs at sea—a dangerous place under the best of conditions. When political problems are the focus of the speech, the "captain" who "steers the ship of state" can reassure us with his or her programs or principles—and make them seem very attractive in the process. In his first inaugural address, George W. Bush said that "through much of the last century, America's faith in freedom and democracy was a rock in a raging sea."[22]

The family. Family metaphors express the dream of a close, loving relationship among people through such images as "the family of humanity."[23]

Light and darkness, storms, and the sea are often sources of enduring metaphors that can magnify meaning in a speech.

As he asked listeners to rise above race, Barack Obama appealed to such images: "Let us be our brother's keeper, Scripture tells us. Let us be our sister's keeper."[24] Such metaphors can be very useful when listeners feel alienated from each other. Family metaphors can then be a powerful force to bring listeners together and to develop identification. Wade Steck demonstrated the potential of such metaphors as he was describing his experiences at the University of Memphis Frosh Camp Program, his introduction to college life:

> When I got to Frosh Camp, they made me feel at home. First thing they did was to break us into "families" of ten to twelve people who would share the same cabin for those few days. Each "family" had its counselors, carefully selected juniors and seniors who were actually called your "mom" or "dad." . . . The thing I liked most were the Fireside Chats. At night under the stars, watching the logs burn . . ., people would just relax and talk. I discovered that many of those in my family shared my concerns and anxieties.

Similarly, the *disease* metaphor pictures our problems as illness and offers solutions in the form of cures.[25] Metaphors of *war and peace* can frame conflict situations, urging us to battle for our beliefs or to find the path of peace.[26] A *building* metaphor, such as "laying the foundation" for the future, emphasizes our impulse to control our lives. And *spatial* metaphors often reflect striving upward and moving forward toward goals.[27]

Handle with care. The special power enduring metaphors have to move listeners deeply should cause a red light to flash on in their minds: *Handle with care!* We have already noted how animal metaphors can express and invite dehumanizing attitudes when used to represent human beings. These dangerous tendencies accompany enduring metaphors as well.

The image of the ship of state launched on dangerous and stormy seas can carry with it an endorsement of a strong central government, of blind obedience to the authority of the captain, and of the loss of individual liberties typically suffered by members of the crew. The image can give a romantic, attractive appear-

FINDING YOUR

voice   Enduring Metaphors in Contemporary Communication

Look for examples of enduring metaphors as used in contemporary public communication (speeches, editorials, blogs, advertising, visual, and televisual communication). Why
do you think they were chosen to illustrate or make the point? What work do they do?
Might they connect with motivation as it is explained in Chapter 5? Can you see any
ethical problems with their use?

ance to authoritarian government and is definitely not sympathetic to democratic systems.

Light and darkness by its nature encourages two-dimensional, even melodramatic thinking, in which the good (light) is always clear, bright, and radiant and evil (darkness) is the opposite. The image does not acknowledge that there may be shades of gray in the choices people must make. Moral choices can be made to appear easy and simple. The speaker's solutions may be offered as the "dawn of hope," when actually they are riddled with difficulties. Thus, the image by its nature may deceive us into simplistic thinking about issues that might be quite complicated.

Metaphors based on the family can give an artificially attractive appearance to abusive and exploitive relationships. Parent–child images suggest loving and caring but may also disguise power relationships that empower one group at the expense of another. Back before the American Revolution, for example, British politicians used to describe Great Britain as the "mother country" and threatened to punish the colonies in America as "rebellious children." They used the image to justify their tyranny. The problem with such images is that they can be absorbed by those who are belittled by them. Until the colonists themselves were freed from the idea that they "belonged" to the mother country, they could never hope to be free.

Other enduring metaphors carry their own dangers as well. As both speaker and listener, you should be especially careful not to use or accept them without closely inspecting the consequences.

Watch at
MyCommunicationLab
Video: "My Twenty-First
Birthday Party"

Similes.   A **simile** is a variation of metaphor that warns listeners when a comparison is coming. Words such as *like* and *as* are signals that alert listeners and introduce the comparison. One of the most memorable similes we have heard was framed by a student who had once been wounded while parachuting in a war zone. He described the tracer bullet as "a force that spun me around like a twisted yo-yo at the end of a string." Very few of us had shared that experience, but most of us were familiar with yo-yos. Aided by the simile, we could easily imagine the moment. View the speech by Scott Champlin in MyCommunicationLab.

Synecdoche.   One of the classic forms of figurative language, **synecdoche** (sin-eck'-duh-key), is grounded in an ancient tendency to represent a subject by focusing on a part of it or on something closely associated with it. Thus, the nautical expression "all hands on deck" represents a group of people by focusing on a useful part of them. "The pen is mightier than the sword" compares two activities, communication and warfare, by focusing on instruments traditionally associated with both.

▶ **simile** A language tool that clarifies something abstract by comparing it with something concrete; usually introduced by "as" or "like."

▶ **synecdoche** Represents a subject by focusing on a vivid part of it or on something clearly associated with it.

Synecdoche can be easily abused. If we focus on one feature of a subject and ignore others, we may distort the picture we present about the subject and cause listeners to draw warped or incomplete conclusions. Thus, "all hands on deck" may cause us to miss a larger picture—that these are human beings who also have hearts and heads, thoughts and feelings, and who deserve to be treated as such. We are left contemplating an even larger question: *Can the part ever really stand for the whole without distorting it?*

Personification.

Personification treats inanimate subjects, such as ideas or institutions, as though they had human form or feeling. Personification makes it easier to arouse feelings about people and values that might otherwise seem abstract and distant. Here is how one student used personification effectively in a classroom speech:

> The university must be more caring. It must see that its investments make a statement to others about its morality. When it supports companies that are destroying the environment, it endorses what they are doing. It becomes a silent partner in that destruction, and might as well be cutting down rain forests itself.

Culturetypes.

Culturetypes express the values, identity, and goals of a particular group at a particular time.[28] In 1960, John F. Kennedy dramatized his presidential campaign by inviting Americans to explore with him "new frontiers" of national progress. That expression worked well in American culture, but it probably would not have made much sense in other countries. For Americans, the frontier is a unique symbol that stands for freedom, challenge, and opportunity.

Some culturetypes include what rhetorical critic Richard Weaver once described as "god and devil terms."[29] Weaver suggested that *progress* has been a primary "god term" of American culture. People often seem willing to follow that word as though it were some kind of divine summons. Tell us to do something in the name of "progress," and we may feel an urge to go along. Other terms, such as *modern* and *efficient,* are similarly powerful, Weaver argued, because they seem rooted in American values. If something is described as "efficient," we are apt to listen respectfully. If something is "modern," many of us think it is better, probably because it has benefitted from "progress."

In her speech, "The Price of Bottled Water" (see Appendix B), Katie Lovett argues that the bottled water industry has co-opted emerging god terms from the environmental movement to advertise its products.

> Bottlers seize upon public anxiety over municipal tap water supplies, supposedly offering us the safety that tap water cannot. As a result, the National Resources Defense Council has found that "pure," "pristine," and "natural" are some of the most commonly used god-terms found in marketing and on labels.

Katie offers evidence indicating that any assumption concerning the superior safety of bottled water is not justified.

Clearly, we need to be wary of god terms and their power to deceive. Similarly, we should be careful of devil terms like *terrorist* and *terrorism.* They can make a person, group, or action seem repulsive and threatening. Developing caution with respect to god and devil terms is an important dimension of critical listening and thinking.

Culturetypes can change over time and within certain subsets of a culture. In recent years, words like *conservative* and *environment* have become more compelling, while *liberalism* and *pollution,* if not devil terms, seem increasingly undesirable to many people.

▶ **personification**   A figure of speech in which nonhuman or abstract subjects are given human qualities.

▶ **culturetypes**   Terms that express the values and goals of a group's culture.

FINDING YOUR

voice   The Culturetypes of Our Time

What words would you nominate as culturetypes in contemporary society? Find examples of the use of these words in public communication. What work do they perform? Are there ethical problems with their use?

Ideographs.   Communication scholar Michael Calvin McGee identified an especially potent group of culturetypes that he called **ideographs.** These words express in a succinct way a country's basic political values.[30] McGee suggested that words like *freedom, liberty,* and *democracy* are important because they are shorthand expressions of political identity. It is inconceivable to us that other nations might not wish to have a "democratic" form of government or that they might not prize "liberty" over every other value. Expressions such as "*freedom* fighters" and "*democracy* in action" have unusual power for us because they are ideographs.

As an audience, we can be especially vulnerable to such language, and it can be dangerous. After all, one person's "freedom fighter" can be another person's "terrorist." We must look beyond such generalities to uncover the hidden agendas of the speaker. Ideographs and culturetypes also can function as trigger words (discussed in Chapter 4). They often do ethical work by reminding us of our heritage and suggesting that we must be true to our values. But there is a potential for abusing such words. You must show that ideographs truly apply to your topic. As a speaker, you should use them sparingly, and as a listener, you should inspect them carefully.

To develop resistance to the unethical use of culturetypes and ideographs, we should apply the following questions:

1. *Is this really what it claims to be?* Does the development of weapons of mass destruction really represent "progress"? Are "freedom fighters" actually thugs?

2. *Are those who use these claims credible sources of information?* For example, are those who advance the "science" of cryonics, the preservation of bodies by freezing them in hopes of discovering how to restore life to them on some future occasion, really "scientists"? Or are they simply exploiters out to take your money?

3. *Do these claims reflect an ethical sense of values?* For example, lopping off the top of a mountain to strip-mine coal may be a highly "efficient" form of mining, but what about the environment?

4. *What kinds of actions are these words urging us to endorse or undertake?* For example, should we be asked to support or even die for "democracy" in a nation whose citizens may prefer some other form of government?

Changing the Order of Words

We expect to find words in certain predictable patterns. *Antithesis, inversion,* and *parallel construction* are techniques that deliberately change the ways words are

▶ **ideographs** Compact expressions of a group's basic political faith.

normally ordered in messages. Their primary functions are to draw attention to the thoughts they express and to reveal the speaker in a favorable light.

Antithesis.

Antithesis arranges different or opposing ideas in the same or adjoining sentences to create a striking contrast. Beth Tidmore used the technique well in her speech on Special Olympics: "With the proper instruction, environment, and encouragement, Special Olympians can learn not only sport skills, but life skills."

Antithesis can suggest that the speaker has a clear, decisive grasp of options. It can magnify the ethos of a speaker as a person of vision, leadership, and action. Consider, for example, how President John F. Kennedy used antithesis in his inaugural address: "Ask not what your country can do for you—ask what you can do for your country." Kennedy said essentially the same thing during a campaign speech before the election: "The new frontier is not what I promise I am going to do for you. The new frontier is what I ask you to do for your country." Same message, different words. The first is memorable, the second is not.

Inversion.

Inversion reverses the expected order of words in a phrase or sentence to make ideas more memorable. The "Ask not" in the Kennedy example illustrates the technique. But inversion goes beyond reversing the expected order of words. In a baccalaureate address presented at Hamilton College, Bill Moyers commented on the many contradictions in contemporary life and concluded: "Life is where you get your answers questioned."[31] Here, the inversion of the conventional order of thoughts in which answers usually follow questions makes a witty, striking observation.

Parallel Construction.

Parallel construction repeats the same pattern of words in a sequence of phrases or sentences for the sake of impact. We discussed the use of parallel construction for framing the main points in a speech in Chapter 9, but parallel construction can occur at any critical moment in a speech. When used in the conclusion of a speech, the repetition of the pattern of words can stamp its message into the mind and make its statement memorable. Lindsey Yoder ended her speech on human trafficking with the following eloquent parallel construction:

> The quiet screams of our people call for us desperately. Let us be the generation to hear them. Let us be the generation to change the world. Let us be the generation to end modern slavery.

Watch at **MyCommunicationLab** **Video:** "Franklin D. Roosevelt's New Deal"

Using the Sounds of Words to Reinforce Their Meaning

As they are pronounced, words have distinctive sounds. At least two techniques, alliteration and onomatopoeia, arrange these sounds in ways that draw special attention to the ideas they contain.

Alliteration.

Alliteration repeats the initial sounds in a closely connected pattern of words. One student speaker who criticized the lowering of educational standards paused near the end of her speech to draw the following conclusion: "We don't need to be dumbing down." Her repetition of the *d* sound was distinctive and helped listeners remember her point. A similar example on an international scale occurred in the ongoing political battle in Great Britain over how closely British economic policy should be tied to the European Union. One Conservative Party leader expressed his position by combining alliteration with animal

---

▶ **antithesis** A language technique that combines opposing elements in the same sentence or adjoining sentences.

▶ **inversion** Changing the normal order of words to make statements memorable.

▶ **parallel construction** Wording points in a repeated pattern to emphasize their importance and to show how they are both related and contrasted.

▶ **alliteration** The repetition of initial consonant sounds in closely connected words.

FIGURE 11.4
Magnifying the Power of Language

Using Figurative Language

Technique	Definition	Example
Metaphors	Unexpected figurative comparisons	An *iron curtain* has descended across the continent.
Enduring metaphors	Metaphors that transcend time and cultural boundaries	The development of the Internet marked the *dawn* of a new way of learning.
Similes	Figurative comparisons using *like* or *as*	The jellyfish is *like a living lava lamp.*
Synecdoche	Focusing on part to represent the whole	All *hands* on deck.
Personifications	Attributing human characteristics to things or events	Liberty *raises her flame* as a beacon.
Culturetypes	Words that express the values, identity, and goals of a group	This company is devoted to the ideals of *modern, efficient, progressive science.*
Ideographs	Words that express a country's basic political beliefs	All we ask is *liberty* and *justice.*

Manipulating the Order of Words

Technique	Definition	Example
Antithesis	Presenting contrasting ideas in parallel phrases	There is a *time to sow* and a *time to reap.*
Inversion	Changing the expected word order	This insult *we did not deserve,* and this result *we will not accept.*
Parallel construction	Repetition of words/phrases at beginning or end of sentences	*It's a program that … It's a program that … It's a program that …*

Exploiting the Sounds of Words

Technique	Definition	Example
Alliteration	Repetition of initial sounds in closely connected words	Beware the *nattering nabobs* of *negativism.*
Onomatopoeia	Words that imitate natural sounds	The creek *gurgled* and *babbled* down to the river.

metaphors and a distinctly British culturetype: "Better to be a British bulldog than a Brussels poodle."[32] His expression made a striking impression and was featured in media accounts.

Onomatopoeia.   **Onomatopoeia** (on uh mah tuh pay′ uh) is the tendency of certain words to imitate the sounds of what they represent. Onomatopoeia has this quality of conveying listeners into a scene by allowing them to hear its noises, smell its odors, taste its flavors, or touch its surfaces. The technique awakens sensory experience.

Suppose you were trying to describe a scene of refugees fleeing from war and starvation. You might describe an old woman and her grandson as they *trudge* down a road to nowhere. The very sound of the word *trudge* suggests the weary, dusty, discouraged walk of the refugees. Similarly, *growl* might suggest the noise made by an angry dog, or *thud* might express the resounding sound of a heavy backpack hitting the ground. Because it invokes an actual sense of the experience it signifies, onomatopoeia offers a kind of "3-D" experience with language and tends to stick in the memory.

These various ways to magnify the power of language are summarized in Figure 11.4. As you consider how you might use them, remember that your language must not seem forced or artificial. For these techniques to work, they must seem to arise naturally and spontaneously in your speaking, and they must seem to fit both

▶ **onomatopoeia** Words that sound like the subjects they signify.

FINDING YOUR voice Do Words Work for You?

Analyze how you used the power of language in your last speech. Did you have to overcome any barriers to perception or feeling among your listeners? Did you measure up to the standards suggested by the six C's? Did listeners respond to your message? What special techniques did you use? Could you have done better? How?

you and your subject. Use them sparingly so that they stand out from the rest of what you say. When artfully employed they can harness and increase the power of words so that they reinforce your message and help make your voice significant.

FINAL reflections Give Me the Right Word

We end this chapter where we began it, reflecting on Joseph Conrad's eloquent, "Give me the right word and the right accent, and I will move the world." Most of us have little desire to move the world, but we would like to convince others to give our thoughts serious consideration.

Words, we now see, can enlighten us or blind us, enflame us or benumb us, bring us together or drive us apart, inspire us to act or discourage action, and define who we are and are not. Words can heal or injure us: There is no greater lie than the nursery maxim you may have chanted as a child, "Sticks and stones may break my bones but words can never harm me."

Words can indeed harm, but developing how well we use words can make us more effective both as people and as communicators. When we acknowledge that powerful words can affect how we see and feel about our world, whether we come together in effective action groups, or whether we nurture our shared values and identity, we have taken a major step toward developing our ways with words.

The next step is to set the standards and guidelines of growth. The goals of clarity, color, concreteness, correctness, conciseness, and cultural sensitivity can light our path toward language development. We should become curious about words: As you study and read, keep a dictionary at your side. Look up words that are unfamiliar to you. Try them on for size to see what they can do. As you expand your language capacity, you enhance your potential for communication.

Finally, experiment with the techniques we have identified. Framing metaphors and similes, for example, exercises your capacity for analogical, creative thinking. Indeed, each of the basic techniques brings unique, important possibilities to communication—that is why they are basic.

In short, words can help us develop awareness, find our voice, and give it power.

After Reading This Chapter, You Should Be Able To Answer These Questions

Study and
Review at
MyCommunicationLab

1 What makes oral language special?

2 What is the spoken word capable of accomplishing?

3 What standards should govern our choice of words?

4 Define the following techniques and describe their functions:

  a. Metaphor

  b. Enduring metaphor

  c. Simile

  d. Synecdoche

  e. Personification

  f. Culturetype

  g. Ideograph

5 What advantages can inversion, antithesis, and parallel construction bring to public speaking?

6 What work can alliteration and onomatopoeia perform for the speaker?

For Discussion and Further Exploration

1 The example that opens this chapter presents arguments for and against the consumption of whiskey. Rephrase these arguments using denotative language. How does this affect the power of the arguments?

2 Develop a metaphor to express an idea about the following abstract concepts: *love, freedom, justice, poverty*. Do these metaphors help communicate the ideas? How? Discuss in class.

3 View a speech in MyCommunicationLab or on YouTube. Does it demonstrate how language can shape perceptions, arouse feelings, bring people together, or incite action? How well does the speech perform these functions? Present your thoughts in class discussion.

4 Look for examples of the use of maxims in political rhetoric (speeches, ads, position statements, etc.). Are the maxims effective? Why or why not?

5 Watch the evening news, and be on the alert for examples of the special language techniques we have discussed. What work do these forms of expression perform?

6 Did you grow up in a cultural background that differs from mainstream American culture? If so, what culturetypes or ideographs can you identify that were distinctive in that different culture? Can you remember what functions these forms of expression performed?

7 Ohio State University President Gordon Gee had a problem with cultural sensitivity as he explained at a public meeting why Notre Dame had not been invited to join the Big Ten: "You can't trust those damn Catholics. . . . The fathers are holy on Sunday and they're holy hell the rest of the week." After his remarks were widely published, he apologized, explaining "They were a poor attempt at humor." Shortly thereafter, he resigned. Can you find other examples of the lack of cultural sensitivity in public communication?

A SAMPLE SPEECH

In her self-introduction presented at Vanderbilt University, Ashley Smith used three contrasting photographs—each representing a different lifestyle—to structure her speech. This device also illustrates the cooperation of the visual and the verbal—pictures and words—to complete her message. The photographs offer the surface details, but the words explain how they are representative of ways of life and what she learned from these exposures. In effect, they bring the photographs into focus for her speech.

Three Photographs

ASHLEY SMITH

Photographs often tell stories that only a few can hear. I would like to tell you the story told to me by three snapshots that hang in my room in suburban Jacksonville, Florida. If you saw them, you might think them totally unrelated; together, they tell a powerful tale.

"Ashley, *levantete!*" I heard each morning for the month that I spent in Costa Rica as an exchange student. I would wake up at 5:30 to get ready for school and would stumble off to the one shower that the family of five shared. I had to wash myself in cold water because there was no warm water—that usually woke me up pretty fast! I then got dressed and breakfast would be waiting on the table. Predictably it would be fruit, coffee, and gallo pinto, a black bean and rice dish usually served at every meal.

We would then walk to school and begin the day with an hour and a half of shop class. After shop we would have about 15- to 20-minute classes in what you and I might call "regular" academic subjects: math and Spanish, for example. Those classes had frequent interruptions and were not taken very seriously. The socialization process was quite clear: These children were being prepared for jobs in the labor force instead of for higher education. Each afternoon as we walked home we passed the elite school where students were still busy working and studying. The picture in my room of my Costa Rican classmates painting picnic tables in the schoolyard reminds me of their narrow opportunities.

The second photograph on my wall is of a little girl in Botswana. She's nearing the end of her education and has finished up to the equivalent of the sixth grade. She will now return to a rural setting because her family cannot afford to continue her schooling. To add to the problem, the family goat was eaten by a lion, so she had to return to help them over this crisis.

But she didn't miss out on much—most likely, she would have gone on into the city and ended up in one of the shantytowns, one more victim of the unemployment, poverty, even starvation endured by the people. Her lack of opportunity is due not so much to class inequalities as in Costa Rica, but more to the cultural tradition of several hundred years of European exploitation. Recently there has been extensive growth there, but the natives have been left far behind.

The third photograph in my room is of four high school students, taken where I went to school in Jacksonville, Florida. We're all sitting on the lawn outside school, overlooking the parking lot full of new cars that will take us home to warm dinners and comfortable beds and large homes and privileged

◀ Ashley's sharp, clear use of images helps shape listener *perceptions* and arouses *feelings* by overcoming barriers of distance. The touch of dialogue adds action to the picture.

◀ The Botswana picture personifies the cultural deprivation Ashley criticizes. Again, the combination of picture and words magnifies and explains her feelings and invites identification from her listeners.

The third photograph offers ▶
a transition into Ashley's
personal plan of action. We
see that for her it reflects
a way of life that hides the
reality she had found elsewhere that now calls her
into a life commitment.

Again, Ashley uses synec- ▶
doche and personification
to focus sharply on her
life goals and to represent
them to her listeners.

lives. Many of us—including myself for most of my life—took this world for
granted. But now, for me, no more. I may have gained a lot in my travels, but I
lost my political innocence.

One thing I gained is an intense desire to become an educator. I want to
teach people to succeed on their merits despite the social and economic inequalities that they're faced with. And I want to learn from them as well. I want
to teach the boy who never mastered welding that he could own the factory.
And I want him to teach me how to use a rice cooker. I want to teach the girl
who is exhausted each afternoon after walking to the river with a jar on her
head to gather water that she could design an irrigation system. But I also want
her to teach me how to weave a thatched roof. I want to travel and teach and
learn.

Three photographs, hanging on my wall. They are silent, mute, and the
photographer was not very skillful. But together they tell a powerful story in
my life.

12 Presenting Your Speech

Listen to Chapter 12 at MyCommunicationLab

LaVonia stood in the front of the room with shoulders hunched, arms crossed, leg jiggling, eyes on the floor, voice breathless. She was terrified.

By the middle of the semester, she stood tall, gestured freely, looked at all of the audience, and spoke in a clear, firm voice. She spoke with such energy and enthusiasm, with such joy and passion, that we *wanted* to listen to her and to take her ideas seriously. She communicated in ways that magnified her ethos, exhibiting the qualities of competence, character, goodwill, and forcefulness that we described in Chapter 3. Her improvement proved so impressive that she became a tutor in the Speaking Center.

LaVonia has gone on to graduate school in counseling, taking her confidence in presenting her voice with her and leaving fond memories with us.

"Finding your voice" means far more than simply sounding good and looking good at the lectern. Rather, finding your voice means finding the causes that call you to speak, discovering what you want to say about them, and framing these messages with all the skill and power they deserve. Nevertheless, all your reflection, investigation, and planning will come to naught unless your speeches come to life in the actual **presentation**.

That's what this chapter is about—preparing you for presentation by helping you develop two great resources, your physical voice and your body language. We also want to help you become versatile in using certain types of presentation and flexible in handling special communication situations. Finally, we show you how to practice for success.

The Power of Presentation

LaVonia showed how you can improve your delivery to really sell a speech. Yet we also remember another student speaker who described her childhood in these terms: "I was always getting into trouble." But as she said these words, she seemed listless; she slouched at the podium and avoided eye contact. Her passive manner did not reinforce her self-portrait as a boisterous child. Instead, *there was a disconnect between what she said and what she showed.* Law enforcement interviewers often refer to such moments as "discrepancies, places where words, facial expressions, and body language do not jibe."[1]

Whenever verbal and nonverbal symbols seem out of sync, listeners typically assign more importance to the nonverbal message. As specialists in relationships observe,

> The way you listen, look, move, and react tells the other person whether or not you care, if you're being truthful, and how well you're listening. When your nonverbal signals match up with the words you're saying, they increase trust, clarity, and rapport. When they don't, they generate tension, mistrust, and confusion.[2]

▶ **presentation** Delivering a speech to an audience, integrating the skills of nonverbal communication with the speech content.

Clearly, communication goes far beyond the mere exchange of words. For presentations to be effective, listeners must be able to hear you easily and to understand your words as you pronounce them. They should enjoy listening to your voice and see your gestures as underscoring your message rather than detracting from it. Nonverbal communication scholars agree that "we are biased in favor of expressive behavior" because it increases liking, authority, and affiliation.[3]

An effective presentation should sound natural and conversational—so that you are talking *with* listeners, not *at* them. Your goal should be an **expanded conversational style** that is direct, spontaneous, colorful, and tuned to the responses of listeners.[4] Although a bit more formal than everyday conversation, such a style sounds natural. Approach your presentation not from a *performance* orientation but from a *communication* orientation: Set aside expectations that "speaking publicly requires formal eloquence, a polished delivery, and perfection," and instead embrace the goal of "help[ing] your audience understand your message."[5] Finding your voice means figuring out how to use your personal style effectively in public settings.

Underlying the obvious requirements for an effective presentation are deeper requirements of *attitude*. As both speaker and listener, *you should want to communicate*. This point may seem obvious, but we remember another student in whom this desire to communicate seemed oddly lacking. She had done well in high school speaking contests, she told us in her first speech, and thought of herself as a good speaker. And in a technical sense, she was right. Her voice was pleasant and expressive, her manner direct and competent. But there was a false note, an overtone of artificiality. As a result, her listeners gave her a rather chilly reception. It was clear that, for her, speaking was an exhibition. *She* was more important than her audience and her ideas. Listeners sensed that she had her priorities wrong.

The desire to communicate produces a sense of **immediacy**, a closeness between speaker and listeners.[6] Immediacy relates to the likableness dimension of ethos, which we discussed in Chapter 3. It encourages listeners to open their minds to you and to be influenced by what you say.[7]

You can encourage immediacy by reducing the actual distance between yourself and listeners. If possible, move closer to them. Smile at them when appropriate, maintain eye contact, use gestures to clarify and reinforce ideas, and let your voice express your feelings. Even if your heart is pumping, your hands are a little sweaty, and your knees feel wobbly, the self you show listeners should be a person in control of the situation. Focus on engaging your audience with your ideas.

To summarize, *an effective presentation makes your ideas come alive while you are speaking*. It blends nonverbal with verbal symbols so that reason and emotion, heart and head, mind and body all work together to advance your message. The remainder of this chapter helps you move closer to a presentation that reaches this goal.

Mariska Hargitay of TV's *Law and Order* varied her rate of speech to add texture to her speech on domestic violence and the founding of the Joyful Heart Foundation.

Developing Your Physical Voice

It may seem strange to say that to find your voice you must develop your voice. But when utilized properly, the human vocal apparatus can be a rich and expressive instrument of communication. Consider the following simple statements:

Explore at **MyCommunicationLab Activity:** "Speech Delivery"

▶ **expanded conversational style** A presentational quality that, while more formal than everyday conversation, preserves its directness and spontaneity.

▶ **immediacy** A quality of successful communication achieved when the speaker and audience experience a sense of closeness.

I don't believe it.

You did that.

Give me a break.

How many different meanings can you create as you speak these words, just by changing the ways you say them?

The quality of your voice affects your ethos as well as your message. If you sound confident and comfortable with your own identity and if listening to you is a pleasant experience for your audience, listeners are likely to raise their estimation of you. But if you sound tentative, people may think you are not very decisive, perhaps not even convinced by your own message. If you mumble, they may think you are trying to hide something. If you are overly loud or strident, they may conclude you are not very likable. In the first semester of her freshman year, the student in our opening scenario discovered that a faculty member (who shall remain nameless) lowered her grade on a presentation because the professor did not think she demonstrated sufficient confidence and projection. Determined to combat that perception, LaVonia took our course in public speaking to learn how to project her soft, breathy voice confidently and assertively—and she succeeded.

Although you may not want to make radical changes in your speaking voice, minor improvements can produce big dividends. As poet and author Maya Angelou observed, "Words mean more than just what is set down on paper. It takes the human voice to infuse them with deeper meaning."[8] With a little effort and practice, most of us can make positive changes. However, not all physical impairments can be fixed with simple vocal exercises. If you have a serious vocal problem, contact a speech therapy clinic for professional help.

Think of your voice as providing the music to the lyrics of your words. Your favorite performers vary their delivery, using a range of notes, tempos, and volume levels juxtaposed with the language of their songs to create meaning. You have an opportunity to convey layers of meaning in your message as your voice brings your speech to life. In her commencement speech at the Berklee College of Music in Boston, singer Annie Lennox not only used rich vocal textures and tones in her presentation but also sang snippets of the songs that had influenced her career. Her mix of pitch, rate, and volume added both zest and interest to a speech well tailored to the audience and the occasion.[9]

The first step in learning to use your voice more effectively is to evaluate how you usually talk. Record yourself while speaking and reading aloud. As you listen to yourself, ask these questions:

- Does my voice convey the meaning I intend?

- Would I want to listen to me if I were in the audience?

- Does my voice present me at my best?

If your answers are negative or uncertain, look at how the concepts in this section can help you discover ways to better find your voice. Save your original recording so that you can hear yourself improve as you practice.

Pitch

Pitch is the placement of your voice on a scale ranging from low and deep to high and shrill. Like singers, speakers can use a wealth of tones to be expressive. For effective speaking, find a pitch level that is comfortable and that allows maximum flexibility and variety. Each of us has a **habitual pitch**, the level at which we speak most

▶ **pitch** The position of the human voice on a scale ranging from low and deep to high and shrill.

▶ **habitual pitch** The vocal level at which people speak most frequently.

FINDING YOUR

voice Using Pitch Effectively

You can use the following exercise to help determine your optimum pitch.
Sing the sound *la* down to the lowest pitch you can produce without feeling strain or having your voice break or become rough. Now count each note as you sing up the scale to the highest tone you can comfortably produce. Most people have a range of approximately sixteen notes. Your optimum pitch will be about one-fourth of the way up your range. For example, if your range extends twelve notes, your optimum pitch would be at the third note up the scale. Again, sing down to your lowest comfortable pitch, and then sing up to your optimum pitch level.[10]

Record this exercise (perhaps on a cell phone, computer, or digital camera), and compare your optimum pitch to the habitual pitch revealed during your first recording. If your optimum pitch is within one or two notes of your habitual pitch, you should not experience vocal problems related to pitch level. If your habitual pitch is much higher or lower than your optimum pitch, you may not have sufficient flexibility to raise or lower the pitch of your voice to communicate changes in meaning and emphasis. You can change your habitual pitch by practicing speaking and reading at your optimum pitch.

frequently. We also have an **optimum pitch**, the level that allows us to produce our strongest voice with minimal effort and that permits variation up and down the scale.

To experiment with how to use pitch effectively, read the following paragraphs from N. Scott Momaday's *The Way to Rainy Mountain*. Use your optimum pitch level, with pitch changes to provide meaning and feeling. To make the most of your practice, record yourself so you can observe both problems and progress.

> A single knoll rises out of the plain in Oklahoma, north and west of the Wichita Range. For my people, the Kiowas, it is an old landmark, and they gave it the name Rainy Mountain. The hardest weather in the world is there. Winter brings blizzards, hot tornadic winds arise in the spring, and in the summer the prairie is an anvil's edge. The grass turns brittle and brown, and it cracks beneath your feet. There are green belts along the rivers and creeks, linear groves of hickory and pecan, willow, and witch hazel. At a distance in July or August the steaming foliage seems almost to writhe in fire. . . . Loneliness is an aspect of the land. All things in the plain are isolate: There is no confusion of objects in the eye, but one hill or one tree or one man. To look upon that landscape in the early morning, with the sun at your back, is to lose the sense of proportion. Your imagination comes to life, and this, you think, is where Creation was begun.[11]

Use the exercise to explore the full range of variation around your optimum pitch and make you more conscious of the relationship between pitch and effective communication. Then record yourself reading the passage again, this time exaggerating the pitch variations as you read it—even to the point of feeling silly. If you have a narrow pitch range, you may discover that exaggeration makes you sound more effective.

When you speak before a group, don't be surprised if your pitch seems higher than usual. Pitch is sensitive to emotions and usually goes up when you are under

▶ **optimum pitch** The level at which people can produce their strongest voice with minimal effort and that allows variation up and down the musical scale.

pressure. You can follow the professionals' practice of warming up your voice before you speak, including humming your optimum pitch softly to yourself, so that you start out on the right level.

Rate

Your **rate**, or the speed at which you speak, helps set the mood of your speech. Just as vocalists may sing *largo* or *presto, accelerando* or *ritardando*, with rests and fermatas, you can speak slowly or quickly, speed up or slow down, with pauses and sustained sounds to give texture to your presentation. For example, when *Law and Order: SVU* star Mariska Hargitay spoke on domestic violence to the National Press Club, she used a fast, light pace as she talked about whipping out her cell phone to take a photograph of the vice president when she met him. When she moved to delineating the statistics on domestic violence, however, she used a slower, more deliberate rate.[12] These variations involved the duration of syllables, the use of pauses, and the overall speed of presentation.

The rate and stress patterns within a speech produce its **rhythm**, an essential component of all communication.[13] With rhythmic variations, you point out what is important and make it easier for listeners to comprehend your message. For example, if you have been speaking rapidly and then suddenly slow your pace, pausing to highlight the contrast, you will call attention to what you are saying. This, your vocal change suggests, is important.

People who feel intimidated by the speaking situation often speed up their presentations and run their words together—a rapid-fire delivery suggesting the speaker's desire to get it over with and sit down! At the other extreme, some speakers become so slow and deliberate that they almost put themselves and their audiences to sleep. Neither machine-gun speed nor snail's pace slowness encourages your audience to listen carefully.

As we noted in Chapter 3, the typical rate for extemporaneous speaking is approximately 125 words per minute. You can check your speed by timing your reading of the excerpt from *Rainy Mountain*. If you were reading at the average rate, you would have taken about sixty seconds to complete that material. If you allowed time for pauses between phrases, which is appropriate for such formal material, your reading may have run slightly longer. If you took less than fifty seconds, you were probably speaking too rapidly or not using pauses effectively.

Pausing before or after a word or phrase highlights its importance. Pauses also give your listeners time to contemplate what you have said. They can build suspense and maintain interest as listeners anticipate what you will say next. Moreover, pauses can clarify the relationships among ideas, phrases, and sentences. They are oral punctuation marks, taking the place of the commas and periods, underlines, and exclamation marks that occur in written communication. Experienced speakers learn how to use pauses to maximum advantage. Humorist William Price Fox once wrote of Eugene Talmadge, a colorful Georgia governor and fabled stump-speaker, "That rascal knew how to wait. He had the longest pause in the state."[14] Use pauses and vocal emphasis to state your main ideas most forcefully.

In her speech "Pulling a Cat out of a Hat," reprinted at the end of Chapter 6, Jessica Bradshaw began by reading a poem written about Dr. Seuss's writing. Try your hand at reading the following passage, deliberately using rate and pitch variations, including pauses, to communicate the mood of the material. To fully explore and exercise your capacity to use variations in pace effectively, remember to exaggerate for effect. (It helps to actually read the material to young children. They usually make a wonderful audience!)

▶ **rate**   The speed at which words are uttered.

▶ **rhythm**   Rate and stress patterns of vocal presentation within a speech.

Have you read *The Cat in the Hat?*
Of course you have. I'm sure of that!
And how about *Green Eggs and Ham?* Did you dig that Sam-I-Am?
Or *Yertle, the Turtle* you got from Aunt Myrtle?
And, did you like the book 'bout the Grinch?
You silly goose, that was a cinch!

If your natural tendency is to speak slowly, you can practice developing a faster, more lively rate by reading light material aloud. Try reading other stories by Dr. Seuss. Such tales as *Green Eggs and Ham* should bring out the ham in you!

Although pausing can work for you, the wrong use of silence within a speech can work against you. *A short, deliberate pause conveys meaning; a long hesitation signals confusion, uncertainty, and/or a lack of preparation.* Some speakers habitually use "ers" and "ums," "wells" and "okays," "likes" and "you knows" in the place of pauses without being aware of it. These **vocal distractions** may fill in the silence while the speaker thinks about what to say next, or they may be signs of nervousness. They may also be signals that speakers lack confidence in themselves or their messages.

Sometimes simply becoming aware of such vocal distractions is enough to help you control them. Work to eliminate such fillers from your daily conversations so that you do not have to worry about cutting them out during presentations. Your friends likely won't notice, but those you want to impress—from professors to employers—will.

Practicing your presentation also diminishes vocal distractions. When you are comfortable with what you're going to say and how you're going to say it, you are much less likely to need those vocalized pauses or to use "okay," "well," or "you know" as transitions instead of language that will help your listeners follow your points.

Remember, the goal is to decrease your vocal distractions, not to get rid of every single one. A few are natural; many affect your credibility.

FINDING YOUR voice
Minimizing, Um, Vocal Distractions

Worried that you might be including too many vocal distractions in your presentations? Try this exercise, adapted from one developed by Professor Pat Baker of Davidson College:

1. Record your presentation as you practice one of the major points for your speech.
2. Then play it back, counting the "uhs" (or "likes" or whatever). Write the total number here: _____
3. Divide by the number of minutes you spoke to determine your baseline per minute. Baseline per minute _____
   Divide this number by two to get your baseline per 30 seconds _____
4. Record your presentation again, focusing on delivering 30 seconds' worth. Play it back, and again count the vocal distractions for that period.
5. Do this several times, trying to decrease the number of vocal distractions each time. Then consider increasing the time to 45 seconds or 1 minute.

▶ **vocal distractions** Filler words, such as "er," "um," and "you know," used in the place of a pause.

Different cultures have different speech rhythms. In the United States, for example, northerners often speak more rapidly than southerners. These variations in the patterns of speech can create misunderstandings. Californians, who use longer pauses than New Yorkers, may perceive the latter as rude and aggressive. New Yorkers may see Californians as too laid back or as not having much to say. Be generous in reading the speech patterns of others to avoid stereotyping individuals on the basis of what may be culturally based speech rate variations.

Volume

Like songs, no presentation can be effective if the audience can't hear you. Nor will your presentation be successful if you overwhelm listeners with a voice that is too loud. When you speak before a group, you usually need to speak louder than you do in general conversation. The size of the room, the presence or absence of a microphone, and background noise may also call for adjustments. To develop the capacity to deal with such noise, speech teachers of ancient Greece often took their students to the beach and had them practice over the sound of crashing waves. To adjust your loudness, take your cues from audience feedback. If you are not loud enough, you may see listeners leaning forward, straining to hear. If you speak too loudly, they may unconsciously lean back, pulling away from the noise.

As with culturally influenced speech rates, different cultures have different norms and expectations concerning appropriate volume. For example, in some Mediterranean cultures, a loud voice signifies strength and sincerity, whereas in some Asian and Native American cultures, a soft voice is associated with good manners and education.[15] When members of your audience come from a variety of cultural and ethnic groups, try to moderate your delivery and be sensitive to your listeners' responses.

To speak with proper volume, you must have good breath control. You need enough force to project your voice so that you can be heard at the back of a room. You also need enough breath to finish phrases and provide appropriate pauses.

FINDING YOUR

voice   Take a Deep Breath

To check whether you are breathing properly for speaking, stand with your feet approximately 8 inches apart. Place your hands on your lower rib cage, thumbs to the front, fingers to the back. Take a deep breath—in through your nose and out through slightly parted lips. If you are breathing correctly, you should feel your ribs moving up and out as you inhale.

Then take a normal breath and see how long you can count while exhaling. If you cannot reach fifteen without losing volume or feeling the need to breathe, you need to work on extending your breath control. Begin by counting in one breath to a number comfortable for you, and then gradually increase the count over successive tries. Do not try to compensate by breathing too deeply. Deep breathing takes too much time and attracts too much attention while you are speaking. Use the longer pauses in your speech to breathe, and make note of your breathing pattern as you practice your speech.

Breathing improperly affects more than just the volume of your speech. If you breathe by raising your shoulders, the muscles in your neck and throat tense up. This can result in a harsh, strained vocal quality. Moreover, you probably will not take in enough air to sustain your phrasing, and the release of air will be difficult to control. The air and sound will all come out with a rush when you drop your shoulders, leading to unfortunate oral punctuation marks when you don't want or need them. Yoga and singing both encourage proper breathing, deep into your diaphragm—roughly behind your belly button.

Vary the volume of words and phrases in your speech, just as you change your pitch and rate of speaking to express ideas more effectively. Changes in volume are often used to express emotion. The more excited or angry we are, the louder we tend to become. But don't let yourself get caught in the trap of having only two options: loud and louder. Decreasing your volume, slowing your rate, pausing, or dropping your pitch can also express emotion quite effectively.

Davidson student BJ Youngerman demonstrated the importance of variations in volume as he reenacted a scene from his experience as a baseball umpire. In the confrontation between himself and a coach, BJ contrasted the angry loudness of the coach with his own quieter, more controlled vocal mannerisms as an umpire. Read the scene aloud, and as you play both roles, explore your own capacity to produce both louder and quieter speech:

BJ Youngerman used changes in loudness effectively in his speech about his experience as a baseball umpire.

Me: "He's out!" (with hand motion)
Coach: "You've got to be kidding me, Blue! He was a good 10 feet beyond the base before the ball got there. That's horrible!"
Me: "Coach, it's a judgment call. I called it like I saw it. Please get back to your dugout."
Coach: "Blue, that was the worst call I've ever seen. You're totally blind."
Me: "Coach, this is your final warning: Get in the dugout."
Coach: "Well just because you got cut in Little League doesn't mean you have to take it out on these kids!"
Me: "That's it! You're done!" (waves arms to signify ejection of coach)

Had BJ delivered this entire exchange *forte* (loud) or *pianissimo* (soft), the lack of contrast would have robbed the example of much of its power. Instead, the vocal contrasts accompanied his vigorous gestures to stimulate interest in his presentation on being an umpire.

FINDING YOUR voice   Can You Hear Me Now?

To acquire more variety in volume, practice the following exercise recommended by Ralph Hillman: "First, count to five at a soft volume, as if you were speaking to one person. Then, count to five at medium volume, as if speaking to ten or fifteen people. Finally, count to five, as if speaking to thirty or more people."[16] If you record this exercise, you should be able to hear the clear progression in loudness.

Variety

Have you noticed a continuing refrain in these discussions of pitch, rate, and volume? Variety is the spice of life, including public speaking. You recognize the importance of vocal variety when you hear speeches that lack it. Speakers who drone on in a monotone convey that they have little interest in their topic or their listeners or that they fear the situation they are in. Variety can make speeches come to life by adding color and interest.

One of the best ways to develop an array of vocal qualities is to express meaning and feeling by reading aloud lively writings. As you read the following selection from Betty Ren Wright's *Johnny Go Round*, strive for maximum variation of pitch, rate, and volume:

> Johnny Go Round was a tan tom cat.
> Would you like to know why we called him that?
> Because Johnny goes round when he's chasing a ball,
> And Johnny goes round after nothing at all.
> Silly old Johnny Go Round![17]

Record yourself while reading this and other favorite poems or dramatic scenes aloud. Compare these practices with your initial self-evaluation recording to see if you are developing variety in your presentations.

Vocal Problems

People often make judgments about others on the basis of their speech patterns. If you slur your words, mispronounce familiar words, or speak with a dialect that sounds unfamiliar to your audience, you may be seen as uneducated or distant. When you sound "odd" to your listeners, their attention will be distracted from what you are saying to the way you are saying it. In this section, we cover articulation, enunciation, pronunciation, and dialect, as they can detract from speaking effectiveness.

Articulation. **Articulation** is the way you produce individual speech sounds. Some people have trouble making certain sounds. For example, they may substitute a *d* for a *th*, saying "dem" instead of "them." Other sounds that are often misarticulated include *s, l,* and *r.* Severe articulation problems can interfere with effective communication, especially if the audience cannot understand the speaker or if the variations suggest low social or educational status. Many of these problems may be best treated by a speech therapist, who can retrain the individual to produce the sound in a more commonly understood manner.

Enunciation. **Enunciation** is the way you pronounce words in context. In casual conversation, it is not unusual for people to slur their words—for example, saying "gimme" for "give me." However, careless enunciation causes credibility problems for public speakers. Do you say, "Swatuh thought" for "That's what I thought"? "Harya?" for "How are you?" or "Howjado?" for "How did you do?" In public speaking, these enunciation patterns are likely to diminish your ethos. Check your enunciation patterns on the recordings you have made to determine whether you should articulate words more clearly. If you do, concentrate on careful enunciation as you practice your speech. Be careful, however, to avoid the opposite problem of inflated, pompous, and pretentious enunciation, which sounds phony. Strike the balance between sloppy slurring and overly precise articulation.

▶ **articulation** The manner in which individual speech sounds are produced.

▶ **enunciation** The manner in which individual words are articulated and pronounced in context.

Pronunciation. **Pronunciation** involves saying words correctly. It includes both using the correct sounds and placing the proper accent on syllables. Because written English does not always indicate the correct pronunciation, we may not be sure how to pronounce words that we first encounter in print. For instance, does the word *chiropodist* begin with a *sh*, a *ch*, or a *k* sound? What syllables should be emphasized?

If you are not certain how to pronounce a word, consult a dictionary. An especially useful reference is the *NBC Handbook of Pronunciation*, which contains 21,000 words and proper names that sometimes cause problems.[18] When international stories and new foreign leaders first appear in the news, newspapers frequently indicate the correct pronunciation of their names. Check front-page stories in the *New York Times* for guidance with such words. Then again, you can follow the advice given to one of the authors. Before giving a presentation, she sought to verify the pronunciation of "trompe l'oeil," a French term meaning "trick of the eye." A colleague brightly offered, "I know! It's pronounced '*synonym*'!"

In addition to problems pronouncing unfamiliar words, you may find that there are certain words you habitually mispronounce. For example, how do you pronounce the following words?

government	athlete
ask	library
nuclear	picture

Unless you are careful, you may find yourself slipping into these common mispronunciations:

goverment	athalete
axe	liberry
nuculer	pitchur

Mispronunciation of such common words can damage your ethos. Be sure to verify your pronunciation of troublesome words as you practice your speech and become comfortable with their correct form.

Dialect. A **dialect** is a speech pattern typical of a geographic region or ethnic group. Your dialect usually reflects the area of the country where you were raised or lived for any length of time or your cultural and ethnic identity.[19] In the United States, there are three commonly recognized dialects: eastern, southern, and midwestern. Additionally, there are local variations within the broader dialects. For example, South Carolina boasts the Gullah dialect from the islands off the coast, the low-country or Charlestonian accent, the Piedmont variation, and the Appalachian twang.[20] And then there's always "Bah-stahn" [Boston], where you can buy a "lodge budded pup con" [large, buttered popcorn] at the movies!

There is no such thing in nature as a superior or an inferior dialect. There are, however, occasions when a distinct dialect is a definite disadvantage or advantage. Listeners prefer speech patterns that are familiar to their ears. Audiences may also have stereotyped preconceptions about people who speak with certain dialects. For example, those raised in the South often associate a northeastern dialect with brusqueness and abrasiveness, and midwesterners may associate a southern dialect with slowness of action and mind. When inaugurated as president at a southern institution, Dr. Carol Quillen used effective self-deprecating humor by sharing advice she'd received: "we know you are from the northeast—bless your heart!—but let us finish our *own* sentences."[21]

Matt Damon made effective use of his natural Boston accent when speaking in New England.

▶ **pronunciation** The use of correct sounds and of proper stress on syllables when saying words.

▶ **dialect** A speech pattern associated with an area of the country or with a cultural or ethnic background.

If you sound like southern comic Jeff Foxworthy or like Will Ferrell's pompous Ron Burgundy from *Anchorman,* you want to be aware of potential misperceptions based on your dialect. In those situations, work to build your competence, integrity, and goodwill more explicitly.

Your dialect should reflect the standard for educated people from your geographic area or ethnic group. You should be concerned about tempering it only if it creates barriers to understanding and identification between you and your audience. Then you may want to work toward softening your dialect so that you can lower these barriers for the sake of connecting your message with your audience.

Developing Your Body Language

Explore at **MyCommunicationLab** Activity: "Physical Delivery"

Remember the student whose lackadaisical delivery contradicted her words about being a boisterous child? Communication with your audience begins before you ever open your mouth. Your facial expression, personal appearance, and manner of movement all convey a message. Do you seem confident and determined as you walk to the front of the room to give your speech, or do you stumble and shuffle? As you begin your speech, do you look listeners directly in the eye, or do you stare at the ceiling as if you are seeking divine intervention?

Watch at **MyCommunicationLab** Video: "Tips for Speech Delivery"

Body language is a second great resource that will enable you to achieve a successful presentation.[22] In his classic book *The Presentation of Self in Everyday Life,* Erving Goffman emphasizes the importance of creating consistency among the verbal and nonverbal elements of expression. To achieve a harmony of impressions, *your body language must reinforce your verbal language.*[23] If your face is expressionless as you urge your listeners to action, you are sending inconsistent messages. If you seem flustered and uncertain as you urge listeners to be confident and calm, your impressions will be badly out of sync. Be sure that your body and words both "say" the same thing, and that your body gives voice to the concepts you want to express. As you study this section, remember that, although we discuss separate types of body language, in practice they all work together and are interpreted as a totality by audiences.[24]

Facial Expression and Eye Contact

Watch at **MyCommunicationLab** Video: "Untreated Depression"

I knew she was lying the minute she said it. There was guilt written all over her face!

He sure is shifty! Did you see how his eyes darted back and forth? He never did look us straight in the eye!

Most of us believe we can judge people's character, determine their true feelings, and tell whether they are honest by watching their facial expressions. If there is a conflict between what we see and what we hear, we usually believe our eyes rather than our ears.

The eyes are the most important element of facial expressiveness. In mainstream American culture, frequent and sustained eye contact suggests honesty, openness, and respect. We may think of a person's eyes as windows into the self. If you avoid looking at your audience while you are talking, you are drawing the shades on these windows. A lack of eye contact suggests that you do not care about listeners, that you are putting something over on them, or that you are afraid of them. Other cultures view eye contact differently. In China, Indonesia, and rural Mexico, traditionally people lower their eyes as a sign of deference. In general, people from Asian and some African countries engage in less eye contact than those

▶ **body language** Communication achieved using facial expressions, eye contact, movements, and gestures.

from the mainstream American culture.[25] Some Native Americans may even find direct eye contact offensive or aggressive. Therefore, with culturally diverse audiences especially, don't conclude that listeners who resist eye contact are necessarily expressing their distrust or refusal to communicate.

Watch at
MyCommunicationLab
Video: "Sweat"

When you reach the lectern, turn, pause, and engage the eyes of your audience. This signals that you want to communicate and prepares people to listen. During your speech, try to make eye contact with all sectors of the audience. First, look at people at the front of the room, then shift your focus to the middle and sides, and, finally, look at those in the rear. You may find that those sitting in the back of the room are the most difficult to reach. They may have taken a rear seat because they don't want to listen or be involved. Eye contact is one way you can gain and hold their attention. Don't just stare at one or two people. You will make them uncomfortable, and other audience members will feel left out.

Smile as you start your speech unless a smile is inappropriate to your message. A smile signals your goodwill toward listeners and your ease in the speaking situation—qualities that should help your ethos.[26] From your very first words, your face should reflect and reinforce the meanings of your words. An expressionless face suggests that the speaker is afraid or indifferent. A frozen face may be a mask behind which the speaker hides. The solution lies in selecting a topic that excites you, concentrating on sharing your message, and having the confidence that comes from being well prepared.

You can also try the following exercise. Utter these statements using a dull monotone and keeping your face as expressionless as possible:

I am absolutely delighted by your gift.

I don't know when I've ever been this excited.

We don't need to beg for change—we need to demand change.

All this puts me in a very bad mood.

Now repeat them with *exaggerated* vocal variety and facial expression. You may find that your hands and body also want to get involved. Encourage such impulses so that you develop an integrated system of body language.

Movement and Gestures

Most actors learn—often the hard way—that, if you want to steal a scene from someone, all you have to do is move around, develop a twitch, or swing a leg. Before long, all eyes will be focused on that movement. This cheap theatrical trick shows that physical movement sometimes can attract more attention than words. All the more reason that your words and gestures should work in harmony and not at cross-purposes! This also means you should avoid random movements, such as pacing back and forth, twirling your hair, rubbing your eyes, jingling change in your pockets, or "driving" the lectern. Once you are aware of such mannerisms, it is easier to control them. Try a video recording (perhaps with a cell phone or digital camera) as you practice for your next speech. Just as audio recording can reveal aspects of your voice that are surprising, so can video recording reveal unsuspected habits of movement that you should correct.

Your gestures and movement should be consistent with, and complement, what you are saying. You may have developed a strategic awareness of body language as you practice—for example: "When I reach this moment in the speech, I've got to stop, pause, look hard at listeners, and use gestures to really drive home my

Bishop Desmond Tutu uses strong gestures that seem natural.

point." But body language should always *appear* natural and spontaneous. Gestures should never *look* contrived or artificial. For example, you should avoid framing a gesture to fit each word or sequence of words you utter. Perhaps every speech instructor has encountered speakers like the one who stood with arms circled above him as he said, "We need to get *around* this problem." That's not good body language!

Let your gestures grow out of your message naturally. Stand tall with good posture so that you can breathe easily and project confidence. Start with your hands and body in a position that allows free action. For example, you cannot gesture if your hands are locked behind your back or jammed into your pockets or if you are grasping the lectern as a life preserver. Instead, let your hands rest in a relaxed position—at your sides, on the lectern, or in front of you at waist level. As you execute a gesture, let yourself move naturally and fully. Don't raise your hand halfway and then stop with your arm frozen awkwardly in space. When you have completed a gesture, let your hands return to the starting point, ready to emphasize the next important point.

Do not assume that there is a universal language of gesture. Rwandans, for example, learn an elaborate code of gestures that is a direct extension of their spoken language.[27] In contrast, our "gestural language" is far less complex and sophisticated. Still, it can perform important communication functions, such as reinforcing, amplifying, and clarifying the spoken word and signaling your feelings and intentions.

The Factor of Distance.

From **proxemics**, the study of how humans use space during communication, we can derive two additional principles that help explain the effective use of movement during speeches. The first suggests that *the actual* **distance** *between speakers and listeners affects their sense of closeness or immediacy.* Barack Obama's speeches offer an interesting illustration of this principle. At times, Obama speaks in formal settings that seem to place him *above* and somewhat *distant from* his listeners. An obvious example occurs when he makes formal speeches to Congress such as the State of the Union address. These manipulations of space emphasize the power and formality of his office and enhance his presidential qualities. At other moments, we see him in less formal settings, responding to question-and-answer sessions or conducting town hall meetings. In these moments, he comes closer to listeners, approaches them more on their own level, and comes across more as a "regular guy" with a charming smile and appealing sense of humor. Control of proxemics in all such cases helps to establish his well-rounded identity as a citizen-leader who enjoys unusual power but is also "one of us." You can be very sure that his advisers are aware of these proxemic effects!

FINDING YOUR

voice   Toward a Livelier Presentation

As you practice your next speech, record yourself or work with a partner and deliberately try to speak in as dull a voice as possible. Stifle all impulses to gesture. Then practice speaking with as colorful a voice as possible, giving full freedom to movement and gesture. Then analyze the two versions. Which aspects create a colorful and expressive presentation that makes your ideas seem more lively and vivid? How can you incorporate these aspects into your presentation to your audience?

▶ **proxemics**   The study of how human beings use space during communication.

▶ **distance**   Principle of proxemics involving the control of the space that separates speaker and audience.

The greater the physical distance between speaker and audience is, the harder it is to achieve identification between them. This problem gets worse when a lectern acts as a physical barrier. Short speakers can almost disappear behind it! One judge counsels attorneys to avoid lecterns altogether, arguing that "they create artificial barriers between lawyer and juror."[28] Try speaking either beside or in front of the lectern so that your body language can work for you.

At the same time, you don't want to move so close to listeners that you make them feel uncomfortable. If they pull back involuntarily in their chairs, you know you have violated their sense of personal space. A Goldilocks distance that's "just right" can be achieved by watching your audience's responses. In addition, moving purposefully—without pacing—can engage your audience and provide an appropriate outlet for your energy.

The Factor of Elevation.   The second principle of proxemics suggests that **elevation** *also affects the sense of closeness between speakers and listeners.* When you speak, you often stand above your seated listeners in a "power position." Because we tend to associate *above* us with power over us, speakers may find that this arrangement discourages identification with some listeners. Often, they will sit on the edge of the desk or stand in front of the lectern in a more relaxed and less elevated stance. If your message is informal and requires close identification or if you are especially tall, you might try this approach.

Reducing the physical distance between the speaker and audience can help increase identification with the speaker, as being "one of us."

Explore at **MyCommunicationLab** **Activity:** "Professional Appearance"

Personal Appearance

Your clothing and grooming affect how you are perceived and how your message is received.[29] Again, as Goffman notes, one's personal appearance should be consistent with the overall impression one wishes to give.[30] How we dress can even influence how we see ourselves and how we behave. A police officer out of uniform may not act as authoritatively as when dressed in blue. A doctor without a white jacket may behave like just another person. You may have a certain type of clothing that makes you feel comfortable and relaxed. You may even have a special "good luck" outfit that raises your confidence.

When you are scheduled to speak, dress in a way that makes you feel good about yourself, and that respects the audience and the occasion. How you dress reflects how you feel about the importance of the event. Guy Kawasaki, who played a key role in marketing Apple products and now has an active career as a speaker and consultant, suggests that "to underdress is to communicate . . . 'I'm smarter/richer/more powerful than you. I can insult you and not take you serious[ly], and there's nothing you can do about it.' This is hardly the way to get an audience to like you."[31] Think of your speech as a *professional* situation, and dress accordingly. If your outfit feels perfect for an afternoon of watching sports or could be described as "hot and sexy," it probably won't emphasize either to yourself or to the audience that your message is important. As we noted in Chapter 10, your appearance can serve as a presentation aid that complements your message. Like any other aid, it should never compete with your words for attention or be distracting.

Learning to use your body language effectively will enhance your impact beyond public speaking. From courtrooms to business to personal relationships, understanding the value of coordinating message and delivery will improve communication

▶ **elevation**   Principle of proxemics dealing with power relationships implied when speakers stand above listeners.

in your life.[32] Emmy-winning actor Alan Alda believes so strongly in the power of connecting voice, body, and ideas that he has started a program at SUNY–Stony Brook University for communicating in the sciences. Using impromptu and role-playing exercises, he helps everyone from physicians to physicists learn how to strengthen their voice by improving their presentation.

Developing Versatility in Presentation

Explore at MyCommunicationLab Activity: "Methods of Delivery"

Finding your voice means more than developing your natural resources of voice and body language. It also means understanding how those resources can enhance the four types of presentation: impromptu speaking, extemporaneous speaking, reading from a manuscript, and memorized text presentation (see Figure 12.1). Although classrooms frequently emphasize impromptu and extemporaneous delivery, you may encounter situations in which you need to use a manuscript or offer a memorized presentation, particularly in situations outside of the classroom.

Impromptu Speaking

Impromptu speaking is speaking on the spur of the moment in response to unpredictable situations with limited time for preparation. Such speaking is sometimes called "speaking off the cuff," a phrase that suggests you could put all your notes on the cuff of your shirt or, if you followed the practice of a recent political speaker, in the palm of your hand (we don't recommend either practice!). Even in a carefully prepared speech, there may be moments of impromptu presentation—times when you must make on-the-spot adjustments to audience feedback or respond to questions at the end of your speech.

Many situations call for impromptu speaking. At work, you might be asked to make a presentation "in five minutes." Or in meetings, you may decide to say a few words about a new product. During class, you often answer a question or comment on a point just made by your professor. In these cases, you make impromptu speeches.

When you have just a few minutes to prepare, don't waste time and mental energy panicking. Instead, focus on the task at hand. If you can find a quiet place, that will help; one author prepared a short presentation in a restroom. Start by *determining your purpose*. What do you want the audience to know? Why is this important? Next, *decide on your main points*. You may have time for only one main point; you should not tackle more than three. Don't try to cover too much. If you can, jot down a memory-jogging word for each idea in a skeletal outline that will help keep you focused.

As you speak, don't dash through your remarks. A slower delivery gives you time to think ahead, allows your audience time to absorb what you're saying, and minimizes "ums" and "likes" and "you knows." Stick to your main point or points. Use the **PREP formula** to develop each one: State the *p*oint, give a *r*eason or *ex*ample, and then restate the *p*oint.

Point:	You should buy a hybrid car.
Reason(s):	Hybrid cars are good for the environment—and good for your pocketbook!
Example:	If you drive 10,000 miles a year, you could easily save $600 a year on gas alone.
Restatement of *Point*:	Drive green and keep more green. Buy a hybrid!

▶ **impromptu speaking** Speaking on the spur of the moment in response to an unpredictable situation with limited time for preparation.

▶ **PREP formula** A technique for making an impromptu speech: State a point, give a reason or example, and restate the point.

If you have more than one point, incorporate simple transitions as you go: "My first point is . . . . Second, it is important to . . . . Finally, it is clear that . . . ." Keep your presentation short, and end with a summary of your remarks.

An impromptu speech often is one of several such speeches as people express their ideas in meetings. The preceding speeches create the context for your presentation. If earlier speakers stood at the front of the room to speak, you should do so as well. If they remained seated, you may wish to do the same. On the other hand, if earlier speakers offended listeners while making standing presentations, you may wish to remain seated to differentiate yourself from them. If seated speakers made trivial presentations, standing would signal that what you are going to say is important.

Most impromptu speaking situations are relatively casual. No one expects a polished presentation on a moment's notice. However, the ability to organize your ideas quickly and effectively and to present them confidently puts you at a great advantage, both inside and outside of the classroom. The principles of preparing speeches that you are learning in this course will help you become a more effective impromptu speaker in a variety of contexts.

Extemporaneous Speaking

Extemporaneous speaking *is prepared and practiced, but not written out or memorized.* Rather than focusing on the exact wording of the speech, the speaker concentrates

FIGURE 12.1
Methods of Presentation

Method	Use	Advantages	Disadvantages
Impromptu	When you have no time for preparation or practice	Is spontaneous; can meet demands of the situation; is open to feedback.	Is less polished, less well researched, less organized; allows less use of supporting material.
Extemporaneous	For most public speaking occasions	Is spontaneous; encourages responding to audience feedback; encourages focusing on the essence of your message.	Requires considerable preparation and practice; experience leads to excellence.
Manuscript	When exact wording is important, time constraints are strict, or your speech will be telecast	Allows planning of precise wording; can be timed down to seconds.	Requires practice and an ability to read well; inhibits response to feedback.
Memorized	When you will be making a brief remark, such as a toast or award acceptance, or when the wording of your introduction or conclusion is important	Allows planning of eloquent wording; can sound well polished.	Must be written out in advance; can make you forget to communicate; can sound sing-songy.

▶ **extemporaneous speaking** A form of presentation in which a speech, although carefully prepared and practiced, is not written out or memorized.

on the sequence of ideas that will develop in the speech, on its underlying message, and on the final impression the speech should leave with listeners. Extemporaneous speaking features a spontaneous and natural-sounding presentation and makes it easier to establish immediacy with an audience. The speaker is not the prisoner of a text, and each presentation will vary according to the audience, occasion, and inspiration of the moment.

Because extemporaneous speaking focuses on the ideas and the listeners, it encourages interaction with an audience. A Vanderbilt student who distributed photographs and then instructed listeners on how to view them and another student who asked listeners to close their eyes and imagine themselves living as dwarfs were playing up these advantages. Such interaction encourages the audience to participate in constructing the message of the speech. It becomes their creation as well, which is especially important when persuading listeners.

Because it requires speakers to master the overall pattern of thought within their speeches, extemporaneous speaking emphasizes the importance of *preparation and practice*. As you rehearse for your extemporaneous speech, move from any manuscript or full-sentence outline you may have prepared to a key-word outline such as we discussed in Chapter 3. Both in practice and in actual presentation, the key-word outline will not only keep you on track but also keep your focus where it belongs: on your ideas and your listeners.

At its best, such speaking combines the spontaneity and immediacy of impromptu speeches and the careful preparation of manuscript and memorized presentations. *It is therefore the master mode of speaking,* the best for most speaking situations and the one preferred by most instructors for most classroom speeches. Its special advantage is that it encourages you to adapt to audience feedback in creative and constructive ways.

Responding to Feedback from Your Audience

As we saw in Chapter 1, **feedback** is the message listeners send back to you as you speak. Facial expressions, gestures, or sounds of agreement or disagreement let you know how you are coming across. Since most feedback is nonverbal, you should maintain eye contact with your audience so that you can respond to these signals. Use feedback to monitor whether listeners understand you, are interested, and agree with what you are saying. Negative feedback in particular can alert you that you need to make on-the-spot adjustments.

Feedback That Signals Misunderstanding. Listeners' puzzled expressions can signal that they don't understand what you are saying. You may need to define an unfamiliar word or rephrase an idea to make it simpler. You could add an example or story to make an abstract concept more concrete. It might help to compare or contrast an unfamiliar idea with something the audience already knows and understands. When you detect signs of misunderstanding, you can say, "Let me put it another way." Then provide a different explanation that might be clearer to them.

Feedback That Signals Loss of Interest. Bored listeners wiggle in their seats, drum their fingers, or develop a glazed look. To get them to reengage, you can provide an example or story that makes your message come to life, or you can involve listeners by asking a question that calls for a show of hands. You can startle them with a bold statement and remind them of the importance of your topic. Keep in mind that enthusiasm is contagious: *your* interest can arouse *theirs*. Move from behind the lectern and come closer to them. Whatever happens, do not become

▶ **feedback** Your perception of how audience members react to the message as you speak.

YOUR ethical VOICE Persistent Questions about Presentation

Audiences often raise ethical and practical questions concerning the presentation aspects of public speaking. The following mini-scenarios offer a sampling of such questions and doubts:

1. "He talks so slowly. Does he *think* slowly, too?"

2. "She talks so fast. Is she trying to put something over on me?"

3. "I don't like how he dresses or his hairstyle, either. Can a person with such bad taste be telling the truth?"

4. "She has a peculiar accent. Probably foreign. How can she possibly understand my problems?"

5. "He just mispronounced a word. Could his thinking be flawed as well? Can I trust such an ignoramus?"

6. "She looks uncomfortable. Kind of buried in her notes and not looking us in the eye. If she's not confident as a speaker, should I be confident in following her advice?"

7. "He sounds too good, too polished. Can I trust him?"

Assuming that you are the person to whom such questions are asked, how would you answer them? What advice would you offer to counter such distrust?

disheartened or lose faith in your speech. In all likelihood, some people—probably more than you think—find the speech interesting.

Feedback That Signals Disagreement.   Listeners who disagree with you may frown or shake their heads to indicate how they feel about what you are saying. A number of techniques can help you soften disagreement. If you anticipate resistance, work hard to establish your ethos in the introduction of your speech. Listeners should see you as a competent, trustworthy, strong, and likable person who has their best interests at heart.

To be perceived as competent, you need to *be* competent. Practice your presentation until you are comfortable with it. Arm yourself with a surplus of information, examples, and testimony from sources your audience will respect. Set an example of tolerance by respecting positions different from your own.

You may find that, although you differ with listeners on issues, you agree with them on goals. Stress the values that you share. Appeal to their sense of fair play and their respect for your right to speak. You should be the model of civility in the situation. Avoid angry reactions and the use of inflammatory language. Think of these listeners as offering an opportunity for your ideas to have impact.

Reading from a Manuscript

When you make a **manuscript presentation**, you read to an audience from either a text or a teleprompter. Manuscript presentations pose challenges. The first begins with the preparation of the manuscript. Many people do not write in a natural oral style. The major differences between oral and written language, covered in Chapter 11, bear repeating. Good oral style uses short, direct, conversational speech patterns. Even sentence fragments can be acceptable. Speakers need to use repetition, rephrasing, and amplification more than writers. Developing a sense of rhythm and using imagery are especially important in oral style.

Delivery of a manuscript presentation poses additional challenges. When people plan to read a speech, they often do not practice enough. Unless speakers are

▶ **manuscript presentation**   A speech read from a prepared text or teleprompter.

Annie Lennox, British singer-songwriter, gave such a skillful manuscript speech at Berklee College of Music that many thought she was using extemporaneous delivery.

comfortable with the material, they can end up glued to their manuscript rather than communicating with listeners through eye contact and adaptation to feedback. A lack of practice also inhibits a lively delivery with vocal variety.

President George W. Bush, for example, struggled with manuscript presentations early in his presidency. Yet when he spoke to rescue workers at the still-smoking ruins of the World Trade Center in the wake of the terrorist attacks of 9/11, his impromptu remarks responded to the concerns of his audiences, both immediate and removed. As a result, Bush had met the "challenge of a leader," which was to have his speech "capture the needs and mood of his country," for the first time.[33] Later Bush would give successful manuscript speeches, but it is interesting that he should find his voice in the give-and-take of impromptu speaking.

Successful manuscript speeches retain the conversational, communicative flavor of impromptu and extemporaneous speaking while working from prepared, scripted remarks. When singer Annie Lennox gave the 2013 commencement speech at Berklee College of Music in Boston, she presented the address so well that those of us hearing it on the radio did not even realize that she was not using extemporaneous delivery. Viewing the video of the speech revealed that she did indeed have a manuscript. Her oral style, familiarity with the speech, and connection to the audience made her presentation effective.

Manuscript presentations are most useful when the speaker seeks accuracy or eloquence or when time constraints are severe: Many media presentations, for example, must be timed within seconds. Extemporaneous presentations may also include quotations or technical information that must be read if the speeches are to achieve their effect. Because you will need to read material from time to time, we offer the following suggestions:

- Use a large font to prepare your manuscript so you can see it without straining.
- Use light pastel rather than white paper to reduce glare from lights.
- Double- or triple-space the manuscript.
- Use the top two-thirds to three-quarters of the page to facilitate eye contact.
- Mark pauses with slashes, or break phrases into bullet points.
- Highlight material you want to emphasize by capitalizing or italicizing it.
- Practice speaking from your manuscript so that you can deliver it well and maintain as much eye contact as possible with your audience.
- Think about incorporating some "planned ad libs" that will seem spontaneous and help connect with your audience.
- Don't panic if you stray a bit from the manuscript in delivery; your audience won't know unless you signal it to them, and some spontaneity helps enliven the presentation.

As you make final preparations, ask a friend to make a video recording of your rehearsal. Review the recording and ask yourself, Do I sound as though I'm *talking with* someone or as if I'm reading a text? Do I maintain eye contact with my imaginary audience? Do I pause effectively to emphasize the most important points? Does my body language reinforce my message? Revise and continue practicing until you are satisfied.

Memorized Text Presentation

Memorized text presentations are committed to memory and delivered word for word. Because the introduction and conclusion of a speech are especially important—the introduction for gaining audience attention and the conclusion for leaving a lasting impression—their wording should be carefully planned and rehearsed. You might also want to memorize short congratulatory remarks, a toast, or a brief award-acceptance speech.

In general, you should avoid trying to memorize anything much longer than a minute or two because this method of presentation poses many problems. Speakers who try to memorize their speeches can get so caught up with *remembering* that they forget about *communicating*. The result often sounds stilted or sing-songy. Speaking from memory also inhibits adapting to feedback. It can keep you from clarifying points when audience members signal that they don't understand or from following up on ideas that seem especially effective. Another problem with memorized speeches is that they often must be scripted word for word in advance. As we noted with manuscript speaking, people often struggle to write in an oral style.

If you must memorize a speech, commit it so thoroughly to memory that you can concentrate on communicating with your audience. If you experience a "mental block," keep talking. Restate or rephrase your last point to put your mind back on track. If this doesn't work, you may find yourself forced into an extemporaneous style and discover that you can actually express your ideas better without the constraints of exact wording.

Practicing for Presentation

It takes a lot of practice to sound natural. Although this statement may seem contradictory, it should not be surprising. Speaking before a group is not your typical way of communicating. Even though most people seem spontaneous and relaxed when talking with a small group of friends, something happens when they walk to the front of a room and face a larger audience of less familiar faces. They often freeze or become stilted and awkward, which is uncomfortable for everyone.

The key to overcoming this problem is to *prepare and practice* until you can respond fully to your ideas as you present them. Remember that public speaking is a process, not a product: Start by developing your presentation sufficiently in advance of the scheduled date so that you have the opportunity to refine and grow comfortable with your message. Then follow the advice on how to get to Carnegie Hall: Practice, practice, practice! Steve Jobs' renowned presentations of Apple products succeeded because he started working on the event well in advance and then devoted the forty-eight hours before each one to polishing the presentation. His engaging, nonchalant informality came "after grueling hours of practice."[34]

Don't fall into the trap of avoiding practice because it reminds you that you are not confident about your upcoming speech: That is a recipe for a self-fulfilling prophecy![35] Instead, rehearse your speech until your voice, face, and body can express your feelings as well as your thoughts. Constance Bernstein, founder of Synchronics Group Trial Consultants, advises lawyers to be so familiar with their

▶ **memorized text presentation**
Speeches that are committed to memory and delivered word for word.

arguments that "you will be able to deliver them without faltering—without losing eye contact."[36]

Reading over your notes helps your familiarity with the outline, but go a step further: Say the words *out loud* using your key-word outline. "Speaking the speech" will provide several benefits:

- **It will enhance your memory.** Actually vocalizing the words engages your brain in ways that simply reading them will not and helps you become more comfortable with the message.

- **It will provide a more accurate estimation of time.** You can think through a presentation in about three-quarters of the time you need to deliver it. Think of how you feel when an instructor keeps you beyond the allotted class time, and use that to help you stay within the specified limits.

- **It will enable you to make adjustments to enhance orality.** That compound-complex sentence that looked so good on paper leaves you breathless and confused when you say it out loud. It's better to discover that during practice than during delivery.

You will probably want privacy the first two or three times you practice. Even then, you should try to simulate the conditions under which the speech will be given. Stand up while you practice. Imagine your listeners in front of you. Picture them responding positively to what you have to say. Address your ideas to them, and visualize your ideas having impact. In addition, think about your speech as you walk to class, brush your teeth, and stand in line; that will help you become comfortable with its content and with how you want to express it.

Then use the help of others—your roommate, your friends, and anyone else who will listen. If your campus has a Communication Center, visit it for the advice and support of peer coaches. Research confirms that speakers who practice before audiences receive higher evaluation scores later.[37] The suggestions of others may be more objective than your self-evaluation, and you will get a feel for speaking to real people rather than to an imagined audience. Seek constructive feedback from your friends by asking them specific questions: Was it easy for them to follow you? Did your ideas seem clear and soundly supported? Were you speaking loudly and slowly enough? Do you have any mannerisms (such as twisting your hair or saying "you know" after every other sentence) that distracted them? Recording your practice can also be beneficial—as long as you remember to look for *both* strengths and areas to improve.

If possible, go to your classroom to practice. If this is not possible, find another empty room where the speaking arrangements are similar. Such onsite rehearsal helps you get a better feel for the situation you will face, reducing its strangeness when you make your actual presentation. Make sure your key-word cards are concise and easy to see. Type or print quotations in large letters so you can read them easily, and put each quotation on a single index card. If using a lectern, position this material so that you can maintain frequent eye contact with your audience even while referring to it. If you will speak beside or in front of the lectern, hold your cards in your hand and raise them when it is time to read. Practice reading your quotation until you can present it naturally while only glancing at your notes. If your speech includes presentation aids, practice handling them until they are smoothly integrated into your presentation. They should seem a natural extension of your verbal message.

On the day that you are assigned to speak, get to class early enough to look over your outline one last time so that it is fresh in your mind. Take the time to focus on your speech. Although financial consultant-cum-star Suze Orman regularly goes on the speaking circuit, she insists that "when I'm on my way to a speaking engagement, you cannot talk to me about another project. All I'm doing is thinking about that speech. That way, when I get there, everything is clear."[38]

Visualize yourself presenting a successful speech. If you have devoted sufficient time and energy to your preparation and practice, you should feel confident about communicating with your audience. Breathe deeply, and enjoy the experience of sharing your ideas with your audience. Remember the perspective of Jody Cross, owner of the consulting firm Leaders Speak: "Perfection is not the goal—connection is!"[39] With practice, you will be able to achieve that connection.

The "Speaker's Notes: Practicing for Presentation" checklist summarizes our suggestions for practicing.

SPEAKER'S notes   Practicing for Presentation

To practice your presentation, follow these suggestions:

1. Practice standing up and speaking aloud, if possible in the room where you will be making your presentation.

2. Practice first from your formal outline; then gradually work your way to your key-word outline as you master your material.

3. Work on maintaining eye contact with an imaginary audience.

4. Practice integrating your presentation aids into your message.

5. Check the timing of your speech. Add or cut as necessary.

6. Continue practicing until you feel comfortable and confident.

7. Present your speech in a "dress rehearsal" before friends. Make final changes in light of their suggestions.

FINDING YOUR voice   Critiquing Presentation Practices

Attend a guest lecture or speech or view a presentation on YouTube (such as Michelle Obama's commencement speech to the Martin Luther King, Jr., Magnet School or Betty White's acceptance speech at the Screen Actors Guild awards). Was the speaker's voice effective or ineffective? Why? How would you evaluate the speaker's body language? Did the speaker read from a manuscript, make a memorized presentation, or speak extemporaneously? Was the speaker adept at moving from one mode of presentation to another? How flexible was the speaker in answering questions? Report your observations in class.

Developing Flexibility in Special Situations

To the versatility you develop as you master and integrate the various modes of speaking, you should add flexibility in special speaking situations. We address two such situations: question-and-answer sessions and mediated presentations.

Handling Questions and Answers

If you are successful in arousing interest and stimulating thinking, your listeners may want to ask questions at the end of your speech. You should welcome and encourage this sign of success. The following suggestions should make handling questions easier for you.[40]

Watch at **MyCommunicationLab** Video: "Questions and Answers"

- **Prepare for questions.** Try to anticipate what you might be asked, think about how you will answer these questions, and do the research required to answer them authoritatively. Practice your speech before friends, and urge them to ask you tough questions.

- **Paraphrase the question as the beginning of your answer.** This is especially important if the question was long or complicated and your audience is large. Paraphrasing ensures that everyone in the audience hears the question. It gives you time to plan your answer, and it helps verify that you have understood the question. Paraphrasing also enables you to steer the question to the type of answer you are prepared to give.

- **Maintain eye contact with the audience as you answer.** Note that we say, "with the *audience*," not just "with the questioner." Look first at the questioner, and then make eye contact with other audience members, returning your gaze to the questioner as you finish your answer. The purpose of a question-and-answer period should be to extend the understanding of the entire audience, not to carry on a conversation with one person.

- **Defuse hostile questions.** Reword emotional questions in more neutral language. For example, if you are asked, "Why do you want to throw our money away on people who are too lazy to work?" you might respond with something like, "I understand your frustration with the current programs; we need to explore why they aren't helping people break out of the cycle of unemployment." Don't be afraid to use such questions to help you make a closely related point.[41]

- **Don't be afraid to concede a point or to say, "I don't know."** Such tactics can earn you points for honesty and can also help defuse a difficult question or hostile questioner. You can offer to find the information and get in touch with the questioner later, or you can indicate that that particular aspect was outside the realm of your research. Or you can use the next tactic.

- **Keep your answers short and direct.** Don't give another speech. Vice President Joe Biden of Delaware, while highly regarded as a foreign policy expert, entered the 2008 presidential sweepstakes with a reputation for being a compulsive talker and for putting his foot in his mouth. At the first nationally televised debate for Democratic Party hopefuls, the moderator skewered him with an unfriendly question:

Moderator: An editorial in the *Los Angeles Times* said, "In addition to his uncontrolled verbosity, Biden is a gaffe machine." Can you reassure voters in this country that you would have the discipline you would need on the world stage, Senator?
Senator Biden: Yes.
(Audience laughter. Long moment of silence)
Moderator: Thank you, Senator Biden.
(More laughter)[42]

Stepping into the audience to take questions, as celebrity chef Robert Irvine did during a demonstration, gives the speaker a chance to extend and increase the influence of the speech.

As the *New York Times* described the moment, "The audience laughed at his brevity. Mr. Biden, looking proud of himself, said nothing else, as Mr. [Brian] Williams silently if slightly uncomfortably waited for him to expand on his remarks."[43] Commentator Chris Matthews described it as "a Johnny Carson moment." Fellow commentator Margaret Carlson added, "In a debate with that many [eight] people, a one-liner stands out. And the best one-liner is a one-word one-liner."[44] Especially, she might have added, when the one-liner comes from Senator Biden! While the vice president seemed on the surface to concede the assumption behind the question, the brevity of his answer really worked as a refutation to the charge that he was uncontrollably verbose. His lightheartedness also drew a lot of the poison out of the question.

- **Handle nonquestions politely.** If someone starts to give a speech rather than asking a question, wait until he or she pauses for breath, and then intervene with something like, "Thank you for your comment," or, "I appreciate your remarks." Continue with, "Your question, then, is . . .," and select one aspect of the statement to which you want to respond. You might also respond, "That's an interesting perspective. Can we have another question?" Maintaining eye contact with the entire audience will facilitate this goal. Stay in command of the situation.

In a question-and-answer session he had with Congressional Republicans, President Obama was confronted with a "questioner" who actually made a long, hostile political speech. When he finally paused for a moment, the president commented, "I know there's a question in there somewhere . . . . [and at] some point I know you're going to let me answer." This rather blunt (but polite) interruption allowed Obama to control the remainder of the exchange.[45]

- **Bring the question-and-answer session to a close.** Call for one or two final questions, so that you have flexibility in how you handle the situation.

As you complete the answer, summarize your message again to refocus listeners on your central points. When Tom Ross, former president of Davidson College, met with a group of parents and alumni, one parent of a current student offered a heartfelt tribute to the quality of her daughter's education. Ross smiled at his audience and said, "I can't think of a better way to end this evening than with that!"[46]

Making Mediated Presentations

From YouTube to teleconferences, at some time in your life you are likely to make a mediated presentation. You may find yourself creating an online training program, speaking on closed-circuit television, Skyping an interview, recording instructions at work, using community access cable channels to promote a cause, running for public office, or even appearing on commercial television. Each of these mediated formats requires not only developing your physical voice and your body language but also making particular adaptations to deliver your messages well.[47]

With most mediated presentations, you cannot see your audience because of separations of time, distance, or both. In fact, with today's Internet, you may not even know who your audiences may eventually be. You won't be able to adapt to feedback, so as you develop your presentation, you must work to keep the message clear. Use concrete, colorful language so that your audience remembers your points. Use previews and internal summaries to keep viewers on track. If you want to incorporate presentation aids, make sure they are appropriate to the medium. Large easel posters, for example, are likely to be unwieldy online, whereas videos may be effectively incorporated. (See related considerations in Chapter 10.)

Despite the fact that you cannot see the faces of your viewers, you want to keep a conversational tone. Imagine yourself speaking to individuals, but be sure to speak slowly enough that your audience can follow you. Use those extemporaneous skills to good effect; if you must use a teleprompter to stay within a time limit, practice using the guidelines for manuscript speaking.

The camera magnifies all your movements and vocal changes, so use restrained head movements and underplayed facial expressions as well as moderate changes in volume. Rely on pauses and on subtle changes in tempo, pitch, and inflection to drive your points home. At the same time, you don't want to be a talking head; you want your voice and facial expressions to convey your interest in the topic.

Because the camera bring you close to viewers, it also magnifies every aspect of your appearance. Consider what the backdrop will be. If you can, minimize the distractions; many a YouTube presentation has been marred as viewers try to figure out what's posted on the refrigerator or what clothes are hanging in the closet. The backdrop will influence your choice of dress: If you have light hair or if the backdrop will be light, wear dark clothing for contrast. If you have a dark skin tone, consider a light or neutral background and light-colored clothes. Dressing conservatively will keep the focus on you and your message. Avoid shiny fabrics, glittery or dangling jewelry, and flashy prints and stripes that might "swim" on the screen and distract viewers. Avoid white or light pastels, which could reflect lights and create glare. Both men and women need makeup to achieve a natural look on camera. Have powder available to reduce skin shine or to hide a five o'clock shadow. Use makeup conservatively because the camera will intensify it.

Remember that the microphone picks up *all* sounds, including shuffling papers and tapping on a lectern. If you use a stand or handheld microphone, position it about 10 inches below your mouth. The closer the microphone is to your mouth, the more it picks up unwanted noises like whistled *s* sounds or tongue clicks. Before you begin your speech and after you finish, always assume that any microphone or camera near you is "live." Don't say or do anything you wouldn't want your audience to hear or see.

All of the advice about preparation and practice, from rehearsing in the space if possible to being fully comfortable with your message, applies to mediated presentations as well. Keep your voice conversational, your body relaxed, and your face friendly even as you look into the eye of the camera.

Certain media, such as television, require strict time limits; if the producer tells you that you have five minutes, it does not mean that you have five minutes and five seconds. In such cases, use either a teleprompter (which is best used with practice) or extemporaneous delivery (with an eye toward which portions might be condensed or extended as necessary).

If you make a mistake, keep going. Sometimes "mistakes" are improvements. If appropriate, smile when you finish and continue looking at the camera to allow time for a fade-out.

FINAL reflections   Holding Court

It is now clear that no one is going to give you your voice. You have to find it for yourself—and to convince others that you have found it as you stand before them. As you step to the front of the room when you are asked to speak, you should do so confidently. You should project the realization that you have something worthwhile and important to say that listeners should consider carefully.

In the courtroom, lawyers strive to convey this air of confidence and leadership. Trial consultant Constance Bernstein advises attorneys to "win trials nonverbally" through strong presentations of their case and themselves. She emphasizes the importance of eye contact as a way to "address each juror individually." She stresses standing tall and firm so that "you will feel more grounded." She advocates using gestures "to anchor your message," both because they are memorable and because "your hands are invisible connections to jurors." And she recommends speaking in a way that conveys assurance and poise:

> When you are in the courtroom fearing the worst, do not let anyone sense your anxiety. Take a deep breath and relax. . . . Opposing counsel will be dismayed by your confidence; the judge will be impressed by your calmness; and the jurors will view you as self-confident and thoroughly prepared.[48]

Attorneys seek Bernstein's counsel to help craft and deliver successful presentations. Note how her advice echoes ours for public speaking. Using your facial expressions and eye contact, your movement and gestures, and your personal appearance can amplify your voice by underscoring and magnifying your message.

What Bernstein did not consider here is how to use your physical voice to underscore and magnify your message. As a speaker, you present a total package, so your pitch, rate, volume, and variation need to elaborate on the meaning of your body language as well as your words. As LaVonia discovered in our opening scenario, more confident presentational styles lead to more confident presentations, which in turn lead to even more confident presentational styles—whether speaking in front of the class, interviewing for an internship, or addressing a convention. Extemporaneous or manuscript, presentation or question-and-answer session, face-to-face or mediated, effective delivery forms an essential part of finding your voice.

After Reading This Chapter, You Should Be Able To Answer These Questions

1 How can your physical voice enliven your message?

2 What can body language contribute to your presentation? How can it detract?

3 What are the advantages and disadvantages of impromptu, extemporaneous, manuscript, and memorized presentations?

4 How can you prepare effectively for your presentation?

5 What steps will enhance your question-and-answer sessions?

6 How does giving a presentation in a mediated format affect your approach?

For Discussion and Further Exploration

1 Find a children's book, such as Judith Viorst's *Alexander and His Terrible, Horrible, No Good, Very Bad Day*. Read it aloud, exaggerating your pitch, rate, and volume in the process. How does vocal variety help give the words new meanings? Is there a point at which the exaggeration is problematic?

2 Develop a list of statements, such as, "I'm tired," "That's hilarious," and "What a wonderful story you have told." Read these statements in a manner that is deliberately discrepant (for example, "That's very interesting," in an utterly bored voice). Then experiment with how many meanings you can generate for these statements with different uses of your voice.

3 During a conversation with a friend, try limiting your facial expressions, eye contact, movement, and gestures. How long does it take your friend to become aware that something is different? How do you feel when you are talking conversationally but limiting your body language? How can you develop your body language appropriately when giving a speech?

4 Find a speech that uses a manuscript or memorized delivery (e.g., at C-SPAN or Annie Lennox's 2013 commencement speech at Berklee College of Music). What did the speaker do to enhance the presentation? What did the speaker do that distracted from the presentation? What could the speaker have done to improve? Then find a speech that uses extemporaneous delivery (e.g., at TED.com). What did the speaker do to enhance the presentation? What did the speaker do that distracted from the presentation? What could the speaker have done to improve?

5 Map out a practice schedule for your next speech. How can you use practice to encourage using your voice clearly in your presentation?

6 Consider your last speech. If you had a question-and-answer session afterward, how could the guidelines in this chapter have helped? If you did not, consider how the guidelines in this chapter might have prepared you for one.

7 Say one of your presentations is so good that your professor would like you to give it again, this time to be posted on MyCommunicationLab. How would you modify your presentation for the mediated form?

13 Informative Speaking

Listen to **Chapter 13** at **MyCommunicationLab**

> *The improvement of understanding is for two ends: first our own increase of knowledge; secondly, to enable us to deliver that knowledge to others.*
>
> —JOHN LOCKE

Cell phones! Twitter! Skype! Radio! Textbooks! Facebook! Newspapers! Bulletin Boards! Lectures! Newsletters! Television! TED talks! They all inundate us with information. No wonder many of us suffer sometimes from "information overload." No wonder many of us may at moments want to turn it all off, to hit the "delete" key in our minds. Although we may sometimes feel as though we are drowning in information, we need it to make sense of our world and to make vital connections with others to survive.

Without the sharing of information, there would be no civilization as we know it. Although other animals may share food, engage in primitive social behavior, and use signal language to warn of dangers or express feelings, humans alone have developed a complex language that allows knowledge to accumulate and be shared across generations. Information empowers us to survive and thrive in our world. Advances such as breakthroughs in medical research, new ways to safeguard the environment, and early detection systems that alert us to natural disasters help us cope with challenges to our existence and contribute to the quality of our lives. Free and open exchange of information is especially crucial to democratic societies in which our fate depends on the will of *enlightened citizens*.

Learning to make effective and ethical informative presentations will contribute substantially to finding your voice as a public speaker. As discussed in Chapter 8, presenting substantive information in a balanced and responsible way is a skill that will benefit you regardless of whether your general purpose is to inform, persuade, or celebrate. Responsible informative speaking reinforces respect for the integrity of ideas and sound information, a respect that is vital to the standards of ethical speaking discussed in Chapter 1.

Informative speaking is especially important in the work environment. If you become a journalist, you must know how to convey information accurately and succinctly. If you choose to be a teacher, effectively presenting material that your students need to learn may be vital to their success throughout life. Working as a manager, you may need to present oral reports or briefings as well as train new employees. Also within the business world, there is an increasing desire to share ideas and methods of doing things. Companies are bringing in outside speakers to provide new information and ideas to employees rather than just to motivate them.

In this chapter, we examine the nature, types, and functions of informative speaking. We also offer advice for motivating your listeners to listen to and remember your messages. We then cover the major design formats used to structure informative presentations. We end by considering the *briefing*, a special form vital to many business and professional settings.

Biz Stone, Twitter co-founder, considered a great storyteller, speaks to corporate groups to provide new information and ideas to employees.

Informative Speaking: An Overview

Informative speaking enlightens listeners by sharing ideas and information so that they can make judicious decisions. As an informative speaker, you want listeners to pay attention to your message and understand it. Your purpose is not to convince them to change their minds or behavior but to offer a balanced presentation of relevant information so that they can more responsibly reach their own conclusions. For instance, Jessica Floyd presented an informative speech on the dangers of the West Nile virus carried by mosquitoes. The dangers were vivid, but Jessica only suggested ways that listeners might avoid the disease. What they did in response to this new knowledge was up to them.

By sharing information, an informative speech reduces ignorance. It does not simply repeat something the audience already knows. Rather, the **informative value** of a speech is measured by *how much new and important information or understanding it provides the audience.* As you prepare your informative speech, ask yourself the following questions:

- Is my topic significant enough to merit an informative speech?

- What do my listeners already know about my topic?

- What more do they need to know to accomplish my purpose?

- Do I understand my topic well enough to help others understand it?

The answers to these questions should help you plan a speech with high informative value.

It is clear that informative speakers carry a large ethical burden to communicate responsible knowledge of their topics. A responsible informative speech should cover all major positions on a topic and present all vital information. Although informative speakers may have strong feelings on a subject, it is unethical for them to deliberately omit or distort information. Speakers who are unaware of information because they have not done sufficient research are also irresponsible. As you prepare your speech, you should seek out material from sources that offer different perspectives on your subject.

YOUR ethical VOICE   The Ethics of Informative Speaking

As you prepare your informative speech, keep these ethical considerations in mind.

1. Be sure you can defend the morality of your choice of topic.

2. Mention all major positions on a topic when there are different perspectives.

3. Present all information that is important for audience understanding.

4. Do not distort information.

5. Do sufficient research to speak responsibly.

6. Do not omit relevant information because it is inconsistent with your perspective.

7. Strive to be as objective as possible.

▶ **informative speaking** Functions to enlighten by sharing ideas and information.

▶ **informative value** A measure of how much new and important information or understanding a speech conveys to an audience.

Forms of Informative Speaking

If it's true that we live in an Age of Information, the importance of informative speaking can hardly be exaggerated. Informative speaking arises from three basic needs.

1. We want to expand our knowledge of the world. We may believe that stretching our horizons helps us become more powerful. This may account for the value of speeches of description.

2. We want to learn skills that are helpful or enjoyable. This may account for the importance of speeches of demonstration.

3. We are curious about how things work and how they are made. This is especially true when these things are important to our quality of life. This may account for the importance of speeches of explanation.

Speeches of Description

Often the specific purpose of a speech is to describe what's "out there" with respect to a given activity, event, object, person, or place. A **speech of description** should give the audience a clear image of your subject. The words should be concrete and colorful so they describe the subject precisely and convey the feeling of the message. The speech "The Monument at Wounded Knee" in Appendix B describes a *place* and *object* by providing vivid word-pictures. Thus, the landscape is not simply desolate; it is characterized by "flat, sun-baked fields and an occasional eroded gully." Cecile Larson goes on to describe the monument:

> The monument itself rests on a concrete slab to the right of the grave. It's a typical, large, old-fashioned granite cemetery marker, a pillar about six feet high topped with an urn—the kind of gravestone you might see in any cemetery with graves from the turn of the century. The inscription tells us that it was erected by the families of those who were killed at Wounded Knee. Weeds grow through the cracks in the concrete at its base.

Can you "see" the monument? If so, Cecile's pictorial language has done its descriptive work. While she describes a place and an object, Cecile's purpose is also to deepen historical understanding of an *event* that occurred there.

As Cecile's vivid example makes clear, the key to descriptive speaking is creating an image of what your subject looks like in the minds of your listeners. The effective use of presentation aids can be very helpful, as can concrete, colorful language as discussed in Chapter 11. Your topic and purpose should suggest the appropriate design to use. The "Monument" speech follows a spatial pattern, in that it develops a verbal map of the monument site.

Speeches of Demonstration

The **speech of demonstration** shows an audience how to do something. Dance instructors teach us the Texas two-step. CPR instructors teach us procedures that save lives. Cooking shows offer demonstrations. One of our students, Jeffrey O'Connor, showed his classmates how to read a textbook effectively. The tip-off to the speech

► **speech of description** An informative speech that uses vivid language to illustrate an activity, object, person, or place.

► **speech of demonstration** An informative speech that shows the audience how to do something or how something works.

of demonstration is the phrase *"how to."* What these examples have in common is that they demonstrate a process and empower listeners by showing them how to perform it.

Speeches of demonstration are often helped by the use of presentation aids (see Chapter 10). Speakers can present and discuss the objects that must be used or steps that must be taken to accomplish some purpose. They might use PowerPoint to show the steps to be followed or actually demonstrate how to perform an activity. When you are making a speech of demonstration, "show and tell" is usually much more effective than just telling.

Speeches of Explanation

A **speech of explanation** offers information about subjects that are abstract or complicated. Because understanding is the object of such a speech, a speech of explanation should present the critical characteristics of a subject and offer many good examples.[1] Speeches of explanation sometimes incorporate characteristics of speeches of description and demonstration. In "Descent into Darkness," her powerful speech explaining Alzheimer's disease that concludes this chapter, Olivia Jackson organized her subject in the following way:

Speeches of demonstration show the audience how to do something.

1. She opened her speech with the story of her grandfather who had contracted Alzheimer's disease.

2. She defined the disease.

3. She explained the significance of the disease for those afflicted with it and their families.

4. She described how the disease develops.

5. She explained how to reduce susceptibility to it.

Speeches of explanation face an additional challenge when their information runs counter to common misconceptions. Professor Katherine Rowan provides an example of how this can work in public service campaigns:

> A particularly resilient obstacle to [seat] belt use is the erroneous but prevalent belief that hitting one's head on a windshield while traveling at 30 miles per hour is an experience much like doing so when a car is stationary. . . . If people understood that the experience would be much more similar to falling from a three-story building and hitting the pavement face first, one obstacle to the wearing of seat belts would be easier to overcome.[2]

As her example indicates, analogies—such as comparing an auto accident at thirty miles per hour to falling from a building—can help break through our resistance to new ideas and behaviors. The use of such strategic comparisons and contrasts can help listeners accept new information and use it in their lives, perhaps even to *save* their lives.

▶ **speech of explanation** An informative speech that offers information about abstract and complex subjects.

SPEAKER'S notes
Guidelines for Effective Informative Speaking

Keep these tips in mind as you develop an informative speech.

1. Speeches of description require colorful language.
2. Speeches of demonstration need an orderly sequence of steps.
3. Speeches of demonstration are helped by presentation aids.
4. Speeches of explanation need clear definitions of important terms.
5. Speeches of explanation require good examples.
6. Speeches of explanation can make effective use of analogies.

Helping Listeners Learn

Explore at **MyCommunicationLab Activity:** "Informative Speeches"

Having been a student for most of your life, chances are you've suffered the misfortune of taking a class from a boring teacher or professor. She was obviously well qualified and well prepared, but every time she started to lecture, you found yourself drifting away.

As we noted in Chapter 4, we "hear" a lot every day, yet we only listen to a small part of it. We selectively attend to messages that interest us, concern us, engage us, or even alarm us. Much of the rest of what we "hear" doesn't penetrate our listening barriers.

So how can you improve the odds that audience members will listen to and remember your informative messages? You can start by considering some basic audience characteristics, as discussed in Chapter 5. How much do your listeners already know about your topic? How interested might they be in your topic? What preconceptions might they have about your topic that might help or hinder your ability to reach them? How do they regard you as a speaker on this topic? Figure 13.1 charts these audience considerations and directs you to possible strategies you can use.

Motivating Audiences to Listen

To motivate listeners, especially those who are not initially interested in your subject, you must tell them why your message is important to them. As you consider your audience in relation to your topic, ask yourself why they would want to know what you have to tell them:

- Will it help them understand and control the world around them?
- Will it improve their health, safety, or general well-being?
- Will it give them a sense of making a contribution to society?
- Will it help them get along better with family and friends?
- Will it give them a feeling of accomplishment?
- Will it contribute to the revival of moral balance and fairness?
- Will it provide them with enjoyment?

Audience Type	Strategies
Interested but uninformed	• Provide basic information in clear, simple language. • Avoid jargon; define technical terms. • Use examples and narratives for amplification. • When communicating complicated information, use analogies, metaphors, and/or presentation aids. • Use voice, gestures, and eye contact to reinforce meaning.
Interested and knowledgeable	• Establish your credibility early in the speech. • Acknowledge diverse perspectives on topic. • Go into depth with information and expert testimony. • Offer engaging presentation that keeps focus on content.
Uninterested	• Show listeners what's in it for them. • Keep presentation short and to the point. • Use sufficient examples and narratives to arouse and sustain interest. • Use eye-catching presentation aids and colorful language. • Make a dynamic presentation.
Unsympathetic (toward topic)	• Show respect for listeners and their point of view. • Cite sources the audience will respect. • Present information to enlarge listeners' understanding. • Develop stories and examples to arouse favorable feeling. • Make a warm, engaging presentation.
Distrustful (of speaker)	• Establish your credibility early in the speech. • Rely heavily on factual examples and expert testimony. • Cite sources of information in your presentation. • Be straightforward, businesslike, and personable. • Keep good eye contact with listeners.

FIGURE 13.1
Audience Considerations for Informative Speeches

For example, a speech offering advice for having a perfect job interview would appeal to your listeners' need for achievement, whereas a speech documenting the suffering of those on the Jersey shore in the wake of Hurricane Sandy would address their need to care for others.

Hannah Johnston opened her speech on the fast-food industry by appealing to health and safety motivations: "If you had a choice, I'm sure you wouldn't choose to eat some of the stuff that can end up in processed meat." Hannah ruined lunch for some of her classmates, but they could not help but listen closely.

Maintaining Audience Attention

In Chapter 9, we discussed how to attract audience attention in the introduction of your speech. Here, we focus on how to sustain that interest. You can do so by making good use of one or more of the five factors that affect attention: relevance, intensity, contrast, repetition, and novelty.

To organize groups of volunteers such as those assembling to clean up Staten Island and the New Jersey shore after Hurricane Sandy, you might appeal to listeners' need to care for others.

Relevance. A speech that relates to an audience's needs, interests, or concerns will hold its attention. You should point out the **relevance** of your topic for uninterested listeners. Nick Orobello had to work to make his speech on electronic health records relevant to his young and healthy audience at Davidson College. He grabbed their attention in his introduction by relating a common experience: having to answer the same questions over and over in the same visit to medical personnel. Then he sustained interest by showing listeners how electronic medical records would increase the efficiency and effectiveness of their own health care throughout their lives. He used vivid narratives and examples to help him keep their attention.

Intensity. **Intensity** in a speech can refer to its boldness, colorful language, or passionate presentation. Riveting examples and the effective use of presentation aids can also add intensity.

Recently, we heard a worker describe spectacular results he had achieved in his company's wellness program. At the beginning of the program, he said, he was severely overweight and suffered from high blood pressure, diabetes, and elevated triglyceride levels. He really got our attention when he summarized his situation this way: "I was a tickin' time bomb."

This colorful expression, which seems so simple and straightforward, actually illustrates how a number of the language techniques discussed in Chapter 11 can come together to create intensity. First, it illustrates *metaphor*. Literally, our bodies are not bombs, but to think of them that way stresses the dangers of obesity and an unhealthy lifestyle. The metaphor makes us think of heart attacks and strokes as explosions that can quite literally destroy us from within. Second, the example illustrates *alliteration*, the repetition of initial sounds in adjoining words to create a striking effect. The repetition of the *t* sound drives the point home. Third, the example represents *onomatopoeia*, the use of words that sound like what they signify. "Tickin'" sounds like an ominous clock. Time was running out for this worker if he did not act.

Contrast. **Contrast** attracts and sustains attention by highlighting the differences between opposites. In this textbook, we print important terms in boldface so that they will grab your attention. During your presentation, you can show contrast through abrupt changes in pitch, volume, movement, and rate of speech. Contrasting views can help dramatize disputed issues in a way that listeners often find engaging. Speakers may define abstract concepts by contrast in a manner that attracts attention; for example, "We Americans are definitely *not* socialists!" Finally, you can highlight contrasts by simply speaking in terms of oppositions, such as life and death, or by highlighting the highs and lows of a situation.

Alexandra McArthur used contrast as she compared the "dream" Honduras painted in tourist brochures with the "reality" she had experienced during a longer stay in that country (see the text of her speech in Appendix B).

Repetition. The **repetition** of sounds, words, and phrases during a speech can attract and hold attention. Skillful speakers use repetition to emphasize points, help

---

▶ **relevance**   Refers to the extent to which a speech relates to an audience's specific needs, interests, or concerns.

▶ **intensity**   Refers to the extent to which aspects of a speech are striking or stand out.

▶ **contrast**   Attracts attention and sharpens perspective by highlighting the differences between opposites.

listeners follow the flow of ideas, and embed messages in audience memory. As we saw in Chapter 11, repetition is the basis of alliteration and parallel construction. Alliteration lends vividness to main ideas: "Today, I will discuss how the *Mississippi* River *meanders* from *Minnesota* to the sea." The repetition of the *m* sound catches attention and emphasizes the statement. Similarly, parallel construction establishes a pattern that sticks in the mind. Repeated questions and answers—such as, "What is our goal? It is to . . ." —sustain attention.

Novelty. **Novelty** refers to the quality of being new or unusual. If you have a fresh way of seeing and saying things, uninterested or distrustful listeners may increase both their respect for you and their interest in your subject. A novel phrase can fascinate listeners and hold their attention. In a speech on environmental steward-ship, Jim Cardoza found a novel way to describe the magnitude of pollution. After reporting that 19 million tons of garbage are picked up each year along the nation's beaches, he concluded: "And that's just the tip of the *wasteberg*." His invented word, *wasteberg*, reminded listeners of *iceberg* and suggested the enormity of the problem.

SPEAKER'S
notes   Attention Techniques

Use the following strategies to attract and sustain the attention of your listeners.

1. *Motivate* listeners by showing them how they can benefit from your message.

2. *Speak with intensity*—develop word-pictures that vividly depict your topic.

3. *Use strategic repetition* to amplify your message.

4. *Rely on novelty* by using fresh wording and new examples.

5. *Present contrasts* to show what your topic is not.

6. *Highlight relevance* to connect your subject directly to the experience of listeners.

Promoting Audience Retention

Even the best information is useless unless your listeners remember it. Repetition, relevance, and structural factors can all be used to promote audience **retention**. The more frequently we hear anything, the more likely we are to retain it. This is why advertisers bombard us with slogans that appear repeatedly in their advertisements. The repetition of key words or phrases in a speech also helps the audience remem-ber. In his famous civil rights speech in Washington, D.C., Martin Luther King, Jr.'s repetition of the phrase "I have a dream . . ." became the hallmark of the speech and is now used as its title.

Relevance is also important to retention. Our minds filter incoming informa-tion, associate it with things we already know, and evaluate it for its potential use-fulness. *If you want listeners to remember your message, tell them why and how it relates to their lives.*

▶ **repetition**   Repeating sounds, words, or phrases to attract and hold attention.

▶ **novelty**   The quality of being new or unusual.

▶ **retention**   The extent to which listeners remember and use a message.

FINDING YOUR

voice Your Favorite Teacher

You can probably recall one or several outstanding teachers who have helped inspire you to want to learn. How did that teacher do this? What techniques did he or she use to motivate you to listen, maintain attention, and retain the main ideas? How can you use these techniques to assure that listeners hear you as well, that you have found your voice?

Structural factors also affect how well a message is retained. Previews, summaries, clear transitions, and a well-organized speech, as discussed in Chapter 9, can help your audience retain and remember your message. Suppose you were given the following list of words to memorize:

> north, man, hat, daffodil, green, tulip, coat, boy, south, red, east, shoes, gardenia, woman, purple, marigold, gloves, girl, yellow, west

Memorizing this list might be quite a challenge, but what if the words were rearranged like this?

> north, south, east, west
>
> man, boy, woman, girl
>
> daffodil, tulip, gardenia, marigold
>
> green, red, purple, yellow
>
> hat, coat, shoes, gloves

In the first example, you have what looks like a random list of words. In the second, the words have been organized by categories. Now you have five groups of four related words to remember. Material that is presented in a consistent and orderly pattern is much easier for your audience to retain.

Speech Designs

Explore at MyCommunicationLab Activity: "Scrambled Speech: Snuggies"

Once you have selected your topic, conducted research, determined your main points, and considered how you can motivate listeners, you need to select a design for your speech. In Chapter 9, we offered an overview of some of the major speech designs. Here, we offer a detailed discussion of six major speech designs that are well suited for informative speeches: categorical, comparative, spatial, sequential, chronological, and causation.

Categorical Design

Watch at MyCommunicationLab Video: "Roommates"

A **categorical design** arranges the main ideas and materials of a speech by natural or customary divisions. Natural divisions exist within the subject itself, such as three important early warning symptoms for detecting breast cancer. Customary

▶ **categorical design** Arranges the main ideas and materials of a speech by natural or customary divisions.

divisions represent conventional ways of thinking about a subject, such as past, present, and future views of it. Categories help us sort information so that we can make sense of it.

Each category in the design becomes a main point for development. You should limit the number of your categories to no more than five. Three works better for a short speech. Remember, you have to develop each point with supporting material. That takes time! You don't want to go beyond the time limits set by your instructor. Nor do you want to overtax your listeners' ability to remember and their willingness to give you their attention.

In her informative speech, Nicolette Fisk described architectural answers to a dilemma posed by terrorist attacks: how to keep our greatest monuments and buildings safe but still beautiful. Here is an abbreviated outline of the categorical design of her speech:

Preview: Architects have developed three innovative answers to the question of how to both guard and beautify our greatest buildings and shrines.

I. Retaining walls provide one such answer.

   A. Overlapping stone walls can provide a picturesque barrier to explosive-laden vehicles.

   B. Retaining walls have been erected to protect the Washington Monument.

   C. Architect Laurie Olin said, "The point is to turn this security thing into a beautiful walk."

II. Collapsible concrete is a second answer to the challenge.

   A. It is strong enough to support pedestrians, but collapses under the weight of heavier vehicles.

   B. It both preserves open public space and creates an urban booby trap for terrorists.

   C. It is widely used in New York City.

III. Adding street furniture offers a third answer to protect pedestrians along sidewalks.

   A. Bollards are designed to absorb huge vehicular impacts.

     1. They were first designed for military security measures.

     2. Now they function as fashionable, decorative features around buildings.

   B. Heavy benches and boulders along the street provide seating as well as protection for strollers.

To conclude, *categories are the mind's way of ordering the world by seeking patterns within it or by supplying patterns to arrange it.* Speech designs based upon these patterns are a very effective way to convey information.

Comparative Design

A **comparative design** explores the similarities or differences among things, events, and ideas. Comparing the unknown to the known can be especially useful when

Watch at **MyCommunicationLab** Video: "AED: The Automated External Defibrillator"

Watch at **MyCommunicationLab** Video: "Brain Research of the Sexes"

▶ **comparative design** Arranges a speech by exploring the similarities or differences among things.

your topic is unfamiliar, abstract, technical, or difficult to understand. Two basic variations of comparative design are literal and figurative analogies.

In a **literal analogy**, the subjects compared are drawn from the same field of experience. For instance, you might track the voting records of two different politicians on an important issue such as campaign finance reform. "The French Paradox," printed in Appendix B, illustrates a literal analogy, comparing French and American styles of eating.

In a **figurative analogy**, the subjects are drawn from different fields of experience. For example, you might describe the complexities of the human circulatory system by comparing it to a city traffic system. Paul Ashdown, a professor of journalism at the University of Tennessee, used an extended figurative analogy comparing the World Wide Web to America's "Wild West."[3] Both literal and figurative analogy designs can be insightful and imaginative, helping listeners see subjects in surprising, revealing ways. But if the comparison seems strained, the speech will collapse, and the speaker's ethos will be damaged.

Comparative designs often contain contrasts, in which case each point of difference becomes a main point. In the interest of simplicity, you should limit yourself to just a few points of similarity or difference in a short presentation.

In her speech on healthy eating, Thressia Taylor used a figurative analogy comparing caring for a classic car to healthy eating:

Preview: Providing your body with the healthy food is as important as providing a classic car with the right fuels and lubricants.

I. Getting the right proteins is like having the right octane in your gasoline.

 A. Protein builds, maintains, and repairs the tissues that keep your engine from sputtering.

 B. Three or more servings a day will act as an octane booster to keep your engine running smoothly.

II. You need carbohydrates for energy and quick acceleration.

 A. Your carbohydrates should come from whole grains, fruits, and vegetables.

 B. Eat four servings daily to keep your engine humming.

III. Finally, you need fat to keep your body well lubricated.

 A. Bad fats can gum up our systems and land us in the junkyard before our time.

 B. Good fats are necessary for the long haul.

Spatial Design

A **spatial design** is appropriate for speeches that develop their topics within a physical setting. The main points are arranged as they occur in physical space. Most people are familiar with maps and can visualize directions. A speech using a spatial design provides listeners with a descriptive oral map, such as we see in Cecile Larson's "Wounded Knee" speech (see Appendix B).

To develop a spatial design that is easy to follow, select a starting point and then take your audience on an orderly journey to a destination. Once you begin a pattern of movement, stay with it to the end of the speech. If you change direction in the middle, the audience may get lost.

▶ **literal analogy**   A comparison of subjects drawn from the same field of experience.

▶ **figurative analogy**   A comparison of subjects drawn from essentially different fields of experience.

▶ **spatial design**   Arranges the main points of a speech as they occur in actual space, thus creating an oral map.

Landmarks, such as these statues of Elvis and WC Handy in downtown Memphis, help listeners identify the places in a spatial design.

Belinda Phillip's informative speech on Downtown Memphis Music followed a spatial design:

Preview: When you visit Downtown Memphis, begin at the Peabody; then stroll down Beale Street to the FedEx Forum.

I. Your first stop should be at the Peabody Hotel.

    A. Watch the ducks march through the lobby to a Sousa March.

    B. Visit the Sky Room on the roof, home of big band dances.

II. Stroll over to Beale Street, "The Home of the Blues."

    A. See the Elvis statue at the west end of Beale.

    B. Proceed east to Lansky's, "Clothier to the King," where Elvis shopped.

    C. Drop in to B.B. King's to see if he is around.

    D. Visit A. Schwab's on Beale for music souvenirs.

    E. See the W. C. Handy statue at the east end of Beale.

III. Cross the Street to the FedEx Forum

    A. Visit the "Rock and Soul" Smithsonian Museum.

    B. Tour the Gibson Guitar factory.

Belinda's spatial design followed a linear pattern that was orderly and provided listeners with a good sense of the location of important places. Each of her main points received about the same amount of attention, so that her speech seemed well balanced.

Speakers using a spatial pattern often use presentation aids, such as photographs or maps, to reinforce the sense of space created in their speeches.

Sequential Design

Watch at
MyCommunicationLab
Video: "Learn CPR"

Watch at
MyCommunicationLab
Video: "How to Use PowerPoint"

A **sequential design** explains the steps of a process in the order in which they should be taken. This design is especially useful for "how to" speeches of demonstration. You begin by identifying the necessary steps in the process and the order in which they should take place. These steps become the main points of your speech. In a short presentation, you should have no more than five steps as main points. You can assign numbers to these steps as you make your presentation.

The following brief outline, developed by Jeffrey O'Connor, illustrates a sequential design:

Preview: The five steps of efficient textbook reading include skimming, reading, rereading, reciting, and reviewing.

 I. First, *skim* through the chapter to get the overall picture.
   A. Identify the major ideas from the section headings.
   B. Read summary statements.
   C. Read boxed materials.
   D. Make a key-word outline of major topics.

 II. Second, *read* the chapter a section at a time.
   A. Note questions on the material in the margins.
   B. Check definitions of unfamiliar words.
   C. Go back and highlight the major ideas.

 III. Third, *reread* the chapter.
   A. Fill in your key-word outline with more detail.
   B. Try to answer the questions you posed.
   C. Prepare questions for your instructor on things you don't understand.

 IV. Fourth, *recite* what you have read.
   A. Use your outline to make an oral presentation to yourself.
   B. Explain the material to someone else.

 V. Finally, *review* the material within twenty-four hours.
   A. Review your outline.
   B. Reread the highlighted material.

▶ **sequential design** Explains the steps of a process in the order in which they should be taken.

Presenting the steps in this orderly, sequential way helped Jeffrey "walk" his University of New Mexico classmates through the process.

Chronological Design

A **chronological design** explains events or historical developments in the order in which they occurred. Using the chronological design, you may start with the beginnings of the subject and trace it up to the present through its defining moments. Or you may start with the present and trace the subject back to its origins. In either case, chronological presentations are generally more effective when speakers keep their presentation of events simple, in the order in which they occurred, and related to the specific purpose of the speech. Never discuss history for its own sake. Use the past to illuminate your purpose for speaking in the present.

Watch at **MyCommunicationLab**
Video: "History of the Circus"

To keep your listeners' attention and meet time requirements, you must be selective. Choose landmark events for your main points, and then arrange them in their natural order.

Robert Rozinski presented a speech on the evolution of cell phones based on the following chronological design:

Preview: Cell phones grew out of field radios and pagers, were then developed for use in cars, next evolved into portable models, and finally emerged as the smart phones we have today.

I. The first wireless means of voice communication were the field radios, walkie-talkies, and pagers widely used for military communication in World War II.

    A. These "phones" were heavy and bulky.

    B. They had a limited range of effectiveness.

II. In the 1980s mobile car phones were manufactured.

    A. They were still bulky and heavy.

    B. Some connected the caller to an operator who redirected the call.

III. In 1993 the first handheld phone was produced by Motorola.

    A. It was 9" long, 5" deep, and 2" wide and weighed 2.5 lbs.

    B. It had a talk time of 30 minutes and took 10 hours to recharge.

    C. It cost up to $8,700 in today's money.

IV. The prototypes of the cell phones of today became available around the turn of the century.

    A. The clam-shell model was developed.

    B. Touch pad phones were produced.

    C. Computer capabilities and applications were added.

The causation design used by Alexandra McArthur exposed the negative side of tourism.

▶ **chronological design** Explains events or historical developments in the order in which they occurred.

Causation Design

Watch at
MyCommunicationLab
Video: "Fast Foods"

Watch at
MyCommunicationLab
Video: "Sleep-Deprived
College Students"

Explore at
MyCommunicationLab
Activity: "Annotated
Outline: Bethel Ministries"

A **causation design** addresses the origins or consequences of a situation or event, proceeding from cause to effect or from effect to cause. The most important points of focus are the subject and either how it came about or what its results might be. The major causes or consequences become main points in the body of the speech.

In her speech "Honduras: Paradise or . . .," Alexandra McArthur held the tourism industry up for close critical inspection. Although the industry is typically accepted without question as a blessing for underdeveloped nations, Alexandra revealed a seamier side of it. Her speech developed in the following cause-effect pattern:

Preview: While it offers some benefits, tourism also has a downside because of its economic, sociological, and political impact.

I. Economic impact: the dollars generated by tourism are not an unmixed blessing.

   A. Tourism contributes to unequal distribution of wealth: the rich get richer, the poor poorer.

   B. Tourism can take money out of a country and put it into the pockets of foreign investors.

II. Sociological impact: native populations can suffer.

   A. Native workers are often overqualified and underpaid.

   B. Encourages child labor: tourists are more likely to buy souvenirs and crafts from children.

III. Political impact: tourism encourages class and foreign resentment.

   A. Natives are often forced off land wanted for tourist attractions.

   B. Natives may be banned from the beaches and restaurants created on their own land.

   C. Natives can't afford the luxuries available.

IV. So what our tourism dollars earn for us can be a bitter dividend.

Speeches using a causation design are subject to one major drawback—the tendency to oversimplify. Any complex situation will generally have many underlying causes, and any given set of conditions may lead to many different future effects. Be wary of overly simple explanations and overly confident predictions. Such simplified explanations and predictions are one form of fallacy (discussed further in Chapter 15).

As noted in Chapter 9, the design for your speech should fit the material you have found and your specific purpose. The designs discussed in this chapter are often combined within a single speech. For instance, Maria Tomasso's speech on sabermetrics, the mathematical assessment of the worth of ballplayers, began by defining the subject, traced its development chronologically, and then explained how it is often applied in college and major league baseball. Landon West's speech "The Battle of the Bulge" first described the extent of obesity in America and then

▶ **causation design** Addresses the origins or consequences of a situation or event, proceeding from cause to effect or from effect to cause.

Design	Use When
Categorical	Your topic has natural or customary divisions. Each category becomes a main point for development. It is useful when you need to organize large amounts of material.
Comparative	Your topic is new to your audience, abstract, technical, or simply difficult to comprehend. It helps make material more meaningful by comparing or contrasting it with something the audience already knows and understands.
Spatial	Your topic can be discussed by how it is positioned in a physical setting or natural environment. It allows you to take your audience on an orderly "oral tour" of your topic.
Sequential	Your topic can be arranged by time. It is useful for describing a process as a series of steps or explaining a subject as a series of developments.
Chronological	Your topic can be discussed as a historical development through certain defining moments.
Causation	Your topic is best understood in terms of its underlying causes or consequences. May be used to account for the present or predict future possibilities.

FIGURE 13.2
Which Speech Design to Use When

discussed ways to combat it. See Figure 13.2 for an overview of what designs to use and when to use them.

Rising to the Challenge of the Informative Speech

Informative speaking can pose a special challenge for speakers. Self-introductory speeches often reveal fascinating insights into the personalities of speakers. Persuasive speeches offer the drama of controversy surrounding issues. Ceremonial speeches can entertain and inspire. In contrast, informative speeches can sometimes seem rather dull, perhaps because we hear so many of them. On the other hand, many of the informative speeches we have heard in class, including those cited here, were very interesting. What can we learn from the successful speakers cited in this chapter to help us avoid information doldrums?

First, these speakers selected good topics. They chose topics they were genuinely interested in that they could also make interesting to listeners.

As you complete the preparation of your informative speech, consider the following:

- What have I learned in the preparation of this speech?
- Has this experience changed my perspective on my topic?
- What have I learned about tailoring my speech to fit my audience?
- Has this experience deepened my knowledge of the subject and my sensitivity to others' needs?
- Has this experience helped me find my voice? In what ways?

Watch at
MyCommunicationLab
Video: "Nigerian Fashion"

Second, these speakers used their time well. They selected topics early in their preparation and had enough time to do research and reflect on what they learned.

Third, these speakers carefully chose the designs for their speeches. They introduced topics in ways that grabbed and held attention. They had a clear specific purpose for speaking. They kept in mind what the audience needed, and they prepared a conclusion that would make it hard for audiences to forget their most important ideas.

Fourth, these speakers provided colorful, striking content. They used facts, figures, and testimony to confront their listeners with unexpected information. They used examples and stories to awaken feelings and stir the imagination of listeners. They used language in ways that made their ideas come alive.

Fifth, they put a lot of energy into their presentations. They set a varied pace in their presentation style. They used pauses for emphasis. Their voices reflected the importance of their messages. Their gestures complemented what they were saying.

Every day we are bombarded with information, both in and out of the classroom. Although we may become jaded and want to tune things out, we really need to pay attention—to listen and learn from what we hear. You will encounter most of this information outside of the classroom—in the workplace, on television, on the Internet. You might attend a lecture at the local library, view a TED talk on YouTube, or participate in a training session at your job. You may also be in a position to educate others. Use what you have learned here to take full advantage of these opportunities to learn and to share your interests and expertise.

Briefings: An Application

A **briefing** is a specialized form of informative speaking offered in an organizational setting. It may involve description and demonstration, but it usually emphasizes explanation. Briefings often take place during meetings, as when employees gather at the beginning of a workday to learn about plans or policy changes.[4] At such

▶ **briefing** A short informative presentation offered in an organizational setting that focuses on plans, policies, or reports.

meetings, you might be asked to give a status report on a project. Briefings also take place in one-on-one situations, as when you report to your supervisor at work. They can take the form of a press briefing that follows a crisis or major event.[5] Often a question-and-answer period will follow the briefing.

Being asked to present briefings at school or at work provides you with the opportunity to demonstrate your leadership potential. Unfortunately, briefings are not often done well. Most "how to" books on communicating in organizations deplore the lack of brevity, clarity, and directness in such presentations.[6] When executives in eighteen organizations were asked "What makes a presentation poor?" they offered the following answers:

- It is badly organized.

- It is not presented well.

- It contains too much jargon.

- It is too long.

- It lacks examples or comparisons.[7]

The following guidelines can help you prepare and present more effective briefings:

1. *A briefing should be what its name suggests: brief.* Cut out any material that is not related directly to your main points. Keep your introduction and conclusion short. Begin with a preview and end with a summary.

2. *Organize your ideas before you open your mouth.* How can you possibly be organized when you are called on without warning in a meeting to "tell us about your project"? The answer is simple: Prepare in advance (also review our guidelines for making impromptu speeches in Chapter 12). *Never go into any meeting in which there is even the slightest chance that you might be asked to report without a skeleton outline of a presentation.* Select a simple design, and make a key-word outline of points you would cover. Put this on a single note card or a smart phone, and take it to the meeting with you.

3. *Rely heavily on facts and figures, expert testimony, and short examples for supporting materials.* Don't drift off into extended examples and long stories. Use comparison and contrast to make your points stand out and come alive.

4. *Adapt your language to your audience.* If you are an engineer reporting on a project to a group of managers, use the language of management, not the language of engineering. Tell them what they need to know in language they can understand. Relate the subject to what they already know.

5. *Present your message with confidence.* Be sure everyone can see and hear you. Stand up, if necessary. Look listeners in the eye. Speak firmly with an air of assurance. After all, the project is yours, and you are the expert on it.

6. *Be prepared to answer tough questions.* Be prepared to respond to questions openly and honestly. No one likes bad news, but worse news will come if you don't deliver the bad news to those who need to know it *when* they need to know it. Review our suggestions for handling question-and-answer sessions in Chapter 12.

FINAL reflections

Bringing Fire to Your Listeners

According to ancient Greek legend, the god Prometheus was punished severely by the other gods for teaching humans how to make fire. These other, jealous gods feared that humans would now be able to warm themselves, cook their food, gather safely around campfires, and share knowledge in the stories they told. Eventually, they would build civilizations and challenge the gods themselves with the power of their new learning. His fellow gods had every right to be angry with Prometheus. He had just given the first informative speech.

Learning how to give effective informative speeches that describe, demonstrate, and explain is still a key to finding one's voice and developing one's power as a communicator. Beyond acquiring technical skill, the ability to speak informatively implies that you have learned much about people: how to motivate them to listen and learn, how to gain and hold their attention, and how to help them retain your message. It suggests also that you understand how to design messages that will reach out to others, how to earn their trust, and how to transfer knowledge effectively.

Mastering the art of informative speaking is a necessary step in acquiring your voice. It enables you to bring fire to your listeners.

After Reading This Chapter, You Should Be Able To Answer These Questions

Study and **Review** at **MyCommunicationLab**

1 Why is informative speaking important?

2 What must successful speeches of description accomplish? How do they do their work?

3 How must speeches that demonstrate a process proceed? What design is appropriate for them?

4 What goals, techniques, and designs are appropriate for speeches of explanation?

5 How can you assist the learning process in your informative speech?

6 What are the major design options for informative speaking?

7 How can you meet the challenge of informative speaking?

8 How can you prepare and present effective briefings?

For Discussion and Further Exploration

1 Develop an oral description of an interesting place in your hometown, and present it to your class. Are listeners able to "see" the place in their minds? What words work best to create this image for them? What might you have done better?

2 Have you recently used a manual or computer instructions that explained how to program, operate, or repair something? How clear and helpful were the instructions? How might they be improved? Bring them to class and explain your ideas.

3 One testimonial to the power of information is how upset individuals, companies, and countries become when secret and private data are stolen or leaked through hacking or unauthorized disclosures, as happened in the Snowden case. How much secrecy of government information can be tolerated in a society that depends on well-informed citizens? At what point does the secret surveillance of citizens violate their constitutional right to privacy? How do we resolve the conflict between individual rights and our government's need for vital information about us?

4 Download an informative speech found on TED or YouTube. Analyze it in terms of function, type, and design. Consider how it gains and holds attention and how it motivates learning. Can you suggest a different design for the speech? How might you improve its informative value?

5 Select an informative topic, determine a specific purpose, and develop two different outlines for the speech you might give, each illustrating one of the design options covered in this chapter. For each design, explain the motivational techniques you might use to engage your audience. Which do you prefer, and why?

SAMPLE INFORMATIVE SPEECH

This powerful and moving speech was presented by Olivia Jackson to her class at Phillips Exeter Academy in New Hampshire. It develops in a categorical pattern and illustrates effective use of expert testimony and narrative. Olivia's speech opens with the story of her grandfather, a brilliant man now suffering from the slow ravages of Alzheimer's. The story gives Olivia personal credibility to speak on the subject: She is personally invested in it. She presents her speech in MyCommunicationLab.

Watch at **MyCommunicationLab** Video: "Descent into Darkness"

Descent Into Darkness by

OLIVIA JACKSON

My grandfather is the smartest man I know. After skipping two grades in elementary school, my grandfather enrolled at Phillips Exeter. He was the youngest member of the class of 1948, and excelled academically, graduating *cum laude*. He went on to Harvard, and then pursued a career in finance at the Bank of Boston, where he established himself as an expert in the transportation industry. He married my grandmother, Diana Cameron, in 1959.

All his life, grandfather kept his mind active by being treasurer for a number of organizations, running balance sheets and analyzing numbers, doing crossword puzzles and Sudoku, and playing bridge, ultimately becoming a Life Master.

In 1989, just six months after he had accepted an early retirement package from the bank and begun doing consulting work for his former transportation clients, my grandmother was diagnosed with an inoperable brain tumor. From 1994 until 2008, her condition got progressively worse. By 2006 she was bedridden, relying solely on my grandfather to care for her until she passed away.

Olivia defines her topic and demonstrates through her grandfather's example how devastating it can be. She uses the enduring metaphor of light and darkness, combined with ◄ a metaphor based on spatial orientation (**descent**), to give memorable expression to the consequences of the disease.

He now lives in a small house in New Hampshire, taking long walks with his dog, reading historical books, and slowly forgetting who his family is, where he is from, and who he is.

This past winter my grandfather was diagnosed with Alzheimer's disease. Alzheimer's disease, according to the *Encyclopedia of Alzheimer's Disease*, is "a progressive, degenerative disease characterized by the death of nerve cells in several areas of the brain. It is the most common of the more than 70 forms of dementia, a condition that leads to the loss of mental and physical functions." It has been incredibly hard to watch my grandfather forget how to balance his checkbook, forget information my Mom has told him several times before, and forget key family details. Something is erasing and eating away at his memory, creating a dark abyss of emptiness and forgetfulness; a world that used to be so familiar is now slipping away from him.

Today, I want to discuss four potential preventatives for Alzheimer's disease. According to Dash and Villemarette-Pitman, in their book, *Alzheimer's Disease*, the "lifestyle factors" that may possibly prevent this disease include education, physical fitness, social activity, and continual intellectual challenges. Each one of these factors plays an important role in the attempt to decrease one's chances of developing the disease or delaying the onset of Alzheimer's.

Education and its effect on developing Alzheimer's have been studied closely. According to Dash and Villemarette-Pitman, "people with lower levels of education have higher rates of Alzheimer's," also referred to as "AD." They support this hypothesis with several theories. One is the "synaptic reserve hypothesis," which states that a more highly educated person has more nerve cell connections in the brain because their minds have been more active. When the disease begins to deteriorate and destroy these connections, new ones can form more easily and faster due to the higher activity. It is also believed that educated people are better able to mask the dementia because, over the course of their education, they have developed strategies and skills that will help them "better compensate for any loss of ability." Education is one factor that may help prevent Alzheimer's, although it is not a guarantee, as in my grandfather's case. No matter how many years of education you have, or how little, you are still at risk of getting the disease.

Physical fitness is a second factor that is beneficial for all health concerns, lowering cholesterol, maintaining a healthy heart, and potentially preventing Alzheimer's. Dash and Villemarette-Pitman write, "exercise affects both brain structure and function." Everyone should exercise regularly, because, as the authors say, "a program of regular exercise in midlife is protective against developing AD later in life. Elderly people who exercise regularly are at a lower risk of developing AD." It is still uncertain whether physical fitness directly correlates to preventing Alzheimer's or if the exercise helps decrease the chance of getting another disease, which in turn benefits both the body and the mind. However, there appears to be some connection between the physical activity that one participates in throughout the latter half of their life and the prevention of both mental and physical diseases, AD included.

The last two preventative measures include social activity and continuing to be intellectually challenged. Social activity keeps the mind active and alert, whereas an insular person, who is not interacting with others and thus not listening and sharing ideas, is less likely to fully engage their brain all

Olivia previews a discussion of preventative measures, indicating that the body of her speech will follow a categorical design. She makes good use of expert testimony, sustaining the credibility of her speech. She also demonstrates the ability to explain complex ideas with clarity and simplicity.

the time. Similarly, intellectual challenges keep the brain active and engaged. R. S. Wilson, from the Chicago Health and Aging Project, conducted a study of 4,000, sixty-five and older aged residents of South Chicago. He concluded, according to Dash and Villemarette-Pitman, that "those who were more intellectually active were less likely to develop AD. Those who did crossword puzzles and read books showed less cognitive decline as they aged than those who preferred less cognitively engaging activities, such as watching television." Such research suggests that maintaining an active mind for the duration of your life, as well as continuing social connections and interaction, should keep your brain alert, busy, and healthier far longer.

After reading about all of these things, I can't help but wonder why these things didn't help my grandfather. He is highly educated, physically fit, socially active, and still intellectually challenges himself, so how did it happen to him? Why? According to a *Time* Magazine article in 2010, "the therapies that exist—drugs and lifestyle behaviors such as keeping the mind sharp with enriching social relationships and stimulating the brain with games and puzzles—can only *delay*, not stop, the onset of memory loss, confusion and cognitive decline that generally extend over a period of several years or, more often, decades." Having to care for my grandmother for over 15 years really took its toll on my grandfather. He spent much of his time caring for her, worrying about her constantly, and losing much of the social connection they had shared with friends, as well as the stimulation of conversation with her, something they had always enjoyed.

More than five million Americans are affected by Alzheimer's disease, according to *Time*. Every case is a bit different. But the disease always inevitably progresses and is eventually fatal. There are currently no cures for the disease, although researchers are frantically working to find one, and one is desperately needed because over 100,000 people die from Alzheimer's every year. The only thing a caregiver can do is watch the slow decline and make the patient as comfortable as possible. It must be terrifying to lose one's memory, although in my grandfather's case, he seems blissfully unaware of his diagnosis, which is both good and sad at the same time. My grandfather seemed to do everything right in terms of the suggested "lifestyle behaviors" that would prevent AD; we cannot know for sure whether he simply *delayed* the onset of the disease or if my grandmother's long illness also played a role. It still seems worth it to do everything possible to delay or prevent Alzheimer's by keeping one's mind active, socially and intellectually engaged, and by staying physically fit, and hope for a medical breakthrough in preventing and curing this disease. Although this will come too late to help my grandfather, hopefully others can be spared the descent into such darkness.

◀ Olivia ponders why the various measures she has discussed did not protect her grandfather from AD. She suggests that such measures may be able only to delay, not prevent, the onset of the disease. She also wonders whether the many years of caring for her grandmother may have taken their toll, reducing his social connections with friends as well as depriving him of the stimulating conversation he had once enjoyed with his wife.

◀ Olivia concludes that the example of her grandfather underscores the importance of finding a cure for Alzheimer's. That hope—along with the various measures that might delay, if not prevent, the disease—are what we can cling to. As she concludes, Olivia returns to the vivid composite image of darkness and descent to end her speech.

14 Persuasive Speaking

Over a lengthy career, we have heard thousands of student persuasive speeches. A few of them stand out in our minds. What makes them so memorable? *All of them arose out of strong feelings and convictions.*

Lindsey Yoder spoke from both the heart and the head as she indicted human trafficking and called for listeners to join the campaign against that evil commerce. She first presented her speech to her class and then to a wider audience, as she won the Osborn Public Speaking contest at the University of Memphis. News of her speech then reached local activists, and soon she was speaking again at a community rally sponsored by churches and the police department. You can read a text of her speech at the end of this chapter. In MyCommunicationLab, you can also see a rough tape of her speaking at the outdoor rally in a neighborhood where human trafficking abounds. Some words seem destined to live on!

Dolapo Olushola was obviously moved as she described the plight of orphans at the Open Arms Orphanage in her native Nigeria, asking her Davidson College listeners to contribute to their cause. Her listeners responded with strong support. We cite her powerful speech at various moments in this text. You can view this speech in MyCommunicationLab.

Austin Wright of the University of Texas expressed outrage as he described the government's misuse of faulty databases, urging listeners to "help keep Big Brother off your back." His speech appears at the end of Chapter 15.

These and other fine speeches make clear that there is a real difference between having to give a persuasive speech and speaking persuasively because you feel compelled to share your deep concern with others. Through their speeches, these students demonstrated dramatically that they had found their voices.

Because there has been implanted in us the power to persuade each other ..., not only have we escaped the life of the wild beasts but we have come together and founded cities and made laws and invented arts.

—ISOCRATES

 Watch at **MyCommunicationLab Video:** "Open Pockets, Open Arms, Open Futures"

When we speak persuasively, we want others to see the world as we see it and to join in correcting its wrongs. We want to influence both attitudes and actions. **Persuasion** therefore is the *art of gaining fair and favorable consideration for our points of view.* Ethical persuasion is grounded in sound reasoning and is sensitive to the needs and interests of listeners. Such persuasion gives us the chance to make the world a little better.

▶ **persuasion** The art of gaining fair and favorable consideration for our points of view.

Many people still ask, "What difference can one person make? My words don't carry much weight." Perhaps not, but words make ripples, and ripples can come together to make waves. Such was the case with Anna Aley, who first gave her speech condemning substandard off-campus student housing to her public speaking class. Her speech was later presented in a public forum on campus. Its text, which appears in Appendix B, was reprinted in the local newspaper, which followed it up with investigative reports and a supportive editorial. Brought to the attention of the mayor and city commission, Anna's speech helped promote reforms in the city's rental housing policies. When last we checked, her words were still reverberating in Manhattan, Kansas.

Perhaps your classroom speech will not have that kind of impact, but you never know who or what may be changed by it. In this chapter, we explore the nature of persuasive speaking in contrast with informative speaking. Then we will identify the major types of persuasive speaking, how the persuasive process works, challenges that persuaders must confront, and the major designs that serve persuasive speaking.

The Nature of Persuasive Speaking

Persuasive speaking differs from informative speaking in seven basic ways:

First, while informative speeches reveal options, persuasive speeches urge a choice among them. For example, an informative speaker might say: "There are three different ways we can deal with the budget deficit. Let me explain them." In contrast, a persuasive speaker would urge support for one of the options.

Second, informative speakers act as teachers; persuaders act as advocates. The difference is often one of passion and engagement. Persuasive speakers are more vitally committed to a cause. This does not necessarily mean that persuaders are loud; the most passionate and intense moments of a speech can be very quiet.

Third, informative speeches offer supporting material to illustrate points; persuasive speeches use the same material as evidence that justifies advice. An ethical persuader interweaves facts and statistics, testimony, examples, and narratives into a compelling case based on responsible knowledge and sensitivity to the best interests of listeners.

Fourth, the role of the audience changes dramatically from information to persuasion. Informed listeners expand their knowledge, but persuaded listeners make commitments and become *agents of change.* Their new attitudes, beliefs, and actions will affect themselves and others. Clearly, persuasive speeches ask for more audience commitment than do informative speeches. Although there is some risk in being exposed to new ideas, more is at stake when listening to a persuasive message. What if a persuasive speaker is mistaken or even dishonest? What if her proposed plan of action is defective? Doing always involves a greater risk than knowing. Your commitment could cost you—and those who may be influenced by your actions—dearly.

Fifth, speaker credibility is even more important in persuasive than in informative speeches. Because persuasive speeches involve risk, listeners weigh the character and competence of speakers closely. Do they really know what they are talking about? Do they have their listeners' interests at heart? As a persuasive speaker, your ethos will be on public display and will be scrutinized carefully.

Sixth, appeals to feelings are more useful in persuasive than in informative speeches. Because of the risk involved, listeners may balk at accepting recommendations, even when those recommendations are supported by good reasons. To overcome such inertia, persuaders must sometimes appeal to feelings,[1] which is why they often use emotional appeals to open their speeches. For example, the informative statement "A 10 percent rise in tuition will reduce the student population by about 5 percent next term" might take the following form in a persuasive speech:

> The people pushing for the tuition increase don't think a few hundred dollars more each semester will have that much effect. They think we can handle it.
>
> Let me tell you about my friend Tricia. She's on the Dean's List in chemistry, the pride and hope of her family. Tricia will get a great job when she graduates—if she graduates! But if this increase goes through, Tricia won't be back next term. Her dreams of success will be delayed—and perhaps denied!
>
> Perhaps you're in the same boat as Tricia—paddling against the current. We all need to work together to defeat this tuition increase.

Emotional and graphic language, developed through examples or narratives, can help people see the human dimension of problems and move these listeners to the right action.

Seventh, the ethical obligation for persuasive speeches is even greater than for informative speeches. Persuasion that arises out of selfishness or carelessness or malignant motives can be a great curse. But as Isocrates said in this chapter's opening quotation, persuasion can also be a blessing to humankind. This great educator of the Golden Age of Greece knew that at their best, persuasive speakers make us confront our obligation to believe and act in socially and morally responsible ways. By describing how they themselves became persuaded, they model how we should deliberate in difficult situations. By making intelligence and morality effective in public affairs, they can help the world evolve in more enlightened ways.

The major differences between informative and persuasive speaking are summarized in Figure 14.1.

Informative Speaking	Persuasive Speaking
1. Reveals options.	1. Urges a choice among options.
2. Speaker acts as teacher.	2. Speaker acts as advocate.
3. Uses supporting material to enlighten listeners.	3. Uses supporting material to justify advice.
4. Audience expands knowledge.	4. Audience becomes agent of change.
5. Asks for little audience commitment.	5. Asks for strong audience commitment.
6. Speaker's credibility is important.	6. Speaker's credibility more important.
7. Fewer appeals to feelings.	7. More appeals to feelings.
8. High ethical obligation.	8. Higher ethical obligation.

FIGURE 14.1
Informative Versus Persuasive Speaking

The Types of Persuasive Speaking

Persuasion helps us deal with the uncertainties reflected in the following three questions:

- What is the truth about a situation?

- How should I evaluate the situation?

- What should I do about it?

These questions in turn invite three basic types of persuasive speaking: speeches that focus on facts, speeches that address attitudes and values, and speeches that advocate action and policy. At times, these types can be related: You may find them in the same speech or in a series of speeches.

Speeches That Focus on Facts

People argue constantly over what the true state of affairs was, is, and will be. Such arguments generate **speeches that focus on facts.** Our assumptions about facts support our *beliefs*, what we know or think we know about people and events. Uncertainty can surround questions of past, current, and future facts.

Past Facts. Did something actually happen? And if so, how should we evaluate it? Did George Zimmerman shoot Trayvon Martin? If so, was it self-defense, or was it murder? Have human activities led to global warming? Should we be worried about it? Persuaders argue questions of past facts before juries in courtrooms and on newspaper editorial pages as well as on the public platform. Speeches concerning past facts try to shape audience memories of people and events. They will be successful if they do the following:

- **Present other facts that confirm what they claim.** In the text of his speech "Global Burning," reprinted in Appendix B, note how Josh Logan uses charts and statistics to confirm the growth of greenhouse gases over the past thousand years.

- **Present supporting testimony from recent, respected expert sources.** To support his factual claims about global warming, Josh cites the "United Nations Intergovernmental Panel on Climate Change, reporting during the early part of this year." He describes this study as an "authoritative, thousand-page report, which correlates and tests the work of hundreds of environmental scientists from countries all around the globe."

- **Re-create a dramatic, credible narrative of how events in a dispute may have happened.** The renowned Roman orator Cicero, who was also one of history's greatest courtroom lawyers, was superb in creating narratives of past events that seemed to establish their reality. For a spicy example, which also implies the moral depravity of many people in the Rome of several thousand years ago, see his forensic speech *Pro Caelius.*[2]

Current Facts. What is actually going on? Is Iran attempting to develop nuclear weapons? Do North Korea's missiles constitute a threat to the U.S. mainland? Are recent extreme weather events from southern tornadoes to western wildfires to

▶ **speeches that focus on facts** Speeches designed to establish the validity of past or present information or to make predictions about what is likely to occur in the future.

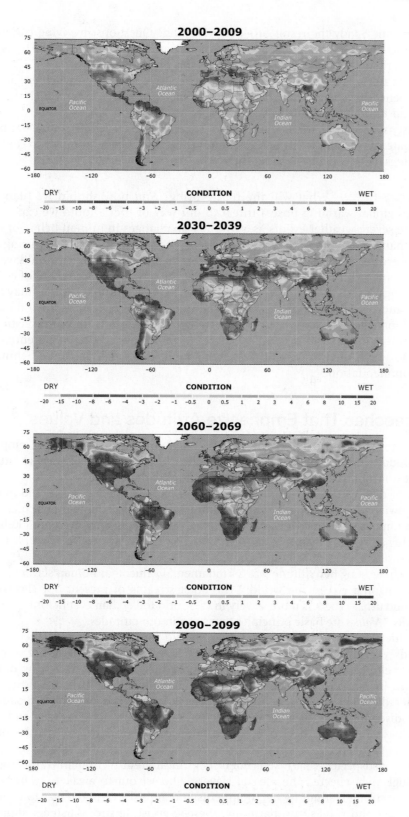

Speeches that focus on facts may need visual supporting materials to strengthen their claims.

Hurricane Sandy the result of global warming? Questions involving current facts are incredibly important to the fate of nations and individuals. On the basis of our perceptions of current facts, we develop plans of action.

At times, questions of past and current facts turn not on whether something happened or is happening but on the *definition* of events. Yes, sexual activity occurred in the encounter between the sports star and the woman, but was the sex consensual, or did it constitute rape? How does one define global warming or climate change and its scope? To control the definitions of events is to control the feelings that people have about them.

Future Facts. What will the future bring? And how should we plan for it? Does global warming pose a threat to our way of life? Should we expect to see more severe weather events as a result? Can changes in human behavior impact or change the course of climate change? Persuasive speeches regarding future facts are **predictions** based on readings of the past and present. Should we invest in a certain company? One persuader may argue that the past record of company earnings justifies a strong vote of confidence in the future. Another may answer that much of this past success occurred under different leadership and that current management has yet to prove itself. The first offers an enthusiastic "buy" recommendation; the second advises caution. It's up to you as a potential investor to weigh the evidence and test the soundness of the reasoning behind each recommendation.

Speeches That Emphasize Attitudes and Values

The troubled world in which we live often invites **speeches that emphasize attitudes and values**. These speeches ask us to react in certain ways to situations that confront us and to connect these reactions with our values.

At the heart of our attitudes are intense feelings. Lindsey Yoder did not make her own commitment against human trafficking until she became close friends with a victim of sex slavery. "It was easy for me to avoid getting involved until Kelley told me her story and I realized it is all around me." It took a powerful example to ignite her strong feelings about this issue.

Underlying her attitude was a fundamental value: that human slavery is a great and ongoing evil in the world: *"The quiet screams of present day slaves are all around us.... There is more slavery in the world today than ever before.... It is our reality." Values* are basic principles that support our attitudes.

Ideally, our attitudes and values should be in harmony, as they were for Lindsey, creating a coherent worldview. However, these elements are sometimes undeveloped, disconnected, or even opposed to one another, leaving our inner world incomplete or fragmented or confused. When we become aware of this inner disarray, we experience what psychologists call **cognitive dissonance**, the discomfort we feel because of conflict between our attitudes and values. Persuasive speakers have the opportunity to create or restore consistency and harmony for us by recommending appropriate changes in attitude. For example, Lindsey suspected that her listeners were indifferent to human trafficking, even though they rejected the idea of slavery. She set out to awaken awareness and arouse strong feelings by her arguments and appeals. Her goal was to bring their attitudes and values into harmony, thereby enlisting strong listener support for her cause.[3]

▶ **predictions**   Forecasts of what we can expect in the future, often based on trends from past events.

▶ **speeches that emphasize attitudes and values**   Speeches designed to modify and apply these elements and to help listeners find harmony among them.

▶ **cognitive dissonance**   The discomfort we feel because of conflict among our attitudes and values.

FINDING YOUR

voice

Harmonizing Attitudes and Values

Can you think of situations that might represent inconsistency between attitudes and values? How might you frame persuasive speeches that could restore harmony between these elements? Report your thoughts in class discussion.

Because values are an integral part of our personality, major changes in them can have a real impact on how we live. Therefore, we don't change values as readily as we change attitudes and beliefs. Speeches that attempt to change values may seem radical and extreme. For this reason, such speeches are rare, usually occurring only in desperate times and situations when existing values seem to have failed us. The Great Depression of the 1930s, the civil rights struggle of the 1950s and 1960s, the Vietnam War of the 1960s and 1970s, and more recent conflicts over government surveillance policies and the power of money in controlling American politics have all raised questions about American values and have inspired persuasive speeches critical of them.

Speeches That Advocate Action and Policy

Speeches that advocate action and policy often build on earlier speeches that affirm facts or activate values. Therefore, in addition to bringing harmony to our inner world of attitudes and values, persuasive speeches can promote coherence between what we say and what we do. Persuasive speakers remind us that we should practice what we preach.

Such was the goal of Amanda Miller, who presented a powerful indictment of the Western Hemisphere Institute for Security Cooperation, better known as the "School of the Americas." Amanda argued that this institute, conducted for many years at Fort Benning, Georgia, under U.S. sponsorship, had been "implicated in gross human rights violations in Latin America." The school, she said, trained its students in "techniques for torture, false imprisonment, extortion, and intimidation" and had been "responsible for the deaths of many thousands of people and countless acts of terrorism." Amanda painted a vivid picture of the contradiction between American values and American actions and urged her listeners to "support the cause" of shutting down the institute. In the process, they would be restoring coherence to the world of morality and action.

The actions proposed by such speeches can be simple and direct, or they can involve complex policy plans, depending on the nature of the problem. To meet the challenge of global warming, Josh Logan proposed a solution that called for listeners' direct personal action as well as their support for changes in government policy. On a less complex issue, Betsy Lyles urged her listeners to donate hair to Locks of Love, an organization that offers hairpieces to impoverished children who are suffering from long-term medical hair loss.

When a speech advocates group action, the audience must see itself as having a common identity and purpose. As we noted in Chapter 11, a speaker can reinforce group identity by using inclusive pronouns (*we, our, us*), by telling stories that

Watch at
MyCommunicationLab
Video: "Tobacco Ordinance Public Hearing: Shirley Lindsey Sears"

Watch at
MyCommunicationLab
Video: "Grant Proposal Presentation: Joel Rekas"

Watch at
MyCommunicationLab
Video: "Tobacco Ordinance Public Hearing: Paul Hager"

▶ **speeches that advocate action and policy** Speeches that encourage listeners to change their behavior either as individuals or as members of a group.

emphasize group achievements, and by referring to common heroes, opponents, or martyrs. Anna Aley used an effective appeal to group identity as she proposed specific actions:

What can one student do to change the practices of numerous Manhattan landlords? Nothing, if that student is alone. But just think of what we could accomplish if we got all 13,600 off-campus students involved in this issue! Think what we could accomplish if we got even a fraction of those students involved!

By identifying and uniting them as victims of unscrupulous landlords, Anna encouraged her listeners to act as members of a group. Figure 14.2 summarizes the ways persuasive speeches work.

The actions advocated in persuasive speeches can involve some risk and inconvenience. Therefore, you must present good reasons to overcome your audience's natural caution. The consequences of acting and not acting must be clearly spelled out. Your plan must be practical and reasonable, and your listeners should be able to see themselves enacting it successfully.

Speeches that advocate action can help raise awareness and support for worthy causes. Here Condoleezza Rice speaks at the Susan G. Komen Breast Cancer Foundation annual National Race for the Cure.

The Persuasive Process

William J. McGuire, professor of psychology at Yale University, suggested that successful persuasion is a process involving up to twelve phases.[4] For our purposes, these phases may be grouped into five stages: aware-

FIGURE 14.2
The Work of Persuasive Speeches

Type	Function	Techniques
Speeches that focus on facts	Establish true state of affairs	Strengthen claims of past, present, and future fact by citing experts and other supporting evidence. Create lively pictures of the contested facts that reinforce their reality.
Speeches that emphasize attitudes and values	Apply attitudes and values to present problems	Reawaken appreciation for values through stories, examples, and vivid language. Show listeners how to apply values. Encourage them to form and re-form attitudes consistent with these values.
Speeches that advocate action and policy	Propose programs to remedy problems and put values into action	Show that the program of action will solve the problem by mentioning previous successes in similar situations. Prove that the plan is practical and workable. Picture the audience enacting the plan of action. Show the consequences of acting and not acting. Visualize success.

ness, understanding, agreement, enactment, and integration (see Figure 14.3). Familiarity with these stages helps us see that persuasion is not an all-or-nothing proposition. A persuasive message can be successful if it moves people through the process toward a goal.

Awareness

Awareness involves knowing about a problem and paying attention to it. This phase is sometimes called *consciousness raising*.[5] In her speech "Honduras: Paradise or . . .?" Alexandra McArthur raised awareness for her cultural critique of the tourism industry in Honduras by creating a vivid contrast between the dream picture painted for tourists and the reality she had experienced:

> The magazine written by the Institute of Tourism highlighted Honduras' hotels, beaches, restaurants, and shopping, while never mentioning the extreme poverty or violence in the country. It described Honduras as "One Small Country: Three Wide Worlds (Tropical Nature, Maya Renaissance, and Caribbean Creation)." In contrast, the land I knew combined the three worlds of superficial tourism, underdeveloped lands, and unequal distribution of wealth.
>
> The people I met on service trips were not the happy, smiling faces on tourist brochures. Instead, far too many of them suffer from malnutrition, and have little access to medicines, running water, or electricity.

Creating awareness is especially important when people do not believe that there actually is a problem. Before advocates could change the way females were depicted in children's books, they first had to convince listeners that always showing boys in active roles and girls in passive roles could thwart the development of self-esteem and ambition in young girls.[6]

Understanding

The second phase of the persuasive process is **understanding**. Listeners must grasp what you are telling them and know how to carry out your proposals. Amanda Miller encouraged understanding of her School of the Americas message by citing a number of examples:

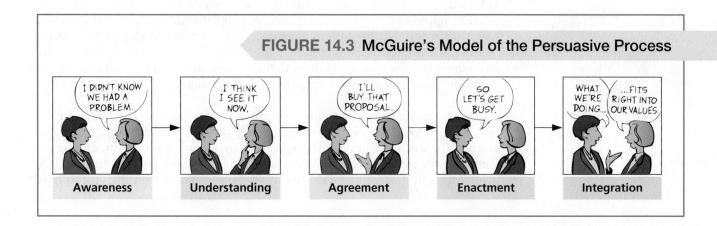

FIGURE 14.3 McGuire's Model of the Persuasive Process

Awareness | Understanding | Agreement | Enactment | Integration

▶ **awareness** This first stage in the persuasive process includes knowing about a problem and paying attention to it.

▶ **understanding** This second phase in the persuasive process requires that listeners grasp the meaning of the speaker's message.

In El Salvador, the United Nations Truth Commission found that of twelve officers responsible for the massacre of nine hundred villagers at El Mozote, ten of them were graduates of the School of the Americas.

I wish this were a solitary case. But according to an Inter-American Commission on Human Rights, School of the Americas graduate Raphael Samundio Molina led a massacre at the Colombian Palace of Justice, and three years later was inducted into the School of the Americas hall of fame. In the same country, an International Human Rights Tribunal found that of two hundred and forty-six officers cited for various crimes, one hundred and five of them were School of the Americas graduates.

Finally, the School has produced at least twelve Latin American dictators in countries such as Peru, Bolivia, Argentina, and Ecuador. This is the distinguished record of the School of the Americas that we continue to fund with our taxpayer dollars.

Because her examples were so controversial, Amanda had to document them carefully, using a variety of sources to heighten their credibility.

Agreement

The third stage in the persuasive process is **agreement**, which occurs when listeners accept your position. As they listen to you, audience members should go through a series of *affirmations*, such as these: "He's right, this is a serious problem. . . . That's striking evidence; I didn't know about that. . . . I see how this can affect my life. . . . I've got to do something about this. . . . This plan makes sense. I believe it will work." These affirmations should build on each other, developing momentum toward agreement at the end of the speech. Any doubt or any hesitation about the validity of a claim or the soundness of the evidence or the accuracy of the reasoning will weaken the process of agreement.

Speakers themselves become important models for agreement. When Dolapo Olushola described the plight of orphans in her native Nigeria, she seemed a strikingly authentic spokesperson as she asked for audience support:

Did you know the current number of orphans in the world would make a circle around the world's equator three times, if they were all holding hands? Do you know that every 15 seconds another child in Africa becomes an AIDS orphan?

Then when listeners learned that Dolapo had helped form a service club dedicated to relieving the plight of orphans in sub-Saharan Africa, it was clear she had already walked the path she wanted them to take. As she painted word-pictures of these abandoned children, she invited listeners to share her passion and sympathy. She convinced them that her cause deserved not just their agreement but also their commitment. She had given them a living model for their response.

Agreement can range from small concessions to total acceptance. Lesser degrees of agreement could represent success, especially when listeners have to change their attitudes, beliefs, or values or risk a great deal by accepting your ideas. During the Vietnam War, we often heard classroom speeches attacking or defending the U.S. involvement in that conflict. Feelings about the war ran so high that just to have

▶ **agreement**   This third stage in the persuasive process requires that listeners accept a speaker's recommendations and remember their reasons for doing so.

a speech listened to without interruption was an accomplishment. If a reluctant listener were to nod agreement or concede, "I guess you have a point," then one could truly claim victory.

Enactment

The fourth stage in the persuasive process is **enactment**. It is one thing to get listeners to accept what you say. It is quite another to get them to act on it. If you invite listeners to sign a petition, raise their hands, or voice agreement, you give them a way to enact agreement and to confirm a commitment. The speaker who mobilized his audience against a proposed tuition increase brought a petition to be signed, distributed the addresses of local legislators to contact, and urged listeners to write letters to campus and local newspapers. He helped transform their agreement into constructive action.

Converting agreement to action may require the use of emotional appeals. Stirring stories and examples, vivid images, and colorful language can arouse sympathy. In an especially interesting use of narrative technique, Lindsey Yoder asked her listeners to imagine themselves as victims of sex slavery, isolated, helpless, and doomed to a life of abuse. Her graphic word-pictures made listeners want to join the cause of eradicating this evil.

Integration

The final stage in the persuasive process is the **integration** of new commitments into listeners' previous beliefs and values. For a persuasive speech to have lasting effect, listeners must see the connection between what you propose and their core values. Josh Logan urged listeners not just to accept his recommendations but also to *become* the solution he advocated. He asked for total integration of beliefs, attitudes, values, and actions.

All of us seek consistency between our values and behaviors. For example, it would be inconsistent for us to march against substandard housing on Monday and contribute to a landlord's defense fund on Tuesday. This is why people sometimes seem to agree with a persuasive message and then change their minds. It dawns on them later that this new commitment means that they must rearrange other cherished beliefs and attitudes.

To avoid a delayed counterreaction, try to anticipate such problems as you design your speech. Don't attempt too much persuasion in a single message. Remember that dramatic change may require a campaign of persuasion in which any single speech plays a small but vital role. Be content if you can move listeners just a small distance in a desirable direction. To learn more about how speakers persuade, see the persuasion website developed by Kelton Rhoads, University of Southern California.

Persuasion, it is now clear, can be a complicated process. Any persuasive message must focus on the stage at which it can make its most effective contribution: raising awareness, building understanding, seeking agreement, encouraging action, or promoting the integration of beliefs, attitudes, and values. To determine where to focus your persuasive efforts, you must consider the challenges of the specific situation.

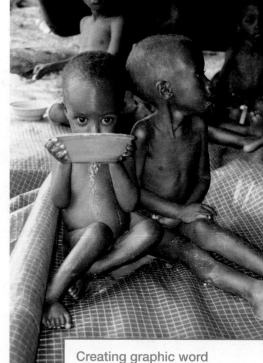

Creating graphic word pictures in a speech can arouse listeners' concern and spur them to join a cause such as aiding starving orphans in Africa.

▶ **enactment** This fourth stage of the persuasive process requires that listeners take appropriate action as the result of agreement.

▶ **integration** This final stage of the persuasive process requires that listeners connect new attitudes and commitments with previous beliefs and values to ensure lasting change.

The Challenges of Persuasive Speaking

The challenges that persuaders face range from confronting a reluctant audience to satisfying strong ethical requirements. As you plan a persuasive speech, you must consider audience members' position on the topic, how they might react to you as an advocate, and the situation in which the speech will be presented. Using the techniques of audience analysis that we introduced in Chapter 5 is crucial to success.

Begin preparing your speech by considering where your listeners stand on the issue. Might they hold differing attitudes about the topic, or are they more likely to be united? If listeners are divided, you might hope to unify them around your position. If listeners are already united—but in opposition—you might try to divide them and attract some toward your position.

Also consider how your listeners regard you as a speaker on the subject. If you do not have their respect, trust, and goodwill, use an abundance of supporting testimony from sources they do trust. Evaluating the relationships among the audience, the topic, and you as the speaker will point you to strategies for effective persuasion.

SPEAKER'S

notes Uniting a Divided Group

Use the following strategies to unite a divided group:

1. Bring to life images of common heroes and enemies.
2. Describe group traditions they may have forgotten.
3. Depict the deeper values they share.
4. Picture common problems.
5. Illustrate goals they share.
6. Spell out the first step they can take together, and urge them to take it.
7. Speak the language of inclusion, such as using family or team metaphors.

Convincing a Reluctant Audience to Listen

If you face an audience that opposes your position, you should be happy with small achievements, such as simply getting thoughtful and fair attention. One way to handle a reluctant audience is to adopt a **co-active approach**, which seeks to bridge the differences between you and your listeners.[7] The major steps in this approach are as follows:

Watch at **MyCommunicationLab** **Video:** "Mandatory Minimums (Problem Cause Solution)"

1. *Establish identification and goodwill early in the speech.* Emphasize experiences, background, beliefs, and values that you share with listeners. Communication consultant Larry Tracy suggests you should try to meet with or telephone key members of your audience before you speak, establishing personal contact and seeking their advice. Then you should mention them favorably as you speak: "Nothing is so sweet to the human ear as the sound of his or her name, especially if it is mentioned positively before others."[8]

2. *Start with areas of agreement before you tackle areas of disagreement.* Otherwise, listeners may simply "turn off and tune out" before you have a chance to state your position.

3. *Emphasize explanation over argument.* By explaining your position more than refuting theirs, you avoid provoking defensive behavior and invite listeners to consider the merits of your position. As Tracy notes, "You cannot persuade people to change their mind; they must persuade themselves." Help them by providing the information they need.

4. *Cite authorities that the audience will respect and accept.* If you can find statements by authorities that are favorably regarded, you can gain "borrowed ethos" for your case. On the other hand, if you cite authorities not respected by your particular listeners, they may react negatively to both you and your cause.

5. *Set modest goals for change.* Don't try to push your audience too far too fast. If reluctant listeners have listened to you—if you have raised their awareness and built a basis for understanding—you have accomplished a good deal.

6. *Make a multisided presentation that compares your position with others in a favorable way.* Show respect for opposing positions and understanding of the reasons why others might have supported them. Then reveal how these positions may not merit such support. Your attitude should be not to challenge listeners but to help them see the situation in a new light. Keep your goals modest. Ask only for a fair hearing. Be aware that reluctant listeners may not *want* to give you a fair hearing. Such listeners may distort your message so that it seems to fit what they already believe. Or they may simply deny or dismiss it, saying that it doesn't apply to them. Or they may discredit a source you cite in your speech, believing that any message that relies on *that* source cannot be taken seriously. Remember also that if you propose too much change, you may create a **boomerang effect**, in which the audience reacts by opposing your position even more strongly.[9]

For all these reasons, to hope for a major change on the basis of any single persuasive effort is what McGuire calls the **great expectation fallacy**.[10] Be patient with reluctant listeners. Try to move them a step at a time in the direction you would like them to go. Give them information that may eventually change their minds.

▶ **co-active approach** A way of approaching reluctant audiences in which the speaker attempts to establish goodwill, emphasizes shared values, and sets modest goals for persuasion.

▶ **boomerang effect** A possible negative reaction to a speech that advocates too much change.

▶ **great expectation fallacy** The mistaken idea that major change can usually be accomplished by a single persuasive effort.

Make a **multisided presentation**. Acknowledge the arguments in favor of opposed positions, showing that you respect and understand those positions, even though you do not accept them.

A multisided approach helps make those you do persuade resistant to later counterattacks because you show them in effect how to answer such arguments. This is called an **inoculation effect** because you "inject" your listeners with a milder form of the arguments they may hear later in more vehement forms from others.[11]

When you acknowledge and then refute arguments, you also help your credibility in two ways. First, you enhance your trustworthiness by showing respect for your opposition. You suggest that the opposing position deserves consideration, even though you have a better option. Second, you enhance your competence by showing your knowledge of the opposing position—of the reasons that explain why people may find it attractive and the reasons that reveal how it is defective.

After your speech, you should continue to show respect for the audience. Even if some listeners want to argue or heckle, keep your composure. To help you through such difficult moments, rehearse your speech before friends who pepper you with tough questions after your presentation. Try to anticipate and prepare for these questions. Listeners may be impressed by your self-control and may be encouraged to rethink their position in light of your example.

We once heard a student speak against abortion to a class that was sharply divided on that issue. She began with a personal narrative, the story of how her mother had been given a drug that was later found to induce birth defects. Her mother was then faced with a decision on terminating the pregnancy. The student concluded by saying that if her mother had chosen the abortion option, she would not be there speaking to them that day. She paused, smiled, and said, "Although I know some of you may disagree with my views, I must say I am glad that you are here to listen and that I am here to speak. Think about it." If your reasons are compelling and your evidence is strong, you may soften the opposition and move waverers toward your position.

Do not worry if the change you want does not show up immediately. There often is a delayed reaction to persuasion, a **sleeper effect** in which change shows up only after listeners have had time to think about and integrate the message into their belief systems.[12] Even if no change is apparent, your message may sensitize your listeners to the issue and make them more receptive to future persuasion.

FINDING YOUR

voice   Persuasive Confrontations

Are there ever times when a speaker should give up trying to persuade a hostile audience and simply confront listeners directly with the position they appear to oppose? Why would a speaker bother to do this? Might speaker and audience gain anything from such a confrontation? Look for an example of such a speech, consulting YouTube and other online sources or watching C-SPAN or other televised presentations. Do you agree with the strategy used in it? Discuss in class.

▶ **multisided presentation** A speech in which the speaker's position is compared favorably to other positions.

▶ **inoculation effect** Preparing an audience for an opposing argument by answering it before listeners have been exposed to it.

▶ **sleeper effect** A delayed reaction to persuasion.

Finally, there is one special technique that can sometimes create identification between speakers and reluctant, even hostile, audiences. That technique is laughter. The French philosopher Henri Bergson has pointed out that shared laughter can be the beginnings of community. The late Ann Richards, former governor of Texas, told a story that illustrates how this technique can work. After she had been elected early in her career to the Travis County Commission, Ann paid a visit to a road maintenance crew at their worksite. As she entered the crew office, Ann noticed a particularly ugly dog stretched across the front door. She proceeded to make her presentation to a group of men whose popular male boss she had just defeated. After her speech, no one responded when she asked for questions. As she told the story:

> Finally, just to break the ice and get them talking, I asked them about their dog. Texas men will always talk about their dogs. Nothing. No one said a word. There was some shuffling of feet. I thought, "There must be something unseemly about the dog's name, it's the only answer." I looked around the room and they were ducking my gaze. "Let me tell you," I said, "that I am the only child of a very rough-talking father. So don't be embarrassed about your language. I've either heard it or I can top it. So what's the dog's name?"
>
> An old hand in the back row with a big wide belt and big wide belt buckle sat up and said in a gravel bass, "Well, you're gonna find out sooner or later." He looked right at me. "Her name is Ann Richards." I laughed. And when I laughed they roared. And a little guy in the front row who was a lot younger and smarter than most, said in a wonderfully hopeful tenor, "But we call her Miss Ann!" From then on those guys and I were good friends.[13]

Facing a reluctant audience is never easy. But you can't predict what new thoughts your speech might stimulate among listeners or what delayed positive reactions to it there might be.

Difficult Audiences in Organizational Settings: A Case Study.

Difficult audiences occur in more than one form. The co-active approach outlined above is useful for approaching sensitive issues of public policy. In organizational settings, the challenge may be to convince reluctant audiences to undertake difficult, demanding initiatives.

Recently, the largest construction company in Arkansas, Nabholz Construction, enjoyed spectacular success in establishing a Wellness Program to counter the widespread and deeply rooted problems of obesity, smoking, and excessive drinking among its employees. As outlined in an HBO documentary, the Nabholz program has redeemed many lives and, in the process, saved the company more than $600,000 annually in runaway health care costs. It has become a national model of excellence as the country confronts an obesity epidemic that imperils millions of lives and costs American business about $70 billion every year in excessive health care costs, lost workdays, and reduced productivity.[14]

The Nabholz initiative began when the company had to confront the tidal wave of rising costs. Then an incident occurred that brought the problem home in a very personal way. Chris Goldsby, vice president of operations, describes the event and its effect upon him. Speaking of construction people, he says: "We don't go to the doctor. That's not tough. And we don't take meds. But we care about each other."[15] Then an employee died of cancer—he just didn't go to the doctor. Might he have been saved if he had gone earlier? This weighed on Chris.

An employee of Nabholz Construction demonstrates his dramatic weight loss in the company's "wellness" program.

Chris's description of construction people suggests the challenge the company had to confront. Jayme Mayo, the dynamic person chosen to lead the program, elaborates this problem and how the company went about meeting it:

We had to go beyond the dry, abstract statistics. We had to meet and test the men individually, and help them understand what this all meant to them personally. At first, many of them resisted what we were trying to do. Some were in denial, others were suspicious or even resentful about the company's intrusion (so they thought) into their private lives. But many of them were at high risk from diseases like diabetes and hypertension and from life-threatening events like heart attacks and strokes. Many of them knew in their hearts that they needed to do something to improve the quality of their lives. We had to show them what was at stake for them and their families if they improved and if they did *not* improve. We had to scare them a little, and then we had to reassure them. As we put it, sometimes we had to hug them, and sometimes kick them in the butt. But they also needed to know they were not alone. The company "had a dog in this fight" and was ready to help them. If they would just work with us, they could and would succeed![16]

Slowly, grudgingly, the employees began to respond, and some of them began to enjoy spectacular success. This is one such person's story:

Wayne is 32 years old, a millwright with Nabholz Construction for eleven years. Several years ago his father died from a massive stroke and a few months later, a close friend died from a heart attack. His mother is 5' 4" and weighs 325 pounds. Wayne started drinking a lot and gaining weight, up to 245 pounds (he is 6' 1"). He was "comfortable in my skin," as he put it, but also realized, "I shouldn't be this tired" all the time. Also, he had two young children, and he started to worry about whether he would be around to see them grow up.

He knew Jayme Mayo from some time back and liked her, but he did have initial doubts as to whether he could lose the weight. Jayme urged him to give the wellness program a try, and designed a simple program for him to reduce calories and work out. "I'll give you six weeks," he told her. "And if it doesn't work, I'm going to quit."

After three weeks, he started to feel better, and after 6 weeks, he had lost 10 pounds. As he put it, "the weight started to roll off." After 10 months, he had lost 60 pounds, down to 185. Now, two years later, he has kept his weight off. He spends four exercise periods each week in the gym. He has so much more energy and zest for life.

The hardest thing, he said, was "giving up Dr. Peppers." The best thing, he says, came when he changed waist sizes, "when I bought those 34's" (waist size of his trousers). His greatest satisfaction is how he has become an example to his family. His sister is now going to the gym, and his brother seems ready to go. His children have become calorie conscious. Recently his son was thinking of buying a candy bar, and asked him, "Dad, how many calories are in this?[17]

There is a great deal to be learned about persuasion from the Nabholz experience. It is clear that when confronted by reluctant audiences, such as their own employees, companies must establish a larger context in which persuasive messages, both oral and written, can have a chance at success. This context includes the following:

- **Committed company leadership.** When Bill Hannah, the widely respected CEO of Nabholz Construction, endorsed the Wellness Program of his company, employees knew that the company meant business. As he and other company executives wrote in newsletters and appeared in person to support project initiatives, they extended the power and *authority* of their offices to the project. In the case of Chris Goldsby, this commitment extended to his own personal example:

    Early in the program he decided to take the health tests it offered: "I had to do something. I had to walk-the-walk as well as talk-the-talk. I couldn't be a leader and skip it." The results, he said, opened his eyes. "I went on a mission. Over the next three years, I went from 292 pounds to 211. I stopped using tobacco and I fell in love with bicycling." That became a huge social thing for him, connecting him with others in the community, especially the health community. They participated in the "Hotter than Hell 100" and the "Ride Across Oklahoma," raising money for hospitals and creating other wellness events.

- **Dedicated Program Management.** Talk to persons successful in the program, and you encounter a litany of praise for the program director. One employee described himself as initially skeptical: "We wuz just a bunch of beer-drinkin' rednecks sittin' around eatin' fried foods and developing heart trouble, high blood pressure, and diabetes." He himself was badly overweight and was diagnosed with diabetes. But he has now lost 50 pounds, and his blood pressure and blood sugar are down. "Jayme," he says, "was with me every step of the way. She's so easy to talk to. Had it not been for the program and her help, I would be a dead man."[18] Another worker, who had lost 60 pounds in the program and was working out daily, commented: "Wasn't for Jayme I wouldn't have done it." At one point in our interviews with her, Jayme confessed that "trust" was the most important ingredient in her interactions with workers. "I make home and gym visits if necessary to meet the needs of my people," she said.

- **Authentic Examples.** Whenever employees went to work at Nabholz, they might meet coworkers like Wayne, who had gone from a size 46 waist to a size 34 waist and gained a great new zest for life; or Michael, who had lost 60 pounds, worked out every day, and "felt a whole lot better"; or Carl, who was just happy to be alive. These are **authentic examples**, always available to persuaders, of the program's effectiveness. They also are a constant challenge: If they can achieve such great results, why can't others? It is hard to overestimate the importance of such authentic examples.

- **Aggressive Program of Incentives.** Incentives ranging from extra vacation days to monetary awards at successful intervals encouraged employees to begin and continue in the program. These were described by some workers as "nice but not decisive." Nevertheless, employees could earn up to $500 for tobacco cessation and $1,000 for weight loss. These "super incentives" were part of the positive context of persuasion we are describing.

▶ **authentic examples** Persons or events close to the lives of audience members. They have great persuasive power, because personal experience confirms they are genuine and true.

■ **Recognition, Rewards, and Support Services.** In case there is any doubt of company commitment, Nabholz provides an onsite medical clinic and small workout rooms for employees and their spouses twenty-four hours a day. There are blood pressure machines in every office and on most large jobsites. Also conspicuous at those sites is the constant presence of the program director. The message is clear: These folks mean business!

At the beginning of Chapter 16, we describe an important holiday event at Nabholz. Each Christmas at its Oklahoma City office, employees and their families gather to celebrate successes in the Wellness Program. Little statues of bulldogs, called "Wellies," are presented to those who have achieved outstanding results. These are the heroes and heroines of Nabholz, whose handprints are added to a "hall of fame."

Clearly, the persuasive messages relating to the Wellness Program, whether in the form of speeches, newsletters, or one-on-one interactions, have occurred within a context that has enabled and promoted their effectiveness. Nabholz has achieved outstanding results in selling its Wellness Program to its own reluctant audience.

Removing Barriers to Commitment

Watch at **MyCommunicationLab** **Video:** "Secondhand Smoke"

If you sense that your audience is largely uncommitted, you have to ask yourself these questions: Are my listeners undecided because they need more information? Do they not yet see the connection between the issue and their own interests? Are they not certain that they can trust my judgment?

Provide Needed Information. Often, a missing fact or unanswered question stands in the way of commitment. "I know that many of you agree with me but are asking, 'How much will this cost?'" Supplying the necessary information can help move listeners toward your position.

Apply Audience Values. You must show listeners that your proposal agrees with principles they already accept. For example, if your listeners resist an educational program for the financially disadvantaged because they think that people ought to take care of themselves, you may have to show them that your program represents "a hand up, not a handout." Show them that your proposal will lead to other favorable outcomes, such as reductions in welfare and unemployment.

As we noted earlier, values are resistant to change. If you can reason from the perspective of your listeners' values, using them as the basis for your arguments, you will encourage their commitment to your position.

Strengthen Your Credibility. When audiences hesitate because they question your credibility, you can "borrow ethos" by citing expert testimony. Call on sources that your listeners trust and respect. Uncommitted audiences will scrutinize both you and your arguments carefully. Reason with such listeners, leading them gradually and carefully to the conclusion you would like them to reach and providing supporting material each step of the way. Adopt a multisided approach, in which you consider all options fairly, to confirm your ethos as a trustworthy and competent speaker.

When addressing uncommitted listeners, don't overstate your case. Let your personal commitment be evident through your sincerity and conviction, but be careful about using overly strong appeals to guilt or fear. Such appeals might cause cautious listeners to resist, resent, and reject both you and your message.[19] Don't push uncommitted listeners too hard. Help them move in the desired direction, but let them take the final step themselves.

Moving from Attitude to Action

Just as opponents may be reluctant to listen, sympathetic audiences may be reluctant to act. It is one thing to agree with a speaker and quite another to accept the inconvenience and risk that action may require. Listeners may believe that the problem does not affect them personally. They may not know what they should do or how they should do it.[20]

Persuasive speeches often must arouse strong feelings to move people to action.

To move people to action, you must give them reasons to act. You may have to arouse their enthusiasm, remind them of their beliefs, demonstrate the need for their involvement, present a clear plan of action, and make it easy for them to comply.

 Watch at **MyCommunicationLab** **Video:** "Starbucks"

Spark Their Enthusiasm. To move people to action, you may have to arouse feelings. Announce your own commitment, and ask listeners to join you. Once people have voiced their commitment, they are more likely to follow through on it. In her speech inviting listeners to become Special Olympics volunteers, Beth Tidmore anticipated that her listeners already agreed with her—*in principle*. But she had not yet won their hearts. Beth decided that the best way to arouse enthusiasm would be to help listeners imagine themselves enacting her proposal. Here is the way she approached this challenge:

> I've had so many great experiences, but these are hard to describe without overworking words like "fulfilling" and "rewarding." So I'm going to let you experience it for yourself. I want everybody to pack your bags—we're going to the Special Olympics summer games in Georgia! . . .
>
> Some of the athletes will be a little bit scared—it will be their first time away from home. All you've got to do is smile and reassure them that they'll have a great time—and you know they will. . . .
>
> Now we'll go to opening ceremonies. You walk onto a big field, and there's a huge tent, and they're playing loud music. All of the kids start dancing—they've never had such a moment! After that, each county marches by with a banner, and when your county comes by, you'd better be up and cheering.
>
> And then you hear something in the distance: a siren. Police cars and fire engines . . . and it's getting louder and louder. Soon it comes into the courtyard, and you catch your first glimpse of the Olympic torch runner. And as the runner gets closer, the Special Olympics theme blares louder on the speakers, and the sirens are just absolutely piercing. They make a final hand-off, and one chosen athlete will light the cauldron. And the flame goes up in this huge whoosh. It's just incredible. All of the athletes cheer, and they're so proud to be part of this moment. . . . Then the athletes get very serious, because they know it's time to take the Special Olympics oath. . . .

After the games are over, you get to see them all on the podium, because everyone gets a medal or a ribbon, everyone places. And it's great, because they're smiling and they're so proud, and there are flashbulbs going off, and the anthem is playing. And they turn and they congratulate their fellow competitors. . . .

Sunday is a sad time, because you have to send them back home to their parents. But when they run off the buses to show their parents their medals, and their parents walk up to you, their simplest "thank you" is a great reward. And in the end your vocal chords are shot, you have a second degree sunburn on most of your body. Your feet hurt, your back aches, and you feel like you could sleep for a week. But you just can't stop smiling, because you know that you've just taken part in something very special.

When Beth distributed commitment cards to her listeners at the end of her speech, it was clear that she had moved her listeners to action.

Revitalize Shared Beliefs and Values. When speakers and audiences celebrate shared beliefs and values, the result is often a renewed sense of commitment. Such occasions may involve telling stories that resurrect heroes and heroines, giving shared beliefs new meaning. At political conventions, Jefferson, Lincoln, Roosevelt, Kennedy, and Reagan are often invoked in speeches. These symbolic heroes can help bridge audience diversity by bringing different factions together. Recently, Lincoln has even been invoked by motivational speakers for business executives at Starbucks and Estee Lauder, to demonstrate leadership in times of crisis. The executives "take comfort in knowing that even Mr. Lincoln doubted himself sometimes."[21]

In her speech, Beth Tidmore relied on and revitalized the values of benevolence, generosity, and magnanimity—those large-hearted virtues that come into play when we reach out to those who do not share all of our blessings.

Demonstrate the Need for Involvement. Show your listeners how the quality of their lives depends on action, and demonstrate that the results will be satisfying. It often helps if you can associate the change with a vision of the future. In his final speech, Martin Luther King, Jr., offered a vision of the Promised Land to help justify the sacrifice called for in his plan of action.

Present a Clear Plan of Action. Listeners may exaggerate the difficulty of enacting a proposal or insist that it is impossible. To overcome such resistance, the plan of action you present should be clear, simple, and well adapted to the problem at hand. Developing such a plan was a key to the success of the Nabholz Wellness Program discussed previously: The program was carefully crafted to meet the problems confronted by employees, was adapted to the individual needs of each employee, was carefully monitored, and was adjusted to changing circumstances. Similarly, construction company Skanska AB's U.S. arm hired two former fighter pilots to discuss at its annual management meeting, "the steps needed to successfully execute a mission, including how to define a project, analyze progress, celebrate success, and debrief at the end."[22]

As you present a plan to your audience, stress that, "we can do it, and this is how we can do it." Develop examples or narratives that show listeners completing the project successfully.

SPEAKER'S notes   Moving People to Action

To move listeners to action, follow these guidelines:

1. Remind listeners of what is at stake.
2. Provide a clear plan of action.
3. Use examples and stories as models for action.
4. Visualize the consequences of acting and not acting.

5. Demonstrate that you practice what you preach.
6. Ask for public commitments.
7. Make it easy for listeners to take the first step.

Be Specific in Your Instructions, and Make It Easy to Comply. Your plan must show listeners what to do and how to do it. Instead of simply urging listeners to write their congressional representatives, provide them with addresses and telephone numbers, a petition to sign, or preprinted and addressed postcards to complete and return. Beth Tidmore passed out information and cards at the end of her speech to help listeners confirm their commitment.

Figure 14.4 offers an overview of these various challenges to persuasion offered by different types of audiences and how to cope with them.

The Challenge of Ethical Persuasion

Ours is a skeptical and cynical age, made more so by large-scale abuses of communication ethics. Advertisers assure us that their products will make us sexier or richer, often with no foundation in fact. Persuasive messages disguised as information

Audience Type	Strategies
Reluctant to listen, possibly hostile	Seek common ground and establish goodwill. Quote sources they respect. Emphasize explanation over argument. Limit your goals: Try for a fair hearing, and ask little from listeners. Try to weaken their resistance. Acknowledge opposing arguments, but show tactfully why you have a different commitment.
Uncommitted, even uninterested	Provide information needed to arouse their interest and encourage their commitment. Connect their values with your position. Become a model of commitment for them to follow.
Friendly, but not yet committed	Remind them of what is at stake. Show them why action is necessary now. Give them clear instructions, and help them take the first step. Picture them undertaking this action successfully.

FIGURE 14.4
Audience Considerations for Persuasive Speaking

appear in "infomercials" on television. They try to slip into our minds under the radar of critical listening. So-called think tanks try to bribe experts into supporting their points of view, thereby contaminating a major source of responsible knowledge.[23] Public officials may present suspicious statistics, make dubious denials, or dance around questions they really don't want to answer. Little wonder that many people have lost trust in society's major sources of communication.

As a consumer of persuasive messages, you can at least partially protect yourself by applying the critical thinking skills we discussed in Chapter 4. As a producer of persuasive messages, you can help counter this trend toward unethical communication. Keep three simple questions in mind as you prepare your persuasive speech:[24]

- What is my ethical responsibility to my audience?

- Could I publicly defend the ethics of my message?

- What does this message say about my character?

As we noted in Chapter 1, an ethical speech is based fundamentally on respect for the audience, responsible knowledge of the topic, and concern for the consequences of your words.

Designs for Persuasive Speeches

As we noted in Chapter 9, evidence, proof, and patterns of reasoning are not effective until they are arranged in a strategic design for your speech.

Many of the designs used for informative speeches are also appropriate for persuasive speeches. Josh Logan used a categorical design when he proposed three categories of technological improvements in his plan to counter global warming. In addition, the sequential design can outline the steps in a plan of action to make it seem practical. The comparative design works well for speeches that concentrate on developing proposals for action. Following this pattern, you might compare the superior features of your proposal with the less adequate features of competing proposals.

YOUR *ethical* VOICE   Guidelines for Ethical Persuasion

To earn a reputation as an ethical persuader, follow these guidelines:

1. Avoid name-calling: Attack problems, proposals, and ideas—not people.

2. Be open about your personal interest in the topic.

3. Don't adapt to the point of compromising your convictions.

4. Argue from responsible knowledge.

5. Don't try to pass off opinions as facts.

6. Don't use inflammatory language to hide a lack of evidence.

7. Be sure your proposal is in the best interest of your audience.

8. Remember, words can hurt.

Three designs, however, are especially suited to persuasive speeches. We will deal with two of them here, the problem–solution design and the motivated sequence design. The third, refutative design, we shall discuss in the next chapter as we discuss persuasion in controversy.

Problem–Solution Design

The **problem–solution design** first convinces listeners that there is a problem and then shows them how to deal with it. The solution can involve changing attitudes, beliefs, and values, or taking action.

It is sometimes hard to convince listeners that a problem exists or that it is serious. People have an unfortunate tendency to ignore problems until they reach a critical stage. You can counteract this tendency by vividly depicting the crisis that will surely occur unless your audience makes a change.

As you focus on the problem, use substantive evidence and combinations of proof to demonstrate that a serious problem exists. Reason from the reality of the situation by using presentation aids, dramatic examples, and colorful imagery to make the problem loom large in the minds of listeners. Reasoning from principle can help justify a solution ("Because better health care means a better future for our children, we must pass health care reform."). Analogical reasoning can help convince listeners that a proposed solution will work ("Here's how Massachusetts addressed this problem. . . ."). We shall say more about persuasive uses of these patterns of reasoning in the next chapter.

When a problem is complex, you must examine its causes. Doing so enables you to argue that your solution will work because it deals with the underlying causes.

A problem–solution speech opposing a tuition increase at your university might build on the following general design:

Thesis statement: We must defeat the proposed tuition increase.

I. Problem: The proposal to raise tuition is a bad idea!

    A. The increase will create hardships for many students.

        1. Many current students will have to drop out.

        2. New students will be discouraged from enrolling.

    B. The increase will create additional problems for the university and the community.

        1. Decreased attendance will mean decreased revenue.

        2. Decreased revenue will reduce the university's community services.

        3. Reduced services will mean reduced support from contributors.

        4. The ironic result will be another tuition increase!

II. Solution: Defeat the proposal to raise tuition.

    A. Sign our petition against the tuition increase.

    B. Write letters to your state legislators.

    C. Write a letter to our local newspaper.

    D. Attend our campus rally next Wednesday, and bring your marching shoes!

Watch at **MyCommunicationLab Video:** "Mass Transit"

Explore at **MyCommunicationLab Activity:** "Annotated Outline: Untreated Depression"

▶ **problem–solution design** A persuasive speech pattern in which listeners are first persuaded that they have a problem and then are shown how to solve it.

When the problem can be identified clearly and the solution is concrete and simple, the problem–solution design works well in persuasive speeches.

As you are planning your problem–solution speech, be sure to take into account **stock issues**, those generic questions that a thoughtful person will ask before agreeing to a change in policies or procedures. Be certain that your speech can answer these questions to the satisfaction of such critical listeners. Stock issues are explored in Figure 14.5.

Motivated Sequence Design

Watch at **MyCommunicationLab**
Video: "Mandatory Minimums (Monroe Version)"

The **motivated sequence design** offers a practical, step-by-step approach when speakers wish to move from the awareness through the enactment phases of the persuasive process in a single speech.[25] The design offers five steps to persuasive success:

1. *Arouse attention.* As in any speech, you begin by stimulating interest in your subject. Vivid stories or examples, surprising claims, striking facts and statistics, eloquent statements from admired leaders—all can arouse the interest of your listeners.

2. *Demonstrate a need.* Show your listeners that the situation you want to change is urgent. Arrange evidence so that it builds in intensity and taps into audience motivations to help listeners see what they have to win and lose with regard to your proposal. By the end of this demonstration, listeners should be eager to hear your ideas for change.

3. *Satisfy the need.* Present a way to satisfy the need you have demonstrated. Set out a clear plan of action, and explain how it will work. Show how this plan agrees with audience principles and values. Offer examples that show how your plan has already worked successfully in other situations.

FIGURE 14.5
Stock Issues in Persuasion

The stock issues in persuasion center around the following questions:

I. Is there a significant problem?
   A. How did the problem originate?
   B. What caused the problem?
   C. How widespread is the problem?
   D. How long has the problem persisted?
   E. What harms are associated with the problem?
   F. Will these harms continue and grow unless there is change?

II. What is the solution to this problem?
   A. Will the solution actually solve the problem?
   B. Is the solution practical?
   C. Would the cost of the solution be reasonable?
   D. Might there be other consequences to the solution?

III. Who will put the solution into effect?
   A. Are these people responsible and competent?
   B. What role might listeners play?[26]

▶ **stock issues**   The major general questions a reasonable person would ask before agreeing to a change in policies or procedures.

▶ **motivated sequence design**   A persuasive speech design that proceeds by arousing attention, demonstrating a need, satisfying the need, visualizing results, and calling for action.

4. *Visualize the results.* Paint verbal pictures that illustrate the positive results listeners can expect. Show them how their lives will be better when they have enacted your plan. A dramatic picture of the future can help overcome resistance to action. You could also paint a picture of what life will be like if listeners *don't* enact your suggestions. Place these positive and negative verbal pictures side by side to strengthen their impact through contrast.

5. *Call for action.* Your call for action may be a challenge, an appeal, or a statement of personal commitment. The call for action should be short and to the point. Give your listeners something specific that they can do right away. If you can get them to take the first step, the next will come more easily.

Simone Mullinax used a motivated sequence design to convince her University of Arkansas listeners to become mentors:

Big Brothers is an effective mentoring program staffed by volunteers.

1. *Arouse attention*	Let me share with you a simple statistic: 20 percent of our nation's children—that's one in every five kids—is now "at risk." What does that mean? It means they have no one to trust, no one to turn to. It means expectations for them are low—our expectations, and more importantly, theirs for themselves.
2. *Demonstrate a need*	These are the so-called problem kids—the ones who drop out of school, and drop into lives that are unproductive, unsuccessful, and often mired in crime. These are wasted lives, wasted humanity, and we all have to pay for their failures.
3. *Satisfy the need*	So what is the answer? I'll tell you about one I know that works because I've tried it. It's called "mentoring," a person-to-person program to become that friend someone doesn't have, that person who cares. It may involve only an hour or two a week, but the mentor is a troubled child's connection to a more healthy and hopeful world.
4. *Visualize the results*	Put yourself in this picture. (She tells the story of her mentoring relationship with one child.) Mentoring helps us reclaim our children, one child at a time. I'll tell you someone else who has benefited—me!
5. *Call for action*	Best part about mentoring is that it's so easy: Can you send an e-mail? Can you make a phone call? Can you talk to your younger sibling's friends? Can you take a child to a ball game or to the movies? Then you have the qualifications to be a mentor! Here's how you can get started (she names an organization, address, and phone number and hands out material). I urge you,

FIGURE 14.6
Selecting Persuasive Speech Designs

Design	Use When
Categorical	• Your topic invites thinking in familiar patterns, such as proving a plan will be safe, inexpensive, and effective. Can be used to change attitudes or to urge action.
Comparative/ Contrast	• You want to demonstrate why your proposal is superior to another. Especially good for speeches in which you contend with opposing views.
Sequential	• Your speech contains a plan of action that must be carried out in specific order.
Problem–Solution	• Your topic presents a problem that needs to be solved and a solution that will solve it. Good for speeches involving attitudes and urging action.
Motivated Sequence	• Your topic calls for action as the final phase of a five-step process that involves, in order, arousing attention, demonstrating need, satisfying need, visualizing the results, and calling for action.
Refutative	• You must answer strong opposition on a topic before you can establish your position. The opposing claims become main points for development. Attack weakest points first, and avoid personal attacks.

join me in this program. The good things we do in our lives radiate out from us and become magnified. The little fires we light can come together to warm the world!

The motivated sequence design has helped generations of persuasive speakers achieve success.

Figure 14.6 summarizes how to select a design for a persuasive speech.

FINAL
reflections   The Case for Persuasion

Some people seem reluctant to persuade others. It's not right, they argue, for me to impose my views on someone else. How can I justify asking them to change because *I think* I know a better way? The argument is interesting—but shaky. If my friends are ignorant of knowledge I possess and that ignorance could cost them dearly, how can I justify *not* persuading them to consider and possibly apply what I have learned?

Recall the words of Isocrates that began this chapter. For Isocrates, the impulse to persuade was vital to the emerging nature of humanity, making possible what we now call *cultural evolution*. Persuasion, he felt, lifts us above the "wild beasts" in that it allows us to inspire others and resolve our disputes by words rather than by fists. Persuasion encourages cooperation and consent to come together and live in communities governed by laws rather than by brute force. Persuasion promotes commercial enterprises, social arrangements, and the advancement of knowledge. For Isocrates, persuasion was the key to civilization.

With the help of this chapter, we can now make an even more specific case for persuasion. Ethical persuasion helps us decide conflicts over facts, encourages more humane attitudes, helps correct flawed beliefs, and makes us take our values more seriously. Improving as persuaders requires that we develop a practical understanding of listeners' needs that allows us to soften opposition, convert doubters, and energize partisans. We become, as Isocrates would say, more effective human beings.

A final justification for persuasion is that we persuade because we have an ethical duty and imperative to speak. In finding our voice, we find causes to support and meaning for our lives. Not to speak, not to persuade, would deny our reasons for being.

After Reading This Chapter, You Should Be Able To Answer These Questions

Study and **Review** at **MyCommunicationLab**

1 How does persuasive speaking differ from informative speaking?

2 What are the three major types of persuasive speaking?

3 What are the five phases of the persuasive process?

4 What strategies might you use to speak constructively to listeners who are initially opposed to your position?

5 How would you persuade listeners who are neutral on an issue to accept your arguments?

6 How would you convince listeners who say they agree with you to take action?

7 What ethical guidelines should persuaders follow?

8 What design options are especially appropriate for persuasive speaking?

For Discussion and Further Exploration

1 Keep a log for one day, and record all moments when you persuade or are persuaded. Prepare a report to the class in which you analyze these moments. Consider the following questions:
   a. What kinds of messages do the work of persuasion?
   b. How effective was the persuasion?
   c. What kinds of appeals work best for you?
   d. When are you most resistant to persuasion?
   e. How important is persuasion in your life?

2 Attend a local government meeting (city or county council, zoning board, etc.), and analyze the persuasive speeches you hear. Do the speakers argue over past, present, or future facts? Do their speeches concern attitudes, beliefs,

and values? Do they propose actions? How effective are they, and why? Report to your class.

3 Watch the video of a persuasive speech on TED or YouTube. Identify the stages of the persuasive process activated during the speech. How effective was the speaker in moving the process along and making persuasion work? Might he or she have done a better job? Explain to the class.

4 Look for examples in the social media of persuasion you think may be unethical. Apply the guidelines offered in "Your Ethical Voice: Guidelines for Ethical Persuasion" (p. 328) to critique these materials. Report your findings in class.

5 Tape a sampling of television commercials, and show them in class. Identify the persuasive designs used in the commercials. What other design options might have been used?

6 Identify a controversial topic on which you have strong feelings. Find and read at least two articles that oppose your position. Which of the ideas in these articles might you incorporate in a multisided presentation? How would you present these ideas? (For example, would you minimize them? Refute them?) Explain your strategy.

7 Watch a sampling of speeches offered at a political convention. What heroes and heroines are celebrated? Why do the speakers invoke these icons, and what is the impact on persuasion? Discuss your thoughts in class.

SAMPLE PERSUASIVE SPEECH

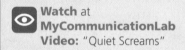
Watch at
MyCommunicationLab
Video: "Quiet Screams"

Lindsey Yoder was a junior at the University of Memphis when she gave the following speech to her public speaking class. The speech, selected for the Osborn Public Speaking contest, won first prize in that competition. Soon word of its quality reached community organizers active in the campaign against human trafficking. Lindsey was invited to speak at a rally sponsored by the local police department and area churches, right in the heart of territory notorious for such activities. A rough videotape of her speech, pieced together from field cameras on the scene, can be viewed in MyCommunicationLab. What had started as a simple class assignment had become magnified beyond the moment: in terms used in her speech, the words that started as ripples had now become waves.

Lindsey's speech begins ▶
by framing an analogy
between the slavery suf-
fered by African Americans
before the Civil War and
modern-day sex slavery
as endured by victims of
human trafficking. Her
appeal is to deep values
of listeners; consequently,
the speech can be viewed
as an appeal to attitudes
and values.

Quiet Screams

LINDSEY YODER

Imagine yourself living during the time of slavery when African Americans were tortured, beaten, and lynched. Surely we all would be a part of the abolitionist movement that fought for their freedom. We would not leave human injustice in the dark.

Today, we are taught in our history classes that slavery ended with the Civil War. However, the quiet screams of present day slaves are all around us. According to enditmovement.com, there is more slavery in the world today than ever before. What we just imagined is not a hypothetical situation: it is our reality!

In January of this year, I attended an annual Christian conference in Atlanta called Passion. I walked into the Georgia Dome expecting to hear some of my favorite speakers and performers. I had no idea that I would soon become part of something much bigger than myself. Louie Giglio, the leader of the Passion movement, informed us—66,000 of us—about modern slavery.

There are, he said, 27 million slaves in the world today. In America alone, there are approximately 200,000, and every year 17,500 more will be sold in sex trafficking. I want you to imagine now being forced to work for someone day in and day out, only to get in return verbal, physical, and sexual abuse. No family to turn to, no friends, no one even knows you are there. Nothing belongs to you. You belong to someone else. Hundreds of thousands are trapped in this scenario.

You may not care about modern slavery, but what if it were your mom? Brother? Best friend? What if it were you? If your heart does not hurt yet for these modern slaves, I hope it will by the end of my presentation.

Modern slavery is not sexy or appealing. There are no beautiful pictures to show, no humor to enjoy. Many want to avoid this issue because it doesn't make us feel good. It would be much easier to ignore it. But we can avoid this no longer. I am going to tell you how victims get caught up in modern slavery, why it is such a huge market in the U.S., and where exactly this is going on.

I would like you to meet a dear friend of mine, I will call her Kelley. When she was a child, her father began abusing her mentally and physically. By the time she was twelve, he was molesting her. He would tell her she was nothing and would never amount to anything. By the age of twenty, she was a modern slave. During that dark time, no one heard her quiet screams.

I shared Kelley's testimony so that you would understand how people just like you and me are caught up in slavery each day. People who feel unnoticed, alone, and abused. They search for acceptance, and the twenty-first-century slave traders find them. They seek them out like predators on prey. They are looking for these lost and unhappy souls that are everywhere. They find, persuade, and trick victims into believing they can provide a glamorous lifestyle. These slave traders *are* appealing and sexy. They reel the unsuspecting lost souls in by promising happiness, money, and companionship. Soon, we have yet another slave in today's world.

On *womensfundingnetwork.org,* you can find information on the Polaris Project, a nonprofit anti-trafficking organization. The Project described a man in Washington, D.C., who "owned" three slaves. Every day they would bring home to him $500 to $2,000, approximately $24,000 every month, *all cash— tax free!* On *harrahpolicedept.com,* the FBI estimates human trafficking annually generates $9.5 billion worldwide. The demand is high because the resale value is high. You can only sell drugs once, but humans, you can sell over and over.

Furthermore, modern slavery is going on all over the world. It was easy for me to avoid getting involved until Kelley told me her story, and I suddenly realized it is all around me. She is part of an organization, Ashes to Beauty, that works here in Memphis. Yes, right here in Memphis! She is saving girls from exactly what she went through. Television website *abc24.com* recently highlighted the local hot spots for sex trafficking: Sam Cooper Boulevard, Memphis International Airport, and Wolfchase Mall Galleria. These are the top three areas where people are being picked up, transported, and sold. *Wmctv.com* says

◄ Lindsey assumed that her audience was initially uncommitted on her topic; that listeners were indifferent because they lacked information and had not yet connected her cause to their feelings and beliefs. Here she offers vital information on the magnitude of the problem, and appeals to listeners' imaginations to picture themselves as victims. In short, her major supporting materials were statistics and narratives to heighten the importance and emotional impact of her topic.

◄ Having raised awareness of the problem, Lindsey extends the persuasive process by increasing audience understanding of how it comes about: how people can become sex slaves and what the motivations are that drive modern slave traders. Her story of her friend is especially compelling.

It is one thing to know that ▶ a serious problem exists, quite another to know that it exists in your neighborhood. That awareness is often the motivation for listeners to act. As she moves to her conclusion, Lindsey asks for audience involvement. But her program for action seems a bit scattered and vague. She needs to tell listeners in clearer terms what they can do: What action, for example, should they urge the university to take? How exactly could listeners join and participate in the "End It Movement"?

Lindsey concludes her ▶ speech with an eloquent quotation that develops the enduring metaphor of light and darkness introduced in her opening. She makes effective use of parallel construction to end the speech with a powerful and graceful plea.

that in the last quarter of 2010 over 1,900 ads were posted on *backpage.com* listing women for sale *right here in Memphis.*

Modern slavery exists without the majority of us even being aware of it. But some of us are fighting to free these slaves. This year at Passion our youth group raised over $3 million to support seven organizations fighting the fight in different ways. You can learn more about these organizations on the Enditmovement website. In addition, the Clinton Global Initiative is now interceding for today's slaves, and President Obama has signed an executive order to strengthen our hand against trafficking.

Still, the battle to end human trafficking is hard and uphill. These organizations can't do it without our help. As the Osborn textbook says, "words make ripples, and ripples can come together to make waves." My words alone will not have much effect, but when we all speak together, the impact can be great. Think of what we, as a university, could do to help end modern slavery. We can keep these organizations going by supporting them as much as we can, but we can also take an active part. Join the "End It Movement." Draw a red X on your hand symbolizing your stand on modern slavery. On Instagram, Twitter, and Facebook, use the hashtag *enditmovement.* The more people who become aware of this injustice, the sooner modern slavery will come to an end.

I wish I could end slavery today, but I cannot. Not alone. Change begins with one person, but it cannot stop there. Norman B. Rice, mayor of Seattle, once said, "Dare to reach out your hand into the darkness, to pull another hand into the light." The quiet screams of our people call to us desperately. Let us be the generation to hear them. Let us be the generation to change the world. Let us be the generation to end modern slavery.

15 Persuasion in Controversy

Listen to
Chapter 15 at
MyCommunicationLab

> *We can't solve problems by using the same kind of thinking that created them.*
>
> —ALBERT EINSTEIN

You leave your afternoon class and go back to your dorm to rest before the Student Council meeting. You go online to check Facebook and a YouTube video a friend has recommended, and ads pop up on the screen, including a car ad you have to view or skip before you can watch the video. You then turn on the television to watch a little baseball, and between innings you watch ads that warn you of the social disgrace of bad breath and body odor and that offer products that will prevent such debacles. As you watch, your mind on "idle," you remember that this is the day of the big debate. Council is going to vote on a hot issue: whether to endorse the administration's call for a tuition increase for the fall term. Student speakers on different sides of this question will build cases to support their positions. You are on the Council, and as you leave for the meeting you anticipate a lively exchange of ideas.

Explore at **MyCommunicationLab** **Activity:** "Persuasion"

Chapter 14 placed persuasive speaking under a microscope. We explored the nature of persuasion, its processes, how different audiences can affect it, and the forms it can take. In this chapter, we take a wider view of persuasion—to see how it works in the social setting, the public sphere of controversial issues and contending interests and conflicting points of view.

The emotional reactions created by these conflicts places a great deal of pressure on persuasion: Much is at stake. Should we extend our military presence in the Middle East? Should laws prohibiting the use of marijuana be changed? Should gun control laws be extended? After the next election, which political party will have the upper hand? We live in a contentious age.

Persuaders can react to these pressures in several ways. One is to surrender to an impulse that may originate in the advertising practices of corporate America. There is, of course, nothing that is inherently wrong with such advertising and much that can be said on its behalf. Often, the ads are the best things about the programs in which they occur; some people, for example, who could care less about the game, tune in the Super Bowl each year to enjoy the carnival of ads and the competition among them. In many cases, these ads are colorful, funny minidramas that stimulate consumer behavior in positive ways. They can help the economy hum.

But there can be a dark side to these ads. They often short-circuit or avoid the critical thinking process. They catch us when our guard is down, when we, as in the opening anecdote, are in "idle" mode. They encourage a cynical attitude toward their audience, which becomes simply a target for manipulation. We call this kind of behavior **manipulative persuasion**.

Manipulative persuasion creates a fantasy world of images, music, and celebrity spokespersons to influence our buying behaviors. In his book *The Assault on Reason*,

---

▶ **manipulative persuasion** Persuasion that works through suggestion, colorful images, music, and attractive spokespersons. It avoids evidence and reasoning and the burden of justifying itself.

Al Gore argues that contemporary politics attracts the manipulator and often supplants reasoned discourse:

> Voters are often viewed mainly as targets for easy manipulation by those seeking their "consent" to exercise power. By using focus groups and elaborate polling techniques, those who design these messages are able to derive the only information they're interested in receiving *from* citizens—feedback useful in fine-tuning their efforts at manipulation.[1]

Such persuasion does not include careful consideration of supporting evidence and proofs. *It avoids the ethical burden of justifying itself.*

Fortunately, realizing that we must compete for the agreement and commitment of our listeners can lead us in a more positive, constructive direction. The path to this better option was mapped long ago by communication theorists in ancient Greece. It is the path of reasoned persuasion.

Reasoned Persuasion Versus Manipulative Persuasion

Reasoned persuasion concentrates on building a case that will justify taking some action or adopting some point of view with regard to a public controversy. The case rests upon arguments carefully constructed out of evidence and patterns of reasoning that make good sense when carefully examined. Reasoned persuasion invites rather than avoids careful inspection. It appeals to our judgment rather than to our impulses. It aims for long-range commitments that will endure in the face of counterattacks. It honors civilized deliberation over verbal mudslinging.

Yet reasoned persuasion does not turn us into robotic thinking machines. It addresses us in our full humanity as thinking as well as feeling beings. Reason without feeling can seem cold and heartless, but feeling without reason is shallow and fleeting. It is the *blend* of passion and reason that can help you find your voice.

The rest of this chapter will help you meet the challenge and enjoy the consequences of reasoned persuasion. We show how to develop compelling evidence and proofs, build patterns of effective reasoning, and avoid defects of evidence, proof, and reasoning.

Forming Evidence

Supporting materials are transformed in the heat of controversy into **evidence**, the foundation of reasoned persuasion.

Facts and Figures.   In controversy, facts and figures loom important. They help answer a crucial question: *Which of the contending sides has the better grasp of reality?*[2] Be sure you supply enough facts to answer that question in your favor. Moreover, Americans have always been practical people who have a special respect for numbers. Recent research confirms the ongoing importance of statistical evidence in persuasion.[3]

Examples.   Examples put a human face on situations. They bring it into focus for us. At the beginning of his speech at the end of this chapter, Austin Wright uses an

Explore at **MyCommunicationLab**
Activity: "Build a Speech: Persuasive Speech"

Watch at **MyCommunicationLab**
Video: "Tobacco Ordinance Public Hearing: Cardiologist"

Watch at **MyCommunicationLab**
Video: "S.A.D.D."

▶ **reasoned persuasion**   Persuasion that builds a case to justify its recommendations.

▶ **evidence**   Supporting materials used in persuasive speeches, including facts and figures, examples, narratives, and testimony.

example to reveal the importance of his subject. He illustrates how examples can reinforce facts by making a situation clearer. When listeners ask, "Can you give me an example?" they are seeking this kind of clarification and authentication.

Narratives.   Good stories bring a situation to life, often in amusing and exciting ways. Recent research confirms the importance of narratives in proving points on controversial issues.[4] Companies that are tuned into persuasion in the marketplace have confirmed the importance of narrative:

> In April 2013, 150 staffers from the marketing team at liquor company Beam Inc. met in Los Angeles for a biannual conference. To kick off the three day event, Beam hired The Moth, a group of professional storytellers best known for a weekly public radio broadcast.
>
> "They are the best at teaching people how to tell better stories," says Chief Marketing Officer Kevin George. And with just a few seconds or minutes to convey messages about brands including Jim Beam and Maker's Mark, Beam's stories need to be sharp.
>
> The Moth team broke down the structure of a story, pointing out why certain parts were more compelling than other parts, and then had Beam staffers tell tales to one another.
>
> Mr. George declined to say how much Beam spent on the April event, but says the payoff was obvious. Company representatives met to discuss new product innovation in May, and rather than just discuss the product's function, Mr. George says they asked one another, "What's the story that goes with this product? How do we tell consumers?"[5]

Similarly, you should consider what's the story that goes with your message, the idea you are selling?

One final point: Both effective examples and stories are hard for opponents to refute.[6] We can argue over the meaning of facts and figures, but a good example or story is harder to deny.

Testimony.   Imagine your ideas are being put on trial. How would you defend them? One way would be to summon witnesses. When you use testimony, you are calling on experts to speak in support of your position. Expert testimony is most effective when the audience knows little about the issue or when listeners lack the ability or motivation to analyze the situation independently.[7] Introduce your witnesses carefully, pointing out their qualifications. Witnesses who testify *against* their self-interest are called **reluctant witnesses**. They provide some of the most powerful evidence available in persuasion. Democratic critics of President Obama's policies often have more impact because they appear to be speaking against their own political affiliations and thus appear less partisan or biased.

In persuasive speaking that is both reasoned and ethical, you should rely mainly on expert testimony, especially with controversial issues. Use prestige or lay testimony as secondary sources of evidence. These three types of testimony are discussed in detail in Chapter 8. You can use prestige testimony to stress values you want listeners to embrace. You can use lay testimony to relate an issue to their lives. Keep in mind that when you quote others, you are linking yourself to them. Be careful with whom you associate!

Keep an open mind as you search for evidence. Look for different positions so that you don't just present one perspective without being aware of others.

Watch at **MyCommunicationLab** Video: "Experience Diversity"

▶ **reluctant witnesses** Witnesses who testify against their apparent self-interest.

Gather more evidence than you think you will need so that you have a wide range of material to choose from. Be sure you have facts, figures, or expert testimony for each of your major points. Use multiple sources and types of evidence to strengthen your case.

Developing Proofs

As persuaders representing different interests and agendas struggle to win in the competition of ideas, four questions loom as vital to their success or failure:

- Which speaker can we most trust?

- Which speech best arouses emotions favorable to its cause?

- Which advocated action best fits with our society's values, dreams, and aspirations?

- Which position offers the best grasp and understanding of reality?

In order to answer these questions, persuaders must develop what the ancient writers called **proofs**, which manage the persuasive resources available in each particular situation. Out of these proofs, you will weave your arguments into a case that justifies your position. Much of the rest of this chapter will focus on how you can develop proofs successfully.

Developing Ethos.   What the ancient writers called **ethos** is based on our perception of a speaker's competence, character, goodwill, and dynamism. If listeners believe that you know what you are talking about and that you are trustworthy, they will listen respectfully to what you have to say. Therefore, you should work ethos-building material into the introduction of your speech whenever you can. You should explain, for example, your personal connection with the topic or what special things you have done to

Reasoned persuasion often depends on expert testimony.

YOUR ethical VOICE   Guidelines for the Ethical Use of Evidence

To use evidence ethically follow these guidelines:

1. Provide evidence from credible sources.

2. Identify your sources of evidence.

3. Use evidence that can stand up under critical scrutiny.

4. Be sure evidence has not been tainted by self-interest.

5. Acknowledge disagreements among experts.

6. Do not withhold important evidence.

7. Use expert testimony to establish facts, prestige testimony to enhance credibility, and lay testimony to create identification.

8. Quote or paraphrase testimony accurately.

▶ **proof**   An arrangement of the resources of persuasion so that it satisfies a basic requirement for success and drives thoughtful listeners toward a conclusion.

▶ **ethos**   A form of proof that relies on the audience's perceptions of a speaker's leadership qualities of competence, character, goodwill, and dynamism.

Watch at **MyCommunicationLab** **Video:** "Generating Credibility"

prepare for the speech. In effect, you say, "I have walked the walk. Therefore, I am qualified to talk the talk."

When a speaker explains the personal problems she faced navigating new health care systems, it makes a much bigger impact on listeners than if the problems are simply listed on a PowerPoint slide:

> In our office, workdays have become even more chaotic. With our older patients we used to be able to simply send a bill to a patient's insurer. Now we have much more paperwork to do. We need to determine whether a procedure is covered and who is covering it. Is it Medicare? Medicaid? Their supplemental insurer? Often we need to send forms to each of these insurers. If a claim is not allowed, we may have to petition each insurer for a waiver to perform needed tests or provide needed medication. This puts a drain on both the medical staff and the patients who need treatment.

Your ethos is dynamic: It can change over time and across subjects, depending on your success as you speak.

Ethos also relates to the sources of information you cite. If listeners view these sources as knowledgeable, trustworthy, and having their best interests in mind, they will be receptive to the source's recommendations. That's why it is so important to identify your sources *and point out why they are qualified to speak on the subject.* Be careful to cite sources you know your audience will respect.

Appealing to Emotions.

What the ancients called **pathos** includes appeals to personal feelings such as fear, pity, and anger. People typically react strongly when they feel angry, afraid, excited, guilty, or compassionate toward others. If used ethically in a context of reasoned persuasion, appeals to personal feelings can help change attitudes or move people to action.[8]

Narratives and examples are often the evidence of choice for emotional appeals. For example, Austin Wright aroused feelings of indignation in the speech that concludes this chapter when he described the unfair treatment received by Maher Arar, a Canadian citizen illegally detained by American authorities on suspicion of Al Qaeda connections. Sixty-second commercials that depict the fate of starving children in less developed countries can likewise become a powerful motivator to action.

Many times, emotional appeals are the only way to show the human dimensions of a problem or the need for immediate action. So how can you use proof by pathos ethically and persuasively? Use these appeals to add color and life to reasoned persuasion, not to replace it.

You should use pathos with caution. If an emotional appeal is too obvious, audiences may think you are trying to manipulate them. Appeals to negative emotions such as fear or guilt are especially tricky because they can boomerang, causing listeners to discredit both you and your speech. When you use appeals to feeling, justify them with solid factual evidence. During your presentation, understate rather than overstate the emotional appeal. Don't engage in theatrics.

Appealing to Group Traditions.

In recent years, many rhetorical scholars have suggested an additional type of proof. **Mythos** appeals to the values and feelings of our social identity based on the feelings we develop as members of groups, communities, and nations. These feelings of group pride, loyalty, heritage, and patriotism are

---

often expressed in sayings, symbols, legends, and folktales. They anchor our traditions and values.[9] As communication scholar Martha Solomon Watson has noted, "Rhetoric which incorporates mythical elements taps into rich cultural reservoirs."[10] When Alexandra McArthur argued that ignoring the poverty that afflicts many nations is behavior unworthy of Americans, she was appealing to these feelings of social identity.

Appeals to cultural identity can remind us of our heroes or enemies. Such appeals gain power from political narratives, such as the story of George Washington's harsh winter at Valley Forge. Or they may be embedded in folk sayings, as when speakers remind us that we live in "the land of opportunity."[11] Appeals to mythos also may reflect economic legends, such as the Horatio Alger stories of success through hard work.

Mythos may also draw on religious narratives. Sacred documents, such as the Bible, provide a rich storehouse of parables, used not only in sermons but also in political speeches.[12] For example, references to the Good Samaritan are often used to justify efforts to help those who are in need.

Stories need not be retold in their entirety each time they are invoked. Because they are so familiar, allusions to them may be sufficient. In his speech accepting the Democratic presidential nomination in 1960, John F. Kennedy called on the myth of the American frontier to move Americans to action:

> The New Frontier of which I speak is not a set of promises—it is a set of challenges. It sums up not what I intend to offer the American people, but what I intend to ask of them.[13]

This appeal became a central theme of Kennedy's presidency. He didn't need to refer directly to the legends of Daniel Boone and Davy Crockett or to the tales of the Oregon Trail when he called on citizens to meet the challenges that lay ahead—he was able to conjure up such thoughts with the phrase "the New Frontier."

One unique value of mythos is that it helps listeners see how the speaker's recommendations fit into the belief and value patterns of their group. An appeal that accomplishes this goal gives such proof a special role in the persuasive process we discussed in Chapter 14. It can help integrate new attitudes and action into the group's culture.

Like appeals to personal feeling, appeals to cultural identity can be misused. At best, they heighten our appreciation of who we are *as a people* and promote consistency between cultural values and public policy. However, when misused, these appeals can make it seem that *there is only one legitimate culture*. Some of those who argued for introducing democratic government to Iraq and Afghanistan seemed to base their arguments on the United States' model. They seemed to imply that our system was superior to all others. Appeals to cultural identity can also devalue those who choose *not* to conform to the dominant values or who belong to marginalized groups. Be aware of these possible drawbacks.

A persuasive speech rarely relies on a single kind of proof. Each type of proof brings its own strength to persuasion. In manipulative persuasion, ethos, pathos, and mythos are usually used more frequently than logos. Fast-food and automobile ads rarely treat us as reasoning beings.

Appeals to cultural identity often call on patriotism and remind us of our heroes, as in this iconic image of Washington crossing the Delaware.

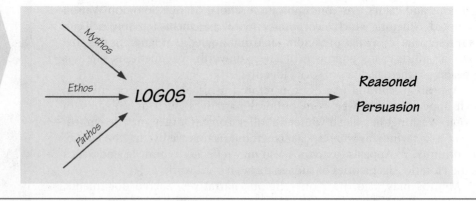

FIGURE 15.1
Proof Priorities in Reasoned Persuasion

Reasoned persuasion relies heavily on what the ancient writers called **logos**, which focuses on one critical question: *Is this a logical speech?* Do the evidence and proofs that the speech develops fit together into patterns of reasoning that thoughtful listeners find acceptable, convincing, and compelling? Such persuasion assigns lesser roles to ethos, pathos, and mythos. Although these latter forms of proof can add energy, color, and human interest, they should supplement rational appeals, not replace them. The relationships among these forms of proof are indicated in Figure 15.1.

FINDING YOUR voice   Understanding Reasoned Persuasion

Find a news story that interests you. Consider the information in the story:

- Determine how you might use this information as evidence,
- Develop this evidence into a proof, and
- Explain how this proof might function as part of a pattern of reasoned persuasion.

How can this exercise help you find your voice as a persuasive speaker?

SPEAKER'S notes   When and How to Use Proof

As you consider which proofs to use in your speech, follow these guidelines:

1. To reassure listeners that you are credible, convince them that you know what you are talking about, that you are fair and honest, and that you have their interests at heart (*ethos*).

2. To convey the human dimensions of a problem, use moving examples and stories (*pathos*).

3. To connect a problem with the culture of listeners, show how it relates to popular traditions, legends, and symbols (*mythos*).

4. To increase understanding, use rational appeals based on facts, statistics, and expert testimony (*logos*).

▶ **logos**   A form of proof that appeals to reason based largely on facts and expert testimony presented logically.

The Master Proof

At the heart of reasoned persuasion, as we noted earlier, is *logos*, based on the purported truth of a situation: what it is, how it originated, where it is tending, its consequences for listeners, and what must be done in response to it. We call this the *master proof* because everything else depends on it. The side in a controversy that demonstrates command of the logos will normally prevail.

To evaluate the truth value of a message, critical listeners will want answers to the following questions:

■ Are the major issues and terms clearly defined?

■ Is the reasoning based on sound principles?

■ Is the reasoning anchored in reality?

■ Are comparisons to similar cases reasonable?

We will consider each of these questions, explain its relevance, and demonstrate how to deal with it as you prepare the arguments for your case.

When persuaders find their voices, the moment is often quite dramatic and illuminating.

👁 **Watch** at **MyCommunicationLab Video:** "Building a Persuasive Argument"

Defining Major Issues

Have you ever had a heated discussion with someone, only to discover later that the two of you were not even talking about the same thing? When speakers and listeners don't share a common understanding, it is difficult to communicate effectively. If speakers and audiences come from different backgrounds, careful definitions are very important. Opening his speech on "gender bending," Brandon Rader was careful to offer the following definition: "If you are a gender bender, you dress or act or think or talk like people in your community assume someone of the opposite sex would act or dress or talk." Having shared this understanding, Brandon went on to argue that most assumptions about gender benders are wrong. Brandon's definition at the start of his speech was essential.

Definitions are sometimes used to change listeners' perceptions and make them more sympathetic to the speaker's position. For example, should alcohol be defined as a drug? Should a fetus be defined as a human being? Definitions that answer such questions can prepare the way for arguments advocating different policies.

In the 1968 Memphis sanitation workers' strike, which led to the assassination of Dr. Martin Luther King, Jr., the workers carried signs stating "I AM A MAN." This simple definition was the basis of a complex moral argument. The strikers were claiming they had *not* been treated like men in social, political, and economic terms.

FINDING YOUR
voice   Controversies over Definitions

In *The Ethics of Rhetoric*, Richard Weaver observed that controversy over definitions of basic terms is a sign of social and cultural division. Consider examples of disagreement over the definitions of the following terms in contemporary arguments:

1. liberalism   **4.** abortion

2. marijuana   **5.** the role of government

3. gun rights

Do these disagreements reflect the kind of social division Weaver suggested? Can understanding these disagreements help you find your voice?

The sanitation workers whose strike provided the setting for Dr. King's assassination wore their arguments defining themselves around their necks.

Deductive Reasoning

In **deductive reasoning**, we reason on the basis of principles, using commonly accepted beliefs to ground and justify our conclusions.[14] We start with a principle, relate some specific subject to it, and draw from that relationship a conclusion about what we should do or think about the subject. A speaker begins by reminding listeners of a principle she believes they all accept: "We believe in freedom of speech." This statement of principle is called the **major premise** of an argument. Next, the speaker offers a specific case related to the principle, which becomes the **minor premise**: "Carolyn would like to speak." Finally, the speaker presents her **conclusion**: "We should let Carolyn speak." Because they accept the major premise, listeners tend to agree (even if they don't particularly care for Carolyn!).

This pattern of major premise/minor premise/conclusion is called a **syllogism**. Carmen Johnson based the reasoning in her speech praising the United Negro College Fund on this major premise: *The mind is a terrible thing to waste.* She assumed her University of Nevada, Las Vegas, audience would accept that premise without question. Dolapo Olushola based her argument in defense of Nigerian orphans on this major premise: *Children have the right to food, clothing, medical care, and loving care.* Again, she assumed her listeners would agree with this principle.

Reasoning from a general principle helps establish common ground. It can also point out inconsistencies between beliefs and behaviors—the gap between what we practice and what we preach. For example, if you can show that the censorship of song lyrics is inconsistent with freedom of speech, then you will have presented a good reason for people to be against such censorship. *We are more likely to change a practice that is inconsistent with our principles or values than we are to change our principles or values.*

At times, the pattern of reasoning in a syllogism may not be completely stated. For example, the major premise may not be presented because speakers assume

---

▶ **deductive reasoning** Arguing from a general principle to a specific conclusion.

▶ **major premise** The general principle on which an argument is based.

▶ **minor premise** Relating a specific subject to the general principle that supports an argument.

▶ **conclusion** Meaning drawn from the relationship between the major and minor premises.

▶ **syllogism** Pattern of deductive reasoning as it develops in reasoned persuasion.

that the principle is already accepted by listeners and that they will think of it on their own. As she spoke of the problems of Native Americans, Ashley Roberson spent much of her time providing examples of the reality of social injustice on reservations—her minor premise. She did not think it necessary to state or defend the major premise: *Social injustice in the United States should not be tolerated*. Instead, she concluded, "We must eradicate social injustice on reservations."

One point that is critical to deductive reasoning is that the speaker must show that a certain situation actually exists. People may not argue against the *principle* of environmental protection, but assertions about a specific case of pollution can create strong and divisive reactions. Your persuasive efforts should focus on that issue, citing evidence to demonstrate that your claims are based in reality.

As you develop a deductive argument, keep these cautions in mind:

- Be certain your audience will accept your major premise.

- Demonstrate the existence of relevant conditions through the use of evidence.

- Explain how the major and minor premises are related so listeners don't miss the point.

- Be sure your conclusion offers a clear course of action for listeners.

- Be certain your reasoning is free from logical errors and fallacies.

Inductive Reasoning

While deductive reasoning starts from some general principle and travels to a specific conclusion, inductive reasoning follows just the opposite track. **Inductive reasoning** starts with a close examination of the particulars—the facts and the exact circumstances—relevant to the case. We either make these observations ourselves or depend on experts who have made them for us. Inductive reasoning is the classic method of scientific investigation, and science still remains a "god term" for many listeners in our culture.[15] If you can show that science supports your argument, you will have strengthened your case for many audiences.

The speech by Austin Wright at the end of this chapter demonstrates inductive reasoning. He showed that he was familiar with information about the use and misuse of faulty databases. He highlighted this information with startling statistical comparisons and contrasts. The following passage reflects this skill:

> The *Los Angeles Times* of January 27, 2006, explains that these companies also have a reputation for losing information. In 2005, for instance, Choicepoint's data system was breached by con artists, compromising more than 19 billion individual files, including social security numbers and financial histories. Although a 2007 Javelin Strategy and Research report finds that identity theft costs victims an average of $5,000, the government forced Choicepoint to pay out a mere $15 million in damages. That's an average of less than one tenth of one cent for each person whose private information was leaked by Choicepoint.

Deductive reasoning and inductive reasoning work together. Reasoning from the reality of specific cases can strengthen principles so that they don't seem to be just items of faith. Such reasoning is also critical to establishing the truth of the minor premise in a syllogism. Is the censorship of song lyrics an actual threat, or is it merely an invented bogeyman in the minds of liberals? Ashley Roberson provided

▶ **inductive reasoning** Reasoning from specific factual instances to reach a general conclusion.

facts, statistics, and examples to demonstrate the extent of the problems on Native American reservations and to show how they constituted social injustice.

Another important point of focus in inductive reasoning is how subjects originate and where they appear to be going—their probable causes and consequences. As you use inductive reasoning in your arguments, keep in mind these basic requirements:

- You must be personally objective. Do not let biases warp your perceptions. Look at an issue from as many perspectives as possible.

- You must present a reasonable number of observations. One or two isolated incidents cannot justify claims.

- You must be sure your observations are up-to-date.

- Your observations must accurately represent the situation. The exception does not prove the rule.

- Your observations must justify your conclusion.

- As you present evidence, introduce the experts you cite, and establish their credentials.

Analogical Reasoning

When we deal with a problem by considering a similar situation and drawing lessons from it, we are reasoning from analogy. Such **analogical reasoning** can help you present an unfamiliar or abstract problem in terms of something listeners find more familiar, more concrete, or more easily understood.

Dr. Richard Corlin, in a presidential address to the American Medical Association on gun violence, used a vivid analogy to demonstrate how video games set the stage for a culture of gun violence. His use of analogical reasoning helped listeners understand his view of the problem:

> I want you to imagine with me a computer game called "Puppy Shoot." In this game, puppies run across the screen. Using a joystick, the game player aims a gun that shoots the puppies. The player is awarded one point for a flesh wound, three points for a body shot, and ten points for a head shot. Blood spurts out each time a puppy is hit—and brain tissue splatters all over whenever there's a head shot. The dead puppies pile up at the bottom of the screen. When the shooter gets to 1,000 points, he gets to exchange his pistol for an Uzi, and the point values go up.

FINDING YOUR voice   Adapting to Controversy

Select a controversial subject for your persuasive speech. How will you build a case for your position? What kinds of evidence will you use? What language resources and forms of proof will you employ? How will you develop compelling arguments out of patterns of reasoning? Explain your strategy at the end of the formal outline you prepare for your speech.

▶ **analogical reasoning** Creating a strategic perspective on a subject by relating it to something similar to it.

If a game as disgusting as that were to be developed, every animal rights group in the country, along with a lot of other organizations, would protest, and there would be all sorts of attempts made to get the game taken off the market. Yet, if you just change puppies to people in the game I described, there are dozens of them already on the market—sold under such names as "Blood Bath," "Psycho Toxic," "Redneck Rampage," and "Soldier of Fortune."[16]

Just as analogical reasoning can dramatize arguments, it can also be used to persuade listeners to accept solutions. For example, those who favor legalizing "recreational" drugs often base their arguments on an analogy to Prohibition.[17] They claim that Prohibition caused more problems than it solved because it made drinking an adventure and led to the rise of a criminal empire. Moreover, they assert that legalizing drugs would help put the international drug dealers out of business, just as the repeal of Prohibition helped bring about the downfall of the gangster empires of the 1930s.

What makes analogical reasoning work? It is similar to inductive reasoning in that it seeks insight through observation, but it concentrates *on one similar situation rather than many.* This means that, although it seems more concrete than some forms of inductive reasoning, it can also be less reliable. Before you decide to use an analogy as part of your argument, be sure that the similarities outweigh the dissimilarities. If you must strain to make an analogy fit, use another form of reasoning.

Out of these various patterns of reasoning—deductive, inductive, and analogical—you should be able to weave compelling arguments that make your case for the position you are defending.

SPEAKER'S notes   Developing Powerful Arguments

To build reasoned arguments, follow these guidelines:

1. Provide clear definitions of basic terms.
2. Justify arguments with deductive reasoning based on accepted principles.
3. Use inductive reasoning to demonstrate the reality of your argument.
4. Use analogical reasoning to draw comparisons that favor your position.

YOUR ethical VOICE   Building Ethical Arguments

To demonstrate that your arguments are ethical, observe the following guidelines:

1. Emphasize logical reasoning built on evidence.
2. Always supplement proof by ethos, pathos, or mythos with proof by logos.
3. Do not use mythos to mask intolerance.
4. Consider how your persuasive strategy will be judged by thoughtful listeners.
5. Acknowledge conditions that might disprove your argument.
6. Understand and respect different positions.

Refutative Design

Watch at
MyCommunicationLab
Video: "Courting
Responsibility"

In the heat of controversy, speakers must at times confront directly an opposing position. The **refutative design** is appropriate when you need to challenge other views. You raise doubts about an opposing position by revealing its inconsistencies and weaknesses. The point of attack may be illogical reasoning, flimsy evidence, or hidden agendas. However, you should avoid personal attacks unless credibility issues are inescapable. Above all, maintain civility, and be fair.

At a recent property owners' association meeting, one of your co-authors had to confront an opposing view that had just been expressed on a fairly heated issue. He had, he thought, a good personal relationship with the opponent and believed she was fairly well liked in the neighborhood. Therefore, he began his refutation very carefully. He complimented the opponent and praised her contributions. "But on this issue," he said, "we see things differently." He then proceeded item by item to identify these points of difference, being careful to avoid personal attacks and to build a positive case for his position. In the end, his side prevailed.

Four steps in developing an effective refutation are as follows:

1. State the point you are going to refute, and explain why it is important.

2. Present your evidence, using facts and figures, examples, and testimony. Cite sources and authorities that the audience will respect.

3. Spell out the conclusion. Don't assume that listeners will interpret correctly what the evidence means. Tell them directly.

4. Explain the significance of your refutation—show how it discredits or damages the opposing position.

In her speech "The Price of Bottled Water," the text of which appears in Appendix B, Katie Lovett offers an excellent illustration of the refutative design in action. She makes exceptional use of expert testimony combined with a special technique: She thought that the self-evident absurdity of the justifications offered for bottled water was so obvious that it would make the case for her. Whenever you can cite the opposition against itself, that is especially damaging! Here is a sampling of how she proceeded:

> Consumers gravitate towards bottled water instead of tap water for two reasons: what's in it and what's not in it. What could possibly be inside a 20-ounce bottle of water that would compel someone to pay $3 and beyond for it? According to *The Journal of Consumer Culture*, "bottled water is a form of cultural consumption, driven by everything from status competition to a belief in magical curing." Clever advertisers feed these feelings. Since bottled water has become an affordable status symbol in today's society, companies can appeal to social distinctions of wealth and class to sell their product.
>
> Take a look at some of the brands currently on the market: There are vitamin waters, nicotine waters, caffeine waters, electrolyte enhanced SmartWater, the "orbtastic" Aquapods that target kids, Bling H_2O which sells for $35 a bottle, "Hello Kitty" water for cats, and yes, even a "diet" water called "Skinny."
>
> Another main reason people want to buy bottled water is for what is *not* in it. The purity of water is the key theme for the bottled water industry. Bottlers seize upon public anxiety over municipal tap water supplies, supposedly

▶ **refutative design** A persuasive design in which the speaker challenges other views.

offering us the safety that tap water cannot. As a result, the National Resources Defense Council has found that "pure," "pristine," and "natural" are some of the most commonly used god-terms found in marketing and on labels.

So these are some of the fantasies and feelings that support the bottled water industry. Are they justified? Unfortunately, contrary to widespread belief, bottled water is not necessarily cleaner, safer, or purer than the water you get from your faucet. The perception is that if it is off the shelf, it is somehow cleaner and tastier. But *The Bulletin of Science, Technology & Society* argues that bottles of water become "petri dishes of germs." The bottles are loaded into trucks, driven down polluted highways, and transported by many different sets of hands before sitting around gathering dust and germs in storage houses.

In a recent four-year scientific study, the Natural Resources Defense Council tested more than 1,000 bottles of 103 brands of bottled water. In its publication, "Bottled Water or Tap Water?" the Council concluded that "there is no assurance that bottled water is any safer than tap water." In fact, a third of the brands tested were found to contain contaminants such as arsenic and carcinogenic compounds. Some of these samples contained levels of these harmful contaminants that exceeded state or industry standards. So much for "pure" and "pristine"!

Design Combinations

The refutative design often works well when speaking about controversial issues, but other designs, such as the problem–solution pattern discussed in Chapter 14, can be used as well. Combinations of designs also often work well in persuasive speeches. Amanda Miller's speech urging the close of the School of the Americas developed primarily in a problem–solution pattern, with the school itself constituting the problem and legislative proposals to close it providing the solution. But as she depicted what a serious problem the school had become, Amanda found it necessary to answer those who continued to defend it. In this section of her speech, she developed a refutative pattern within the larger problem–solution design:

> Those who argue in favor of the School claim that for many it is their only source of military education. But what kind of education are we providing?
>
> I've already shown you what the textbooks teach—and that does not fit my idea of education. The School began as a line of defense against the U.S.S.R. in the Cold War. And with the Cold War long since completed, I can see little reason to continue spending millions of dollars each year funding a school that produces such negative results. That money might better be spent on real education, or health care, or the environment.
>
> A second argument in favor of the School is that the techniques taught are necessary for "self-defense" against civil wars. But what kinds of selves are these people defending? Are they themselves civil? In 1993, an International Human Rights Tribunal revealed that over one hundred School of the Americas graduates had committed war crimes. Among these crimes were heading the concentration camps in Villa Grimaldi in Chile, organizing the Ocosingo Massacre in Mexico, and participating in drug trafficking and assassinations. How exactly do these activities qualify as "self-defense," in any legitimate sense of the word?

Having completed the refutative part of her speech, Amanda was ready to move on to her solution.

Avoiding Defective Persuasion

It takes a lot of work to prepare a persuasive speech—analyzing your audience, researching your topic, designing your speech, and developing powerful arguments. Don't ruin all your hard work by committing **fallacies**, or errors of reasoning. At best, fallacies can destroy your reputation and make you seem incompetent or untrustworthy. At worst, they can destroy all the work you have done in preparation for your persuasive presentation.

The Gallery of Fallacies

Fallacies can contaminate the evidence you use, the, proofs you develop, or the reasoning you employ. Recognizing common fallacies will help you guard against them both as a consumer and as a producer of persuasion.

Slippery Slope.   The **slippery slope fallacy** assumes that once something bad happens, it will establish an irreversible trend leading to disaster. It often involves over simplification and outlandish exaggeration. For example, a prominent religious leader once suggested that feminism was "a socialist, antifamily political movement that encourages women to leave their husbands, kill their children, practice witchcraft, destroy capitalism, and become lesbians."[18] In the slippery slope fallacy, it is not logic but rather our darkest fears that drive our prediction of events.

Red Herring.   The **red herring fallacy** occurs when irrelevant material is injected into an argument to divert attention away from the real issue. It sets up a "wild goose chase." The "red herring" is often a sensational allegation. In the ongoing environmental controversy over fracking, those who favor the practice often suggest that our government wants to put oil companies out of business. In return, those who oppose fracking suggest that the oil companies are trying to take over our country. Such charges from both sides divert attention from the main issues of the controversy.

Bandwagon.   The **bandwagon fallacy** assumes that, because everybody is doing something, it must be the right thing to do. Advertising is a fertile source of bandwagon fallacies. You may be urged to take Brand X for pain relief because

FINDING YOUR

voice   Proofs in Advertising

Look for advertisements that emphasize each of the four forms of persuasive proof: logos, pathos, ethos, and mythos. Consider what factors in the product, advertising medium, or target audience might explain the emphasis in each example? How effective are they? Do you detect any fallacies?

▶ **fallacies**   Errors in reasoning that make persuasion unreliable.
▶ **slippery slope fallacy**   The assumption that once something happens, an inevitable trend is established that will lead to disastrous results.

▶ **red herring fallacy**   The use of irrelevant material to divert attention.
▶ **bandwagon fallacy**   Urges listeners to climb aboard the bandwagon, arguing that because others are doing something, it might be right.

▶ **ad hominem fallacy**   Name-calling rather than arguing.
▶ **myth of the mean fallacy**   The deceptive use of statistical averages in speeches.

more people use it than Brand Y. Spin doctors tout the candidates with the highest poll rating (in polls they themselves conducted). Don't be sucked in by such appeals. Just because something is popular doesn't make it right. Think for yourself, and respect the right of others to do the same.

Ad Hominem.   The **ad hominem fallacy** attacks people rather than problems. Rather than focusing on issues, this fallacy relies on name-calling. An example of ad hominem might take the following form: "Don't listen to those environmentalists who oppose fracking. They're just a bunch of hippies."

Myth of the Mean.   The **myth of the mean fallacy** misuses statistics to befuddle an audience. We've all been taught that "figures don't lie," without being reminded

When listening to spectacular speakers, be on the alert for fallacies.

that "liars figure." For example, a speaker could tell you not to worry about poverty in Tunica, Mississippi, because the average income is well above the poverty level. This average could be skewed by the fact that a few families are very wealthy, creating an illusion of well-being that is not true for most people. Averages are useful to summarize statistical information but should not be used to mask the reality of a situation.

Post Hoc.   The **post hoc fallacy** starts with the assumption that, if one thing comes before another in time, the first is the cause of the second. It confuses simple association with causation. It is the basis of many superstitious beliefs. For example, if you wore a particular school t-shirt when your team won a close and important ball game, that becomes your "lucky shirt" that you wear to all future ball games. Sadly, wearing a "lucky" shirt doesn't guarantee a win.

On more serious public issues, some people once argued that because John F. Kennedy was Catholic, to elect him would mean that the Pope would rule the United States. Those who promoted Prohibition in times past argued that making alcoholic beverages illegal would improve the quality of home life in America. Their post hoc predictions were quite unreliable. Others argued that to "give" women the right to vote would destroy the American electoral system. It's harder to see the post hoc fallacy when it is right under our noses, but be wary: It most assuredly remains a threat to public deliberation.

Non Sequitur.   The words *non sequitur* are Latin for "it does not follow." The **non sequitur fallacy** occurs when the major premise and the minor premise are not really related to each other, when the conclusion does not follow from the relationship between the major and minor premises, or when the evidence presented is irrelevant. For example, Dixy Lee Ray, former chair of the Atomic Energy Commission, offered this defense for the use of atomic energy: "A nuclear power plant is infinitely safer than eating because 300 people choke to death on food every year."

Faulty Analogy.   A **faulty analogy fallacy** occurs when speakers compare things that are dissimilar in important ways. For example, assume that you have transferred

---

▶ **post hoc fallacy** An inductive error in which one event is assumed to be the cause of another simply because the first preceded the second.

▶ **non sequitur fallacy** Occurs when conclusions do not follow from the premises that precede them or from irrelevant evidence.

▶ **faulty analogy fallacy** A comparison drawn between things that are dissimilar in some important way.

to an urban university with 15,000 students from a small-town college that served 1,500 students. You base your persuasive speech on campus security measures on a program that was used at your previous school, arguing that, since it worked at College A, it should work at University A. Might the size differences be important? Should the urban versus rural setting be taken into consideration? Dissimilarities on any major factors can result in a faulty analogy.

Hasty Generalization.

A **hasty generalization fallacy** occurs when you base a conclusion on insufficient or nonrepresentative observations. For example, a student might reason, "My roommate got a D from Professor Osborn. The guy who sits next to me in history got an F from him. I'm struggling to make a C in his class; therefore, Professor Osborn is a tough grader." To avoid a hasty generalization, you would need to know what his grade distribution looks like over an extended period of time.

Either-Or.

An **either-or fallacy** creates a false dilemma. It makes listeners think they have only two mutually exclusive choices. Either-or thinking is attractive because it is dramatic, but it is also an example of oversimplification. It creeps into civic issues with statements such as "It's either jobs or the environment" or "To pay off the debt we must cut social security." Such claims blind listeners to other options—the possibilities of compromises or creative alternatives.

Faulty Testimony.

The **faulty testimony fallacy** takes many different forms. It can occur when a speaker uses "expert" testimony from a source that is not an expert on the topic under consideration. This problem often occurs when titles are used without appropriate explanation, as in, "Dr. Francis Folksworth reported that smoking is not harmful to your health." What the speaker did not reveal was that Dr. Folksworth was a marketing professor who was writing public relations material for the Tobacco Growers Association. As we discussed in Chapter 8, speakers also may quote a person out of context in a way that is not truly representative of that person's position, misuse lay testimony to validate facts, or misrepresent the voice of the people.

Inappropriate Evidence.

Inappropriate evidence fallacies occur when speakers support their points with bizarre or unsubstantiated evidence. Political commentator and former Speaker of the House Newt Gingrich, speaking on why women are less suited than men to traditional military combat roles, once provided this remarkable illustration:

> If combat means living in a ditch, females have biological problems staying in a ditch for 30 days because they get infections . . . . [Moreover,] males are biologically driven to go out and hunt for giraffes.

Representative Pat Schroeder found the perfect answer for this line of reasoning: "I have been working in a male culture for a very long time, and I haven't met the first one who wants to go out and hunt a giraffe."[19]

▶ **hasty generalization fallacy** An error of inductive reasoning in which a claim is made based on insufficient or nonrepresentative information.

▶ **either-or fallacy** Arguing that there are only two options, one of which is desirable.

▶ **faulty testimony fallacy** Using "expert" testimony from a source that is not an expert on the topic under consideration.

▶ **Inappropriate evidence fallacy** Occurs when speakers use one form of evidence when they should be using another.

FINDING YOUR

voice   Find the Fallacies

Look for examples of fallacies in the "Letters to the Editor" section of your local newspaper or in opinions expressed in blogs. Consider how these fallacies affect the credibility or character of the people who commit them. Did you ever commit such an error? Do you think this damaged your credibility? Might personal fallacies be an obstacle to finding your voice?

Begging the Question.   The **begging the question fallacy** occurs when speakers neglect their responsibilities to prove their points. Instead, they make claims and barge ahead as though the claims didn't need to be proven. This fallacy often relies on colorful language to disguise the lack of proof. The words used seem to justify the conclusion. Sometimes this fallacy occurs when speakers rely solely on mythos to support an argument. A conclusion such as "Be patriotic! Support our American way of life. Vote against gun control" begs the question because the speaker has not demonstrated that being against gun control is a form of patriotism.

Straw Man.   The **straw man fallacy** occurs when the persuader creates a likeness of the opposition's position that makes it seem trivial, extreme, or easy to refute. Referring to health care reform as "socialized medicine" and to banking regulations as "a government takeover" are recent examples of such fallacies. As an ethical persuasive speaker, you should represent opposing positions fairly and fully. The straw man fallacy is an implicit admission of weakness or desperation on the part of its user.

Faulty Premise.   The **faulty premise fallacy** occurs when the major premise of an argument is not sound. *If the major premise is faulty, the entire argument may crumble.* We once heard a student begin a line of argument with the following statement of principle: "College athletes are not really here to learn." She was instantly in trouble. When her speech was over, the class assailed her with questions: How did she define *athletes?* Was she talking about intercollegiate or intramural athletes? How about the tennis team? How did she define learning? Was she aware of the negative stereotype at the center of her premise? Wasn't she being unfair, not to mention arrogant? It's safe to say that the speaker did not persuade many people that day.

   To learn more about the fascinating subject of fallacies, go to *Fallacy Files,* an online site containing an extensive collection of fallacies and bad arguments. Developed by Gary N. Curtis, the site offers definitions and examples and is well organized and entertaining. See especially "Stalking the Wild Fallacy," offered under the "Examples" feature on the menu.

▶ **begging the question fallacy**   Assuming that an argument has been proved without actually presenting the evidence.

▶ **straw man fallacy**   Understating, distorting, or otherwise misrepresenting the position of opponents for ease of refutation.

▶ **faulty premise fallacy**   A reasoning error that occurs when an argument is based on a flawed major premise.

Persuasion is constantly threatened by flaws and deception. In a world of competing views, we often see human nature revealed in its petty as well as its finer moments. As you plan and present your arguments or listen to the arguments of others, be on guard against fallacies. Figure 15.2 lists and defines the fallacies we have been discussing.

FIGURE 15.2
Gallery of Fallacies

Gallery of Fallacies	
1. Slippery Slope	argues that one bad thing will inevitably lead to others
2. Red Herring	distracts listeners with sensational, irrelevant information
3. Bandwagon	argues that you should do it because everybody else does
4. Ad Hominem	attacks the person rather than the issue
5. Myth of the Mean	uses an average to hide a problem
6. Post Hoc	confuses proximity with causation
7. Non Sequitur	reasoning in which the conclusion does not follow from the major premise or evidence
8. Faulty Analogy	comparing things that are dissimilar in important ways
9. Hasty Generalization	drawing conclusions based on insufficient evidence
10. Either-Or	presenting choices so that listeners think there are only two options
11. Faulty Testimony	quoting a source out of context or relying on the wrong type of testimony
12. Inappropriate Evidence	using facts when examples are needed or examples when facts are needed
13. Begging the Question	claiming a conclusion that has not been proved with evidence
14. Straw Man	creating a likeness of an opposing position that makes it seem trivial, extreme, and easy to refute
15. Faulty Premise	occurs when the major premise of an argument is not sound

FINAL
reflections   Persuasion That Has Legs

As a response to the pressures of controversy all around us, from global to national to local community issues, reasoned persuasion is both ethical and smart. For one thing, it offers enduring value. The manipulator is interested only in influencing the momentary, shallow commitments that drive our everyday decisions. Some of these commitments may seem of limited consequence—the choice of one shampoo over others, one travel destination over others, perhaps even one automobile over others. But once we enter the arena in which we are asked to support or reject policies or decide among political candidates, such impulsive, shallow commitments are inappropriate, and manipulative persuasion is out of place.

Instead, for these more important decisions, we need persuasion that respects the power of evidence and develops patterns of reasoning into compelling arguments that constitute a case. Such reasoned persuasion is vital to the long-range impact of ideas.

Finding your voice means more than discovering your call to a cause and learning how to make your voice heard. It has to do also with how long your voice will be heard and the extent of its influence. Reasoned persuasion pursues the kind of commitment that endures. It has legs.

There may be an even deeper value. In his book *Decision by Debate*, Douglas Ehninger argued that the value of debate should be judged on more serious grounds than whether one side wins or loses: Debate performs, he said, an *investigative function* [20] If "debate" means the development of contending positions on contentious issues, Ehninger's argument gains resonance. When we build a case to support a position, we also develop a point of view that can reveal something useful about an issue. We can illuminate one facet of what are often many-faceted controversies. The decisions that finally resolve these issues are often compromises that blend elements of the opposed positions. Many of us can "win" in the sense that we are represented in the consensus that emerges. Even when we "lose," our arguments can discipline and improve the decisions that prevail. Therefore, it is important that we seek not so much to "win" an argument but to express our position with all the power and skill we can muster. All persuaders who advance reasoned persuasion on an issue deserve appreciation for contributing to the richness of how controversies are finally resolved.

After Reading This Chapter, You Should Be Able To Answer These Questions

1 What happens to persuasion in controversial settings?

2 What are the differences between manipulative and reasoned persuasion?

3 How can you build a case from evidence and proofs that will stand up in controversies?

4 What are the ethical advantages of reasoned persuasion?

5 What are the strengths and weaknesses of different patterns of reasoning?

6 How can you use the refutative design to deal with opposition?

7 What are the major kinds of fallacies, and how can you avoid them?

Study and **Review** at **MyCommunicationLab**

For Discussion and Further Exploration

1 Search for print advertisements or television and online commercials that rely primarily on emotional appeals. Discuss the ethics of such advertising techniques.

2 Find examples on TED or YouTube of speeches that meet and fail to meet the high standards of reasoned persuasion. Explain and justify your evaluations.

3 Facts and statistics are favored forms of evidence in the United States but may be less valued than sacred and prestige testimony in other countries. Examine the validity of this assumption by investigating samples of public discourse in various countries. What preferences for kinds of evidence do you discover? Discuss the possible impact any differences might have on persuasion across cultures.

4 Compile a list of public figures or sources of information that you respect. Compare these high-ethos sources with those of your classmates, and prepare a master list for possible use in speeches.

5 Find television advertisements that rely primarily on fear appeals. Share these in class, and discuss their effectiveness and ethics.

6 Find a recent persuasive speech in which narrative plays a prominent part. What persuasive work does the narrative perform? How well has the speaker integrated the narrative with other forms of evidence?

7 The western frontier is a major source of mythos in American speeches. *American Progress*, a painting by American artist John Gast, portrays many culturetypes and ideographs. Access this painting online, and see which of these mythic symbols you can identify.

8 Look for examples of syllogisms in a contemporary persuasive speech. Does the speaker detail the major premise, minor premise, and conclusion, or does the speaker depend on the listener to infer any of them to complete the thought structure? How artful and effective is the speaker's work?

A SAMPLE SPEECH

This persuasive speech, presented during Honors Day in the Department of Communication Studies at the University of Texas at Austin, went on to win the National Championship for Persuasive Speaking presented by the National Forensic League. It is noteworthy for its reliance on reasoned persuasion, developing an array of proofs and evidence that emphasize facts and expert testimony, carefully documented to reassure critical listeners. Adding color and human interest to the speech are judicious uses of examples, metaphors, and appeals to fear and fairness.

Keep Big Brother Off Your Back

AUSTIN L. WRIGHT

On September 26, 2002, Canadian citizen Maher Arar boarded a flight home from a family vacation in Tunisia. During a layover in New York City, American authorities detained Arar, interrogating him for the next twelve days. After repeatedly denying any connection to Al Qaeda, Arar was shackled and loaded onto a private, unmarked jet headed for Syria, where he was tortured for the next ten months.

As the *Electronic Privacy Information Center* or EPIC writes in an *amicus* brief presented before the U.S. Supreme Court on May 16, 2008, the U.S. government justified Arar's torture using patently false information. As the brief further explains, two American databases—the Department of Homeland Security's Automated Targeting System and the FBI's National Crime Information Center—track tens of millions of Americans and foreign nationals each year for things as simple as suspicious credit card charges and questionable Internet searches. Indeed, EPIC claims our government uses these databases for searches 2.8 million times every day!

Yet, these databases contain widely documented errors that the government has no intention of fixing. And in 2007 the Department of Justice folded to pressure from the private intelligence companies and granted both databases blanket immunity over the accuracy of their contents, meaning no one can sue the government for the unlawful use of false information provided by private corporations.

In short: the information that our government uses to detain, interrogate and torture suspected terrorists can be fabricated on a whim. But with more Americans being tracked as suspected terrorists than at any other point in our nation's history—writes *The USA Today* of March 10, 2009—the danger of false data to all of us is too grave to ignore.

So today we will discuss how these error-ridden databases are protected, examine the dangers they pose to our personal liberties, and discuss some ways they might be corrected.

According to *The New York Times* of January 15, 2009, the Supreme Court ruled that evidence found in faulty databases may be used to charge someone with a crime, real or imagined. These databases pose a threat to the prohibition on unreasonable search and seizure, but they are protected by the government in two ways: constraints on the exclusionary rule and the use of private companies to sidestep restrictions.

Initially, as the *Wisconsin Law Journal* of January 26, 2009, writes, the Supreme Court passed down a decision seriously limiting the scope of the exclusionary rule in the case of Herring v. United States. The exclusionary rule protects Americans from evidence acquired through an illegal search and seizure. But, in deciding the fate of Bennie Herring—an Alabama man who was pulled over and searched using an erroneous warrant—the Court amended the exclusionary rule, writing off the government's use of false information as "reasonable" since Herring was guilty of a crime. While this new legal doctrine may sound appealing, it does expose innocent Americans as well to unreasonable search, seizure, and detention.

Additionally, the federal government hires private companies, like Choicepoint and LexisNexis, to develop these databases to circumvent legal restrictions on domestic intelligence gathering. *Washington Post* reporter Robert O'Harrow's 2005 book *No Place To Hide* clarifies that the law regulating private intelligence gathering is the Fair Credit Reporting Act. If private companies don't sell credit ratings, however, their techniques do not trigger oversight under the law, meaning that companies can use literally any means to gather information and are not legally required to verify its accuracy. As

◄ The speech opens with an example that raises issues of fairness over the government's use of false information and its complicity in torture. Implied in the example is a sense of violated mythos: Should the United States, which prides itself in protecting individual rights, be engaged in such egregious violations of these rights?

◄ The speech offers a clear preview of what is to come and promises to develop within a categorical design.

a June 1, 2007, Salon.com expose contends, the federal government is outsourcing domestic spying to private companies that can gather any information about anyone, using any means, without any consequences for releasing false information.

The example that follows provides another perspective on false databases: Not only are they dangerous—but also they are sometimes patently absurd. The sardonic humor provides a touch of color and lightness in the otherwise somber wordscape of the speech.

When Ron Peterson, a man from California, asked Choicepoint for his private information in 2005, he was told he was a female prostitute in Florida named Ronnie, an incarcerated murderer in Texas, a stolen goods dealer in New Mexico, a witness tamperer in Oregon, and a sex offender in Nevada. All of which, thankfully, were not true. But just imagine how this so-called "information" might have been misused by a government investigator prepared already to believe the worst about Mr. Peterson!

Beyond such flagrant inaccuracies, these flawed databases threaten each of us in two ways: legal malfeasance and information leaks. Initially, given the Supreme Court's recent decision, false information contained within these databases has the same force of law as accurate information. Since the Department of Justice built a legal force field around these databases in 2007, writes the *Wisconsin Law Journal*, LexisNexis and Choicepoint are legally free to disseminate false information that can be used to fill these databases and to execute searches, seizures, and false arrests, all without a shred of truth or actual legal merit.

These databases and the private companies hired to make them are also dangerously prone to information leaks. The *North Country Gazette* of January 14, 2009, writes that a former NYPD sergeant was able to access a database through his police status and leaked top-secret documents to help a friend win a divorce battle. What's more, the *Los Angeles Times* of January 27, 2006, explains that these companies also have a reputation for losing information. In 2005, for instance, Choicepoint's data system was breached by con artists, compromising more than 19 billion individual files, including social security numbers and financial histories. Although a 2007 Javelin Strategy and Research report finds that identity theft costs victims an average of $5,000, the government forced Choicepoint to pay out a mere $15 million in damages. That's an average of less than one tenth of one cent for each person whose private information was leaked by Choicepoint.

Austin anticipated the question of what listeners might do to counter the vast injustice he had described by offering his own personal action as a model. He also appealed to the pride of his Texas listeners by offering a metaphorical vision of a movement for reform starting on their campus that might then "sweep across the country."

While we may not be able to change the way the Supreme Court treats the use of false information, we can cut this problem off at its source by pressuring the private intelligence companies hired by our government and checking the information they sell. As O'Harrow explains, LexisNexis has built a virtual monopoly on American intelligence gathering. Since 9/11, LexisNexis bought most of the companies hired by the federal government to build the Automated Targeting System and NCIC, including Choicepoint. What's even worse, the CEO of Choicepoint told the *Washington Post* in 2005 that his company won't tolerate regulation under the Fair Credit Reporting Act, meaning LexisNexis subsidiaries are using any means to gather even false information without any legal consequences.

LexisNexis charges our school about a $1.50 fee every time we use their search engine. So here's a radical idea: Let's refuse to use it! And let's ask our librarians and our college officials to cancel their contracts with LexisNexis and its subsidiary companies until they clean up their act. When I found out LexisNexis makes about $5,000 a year off my speech team, I asked my teammates to start using alternative search engines like Google News and Google

Scholar. I prepared this speech using only sources taken from Google News. As an academic community that makes heavy use of their tools, we are in a unique position to pressure LexisNexis for change. And we at the University of Texas—this large and prestigious university—can start a movement for reform that can sweep across this country!

If you want to take more immediate action, send a letter to Choicepoint, demanding access to your information. You can either visit their website or take one of the request forms I have printed off. All you have to do is fill in the blanks and make a copy of your driver's license and a recent bill you have paid that contains your address. If you happen to discover false information in your folder, don't hesitate to send a certified letter to Choicepoint requesting a revision of your file. Choicepoint is legally required to comply with your demands, and correcting even minor errors could help keep Big Brother off your back.

When Maher Arar was illegally detained in 2002, the dual threats posed by the Automated Tracking System and the NCIC may have seemed isolated. But today, the stakes for tens of millions of Americans are greater than ever before. We must act and act now to pressure private intelligence companies to mend the information crisis they have created. With government conducting ten searches every second using faulty data, we literally don't have a second to lose.

◀ Austin concludes by raising a specter of government as a potentially abusive Big Brother, an image that might appeal to both liberals and conservatives. He offers a nice sense of closure by tying back in to his initial example of a tortured citizen and appeals for immediate action.

Listen to
Chapter 16 at
MyCommunicationLab

Objectives

This chapter will help you

1 Appreciate the value of ceremonial speaking

2 Develop the sense of identification between yourself and listeners

3 Magnify important accomplishments and deeds so that listeners can realize their significance

4 Prepare a variety of ceremonial speeches

5 Act as a master of ceremonies

6 Polish your storytelling skills using narrative design

16 Ceremonial Speaking on Special Occasions

Every year the employees of the Nabholz Construction Company hold an annual Christmas party. The mood is lighthearted and festive. During the party, Chris Goldsby, head of the Operations Division, makes award presentations. The featured awards are the "Wellies," represented by small statues of bulldogs, which recognize achievement in the company Wellness Program. This program has won nationwide acclaim for helping its workers stop smoking, get in shape, and lose weight.[1] The recipients of Wellies sometimes make acceptance speeches to express appreciation to co-workers who helped them. Goldsby often ends the ceremony by offering an inspirational message urging others to participate in the program.

> *[People] who celebrate ... are fused with each other and fused with all things in nature.*
>
> —ERNST CASSIRER

Ceremonial speeches are offered on special occasions that are often vital to companies, families, and even nations. Such speeches can occur in a variety of forms. Speakers can offer tributes to people and accomplishments or present or accept awards. They may rise to introduce other featured speakers. After-dinner speeches bring people together in a lighthearted way, and toasts often celebrate happy occasions such as weddings or retirement dinners. Eulogies and memorials bring back fond memories, celebrate achievements, and inspire listeners.

On a deeper level, ceremonial speeches often reinforce the values that bind people together in communities.[2] The philosopher John Dewey observed that people "live in a community in virtue of the things which they have in common; and communication is the way in which they come to possess things in common. What they must have in common . . . are aims, beliefs, aspirations, knowledge—a common understanding."[3] Ceremonial speaking celebrates and reinforces our common goals, beliefs, and aspirations.

Ceremonial speaking often addresses four important questions:

- Who are we?
- Why are we?
- What have we accomplished?
- What can we become together?

From Frederick Douglass's "What to the Slave Is the Fourth of July?" to Lincoln's "Gettysburg Address" to Ronald Reagan's "Challenger Disaster Memorial," many of the most studied speeches in American history were delivered on ceremonial occasions. We remember them because they portray the struggles of American leaders to define, apply, and maintain our nation's values at critical moments when they are being tested.

Your own speaking may not be as momentous, but ceremonial occasions can offer an opportunity for you to celebrate your success in finding your voice. Part of that success is discovering that you can now make a contribution as a speaker, when the occasion arises, to your family, to a mentor or friend, to your company, or to the life of your community.

▶ **ceremonial speeches (ceremonial speaking)**
Speaking that celebrates special occasions, such as speeches of tribute, inspiration, and introduction; eulogies; toasts; award presentations; acceptances; and after-dinner speeches.

Developing your ceremonial speaking skills will have many practical benefits as well as making you a more flexible speaker. You may be asked to "say a few words" at the retirement party of a former teacher or mentor. You might need to present an award to an outstanding coworker. You may wish to celebrate the memory of a beloved friend, to offer a toast at a wedding reception, or to act as the master of ceremonies at a banquet. When you speak effectively on these occasions, you also enhance perceptions of your competence, character, and leadership potential. When you find your voice by presenting such speeches, you often find your future as well. In this chapter, we help you rise to the various speaking challenges posed by the variety of ceremonial occasions.

Techniques of Ceremonial Speaking

Explore at
MyCommunicationLab
Activity: "Build a Speech:
Special Occasional Speech"

Identification and magnification are the two basic techniques used in ceremonial speaking.

Identification

Identification develops when a speech creates a feeling of shared goals, values, emotions, memories, motives, and cultural background between a speaker and listeners. Kenneth Burke, a leading communication theorist of our time, suggested that identification is the key component of public speaking.[4] People who identify with each other are more likely to reason and act together. Because ritual and ceremony draw people together, identification is the heart of ceremonial speaking. Three common strategies for promoting identification in ceremonial speaking are the use of narrative, the recognition of heroes and heroines, and the renewal of group commitment.

Using Narrative.
Storytelling is an effective way of developing identification with an audience.[5] For example, if you were preparing a speech celebrating a fundraising drive at your school, you might tell stories of things that happened when student volunteers were making calls. You might tell about times when volunteers were discouraged or times when they were exhilarated. These vignettes could draw listeners together as they remember the shared experience. Stories that evoke laughter can be especially effective because laughter itself is a shared phenomenon.

Ashlie McMillan's speech of tribute told the inspiring story of a cousin who was a diastrophic dwarf. In her introduction, Ashlie asked listeners to close their eyes and imagine themselves shrinking to help them identify with the challenges faced by her diminutive cousin. This identification prepared the audience to accept Ashlie's eloquent conclusion: "You too may seem too short to grasp your stars, but you never know how far you might reach if you stand upon a dream." We review how to prepare effective narratives later in this chapter.

Recognizing Heroes and Heroines.
Another strategy for promoting identification in ceremonial speaking is to invoke the words and deeds of heroes and heroines as role models. Depending on the nature and purpose of the celebration, a speaker might invoke a figure such as Thomas Jefferson, Martin Luther King, Jr., Mother Theresa, or Elizabeth Cady Stanton. These figures embody and personify such virtues as dedication, steadfastness, sacrifice, and grand achievements against the odds. The lives they lived—as we remember them—represent hope, for having lived once, they can live again in our actions and deeds.

▶ **identification** The feeling of closeness between speakers and listeners that may overcome personal and cultural differences.

FINDING YOUR
voice Heroism

As you consider the use of heroes in ceremonial speeches, focus on how they overcame challenges. What virtues and values do they represent? Think of past and present heroes who are frequently mentioned in such speeches. What qualities do they have that make them admirable or memorable? Why are they so often referenced? Think of others whom you consider heroes, either global figures or people of importance to you personally. What traits make them inspiring? How can you make these values come alive for your audience? In what ways do you think others identify with such heroes? How can such material help you find your voice?

Renewing Group Commitment. Ceremonial speaking is a time both for celebrating what has been accomplished and for renewing commitments. Engage your listeners with a vision of what the future can be like with continued commitment. Urge them to move on. Reinvigorate their identity as a group moving forward.

To renew group commitment, ceremonial speakers often contrast a challenging present to the backdrop of an idealized past. They then create a vision to guide listeners into the future. In his "Gettysburg Address," delivered to commemorate the costliest battle of the costliest war in American history, Abraham Lincoln used this technique to substantially redefine America's moral identity as a nation.

Lincoln opened with a clear reference to an idealized past: "Four score and seven years ago our fathers brought forth on this continent, a new nation, conceived in Liberty, and dedicated to the proposition that all men are created equal." He then moved directly to the troubled present: "Now we are engaged in a great civil war, testing whether that nation, or any nation so conceived and so dedicated, can long endure." After expounding on the sacrifices of the "brave men, living and dead, who struggled here," Lincoln closed by offering a stunning vision to guide the American future: "that this nation, under God, shall have a new birth of freedom—and that government of the people, by the people, for the people, shall not perish from the earth."[6]

SPEAKER'S
notes Promoting Identification

Use the following techniques to develop identification among listeners:

1. Tell stories that remind listeners of shared experiences.

2. Enjoy laughter; it bonds people together.

3. Create portraits of heroes and heroines as shared role models.

4. Revive legends and traditions to remind listeners of what they share.

5. Offer goals and visions to inspire listeners to work together.

Jesse Owens was both a great Olympic hero and a great inspirational speaker.

Magnification

In his *Rhetoric*, Aristotle noted that when speakers select certain features of a person or event and then dwell on those qualities, the effect is to magnify them in the minds of listeners.[7] Such **magnification** comes to represent the meaning of the subject for listeners. It focuses attention on what is relevant, honorable, and praiseworthy.

For example, imagine that you are preparing a speech honoring Jesse Owens's incredible track and field accomplishments in the 1936 Olympic Games. In your research, you come up with a variety of facts:

1.   He had a headache the day he won the medal in the long jump.

2.   He had suffered from racism in America.

3.   He did not like the food served at the Olympic training camp.

4.   He won four gold medals in front of Adolf Hitler, who was preaching the racial superiority of Germans.

5.   Some of his friends did not want him to run for the United States.

6.   After his victories, he returned to further discrimination in America.

If you used all this information, your speech might ramble without a clear purpose. Which of these items should you emphasize? There are certain themes you should focus on to magnify the actions of a person. These themes include

- Triumph over obstacles
- Unusual accomplishment
- Superior performance
- Unselfish motives
- Benefit to society

▶ **magnification**   A speaker's selecting and emphasizing certain qualities of a subject to stress the values they represent.

As you consider these themes, it becomes clearer which facts about Jesse Owens you should magnify. To begin, you should stress that Owens had to overcome obstacles such as racism in America to even make the Olympic team. Then you should point out that his accomplishment was unusual. No one else had ever won four gold medals in Olympic track and field competition. His performances set world records that lasted many years. His motives were unselfish because he received no material gain from his victories. He was driven solely by personal qualities such as courage and determination. Finally, you would show that because his victories repudiated Hitler's racist agenda and caused him public humiliation, Owens's accomplishments benefited our society. The overall effect would be to magnify the meaning of Jesse Owens's great performances, both for himself and for his nation.

Magnification relies on effective language to create dramatic word-pictures. Metaphors and similes can magnify a subject through creative associations, such as, "He struck like a lightning bolt that day." Parallel structure can also help magnify a subject and embed it in our minds. For example, if you were to say of Mother Teresa, "Whenever there was hurt, she was there. Whenever there was hunger, she was there. Whenever there was desperation, she was there," you would be magnifying her dedication and selflessness.

Certain speech designs also promote magnification. Comparison and contrast designs make selected features stand out. For example, you might contrast the purity of Owens's motives with the seemingly greedy motives of today's well-paid athletes. Chronological designs that present the history of a situation magnify the themes you think are important. As Simone Mullinax, whose speech concludes this chapter, sketched certain incidents in her childhood, she gradually revealed the fascinating character of her grandmother. Causation designs magnify a person's accomplishments as the causes of important effects. For example, a speaker might suggest that Jesse Owens's victories refuted Nazi propaganda for many people. Narrative designs help to dramatize events and accomplishments.

Whatever designs ceremonial speeches use, it is important that they build to a conclusion. Speakers should save their best materials and language use for the end of the speech. Ceremonial speeches should never dwindle to a close.

FINDING YOUR voice   Magnification

The way you use magnification reveals a lot about you as a person. The types of successes or accomplishments you use to describe someone reveal what you value. When you describe a person's successes and accomplishments in speeches of tribute, you may be setting goals for your own personal growth and for what you would like to achieve. Consider friends, classmates, and others in your extended family or your community. What qualities and achievements would you be most likely to praise or highlight in a speech of tribute to one or more of them? How would you accomplish magnification of these qualities and accomplishments? How can the magnification of others in a speech contribute to finding your voice?

SPEAKER'S

notes   Magnification

Use the following strategies to magnify a person or accomplishment:

1. Show how people have overcome obstacles to success.
2. Point out how unusual the accomplishments are.
3. Emphasize the superior features of the performance.
4. Describe the unselfish motives behind the achievement.
5. Show how listeners and society have benefited.
6. Use speech designs—comparison, chronological, causation, and narrative—that promote magnification.

Types of Ceremonial Speeches

The ceremonial speeches that you will most likely present in your personal and professional lives include speeches of tribute (award presentations, eulogies, and toasts), acceptance speeches, introductions for other speakers, speeches of inspiration, after-dinner speeches, and speaking as master of ceremonies (see Figure 16.1).

Speeches of Tribute

Watch at **MyCommunicationLab**
Video: "Tribute to Steve Prefontaine"

A **speech of tribute** typically focuses on the values of individual responsibility, striving, and achievement. For example, you might be called on to honor a former teacher at a retirement ceremony, present an award to someone for an outstanding accomplishment, eulogize a person who has died, or propose a toast to a friend who is getting married.

FIGURE 16.1
Types of Ceremonial Speeches

Type	Use When
Tributes	You wish to honor a person, group, occasion, or event. Subtypes include award presentations, eulogies, and toasts.
Acceptance	You need to acknowledge an award or honor.
Introductions	You must introduce a featured speaker in a program.
Inspiration	You want to motivate listeners to appreciate and commit to a goal, purpose, or set of values; this may be religious, commercial, political, or social in nature.
After-Dinner	You want to entertain the audience while leaving a message that can guide future behavior. Here, as elsewhere, brevity is golden.
Master of Ceremonies	You must coordinate a program and see that everything runs smoothly. The master of ceremonies sets the mood for the occasion.

▶ **speech of tribute** A ceremonial speech that recognizes the achievements of individuals or groups or commemorates special events.

Speeches of tribute serve several important purposes. If you have presented a series of speeches on related topics in your class, the speech of tribute gives you a chance to extend your earlier informative and persuasive endeavors.

For example, Holly Carlson chose the banning of books in public schools as the topic area for all her speeches. In her informative speech, she demonstrated how books are banned in schools all over the country, and she cited the books and authors most often targeted. In her persuasive speech, she offered a stirring plea for intellectual freedom, urging her listeners to support the right to read and think for themselves. Then, for her ceremonial speech, she offered a tribute to one of the most frequently banned authors of the twentieth century, J. D. Salinger. Her tribute to Salinger made her listeners want to read his works themselves. It also dramatized how hurtful censorship could be. Thus, all of Holly's speeches were woven into one pattern, which gave focus to her semester's work. She found her voice both cumulatively and forcefully.

The raising of the American flag at Iwo Jima during World War II became an important symbol for courage and fortitude, themes echoed in the similar photograph of the raising of the flag by firefighters over the wreckage of the World Trade Center.

Speeches of tribute blend easily with inspirational speeches. John Bakke's speech accepting the University of Memphis Martin Luther King Jr. Human Rights Award became a speech of tribute to King and then evolved into a speech of inspiration for his listeners. Similarly, student John Scipio paid powerful tribute to King in his "Martin Luther King at the Mountaintop." See his speech in MyCommunicationLab. Finally, Simone Mullinax's tribute to her feisty grandmother offered a conclusion that inspires appreciation for family love and tradition.

Praiseworthy accomplishments, the basis of speeches of tribute, are usually celebrated for two reasons. First, *they are important in themselves:* The influence of a teacher may have contributed to the success of many of her former students. Second, *they are important as symbols.* The planting of the American flag at Iwo Jima during some of the most intense fighting of World War II came to symbolize the fortitude of the entire American war effort; it represented commitment, and it was more important as a symbol than as an actual event. Sometimes the same event may be celebrated for both actual and symbolic reasons. A student speech honoring those who contributed to a fund in memory of the victims of the 2012 school shooting in Newtown, Connecticut, celebrated this achievement both as a symbol of generosity and for the actual help it provided to so many people. When you plan a speech of tribute, you should consider both the actual and the symbolic values that are represented.

 Watch at **MyCommunicationLab**
Video: "Martin Luther King, Jr. at the Mountaintop"

Developing Speeches of Tribute.   As you prepare a speech of tribute, keep the following guidelines in mind:

- **Do not exaggerate the tribute.** If you are too lavish with your praise or use too many superlatives, you may embarrass the recipient and make the praise unbelievable.

 **Watch** at **MyCommunicationLab**
Video: "Tribute to Nike Founder"

■ **Focus on the person being honored, not on yourself.** Even if you know what effort the accomplishment required because you have done something similar, don't mention that at this time. It will come across as conceit when the focus should be on the honoree.

■ **Create vivid images of accomplishment.** Tell stories that make the honoree's accomplishments come to life, using colorful language and concrete examples.

■ **Be sincere.** Speeches of tribute are a time for warmth, pride, and appreciation. Your manner should reflect these qualities as you present the tribute.

When you honor a historical figure, your purpose will often be to promote values represented by the person's life. In his speech accepting the Human Rights Award, John Bakke paid tribute to Dr. King's faith in nonviolence and to his holding fast to that faith, even in the face of criticism from friends as well as enemies. Bakke gave new life to the concept of nonviolence by expanding and exploring its meaning for our time. Note how he used parallel structure and antithesis and how he challenged his listeners to redefine their roles in the political process:

> Taylor Branch has asserted, "Nonviolence is an orphan among democratic ideas," but, "Every ballot is a piece of nonviolence. . . ."
> It's time to make that ballot the effect of full democratic participation. It's time to reclaim our democratic processes. It's time to make the democratic processes work in America just as we are trying to make them work for others.
> That means more than voting. It means informed voting. It means supporting candidates and policies of our choice. It means commitment to the communication processes that give life to democracy. It means thinking of ourselves more as citizens than as just taxpayers. It means full-time citizenship. If campaigns are now permanent, citizenship cannot be cyclical. Democracy and "the vote" will always be open to criticism if people do not vote or do not know what they are voting for.[8]

Award Presentations.   An **award presentation** calls for a speech that

Watch at
MyCommunicationLab
Video: "Presenting a
Dance Award"

■ explains the nature of the award.

■ recognizes those who made it possible.

■ honors the recipients and celebrates their accomplishments.

If an award is already well known, such as the Nobel Peace Prize, you can emphasize why the recipient deserves such prestigious recognition. Thus, when Elie Wiesel received the 1986 Nobel Peace Prize, Egil Aarvik, chairman of the Norwegian Nobel Committee, focused on Wiesel's unique accomplishments. Wiesel had not only survived the Nazi death camps—he had also become a champion of the human spirit (see Wiesel's moving acceptance speech in Appendix B):

> From the abyss of the death camps he has come as a messenger to mankind—not with a message of hate and revenge, but with one of brotherhood and atonement. . . . Elie Wiesel is not only the man who survived—he is also the spirit which has conquered. In him we see a man who has climbed from utter humiliation to become one of our most important spiritual leaders and guides. . . . The Holocaust was a war within a war, a world in itself, a kingdom

▶ **award presentation**   A speech that explains the nature of the award and recognizes the achievements of the award recipient.

of darkness where there existed an evil so monstrous that it shattered all political and moral codes. . . .

His mission is not to gain the world's sympathy for the victims or the survivors. His aim is to awaken our conscience. Our indifference to evil makes us partners in the crime. . . . We know that the unimaginable has happened. What are we doing now to prevent it happening again?. . .

It is in recognition of this particular human spirit's victory over the powers of death and degradation, and as a support to the rebellion of good against the evil in the world, that the Norwegian Nobel Committee today presents the Nobel Peace Prize to Elie Wiesel.[9]

This award presentation demonstrates how you should emphasize the uniqueness, superiority, and benefits of the recipient's achievements.

Eulogies.   A **eulogy** is a short presentation given at a funeral or memorial service. When pop singer Whitney Houston died in 2012, her costar in *The Bodyguard*, Kevin Costner, was invited to speak at her funeral. He suggested to her children that he and their mother had a lot in common. "Really? [laughter from the audience] She's a girl, you're a boy. You're white, she's black." Costner noted that Whitney was driven by questioning whether or not she was good enough, pretty enough. "Whitney if you could hear me now I would tell you, you weren't just good enough—you were great. You sang the whole damn song without a band. You made the picture what it was."[10]

When you are asked to present a eulogy, you face special challenges. In addition to dealing with natural communication anxiety, you must also control your own feelings of grief. Plan your eulogy with these thoughts in mind:

- The primary purpose of a eulogy is to offer comfort to the living. Try to provide words that will continue to warm listeners in the days, months, and years ahead.

- Share stories that highlight the humanity of the person. Use gentle humor to recall his or her endearing qualities.

- Make the eulogy a celebration of life. Focus more on how wonderful it was to have shared the life of the person than on the pain of the loss.

- Emphasize the person's life as a model for those who live on.

Toasts.   A **toast** is a ceremonial speech in miniature. It is offered as a tribute to people, as a blessing for their future, or simply as a bit of lighthearted enjoyment of the present. You might be asked to toast a coworker who has been promoted or a couple at a wedding reception or simply to celebrate the beginning of a new year. The occasion may be formal or informal, but the message should always be eloquent. It simply won't do to mutter, "Here's to Tony, he's a great guy!" or "Cheers!" As one writer has said, such a feeble toast is "a gratuitous betrayal—of the occasion, its honoree, and the desire [of the audience] to clink glasses and murmur, 'Hear, hear,' in appreciation of a compliment well fashioned."[11]

Because toasts should be brief, every word must count. Plan your toast well in advance of the occasion. Memorize it so that you say exactly what you want to say

Watch at **MyCommunicationLab**
Video: "Eulogy for Charlie Brown"

Watch at **MyCommunicationLab**
Video: "Grandmother Swanson: A Toast to You"

A toast, a ceremonial speech in miniature, is offered as a tribute to people, as a blessing for their future, or simply in lighthearted enjoyment of the moment.

▶ **eulogy**   A speech of tribute presented upon a person's death.

▶ **toast**   A short speech of tribute, usually offered at celebration dinners or meetings.

FINDING YOUR

voice

"I propose a toast. . ."

Prepare a toast honoring a classmate whom you feel has made great progress as a speaker this semester or has given a speech you will long remember. Keep these rules in mind: Make it short and sweet, make it striking, and, above all, toast, don't roast!

Watch at
MyCommunicationLab
Video: "A Wedding Toast"

exactly as you want to say it. Practice presenting your toast with glass in hand until it flows easily. If you have difficulty memorizing your toast, it is probably too long. Some years ago we attended a dinner for graduating seniors. One of the speakers offered a memorable toast:

> As you graduate, I'm offering you a gift of wisdom that some say originated with Mark Twain. Twenty years from now you'll be more disappointed by the things you didn't do than by the things you did. So throw off the bowlines, sail away from the safe harbor, and catch the trade winds. Explore, dream, learn, grow, and discover. Here's to the adventurous life that awaits you!

While a touch of humor is often appropriate, a toast should never embarrass or humiliate the honoree.[12] For example, it would certainly be inappropriate at a wedding reception to say, "Here's to John and Mary. I hope they don't end up in divorce court the way I did!" Figure 16.2 offers some additional sample toasts.

FIGURE 16.2
Sample Toasts

- May you have warm words on a cold evening, a full moon on a dark night, and a road downhill all the way to your door. (Irish blessing)

- Here's looking at you, kid. (Humphrey Bogart toasting Ingrid Bergman in *Casablanca*)

- I drink to your charm, your beauty, and your brains—Which gives you a rough idea of how hard up I am for a drink. (Groucho Marx)

- To get the full value of joy, you must have someone to divide it with. (Mark Twain)

- May you have the hindsight to know where you've been, the foresight to know where you're going, and the insight to know when you're going too far.

- As you ramble through life, whatever be your goal, keep your eye upon the doughnut, and not upon the hole. (Offered by Sid Pettigrew)

- May the road rise to meet you.
  May the wind be always at your back.
  May the sun shine warm upon your face.
  And rains fall soft upon your fields.
  And until we meet again,
  May God hold you in the hollow of His hand. (Irish blessing)*

* From "Tom's Toasts: Irish Toasts and Blessings," March 1998.
  http://zinnia.umfacad.maine.edu/~donaghue/toasts01.html (16 Dec. 1998).

Acceptance Speeches

If you are receiving an award or honor, you may be expected to respond with an **acceptance speech**. A speech of acceptance should express your appreciation of the honor and acknowledge others who made it possible. You should be humble, focusing on the values the award represents. Both your language and your manner should reflect the dignity of the occasion.

When Elie Wiesel was awarded the Nobel Peace Prize, he began his acceptance speech with these remarks: "It is with a profound sense of humility that I accept the honor you have chosen to bestow upon me."[13] Follow his lead, and accept an award with grace and modesty. As you accept an award, consider its deeper meaning. In his acceptance speech, Mr. Wiesel stressed the value of freedom and the importance of involvement—of overcoming hatred with loving concern.

Finally, be sure the eloquence of your language fits the dignity of the moment. Wiesel told the story of a "young Jewish boy discovering the kingdom of night" during the Holocaust. This personal, metaphorical narrative was introduced early in the speech and repeated in the conclusion when Mr. Wiesel remarked, "No one is as capable of gratitude as one who has emerged from the kingdom of night." Although you may not be so eloquent, your presentation should befit the dignity of the occasion.

Watch at
MyCommunicationLab
Video: "Accepting a Dance Award"

Watch at
MyCommunicationLab
Video: "Award Acceptance Speech"

Speeches of Introduction

When you are called on to introduce a featured speaker to the audience, you will present a **speech of introduction**. The importance of this speech may vary depending on how well known the speaker is. At times, a formal introduction may be unnecessary. For example, when Madonna introduced Muhammad Ali at a gathering of New York sports personalities, she simply said:

> We are alike in many ways. We have espoused unpopular causes, we are arrogant, we like to have our picture taken, and we are the greatest.[14]

A good speech of introduction usually does three things: It makes the speaker feel welcome, strengthens the ethos of the speaker, and prepares the audience for the speech that will follow. You make a speaker feel welcome by both what you say and how you say it. Deliver your words of welcome with warmth and sincerity.

As soon as you know you will be introducing someone, find out as much as you can about him or her. Talk with the person about what you might emphasize, and avoid making assumptions. One of our favorite stories has to do with the famous western artist and writer Charles M. Russell. Russell did not particularly enjoy public speaking, but on one occasion his wife, Nancy, talked him into speaking at a

---

FINDING YOUR

voice   Your Dream Award

Prepare the acceptance speech you would love to give for the award you would love to receive.

▶ **speech of acceptance** A ceremonial speech expressing gratitude for an honor and acknowledging those who made the accomplishment possible.

▶ **speech of introduction** A ceremonial speech in which a featured speaker is introduced to the audience.

civic gathering in Montana. The toastmaster did not bother to talk to Charlie before the speech, deciding on his own to introduce him as a "famous pioneer." As western historian Bob Doerk described the event, this is how Charlie responded:

> "I have been called a pioneer. In my book a 'pioneer' is a man who comes to a virgin country, traps off all the fur, kills off all the wild meat, cuts down all the trees, grazes off all the grass, plows the roots up, and strings ten million miles of barbed wire. A pioneer destroys things and calls it 'civilization.' I wish to God that this country was just like it was when I first saw it and that none of you folks were here at all."
>
> About this time he realized that he had insulted his audience. He grabbed his hat and, in the boots and desperado sash that he always wore, left the room.[15]

So much for assuming that you know what the speaker values and how he or she would like to be introduced!

Although it may seem obvious, be sure also that you know how to pronounce the speaker's name. We have heard John Bakke speak many times, and we have heard introducers butcher his name on more than one occasion.

The following guidelines will help you build the speaker's ethos and lay the groundwork for speaker–audience identification:

- Create respect by briefly discussing the speaker's main accomplishments.

- Don't be too lavish with your praise. An overblown introduction can be embarrassing to the speaker and can create unreasonable expectations for the speech. We ourselves have been introduced along these lines: "These folks know so much about speaking that I'm sure we can expect a great speech." When that happens, you would just as soon not be introduced!

- Mention achievements that are relevant to the speaker's message, the occasion on which the speech is being presented, or the audience that has assembled.

- Be selective! Introducers who drone on too long can create real problems for the speakers who must follow them.

The final function of an effective introduction is to tune the audience. In Chapter 5, we discussed how preliminary tuning can put listeners in a receptive mood. You tune the audience when you arouse anticipation for the message that will follow. However, don't try to preview what the speaker will say. Let the speaker present the speech.

SPEAKER'S notes   Introducing a Featured Speaker

When you are called on to introduce a featured speaker, keep the following in mind as you prepare your remarks:

1. Be sure you can pronounce the speaker's name.
2. Find out what the speaker would like you to emphasize.
3. Focus on aspects of the speaker's background that are relevant to the topic, audience, and occasion.
4. Announce the title of the speech, and tune the audience for it.
5. Make the speaker feel welcome. Be warm and gracious.
6. Be brief!

Speeches of Inspiration

A **speech of inspiration** helps an audience appreciate, commit to, and pursue a goal or set of values or beliefs. These speeches may be religious, commercial, political, or social. When a sales manager introduces a new product to marketing representatives, pointing up its competitive advantages and its stellar market potential, the speech is both inspirational and persuasive. The marketing reps should feel inspired to push that product with great zeal and enthusiasm. Speeches at political conventions, such as keynote addresses that praise the principles of the party, are inspirational. So also is that great American institution, the commencement address. As different as these speech occasions may seem, they have important points in common.

First, *speeches of inspiration are enthusiastic.* Inspirational speakers set an example through their personal commitment and energy. Both the speaker and the speech must be active and forceful. Speakers offer a model for their audiences through their behavior both on and off the speaking platform. They must practice what they preach.

Second, *speeches of inspiration draw on past successes or frustrations to encourage future accomplishment.* In a commencement speech at Stanford University, the late Steve Jobs, co-founder of Apple, told the story of how he had been fired when he was 30 years old and the company was worth two billion dollars. "It was devastating," he said.

> Then it turned out that getting fired from Apple was the best thing that could have ever happened to me. The heaviness of being successful was replaced by the lightness of being a beginner again, less sure about everything. It freed me to enter one of the most creative periods of my life.
>
> During the next five years, I started a company named NeXT, another company named Pixar, and fell in love with an amazing woman who would become my wife. Pixar went on to create the world's first computer animated feature film, *Toy Story*, and is now the most successful animation studio in the world. In a remarkable turn of events, Apple bought NeXT, I returned to Apple, and the technology we developed at NeXT is at the heart of Apple's current renaissance. And Laurene and I have a wonderful family together.[16]

The implication was clear: Out of apparent failure can arise spectacular success.

Third, *speeches of inspiration revitalize our appreciation for values or beliefs.* In the later years of his life, after his athletic prowess had faded, Jesse Owens became known as a great inspirational speaker. According to a an obituary reported in the *Cogressional Record,* "The Jesse Owens best remembered by many Americans was a public speaker with the ringing, inspirational delivery of an evangelist. . . . [His speeches] praised the virtues of patriotism, clean living and fair play."[17]

The following excerpts, taken from a statement protesting America's withdrawal from the 1980 Summer Olympic Games, illustrate his inspirational style. Jesse Owens was unable to deliver this message personally. He prepared it shortly before his death from cancer.

> What the Berlin games proved . . . was that Hitler's "supermen" could be beaten. Ironically, it was one of his blond, blue-eyed, Aryan athletes who helped do the beating.

Steve Jobs, speaking at Stanford graduation ceremonies, gave an inspiring commencement address that described how past career frustrations ultimately led to his current successes.

Owens's introduction suggests the larger meaning of his victories and sets the stage for identification.

▶ **speech of inspiration** A ceremonial speech directed at awakening or reawakening an audience to a goal, purpose, or set of values.

Note the use of graphic detail to recapture the immediacy of the moment.

I held the world record in the broad jump. Even more than the sprints, it was "my" event. Yet I was one jump from not even making the finals. I fouled on my first try, and playing it safe the second time, I had not jumped far enough.

The broad jump preliminaries came before the finals of my other three events and everything, it seemed then, depended on this jump. Fear swept over me and then panic. I walked off alone, trying to gather myself. I dropped to one knee, closed my eyes, and prayed. I felt a hand on my shoulder. I opened my eyes and there stood my arch enemy, Luz Long, the prize athlete Hitler had kept under wraps while he trained for one purpose only: to beat me. Long had broken the Olympic mark in his very first try in the preliminaries.

Owens's use of dialogue helps listeners feel they are sharing the experience.

"I know about you," he said. "You are like me. You must do it all the way, or you cannot do it. The same that has happened to you today happened to me last year in Cologne. I will tell you what I did then." Luz told me to measure my steps, place my towel 6 inches on back of the takeoff board and jump from there. That way I could give it all I had and be certain not to foul.

As soon as I had qualified, Luz, smiling broadly, came to me and said, "Now we can make each other do our best in the finals."

And that's what we did in the finals. Luz jumped and broke his Olympic record. Then I jumped just a bit further and broke Luz's new record. We each had three leaps in all. On his final jump, Luz went almost 26 feet, 5 inches, a mark that seemed impossible to beat. I went just a bit over that and set an Olympic record that was to last for almost a quarter of a century.

This narrative leaves open the meaning of Owens's "inside" victory: Perhaps it was over self-doubt or over his own stereotype of Germans. Perhaps it was over both.

I won that day, but I'm being straight when I say that even before I made that last jump, I knew I had won a victory of a far greater kind—over something inside myself, thanks to Luz.

This scene presents an inspirational model of international competition.

The instant my record-breaking win was announced, Luz was there, throwing his arms around me and raising my arm to the sky. "Jazze Owenz!" he yelled as loud as he could. More than 100,000 Germans in the stadium joined in. "Jazze Owenz, Jazze Owenz, Jazze Owenz!"

Owens shows how individuals can rise above ideologies, as Long's final message invites identification.

Hitler was there, too, but he was not chanting. He had lost that day. Luz Long was killed in World War II and, although I don't cry often, I wept when I received his last letter—I knew it was his last. In it he asked me to someday find his son, Karl, and to tell him "of how we fought well together, and of the good times, and that any two men can become brothers."

Owens ends with a metaphor of the "road to the Olympics."

That is what the Olympics are all about. The road to the Olympics does not lead to Moscow. It leads to no city, no country. It goes far beyond Lake Placid or Moscow, ancient Greece or Nazi Germany. The road to the Olympics leads, in the end, to the best within us.[18]

After-Dinner Speeches

Watch at
MyCommunicationLab
Video: "After Dinner
Speech"

Occasions that celebrate special events or that mark the beginning or end of something often call for special dinners and provide the setting for an **after-dinner speech**. Political rallies, award banquets, the kickoff for a fund-raising campaign, and the end of the school year are just a few examples of such occasions.

The after-dinner speech is one of the great rituals of American public life. You may be asked to give an after-dinner speech if you are the leader of the group sponsoring the dinner or if you simply have the reputation for being an entertaining speaker. The purpose of an after-dinner speech may range from celebrating group accomplishments to sharing laughter that can enrich lives and bond groups more closely together.

▶ **after-dinner speech** An often humorous ceremonial speech presented after a meal that offers a message without asking for radical changes.

Almost all after-dinner speeches share certain features. In keeping with the nature of the occasion, they should not be too difficult to digest. This is not a time to introduce radical ideas that require listeners to rethink their values or to ask for dramatic changes in belief or behavior. Nor is it a time for anger or negative thoughts. Rather, it is a time for people to savor who they are, what they have done, or what they wish to do. A good after-dinner speech typically leaves a message that guides and inspires future efforts.

The Role of Humor. Humor is appropriate for most after-dinner speeches. In the introduction, humor can place both the speaker and the audience at ease.[19] Enjoying lighter moments can remind us that there is a human element in all situations and that we should not take ourselves too seriously.

Communication scholar Diane Martin has identified a range of functions that humor can serve in speeches.[20] For example, humorous stories can create identification by building an "insider's" relationship between speaker and audience that draws them closer together. In sharing humor, the audience becomes a community of listeners.[21] Another study has discovered that the use of humorous illustrations helps audiences remember the message of the speech.[22]

However, speakers should play to their strengths. Humor should not be forced on a speech. If you decide to begin with a joke simply because you think a speech should start that way, the humor may fall flat. Rather, humor should be functional, relevant, and useful in making a point.

The humor in a speech is best developed out of the immediate situation. Dick Jackman, director of corporate communications at Sun Company, opened an after-dinner speech at a National Football Foundation awards dinner by warning those in the expensive seats under the big chandelier that it "had been installed by the low bidder some time ago."[23] Such references are often made more effective by a touch of self-deprecation.[24] In the spring of 2007, with his approval ratings lower than those of any sitting president in over twenty-five years, President George W. Bush used humor to poke fun at himself and his situation as he spoke at an annual dinner for media correspondents:

Seth MacFarlane, creator of TV's *Family Guy*, used humor, skits, and song when he emceed the Academy Awards Ceremony.

> Well, where should I start? A year ago, my approval rating was in the 30s, my nominee for the Supreme Court had just withdrawn, and my Vice President had shot someone. [laughter] Ahh, those were the good old days. [laughter and applause][25]

Effective humor requires thoughtful planning. If not handled well, it can be a disaster. For example, religious humor is dangerous, and racist or sexist humor is unacceptable. In general, avoid any anecdotes that are funny at the expense of others.

Developing an After-Dinner Speech. After-dinner speeches are more difficult to develop than their lightheartedness might suggest. Like most speeches, they should be carefully planned and practiced. They should have an effective introduction that commands attention because some audience members may be more interested in talking to table companions than listening to the speaker. After-dinner speeches should be more than strings of anecdotes to amuse listeners. The stories told must establish a mood, convey a message, or carry a theme forward. Such speeches should build to a satisfying conclusion that brings home the essence of the message.

Above all, perhaps, after-dinner speeches should be mercifully brief. Long-winded after-dinner speakers can leave the audience fiddling with coffee cups and drawing pictures on napkins. After being subjected to such a speech, Albert Einstein once murmured: "I have just got a new theory of eternity."[26]

Acting as a Master of Ceremonies

Quite often, ceremonial speeches are part of a program of events that must be coordinated with skill and grace if things are to run smoothly. It takes at least as much careful planning, preparation, and practice to function effectively as a **master of ceremonies** as it does to make a major presentation. As the master of ceremonies, you will be expected to keep the program moving, introduce participants, and possibly present awards. You will also set the tone or mood for the program.

If possible, you should be involved in planning the program from the beginning. Being involved will give you a better idea of what is expected of you, what the agenda will be, what the time constraints are, who the featured speakers will be, and what special logistics (such as meal service) you might have to contend with. The following guidelines should help you function effectively as a master of ceremonies:

- **Know what is expected of you.** Remember, as master of ceremonies (emcee), you are not the star of the show. You are the one who brings it all together and makes it work.

- **Plan a good opener for the program.** Your opening remarks as an emcee are as important as the introduction to a major presentation. You should gain the attention of those in the audience and prepare them for the program. Be sure that the mood you set with your opener is consistent with the nature of the occasion.

- **Be prepared to introduce the participants.** Find out all you can about the speakers in advance: Search the Internet, check *Who's Who*, and examine newspaper clipping files. Ask them what they would like you to emphasize, and decide how you might best tune the audience for their speeches. Be sure you know how to pronounce the speakers' names.

- **Know the schedule and timetable so that you can keep the program on track.** You also need to be sure that the participants get this information. They need to know how much time has been allotted for them to speak. Review the schedule with them before the program, and work out some way to cue them in case they are running overtime. If time restrictions are strict, as in a televised program, be ready to edit and adapt your own planned comments if necessary.

- **Make certain that any prizes or awards are kept within reach.** You don't need to be fumbling around looking for a plaque.

- **Plan your comments ahead of time.** Develop a key-word outline for each presentation on a running script of the program. Number these outlines. Print the name of the person or award in large letters at the top of each outline so that you can keep to the schedule.

▶ **master of ceremonies**   A person who coordinates an event or program, sets its mood, introduces, and provides transitions.

- **Practice your presentation.** Although you are not the featured speaker, your words are important (especially to the person whom you will introduce or to the person who will receive the award you present). Practice your comments the same way you would practice a speech.

- **Make advance arrangements for mealtime logistics.** Speak with the maître d' before the program to be sure the waiters know the importance of "silent service."

- **Be ready for the inevitable glitches.** Remember Murphy's Law: If anything can go wrong, it will. Be ready for problems like microphones that don't work or that squeal, trays of dishes being dropped, and people wandering in and out during the course of the program. As you respond to these events, keep your cool and good humor.

- **End the program strongly.** Just as a speech should not dwindle into nothingness, neither should a program. Review the suggestions for speech conclusions in Chapter 9. When ending your presentation, thank those who made the program possible, and then leave the audience with something to remember.[27]

Narrative Design

In Chapters 8 and 9, we discussed how storytelling helps structure and support a speech. In ceremonial speaking, narrative plays an especially important role. Because by nature we are attracted to stories, good narratives can gain and hold our attention. They describe actions, and actions can bring us together and emphasize the moral qualities they illuminate. Thus, narratives are central to identification and magnification, the two basic techniques of ceremonial speaking.

 **Watch** at MyCommunicationLab Video: "Tribute to a Mentor"

As you may recall from Chapter 8, **embedded narratives** are stories within speeches, and **vicarious experience narratives** invite listeners *into* speeches, asking them to imagine themselves participating in the action as it unfolds. The late President Ronald Reagan was a master of both forms. Note how he encouraged listeners to *enter* the story he presented in his second inaugural address:

> Hear again the echoes of our past.
> A general falls to his knees in the harsh snow of Valley Forge; a lonely President paces the darkened hall and ponders his struggle to preserve the Union; the men of the Alamo call out encouragement to each other; a settler pushes West and sings a song, and the song echoes out forever and fills the unknowing air.
> It is the American Sound. It is hopeful, big-hearted, idealistic—daring, decent and fair. That's our heritage. That's our song.[28]

In the **master narrative**, the entire speech becomes a story that reveals some important truth. We saw a good example of this as Jesse Owens told of his experience at the 1936 Olympic Games.

As we noted in Chapter 3, the **narrative design** differs from other speech design formats. Most designs associated with informative and persuasive speaking follow a linear, logical pattern, in which the points develop and follow each other in reasoned sequence. But the narrative design follows a dramatic pattern of development so that the speech presents a sequence of scenes that build a mini-drama. Such a design features three major components: prologue, plot, and epilogue.

▶ **embedded narrative**   A story inserted within a speech that illustrates the speaker's point.

▶ **vicarious experience narrative** Speech strategy in which the speaker invites listeners to imagine themselves enacting a story.

▶ **master narrative**   A speech that is structured around a story that reveals some important truth.
▶ **narrative design**   Speech structure that develops a story from beginning to end through a prologue, plot, and epilogue.

Prologue

The **prologue** in the narrative design sets the scene for what will follow. It is the counterpart of the introduction in other speech designs. The prologue orients listeners to the context of the action so that they can make sense of it. It foreshadows the meaning and importance of the story that will follow. It also introduces the important characters that will be part of the story.

To see these elements in action, consider again the prologue to Jesse Owens's speech on the 1936 Olympics:

> What the Berlin games proved . . . was that Hitler's "supermen" could be beaten. Ironically, it was one of his blond, blue-eyed, Aryan athletes who helped do the beating.
>
> I held the world record in the broad jump. Even more than the sprints, it was "my" event. Yet I was one jump from not even making the finals. I fouled on my first try, and playing it safe the second time, I had not jumped far enough.

The first two sentences of this prologue foreshadow the meaning of the story. They help prepare listeners for the actions that will unfold within the plot. They also anticipate the major character who will develop within the speech, Luz Long. The final four sentences present the context and setting of the story, the fact that Owens held the world record and was favored and the crisis he now had to confront.

Plot

The **plot** acts as the body of a narrative speech. Within the plot, two important things must occur. First, *the action of the story must build suspense, leading up to a climax.* Colorful details and lively dialogue make the action come to life. Second, *the main characters must become three-dimensional as they participate in the action.* This means that they come to stand for things, just as Luz Long, Hitler's hero, ironically comes to stand for fair play, brotherhood, and the virtues of competition.

Let's return to the Owens speech. The plot develops in three closely related scenes: (1) the time immediately before the competition, (2) the competition itself, and (3) the aftermath of the competition.

In the first scene, we watch a crisis of doubt as Owens kneels to pray. We are also introduced to the generous spirit of Luz Long, who appears on cue as though he were the answer to Owens's prayer and who offers the advice Owens needs to qualify for his event. Owens re-creates the immediacy of the moment by using dialogue as Long speaks.

The second scene, which describes the competition itself, is summarized rather quickly. In the third scene, the aftermath, the real business of the speech takes place. Its purpose is to portray Luz Long as an Olympic ideal. The fact that Long is a German, and even that Hitler considers him to be the champion of Nazi ideology, adds deep irony to the portrait.

Owens's message is that sportsmanship transcends both national origin and political affiliation and joins competitors together. Thus, we behold the extraordinary spectacle after the competition when Luz Long joins hands with Owens, raising their arms to the sky as he leads the crowd in chanting, "Jazze Owenz."

▶ **prologue**   An opening that establishes the context and setting of a narrative, foreshadows the meaning, and introduces major characters.

▶ **plot**   The body of a speech that follows a narrative design; it unfolds in a sequence of scenes designed to build suspense.

Epilogue

The **epilogue** of a narrative reflects on the meaning of the action and offers final comments on the character of those who participated in it. It is the counterpart of the conclusion in other speech designs. When used in ceremonial speeches, the epilogue often conveys a moral. In the Owens example, we see the nobility of Luz Long reaffirmed in the final scene of the story:

> Luz Long was killed in World War II and, although I don't cry often, I wept when I received his last letter—I knew it was his last. In it he asked me to someday find his son, Karl, and to tell him "of how we fought well together, and of the good times, and that any two men can become brothers."

What Owens doesn't quite tell us, but we can infer it from what he says, is that Long and Owens had become good friends, that they corresponded often, and that Long knew that his end was near. These inferences only strengthen the underlying lesson for the audience Owens addressed in 1980:

> That is what the Olympics are all about. The road to the Olympics does not lead to Moscow. It leads to no city, no country. It goes far beyond Lake Placid or Moscow, ancient Greece or Nazi Germany. The road to the Olympics leads, in the end, to the best within us.

Just as the Olympic spirit could thrive in the bigoted atmosphere of Nazi Germany in 1936, so also could it blossom in the Cold War atmosphere of Moscow in 1980. Owens's speech became an argument criticizing America's 1980 boycott of the Olympic Games. A video showing this dramatic encounter may be found in the Public Broadcasting System's archive of *American Experience*.

FINAL reflections   "And in Conclusion Let Us Say"

We began our book by encouraging your quest to find your voice. We hope that your quest has been successful and that you have benefited, are benefiting, and will continue to benefit from it. We end our book with our own speech of tribute, this time to you. Public speaking may not have always been easy for you. But it is our hope that you have grown as a person as you have grown as a speaker. Our special wishes, expressed in terms of the underlying vision of our book, are

- that you have learned to climb the barriers that people sometimes erect to separate themselves from each other and that too often prevent meaningful communication.

▶ **epilogue** The final part of a narrative that reflects upon its meaning.

- that you have learned to weave words and evidence into eloquent thoughts and persuasive ideas.

- that you have learned to build and present speeches that enlighten others in responsible and ethical ways.

- above all, that you have found subjects and causes worthy of your voice.

And so we propose a toast: *May you use your new speaking skills to improve the lives and lift the spirits of those who may listen to you.*

After Reading This Chapter, You Should Be Able To Answer These Questions

Study and
Review at
MyCommunicationLab

1 What are the values and uses of ceremonial speaking?

2 How can you develop a sense of identification between yourself and listeners?

3 What purpose does magnification serve, and how can you make it work?

4 What are the different kinds of ceremonial speeches, and how should you prepare for them?

5 What skills are required to be a master of ceremonies?

6 How can you use narrative design to tell an effective story?

For Discussion and Further Exploration

1 Watch the commencement speech "How to Live Before You Die," offered at Stanford University by the late Steve Jobs. (The speech can be found under "Inspirational Speeches" on TED.) Look for the processes of identification and magnification at work in the speech. Do they work effectively?

2 Develop a speech of tribute to yourself as you would like to be remembered. What do you hope to accomplish? What do you stand for? What values give meaning to your life?

3 Prepare a speech of tribute in which you honor a person or group that has contributed to the cause advanced in your persuasive speech.

4 For and against magnification: Some might argue that magnification is distortion, that when you select a person's achievements and accomplishments to praise in speeches of tribute, you are ignoring less desirable features and shortcomings. The effect is to revise and misrepresent reality. What is your position on this issue? Is magnification justifiable? Are there moments in which it might not be desirable?

5 Prepare a speech of introduction for a historical figure you admire, as though that person will then be speaking to the class. Do you use identification and magnification in your introductory remarks?

SAMPLE CEREMONIAL SPEECH

Simone Mullinax presented this speech of tribute to her grandmother in a public speaking class at the University of Arkansas. The speech develops a master narrative based on an extended metaphor and paints an endearing portrait of a complex person who—like key lime pie—combines the qualities of sweetness and tartness.

Baked-In Traditions

SIMONE MULLINAX

Have you ever baked a pie? No, I don't mean one you get from the freezer section at the grocery store—I'm talking about one you bake from scratch. I learned to bake a pie at an early age. And what I learned, early on, is that there are three things you have to master: the crust, the filler, and the topping. You can't have a pie if you lack any of these.

So where do you start? You start of course in the kitchen, which is where I meet my grandmother every time we get together. I would like to tell you she's that sweet, picturesque, grandmotherly grandmother you see on television, but she's not. Rather, she's that opinionated, bold, "her-way-or-the-highway" type that scares some people off. Her salvation is that she's also insanely funny and you fall in love with her stories, her cooking, and her opinions, even when you don't agree with all of them. Just when you're ready to pack up and move on, she does or says something that makes you want to hang around.

She's the woman who marches to the front of the line when her "babies" don't get what they need. She's the woman who sends us care packages made up of "goodies" from Dollar General. She's the woman who offers her opinions to everyone on any occasion, whether they want them or not. She's also the woman who gathered all the family recipes together—some of them unique and over a hundred years old—and gave them to me for a Christmas present. She's my grandmother and my best friend.

But back to baking pies. My signature pie is a key lime pie. It really isn't my signature at all because I frequently forge my grandmother's. People often think of it as a hot weather treat, but every time we are together, even if it's 23 degrees outside, we make that key lime pie. Last year before I competed in the Miss Oklahoma pageant, a reporter called and asked what I was most looking forward to eating after the competition, and I said, "A key lime pie. A whole key lime pie." It was in bold headlines the next day: "Miss Tulsa looking forward to eating a pie." For weeks afterwards people asked me, "So did you get your key lime pie?" And I was able to answer, "Sure did." Because after the pageant my grandmother had two pies sitting on the counter, one for now, and one for later.

Grammy taught me you can't have the pie without the crust. Everything in her life is built on a firm foundation, from the love of her family to the strength of her husband and the companionship of her friends. She stands behind her word, her love, and her family. She is the crust that keeps us all

◀ This brief opening does a great deal of work. Simone opens with a rhetorical question and a definition and establishes her personal ethos. She then hints of a clever categorical design that will follow the three main ingredients of a pie.

◀ This paragraph completes the sketch that introduces Simone's grandmother. Simone paints this portrait by offering a few glimpses of her grandmother in action, small slices of life that depict character.

◀ As she tells us more about pies, Simone also reveals more about herself. We learn that she has been a beauty pageant contestant who has a particular fondness for key lime pies.

This begins an elaboration of the pie as extended metaphor in order to reveal
◀ the value and values of her grandmother. Family connectedness is an underlying theme.

together, and also—I might add—all in line. Many times I have called Grammy with problems or confessions, and then I will hear advice like, "Oh, you don't need to do that, honey." And I know that, but her reminding me makes my own foundation that much stronger. Nothing crumbles in her key lime pie, especially the crust.

These discussions of the filling and the toppings offer Simone an opportunity to develop other aspects of her grandmother's character—her urge to help others build character and her willingness to go beyond the ordinary in order to accomplish worthwhile purposes. ▶

What would a pie be without the filling? Some are lemon or pecan or pumpkin or chocolate or apple or—of course—key lime. But that is what makes each pie unique when you take that first delicious bite. Grammy fills her own life with meaning: one of her favorite sayings is, "Comfort the afflicted and afflict the comfortable." She believes in character-building, and in the value of striving for improvement: "Struggle to get better, struggle to succeed," but "Don't let success prevent you from struggling to get even better." The key lime, like her advice, is sweet—but it definitely has a bite to it!

The best part of the pie is the topping. Sometimes it's another layer of crust, sometimes it's meringue or whipped cream. The topping is that something extra that finishes the pie off. For Grammy, it's doing a little bit more than is necessary, a little bit more than what's expected. Part of it is literally going that extra mile. She and I walk together at 6:30 in the morning, because she says it's the only time of day when the sun doesn't beat you down. I am barely awake for some of these walks, and that extra mile she loves to walk is often uphill! Beyond that, Grammy's favorite toppings are good words, good deeds, and high expectations.

Inspired by her grandmother, Simone can see herself in the distant future baking pies with her own granddaughter and holding the same kinds of conversations. Her conclusion offers extraordinary poetic appreciation for this kind of pie baking. ▶

Years from now I will teach my own granddaughter to build a perfect key lime pie. As we make it I will be thinking about the woman whose love seeps into every crust holding me together. We will mix the fillings together and we will know just what to top it off with to make it perfect. And we will bake pies like friends hold conversations, the intricacies hidden beneath the taste and the impressions lasting beyond the words.

APPENDIX A
Communicating in Small Groups

Many of the important communication interactions in your life will occur while working in small groups. In school, you may be assigned to collaborate with your classmates on group projects. Modern technologies such as Skype and video-conferencing are making it increasingly convenient to schedule regular meetings that include people working from remote locations. Someday you may even find yourself elected to local office or representing the concerns of your neighbors before a gathering of your city council. Sooner or later you will likely participate in task-oriented small group discussions. Alongside the public speaking skills learned throughout this course, developing your ability to communicate in group settings will make a valuable contribution to finding your voice by enhancing your critical skills and nurturing your potential for leadership.

Of course, there are many kinds of human groups. A **small group** typically consists of *three to seven (not more than twelve) people who interact over a period of time in order to achieve a specific goal or set of goals.* For example, small groups may be formed to work on a specific project, to perform regular tasks important to running an organization or business, or to gather ideas and information for dealing with a problem or challenge to the group. Productive small-group interactions are well structured and focused on the task at hand. They follow a well-defined format or agenda, are marked by effective leadership and participation by group members, and occur within a climate of professionalism that fosters a rich and thorough discussion.

In this appendix, we open by considering some advantages and disadvantages of small-group communication. We then discuss some techniques of group problem solving, participating as leaders and members in group discussions, conducting formal meetings using parliamentary procedure, and some rewards and challenges of conducting virtual meetings. We close by considering the various types of presentations that you may be called upon to make in the context of working and communicating in small groups.

Advantages and Disadvantages of Group Problem Solving

There are many advantages to problem solving in small groups. When we listen to a single speaker, we hear one inherently limited version of a situation or problem. Small-group discussions provide a much broader array and cross-fertilization of ideas and perspectives. The process itself can stimulate creative thinking, illuminate misconceptions and biases, and even uncover areas of agreement that can help

▶ **small group** Limited number of people who interact over time to achieve a goal or goals.

385

resolve differences. In short, people who engage in constructive small-group discussions tend to make better, more informed decisions.

Although working in groups has many advantages, it also has some potential disadvantages. Absent the right structure and focus, individuals can be less productive in groups than when working alone. **Cultural gridlock**—communication problems based on deep cultural differences—may arise in groups when members come from different backgrounds. Participants from dissimilar social backgrounds may bring different perspectives, agendas, priorities, procedures, and ways of communicating to meetings. These differences may sidetrack constructive discussions.

Dealing with cultural gridlock is never easy, but the following guidelines will help minimize its impact:

1. Allow time for people to get acquainted before starting to work.

2. Distribute an agenda before the meeting so people know what to expect.

3. Summarize discussions as the meeting progresses. Post key points of agreement.

4. Avoid using jargon that some participants may not understand.

5. Be sensitive to cultural differences in how people relate to one another and to nonverbal communication norms.[1]

Another common drawback of group problem solving is **groupthink**, which occurs when participants uncritically accept and reinforce a single position without adequately considering reservations or alternative views.[2] Groupthink is likely to occur when the group lacks a clear set of procedures for working through problems, when members have not adequately prepared themselves for the discussion, or when harmonious interaction is prioritized over raising and exploring contrasting views and constructive criticisms. It is especially likely to occur when a particularly dynamic or domineering leader prematurely expresses his or her preference for a given position and then communicates in a manner that discourages participants from expressing opposing views and concerns.

Groupthink can be particularly dangerous when it leads people to believe that a given problem or proposal has been thoroughly discussed, when it fact it has not. Dealing with groupthink is difficult, but there are some steps you can take to guard against it. First, groups need to be aware that groupthink can be a problem. The major symptoms of groupthink include pressuring dissidents within the group and censoring their ideas, defending opinions more than exploring alternate ways of thinking, and asserting the group's own moral righteousness while attacking the character of opposing groups.

Once a group is aware that groupthink is a problem, the leader can take action to minimize its effects. The leader should encourage the group to set standards for investigation and appraisal that discourage uncritical thinking and hasty conclusions.

The following leadership behaviors can help reduce groupthink problems:

■ Insist that participants evaluate the support behind recommendations.

■ Urge members to delay decisions until all have expressed their views.

■ Encourage critical questions from participants.

■ Encourage debate of all recommendations.

▶ **cultural gridlock**   A problem that occurs when the cultural differences within a group create tensions that impede constructive discussion.

▶ **groupthink**   Occurs when group members uncritically accept and reinforce a single position on important issues or problems without adequately considering reservations or alternative positions.

Group Problem-Solving Techniques

Group deliberations that are orderly, systematic, and thorough help members reach better decisions. To function effectively, problem-solving groups can use a variety of methods or discussion formats. One of the most influential techniques of group problem-solving is called reflective thinking.

Reflective Thinking and Problem Solving

The reflective-thinking approach to group problem solving is a modification of a technique developed by John Dewey in 1910. This systematic approach has five steps: (1) defining the problem, (2) generating potential solutions, (3) evaluating solution options, (4) developing a plan of action, and (5) evaluating the results.

Step 1: Defining the Problem.   The first step is to define and analyze the problem. For instance, if you were assigned to a group charged with generating ideas for increasing minority enrollment at your university, you would first want to find reliable information on the status of minority enrollment at your university, the extent to which enrollment and retention rates have risen or fallen over the past few years, and whatever measures your university has already implemented to promote and maintain minority enrollment.

The following guidelines can help a group define an issue or problem it needs to work on:

1. Describe the problem as specifically as possible.

2. Gather enough information to understand the problem.

3. Explore the causes of the problem.

4. Investigate the history and duration of the problem.

5. Determine who is affected by the problem.

6. Consider the outcomes if the problem is solved or not solved.

Step 2: Generating Potential Solutions.   Once the problem has been defined, the group can begin looking for solutions. One useful technique for generating possible solutions is **brainstorming**. When brainstorming for ideas, each member contributes every idea she or he can think of, and these are recorded by a person designated by the group. Participants may combine ideas to create new ones, but no criticism or evaluation is allowed at this stage of the process, and no decisions are made regarding preferred solutions. Engaging in creative freewheeling and contributing outrageous ideas are actually encouraged. The point is to generate as many potential solutions as possible for later discussion.[3]

The process of brainstorming proceeds as follows:

1. The leader asks each member in turn to contribute an idea during each round. A member who does not have an idea may pass. At this stage, the emphasis is on full participation and the number of ideas advanced.

2. A recorder writes all ideas on a flip chart or marker board so everyone can see them.

3. Brainstorming continues until *all* members have contributed an idea or passed.

▶ **brainstorming** Technique that encourages the free play of the mind to generate a list of ideas for later careful consideration.

4. The suggestions are reviewed for clarification, new options are added, and options are combined.

5. The group identifies the most promising ideas.

6. The leader appoints members to research each idea and to bring additional information to a later evaluation meeting.

7. The process of gathering solution possibilities should remain open during this break. Additional ideas should be considered during the next phase of the problem-solving process.

To save time, many small groups use **electronic brainstorming**, in which participants generate ideas online before meeting face-to-face.[4] Electronic brainstorming has the advantage of getting group members thinking about potential ideas before the actual meeting. It may also help to elicit more input from members who might feel inhibited in face-to-face meetings due to perceived lack of status or identification with the group. It also gives group leaders a chance to encourage participants to clarify their ideas and research additional supporting materials as necessary.

Step 3: Evaluating Solution Options.   Once your group has generated a list of potential options, another meeting should be scheduled for evaluating, ranking, and choosing the best possible solutions. Members should use the time between meetings to gather more information and clarify their thinking. During the evaluation session, the following criteria should be used:

- Costs of the options

- Probability of success

- Ease or difficulty of enacting options

- Time constraints

- Additional benefits of options

- Potential problems of options

As the discussion proceeds, some proposals will be quickly discarded, others will be strengthened and refined, and still others may be combined to generate new alternatives. After all of the ideas have been considered, group members will often reduce their list to the few most promising options for further discussion. Final agreement on a solution or set of solutions is often reached through consensus or general agreement, although sometimes a vote is necessary when differences of opinion persist among group members.

Participants often become personally caught up with their own solutions. During the evaluation phase, the leader must keep the group focused on the ideas advanced. Differences of opinion and conflict are a natural and necessary part of problem solving. Discussing the strengths of an idea before talking about its weaknesses can help take some of the heat out of the process.

Step 4: Developing a Plan of Action.   Once the group has selected a solution, it should figure out how the solution can be implemented. For example, to improve company morale, a group might recommend a three-step plan:

▶ **electronic brainstorming** A group technique in which participants generate ideas online prior to meeting face-to-face.

1. Provide in-house training programs to increase opportunities for promotion.

2. Create a pay structure that rewards success in training programs.

3. Encourage more employee participation in decision making.

Once again, it is sometimes advisable to schedule a separate follow-up meeting for developing a plan of action. This gives group members more time to consider the logistics of implementing the proposed solution. Participants should consider what resources will be necessary to make their solution work, what factors might help or hinder their effectiveness, a reasonable timetable for achieving their objectives, and who will be responsible for implementing and overseeing the solution. If the group cannot develop a plan of action for the solution or if insurmountable obstacles crop up, they should return to Step 3 and reconsider other options.

Step 5: Evaluating Results.   A problem-solving group must also decide how to evaluate results of the plan's enactment. They should establish evaluation criteria for success, a timetable of when results are expected, and contingency plans to use if the original plan fails. For example, to monitor the ongoing success of the three-part plan to improve employee morale, the group would have to determine benchmarks of progress for each stage. That way the company can detect and correct problems as they occur, before they damage the plan as a whole. Having a scheduled sequence of benchmarks provides a way to determine results while the plan is being enacted rather than having to wait for the entire project to be completed.

Other Approaches to Group Problem Solving

When a group consists of people from very different backgrounds, **collaborative problem solving** may work best.[5] For example, in many urban areas, coalitions of business executives and educators have worked together on plans to train people for jobs in the community. In such situations, the problems are usually important and the resources are typically limited. Because there is no established authority structure and the factions may have different expectations or goals, these diverse participants may have problems working together. To be effective, such groups need to spend time defining the problem and exploring each other's perspectives. This should help them recognize their interdependence, while preserving the independence of each participant. In such groups, the participants must come to see themselves *not* as members of group A (the executives) or group B (the educators), but as members of group C (the coalition). Leadership can be especially difficult in such groups.

One useful approach in such situations is **dialogue groups**. According to William Isaacs, director of the Dialogue Project at the Massachusetts Institute of Technology Center for Organizational Learning (MIT Center), "Dialogue is a discipline of collective thinking and inquiry, a process for transforming the quality of conversation, and, in particular, the thinking that lies beneath it."[6] Rather than establishing a single approach to defining or dealing with a situation or problem, dialogue groups stress understanding the different interpretations and experiences that participants bring to the interaction. Their purpose is to establish a conversation from which common ground and mutual trust can emerge.

▶ **collaborative problem solving** In group communication, an approach that gathers participants from differing backgrounds and social sectors for their input on a problem.

▶ **dialogue group** A group assembled to explore the differing interpretations and experiences that members bring to a given situation or problem.

Leadership is critical in dialogue groups. According to Edgar Schein of the MIT Center, the facilitator must take the following steps:

1. Seat the group in a circle to create a sense of equality.

2. Introduce the problem.

3. Ask people to share an experience in which dialogue led to "good communication."

4. Ask members to consider what leads to good communication.

5. Ask participants to talk about their reactions.

6. Let the conversation flow naturally.

7. Intervene only to clarify problems of communication.

8. Conclude by asking all members to comment however they choose.[7]

The dialogue method is not a substitute for other problem-solving techniques. Instead, it may be used to provide an opportunity for members to understand each other well enough to be talking the same language as they work on solutions to problems.

When an organization wants to explore the feelings or motivations of customers or clients, they often hold a **focus group**.[8] Focus groups typically have six to ten members carefully selected to provide the type of information sought. In a focus group, the moderator asks questions and encourages all of the participants to respond. Advertisements, brochures, or video clips may also be used to stimulate discussion. Interactions between members of the group often provide the most valuable information. The sessions are recorded on either audiotape or videotape for later analysis. Focus groups are typically face-to-face encounters, but they may also be conducted through telephone conference calls, on the Internet, or through videoconferencing.

Participating in Small Groups

To work effectively in a small group, you must understand your individual responsibilities. You should also be prepared to assume leadership when called upon to do so.

Working as a Group Member

Becoming an effective group participant means prioritizing the business of the group and the question at hand over our own individual agendas and concerns. In addition, group members must accept the following responsibilities:

- First, come to meetings prepared to contribute. This means reading background materials and completing any tasks assigned by the group leader before attending a meeting.

- Second, be critically engaged yet open to learning from others. Contribute to discussions without dominating them, and don't get defensive or personal when your ideas are challenged. Finally, be willing to accept the decisions of the group and move on constructively even when your proposals are not accepted.

- Third, listen constructively. Don't interrupt others. Speak up if you feel consensus is forming too quickly. You might save the meeting from groupthink.

▶ **focus group**   A small group formed to reveal the feelings or motivations of customers or clients.

▶ **task leadership behavior**   A leadership emphasis that directs the attention and activity of a group toward a specified goal.

▶ **social leadership behavior**   A leadership emphasis that focuses on building and maintaining positive, productive relationships among group members.

As you participate in group discussions, you should also avoid certain behaviors that can block or distract constructive engagement. For instance, while there is nothing wrong with the occasional humorous comment, "jokers" who use every subject or comment to cue a punch line can prove a major distraction. Participants who talk *too much* or always have to have the last word can hinder participation by other group members. And again, group members should consciously put their egos to rest and avoid getting combative in the face of constructive criticism. The self-analysis form in Figure A.1 can help you assess and improve your group communication skills.

Leading Small Groups

For many years, social scientists have been studying leadership by analyzing group communication patterns. This research suggests that two basic types of leadership behaviors emerge in most groups. The first is **task leadership behavior**, which directs the activity of the group toward a specified goal. The second is **social leadership behavior** (sometimes called maintenance leadership), which helps build and maintain positive relationships among group members.

Task leaders direct group communication toward achieving shared goals. They give and seek information, opinions, and suggestions, and they guide group discussions and keep them on track. Social leaders, on the other hand, promote group cohesion, the constructive resolution of conflicts within the group, and an atmosphere in which group members feel encouraged to participate and appreciated for their contributions. In a healthy communication climate, the two kinds of leadership behavior support each other and keep the group moving toward its goal. When one person combines both styles of leadership, that person is likely to be highly effective.

Leadership has also been studied in terms of the way a leader handles the task and maintenance functions. An **autocratic leader** makes decisions without consultation, issues orders or gives direction, and controls the members of the group through the use of rewards or punishments. A **participative leader** seeks input from group members and gives them an active role in decision making. A **free-rein leader** lets members decide on their own what to do, how to do it, and when to do it. If you were working in an organization, you would probably say you "worked *for*" an autocratic leader, "worked *with*" a participative leader, and "worked *in spite of*" a free-rein leader.

More recent work on leadership suggests that leadership styles are either transactional or transformational. **Transactional leadership** takes place in an environment based on power relationships and relies on reward and punishment to accomplish its ends. **Transformational leadership** appeals to "people's higher levels of motivation to contribute to a cause and add to the quality of life on the planet."[9] It carries overtones of stewardship instead of management. Transformational leaders have the following qualities:

- They have a vision of what needs to be done.

- They are empathetic.

- They are trusted.

- They give credit to others.

- They help others develop.

- They share power.

- They are willing to experiment and learn.

▶ **autocratic leader** A leader who makes decisions without consultation, issues orders or gives direction, and controls the members of the group through the use of rewards or punishments.

▶ **participative leader** A leader who seeks input from group members and gives them an active role in decision making.
▶ **free-rein leader** A leader who leaves members free to decide what, how, and when to act, offering no guidance.

▶ **transactional leadership** A leadership style based on power relationships that relies on reward and punishment to achieve its ends.
▶ **transformational leadership** A leadership style based on mutual respect and stewardship rather than on control.

**Figure A.1
Group Communication
Skills Self-Analysis
Form**

	Need to Do Less	Doing Fine	Need to Do More
1. I make my points concisely.	☐	☐	☐
2. I speak with confidence.	☐	☐	☐
3. I provide specific examples and details.	☐	☐	☐
4. I try to integrate ideas that are expressed.	☐	☐	☐
5. I let others know when I do not understand them.	☐	☐	☐
6. I let others know when I agree with them.	☐	☐	☐
7. I let others know tactfully when I disagree with them.	☐	☐	☐
8. I express my opinions.	☐	☐	☐
9. I suggest solutions to problems.	☐	☐	☐
10. I listen to understand.	☐	☐	☐
11. I try to understand before agreeing or disagreeing.	☐	☐	☐
12. I ask questions to get more information.	☐	☐	☐
13. I ask others for their opinions.	☐	☐	☐
14. I check for group agreement.	☐	☐	☐
15. I try to minimize tension.	☐	☐	☐
16. I accept help from others.	☐	☐	☐
17. I offer help to others.	☐	☐	☐
18. I let others have their say.	☐	☐	☐
19. I stand up for myself.	☐	☐	☐
20. I urge others to speak up.	☐	☐	☐

In short, transformational leaders lead with both their hearts and their heads. According to John Schuster, a management consultant who specializes in transformational leadership training, "The heart is more difficult to develop. It's easier to get smarter than to become more caring."[10] Transformational leadership encourages communication from subordinates because they are less intimidated by their superiors and more willing to ask for advice or help.[11]

Consider how effective leadership relates to the major components of ethos (see the discussion of ethos in Chapter 3). An effective leader is *competent*. This means the leader understands the problem and knows how to steer a group through the problem-solving process. An effective leader has *integrity*. This means the leader is honest and places group success above personal concerns. An effective leader is perceived as a person of *goodwill*, concerned less about the self and more about those the group serves. Finally, an effective leader is *dynamic*. Dynamic leaders are enthusiastic, energetic, and decisive. Most of us have these qualities in varying degrees and can use them when the need for leadership arises. To be an effective leader, remember two simple goals: *Help others be effective* and *get the job done*. Cultivate an open leadership style that encourages all sides to air their views.

Planning Meetings.   In many organizations, meetings are seen as time wasters. This may be because the people who conduct them do not know when to call meetings or how to run them.[12] Meetings should be called when people need to

- discuss the meaning of information face-to-face.
- decide on a common course of action.
- establish a plan of action.
- report on the progress of a plan, evaluate its effectiveness, and revise it if necessary.

More than just knowing when to call meetings, you need to know how to plan them. The following guidelines should help you plan effective meetings:

- *Have a specific purpose for holding a meeting.* Unnecessary meetings waste time. If your goal is simply to increase interaction, plan a social event rather than a meeting.

- *Prepare an agenda, and distribute it to participants before the meeting.* Having an agenda gives members time to prepare and assemble information they might need. Solicit agenda items from participants.

- *Designate tasks for group members that need to be completed in preparation for the meeting.* For instance, members might be asked to research and brief the group on differing aspects of a problem.

- *Keep meetings short.* After about an hour, groups get tired, and the law of diminishing returns sets in. Don't try to do too much in a single meeting.

- *Keep groups small.* You get more participation and interaction in small groups. In larger groups, people may be reluctant to ask questions or contribute ideas.

- *Select participants who will interact easily with each other.* In business settings, the presence of someone's supervisor may inhibit interaction. You will get better participation if group members come from the same or nearly the same working level in the organization.

- *Plan the site of the meeting.* Arrange for privacy and freedom from interruptions. A circular arrangement contributes to participation because there is no power position. A rectangular table or a lectern and classroom arrangement may inhibit interaction.

- *Prepare in advance.* Be certain that you have the necessary supplies, such as chalk, a flip chart, markers, note pads, and pencils. If you will use electronic equipment, be sure it is in working order.

Conducting an Effective Meeting. Group leaders have many responsibilities. They must encourage deliberations that proceed in good faith toward constructive ends. When using a structured discussion format such as the reflective thinking model discussed earlier in this appendix, they should be prepared to guide the group through the various steps of the process. Finally, group leaders should be well informed on the issues so that they can answer questions and keep the group moving toward its objectives.

The following checklist should be helpful in guiding your behavior as a group leader:

- Begin and end the meeting on time.

- Present background information concisely and objectively.

- Facilitate the meeting; don't dominate it.

- Be enthusiastic.

- Get conflict out in the open so that it can be dealt with constructively.

- Urge all members to participate.

- Keep discussion focused on the issue at hand.

- At the close of a meeting, summarize what the group has accomplished.

As a group leader, you may need to present the group's recommendations to others. In this task, you function mainly as an informative speaker. You should present the recommendations offered by the group, along with the major reasons for making these recommendations. You should also mention reservations that may have surfaced during deliberations. Your job in making this report is not to advocate but to educate. Later you may join in any following discussion with persuasive remarks that express your personal convictions on the subject.

Finally, as you conduct meetings, keep in mind behaviors that either advance or impede group effectiveness.[13] Better group decisions are made when all group members participate fully in the process, when members are respectful of each other and leaders are respectful of members, and when negative emotional behaviors are kept in check. More specific details of these findings are listed in Figure A.2.

Guidelines for Formal Meetings

The larger a group is, the more it needs a formal procedure to conduct meetings. Also, if a meeting addresses a controversial or disputed subject, it is wise to have a set of rules to follow. Having clear-cut guidelines helps to keep meetings from becoming

Enhancing Behaviors	Impeding Behaviors
Opinions are sought out.	Members express dislike for others.
Creativity is encouraged.	Members personally attack others.
Participation is encouraged.	Members make sarcastic comments.
Opposing views are encouraged.	Leader sets criteria for solution.
Members provide information.	Leader makes the decision.
Group analyzes suggestions.	Leader intimidates members.
Members listen to one another.	Meeting becomes a gripe session.
Members respect others' ideas.	Disagreements are ignored, not aired.
Members support others' ideas.	Disagreement is discouraged.
Problem is thoroughly researched.	Members pursue personal goals.
Group sets criteria for solution.	
Members are knowledgeable on issue.	
Evidence for suggestions is presented.	
Group focuses on task.	

Figure A.2
Behaviors That Enhance or Impede Decision Making

chaotic and ensures fair treatment for all participants. In such situations, many groups conduct formal meetings by following some variation of **parliamentary procedure**.

Parliamentary procedure establishes an order of business for a meeting and lays out the way the group initiates discussions and reaches decisions. The point is to facilitate discussions that are inclusive and thorough yet structured and task-oriented. Under parliamentary procedure, a formal meeting proceeds as follows:

1. The chair calls the meeting to order.

2. The secretary reads the minutes of the previous meeting, which are corrected, if necessary, and approved.

3. Reports from officers and committees are presented.

4. Unfinished business is considered.

5. New business is introduced.

6. Announcements are made.

7. The meeting is adjourned.

Business in formal meetings goes forward by **motions**, or proposals set before the group. For instance, when the chair asks: "Is there any new business?" a member might respond: "I move that we allot $500 to build a Homecoming float." Before the group can discuss the motion, another group member must say, "I second the motion." The purpose of a **second** is to ensure that more than one person wants to see the motion considered. If no one volunteers a second, the chair may ask, "Is there a second?" Once a motion is made and seconded, it is open for discussion. It must be passed by majority vote, defeated, or otherwise resolved before the group can move on to other business.

▶ **parliamentary procedure** A set of formal rules that establishes an order of business for meetings and encourages the orderly, fair, and full consideration of proposals during group deliberation.

▶ **motions** Formal proposals for group consideration.

▶ **second** A motion must receive a "second" from a member of the group before group discussion can proceed; ensures that more than one member wishes to have the motion considered.

Let us assume that, as the group discusses the motion to build a homecoming float, some members believe the amount of money proposed is insufficient. At this point, another member may say: "I move to amend the motion to provide $750 for the float." The **motion to amend** gives the group a chance to modify a main motion. It must be seconded and, after discussion, must be resolved by majority vote before discussion goes forward. If the motion to amend passes, then the amended main motion must be considered further.

How does a group make a decision on a motion? There usually is a time when discussion begins to lag. At this point, the chair might say, "Do I hear a call for the question?" A motion to **call the question** ends discussion, and it requires a two-thirds vote for approval. Once the group votes to end discussion, it must then vote to accept or reject the motion. No further discussion can take place until the original or amended original motion is voted on.

Sometimes the discussion of a motion may reveal that the group is confused or sharply divided about an issue. At this point, a member may move to **table the motion** instead of calling the question. This can help dispose of a troublesome motion without further divisive or confused discussion. Once a motion is tabled, it can be reconsidered only if the member who called for the table moves to rescind that motion. At other times, the discussion of a motion may reveal that the group lacks information to make an intelligent decision. At that point, we might hear from a member: "In light of the uncertainty over costs, I move we postpone further consideration until next week's meeting." The **motion to postpone consideration** gives the chair a chance to appoint a committee to gather the information needed. The **move to adjourn** presented by a member ends the meeting.

These are just some of the important procedures that can help ensure that formal group communication remains fair and constructive (see Figure A.3). For more information on formal group communication procedures, consult the latest edition of *Robert's Rules of Order*.

Virtual Meetings

In this age of rapidly advancing technology, you will likely be asked to participate in **virtual meetings** that are conducted and mediated using some combination of electronic and computer technology. Businesses and government organizations have used teleconferencing to conduct meetings among employees working from remote locations for decades. Modern software packages for videoconferencing allow for the integration of audio, visual, and written transactions among group members in real time, and there is little doubt that such technologies will continue to improve and become increasingly common in the future.

There are many advantages of using virtual technology for conducting small group meetings. The most obvious, as mentioned above, is allowing group members to interact from remote locations. Virtual meetings are more convenient and less time-consuming for group participants; they minimize travel costs and other related expenses for organizations; and they leave less of a carbon trail, making them more environmentally friendly. The instantaneous exchange of written and audiovisual documents can enhance the substance and efficiency of group communication, and can be especially effective for conducting group brainstorming sessions. What's more, the use of virtual communication technologies can elicit more and better input from group members who might contribute less in face-to-face discussions, and can discourage one or two group members from dominating the entire discussion.

▶ **motion to amend**   A parliamentary move that offers opportunity to modify a motion presently under discussion.

▶ **call the question**   A motion that proposes to end discussion and vote on the original motion.

▶ **table the motion**   A parliamentary move to suspend indefinitely the discussion of a motion.

▶ **motion to postpone consideration** A motion that defers discussion until some specified time.

▶ **move to adjourn**   A motion that calls for the meeting to end.

Figure A.3 **Guide to Parliamentary Procedure**

Action	Requires Second	Can Be Debated	Can Be Amended	Vote Required	Function
Main Motion	Yes	Yes	Yes	Majority	Commits group to a specific action or position.
Second	No	No	No	None	Assures that more than one group member wishes to see idea considered.
Move to Amend	Yes	Yes	Yes	Majority	Allows group to modify and improve an existing motion.
Call the Question	Yes	No	No	Two-thirds	Brings discussion to an end and moves to a vote on the motion in question.
Move to Table the Motion	Yes	No	No	Majority	Stops immediate consideration of the motion until a later unspecified time.
Move to Postpone Consideration	Yes	Yes	Yes	Majority	Stops immediate discussion and allows time for the group to obtain more information on the problem.
Move to Adjourn	Yes	No	No	Majority	Formally ends meeting.

For all the potential advantages of conducting virtual meetings, there are many challenges and potential frustrations that can undermine their effectiveness. Of course, your communication system must be working and interfacing properly, and group members must know how to use it and have access to the right equipment. And while technology is fast closing the gap, virtual communication usually provides for less immediacy and quality feedback than face-to-face interactions, which may cause some members to get confused, lose focus, and quit contributing to group discussions. Finally, virtual meetings are generally less effective for promoting group cohesion and resolving differences of opinion within the group.

These challenges heighten the importance of conducting virtual meetings that are well planned and carefully structured. Because there is usually less opportunity to clarify misunderstandings, it is even more important for everyone to understand the purpose for meeting and to have a well-defined agenda of discussion items. Group leaders may need to be more active in eliciting input from all participants, and group members need to familiarize themselves with the technology and commit themselves to the process without the peer reinforcement of direct engagement.

▶ **virtual meetings** Group meetings that are conducted and mediated using electronic and/or computer technology.

Experts generally recommend supplementing virtual meetings with occasional face-to-face gatherings, especially for making really important decisions or developing long-range plans.[14] See our discussion in Chapter 13 for related advice on making video presentations, and Chapter 10 on using PowerPoint and other forms of multimedia presentation aids.

Making Group Presentations

Small-group communication often overlaps with public speaking. As discussed in Chapter 13, you may be asked to make short informative presentations or "briefings" during work meetings on the status of a project or some aspect of a problem. On other occasions, group members may need to present their findings and recommendations to larger audiences. When preparing for such presentations, group leaders should

- designate which group members will present which parts of the report.
- assign other duties, such as preparing or coordinating presentation aids.
- develop an outline or agenda for the presentation.
- determine who should handle questions and answers.
- schedule and oversee a rehearsal of the group presentation.

Often, a designated spokesperson will simply present an **oral report**. This report is basically an informative speech that follows a specific design. The introduction briefly reviews the problem, introduces the members of the group (including their credentials) if they are not well known to the audience, and describes the process used by the group to study the problem. The body of the report covers the major findings or recommendations for action. The conclusion summarizes the findings and may make suggestions for further work. The report should be as brief as possible and should allow for questions and answers following the formal presentation.

In addition to a simple oral report, group presentations may follow four other formats: a symposium, a panel discussion, a roundtable presentation, or a forum.

A **symposium** features a moderator and members of the problem-solving group as presenters. This group should be selected on the basis of the participants' special competencies and communication skills. The primary role of the moderator is to introduce the topic and speakers at the beginning of the symposium and to summarize the findings as the presentation draws to a close. Each symposium speaker will typically cover one aspect of the topic, making a short (well-prepared and rehearsed) report on the group's findings or recommendations in that area. The moderator enforces time limits and keeps the presentations on track. The symposium is usually followed by a question-and-answer session.

A **panel discussion** is less formal than a symposium. It also has a moderator who introduces the topic and the participants, but it does not feature prepared speeches. Rather, it is a planned pattern of spontaneous exchanges. Following the brief introductions, the moderator asks questions of the group. Participants respond with brief impromptu answers. The moderator guides the discussion and keeps the group in focus. He or she should also see that no single participant dominates the discussion and that all panelists participate.

▶ **oral report** Presentation that summarizes the deliberations of a small group to inform a larger audience of decision makers.

▶ **symposium** Group presentation in which speakers address different areas of an issue.

▶ **panel discussion** A group presentation featuring organized exchanges among speakers, directed by a moderator.

Although responses in a panel discussion are impromptu, the participants should be told in advance what general types of questions may be asked so that they can prepare with these in mind. Panelists should think back through what went on in the group and organize their ideas in advance of the discussion. They should be prepared for tough follow-up questions either from the moderator or from the audience.

A **roundtable** presentation is an interactive way of publicly exchanging information, ideas, or opinions.[15] All members of the group are considered equal and are encouraged to participate openly and fully in the proceedings. There are no formal opening statements or prepared speeches. The leader helps generate discussion, makes certain the speakers stay on track and adhere to time limits, and encourages a nonjudgmental dialogue. In late 2006, the Sierra Club conducted a roundtable on the climate crisis that included business and political leaders as well as environmental activists.[16] An abridged transcript of the proceedings is available in the May/June 2007 issue of *Sierra*.

In a **forum** presentation, questions come from the audience rather than from the moderator. The basic job of the moderator of a forum is to keep the discussion on track. The moderator may introduce the topic and participants, and during the course of the forum, he or she recognizes audience members who wish to ask questions. At times, the moderator may also have to actually "moderate"—act as a referee if questions or answers become heated on emotional topics. If the group anticipates controversy, it may wish to arrange for a parliamentarian to help keep the meeting constructive. Participants should follow the guidelines suggested for handling questions and answers in Chapter 12.

FINAL
reflections Your Group Voice

Over the course of our lives, all of us will develop multiple formal and informal group associations that will exert a tremendous influence on our lives. As you complete your education and pursue a professional or public life beyond college, you will likely be called upon to participate in a variety of task-oriented small groups. Your ability to make constructive contributions to group discussions will distinguish and nurture your potential for leadership and success. In this appendix, we have discussed the nature of small-group communication, the process of group problem-solving, planning and conducting formal meetings, conducting virtual meetings, and some advice for making group presentations before larger audiences. Together with the public speaking skills taught throughout this textbook, developing your group communication skills will make a valuable contribution to finding your voice.

▶ **roundtable** Interactive way of informally exchanging ideas, information, or opinions within a small group before a larger audience.

▶ **forum** Presentational format in which a group of specialists in different areas of a subject respond to questions from an audience.

B Speeches for Analysis

Self-Introductory Speeches

My Three Cultures
SANDRA BALTZ

Sandra Baltz first presented this self-introductory speech many years ago at the University of Memphis. She addressed the themes of cross-culturalism and family values long before these became fashionable. Sandra's deft use of comparison and contrast, and her example of foods illustrating how three cultures can combine harmoniously, are instructive. As her speech developed, she built her ethos as a competent, warm person, highly qualified to give later informative and persuasive speeches on issues involving medical care. Presented at a time when tensions in the Middle East were running high, Sandra's speech served as a gentle reminder that people of goodwill can always find ways to enjoy their differences and to reaffirm their common membership in the human family.

Several years ago I read a newspaper article in the Commercial Appeal in which an American journalist described some of his experiences in the Middle East. He was there a couple of months and had been the guest of several different Arab families. He reported having been very well treated and very well received by everyone that he met there. But it was only later, when he returned home, that he became aware of the intense resentment his hosts held for Americans and our unwelcome involvement in their Middle Eastern affairs. The journalist wrote of feeling somewhat bewildered, if not deceived, by the large discrepancy between his treatment while in the Middle East and the hostile attitude that he learned about later. He labeled this behavior hypocritical. When I reached the end of the article, I was reminded of a phrase spoken often by my mother. "Sandra," she says to me, "respeta tu casa y a todos los que entran en ella, trata a tus enemigos asi como a tus amigos."

This is an Arabic proverb, spoken in Spanish, and roughly it translates into, "Respect your home and all who enter it, treating even an enemy as a friend." This is a philosophy that I have heard often in my home. With this in mind, it seemed to me that the treatment the American journalist received while in the Middle East was not hypocritical behavior on the part of his hosts. Rather, it was an act of respect for their guest, for themselves, and for their home—indeed, a behavior very typical of the Arabic culture.

Since having read that article several years ago, I have become much more aware of how my life is different because of having a mother who is of Palestinian origin but was born and raised in the Central American country of El Salvador.

One of the most obvious differences is that I was raised bilingually—speaking both Spanish and English. In fact, my first words were in Spanish. Growing up speaking two languages has been both an advantage and a disadvantage for me. One clear advantage is that I received straight A's in my Spanish class at Immaculate Conception High School. Certainly, traveling has been made much easier. During visits to Spain, Mexico, and some of the Central American countries, it has been my experience that people are much more open and much more receptive if you can speak their language. In addition, the subtleties of a culture are easier to grasp and much easier to appreciate.

I hope that knowing a second language will continue to be an asset for me in the future. I am currently pursuing a career in medicine. Perhaps by knowing Spanish I can broaden the area in which I can work and increase the number of people that I might reach.

Now one of the disadvantages of growing up bilingually is that I picked up my mother's accent as well as her language. I must have been about four years old before I realized that our feathered friends in the trees are called "birds" not "beers" and that, in fact, we had a "birdbath" in our backyard, not a "beerbath."

Family reunions also tend to be confusing around my home. Most of my relatives speak either Spanish, English, or Arabic, but rarely any combination of the three. So, as a result, deep and involved conversations are almost impossible. But with a little nodding and smiling, I have found that there really is no language barrier among family and friends.

In all, I must say that being exposed to three very different cultures—Latin, Arabic, and American—has been rewarding for me and has made a difference even in the music I enjoy and the food I eat. It is not unusual in my house to sit down to a meal made up of stuffed grape leaves and refried beans and all topped off with apple pie for dessert.

I am fortunate in having had the opportunity to view more closely what makes Arabic and Latin cultures unique. By understanding and appreciating them I have been able to better understand and appreciate my own American culture. In closing, just let me add some words you often hear spoken in my home—*adios* and *allak konn ma'eck*—goodbye, and may God go with you.

Lady with a Gun
ELIZABETH TIDMORE

Beth Tidmore presented this self-introductory speech to her honors class in oral communication at the University of Memphis. The speech, offered as a tribute to her mother's faith in her, describes her dramatic development into a shooting champion. Beth's speech is noteworthy for its use of narrative design, especially dialogue. Her graphic descriptions, engaging her listeners' senses of sight, sound, touch, and smell, also helped her establish a vital, direct contact with her audience and transported them to the scenes she depicted. By the end of that semester, Beth had won the National Junior Olympic Championship Women's Air Rifle competition and had been named to the All-America shooters team.

I'm sure everybody has had an April Fool's joke played on them. My father's favorite one was to wake me up on April first and tell me, "School's been canceled for the day; you don't have to go," and then get all excited and say, "April Fools!" I'd get up and take a shower . . .

Well, on April first, 2000, my mother said three words that I was sure weren't an April Fool's joke. She said, "We'll take it." The "it" she was referring to was a brand-new Anschutz 2002 Air Rifle. Now, this is $2,000 worth of equipment for a sport that I'd been in for maybe three months—not long. That was a big deal! It meant that I would be going from a junior-level to an Olympic-grade rifle.

Someone outside of the sport might think, "Eh, minor upgrade. A gun is a gun, right?" No. Imagine a fifteen-year-old who has been driving a used Toyota and who suddenly gets a new Mercedes for her sixteenth birthday. That's how I felt.

And as she was writing the check, I completely panicked. I thought, "What if I'm not good enough to justify this rifle? What if I decide to quit and we have to sell it, or we can't sell it? What if I let my parents down and I waste their money?" So later in the car I said, "Momma, what if I'm not good enough?" She said, "Don't worry about it—it's my money." Okay . . .

So my journey began. Most shooters start out when they're younger, and they move up through different rifles. Most of my peers had at least four years' experience on me. I had to jump right in and get a scholarship. And to get a scholarship I had to get noticed. And to get noticed I had to win, and to win, I had to shoot great scores immediately.

So my journey was filled with eight-hours-a-day practice, five days a week. On weekends I shot matches and I traveled. I had to take my homework with me to complete it before I got back to school. I had to do physical training, I had dietary restrictions. When all my friends were out at parties and at Cancun for Spring Break, I was at the shooting range. My free time—if I had any—was spent lifting weights and running.

At times I really resented my friends, because I thought they must have all the fun. But you know what, it was worth it! My friends don't know what it's like to feel the cold, smooth wood of the cheekpiece against your face. And they don't know the rich smell of Hoppe's No. 9 [oil] when you're cleaning your rifle. And they've never been to the Olympic Training Center in Colorado and seen how they embroider the little Olympic logo on *everything* from the mattresses to the plates. And they don't know the thrill of shooting in a final and having everyone applaud when you shoot a ten or even a center ten, or standing on the podium and having them put a medal around your neck, and being proud to represent your school, your country. . . .

There's a bumper sticker that says, "A Lady with A Gun Has More Fun." After three years in this sport, I have had so much fun! I've been all over the U.S., I've been captain of a high school rifle team, I've been to matches everywhere, I've won medals, I've been to World Cups and met people from all over the world. And I've gotten to experience so many different people, places, and events through my participation in shooting sports.

So not long ago, I asked my mother, "Mom, how did you know?" She said, "Ah, I just knew." I said, "No, Mom—*really*. How did you know that you weren't going to waste your money?" She got very serious and she took me by the shoulders and she squared me up. She looked me right in the eye and she said, "When you picked up that gun, you just looked like you belonged together. I knew there was a sparkle in your eye, and I knew that you were meant to do great things with that rifle."

So, thanks, Mom.

To Toss or Not to Toss: The Art of Baseball Umpiring

BJ YOUNGERMAN

BJ Youngerman presented this speech in his class at Davidson College. It illustrates the use of an activity as the starting point for a self-introductory speech. BJ combines effective narrative, animated gestures, and vocal contrast to carry listeners to the scene of an umpiring situation and to create the setting for his speech. He offers an impressive array of expert testimony in support of his own extensive experience to create an authentic, highly credible speech.

     Me: "He's out!" [with hand motion].
Coach: "You've got to be kidding me, Blue! He was a good 10 feet beyond the base before the ball got there. That's horrible!"
     Me: "Coach, shut up, you know you're being ridiculous. Get back to your dugout."
Coach: "Blue, that was the worst call I've ever seen. You're totally blind."
     Me: "Coach, you're just a sore loser: Get in the dugout."
Coach: "Well just because you got cut in Little League doesn't mean you have to take it out on these kids!"
     Me: "That's it! You're done!" [*swings arms to signify ejection of coach*].

Although umpiring is often considered to be a job where the sole purpose is to make judgment calls, in fact, the work includes many complexities, especially when you're dealing with angry players, coaches, and spectators. In the next few minutes, I will look into the importance of maintaining order, the importance of professionalism, and the necessity of making the right call the *first* time when working as a baseball umpire. But first let me tell you a little about my background as an umpire.

My first umpiring experience occurred with Little League when I was 13. By the time I was 16, I had been certified by the High School Federation Board and now have umpired three seasons for well over 200 games.

Some of you may be wondering: What exactly is the role of an umpire? According to Kathryn Davis, author of *The Art of Sports Officiating*, "Referees [Umpires] are the decisive directors of the game. They rule, punish, guide, and educate, all in the same split second." The U.S. Department of Labor estimates that there are roughly 16,000 umpires, referees, and other sports officials nationwide. Fred Frick, a writer for *The Baseball Almanac*, provides the "10 Commandments of Umpiring," which include the following: First, keep your personalities out of your work. Second, Forgive and forget and avoid sarcasm. Don't insist on the last word. Third, never charge a player, and above all, no pointing your finger or yelling. Finally, he advises to always keep your temper, as a decision made in anger is never sound.

Another important aspect of the art of umpiring is in maintaining order throughout the game. Rich Coyle and Arnie Mann, president and commissioner respectively for the Greater New Haven Baseball Umpires Association, offer several different techniques to use in maintaining order. Coyle recommends defusing the situation by walking away. Mann also made the infamous comment, "Don't look for boogers," or you'll encounter problems. Both Coyle and Mann agree that if someone starts attacking you personally, then eject him or her. One of the ways to avoid ever getting to the point of potentially having to eject someone is to always remain professional.

Why is it important to maintain professionalism? First and foremost, because image is crucial to success. Davis points out that you must establish your initial image at the pre-game conference. You ought to explain any new or difficult rule interpretations and ask if there are any questions. Another aspect of professionalism is the uniform, as it is a major part of your image. Davis notes, "Groomed appearance exudes competence, confidence and pride in the profession." According to Travis Hamilton, an expert on professionalism, the uniform must be tucked in and shoes must be shined. Rich Coyle jokingly comments that you can get through the first three innings even if you're the most horrible ump in the world, so long as you look good.

Attitude is also a part of image. You should be friendly but reserved. Davis says, "Coaches notice an official's rapport with the players, punctuality to the game, proper game equipment, enthusiasm, and effort." Finally, knowledge and competence are incredibly important as well, as they are components of professionalism. Aside from looking good, the other important part of professionalism is doing your job correctly. This brings up the question: How are you to make the right call and when, if ever, should you make the decision to change it?

In terms of making the right call, Rudy Raffone, rules interpreter for the Greater New Haven Chapter of the High School Umpires Federation board, suggests, "Replay the play in your head so you don't simply react, but instead actually think." Additionally, Rich Coyle recommends selling the call by showing loud verbal and physical signs.

Changing a call is a much more difficult decision. Jay Miner of *Referee* magazine asks, "When is a judgment call not a judgment call? Is it when an umpire second-guesses his own call, consults with a colleague, and changes it?"

I once encountered a similar situation to this. At age 16, I was a new umpire working a game in which the players were also 16. There was a close call at third base from which I was shielded. I made a call, but immediately went to my home plate umpire for help. After discussing the play with my co-umpire, he told me that I made the wrong call, so I did what I thought was the logical and right thing, and reversed the call. Though I probably did end up making the right decision by changing the call, my credibility was immediately gone, as the coaches, fans, and players now assumed I would overturn almost any call. Jerry Crawford, a Major League Baseball umpire says, "You don't waver . . . and that's how I would deal with [a close call]; there was no backing off. You've got to maintain that sense about you all the time. Your job is to maintain control out there and being weak-kneed, there's no place for that on a baseball field." It certainly seems that a Major League umpire should know best, having worked his way through the whole system.

In conclusion, umpiring requires so many different elements that one must constantly stay focused both on the game as well as on maintaining order, remaining professional, and making the right call the first time.

With this information in mind, let's do a little reenactment of the scene I portrayed a few minutes ago:

> *Me:* "He's out!" (*with hand motion*).
> *Coach:* "You've got to be kidding me, Blue! He was a good 10 feet beyond the base before the ball got there. That's horrible!"
> *Me:* "Coach, it's a judgment call. I called it like I saw it. Please get back to your dugout."
> *Coach:* "Blue, that was the worst call I've ever seen. You're totally blind."
> *Me:* "Coach, this is your final warning: Get in the dugout."
> *Coach:* "Well just because you got cut in Little League doesn't mean you have to take it out on these kids!"
> *Me:* "That's it! You're done!" (wave arm)

The first scene was me, rookie umpire. The second is me, veteran umpire. In this case, the result on the field did not change. But I carried away from that second scene the knowledge that I was serving the game I love in just the right way.

Informative Speeches

The "Monument" at Wounded Knee
CECILE LARSON

Cecile Larson's speech informs listeners about a shameful episode in American history. The speech follows a spatial design. Cecile's vivid use of imagery and the skillful contrasts she draws between this "monument" and our "official" monuments create mental pictures that should stay with her listeners long after the words of her speech have been forgotten.

We Americans are big on monuments. We build monuments in memory of our heroes. Washington, Jefferson, and Lincoln live on in our nation's capital. We erect monuments to honor our martyrs. The Minuteman still stands guard at Concord. The flag is ever raised over Iwo Jima. Sometimes we even construct monuments to commemorate victims. In Ashburn Park downtown there is a monument to those who died in the yellow fever epidemics. However, there are some things in our history that we don't memorialize. Perhaps we would just as soon forget what happened. Last summer I visited such a place—the massacre site at Wounded Knee.

In case you have forgotten what happened at Wounded Knee, let me refresh your memory. On December 29, 1890, shortly after Sitting Bull had been murdered by the authorities, about 400 half-frozen, starving, and frightened Indians who had fled the nearby reservation were attacked by the Seventh Cavalry. When the fighting ended, between 200 and 300 Sioux had died—two-thirds of them women and children. Their remains are buried in a common grave at the site of the massacre.

Wounded Knee is located in the Pine Ridge Reservation in southwestern South Dakota— about a three-hour drive from where Presidents Washington, Jefferson, Theodore Roosevelt, and Lincoln are enshrined in the granite face of Mount Rushmore. The reservation is directly south of the Badlands National Park, a magnificently desolate area of wind-eroded buttes and multicolored spires.

We entered the reservation driving south from the Badlands Visitor's Center. The landscape of the Pine Ridge Reservation retains much of the desolation of the Badlands but lacks its magnificence. Flat, sun-baked fields and an occasional eroded gully stretch as far as the eye can see. There are no signs or highway markers to lead the curious tourist to Wounded Knee. Even the *Rand-McNally Atlas* doesn't help you find your way. We got lost three times and had to stop and ask directions.

When we finally arrived at Wounded Knee, there was no official historic marker to tell us what had happened there. Instead there was a large, handmade wooden sign—crudely lettered in white on black. The sign first directed our attention to our left—to the gully where the massacre took place. The mass grave site was to our right—across the road and up a small hill.

Two red-brick columns topped with a wrought-iron arch and a small metal cross form the entrance to the grave site. The column to the right is in bad shape: cinder blocks from the base are missing; the brickwork near the top has deteriorated and tumbled to the ground; graffiti on the columns proclaim an attitude we found repeatedly expressed about the Bureau of Indian Affairs—"The BIA sucks!"

Crumbling concrete steps lead you to the mass grave. The top of the grave is covered with gravel, punctuated by unruly patches of chickweed and crabgrass. These same weeds also grow along the base of the broken chainlink fence that surrounds the grave, the "monument," and a small cemetery.

The "monument" itself rests on a concrete slab to the right of the grave. It's a typical, large, old-fashioned granite cemetery marker, a pillar about six feet high topped with an urn—the kind of gravestone you might see in any cemetery with graves from the turn of the century. The inscription tells us that it was erected by the families of those who were killed at Wounded Knee. Weeds grow through the cracks in the concrete at its base.

There are no granite headstones in the adjacent cemetery, only simple white wooden crosses that tell a story of people who died young. There is no neatly manicured grass. There are no flowers. Only the unrelenting and unforgiving weeds.

Yes, Americans are big on monuments. We build them to memorialize our heroes, to honor our martyrs, and sometimes, even to commemorate victims. But only when it makes us feel good.

Video Games
JOSEPH VAN MATRE

Joseph Van Matre presented this informative speech to his Fundamentals of Communication class at the University of Arkansas, taught by Lynn Meade. He reports that the idea for the speech "just popped into my head" after listening to a report on National Public Radio. The speech opens very effectively by using rhetorical questions, and features timely and interesting research that develops in a categorical pattern.

If I say the word "gamer," what words come to mind? Antisocial? Geek? Dropout? Well, how about fitness guru, educator, or intelligence analyst?

I'm not a hardcore gamer, but I do enjoy a round of Mario Smash Bros. every now and then. So when I heard on National Public Radio one day that video games can actually help in the business world, I was intrigued and did some research. What I discovered was quite surprising.

While there have been many stereotypes associated with video games and those who play them, today I'm going to show you some of the very real benefits video games can bring to the health, education, military, and business worlds. By the end of my presentation, some of you may even be ready to break out your Game Boy!

While many people think that video games contribute to inactivity, and therefore to health problems, video games have actually helped many gamers become more active. In fact, new input systems in the twenty-first century have encouraged many players to climb off the couch. Dance Dance Revolution, for example, has become popular with many physical educators. As the *New York Times* of April 2007 reported, the West Virginia Department of Education and the Los Angeles Unified School System both use DDR as a part of their PE programs. The game "requires players to dance in ever more complicated and strenuous patterns in time with electronic dance music." Dr. Linda Carson, distinguished professor at West Virginia University, reported her first encounter with the game: "I was in a mall walking by the arcade and I saw these kids playing D.D.R., and I was just stunned. There were all these kids dancing and sweating and actually standing in line and paying money to be physically active. . . . It was a physical educator's dream." In followup studies, Dr. Carson and her colleagues have found significant health benefits for overweight children who play the game regularly.

New technologies developed by NASA can also promote mental health. While this is a little complicated, as one plays a video game, the controller gets easier to use when the player brings a healthy brainwave pattern to the game. Thus the game becomes both diagnostic and therapeutic. According to Dr. Olafur Paisson, professor of psychiatry at Eastern Virginia Medical School, "With this new [biofeedback] technology, we have found a way to package this training in an enjoyable and inherently motivating activity."

Now that you know how video games can help keep you healthy, let's consider how they can make you smarter. First, video games can be effective educational tools. A study by the British Government showed that playing games such as SimCity and Rollercoaster Tycoon can help develop creativity, critical thinking, and math skills. When played in a group, they can also develop interpersonal skills. Then if you add correct economic and human behavior algorithms, you can make these games even more effective for economics and business education.

Video games can also help people develop a knowledge of history. For example, many people are fascinated by World War II, but it's hard for them to imagine what fighting in that war must have been like. But if you place them right in the middle of simulated battle situations in which they receive the combat orders just as soldiers of that time received them under actual conditions, their imaginations are stimulated. They must act and think and fight for survival. Playing such battle games makes it so much easier to motivate them to learn about the countries and causes and underlying cultural conditions involved in the many battlefields of that war. All these types of interactive education "games" are being developed right now.

Now that you see how video games can be used in education, let's look at how they also can function in the worlds of business and national defense. Businesses are finding great uses for video games to enhance training. In 2008, for example, UPS spent over $5.5 million on new training centers that integrate "on-line learning, 3-D models, podcasts, and videos with traditional classroom learning." These training programs are effective, according to the *Emerging Technologies Center*, because they are "immersive, require the player to make frequent, important decisions, have clear goals, adapt to other players individually, and involve a social network." Obviously, these cultivate important skills in the business world.

Finally, the military is using video games to enhance training, lower costs, assist in rehabilitation, and perform dangerous tasks. Converting war games into video games allows training to focus on specific goals and can lower costs dramatically. Southern California's Institute for Creative Technologies has shown that using X-box type games can help soldiers returning from the Middle East and Afghanistan to cope with PTSD (Post-traumatic Stress Disorder). Working with video games, trainees develop skills that can help them control drone planes and tanks on the battlefield. As Dr. Alan Pope of Langley Air Force Base has reported, "Flight simulators are essentially very sophisticated video games." By developing such games, training is simplified and accelerated, and mistakes can be corrected without devastating on-site consequences.

So have you begun to change your mind about video games and gamers? We've seen that video games can make us more healthy, smarter, better trained for the business world, and more secure from international threats. The next time you see people playing World of Warcraft or Halo, try not to think of them as "geeks" or as "dropouts." Those "geeks" may have their hands on the future!

The French Paradox: A Delicious Secret Revealed

GABRIELLE WALLACE

This colorful informative speech builds largely upon a comparative design, developing a literal analogy between French and American eating styles. It also offers a model of responsible knowledge, using facts and testimony drawn from numerous sources and experts. Gabrielle connects with audience dreams of a "give us the cake but spare us the consequences" lifestyle. In effect, she shows how these dreams might become reality. She presented her speech originally at Davidson College.

Have any of you ever fought the dreaded "freshman 15"—those unwanted pounds that seem to show up on you out of nowhere—but noticed by everyone as soon as you go home after your first year? What if I told you of a land where people eat this, drink this, and look like this [shows slides revealing delicious foods, elegant wines, and attractive people]? Would you believe me? They live like we wish we could, but don't experience the freshman 15—at least not as many of them do. If this sounds unlikely, it is nonetheless true. I call it "the French paradox." It refers to the fact that the French eat foods on a regular basis that are every bit as rich and fattening as what we eat, yet they are not nearly as prone to rapid weight gain and other negative health consequences. In order to understand the French paradox, we must consider how they combine food choices, beverage consumption, and cultural attitudes towards eating itself.

First, let's take a look at French eating habits. What they eat and how much they eat work together to make an ideal diet. The French eat as little processed food as possible. According to Roger Corder, a professor at St. Bartholomew's Hospital in London who has studied the French diet extensively, the French eat a higher quality and better variety of foods than most Americans. Like us, the French like rich fatty foods—gravies and cream sauces are common. But a much higher percentage of their diet consists of whole grains and vegetables, and they emphasize seasonally fresh and locally grown foods. This richness and variety satiates the palate and is considerably more filling than processed foods.

As a result, perhaps, the French eat smaller portions of food. According to Paul Rozin, a nutritionist at the University of Pennsylvania, French portion sizes on average are about 25% smaller than American portions—which might explain why Americans are roughly three times more likely to become obese than French people.

A factor that might account for this is the French upbringing. Mireille Guiliano, author of *French Women Don't Get Fat*, says that the French are not conditioned to overeat. Instead, they are taught to eat only until they are full, and then stop! A recent University of Pennsylvania study confirmed this tendency. The study compared the eating habits of students from Paris and Chicago. It found that French students stopped eating in response to internal cues, like when they first started feeling full or when they wanted to leave room for dessert. The American students, on the other hand, relied more on external cues. They would, for example, eat until the TV show they were watching ended, or until they ran out of a beverage. There's no question that eating habits are a vital point of difference between the French and American cultures.

The second important factor in explaining the French paradox has to do with beverage consumption. The French drink primarily two beverages: water and wine. Again according to

Mireille Guiliano, they start the day with a glass of water. Water is known to have metabolic benefits: an article in *Prevention* magazine suggests that consuming 16 oz. of water increases the body's calorie burning rate as much as 30% within 40 minutes.

The second beverage of choice is red wine. According to an article published in 2008 in the *Independent*, a prominent London newspaper, the average French person drinks nearly 17 gallons of wine a year, as compared to the 7 gallons a year consumed by the average Briton. Recently scientists have discovered numerous health benefits of red wine. Studies suggest it promotes higher levels of heart-healthy HDL cholesterol, which counters the effects of bad cholesterol by preventing artery blocking plaque deposits. The World Health Organization reported that countries with the highest wine consumption—France, Italy, and Spain—had the lowest rates of heart disease. Indeed, the region of France that drinks the most wine has the highest percentage of men who live to age 90!

The third important factor in explaining the French paradox has to do with their overall attitude and approach to eating itself. Meal time in France is an elaborate event. Meals typically consist of three to four courses, including a separate course for salad, cheese, and fruit. Susan Loomis, writing in *Health* magazine, likened French meals to Thanksgiving. "[W]hat Americans do once a year," she continued, "prepare food linked to ritual and history, then gather with family and friends—the French do often, most of them at least once a week."

A meal being a social event encourages slow eating—which contributes again to less overall consumption. As Dr. Rozin argues, the French tend to eat more slowly and to include more socializing and conversation with their meals. The social etiquette of a French meal also tends to promote gradual eating. The next course is never brought out until everyone at the table has finished. Only then, usually after some delay, does eating resume.

Finally, the French thoroughly enjoy the delight of food itself. They enjoy using all five senses when eating. My stepfather, when tasting a new wine, always sticks his nose in it to take in the smell, swirls it to watch the color, and slowly takes in a small amount to absorb the flavor. The owner of a French bakery where I work back home often puts baguettes up to his ear and squeezes them to hear their crunch and test their quality. Claude Fischler, a French sociologist at the University of Pennsylvania, notes that when asked to respond to the words chocolate cake, Americans say "Guilt" whereas the French say "Celebration."

For the French, eating is about the experience of living. It is engrained in their culture and permeates their daily experience. The three factors of eating correctly, drinking wisely, and making a meal an enjoyable experience are what make the French paradox possible. It appears the French have found the secret to being able to have their cake and eat it too—along with some wine, friends, and celebration. We, as American college students, could learn from their example, especially if we want to avoid the horror of the freshman 15!

Persuasive Speeches

Global Burning
JOSHUA LOGAN

Josh Logan presented this persuasive speech on the theme of global warming in his class at the University of Memphis. "Global Burning" focuses on the problem and attempts to arouse awareness, share understanding, and secure agreement. Its strategy is to magnify the reality of global warming and its meaning for listeners. Its challenge is to remove barriers that might stand in the way of their commitment. To achieve his goals, Josh used colorful, graphic language, a presentation aid, and effective examples. His presentation reflected his passion, sincerity, and commitment on this topic.

Ten years ago, five years ago, reasonable people could still argue and even disagree over some tough environmental questions: Is there really such a thing as "global warming"? Is the world really getting hotter at a rapid pace? And is it being fanned by humans? Are we really responsible for environmental conditions?

Now there's little room left for argument. The answer to all these questions is clearly YES. This definitive answer has been provided by the United Nations Intergovernmental Panel on Climate Change, reporting during the early part of 2007. This authoritative report, which correlates and tests the work of hundreds of environmental scientists from countries around the globe, concludes that the process of global warming is now in motion and is accelerating. And the fire is fed largely by humans: the IPCC supports this conclusion at a 90 to 99% level of confidence. The United States especially, with about 4% of the world's population, accounts for 25% of all global warming. We are the ones with our foot on the accelerator.

Today I want to sketch the dimensions of this problem, and what it might mean for you and your children. I will first track the causes of global warming, then trace its recent path and project its future. As recently as 2006, polls tell us that many people in the United States were in denial about global warming: yes, we believe it exists and, yes, we are concerned, but we're not that much concerned. Fifty-four percent of us think global warming is a problem for the future—but not now! Global warming is still something of an abstract, distant problem for us, and we can't see the future all that clearly.

That's the challenge I want to try to meet today. We must recognize global warming for what it is, the monster we are creating by all our action and inaction. We must become scared—really scared! We must be willing to think green and act green, from the personal everyday decisions we make on disposing trash to the big consumer decisions we make on which cars to buy, to the political decisions we make on which candidates to support. We must understand that this hot world is starting to catch fire—and we must be willing to pay the price to help put the flames out. We must be committed to the proposition that global warming must not become global burning.

Global warming begins with greenhouse gases—the tons of carbon dioxide that belch out of our smokestacks and our automobile exhausts; the vast clouds of methane gas that rise from our farms and ranches and landfills; the nitrous oxide from fertilizers, cattle feed lots, and chemical products. The world's forests are supposed to absorb much of this industrial and agricultural output, but guess what? We've also been busy cutting the rainforests and clear-cutting our own forests. We're tying nature's hands behind her back at just the wrong moment. So all these deadly gases mix and accumulate in the atmosphere, where they magnify the heat of the sun.

Now let's gain some perspective on where we now actually stand. I want to show you a chart that traces the human influence on the atmosphere over the past thousand years of history. This chart summarizes the history of greenhouse gases, according to the IPCC's *Summary for Policymakers*. Notice that the bottom border divides the time frame into two-hundred-year periods. The side frame measures the amount of the gas pouring into the atmosphere. Notice that for about eight hundred of these years, this amount is stable and even—almost a straight line. Then as the nineteenth century dawns on the Industrial Revolution, the lines begin to climb, at first gradually, then increasingly steeper until they almost reach the vertical during the past half-century. The dry technical language of the summary, speaking to carbon dioxide alone, carries the message of this chart with sharp clarity: "The atmospheric concentration of carbon dioxide (CO_2) has increased by 31 percent since 1750. The present CO_2 concentration has not been exceeded during the past 420,000 years and likely not during the past 20 million years. The current rate of increase is unprecedented during at least the past 20,000 years."

Now what does all this mean in human terms, especially if these lines continue to climb on the charts of the future? Well get your fans out, because it's going to be hot. Very hot. According to *National Geographic News* of July, 2006, eleven of the last twelve years have been the hottest on record, probably reaching back for at least a thousand years. But that record won't last for long. The UN congregation of the world's scientists predicts that the earth's surface temperature could rise at least five degrees over the next hundred years—just in the last generation it has already risen two degrees on average. Can you imagine what it will be like to add five degrees to the average summer day in Memphis?

Beyond that, the world's agriculture will be profoundly changed. Fertile lands will become deserts, and vast populations will be forced to relocate. As you might imagine, and as *Time* magazine of April 2006 confirms, it is the poorest and least flexible populations—such as those one finds in Africa—who will be hardest hit initially. *Science* magazine adds that major forest fires in the West and South are more numerous and more devastating than they were a generation ago. The average land burned during a given year is more than six times what it was a generation ago.

Moreover, it will soon get more lonely here on planet earth. The latest word is that more than one-third—that's one-third—of all species in several parts of the world could be destroyed over the next fifty years. Chris Leeds, conservation biologist of the University of Leeds, says: "Our analyses suggest that well over a million species could be threatened with extinction as a result of climate change." That's over a million species.

The story becomes more tragic when we contemplate the fate of the oceans. Some scientists had previously discounted global warming because some of the most dire predictions about rising temperatures had not come true. What they forgot was the capacity of the oceans to absorb heat and smother some of the immediate impact of global warming. But a recent issue of *Science* magazine has published reports that—as they put it—"link a warming trend in the upper 3,000 meters of the world's oceans to global warming caused by human activities."

As the oceans grow warmer, especially in the Gulf of Mexico area, the threat of hurricanes grows more ominous. In its summary of conditions in 2006, *Time* reported that over the past thirty-five years, the number of category 4 & 5 hurricanes has jumped 50%. But these reports truly threaten all living creatures. In particular, they confirm the IPCC predictions that most coral reefs will disappear within thirty to fifty years. And as the oceans continue to warm and melt the great ice shelves in the polar regions, the rise in sea level—as much as three feet over the next century and perhaps even more—will wipe out vast lowland areas such as the Sundarbans in India and Bangladesh, the last, best habitat for the Bengal tiger. Large parts of Florida and Louisiana will surrender to the sea—sell your beach property soon! The barrier islands off Mobile Bay, where my parents took me camping as a boy and where I hope to take my own children, will gradually recede into memory. These are just fragments, mere glimpses, of the future global warming has in store for us, our children, and grandchildren.

Well, I hope I have gained your attention today. We have a problem here that threatens the quality of life here on earth. Can we do anything about it? I would like to give you a happy, simple answer to this question, but it is a complex one. It's not like we can just take our foot off the greenhouse accelerator, and bring the bus to a halt. Once it is heated, the ocean does not cool quickly. Once they have accumulated, greenhouse gases can linger for a long time. But there are things we can do to change this scenario. The future is not an either-or proposition, and we can mitigate some of the worst possibilities. We can cool the fires under global warming to prevent it from becoming global burning. In my next speech I hope to show you how.

The clock is ticking, but I don't think it's too late. I hope that what I've said in the last two speeches has gained your attention. Get involved! Together we can cool the fever, and turn down the heat under our planet.

We Don't Have to Live in Slums
ANNA ALEY

Anna Aley was a student as Kansas State University when she presented this persuasive speech. It is noteworthy for its vivid language; its effective use of supporting materials, especially narrative; and the way in which it focuses listeners on a program of action.

Slumlords—you'd expect them in New York or Chicago, but in Manhattan, Kansas? You'd better believe there are slumlords in Manhattan, and they pose a direct threat to you if you ever plan to rent an off-campus apartment.

I know about slumlords; I rented a basement apartment from one last semester. I guess I first suspected something was wrong when I discovered dead roaches in the refrigerator. I definitely knew something was wrong when I discovered the leaks: the one in the bathroom that kept the bathroom carpet constantly soggy and molding and the one in the kitchen that allowed water from the upstairs neighbor's bathroom to seep into the kitchen cabinets and collect in my dishes.

Then there were the serious problems. The hot water heater and furnace were connected improperly and posed a fire hazard. They were situated next to the only exit. There was no smoke detector or fire extinguisher and no emergency way out—the windows were too small for escape. I was living in an accident waiting to happen—and paying for it.

The worst thing about my ordeal was that I was not an isolated instance; many Kansas State students are living in unsafe housing and paying for it, not only with their money, but their happiness, their grades, their health, and their safety.

We can't be sure how many students are living in substandard housing, housing that does not meet the code specifications required of rental property. We can be sure, however, that a large number of Kansas State students are at risk of being caught in the same situation I was. According to the registrar, approximately 17,800 students are attending Kansas State this semester. Housing claims that 4,200 live in the dorms. This means that approximately 13,600 students live off-campus. Some live in fraternities or sororities, some live at home, but most live in off-campus apartments, as I do.

Many of these 13,600 students share traits that make them likely to settle for substandard housing. For example, many students want to live close to campus. If you've ever driven through the surrounding neighborhoods, you know that much of the available housing is in older houses, houses that were never meant to be divided into separate rental units. Students are also often limited in the amount they can pay for rent; some landlords, such as mine, will use low rent as an excuse not to fix anything and to let the apartment deteriorate. Most importantly, many students are young and, consequently, naive when it comes to selecting an apartment. They don't know the housing codes; but even if they did, they don't know how to check to make sure the apartment is in compliance. Let's face it—how many of us know how to check a hot water heater to make sure it's connected properly?

Adding to the problem of the number of students willing to settle for substandard housing is the number of landlords willing to supply it. Currently, the Consumer Relations Board here at Kansas State has on file student complaints against approximately one hundred landlords. There are surely complaints against many more that have never been formally reported.

There are two main causes of the substandard student housing problem. The first—and most significant—is the simple fact that it is possible for a landlord to lease an apartment that does not meet housing code requirements. The Manhattan Housing Code Inspector will evaluate an apartment, but only after the tenant has given the landlord a written complaint and the landlord has had fourteen days to remedy the situation. In other words, the way things are now, the only way the Housing Code Inspector can evaluate an apartment to see if it's safe to be lived in is if someone has been living in it for at least two weeks!

A second cause of the problem is the fact that campus services designed to help students avoid substandard housing are not well known. The Consumer Relations Board here at Kansas State can help students inspect apartments for safety before they sign a lease, it can provide students with vital information on their rights as tenants, and it can mediate in landlord–tenant disputes. The problem is, many people don't know these services exist. The Consumer Relations Board is not listed in the university catalogue; it is not mentioned in any of the admissions literature. The only places it is mentioned are in alphabetically organized references such as the phone book, but you have to already know it exists to look it up! The Consumer Relations Board does receive money for advertising from the student senate, but it is only enough to run a little two-by-three-inch ad once every month. That is not large enough or frequent enough to be noticed by many who could use these services.

It's clear that we have a problem, but what may not seem so clear is what we can do about it. After all, what can one student do to change the practices of numerous Manhattan landlords? Nothing, if that student is alone. But just think of what we could accomplish if we got all 13,600 off-campus students involved in this issue! Think what we could accomplish if we got even a fraction of those students involved! This is what Wade Whitmer, director of the Consumer Relations Board, is attempting to do. He is reorganizing the Off-Campus Association in an effort to pass a city ordinance requiring landlords to have their apartments inspected for safety before those apartments can be rented out. The Manhattan code inspector has already tried to get just such an ordinance passed, but the only people who showed up at the public forums were known slumlords, who obviously weren't in favor of the proposed ordinance. No one showed up to argue in favor of the ordinance, so the city commissioners figured that no one wanted it and voted it down. If we can get the Off-Campus Association organized and involved, however, the commissioners will see that someone does want the ordinance, and they will be more likely to pass it the next time it is proposed. You can do a great service to your fellow students—and to yourself—by joining the Off-Campus Association.

A second thing you can do to help ensure that no more Kansas State students have to go through what I did is sign my petition asking the student senate to increase the Consumer Relations Board's advertising budget. Let's face it—a service cannot do anybody any good if no one knows about it. The Consumer Relations Board's services are simply too valuable to let go to waste.

An important thing to remember about substandard housing is that it is not only distasteful, it is dangerous. In the end, I was lucky. I got out of my apartment with little more than bad memories. My upstairs neighbor was not so lucky. The main problem with his apartment was that the electrical wiring was done improperly; there were too many outlets for too few circuits, so the fuses were always blowing. One day last November, Jack was at home when a fuse blew—as usual. And, as usual, he went to the fuse box to flip the switch back on. When he touched the switch, it delivered such a shock that it literally threw this guy the size of a football player backwards and down a flight of stairs. He lay there at the bottom, unable to move, for a full hour before his roommate came home and called an ambulance.

Jack was lucky. His back was not broken. But he did rip many of the muscles in his back. Now he has to go to physical therapy, and he is not expected to fully recover.

Kansas State students have been putting up with substandard living conditions for too long. It's time we finally got together to do something about this problem. Join the Off-Campus Association. Sign my petition. Let's send a message to these slumlords that we're not going to put up with this any more. We don't have to live in slums.

The Price of Bottled Water
KATIE LOVETT

The persuasive speech that follows reflects a moment of self-discovery as Katie Lovett found her topic and her voice simultaneously. As Katie tells the story: "My persuasive speech topic came about after I attended a screening of the internationally acclaimed documentary 'Flow: For Love of Water' which addresses the global water crisis. Immediately after the film ended, I knew that I wanted to design a speech persuading people against buying bottled water. The research process for that speech was incredibly interesting and I am actually now getting more involved in the Davidson Environmental Action Coalition (EAC) as a result of our COM 101 speech assignment."

Have you heard the tired old joke about the salesperson who could sell ice cubes to Eskimos? If you think about it, that's not only a tribute to sales skills but also says a lot about our attitudes toward Native peoples—and how superior we feel towards them. These stupid people (it implies) are buying something they have no use for.

But consider this: In today's society, huge corporations like Coca-Cola, Pepsi, and Nestlé are marketing their own "ice cubes" to us with immense success. Water, a natural resource that has historically been viewed as free and open to the public, is now being bottled and sold for profit by large multinational corporations.

Why are we buying water? And what are the consequences of it? These are the questions I want to consider today. We will examine marketing strategies, consumer misconceptions, and the environmental impact of our behavior.

Let's begin by considering how the bottled water industry sells its own "ice cubes" to us. Consumers gravitate towards bottled water instead of tap water for two reasons: what's in it and what's not in it. What could possibly be inside a 20-ounce bottle of water that would compel someone to pay $3 and beyond for it? According to *The Journal of Consumer Culture*, "bottled water is a form of cultural consumption, driven by everything from status competition to a belief in magical curing." Clever advertisers feed these feelings. Since bottled water has become an affordable status symbol in today's society, companies can appeal to social distinctions of wealth and class to sell their product.

Take a look at some of the brands currently on the market: There are vitamin waters, nicotine waters, caffeine waters, electrolyte enhanced SmartWater, the "orbtastic" Aquapods that target kids, Bling H$_2$O which sells for $35 a bottle, "Hello Kitty" water for cats, and yes, even a "diet" water called "Skinny." And according to *The Journal of Consumer Culture*, "new water brands are entering the US market at the rate of about eight per month." Now tell me, how can we possibly feel superior to Eskimos?

Another main reason people want to buy bottled water is for what is *not* in it. The purity of water is the key theme for the bottled water industry. Bottlers seize upon public anxiety over municipal tap water supplies, supposedly offering us the safety that tap water cannot. As a result, the National Resources Defense Council has found that 'pure,' 'pristine,' and 'natural' are some of the most commonly used god-terms found in marketing and on labels.

So these are some of the fantasies and feelings that support the bottled water industry. Are they justified? Unfortunately, contrary to widespread belief, bottled water is not necessarily cleaner, safer, or purer than the water you get from your faucet. The perception is that if it is off the shelf, it is somehow cleaner and tastier. But *The Bulletin of Science, Technology & Society* argues that bottles of water become "petri dishes of germs." The bottles are loaded into trucks, driven down polluted highways, and transported by many different sets of hands before sitting around gathering dust and germs in storage houses.

In a recent four-year scientific study, the Natural Resources Defense Council tested more than 1,000 bottles of 103 brands of bottled water. In its publication, "Bottled Water or Tap Water?" the Council concluded that, "there is no assurance that bottled water is any safer than tap water." In fact, a third of the brands tested were found to contain contaminants such as arsenic and carcinogenic compounds. Some of these samples contained levels of these harmful contaminants that exceeded state or industry standards. So much for "pure" and "pristine"!

Another important misconception involves the regulation of tap water and bottled water. The journal *Environmental Health Perspectives*, in its article "The Price of Bottled Water," reveals the startling fact that city tap water in the United States undergoes more rigorous testing than bottled water. The Environmental Protection Agency (EPA) oversees the treatment of tap water while the Food and Drug Administration (FDA) regulates bottled water. But the FDA's standards for bottled water are actually no stricter than the EPA's health standards for public tap water: the FDA merely adopted the EPA's public drinking standards, which were first set forth in the Clean Water Act of 1978.

You may be asking, what about these reports showing that thousands of people get sick and more than one hundred of them die annually from tap water? Isn't it true that the bottled water industry has a relatively clean record in terms of outbreaks of illnesses?

According to the *Bulletin of Science, Technology & Society*, the reason for this dramatic discrepancy is that while the federal government requires all municipal water authorities to report even the mildest illnesses within 24 hours, there is no requirement for reporting sickness from bottled water. *Flow: For Love of Water*, an internationally acclaimed documentary concerning the global water crisis, also makes the shocking point that there is only one person in the FDA regulating the entire multi-billion dollar bottled water industry.

So while you are laying out the big bucks, thinking that you are protecting your health by drinking bottled instead of tap water, keep in mind that bottled water has not been proven to be any cleaner or better for you.

What about the environmental consequences of the bottled water industry? Consider that it takes an enormous amount of energy to produce a bottle of water. The process of manufacturing, transporting, and recycling plastic bottles drains fossil fuels and contributes to greenhouse gases. The bottles are often filled far away, shipped overseas, transported across the country in trucks, and then stored in refrigerators at your local convenience store. Compare that environmental impact to just turning on your kitchen faucet and we can begin to see the even larger price of bottled water.

The article "5 Reasons Not to Drink Bottled Water" warns that bottled water produces up to 1.5 million tons of plastic waste per year, since over 80% of plastic bottles are simply thrown away rather than recycled. By doing what you can to reduce that enormous pile of plastic bottles, filling a reusable bottle with tap water instead, you can make your own contribution to the quality of the environment.

I hope now, after this speech, that you will be a little less susceptible to the marketing techniques of the bottled water industry. Remember, at the very least bottled water is not safer than tap water, and instead the opposite may be true. And finally, remember the negative impact on the environment.

We pay too much—and in too many ways—for our fantasies concerning bottled water. It's time to put away these childish things. It's time to turn on our faucets instead of opening our wallets!

Fairly Traded Coffee
ELIZABETH LYLES

This persuasive speech by Betsy Lyles was presented in her class at Davidson College. It relies heavily on an impressive array of facts and figures to convince listeners of the ethical importance of buying fairly traded coffee. The speech might have benefited from a greater use of motivational appeals and narratives to make it come alive more powerfully for listeners.

How many of you began the morning with a cup of coffee? Many, if not most of you buy coffee every day. This daily purchase amounts to about $500 a year that you might spend on coffee. Based on a very conservative estimate that 10% of Davidson students drink coffee daily, collectively we as a student body invest more than $75,000 in the coffee industry per year.

The money we spend on coffee can go to either of two markets—the fair trade coffee market and regular trade coffee market. Today I want to urge you to support fairly traded coffee because it promotes both sustainable development and a decent life style for coffee farmers in those regions that are dependent upon the export of coffee for income. I will help you gain an understanding of what fair trade is, the effect of fairly traded coffee on workers and the environment, and how you can support fairly traded coffee here on campus.

Let's start by discussing how most coffee is produced. Most coffee is produced in ways that are harmful to both the farmer and the environment. According to an article by Don Wells in *Herizons* magazine, it is grown on plantations where trees have been cut down to allow more space to plant coffee beans. After the crop is harvested the soil is depleted.

Most coffee produced this way is sold by the farmers to a big supplier. The supplier then sells it separately to importers. This means there are two more people who share the profit and the coffee farmers themselves get very little money for their work. The article in *Herizons* goes on to say that of the $7 we might pay for a pound of coffee, the coffee farmers might get 3 cents while the coffee corporations get 86 cents of every dollar consumers spend on coffee.

With coffee farmers losing most of their profits to the "middle man" it creates a strain on their families, making it hard for them to maintain a sustainable lifestyle.

Now let's look at how being associated with fair trade helps the coffee farmers and the environment. Fair trade helps workers develop a lifestyle that is both sustainable and comfortable. Fair trade pays coffee farmers more per pound than they would be paid otherwise.

Andrew Downie reported in the *New York Times* last month that fair trade coffee farmers in Brazil are paid at least $1.29 a pound, compared with the regular market rate of roughly $1.05 per pound. That might not sound like much to you, but consider it from the point of view of a small farmer in Brazil, trying to raise a family. The difference mounts up into something really substantial! Downie also goes on to say that fair trade policies also create price floors to make sure that farmers will make a reasonable amount even if the coffee prices go down. The price floor is always set above the regular coffee market rate.

Coffee workers can see a noticeable difference in lifestyles as a result of fair trade. As Wells noted, coffee importers who trade fairly provide low-interest loans and credit to farmers, which helps them stay out of debt to local lenders. In a book by Alex Nicholls, *Fair Trade: Market-Driven Ethical Consumption*, a farmer from Belize remarked about how his lifestyle had changed:

> "I used to live in a thatch hut with a mud floor. Now I have two concrete houses and
> I have been able to educate my children. . . . They had to work in a shrimp farm when
> they were younger [to support the family], but now my children only go to school. We
> don't need them to work."

Another benefit of fair trade coffee is that it's grown organically, which means it has a lower environmental impact than mass produced coffee. Organic farming methods are less likely to deplete the soil and do not contribute to pollution and land and water resources.

So far we have learned what constitutes fair trade coffee farming and how it helps both the farmer and the environment. Now let's look at ways that you can personally support fair trade. There are many opportunities, right here in Davidson. To begin, it's not hard for you to buy fairly traded coffee. According to the Davidson College Dining Services web site, both the Commons and the Union serve S&D coffee, which is a fair trade supplier. So we've already supported fair trade coffee, if we've bought our coffee on campus. One hundred percent of Summit Coffee is fairly traded, so by purchasing this coffee you are supporting farmers.

Even if you don't like coffee, even if you never drink coffee, you can still support fair trade enterprises, because our Ben & Jerry's sells fairly traded ice cream.

A second contribution you can make is to promote awareness of fairly traded coffee. Only 3.3 percent of coffee sold in the United States last year was certified fair trade, but even that was more than eight times the level in 2001. The online campaign "Join the Big Noise" has produced a huge part of this increase, and by going online to maketradefair.com you can join the campaign to promote fair trade. Additionally, according to a study conducted last year by the New York based National Coffee Association, 27% of Americans said they were aware of the fair trade movement, up from the 12% claiming to be aware of it just a few years earlier. I challenge every one of you to participate in making those numbers increase even more significantly.

Now you understand how fair trade is an ethical alternative, how it positively affects the workers and the environment, and what you can do to support it right here in Davidson. I will leave you with the words of Bruce Crowther of the Fairtrade Foundation:

> People see [fair trade] as charity, but it is not, it is justice. We have to get rid of the
> charity way of thinking. I see doing fair trade as doing two things: one, it is helping
> people immediately and changing their lives; then there is the bigger picture where it is
> a protest tool, a way of registering your vote. But now we are not boycotting something,
> we are supporting something positive.

Every time you drink coffee remember the coffee farmer. Buy fairly traded coffee.

Ceremonial Speeches

> ## Remarks on Accepting the Martin Luther King Jr. Human Rights Award
>
> JOHN BAKKE

Professor John Bakke presented this thoughtful speech in 2006 in ceremonies held at the University of Memphis. Dr. Bakke used his acceptance speech to breathe new life into Dr. King's principle of nonviolence. Rather than a dated tactic in a long-ago civil rights struggle, nonviolence, by Bakke's interpretation, now demands full participation in the political process and acceptance of one's obligations as a citizen. Thus, what begins as an acceptance speech for an award quickly becomes a speech of tribute to Dr. King and finally a speech of inspiration to his listeners.

Thank you. It seems to me that many acceptance speeches begin with the words, "I've received many awards before, but . . ." Well, the truth is that I have not received many awards before, but of all the awards I have not received, this is the one I always wanted. What is more important in our lives than our rights as human beings? And who in our lifetime has done more to extend human rights than Dr. King? I'm overwhelmed by the honor. So please indulge me for a few minutes while I thank some people who are special to me before I say a few words in honor and memory of the person whom we all have reason to thank today. Dr. Martin Luther King Jr. gave me the courage to practice what he preached as best I could in and out of academia at critical points in my own life and in the life of this university and our community. And for that I am most thankful. . . . [Dr. Bakke acknowledges his family and friends, as well as his colleagues at the University of Memphis who shared his values and supported his work.]

We came to Memphis in 1967 and I was fortunate to be part of a progressive department at a university in a community ready for positive change. It is no accident that four members of that department, then called Speech and Drama, were previous recipients of this Martin Luther King Award. . . . And finally, thanks to all the seekers and holders of elected office who have given me the opportunity to work with them as well as to all the wonderful people whom I have worked with as a partisan in the political process. I got into campaign communication to help good people become more competitive in the campaign arena. I am proud of all these people for what they have done for human rights.

Dr. Martin Luther King Jr. gave to human rights his last full measure of devotion. He was devoted to nonviolence as a political strategy and as a personal philosophy because he knew the effects of violence even on those who commit violent acts as a means of necessary self defense or in a just cause. But when King was nearing his last days on earth, as Taylor Branch has recently written, in his commitment to nonviolence, King "found himself nearly alone among colleagues weary of sacrifice."

In 1968 King was increasingly under attack from all sides, by friends and foes alike. He was criticized by the Johnson Administration for opposing the war in Southeast Asia. He was under intense scrutiny by J. Edgar Hoover and the FBI. He was criticized by the white liberal establishment for his proposed Poor People's March. He was criticized by militant Black Power advocates for his nonviolent tactics and his coalitions with whites. And many of his closest friends just wanted him to back off for a while and by all means stay out of Memphis where a sanitation workers strike had been going on since February 2nd.

All such criticism came together and reached a crescendo after King's march in Memphis on behalf of the sanitation workers was disrupted by violence. The criticism came from all over, from the *New York Times* and *Washington Post* as well as the *Atlanta Constitution*, the *Dallas Morning News*, and, yes, the local *Memphis Commercial Appeal* and *Press Scimitar* newspapers. In editorials entitled "King's Credibility Gap" and "Chicken a la King," the *Commercial Appeal*, for example, said that "King's pose as the leader of a non-violent movement has been shattered" and "The Real Martin Luther King . . . [is] one of the most menacing men in America today." The *Press-Scimitar* said that King's "rhetoric has lost its spell" and the *Dallas Morning News* called him "a headline hunting high-priest on non-violent violence," "a press agent protester," "a marching militant" willing to "wreck everything for a spot on the evening newscast" and a "peripatetic preacher" who "could not allow the troubled -waters to go unfished when there was a chance that the fisher might pick up a little publicity." You can imagine what was being said on the street at the time.

From all corners, the message was clear. "Martin Luther King! Go home! Go back where you came from. Get back in your place! At worst, you're dangerous. At best, you're history." Believe me! James Earl Ray was not the only American who wanted King out of the way. On the eve of April 4, in such a climate of violence in Memphis, Martin Luther delivered his "Mountaintop Speech" at Mason Temple. Like Socrates at his trial, like Jesus before Pilate, like Luther at Worms, King, virtually alone, had to stand up and be who he was: Dr. Martin Luther King Jr., the true apostle of nonviolent direct action.

I spent much time as a graduate student studying great speeches. I also read many treatises on the nature of eloquence. Thus I can say, personally and professionally, history knows no more eloquent speaker than Martin Luther King Jr. I never understood what Longinus meant when he wrote that "eloquence was the concomitant of a great soul" until I heard Dr. King in a context in which I knew what he was up against and what he was asking for. His last speech in Memphis was more than speech. It was "eloquence," once described by the great orator Daniel Webster as "action . . . noble, sublime, godlike action."

In the peroration of what became his last speech, King mentioned the threats and uncertainties that surrounded his life, but announced that he had been to the mountaintop. And from that lofty eminence he had seen "the Promised Land," a vision that would redeem all the years of pain and suffering. He might not get there with them, but assured listeners "that we as a people will get to the Promised Land."

It was perfect communication. All in his presence were filled with King's conviction and what they felt was his "truth." The striking sanitation workers would get what they deserved and so too would they as a people. That WAS more than speech. It WAS action. In Webster's words: "noble, sublime, manly, godlike action." Martin Luther King, you see, was more than just a "dreamer," more than someone who simply walked on troubled waters turning the other cheek. King was America's conscience and a powerful force for change.

In his *Ethics of Rhetoric*, published in 1953 before King became a national figure, Richard Weaver wrote that the discourse of the noble orator is about "real potentiality or possible actuality," whereas that of the "mere exaggerator" is about "unreal potentiality." In his famous "I Have a Dream" speech, King said—remember it was 1963—that he had a dream that the sons of former slaves and former slave owners would be able to sit down together at the table of brotherhood. Unreal potentiality or possible actuality? He said little black boys and black girls would be able to join hands with little white boys and girls and walk together as sisters and brothers. Possible actuality or unreal potentiality? And he said that his four children would one day live in a nation where they would be judged not by the color of their skin but by the content of their character. A dream? Or real vision? And what about "We as a people will get to the promised land"? What about that one? Where are we on that one today? And if we are not where we want to be, whose fault is it? Certainly not Martin Luther King's nor the legitimacy of his vision.

In the last volume of his great trilogy, *America in the King Years*, Taylor Branch begins with the assertion that today "nonviolence is an orphan among democratic ideas." He says, "It has nearly vanished from public discourse even though the basic element—the vote— has no other meaning." In homage to King and for the good of ourselves, Branch strongly suggests that we commit the same time, energy, and resources to the nonviolent means of change as we now commit to the violent ones. "Every ballot is a piece of nonviolence," he says, "signifying hard-won consent to raise politics above fire power and bloody conquest."

It's time to make that ballot the effect of full democratic participation. It's time to reclaim our democratic processes. It's time to make the democratic processes work in America just as we are trying to make them work for Iraq.

That means more than voting. It means informed voting. It means supporting candidates and policies of our choice. It means commitment to the communication processes that give life to democracy. It means thinking of ourselves more as citizens than as just taxpayers. It means full-time citizenship. If campaigns are now permanent, citizenship cannot be cyclical. Democracy and "the vote" will always be open to criticism if people do not vote or do not know what they are voting for.

I don't care how much we spend on voting technology. I don't care how much we restrict campaign contributions. Special interests will always have special influence as long as we the people are not especially interested. Voting two dead people certainly was bad [in a recent local election], but over 90% of live voters staying home was a whole lot worse.

If we work to make the democratic processes work for us at home as well as around the world, we will be on the true path—the nonviolent path—to the kind of homeland security that will keep us moving toward the Promised Land. It is nonviolence that makes civilization civil and it is through the nonviolent participation in democracy that we can live out the true meaning of OUR creed. We will be keeping alive the hope of the American dream of our founding fathers and the real potentiality in the vision of Dr. Martin Luther King Jr.

Nobel Peace Prize Acceptance Speech[1]
ELIE WIESEL

Elie Wiesel delivered the following speech in Oslo, Norway, on December 10, 1986, as he accepted the Nobel Peace Prize. The award recognized his lifelong work for human rights, especially his role as "spiritual archivist of the Holocaust." Wiesel's poetic, intensely personal style as a writer carries over into this ceremonial speech of acceptance. He uses narrative very effectively as he flashes back to what he calls the "kingdom of night" and then flashes forward again into the present. The speech's purpose is to spell out and share the values and concerns of a life committed to the rights of oppressed peoples, in which, as he put it so memorably, "every moment is a moment of grace, every hour an offering."

It is with a profound sense of humility that I accept the honor you have chosen to bestow upon me. I know: your choice transcends me. This both frightens and pleases me.

It frightens me because I wonder: do I have the right to represent the multitudes who have perished? Do I have the right to accept this great honor on their behalf? I do not. That would be presumptuous. No one may speak for the dead, no one may interpret their mutilated dreams and visions.

It pleases me because I may say that this honor belongs to all the survivors and their children, and through us, to the Jewish people with whose destiny I have always been identified.

I remember: it happened yesterday or eternities ago. A young Jewish boy discovering the kingdom of night. I remember his bewilderment, I remember his anguish. It all happened so fast. The ghetto. The deportation. The sealed cattle car. The fiery altar upon which the history of our people and the future of mankind were meant to be sacrificed.

I remember: he asked his father: "Can this be true? This is the 20th century, not the Middle Ages. Who would allow such crimes to be committed? How could the world remain silent?"

And now the boy is turning to me: "Tell me," he asks. "What have you done with your life?"

And I tell him that I have tried. That I have tried to keep memory alive, that I have tried to fight those who would forget. Because if we forget, we are guilty, we are accomplices.

And then I explained to him how naive we were, that the world did know and remain silent. And that is why I swore never to be silent whenever and wherever human beings endure suffering and humiliation. We must always take sides. Neutrality helps the oppressor, never the victim. Silence encourages the tormentor, never the tormented.

Sometimes we must interfere. When human lives are endangered, when human dignity is in jeopardy, national borders and sensitivities become irrelevant. Wherever men or women are persecuted because of their race, religion or political views, that place must—at that moment—become the center of our universe.

Of course, since I am a Jew profoundly rooted in my people's memory and tradition, my first response is to Jewish fears, Jewish needs, Jewish crises. For I belong to a traumatized generation, one that experienced the abandonment and solitude of our people. It would be unnatural for me not to make Jewish priorities my own: Israel, Soviet Jewry, Jews in Arab lands.

But there are others as important to me. Apartheid is, in my view as abhorrent as anti-Semitism. To me, Andrei Sakharov's isolation is as much a disgrace as Iosif Begun's imprisonment. As is the denial of Solidarity and its leader Lech Walesa's right to dissent. And Nelson Mandela's interminable imprisonment.

There is so much injustice and suffering crying out for our attention: victims of hunger, or racism and political persecution, writers and poets, prisoners in so many lands governed by the left and by the right. Human rights are being violated on every continent. More people are oppressed than free.

And then, too, there are the Palestinians to whose plight I am sensitive but whose methods I deplore. Violence and terrorism are not the answer. Something must be done about their suffering, and soon. I trust Israel, for I have faith in the Jewish people. Let Israel be given a chance, let hatred and danger be removed from her horizons, and there will be peace in and around the Holy Land.

Yes, I have the faith. Faith in God and even in His creation. Without it no action would be possible. And action is the only remedy to indifference: the most insidious danger of all. Isn't this the meaning of Alfred Nobel's legacy? Wasn't his fear of war a shield against war?

There is much to be done, there is much that can be done. One person—a Raoul Wallenberg, an Albert Schweitzer, one person of integrity, can make a difference, a difference of life and death. As long as one dissident is in prison, our freedom will not be true. As long as one child is hungry, our lives will be filled with anguish and shame.

What all these victims need above all is to know that they are not alone: that we are not forgetting them, that when their voices are stifled we shall lend them ours, that while their freedom depends on ours, the quality of our freedom depends on theirs.

This is what I say to the young Jewish boy wondering what I have done with his years. It is in his name that I speak to you and that I express to you my deepest gratitude. No one is as capable of gratitude as one who has emerged from the kingdom of night.

We know that every moment is a moment of grace, every hour an offering; not to share them would mean to betray them. Our lives no longer belong to us alone; they belong to all those who need us desperately.

Thank you Chairman Aarvik. Thank you members of the Nobel Committee. Thank you people of Norway, for declaring on this singular occasion that our survival has meaning for mankind.

Reach for the Stars!

ASHLIE MCMILLAN

In her speech of tribute to her cousin, Ashlie McMillan, a student at Vanderbilt University, makes use of both identification and magnification, the major techniques of ceremonial speaking. By asking her listeners to imagine themselves as dwarfs, Ashlie develops a narrative based on vicarious experiences.

Please close your eyes. Imagine now that you are shrinking. Can you feel your hands and feet getting smaller, your arms being pulled in closer to your shoulders? Can you picture your legs now dangling off the edge of your seat as your legs shrink up closer to your hips? Now you are only three feet tall. But don't open your eyes yet. This is your first day of being a diastrophic dwarf.

You wake up and get out of bed, which is quite a drop because the bed is almost as tall as you are. You go to the bathroom to wash your face and brush your teeth, but you must stand on a trash can because the faucet is out of your reach. Now you go back to your dorm room, and you're ready to put on your clothes. But again you can't reach the clothes hanging in your closet because you're too short. You have to struggle to get dressed.

Now you have errands that you must run. But how are you going to do them? If you walk, it will take you a long time because you must take many short steps. And you can't drive a car because you can't reach the pedals, much less see over the steering wheel. Finally you get to the bank. But it takes you about five minutes to get the teller's attention because she can't see you below the counter. Next you go to the grocery store. This takes forever because you can't push a cart. You're forced to use a carry basket and to find people who will reach high items for you. Frustrated yet? Okay, open your eyes.

In 1968 my cousin, Tina McMillan, was born. Today she's in her twenty-ninth year as a diastrophic dwarf. What does that mean? It means that she'll never be taller than three feet. It means that her hands will never be able to bend this way [gestures] because she will never have joints in her fingers or toes. She'll always have club feet, and she had to have a rod put in her spine because all diastrophic dwarfs are plagued with scoliosis.

So what does her dwarfism mean to my cousin? Nothing. When you first meet Tina, you might be a little shocked at how tiny she is. But after a while you forget her physical size because her personality is so large and her spirit is so bright. Today I want to tell you the story of how this small person is reaching for the stars. Her life is a miracle that should teach us never to let obstacles stand in the way of our goals and dreams.

When my aunt and uncle were told that they were going to have a baby who was a diastrophic dwarf, they prepared themselves. They were ready to tell their child that she would never be able to have a Great Dane dog because it would be three times the size that she was. That she would never be able to ride a horse. That she would never be able to drive a car. And that she might not be able to attend college because the dormitories and other facilities were not built for people three feet tall.

What my aunt and uncle were *not* prepared for was a child with a physical disability who refused to see herself as disabled. I can tell you that growing up with Tina was quite an experience. She was always the ham of the cousins, always the center of attention. I remember going over to her house and playing with her *three* Great Dane dogs in the backyard. I remember every Sunday when my grandpa would take us out to the farm and we would fight over who got to ride the horses. And Tina would even fight my grandfather so she could get up on the horse all by herself. And I remember the day, some time after her sixteenth birthday, that she slid behind the wheel of a car. She had teamed up with some engineers down in Texas to have the pedals extended as well as hand gears made on the steering wheel so that she could drive herself. But perhaps my proudest and fondest memory was watching my cousin walk across the graduation stage at Texas Christian University in 1991. She not only got her degree in English, but she went on to get a master's degree in anthropology from TCU. After she graduated, the university invited her to come back to teach in the English Department. But by this time Tina had a new challenge: She declined the teaching job so that she could enter politics as campaign manager for the mayor of Dallas.

Tina has never stopped challenging the perception that she is disabled. Next April she will be marrying a person of normal stature, and once again she will defy society's assumption that something must be wrong about such a marriage. And then in the fall she plans on attending the University of Texas law school. Want to bet against her there?

Somehow, against the odds, my cousin has led a normal life. To many people, what she has accomplished might not seem that exceptional. To me, however, she is an inspiration. Whenever I think I've got problems that are too much for me, I think of her and of what she has done, this large and vital person stuffed into such a small body. I think of how she refuses to use her disability as a scapegoat or excuse. And I remember how she does not even consider quitting if something stands in her way. She simply views the obstacle, decides the best way to get around it, and moves on. And although she will lose the ability to walk, probably by the age of forty, I believe that she will still find the way to keep moving toward her goals.

The next time a large obstacle stands in your way, remember Tina, my small cousin, who has achieved such noteworthy things. You too may seem too short to grasp your stars, but you never know how far you might reach if you stand upon a dream.

Eulogy for Jesse Owens
THOMAS P. O'NEILL

Following the death of Jesse Owens in 1980, many tributes were presented.
The following comments by Thomas P. O'Neill, then speaker of the U.S.
House of Representatives, illustrate this genre. This speech was printed in the
Congressional Record, *1 April 1980, pp. 7459–7460.*

I rise on the occasion of his passing to join my colleagues in tribute to the greatest American sports hero of this century, Jesse Owens. . . . His performances at the Berlin Olympics earned Jesse Owens the title of America's first superstar.

No other athlete symbolized the spirit and motto of the Olympics better than Jesse Owens. "Swifter, higher, stronger" was the credo by which Jesse Owens performed as an athlete and lived as an American. Of his performances in Hitler's Berlin in 1936, Jesse said: "I wasn't running against Hitler, I was running against the world." Owens's view of the Olympics was just that: He was competing against the best athletes in the world without regard to nationality, race, or political view.

Jesse Owens proved by his performances that he was the best among the finest the world had to offer, and in setting the world record in the 100-yard dash, he became the "fastest human" even before that epithet was fashionable.

In life as well as on the athletic field, Jesse Owens was first an American, and second, an internationalist. He loved his country; he loved the opportunity his country gave him to reach the pinnacle of athletic prowess. In his own quiet, unassuming, and modest way—by example, by inspiration, and by performance—he helped other young people to aim for the stars, to develop their God-given potential...

As the world's first superstar, Jesse Owens was not initially overwhelmed by commercial interests and offered the opportunity to become a millionaire overnight. There was no White House reception waiting for him on his return from Berlin, and as Jesse Owens once observed: "I still had to ride in the back of the bus in my hometown in Alabama."

Can one individual make a difference? Clearly in the case of Jesse Owens, the answer is a resounding affirmative, for his whole life was dedicated to the elimination of poverty, totalitarianism, and racial bigotry; and he did it in his own special and modest way, a spokesman for freedom, an American ambassador of goodwill to the athletes of the world, and an inspiration to young Americans. . . . Jesse Owens was a champion all the way in a life of dedication to the principles of the American and Olympic spirit.

Glossary

accuracy   Criterion for evaluating the correctness of information by checking it against other information.

acronym   A word composed of the initial letters of a series of words.

ad hominem fallacy   Name-calling rather than arguing.

advocacy website   A website whose major purpose is to change attitudes or behaviors.

after-dinner speech   An often humorous ceremonial speech presented after a meal that offers a message without asking for radical changes.

agreement   This third stage in the persuasive process requires that listeners accept a speaker's recommendations and remember their reasons for doing so.

alliteration   The repetition of initial consonant sounds in closely connected words

amplification   The art of developing ideas by restating them in a speech.

analogical reasoning   Creating a strategic perspective on a subject by relating it to something similar to it.

analogous color scheme   Colors adjacent on the color wheel; used in a presentation aid to suggest both differences and close relationships among the components.

antithesis   A language technique that combines opposing elements in the same sentence or adjoining sentences.

articulation   The manner in which individual speech sounds are produced.

attitude adjustment   Shifting your focus from yourself to your listeners and message.

attitudes   Feelings we have developed toward specific kinds of subjects.

audience   Includes those that speakers would like to listen, as well as those that actually listen.

audience demographics   General characteristics of listeners, including age, gender, education, sociocultural background, and group affiliations.

audience dynamics   The beliefs, attitudes, values, and motives that influence the behavior of listeners.

authentic examples   Events and experiences known personally by listeners to be true and genuine.

authority   Criterion for evaluation that asks whether the source of information cited in a speech is an expert on the subject.

autocratic leader   A leader who makes decisions without consultation, issues orders or gives direction, and controls the members of the group through the use of rewards or punishments.

award presentation   A speech that explains the nature of the award and recognizes the achievements of the award recipient.

awareness   This first stage in the persuasive process includes knowing about a problem and paying attention to it.

balance   Suggests that the introduction, body, and conclusion receive appropriate development.

bandwagon fallacy   Urges listeners to climb aboard the bandwagon, arguing that because others are doing something, it might be right.

bar graph   A graph that shows comparisons and contrasts between two or more items or groups.

begging the question fallacy   Assuming that an argument has been proved without actually presenting the evidence.

beliefs   What we know or think we know about subjects.

body   The section of a speech that contains your main ideas and the materials that support them.

body language   Communication achieved using facial expressions, eye contact, movements, and gestures.

boomerang effect   A possible negative reaction to a speech that advocates too much change.

brainstorming   Technique that encourages the free play of the mind to generate a list of ideas for later careful consideration.

brief example   A concise reference to an example to illustrate or develop a point.

briefing   A short informative presentation offered in an organizational setting that focuses on plans, policies, or reports.

bulleted list   A presentation aid that highlights ideas by presenting them as a list of brief statements.

call the question   A motion that proposes to end discussion and vote on the original motion.

categorical design   Arranges the main ideas of a speech by natural or customary divisions.

causation design   Considers the origins or consequences of a situation or event, proceeding from cause to effect or from effect to cause.

ceremonial speeches (ceremonial speaking)   Speaking that celebrates special occasions, such as speeches of tribute, inspiration, and introduction; eulogies; toasts; award presentations; acceptances; and after-dinner speeches.

channel   Medium that conveys the message to listeners.

chronological design   Explains events or historical developments in the order in which they occurred.

co-active approach   A way of approaching reluctant audiences in which the speaker attempts to establish goodwill, emphasizes shared values, and sets modest goals for persuasion.

cognitive dissonance   The discomfort we feel because of conflict among our attitudes and values.

cognitive restructuring   Replacing negative thoughts with positive, constructive ones.

collaborative problem solving   In group communication, an approach that gathers participants from differing backgrounds and social sectors for their input on a problem.

communication anxiety   Those unpleasant feelings and fears you may experience before or during a presentation.

comparative design   Arranges a speech by exploring the similarities or differences among things.

competence   The perception of a speaker as being well informed, intelligent, and well prepared.

complementary color scheme   Colors opposite one another on the color wheel; used in a presentation aid to suggest tension and opposition.

comprehensive listening   Listening that focuses on understanding and interpreting the verbal and nonverbal aspects of a message.

computer-generated presentation   The use of commercial presentation software to join audio, visual, textual, graphic, and animated components.

conclusion (in deductive reasoning)   Meaning drawn from the relationship between the major and minor premises.

conclusion (to a speech)   The ending for your speech that reinforces your main ideas and provides your audience with something to remember.

connotative meaning   The emotional, subjective, personal meaning that certain words can evoke in listeners.

context of interpretation   Helps shape the meaning of a fact by offering a way of looking at it.

contrast   Attracts attention and sharpens perspective by highlighting the differences between opposites.

coordination   The requirement that statements equal in importance be placed on the same level in an outline.

critical listening   Listening that carefully evaluates a message.

cultural gridlock   A problem that occurs when the cultural differences within a group create tensions that impede constructive discussion.

cultural sensitivity   The respectful appreciation of diversity within an audience.

culturetypes   Terms that express the values and goals of a group's culture.

deductive reasoning   Arguing from a general principle to a specific conclusion.

deliberative speeches   Used to propose, discuss, debate, and decide future policies and laws.

denotative meaning   The dictionary definition or objective meaning of a word.

design   Standard way to arrange the main points of a speech.

dialect   A speech pattern associated with an area of the country or with a cultural or ethnic background.

dialogue   Having the characters in a narrative speak for themselves rather than paraphrasing what they say.

dialogue group   A group assembled to explore the differing interpretations and experiences that members bring to a given situation or problem.

direct quotation   Repeating the exact words of others to support a point.

discovery phase   Identifying large topic areas that might generate successful speeches.

disinformation   Information that has been fabricated or distorted in order to advance a hidden agenda.

distance   Principle of proxemics involving the control of the space that separates speaker and audience.

documents file   Contains articles downloaded from search engines or pages you have scanned into your computer.

doublespeak   Words that point in the direction opposite from the reality they supposedly describe.

dynamism   The perception of a speaker as confident, decisive, and enthusiastic.

either-or fallacy   Arguing that there are only two options, only one of which is desirable.

electronic brainstorming   A group technique in which participants generate ideas online prior to meeting face-to-face.

elevation   Principle of proxemics dealing with power relationships implied when speakers stand above listeners.

embedded narrative   A story inserted within a speech that illustrates the speaker's points.

empathic listening   Listening that goes beyond rationality to consider the human and humane aspects of a message.

enactment   This fourth stage of the persuasive process requires that listeners take appropriate action as the result of agreement.

enduring metaphors   Metaphors of unusual power and popularity that are based on experience that lasts across time and crosses many cultural boundaries.

enunciation   The manner in which individual words are articulated and pronounced in context.

epilogue The final part of a narrative, reflecting upon its meaning.

ethnocentrism The tendency of any nation, race, religion, or group to believe that its way of looking at and doing things is right and that other perspectives have less value.

ethos Audience impressions of a speaker's competence, integrity, goodwill, and dynamism; in persuasion, a form of proof that relies on the audience's perceptions of a speaker's leadership qualities.

eulogy A speech of tribute presented upon a person's death.

euphemism Words that soften or evade the truth of a situation.

evidence Supporting materials used in persuasive speeches, including facts and figures, examples, narratives, and testimony.

examples Incidents that illustrate a speaker's points.

expanded conversational style A presentational quality that, while more formal than everyday conversation, preserves its directness and spontaneity.

expert testimony Citing the words of people (or institutions) qualified by training or experience to speak as authorities on a subject.

exploration phase Examining large topic areas to pinpoint more precise speech topics.

extemporaneous speaking A form of presentation in which a speech is carefully prepared and practiced but not written out, memorized, or read.

extended example A more detailed example that speakers use to illustrate or develop a point.

facts Descriptive statements that can be verified as true by independent observation.

factual example An example based on something that actually happened or really exists.

fallacies Errors in reasoning that make persuasion unreliable.

faulty analogy A comparison drawn between things that are dissimilar in some important way.

faulty premise fallacy A reasoning error that occurs when an argument is based on a flawed major premise.

faulty testimony Occurs when a speaker offers "expert testimony" when the source is not really an expert on the subject.

feedback Your perception of how audience members react to the message as you speak.

figurative analogy A comparison of subjects drawn from essentially different fields of experience.

figurative language Words used in surprising and unusual ways that magnify the power of their meaning.

flip chart A large, unlined tablet, usually a newsprint pad, that is placed on an easel so that each page can be flipped over the top when it's full.

flowchart A visual method of representing power and responsibility relationships or describing the steps in a process.

focus group A small group formed to reveal the feelings or motivations of customers or clients.

forensic speeches Used to determine the rightness and wrongness of past actions, often in courts of law.

formal outline Represents the final, complete, polished plan of your speech.

forum Presentational format in which a group of specialists in different areas of a subject respond to questions from an audience.

free-rein leader A leader who leaves members free to decide what, how, and when to act, offering no guidance.

gender stereotyping Generalizations based on oversimplified or outmoded assumptions about gender roles.

general purpose The speaker's intention to inform or persuade listeners or to celebrate some person or occasion.

general search engine An Internet search engine that allows you to enter a keyword and find related websites.

goodwill The impression that speakers have their listeners' best interests at heart.

graphics Visual representations of information, such as sketches, maps, graphs, charts, and textual materials.

great expectation fallacy The mistaken idea that major change can usually be accomplished by a single persuasive effort.

groupthink Occurs when a single, uncritical frame of mind dominates group thinking and prevents the full, objective analysis of specific problems.

habitual pitch The vocal level at which people speak most frequently.

hasty generalization An error of inductive reasoning in which a claim is made based on insufficient or nonrepresentative information.

hypothetical example An example offered not as real but as representative of actual people, situations, or events.

identification The feeling of closeness between speakers and listeners that may overcome personal and cultural differences.

ideographs Compact expressions of a group's basic political faith.

immediacy A quality of successful communication achieved when the speaker and audience experience a sense of closeness.

impromptu speaking   Speaking on the spur of the moment in response to an unpredictable situation with limited time for preparation.

inappropriate evidence fallacy   Occurs when speakers use one form of evidence when they should be using another.

inductive reasoning   Reasoning from specific factual instances to reach a general conclusion.

inferences   Assumptions based on incomplete information.

information website   A website designed to provide factual information on a subject.

informative speaking   Functions to enlighten by sharing ideas and information.

informative value   A measure of how much new and important information or understanding a speech conveys to an audience.

inoculation effect   Preparing an audience for an opposing argument by answering it before listeners have been exposed to it.

integration   This final stage of the persuasive process requires that listeners connect new attitudes and commitments with previous beliefs and values to ensure lasting change.

integrity   The quality of being honest, ethical, and dependable.

intensity   Refers to the extent to which aspects of a speech are striking or stand out.

interest charts   Visual displays of speaker or audience interests, as prompted by probe questions.

interference   Distractions that can disrupt the communication process.

internal summary   A transition that reminds listeners of major points already presented in a speech before proceeding to new ideas.

introduction   The opening to your speech that gains attention, previews your message, and establishes a favorable connection with your listeners.

inversion   Changing the normal order of words to make statements memorable.

jargon   Technical language related to a specific field that may be incomprehensible to a general audience.

key-word outline   Abbreviated version of a formal outline used in presenting a speech; focuses on cues and points of emphasis.

lay testimony   Citing the words or views of ordinary people on a subject.

line graph   A visual representation of changes across time; especially useful for indicating trends of growth or decline.

literal analogy   A comparison of subjects drawn from the same field of experience.

logos   Appeals based on logic and evidence; in persuasion, a master form of proof that appeals to reason based largely on facts and expert testimony presented logically.

magnification   A speaker's selecting and emphasizing certain qualities of a subject to stress the values they represent.

main points   The most important ideas developed in support of the thesis statement.

major premise   The general principle on which an argument is based.

malapropisms   Language errors that occur when a word is confused with another word that sounds like it.

manipulative persuasion   Persuasion that works through suggestion, colorful images, music, and attractive spokespersons. It avoids evidence and reasoning and the burden of justifying itself.

manuscript presentation   A speech read from a prepared text or teleprompter.

master narrative   A speech that is structured around a story that reveals some important truth.

master of ceremonies   A person who coordinates an event or program, sets its mood, introduces speakers, and provides transitions.

maxims   Brief and particularly apt sayings.

media and Internet prompts   Sources such as newspapers, magazines, and the electronic media that can suggest ideas for speech topics.

memorized text presentations   Speeches that are committed to memory and delivered word for word.

message   What the speaker wishes to accomplish.

metaphor   An implied comparison that connects subjects not usually related to create a surprising perspective.

mind mapping   Changes customary patterns of thinking to encourage creative exploration.

minor premise   Relating a specific subject to the general principle that supports an argument.

mirror question   A question that repeats part of a previous response to encourage further discussion.

monochromatic color scheme   Use of variations of a single color in a presentation aid to convey the idea of variety within unity.

motion to amend   A parliamentary move that offers opportunity to modify a motion presently under discussion.

motion to postpone consideration   A motion that defers discussion until some specified time.

motions   Formal proposals for group consideration.

motivated sequence   A persuasive speech design that proceeds by arousing attention, demonstrating a need, satisfying the need, visualizing results, and calling for action.

motives   Widely shared psychological needs, desires, and impulses.

move to adjourn   A motion that calls for the meeting to end.

multisided presentation   A speech in which the speaker's position is compared favorably to other positions.

myth of the mean fallacy   The deceptive use of statistical averages in speeches.

mythos   A form of proof grounded in the social feelings that connect us powerfully with group traditions, values, legends, and loyalties.

narrative design   Speech structure that develops a story from beginning to end through a prologue, plot, and epilogue.

narrative fidelity   Measures the authenticity of the story, the likelihood that it happened or might happen.

narrative probability   Measures the skill of the speaker in blending scene, characters, and action into a compelling story.

narratives   Stories that illustrate the ideas or theme of a speech.

neologism   An invented word that combines previous words in a striking new expression.

non sequitur fallacy   Occurs when conclusions do not follow from the premises that precede them or arise from irrelevant evidence.

novelty   The quality of being new or unusual.

objectivity   Criterion for evaluating whether or not a source is free from bias.

onomatopoeia   Words that sound like the subjects they signify.

opinions   Expressions of personal feeling or belief offered without supporting material.

optimum pitch   The level that allows people to produce their strongest voice with minimal effort and that permits variation up and down the scale.

oral citations   References to supporting materials during the speech that strengthen the credibility of the speech and support controversial and surprising claims.

oral report   Presentation that summarizes the deliberations of a small group to inform a larger audience of decision makers.

order   A consistent pattern used to develop a speech.

panel discussion   A group presentation featuring organized exchanges among speakers, directed by a moderator.

parallel construction   Wording points in a repeated pattern to emphasize their importance and to show how they are both related and contrasted.

paraphrase   Rephrasing or summarizing the words of others to support a point.

parliamentary procedure   A set of formal rules that establishes an order of business for meetings and encourages the orderly, fair, and full consideration of proposals during group deliberation.

participative leader   A leader who seeks input from group members and gives them an active role in decision making.

pathos   Appeals based on personal feelings.

peer review   Process by which articles in scholarly journals are checked by experts in the field for quality and accuracy before being approved for publication.

personification   A figure of speech in which nonhuman or abstract subjects are given human qualities.

persuasion   The art of gaining fair and favorable consideration for our points of view.

pie graph   A circle graph that shows the size of a subject's parts in relation to each other and to the whole.

pitch   The placement of the human voice on a scale ranging from low and deep to high and shrill.

plagiarism   Presenting the ideas and words of others as though they were your own.

plot   The body of a narrative that unfolds in a sequence of scenes designed to build suspense.

post hoc fallacy   An inductive error in which one event is assumed to be the cause of another simply because the first preceded the second.

predictions   Forecasts of what we can expect in the future, often based on trends from past events.

preliminary tuning effect   The effect of previous speeches or other situational factors in predisposing an audience to respond positively or negatively to a speech.

PREP formula   A technique for making an impromptu speech: State a point, give a reason or example, and restate the point.

presentation   Delivering a speech to an audience, integrating the skills of nonverbal communication with the speech content.

presentation aids   Visual and auditory materials intended to enhance the clarity and effectiveness of a presentation.

prestige testimony   Citing the words of a person who is highly admired or respected but not necessarily an expert on your topic; similarly, citing a text in this way.

preview   The part of the introduction that identifies the main points to be developed in the body of the speech and presents an overview of the speech to follow.

probe   A question that asks a person to elaborate on an answer.

problem–solution design   A persuasive speech pattern in which listeners are first persuaded that they have a problem and then are shown how to solve it.

prologue   The opening of a narrative that establishes the context and setting, foreshadows the meaning, and introduces major characters.

pronunciation   The use of correct sounds and of proper stress on syllables when saying words.

proof   An arrangement of the resources of persuasion so that it satisfies a basic requirement for success.

proxemics   The study of how human beings use space during communication.

public speaking ethics   Standards for judging the rightness or wrongness of public speaking behaviors.

quoting out of context   An unethical use of a quotation that changes or distorts its original meaning.

racist language   Using disparaging labels and references to race or making irrelevant references to race such as "black doctor."

rate   The speed at which words are uttered.

reality testing   Subjecting negative messages you send yourself to rational scrutiny.

reasoned persuasion   Persuasion that builds a case to justify its recommendations.

red herring fallacy   The use of irrelevant material to divert attention.

refinement phase   Framing the general and specific purposes of a speech topic and a thesis statement.

refutative design   A persuasive design in which the speaker challenges other views.

reinforcer   A comment or action that encourages further communication from someone being interviewed.

relevance   Refers to the extent to which a speech relates to an audience's specific needs, interests, or concerns.

reluctant testimony   Invoking the words of sources who appear to speak against their own interests.

reluctant witnesses   Witnesses who testify against their apparent self-interest.

repetition   Repeating sounds, words, or phrases to attract and hold attention.

research log   Computer file in which you jot down ideas, list key terms, and prioritize readings.

responsible knowledge   An advanced sense of awareness concerning a topic, understanding its major features, issues, latest developments, and local applications.

retention   The extent to which listeners remember and use a message.

rhetorical questions   Questions that have a self-evident answer or that provoke curiosity, which the speech then proceeds to satisfy.

rhythm   Rate and stress patterns of vocal presentation within a speech.

roundtable   Interactive way of informally exchanging ideas, information, or opinions within a small group before a larger audience.

second   A motion must receive a "second" from a member of the group before group discussion can proceed; ensures that more than one member wishes to have the motion considered.

selective relaxation   Practicing muscle control techniques to help you reduce physical tension by relaxing on cue.

self-awareness inventory   A series of questions that allow speakers to explore their individuality so they can prepare a speech of self-introduction.

sequential design   Explains the steps of a process in the order in which they should be taken.

setting   Physical and psychological context in which a speech is presented.

sexism   Allowing gender stereotypes to control interactions with members of the opposite sex.

sexist language   Using disparaging labels and references to gender or using masculine nouns or pronouns when the intended reference is to both sexes.

simile   A language tool that clarifies something abstract by comparing it with something concrete; usually introduced by *as* or *like*.

simplicity   Suggests that a speech has a limited number of main points and that it is short and direct.

slang   The language of the street.

sleeper effect   A delayed reaction to persuasion.

slippery slope fallacy   The assumption that once something happens, an inevitable trend is established that will lead to disastrous results.

small group   Limited number of people who interact over time to achieve a goal or goals.

social leadership behavior   A leadership emphasis that focuses on building and maintaining positive, productive relationships among group members.

source citations   Abbreviated references in a formal outline to research sources that support the points made.

source file   Contains complete information on every source you find helpful.

spatial design   Arranges the main points of a speech as they occur in actual space, creating an oral map.

speaker   Initiates the communication process by framing an oral message for the consideration of others.

speaking situation   The occasion for speaking as well as the physical and psychological settings.

specific purpose   The speaker's particular goal or the response that the speaker wishes to evoke.

speeches that advocate action and policy   Speeches that encourage listeners to change their behavior either as individuals or as members of a group.

speeches that emphasize attitudes and values   Speeches designed to modify and apply these elements and help listeners find harmony among them.

speeches that focus on facts   Speeches designed to establish the validity of past or present information or to make predictions about what is likely to occur in the future.

speech of acceptance   A ceremonial speech expressing gratitude for an honor and acknowledging those who made the accomplishment possible.

speech of demonstration   An informative speech that shows the audience how to do something or how something works.

speech of description   An informative speech that uses vivid language to illustrate an activity, object, person, or place.

speech of explanation   An informative speech that offers information about abstract and complex subjects.

speech of inspiration   A ceremonial speech directed at awakening or reawakening an audience to a goal, purpose, or set of values.

speech of introduction   A ceremonial speech in which a featured speaker is introduced to the audience.

speech of tribute   A ceremonial speech that recognizes the achievements of individuals or groups or commemorates special events.

statistics   Facts that can be measured mathematically.

stereotypes   Generalized pictures of a race, gender, or group that supposedly represent its essential characteristics.

stock issues   The major general questions a reasonable person would ask before agreeing to a change in policies or procedures.

straw man fallacy   Understating, distorting, or otherwise misrepresenting the position of opponents for ease of refutation.

subject directory   An organized list of links to websites on specific topics.

subject files   Main divisions in the information you encounter as you research your topic.

subordination   The requirement that material in an outline descend in importance from the general to the specific—from main points to subpoints to sub-subpoints and so on.

subpoints   The major divisions of a speech's main points.

sub-subpoints   Strengthen subpoints by supplying relevant supporting materials.

supporting materials   The facts and statistics, testimony, examples, and narratives that are the building blocks of substantive speech-making.

syllogism   Pattern of deductive reasoning as it develops in reasoned persuasion.

symbolic racism   Indirect racism that uses code words or subtle contrasts to suggest that one race is superior to another.

symposium   Group presentation in which speakers address different areas of an issue.

synecdoche   Represents a subject by focusing on a vivid part of it or on something clearly associated with it.

table the motion   A parliamentary move to suspend indefinitely the discussion of a motion.

task leadership behavior   A leadership emphasis that directs the attention and activity of a group toward a specified goal.

testimony   Citing the words and ideas of others to support a point.

textual graphics   Visuals that contain words, phrases, or numbers.

thesis statement   Summarizes in a simple declarative sentence the central idea of your speech.

toast   A short speech of tribute, usually offered at celebration dinners or meetings.

topic analysis   Using questions often employed by journalists to explore topic possibilities for speeches (who, what, why, when, where, and how).

topic area inventory chart   A means of determining possible speech topics by listing topics you and your listeners find interesting and matching them.

transactional leadership   A leadership style based on power relationships that relies on reward and punishment to achieve its ends.

transformational leadership   A leadership style based on mutual respect and stewardship rather than on control.

transitions   Connecting elements that cue listeners that you are finished making one point and are moving on to the next.

trigger words   Words that arouse such powerful feelings that they interfere with the ability to listen effectively.

understanding   This second phase in the persuasive process requires that listeners grasp the meaning of the speaker's message.

values   The moral principles that suggest how we should behave or what we should believe.

vicarious experience narrative   Speech strategy in which the speaker invites listeners to imagine themselves enacting a story.

virtual meetings   Group meetings that are conducted and mediated using electronic and/or computer technology.

visualization   Systematically picturing yourself succeeding as a speaker and practicing your speech with that image in mind.

vocal distractions   Filler words, such as "er," "um," and "you know," used in the place of a pause.

working outline   A tentative plan that allows you to see the structure of your message as you develop it.

works cited list   Supplies complete, relevant information about sources of research actually cited in the speech.

works consulted list   Supplies complete, relevant information about all sources of research considered in the preparation of the speech.

Notes

Chapter 1

1. Richard M. Weaver, *Ideas Have Consequences* (Chicago: University of Chicago Press, 1948) and *The Ethics of Rhetoric* (Chicago: Henry Regnery, 1953).
2. Roderick P. Hart, "Why Communication? Why Education? Toward a Politics of Teaching," *Communication Education* 42 (1993): 101.
3. Press Release, National Association of Colleges and Employers, 15 March 2007, www.naceweb.org/press/display.asp?year=2007&prid=254 (accessed 7 May 2007).
4. Press Release, National Association of Colleges and Employers, 8 November 2012, www.naceweb.org/printerFriendly.aspx?printpage=/Press/Release (accessed 6 January 2013).
5. "Employers Complain About Communication Skills," *Pittsburgh Post-Gazette*, 6 February 2005, www.post-gazette.com/pg/pp/05037/453170.stm (accessed 7 May 2007).
6. Jill J. McMillan and Katy J. Harriger, "College Students and Deliberation: A Benchmark Study," *Communication Education* 51 (2002): 237–253.
7. From Kathleen Peterson, ed., *Statements Supporting Speech Communication* (Annandale, VA: Speech Communication Association, 1986).
8. Elizabeth Lozano, "The Cultural Experience of Space and Body: A Reading of Latin American and Anglo American Comportment in Public," in *Our Voices: Essays in Culture, Ethnicity, and Communication*, ed. Alberto Gonzalez, Marsha Houston, and Victoria Chen (Los Angeles: Roxbury, 2004), p. 275.
9. T. Harry Williams, ed., *Abraham Lincoln: Selected Speeches, Messages, and Letters* (New York: Holt, Rinehart & Winston, 1964), p. 148.
10. Pericles, "Funeral Oration," in *Thucydides on Justice, Power, and Human Nature*, ed. and trans. Paul Woodruff (Cambridge, MA: Hackett, 1993), p. 42.
11. Michael Osborn and Suzanne Osborn, *Alliance for a Better Public Voice: The Communication Discipline and the National Issues Forums* (Dayton, OH: National Issues Forums Institute, 1991).
12. "Twitter Turns Six," Twitter.com, 21 March 2012 (accessed 8 January 2013).
13. Michael Scherer and Jay Newton-Small, "Welcome to the Fun House," *Time*, 9 November 2009, pp. 40–41.
14. See especially Burke's discussion of identification and consubstantiality: "The Range of Rhetoric," in *A Rhetoric of Motives* (Berkeley: University of California Press, 1969), pp. 3–43.
15. Martin Luther King, Jr., "I Have a Dream," www.americanrhetoric.com/speeches/mlkihaveadream.htm.
16. "Credo of Ethical Communications," National Communication Association. Reprinted by permission of the National Communication Association. www.natcom.org.
17. Tom Teepen, "Twisting King's Words to Give His Antagonists Comfort," *Minneapolis Star Tribune*, 14 July 1997, p. 9A.
18. Lawrence M. Hinman, "How to Fight College Cheating," *Washington Post*, 3 September 2004, http://ethics.sandiego.edu/LMH/op-ed/CollegeCheating/index.asp (accessed 29 June 2006).
19. *Spectra*, newsletter of the National Communication Association (September 2008), pp. 28–29.
20. This theme develops in Richard L. Johannesen, Kathleen S. Valde, and Karen E. Whedbee, *Ethics in Human Communication*, 6th ed. (Long Grove, IL: Waveland, 2007).
21. Robert A. Caro, *The Path to Power*, vol. 1 of *The Years of Lyndon Johnson* (New York: Vintage Books, 1990), pp. 59–60.

Chapter 2

1. Elizabeth Quinn, "Why Do So Many Athletes Have Superstitions and Rituals?" 28 October 2008, http://sportsmedicine.about.com/od/sportspsychology/a/superstitions.htm (accessed 4 November 2009).
2. Cited in Dave Weiss, "Performance Anxiety—Is It Really a Syndrome?" 6 April 2006, www.healthcentral.com/diet-exercise/c/36/1557/anxiety (accessed 10 November 2009).
3. Anxiety Support Group, "*Panic: A Film About Coping*" undated, http://www.dailystrength.org/c/Anxiety/recs/2795-panic-film-coping (accessed 6 August 2013).
4. "Celebrities with Social Anxiety," undated, http://socialanxietydiisorder.about.com (accessed 23 May 2013).
5. Cited in Scott Berkun and Liz Danzico, "Training the Butterflies: Interview with Scott Berkun," 23 February 2010, http://allstapart.com/article/interview-with-scott-berkum (accessed 8 February 2013).
6. From the National Communication Association.
7. Amber N. Finn, Chris R. Sawyer, and Paul Schrodt, "Examining the Effect of Exposure Therapy on Public Speaking State Anxiety," *Communication Education* 10 (2009): 92–109.
8. John A. Daly, Anita L. Vangelisti, and David J. Weber, "Speech Anxiety Affects How People Prepare Speeches: A Protocol Analysis of the Preparation Processes of Speakers," *Communication Monographs* 62 (1995): 383–397.
9. Therese J. Borchard, "Conquering Performance Anxiety: A Primer for All Phobias," 10 May 2011, http://psychcentral.com/blog/archives/2011/05/10/conquering-performance-anxiety-a-primer-for-all-phobias/ (accessed 6 February 2013).
10. John M. Grohol, "Visualize Your Goal in Order to Attain It," 16 August 2011, http://psychcentral.com/news/2011/08/16/visualize-your-goal-in-order-to-attain-it/28624.html (accessed 6 February 2013).
11. Daly, Vangelisti, and Weber, "Speech Anxiety Affects How People Prepare Speeches."
12. Randolph W. Whitworth and Claudia Cochran, "Evaluation of Integrated Versus Unitary Treatments for Reducing Public Speaking Anxiety," *Communication Education* 45 (1996): 306–314.
13. Chia-Fang (Sandy) Hsu, "The Relationship of Trait Anxiety, Audience Nonverbal Feedback, and Attributions to Public Speaking State Anxiety," *Communication Research Reports* 26 (2009): 237–246.
14. Lou Davidson Tillson, "Building Community and Reducing Communication Apprehension: A Case Study Approach," *Speech Communication Teacher* (Summer 1995): 4–5.

Chapter 3

1. James C. McCroskey and Mason J. Teven, "Goodwill: A Reexamination of the Construct and Its Measurement," *Communication Monographs* 66 (1999): 90–103.
2. Kenneth Burke, *A Rhetoric of Motives* (Berkeley: University of California Press, 1969), pp. 20–23.
3. Barack Obama, "Reclaiming the Promise to the People," *Vital Speeches of the Day* 70 (1 Aug. 2004): 625.

Chapter 4

1. Cited in Clifton Fadiman, ed., *The Little Brown Book of Anecdotes* (Boston: Little Brown, 1985), pp. 475–476.
2. "Listening Skills," *Skills You Need*, undated, http://skillsyouneed.couk/IPS/Listening_Skills.html (accessed 15 February 2013).
3. "The Discipline of Listening," *Harvard Business Review Blog Network*, 21 June 2012, http://blogs/hbr.org/cs/2012/06/the_discipline_of_listening.html (accessed 15 February 2013).
4. Michael Purdey, "The Listener Wins," undated, http://career-advice.monster.comm/in-the-office/workplace-issues/the-listener-wins/article.aspx (accessed 15 February 2013).
5. Amy Kossoff Smith, "Are You a Bad Listener?" *Chicago Tribune*, 16 March 2012, www.chicagotribune.com/features/tribu/sc-fam-0313-listen-month-20120313,0,50772773.story (accessed 15 February 2013).
6. Ibid.
7. Dana Bristol-Smith, "Listening: The Overlooked Communication Skill," *Speak for Success*, undated, www.speakforsuccess.net/a-listng.htm (accessed 15 February 2013).
8. Smith, "Are You a Bad Listener?"
9. Fang-Yi Flora Wei, Y. Ken Wang, and Michael Klausner, "Rethinking College Students' Self-Regulation and Sustained Attention: Does Text Messaging During Class Influence Cognitive Learning?" *Communication Education* 61, no. 3 (July 2012): 185–204.
10. Professor Halley discussed this triggering stimuli assignment on the website of the International Listening Association in 1998. The article is no longer available online.
11. Graham D. Bodie and Susanne M. Jones, "The Nature of Supportive Listening II: The Role of Verbal Person Centeredness and Nonverbal Immediacy," *Western Journal of Communication* 76, no. 3 (May–June 2012): 250–269; and Graham D. Bodie, "The Active-Empathic Listening Scale (AELS): Conceptualization and Evidence of Validity Within the Interpersonal Domain," *Communication Quarterly* 59, no. 3 (July–August 2011): 277–295.

Chapter 5

1. George Kennedy, trans., The Rhetoric of Aristotle (New York: Oxford University Press 1992), bk. 2, chs. 11–14, pp. 163–169.
2. Richard E. Petty and Duane T. Wegener, "Attitude Change: Multiple Roles for Persuasion Variables," in Handbook of Social Psychology, ed. Daniel T. Gilbert, Susan T. Fiske, and Gardener Lindzey, 4th ed. (Boston: McGraw-Hill, 1998), vol. 1, p. 358; Milton Rokeach, The Open and Closed Mind (New York: Basic Books, 1960); and T. R. Tyler and R. A. Schuller, "Aging and Attitude Change," Journal of Personality and Social Psychology 61 (1991): 689–697.
3. Jack W. Germond, "Clinton Was Able to Expand Appeal to Suburbs, Whites, Independents," Baltimore Sun, 5 November 1992, http://articles.baltimoresun.com/1992-11-05/news/1992310208_1_clinton-young-voters-white-voters (accessed 6 June 2013); and Scott Keeter, Juliana Horowitz, and Alec Tyson, "Young Voters in the 2008 Election," Pew Research Center, 13 November 2008, www.pewresearch.org/2008/11/13/young-voters-in-the-2008-election/ (accessed 6 June 2013).
4. Charles U. Larson, Persuasion: Reception and Responsibility, 10th ed. (Boston: Wadsworth, 2004), p. 275.
5. "A Portrait of 'Generation Next': How Young People View Their Lives, Futures, and Politics," Pew Research Center, 9 January 2007, www.people-press.org/2007/01/09/a-portrait-of-generation-next/ (accessed 15 June 2013).
6. See Deborah Tannen, You Just Don't Understand: Women and Men in Conversation (New York: HarperCollins, 2010); and Sonja Foss and Cindy Griffin, "Beyond Persuasion: A Proposal for an Invitational Rhetoric," Communication Monographs 62 (1995): 2–18.
7. "The Gender Gap: Three Decades Old: As Wide as Ever," Pew Research Center, 29 March 2012, www.people-press.org/2012/03/29/the-gender-gap-three-decades-old-as-wide-as-ever/ (accessed 6 June 2013); also see "The Gender Gap: Attitudes on Public Policy Issues," Center for American Women and Politics, 2012, www.cawp.rutgers.edu/fast_facts/voters/gender_gap.php (accessed 6 June 2013).
8. "The Gender Gap: Voting Choices in Presidential Elections," Center for American Women and Politics, 2012, www.cawp.rutgers.edu/fast_facts/voters/documents/GGPresVote.pdf (accessed 6 June 2013).
9. Debra Cassens Weiss, "Have Women's Law School Numbers Peaked? NAWL Report Suggests the Pipeline May Be Shrinking," ABA Journal: Law News Now, 10 November 2011, www.abajournal.com/news/article/have_women_law_school_numbers_peaked_nawl_report_suggest_the_pipeline_is/ (accessed 6 June 2013); and Susanna Kim, "Record Number of Female Breadwinners, According to Pew," ABC News, 29 May 2013, www.abcnews.go.com/Business/record-number-female-primary-bread-winners-according-pew-204228999--abc-news-topstories.html (accessed 6 June 2013).
10. Linda Lowen, "Who's More Likely to Vote—Women or Men? Gender Differences and Voter Turnout," About.com, 30 November 2011, http://womenssues.about.com/od/thepoliticalarena/a/GenderVoting.html (accessed 6 June 2013).
11. "The Gender Gap: Three Decades Old."
12. K. Stenner, The Authoritarian Dynamic (New York: Cambridge University Press, 2005); and J. F. Dovido, P. Glick, and L. A. Rudman, eds., On the Nature of Prejudice: Fifty Years After Allport (Malden, MA: Blackwell, 2005).
13. "Young California Voters Shun Party Affiliation," UC Davis News and Information, 26 December 2012, http://news.ucdavis.edu/search/printable_news.lasso?id=10444&table=news (accessed 28 July 2013); and Kevin Haas, "Many Young Voters Not Picking Political Parties," The State Journal-Register, 19 October 2008, www.sj-r.com/x270971468/Many-young-voters-not-picking-political-parties (accessed 28 July 2013).
14. Henry A. Murray, Explorations in Personality (New York: Oxford University Press, 1938). Interest in Murray's research continues, and the Radcliffe Institute for Advanced Study maintains a website for the Murray Research Center at www.radcliffe.edu/.
15. Abraham H. Maslow, Motivation and Personality, 2nd ed. (New York: Harper & Row, 1970).
16. Jami Zaki, "The Altruism Instinct: An Antidote to the Tragedy of the Commons," Psychology Today, 23 November 2009, www.psychologytoday.com/blog/your-brain-us/200911/the-altruism-instinct (accessed 17 June 2013).
17. Associated Press, "Gore Promotes Benefits of Good Story-telling," Memphis Commercial Appeal, 8 October 1995, B2.
18. Barack Obama, "2004 Democratic National Convention Keynote Address, Delivered 27 July 2004, Fleet Center, Boston," www.americanrhetoric.com/speeches/convention2004/barackobama2004dnc.htm (accessed 6 June 2013).
19. James Joyner, "Romney Bungles Castro Quote in Miami," Outside the Beltway, 19 March 2007, www.outsidethebeltway.com/romney_bungles_castro_quoteP_in_miami/ (accessed 17 June 2013).
20. Humphrey Taylor, "Americans Believe That over Half the World's Population Speaks English," Harris Poll (November 1998) ttp://www.harrisinteractive.com/vault/Harris-Interactive-Poll-Research-AMERICANS-BELIEVE-THAT-OVER-HALF-THE-WORLDS-POPULA-1998-11.pdf (accessed 15 July 2013).

Chapter 6

1. Cited in Judith Humphrey, "Executive Eloquence: A Sevenfold Path to Inspirational Leadership," *Vital Speeches of the Day* 64 (15 May 1998): 469.
2. The concept of mind mapping takes somewhat different directions in books that develop the technique. See, for example, Joyce Wycoff, Steve Cook, and Michael J. Gelb, *Mindmapping: Your Personal Guide to Exploring Creativity and Problem-Solving* (New York: Berkley, 1991); and Tony Buzan and Barry Buzan, *The Mind Map Book: How to Use Radiant Thinking to Maximize Your Brain's Untapped Potential* (New York: Plume Books, 1996). For a judicious summary of recent developments, see "Mind Map," *Wikipedia, undated* http://en.wikipedia.org/wiki/Mind_map (accessed 21 February 2013).
3. Corporate mind mappers often refer to this space as "landscape." They think of the central concept as a tree and its associated ideas as "branches." See, for example, the mind map provided in "Mind Maps: A Powerful Approach to Note-Taking," undated www.mindtools.com/pages/article/newISS_01.htm (accessed 21 February 2013).
4. Rudyard Kipling, *Just So Stories* (Garden City, NY: Doubleday, 1921), p. 85.
5. Wayne C. Booth, Gregory G. Colomb, and Joseph M. Williams, *The Craft of Research* (Chicago: University of Chicago Press, 1995), p. 42.
6. Ibid., p. 38.

Chapter 7

1. "Special Report: Internet Encyclopedias Go Head to Head," *Nature* 438 (15 December 2005): 900–901, www.nature.com/nature/journal/v438/n7070/full/438900a.html

Chapter 8

1. "Regional and State Unemployment, 2012 Annual Average Summary," www.bis.gov/news.release/srgune.nrO.htm (accessed 5 March 2013).
2. Anne P. Mintz, ed., *Web of Deception: Misinformation on the Internet* (Medford, NJ: CyberAge, 2002), p. 8.
3. William L. Benoit and Kimberly A. Kennedy, "On Reluctant Testimony," *Communication Quarterly* 47 (1999): 376–387.
4. Bill Moyers, "Best of Jobs: To Have and Serve the Public's Trust," keynote address at the PBS Annual Meeting, 23 June 1996, reprinted in *Current*, 8 July 1996.
5. Michael Calvin McGee, "In Search of 'The People': A Rhetorical Alternative," *Quarterly Journal of Speech* 61 (1975): 235–249.
6. "Barack Obama's Speech on Race," *The New York Times*, www.nytimes.com/2008/03/18/us//politics/18text-obama.html (accessed 19 March 2008).
7. "On the Campaign Trail," *Reader's Digest*, March 1992, p. 116.
8. Bono, "Remarks to the 2006 National Prayer Breakfast: February 2, 2006," http://usliberals.about.com/od/faithinpubliclife/a/BonoSermon.htm (accessed 15 March 2007).
9. Governor Chris Christie, "State of the State Address," www.nj.com/politics/index.ssf/2013/01/full_text_of_chris_christies_2.html (accessed 5 May 2013).
10. Joseph Jimenez, "When Your Reputation Doesn't Match Your Ideals . . . Something Has to Change," *Vital Speeches of the Day* 78 (July 2012): 230.
11. Ibid., p. 229.
12. Walter R. Fisher, Human Communication as Narration: Toward a Philosophy of Reason, Value, and Action (Columbia: University of South Carolina Press, 1987).
13. From Norman Mailer, *The Spooky Art*, excerpted in *Newsweek*, 27 January 2003, p. 64.
14. Fisher, Human Communication, pp. 62–69.

Chapter 9

1. Patricia Kearney, Timothy G. Plax, Ellis R. Hayes, and Marily J. Ivey, "College Teacher Misbehaviors: What Students Don't Like About What Teachers Say and Do," *Communication Quarterly* 39 (1991): 309–324.
2. Ernest C. Thompson, "An Experimental Investigation of the Relative Effectiveness of Organizational Structure in Oral Communication," *Southern Speech Journal* 26 (1960): 59–69.
3. Harry Sharp, Jr., and Thomas McClung, "Effects of Organization on the Speaker's Ethos," *Speech Monographs* 33 (1966): 182–183.
4. Kimo Ah Yun, Cassie Costantini, and Sarah Billingsley, "The Effect of Taking a Public Speaking Class on One's Writing Abilities," *Communication Research Reports* 29 (October–December 2012): 285–291.
5. The concept was introduced in Alan Monroe, *Principles and Types of Speech* (New York: Scott, Foresman, 1935).
6. Cited in Arthur M. Schlesinger, Jr., *A Thousand Days: John F. Kennedy in the White House* (Boston: Houghton Mifflin, 1965), p. 733.
7. Pope Francis, "Thirst for the Absolute," *Vital Speeches International* v. 79 (20 March 2013): 154.
8. Henri Bergson, *Laughter: An Essay on the Meaning of the Comic*, trans. Cloudsley Brereton and Fred Rothwell (London: Macmillan, 1911), p. 56.

Chapter 10

1. Elisabeth Bumiller, "We Have Met the Enemy and He Is PowerPoint," *New York Times*, 26 April 2010, www.nytimes.com/2010/04/27/world/27powerpoint.html (accessed 18 May 2010).
2. "Dyslexia," *Black's Medical Dictionary*, 42nd ed., (Allen and Unwin, 2010), http://ezproxy.lib.davidson.edu:3668/entry/blackmed/dyslexia (accessed 18 May 2010).
3. Cheryl Hamilton and Cordell Parker, *Communicating for Results*, 9th ed. (Belmont, CA: Wadsworth, 2011), p. 341.
4. Nabil Mzoughi and Samar Abdelhak, "The Impact of Visual and Verbal Rhetoric in Advertising on Mental Imagery and Recall," *International Journal of Business and Social Science* 2, no. 9 (2011): 257.
5. See the classic study conducted by Wharton Business School's Applied Research Center and the Management Information Services Department of the University of Arizona, cited by Robert L. Lindstrom, "The Presentation Power of Multimedia," *Sales and Marketing Management* 51 (September 1994): 7 These findings are reinforced by Gina Poirier, "The Advantages of Multimedia Presentation Aids," (n.d.), www.ehow.com/info_12012601_advantages-multimedia-presentation-aids.html; and ""Presentation Aids," Changing Minds and Persuasion (n.d.), http://changingminds.org/techniques/speaking/preparing_presentation/presentational_aids.html (accessed 20 May 2013).
6. Lisa Collier Cool, "Danger in the Dorm," *Family Circle*, 17 February 2004, p. 15.
7. Jill Bolte-Taylor, "Stroke of Insight," February 2008, www.ted.com/speakers/jill_bolte_taylor.html.
8. Cited in Laurence J. Peter, *Peter's Quotations: Ideas for Our Time* (New York: Bantam, 1979), p. 478.
9. Garr Reynolds, *Presentation Zen Design: Simple Design Principles to Enhance Your Presentations* (Berkeley, CA: New Riders, 2010), p. 139.

10. An excellent resource on understanding, preparing, and using charts and graphs is Gerald Everett Jones, *How to Lie with Charts* (Lincoln, NE: iUniverse, 2000).

11. Jody Cross, *Leaders Speak: How to Transform Your Career and Life Through Public Speaking* (n.p.: Author, 2012), p. 159.

12. Our thanks for this example go to Professor Mary Katherine McHenry, Northwest Mississippi Community College, Senatobia, Mississippi.

13. Rebecca Ganzel, "Power Pointless," *Presentations*, February 2000, pp. 53–58.

14. Franklin N. Tessner, "PowerPoint 2008 vs. Keynote '08," Apr 16, 2008, www.macworld.com/article/1132979/office_presentation.html?page=2 (accessed 21 May, 2013); Robin Williams, *The Non-Designer's Presentation Book: Principles for Effective Presentation Design* (Berkeley, CA: Peachpit Press, 2010), pp. 12–13.

15. Peter Norvig, "The Gettysburg PowerPoint Presentation" and "The Making of the Gettysburg PowerPoint Presentation," 2000, http://norvig.com/Gettysburg/ and http://norvig.com/Gettysburg/making.html (accessed 18 May 2010).

16. Cliff Atkinson, *Beyond Bullet Points*, 3rd ed. (Redmond, WA: Microsoft, 2011), 1–16.

17. Garr Reynolds, *Presentation Zen: Simple Ideas on Presentation Design and Delivery* (Berkeley, CA: New Riders, 2008), p. 68. See also Reynolds' website at www.garrreynolds.com/; and William Earnest, *Save Our Slides: PowerPoint Design That Works* (Dubuque, IA: Kendall/Hunt, 2007).

18. Williams, *The Non-Designer's Presentation Book*, p. 131.

19. Ty Boyd, "Are You Addicted to PowerPoint?" 28 January 2012 e-newsletter.

20. Nancy Duarte, *Slide*ology: The Art and Science of Creating Great Presentations* (Sebastopol, CA: O'Reilly Media, 2008), p. 152.

21. Ibid., p. 140.

22. Farhad Manjoo, "No More Bullet Points, No More Clip Art," 5 May 2010, http://www.slate.com/id/2253050/ (accessed 21 May 2013).

23. Duarte, *Slide*ology*, p. 2.

24. Professor Scott Titsworth, Ohio University, CRTNET posting #11325, 10 May 2010. Reprinted by permission of Scott Titsworth, Director of the School of Communication Studies at Ohio University.

25. Shawn P. Apostel, "Visual Presentation Aids in the Communication Center: Tips and Techniques for Providing Useful Design Feedback," National Association of Communication Centers conference, Eastern Kentucky University, Richmond, KY, 20 April 2012.

26. Shawn P. Apostel, "Avoiding Prezilepsy: Organizational Strategies to Reduce Motion Sickness Caused by Prezi," National Association of Communication Centers conference, Eastern Kentucky University, Richmond, KY, 21 April 2012.

27. Ibid.

28. George Williams, "Use Haiku Deck for Simple, Elegant Presentations," *Chronicle of Higher Education*, 19 June 2013, http://chronicle.com/blogs/profhacker/use-haiku-deck-for-simple-elegant-presentations/50383 (accessed 21 May, 2013).

29. Eric Newton, "Commencement Address," 3 May 2013, http://queens.edu/News-and-Information/Flash-Philanthropy.html (accessed 5 May 2013).

30. Stephanie Diamond, *Prezi for Dummies* (Hoboken, NJ: Wiley, 2010), p. 40; and John Tollett, "Foreward" in Williams, *The Non-Designer's Presentation Book*, p. viii.

31. See, for example, Reynolds, *Presentation Zen Design*, p. 20; Williams, *The Non-Designer's Presentation Book*, p. 19.

32. Dave Paradi, "Latest Annoying PowerPoint Survey Results: Results of the 2011 Annoying PowerPoint Survey," May 2011, www.thinkoutsidetheslide.com/free-resources/latest-annoying-powerpoint-survey-results/ (accessed 22 May 2013).

33. Alex White, *The Elements of Graphic Design: Space, Unity, Page Architecture, and Type* (New York: Allworth Press, 2002), p. ix.

34. Dave Paradi, "Latest Annoying PowerPoint Survey Results: Results of the 2011 Annoying PowerPoint Survey" (May 2011), "Results from the 2009 PowerPoint Survey" (17 May 2010), and "Survey Shows How to Stop Annoying Audience with Bad PowerPoint" (14 March 2004), www.thinkoutsidetheslide.com/articles/ (accessed 22 May 2013).

35. Paradi, "Latest Annoying PowerPoint Survey Results."

36. Reynolds, *Presentation Zen Design*, p. 43

37. Paradi, "Latest Annoying PowerPoint Survey Results."

38. Williams, *The Non-Designer's Presentation Book*, p. 46.

39. Julie Dirksen, *Design for How People Learn* (Berkeley, CA: New Riders, 2012), p. 41.

40. Reynolds, *Presentation Zen Design*, , p. 19.

41. Paradi, "Latest Annoying PowerPoint Survey Results."

42. Jones, *How to Lie with Charts*.

43. Alliance for Board Diversity, "Missing Pieces: Women and Minorities on Fortune 500 Boards—2010 Alliance for Board Diversity Census, (2011), www.catalyst.org/knowledge/people-colors-share-fortune-500-board-seats (accessed 24 May 2013).

44. Cornelia Brunner, "Teaching Visual Literacy," *Electronic Learning*, 16 > (November–December 1994): 16.

45. "NPPA Calls *Newsweek*'s Martha Stewart Cover 'A Major Ethical Breach,'" National Press Photographers Association, 9 March 2005, www.nppa.org/news_and_events/news/2005/03/newsweek.html (accessed 20 May 2010).

46. Gloria Borger, "The Story the Pictures Didn't Tell," *U.S. News & World Report*, 22 February 1993, pp. 6–7; and John Leo, "Lapse or TV News Preview?" *Washington Times*, 3 March 1993, p. G3.

Chapter 11

1. William Raspberry, "Any Candidate Will Drink to That," *Austin American Statesman*, 11 May 1984, p. A–10.

2. Ollie Reed, "Corsicans, Navajo Weave Ties," Scripps Howard News Service, 3 July 2001, *Commercial Appeal* (Memphis), www.gomemphis.com (accessed 5 July 2001).

3. Among recent studies is that reported by Peter A. Andersen and Tammy R. Blackburn, "An Experimental Study of Language Intensity and Response Rate in E-Mail Surveys," *Communication Reports* 17, no. 2 (Summer 2004): 73–82.

4. Jerry Tarver, "Words in Time: Some Reflections on the Language of Speech," *Vital Speeches of the Day* 54 (15 April 1988): 410.

5. "Paula Deen Racist Comments, Use of N-Word Allegedly Caught on Video," 6 June, 2013, www.huffingtonpost.com/2013/06/19/paula-deen-racist comment (accessed 25 June 2013).

6. "Conversations From the Moon," www.v-j-enterprises.com/astro2.html, 5 April 1996 (accessed 17 June 2008).

7. Based on the account in Claire Perkins, "The Many Symbolic Faces of Fred Smith: Charismatic Leadership in the Bureaucracy," *Journal of the Tennessee Speech Communication Association* 11 (1985): 22.

8. Adapted from *The American Heritage Dictionary*, 2nd ed. (Boston: Houghton Mifflin, 1985), p. 92.

9. "President Obama's Address at Boston Memorial Service," 18 April 2013, www.huffingtonpost.com/2013/04/18/obama-boston-address-full (accessed 24 June 2013).

10. Listeners whose lives seem dull and unrewarding are especially susceptible to such dramas. See the discussion in Eric Hoffer, *The True Believer: Thoughts on the Nature of Mass Movements* (New York: Harper, 1951).

11. Ronald Reagan, "Second Inaugural Address," *Vital Speeches of the Day* 51 (1 February 1985): 226–228.

12. "Plain Language," undated, www.plainlanguage.gov (accessed 3 April 2013).

13. "When Will Overhead Won the Indy 500," 11 May 2010, oilpressure.wordpress.com/.../11/when-will-overhead-won-the-Indy-500 (accessed 13 May 2013).

14. Bill Moyers, "Commencement Address," University of Texas, cited in *Time*, 19 June 1985, p. 68.

15. "Wrestling Showman, Innovator Fargo Dies," *Commercial Appeal* (Memphis), 25 June 2013, p. B1.

16. "Malapropisms Live!" *Spectra*, May 1986, p. 6.

17. Haven E. Cockerham, "Conquer the Isms That Stand in Our Way," *Vital Speeches of the Day* (1 February 1998): 240.

18. "Paula Deen Loses Major Endorsement Deal," 25 June 2013, *The New York Times*, www.nytimes.com/2013/06/25/us/paula-deen-loses-major-endorsement (accessed 25 June 2013).

19. "Billie Jean King Serves Up Wisdom to 527 Graduates of Williams College 2013 Class," undated, the http://transcript.com/news/ci_23375335/billie-jean-king-address (accessed 26 June 2013).

20. *Commercial Appeal* (Memphis), 26 January 2010, p. A9.

21. For additional discussion of such metaphors, see Michael Osborn, "Archetypal Metaphor in Rhetoric: The Light-Dark Family," *Quarterly Journal of Speech* 53 (1967): 115–126, and "The Evolution of the Archetypal Sea in Rhetoric and Poetic," *Quarterly Journal of Speech* 63 (1977): 347–363.

22. George W. Bush, "Inaugural Address," *Vital Speeches of the Day* (1 February 2001): 226. .

23. See another side of this image in J. Vernon Jensen, "British Voices on the Eve of the American Revolution: Trapped by the Family Metaphor," *Quarterly Journal of Speech* 63 (1977): 43–50.

24. Barack Obama's Speech on Race, www.npr.org/templates/story/story.php?storyId=8847867

25. For an insightful discussion of the metaphors we use to construct our ideas about illness, see Susan Sontag, *Illness as Metaphor* (New York: Vintage Books, 1979), and *AIDS and Its Metaphors* (New York: Farrar, Straus and Giroux, 1988).

26. See Robert Ivie, "Images of Savagery in American Justifications for War," *Communication Monographs* 47 (1980): 279–294.

27. Michael Osborn, "Patterns of Metaphor Among Early Feminist Orators," in *Rhetoric and Community: Studies in Unity and Fragmentation*, ed. J. Michael Hogan (Columbia: University of South Carolina Press, 1998), pp. 10–11.

28. Osborn, *Orientations to Rhetorical Style*, p. 16.

29. Richard Weaver, "Ultimate Terms in Contemporary Rhetoric," in *The Ethics of Rhetoric* (Chicago: Henry Regnery, 1953), pp. 211–232.

30. Michael Calvin McGee, "The Ideograph: A Link Between Rhetoric and Ideology," *Quarterly Journal of Speech* 66 (1980): 1–16.

31. Bill Moyers, "Pass the Bread," a baccalaureate address presented at Hamilton College, 20 May 2006.

32. "British Officials Divided on EU," *Commercial Appeal* (Memphis), 12 December 2011, p. A5.

Chapter 12

1. Richard Conniff, "Reading Faces," *Smithsonian* 34 (January 2004): 49.

2. Jeanne Segal, Melinda Smith, Greg Boose, and Jaelline Jaffe, "Nonverbal Communication: Improving Your Nonverbal Skills and Reading Body Language," January 2013, www.helpguide.org/mental/eq6_nonverbal_communication.htm (accessed 20 May 2013).

3. Martin S. Remland, *Nonverbal Communication in Everyday Life*, 2nd ed. (Boston: Houghton Mifflin, 2003), pp. 283–285.

4. James A. Winans used the term "enlarged conversation style" in *Speechmaking* (New York: Appleton-Century-Crofts, 1938).

5. Karen Kangas Dwyer, *Conquer Your Speech Anxiety*, 2nd ed. (Belmont, CA: Thomson Wadsworth, 2005), pp. 79–80.

6. James C. McCroskey, *An Introduction to Rhetorical Communication*, 9th ed. (Boston: Allyn & Bacon, 2006).

7. Virginia Peck Richmond, James C. McCroskey, and Mark L. Hickson, *Nonverbal Behavior in Interpersonal Relations*, 7th ed. (Boston: Allyn & Bacon, 2011).

8. Maya Angelou (n.d.) www.brainyquote.com/quotes/quotes/m/mayaangelo140532.html (accessed 20 May 2013).

9. Annie Lennox's 2013 commencement address is available through her website, www.annielennox.com.

10. Adapted from Stuart W. Hyde, *Television and Radio Announcing*, 10th ed. (Boston: Houghton Mifflin, 2003).

11. N. Scott Momaday, *The Way to Rainy Mountain* (Albuquerque: University of New Mexico Press, 1969), p. 5.

12. Mariska Hargitay, "No More!" National Press Club, 13 March 2013, www.youtube.com/watch?v=uOE4x6hfSxE (accessed 18 April 2013).

13. Carole Douglis, "The Beat Goes On: Social Rhythms Underlie All Our Speech and Actions," *Psychology Today*, November 1987, pp. 36–41.

14. William Price Fox, "Eugene Talmadge and Sears Roebuck Co.," in *Southern Fried Plus Six* (New York: Ballantine Books, 1968), p. 36.

15. Michael L. Hecht, Peter A. Andersen, and Sidney A. Ribeau, "The Cultural Dimensions of Nonverbal Communication," in *Handbook of International and Intercultural Communication*, ed. Molefi Kete Asante and William B. Gudykunst (Newbury Park, CA: Sage, 1989), pp. 163–185; and Larry A. Samovar, Richard E. Porter, and Edwin R. McDaniel, *Communication Between Cultures*, 6th ed. (Belmont, CA: Wadsworth, 2007).

16. Ralph Hillman, *Delivering Dynamic Presentations: Using Your Voice and Body for Impact* (Boston: Allyn & Bacon, 1999).

17. Betty Ren Wright, *Johnny Go Round* (New York: Tell a Tale Books, 1960), pp. 1–3.

18. *NBC Handbook of Pronunciation*, 4th ed. (New York: Harper, 1991).

19. Judee K. Burgoon, Laura K. Guerrero, and Kory Floyd, *Nonverbal Communication* (Boston: Allyn & Bacon, 2010), pp. 141–42.

20. Carolanne Griffith-Roberts, "Let's Talk Southern," *Southern Living*, February 1995, p. 82.

21. Carol Quillen, "Inaugural Remarks," Davidson College, Oct. 19, 2011, www3.davidson.edu/cms/x44303.xml (accessed 21 October 2011).

22. Samovar, Porter, and McDaniel, *Communication Between Cultures*, p. 177.

23. See Erving Goffman's discussion in *The Presentation of Self in Everyday Life* (London: Penguin Press, 1969), pp. 1–14.

24. Mark L. Knapp, Judith A. Hall, and Terrence G. Horgan, *Nonverbal Communication in Human Interaction*, 8th ed. (Belmont, CA: Wadsworth, 2014), p. 8.

25. See, for example, Burgoon, Guerrero, and Floyd, *Nonverbal Communication*, pp. 43–44; and Mark P. Orbe and Tina M. Harris, *Interracial Communication: Theory into Practice*, 2nd ed. (Belmont, CA: Wadsworth, 2007), pp. 112–14.

26. Research psychologist Carolyn Copper has found that newscasters influence voters when they smile while speaking of candidates, further evidence of the power of facial expression. "A Certain Smile," *Psychology Today*, January–February 1992, p. 20.

27. Edouard Gasarabwe-Laroche, "Meaningful Gestures: Nonverbal Communication in Rwandan Culture," *UNESCO Courier*, September 1993, pp. 31–33.

28. Richard B. Klein, "Winning Cases with Body Language: Moving Toward Courtroom Success," *Trial* 31 (July 1995): 84.

29. The literature supporting this conclusion is reviewed by Virginia Kidd, "Do Clothes Make the Officer? How Uniforms Impact Communication: A Review of Literature," presented at the Visual Communication Conference at Pray, MT, 8 July 2000.

30. Goffman, *The Presentation of Self*, p. 21.

31. Guy Kawasaki, "How to Get a Standing Ovation," posted 7 September 2010, http://holykaw.alltop.com/how-to-get-a-standing-ovation-O (accessed 21 May 2013).

32. See, for example, Carmine Gallo, "Body Language: A Key to Success in the Workplace," 14 February 2007 http://finance.yahoo.com/news/pf_article_102425.html (accessed 20 May 2013); and Charisse Jones, "Face Off: Hotel Staff Taught to Read Guests' Body Language," USA Today, 24 October 2011, http://travel.usatoday.com/hotels/story/2011-10-24/Face-off-Hotel-staff-taught-to-read-guests-body-language/50896514/1 (accessed 24 November 2011).

33. Ken Ringle, "George Bush and the Words of War," Washington Post, 9 March 2003, http://pqasb.pqarchiver.com/washingtonpost/access/303554101.html?dids=303554101:303 (accessed 18 May 2007).

34. Carmine Gallo, "The Presentation Secrets of Steve Jobs: How to Be Insanely Great in Front of Any Audience," 29 November 2009 www.slideshare.net/cvgallo/the-presentation-secrets-of-steve-jobs-2609477 (accessed 21 May 2013).

35. Ralph R. Behnke and Chris R. Sawyer, "Public Speaking Procrastination as a Correlate of Public Speaking Communication Apprehension and Self-Perceived Public Speaking Competence," Communication Research Reports 16 (1999): 40–47.

36. Constance Bernstein, "Winning Trials Nonverbally: Six Ways to Establish Control in the Courtroom," Trial 30 (January 1994): 61+. Academic OneFile (accessed 23 August 2010).

37. Tony E. Smith and Ann Bainbridge Frymier, "Get 'Real': Does Practicing Speeches Before an Audience Improve Performance?" Communication Quarterly 54 (2006): 113.

38. Claudia Wallis and Sonja Steptoe, "The Case for Doing One Thing at a Time," Time, 16 January 2006, p. 76.

39. Jody Cross, Leaders Speak: How to Transform Your Career and Life Through Public Speaking (n.p.: Author, 2012), p. 167.

40. These guidelines for handling questions and answers are a compendium of ideas from the following sources: Stephen D. Body, "Nine Steps to a Successful Question-and-Answer Session," Management Solutions, May 1988, pp. 16–17; Teresa Brady, "Fielding Abrasive Questions During Presentations," Supervisory Management, February 1993, p. 6; J. Donald Ragsdale and Alan L. Mikels, "Effects of Question Periods on a Speaker's Credibility with a Television Audience," Southern States Communication Journal 40 (1975): 302–312; Dorothy Sarnoff, Never Be Nervous Again (New York: Ballantine, 1987); Laurie Schloff and Marcia Yudkin, Smart Speaking: Sixty-Second Strategies (New York: Holt, 1991); and Alan Zaremba, "Q and A: The Other Part of Your Presentation," Management World, January–February 1989, pp. 8–10.

41. Matthew Hutson, "How to Dodge a Question," Psychology Today, October 2009, p. 24.

42. "South Carolina Democratic Debate transcript," MSNBC, p. 7, 27 April 2007, www.msnbc.msn.com/id/18352397 (accessed 20 May 2007).

43. Adam Nagourney and Jeff Zeleny, "In Mostly Sedate Debate, Democrats Show More Unity than Strife," New York Times, 27 April 2007, http://query.nytimes.com/gst/fullpage.html?res=9400E7DD123EF934A15757C0A9619C8 (accessed 19 May 2007).

44. "Commentaries," Hardball with Chris Matthews, CNBC, 27 April 2007.

45. "Remarks by the President at GOP House Issues Conference," 29 January 2010, www.whitehouse.gov/the-press-office/remarks-president-gop-house-issues-conference (accessed 21 February 2010).

46. Tom Ross to COM 101: Principles of Oral Communication, Davidson College, December 2, 2008.

47. The authors are indebted to Professor Roxanne Gee of the television and film area in the Department of Communication at the University of Memphis; much of this section rests on her observations and suggestions.

48. Bernstein, "Winning Trials Nonverbally," 61+.

Chapter 13

1. Katherine E. Rowan, "Goals, Obstacles, and Strategies in Risk Communication: A Problem-Solving Approach to Improving Communication About Risks," Journal of Applied Communication Research 19 (1991): 314.

2. Ibid.

3. Paul Ashdown, "From Wild West to Wild Web," Vital Speeches of the Day 65 1 September 2000): 699–701.

4. Paul R. Gamble and Clare E. Kelliher, "Imparting Information and Influencing Behavior: An Examination of Staff Briefing Sessions," Journal of Business Communication v. 36 (July 1999): 261.

5. Ancil B. Sparks and Dennis D. Staszak, "Fine Tuning Your News Briefing: Law Enforcement Agency Media Relations," FBI Law Enforcement Bulletin http://www.highbeam.com/doc/1G1-69441917.html (posted December 2000): accessed 10 July 2013.

6. Howard Gardner, Changing Minds: The Art and Science of Changing Our Own and Other People's Minds (Cambridge, MA: Harvard Business School Publishing, 2006).

7. Representative is Timothy J. Koegel, The Exceptional Presenter (Austin, TX: Greenleaf Book Group Press, 2007).

Chapter 14

1. Mark A. Hamilton and John E. Hunter, "The Effect of Language Intensity on Receiver Attitudes Toward Message, Source, and Topic," in Persuasion: Advances Through Meta-Analysis, ed. M. Allen and R. W. Preiss (Beverly Hills, CA: Sage, 1998).

2. This speech is made available in English translation by the Perseus Digital Library, sponsored by Tufts University, www.perseus.tufts.edu/cgi-bin/ptext?doc=Perseus:text1999.02.0020:text=Cael.:section=1.

3. For a different view, which depicts persuasion in terms of manipulation and domination, see Sonja K. Foss and Cindy L. Griffin, "Beyond Persuasion: A Proposal for an Invitational Rhetoric," Communication Monographs 62 (1995): 2–18.

4. William J. McGuire, "Attitudes and Attitude Change," in The Handbook of Social Psychology, ed. Gardner Lindzey and Elliot Aronson (New York: Random House, 1985), vol. 1, pp. 258–261.

5. Roger Brown, Social Psychology: The Second Edition (New York: Free Press, 1986).

6. Gloria Steinem, Revolution from Within: A Book of Self-Esteem (New York: Little, Brown, 1992), p. 120.

7. Adapted from Herbert W. Simons, Persuasion in Society (Thousand Oaks, CA: Sage, 2001).

8. Larry Tracy, "Taming Hostile Audiences: Persuading Those Who Would Rather Jeer than Cheer," Vital Speeches of the Day 71(1 March 2005): 311.

9. N. H. Anderson, "Integration Theory and Attitude Change," Psychological Review 78 (1971): 171–206.

10. McGuire, "Attitudes and Attitude Change," 260.

11. Joshua A. Compton and Michael W. Pfau, "Inoculation Theory of Resistance to Influence at Maturity," in Communication Yearbook 29, ed. P. J. Kalbfleisch (Mahwah, NJ: Erlbaum, 2005), pp. 97–145.

12. Mike Allen and James B. Stiff, "Testing Three Models for the Sleeper Effect," Western Journal of Speech Communication 53 (1989): 411–426.

13. As recounted in Diane M. Martin, "Balancing on the Political High Wire: The Role of Humor in the Rhetoric of Ann Richards," Southern Communication Journal 69 (2004): 278.

14. The Nabholz experience was documented in an HBO television program, "Overweight in the Workplace: How Wellness Programs Can Help the American Workforce," in the series, The Weight of the Nation: Confronting America's Obesity Epidemic

(www.theweightof the nation.hbo.com/films/bonus-shorts/
overweight-in-the-workplace-how-wellness-programs-can-help-
the-american-workforce), shown in May, 2012.

15. Interview with Chris Goldsby, Sept. 18, 2012.

16. Interview with Jayme Mayo, June 17, 2012.

17. Interview with Wayne Robinson, July 17, 2012.

18. Interview with Carlile Baker, July 28, 2013.

19. Franklin J. Boster and Paul Mongeau, "Fear-Arousing Persuasive Messages," in *Communication Yearbook 8*, ed. R. Bostrom (Beverly Hills, CA: Sage, 1984), pp. 330–377; and Richard E. Petty and Duane T. Wegener, "Attitude Change: Multiple Roles for Persuasion Variables," in *The Handbook of Social Psychology*, 4th ed., ed. Daniel T. Gilbert, Susan T. Fiske, and Gardner Lindzey (Boston: McGraw-Hill, 1998), pp. 353–354.

20. Katherine E. Rowan, "Goals, Obstacles, and Strategies in Risk Communication: A Problem-Solving Approach to Improving Communication About Risks," *Journal of Applied Communication Research* 19 (1991): 322.

21. "Wanted: Gurus With Actual Experience," *The Wall Street Journal*, July 3, 2013, B6.

22. "Wanted: Gurus with Actual Experience," *Wall Street Journal*, 3 July 2013, p. B6.

23. Steve Hargreaves, "Exxon Linked to Climate Change Pay Out," *Fortune* (CNN.Money), 2 February 2007, http://money.cnn.com/2007/02/02/news/companies/exxon_science/index.htm?cnn=yes (accessed 23 May 2007).

24. Adapted from Richard L. Johannesen, Kathleen S. Valde, and Karen E. Whedbee, *Ethics in Communication*, 6th ed. (Prospect Heights, IL: Waveland, 2007).

25. The motivated sequence design was introduced in Alan Monroe's *Principles and Types of Speech* (New York: Scott, Foresman, 1935) and has been refined in later editions.

26. The structure of the stock issues design has been adapted from Charles U. Larson, *Persuasion: Reception and Responsibility*, 13th ed. (Belmont, CA: Wadsworth, 2012); and Charles S. Mudd and Malcolm O. Sillars, *Public Speaking: Content and Communication* (Prospect Heights, IL: Waveland, 1991), pp. 100–102.

Chapter 15

1. Al Gore, *The Assault on Reason* (New York: Penguin Press, 2007), pp. 245–246.

2. Franklin J. Boster, Kenzie A. Cameron, Shelly Campo, Janet K Lillie, Esther M. Baker, and Kimo Ah Yun, "The Persuasive Effects of Statistical Evidence in the Presence of Exemplars," *Communication Studies* 51 (2000): 296–306.

3. M. Sean Limon and Dean C. Kazoleas, "A Comparison of Exemplar and Statistical Evidence in Reducing Counter-Arguments and Responses to a Message," *Communication Research Reports* 21 (2004): 291–298.

4. Thomas Hugh Feeley, Heather M. Marshall, and Amber M. Reinhart, "Reactions to Narrative and Statistical Written Messages Promoting Organ Donation," *Communication Reports* 10 (2006): 89–100.

5. "Wanted: Gurus with Actual Experience," *Wall Street Journal*, 3 July 2013, p. B6.

6. Limon and Kazoleas, "A Comparison of Exemplar and Statistical Evidence," 291–298.

7. Shelly Chaiken, Wendy Wood, and Alice H. Eagly, "Principles of Persuasion," in *Social Psychology: Handbook of Basic Principles*, ed. E. Tory Higgins and Arie W. Kruglanki (New York: Guilford, 1996), pp. 702–742.

8. Antonio R. Damasio, *Descartes' Error: Emotion, Reason, and the Human Brain* (New York: Putnam, 1994).

9. Representative of this scholarship is Ernest G. Bormann, "Fantasy and Rhetorical Vision: The Rhetorical Criticism of Social Reality," *Quarterly Journal of Speech* 58 (1972): 396–407; Walter F. Fisher, "Narration as a Human Communication Paradigm: The Case of Public Moral Argument," *Communication Monographs* 51 (1984); 1–22; Michael C. McGee, "In Search of 'The People': A Rhetorical Alternative," *Quarterly Journal of Speech* 61 (1975): 235–249; Michael Osborn, "Rhetorical Depiction," in *Form, Genre and the Study of Political Discourse*, ed. Herbert W. Simons and Aram A. Aghazarian (Columbia: University of South Carolina Press, 1986), pp. 79–107; and Janice Hocker Rushing, "The Rhetoric of the American Western Myth," *Communication Monographs* 50 (1983): 14–32.

10. Martha Solomon, "The 'Positive Woman's' Journey: A Mythic Analysis of the Rhetoric of STOP ERA," *Quarterly Journal of Speech* 65 (1979): 262–274.

11. Rushing, "The Rhetoric of the American Western Myth," 14–32.

12. Roderick P. Hart, *The Political Pulpit* (West Lafayette, IN: Purdue University Press, 1977).

13. John Fitzgerald Kennedy, "Acceptance Address, 1960," in *The Great Society: A Sourcebook of Speeches*, ed. Glenn R. Capp (Belmont, CA: Dickenson 1969), p. 14.

14. Some argue that the terms *deduction* and *induction* should no longer be used in speech textbooks because modern logic has changed its use of these words. Such logicians are concerned with accounting for certainty in conclusions, such as one seeks in mathematical reasoning. Since the time of Aristotle, rhetorical theorists have recognized that speakers deal with a world of contingency in which degrees of uncertainty and probability are the sole concerns. Systems of nomenclature such as *induction* and *deduction* should be measured by their usefulness in specific fields of inquiry and are not subject to decree by any other privileged field.

15. Richard M. Weaver, "Ultimate Terms in Contemporary Rhetoric," in *Language Is Sermonic: Richard M. Weaver on the Nature of Rhetoric*, ed. Richard L. Johannesen, Rennard Strickland, and Ralph T. Eubanks (Baton Rouge: Louisiana State University Press, 1970), pp. 92–93.

16. Richard F. Corlin, "The Secrets of Gun Violence in America," *Vital Speeches of the Day* 67 (1 August 2001): 611. Reprinted by permission of Richard Corlin.

17. Lisa M. Ross, "Buckley Says Drug Attack Won't Work," *Commercial Appeal* (Memphis), 14 September 1989, p. B2.

18. Gilbert Cranberg, "Even Sensible Iowa Bows to the Religious Right," *Los Angeles Times*, 17 August 1992, p. B5.

19. *The Commercial Appeal* (Memphis), 6 Sept. 1996, p. C1.

20. Douglas Ehninger and Wayne Brockriede, *Decision By Debate*, (New York: Dodd Mead & Company, 1963).

Chapter 16

1. "Overweight in the Workplace: How Wellness Programs Can Help the American Workforce," in the series *The Weight of the Nation: Confronting America's Obesity Epidemic*, HBO, May 2012. This description of the "Wellies" ceremony was reconstructed from an interview with Chris Goldsby, 18 September 2012.

2. Celeste Michelle Condit, "The Functions of Epideictic: The Boston Massacre Orations as Exemplar," *Communication Quarterly* 33 (1985): 284–299; Gray Matthews, "Epideictic Rhetoric and Baseball: Nurturing Community Through Controversy," *Southern Communication Journal* 60 (1995): 275–291; Randall Parrish Osborn, "Jimmy Carter's Rhetorical Campaign for the Presidency: An Epideictic of American Renewal," Paper presented at the Southern States Communication Association Convention, Memphis, TN,

March 1996; C. Perelman and L. Olbrechts-Tyteca, *The New Rhetoric: A Treatise on Argumentation* (South Bend, IN: University of Notre Dame Press, 1971), pp. 47–54; and Richard M. Weaver, *The Ethics of Rhetoric* (Chicago: Henry Regnery, 1953), pp. 164–185.

3. John Dewey, *Democracy and Education* (New York: Macmillan, 1916), p. 4.

4. See Burke's discussion in "The Range of Rhetoric," in *A Rhetoric of Motives* (Berkeley: University of California Press, 1969), pp. 3–43.

5. Walter R. Fisher, *Human Communication as Narration: Toward a Philosophy of Reason, Value, and Action* (Columbia: University of South Carolina Press, 1989).

6. *Selected Speeches and Writings by Abraham Lincoln* (New York: Vintage Books, 1992), p. 405.

7. See the discussion in *The Rhetoric of Aristotle*, trans. Lane Cooper (New York: Appleton-Century-Crofts, 1932), I.7, I.9, I.14 (pp. 34–44, 46–55, 78–79).

8. John Bakke, "Remarks on Accepting the Martin Luther King, Jr., Human Rights Award," presented in April 2006, at the University of Memphis, Memphis, TN.

9. Egil Aarvik, "Nobel Peace Prize 1986 Presentation Speech," www.pbs.org/eliewiesel/nobel/presentation.html.

10. Kevin Costner, "Eulogy for Whitney Houston Presented February 19, 2012," posted 19 February 2012, http://transcripts.cnn.com/TRANSCRIPTS/1202/18/se.07.html (downloaded 1 July 2013).

11. Owen Edwards, "What Every Man Should Know: How to Make a Toast," *Esquire*, January 1984, p. 37.

12. The advice that follows is adapted from Jacob M. Braude, *Complete Speaker's and Toastmaster's Library: Definitions and Toasts* (Englewood Cliffs, NJ: Prentice Hall, 1965), pp. 88–123; and Wendy Lin, "Let's Lift a Glass, Say a Few Words, and Toast 1996," *Commercial Appeal* (Memphis), 28 December 1995, p. C3.

13. Elie Wiesel, "Nobel Peace Prize Acceptance Speech," *New York Times*, 11 December 1986, p. A8.

14. *Commercial Appeal* (Memphis), 23 October 1995, p. D2.

15. Frank Dobie, "The Conservatism of Charles M. Russell," in *Charlie Russell Roundup: Essays on America's Favorite Cowboy Artist*, ed. Brian Dippie (Helena, MT: Montana Historical Society Press, 1999), p. 256.

16. Steve Jobs, "Commencement Address at Stanford University," *Stanford Report*, 14 June 2005

17. *Congressional Record*, 1 April 1980, p. 7249.

18. Ibid., p. 7248.

19. Roger Ailes, *You Are the Message* (New York: Doubleday, 1988), pp. 71–74.

20. Diane M. Martin, "Balancing on the Political High Wire: The Role of Humor in the Rhetoric of Ann Richards," *Southern Communication Journal* 69 (2004): 273–288.

21. For more on the social function of laughter, see Henri Bergson, *Laughter: An Essay on the Meaning of the Comic*, trans. Cloudsley Brereton and Fred Rothwell (London: Macmillan, 1911).

22. Robert M. Kaplan and Gregory C. Pascoe, "Humorous Lectures and Humorous Examples: Some Effects upon Comprehension and Retention," *Journal of Educational Psychology* 69 (1977): 61–65.

23. Dick Jackman, "Awards Dinner of the National Football Foundation and the Hall of Fame," *Harper's Magazine*, March 1985.

24. Charles R. Gruner, "Advice to the Beginning Speaker on Using Humor—What the Research Tells Us," *Communication Education* 34 (1985): 142–147; and Christie McGuffee Smith and Larry Powell, "The Use of Disparaging Humor by Group Leaders," *Southern Speech Communication Journal* 53 (1988): 279–292.

25. "President Bush Attends Radio and Television Correspondents' Annual Dinner," 28 March 2007, www.whitehouse.gov/news/releases/2007/03/20070328-6.html (accessed 23 May 2007).

26. *Washington Post*, 12 December 1978.

27. Adapted from Joan Detz, *Can You Say a Few Words?* (New York: St. Martins, 1991), pp. 77–78.

28. Ronald Reagan, "Second Inauguration Address," *Vital Speeches of the Day* 51 (1 February 1985): 226–228.

Appendix A

1. Adapted from Marc Hequet, "The Fine Art of Multicultural Meetings," *Training* (July 1993): 29–33.

2. For additional insights on groupthink, see the following articles: Judith Chap Chapman, "Anxiety and Defective Decision Making: An Elaboration of the Groupthink Model," *Management Decision* 44 (2006): 1391–1404; Jack Eaton, "Management Communication: The Threat of Groupthink," *Corporate Communications* 6 (2001): 183–192; and Steve A. Yetiv, "Groupthink and the Gulf Crisis," *British Journal of Political Science* 33 (2003): 419–442.

3. For more information on face-to-face brainstorming, see J. M. Hender, et al., "Improving Group Creativity: Brainstorming versus Non-brainstorming Techniques in a GSS Environment," *Proceedings of the 24th Annual Hawaii International Conference of Systems Sciences, 2001*; Thomas J. Kramer, Geral P. Fleming, and Scott M. Mannis, "Improving Face-to-Face Brainstorming Through Modeling and Facilitation," *Small Group Research* 32 (2001); and Paul A. Paulus, et al., "Social and Cognitive Influences in Group Brainstorming: Predicting Production Gains and Losses," *European Review of Social Psychology*, 12 (January 2002).

4. For additional information on electronic brainstorming, see Nicolas Michinov and Corine Primois, "Improving Productivity and Creativity in Online Groups Through Social Comparison Process: New Evidence for Asynchronous Electronic Brainstorming," *Computers in Human Behavior* 21 (2005): 11–28.

5. Roz D. Lasker and Elisa S. Weiss. "Broadening Participation in Community Problem-Solving: A Multidisciplinary Model to Supportive Collaborative Practice and Research," *Journal of Urban Health* (March 2003): 14–47; Nikol Rummel and Hans Spada, "Learning to Collaborate: An Instructional Approach to Promoting Collaborative Problem Solving in Computer-Mediated Settings," *Journal of the Learning Sciences*, 14 (2005): 201–241.

6. William M. Issacs, "Taking Flight: Dialogue, Collective Thinking, and Organizational Learning," *Organizational Dynamics* (Autumn 1993): 24–39.

7. Edgar H. Schein, "On Dialogue, Culture, and Organizational Learning," *Organizational Dynamics* (Autumn 1993): 40–41. For additional information on dialogue groups, see Joseph H. Albeck, Sami Adwan, and Dan Bar-on, "Dialogue Groups: TRT's Guidelines for Working Through Intractable Conflicts by Personal Story Telling," *Peace and Conflict: Journal of Peace Psychology* 8 (2002): 301–322.

8. David W. Stewart, Prem N. Shamdassani, and Dennis W. Rook, *Focus Groups: Theory and Practice*, 2nd ed. (Thousand Oaks, CA: Sage, 2006); Thomas L. Greenbaum, *Moderating Focus Groups: A Practical Guide for Group Facilitation* (Thousand Oaks, CA: Sage, 2000); and Claudia Puchta and Jonathan Potter, *Focus Group Practice* (Thousand Oaks, CA: Sage, 2004).

9. John P. Schuster, "Transforming Your Leadership Style," *Association Management* (January 1994): 39–43.

10. *Ibid.*

11. Svjetlana Madzar, "Subordinate's Information Inquiry: Exploring the Effective of Perceived Leadership Style and Individual Differences," *Journal of Occupational and Organizational Psychology* (June 2001): 221–232.

12. Much of the material in this section is adapted from Gregorio Billikopf, "Conducting Effective Meetings," August 2005,

www.cnr.berkeley.edu/ucce50/ag-labor/7labor/11.pdf (accessed 30 June 2007); Don Clark, "Meetings," 20 May 2007, www.nwlink .com/~donclark/leader/leadmet.html (accessed 30 June 2007); and Carter McNamara, "Basic Guide to Conducting Effective Meetings," copyright 1997–2007, www.managementhelp.org/ misc/mtgmgmnt.htm (accessed 30 June 2007).

13. Michael E. Mayer, "Behaviors Leading to More Effective Decisions in Small Groups Embedded in Organizations," *Communication Reports* (Summer 1988): 123–132.

14. Christopher Niesche, "Virtual Meetings on the Rise," *The Sydney Morning Herald*, 1 Nov. 2012, www.smh.com.au/business/ momentum/virtual-meetings-on-the-rise-20121023-2832v.html

(accessed 9 Aug. 2013); J. Dan Rothwell, *In the Company of Others: An Introduction to Communication*, 3rd ed. (New York: Oxford University Press, 2010) 328–329.

15. "Roundtables," 4 Dec. 2003, www.sdanys.org/Archive_Round/ NYPWAGuidelines.htm (accessed 30 June 2007).

16. Marilyn Berlin Snell, "Climate Exchange," *Sierra*, May/June 2007, 44–53, 73–74.

Appendix B

1. Page 410, Nobel Peace Prize Acceptance Speech, December 10, 1986. © The Nobel Foundation 1986.

Photo Credits

Index

Note: *f* indicates figures.